THE
BRITISH
POLITY

Other Books by Philip Norton:

Dissension in the House of Commons 1945-74 (1975)
Conservative Dissidents (1978)
Dissension in the House of Commons 1974-1979 (1980)
The Commons in Perspective (1981)
Conservatives and Conservatism (with A. Aughey) (1981)
The Constitution in Flux (1982)
Law and Order and British Politics (editor) (1984)
Parliament in the 1980s (editor) (1985)
The Political Science of British Politics (edited with J. Hayward) (1986)
Legislatures (editor) (1990)
Parliaments in Western Europe (editor) (1990)
New Directions in British Politics? (editor) (1991)
Parliamentary Questions (edited with M. Franklin) (1993)
Back From Westminster (with D. Wood) (1993)
Does Parliament Matter? (1993)
National Parliaments and the European Union (editor) (1996)
The New Parliaments of Central and Eastern Europe (edited with D. M. Olson) (1996)
The Conservative Party (editor) (1996)
Legislatures and Legislators (1998)
Parliaments and Governments in Western Europe (editor) (1998)
Parliaments and Pressure Groups in Western Europe (editor) (1999)
Parliaments in Asia (edited with N. Ahmed) (1999)
Politics UK (with Bill Jones and others), 4th ed. (2000)

THE
BRITISH
POLITY
FOURTH EDITION

PHILIP NORTON
The University of Hull

New York   San Francisco   Boston
London   Toronto   Sydney   Tokyo   Singapore   Madrid
Mexico City   Munich   Paris   Cape Town   Hong Kong   Montreal

Publisher: Priscilla McGeehon
Senior Acquisitions Editor: Eric Stano
Associate Editor: Anita Castro
Marketing Manager: Megan Galvin-Fak
Supplements Editor: Mark Toews
Production Manager: Ellen MacElree
Project Coordination, Text Design, and Electronic Page Makeup: Pre-Press Company, Inc.
Cover Designer/Manager: Nancy Danahy
Cover Image: © PhotoDisc, Inc.
Manufacturing Buyer: Roy Pickering
Printer and Binder: Courier
Cover Printer: Phoenix Color Corp.

Library of Congress Cataloging-in-Publication Data

Norton Philip.
 The British polity / Philip Norton.—4th ed.
   p. cm.
 Includes bibliographical references and index.
 ISBN 0-8013-1844-0
 1. Great Britain—Politics and government. I. Title.

 JN231 .N669 2000
 320.941—dc21   00-046137

Please visit our website at http://www.ablongman.com

0-8013-1844-0

1 2 3 4 5 6 7 8 9 10—CRS—03 02 01 00

To Mr. and Mrs. R. A. Bradel

Contents

Illustrations and Tables

MAPS

TABLES

FIGURES

Preface

The past decade has witnessed tremendous changes in British politics. The period from 1992 to 1997 saw a Conservative government under pressure. The government's parliamentary majority had disappeared by the end of the Parliament and its parliamentary supporters were badly divided on the issue of European integration. The general election of 1997 produced a remarkable victory for the Labour party—the "out" party in British politics for 18 years. It was swept into office with a massive parliamentary majority—the size of its majority exceeding the size of the parliamentary Conservative party. Since its return to office, the Labour government has achieved passage of several major pieces of constitutional reform. Following referendums, new assemblies have been created in Scotland, Wales, and Northern Ireland. A Human Rights Act has been passed, incorporating the European Convention on Human Rights into British law. The second chamber of Parliament, the House of Lords, has seen a fundamental change in its membership. The contours of the British constitution have undergone remarkable change and may see further change; there are demands for further reforms, including the introduction of a new method of electing members of Parliament.

Changes have also occurred as a consequence of British membership in the European Union: The Conservative government took part in negotiations for the Treaty on European Union (the Maastricht Treaty), which took effect in 1993. Its successor Labour government was involved in negotiations for the Amsterdam Treaty, which took effect in 1999. Further changes in the structures of the European Union are planned, along with an enlargement as more states apply for membership. Political parties in the U.K. have also become embroiled in a growing debate as to whether or not the U.K. should join the single European currency (the "euro") created by most member states of the European Union.

Membership in the European Union (EU), along with the incorporation of the European Convention on Human Rights, and the devolution of powers to elected assemblies in different parts of the U.K., have added a substantial judicial dimension to the constitution. Judges have had to adapt to a new role.

The changing nature of society has also had consequences for the monarch and members of the royal family. They have had to respond to a series of unrelated events that at various points undermined the standing of the monarchy in the U.K. They have had to contend with a new situation created by the death in a car accident in 1997 of Diana, Princess of Wales.

The changes in the British polity have not been confined to the formal structures. The political parties have undergone remarkable changes. The Labour party has become "New Labour." The Conservative party has sought to adapt itself to changed political circumstances under a new leader. The Liberal Democratic party has also sought to adapt to a new political environment, also now under a new leader. The parties have had to contend with a more crowded political environment, not only as a consequence of U.K. membership in the EU and a more active judiciary, but also because of the continuing growth of organized interests. Citizens are channelling their political energies through interest groups rather than through political parties. The parties have also had to contend with changes in the mass media. The media are now more pervasive as well as more fragmented. Technological change has facilitated a 24-hour news service as well as more means of transmitting information. Politicians have had to cope with a political environment that is undergoing remarkable change.

The last edition of *The British Polity* was published in 1993. Since then, the polity has been subject to all these changes. As a result, the chapters have been subjected to extensive revision and, in many cases, a complete rewriting. The number of chapters has increased—there is a new chapter on the new assemblies in the different parts of the U.K.—and local government is now dealt with in a chapter devoted exclusively to it. No chapter has emerged unscathed. The nature of the changes over the past decade has also resulted in the conclusion being written anew for this volume. The theme of the last chapter remains that of continuity and change. The same theme could equally apply to succeeding editions of *The British Polity*. Though there is much continuity, there is also a great deal of change. This edition records far more change than earlier editions. Whether much of the change is desirable or not is something that is addressed in the concluding chapter.

In preparing this edition, I have incurred a number of debts. Craig Beaumont, Peter Just, and Ben Pearson have assisted in researching data. Anita Castro at Addison Wesley Longman has combined persistence and enthusiasm in ensuring that the text was delivered. I am also grateful to various readers who reviewed some of the manuscript for this edition and made some extremely helpful comments: Adrian Clark at James Madison University; Lewis John at Washington and Lee University; Gerard Rutan at Western Washington University; Andreas Sobisch at John Carroll University; Gordon Tolle at South Dakota State University; and Sondra Zeff at SUNY Binghamton.

Since the third edition, exchange rates have fluctuated. They have also fluctuated during the period that the manuscript was being written. In this edition, dollar equivalents are calculated on an exchange rate of £1 = $1.60.

A number of changes have been made in succeeding editions as a result of comments from readers. I am again happy to invite comments; those from colleagues and readers have been extremely helpful. I alone, though, am responsible for any errors, omissions, or misinterpretations that remain.

Philip Norton

About the Author

Philip Norton (Lord Norton of Louth) is professor of government and director of the Centre for Legislative Studies at the University of Hull. He became a full professor in 1986 at the age of 35—making him, at the time, the youngest professor of politics in the United Kingdom. He was elevated to the peerage, as Lord Norton of Louth, in 1998 at the age of 47.

He is the author or editor of more than 20 books. He is president of the Politics Association in the United Kingdom. He is also vice president of the Political Studies Association, editor of *The Journal of Legislative Studies,* and cochair of the Research Committee of Legislative Specialists of the International Political Science Association. In 1999 he was appointed to chair the Conservative Party Commission to Strengthen Parliament, which reported in July 2000. He is a former president of the British Politics Group in the United States.

Professor Lord Norton divides his time between teaching at the University of Hull and serving in the House of Lords.

Useful Internet Sites

The following is a selection of web sites that provide useful material. Readers should bear in mind that web sites may not always remain active or retain the same address.

PART II: THE POLITICAL ENVIRONMENT

Constitution:

www.charter88.org.uk

   Charter88 constitutional reform movement

www.ucl.ac.uk/constitution-unit

   Constitution Unit. Academic research organization that produces material on constitutional change.

Political parties:

www.conservative-party.org.uk

   Conservative party

www.labour.org.uk

   Labour party

www.libdems.org.uk

   Liberal Democratic party

www.snp.org.uk

> Scottish National party

www.plaid-cymru.wales.com

> Plaid Cymru party

www.uup.org

> Ulster Unionist party

www.dup.org.uk

> Democratic Unionist party

www.indigo.ie/sdlp

> Social Democratic and Labour party (SDLP)

www.sinfein.ie/index.html

> Sinn Fein

Organized interests:

www.cbi.org.uk

> Confederation of British Industry

www.nfu.org.uk

> National Farmers' Union

www.tuc.org.uk

> Trades Union Congress (TUC)

www.foe.co.uk

> Friends of the Earth

PART III: GOVERNMENTAL DECISION MAKING

www.number-10.gov.uk

> No. 10 Downing Street. Has a mass of material.

www.cabinet-office.gov.uk

> Cabinet Office. Includes data on the civil service.

www.open.gov.uk

> Contains links to all government departments as well as to much of local government.

www.open.gov.uk/lcd/index.htm

> Lord Chancellor's Department

www.gnet.goc.uk/lawcomm/homepage/htm

> Law Commission. Makes recommendations on changes in the law.

www.europa.eu.it

> Most useful site to access information on the European Union

www.nio.gov.uk

> Northern Ireland Office

www.scotland.gov.uk

> The Scottish Executive

www.scottish.parliament.uk

www.wales.org.uk

www.ni-assembly.gov.uk

> Web sites of the devolved assemblies

www.local.detr.gov.uk

> Department of the Environment's guide to local government finance

www.loc.gov.uk

> Local Government Association

PART IV: SCRUTINY AND LEGITIMATION

www.parliament.uk

> Web site of the Houses of Parliament. Contains debates of both Houses as well as texts of bills, amendments, committee reports, and other valuable data

www.lords-reform.org.uk

> Web site of the Royal Commission on the Reform of the House of Lords

www.hmso.gov.uk/acts.htm

> Texts of Acts of Parliament

Royal family:

www.royal.gov.uk

> The royal family. The site attracts a large number of "hits."

www.princeofwales.gov.uk

> The Prince of Wales

www.monarchy.net

> The Constitutional Monarchy Association

www.republic.org.uk

> Web site of Republic

PART V: ENFORCEMENT AND FEEDBACK

www.dhcour.coe.fr

> European Court of Human Rights

www.cps.gov.uk

> Crown Prosecution Service

www.mediauk.com

> Provides links to newspapers and other media in the United Kingdom

www.ananova.com

> Formerly PA News Centre, covers breaking news stories in the United Kingdom

Part I

Introduction

Chapter 1

The Contemporary Landscape

Continuity and change are features of every political system. What makes each system significant is the nature and the extent of that change. Some systems are characterized by rapid and sometimes revolutionary change. Others are noted for continuity with past experience and structures. The task of the student of politics is to discern the distinctive features of that continuity and change; to generate concepts; and, if possible, to construct models and theories that will aid understanding of and serve to explain those distinctive features and the relationship among them.

The distinctive features of a political system can be recognized by comparing that system with another or, better still, with many others. In discussing the merits of comparative politics, a student in a class of mine once objected to the whole exercise. "There's no point in comparing one country with another," he argued. "Every country is unique." As others in the class were quick to respond, the only way by which one knows that a country is unique is by comparing it with others. Just as one can know whether one is short or tall only by comparing oneself with others, so one can know whether one's own political system is "short" or "tall" only by putting it alongside other systems and noting the differences.

Space and resources preclude an exhaustive or even an extensive comparative study in this work. Instead, I will illustrate the distinctive nature of the British polity by comparing it, where appropriate, with the American. They are similar in many respects, with a shared language; advanced industrial economies; similar but not always identical political, social, and economic values; and some mutual needs. Each has a sense of affinity with the other. As we shall see, however, there are significant dissimilarities, which make a comparative exercise useful. Such an exercise will serve not only to sensitize the American reader to the distinctive features of the British polity, but also to make readers more aware of the features of their own polity. That, at least, is the hope.

To help the reader understand continuity and change within the British polity, I will stress the significance of the political culture. This emphasis will form the basis of the next chapter as well as the book's conclusion. Before we proceed to an analysis of that culture, a brief sketch of the salient features of contemporary Britain is necessary. This outline is especially pertinent for comparative purposes. There are important dissimilarities between the United States and Britain in terms of geography, demography, and social history. Britain is a small, crowded island, largely oriented in terms of industry and population to England (and especially the southeast of England), with a class-based society that has superseded, but by no means discarded altogether the characteristics of, a feudal society. The purpose of this chapter is to highlight those features. Such a study is a prerequisite for a consideration of the political culture and the institutions and processes that culture nurtures.

LAND AND POPULATION

From the perspective of land distribution and usage, Great Britain could be described as a predominantly agricultural kingdom, based on the three countries of England, Scotland, and Wales. (The United Kingdom comprises these three countries plus Northern Ireland: See Map 1.1.) In terms of the distribution and activities of the population, it is predominantly English, nonagricultural, and town- or suburban-based.

Great Britain occupies a total area of 88,798 square miles. This compares with an area of 3,615,123 square miles for the United States. Within the United States, ten states each have a greater land area than Britain. Alaska (586,412 square miles), Texas (267,339), and California (158,693) are the most notable. England has approximately the same land area as New York State, Scotland the same as South Carolina, and Wales the same as Massachusetts.

The disparity in population size is also substantial, though not quite so extreme. In 1998 the U.K. population was 59.2 million, up from 38.2 million at the turn of the century. The U.S. population in 1998 was 270.6 million, up from 76 million in 1900 (see Table 1.1). There is also a significant difference in population growth. Between 1970 and 1998, the United Kingdom population increased by just over 6 percent. In the same time period the United States population increased by a little under 30 percent. A continuation of a slow United Kingdom growth rate is also anticipated, with the population projected to be 61.5 million in 2025. The projection for the United States is 331 million by 2025. In terms of growth rates, Britain is a typical West European country. The United States is closer to growth rates of Asia.

When the population is put in the context of land size, Britain emerges as a crowded island. The number of people per square mile in 1997 was just under 660 (or just over 240 per square kilometer). By European standards, this is high but not exceptional: The Netherlands, Belgium, and Germany are even more densely populated. The number of people per square mile in the United States in 1997 was just over 7. By worldwide standards, this is a low but not exceptional

MAP 1.1   The United Kingdom

TABLE 1.1 United Kingdom and United States populations, 1900–1998

Year	U.K. Population (millions)	U.S. Population (millions)
1900	38.2	75.9
1910	42.1	92.0
1920	44.0	105.7
1930	46.1	122.8
1940	48.3	131.7
1950	50.6	150.7
1960	53.0	179.3
1970	55.7	203.3
1980	56.0	226.5
1990	57.4	248.7
1998	59.2	270.6

SOURCE: *Statistical Abstracts of the United States*, 19th ed. (Hoover Business Press, 1999), *Social Trends* (National Statistics); *Population Trends* (National Statistics).

figure. Russia, Brazil, New Zealand, Australia, and Canada are among the nations with lower population density.

Within the United Kingdom, the population is heavily concentrated in one country. In 1997, 49.3 million people lived in England, compared with a little over 5 million in Scotland, 2.9 million in Wales, and 1.7 million in Northern Ireland. The number of people per square kilometer in England in 1997 was 376—the highest population density of any European country and greater even than that of Japan. Within England, the greatest concentration of inhabitants is in the southeast of the country (that is, Greater London and the surrounding counties); just under one-third of the population of the United Kingdom resides there.

The population resides predominantly in areas classified, for local government purposes, as urban. Over 80 percent of the population in England, and more than 70 percent in Scotland and Wales, live in urban areas. Just over half the population lives in 66 urban areas with populations in excess of 100,000 people. The largest concentration in urban areas is shown in Table 1.2. The shift from rural to urban areas has been marked in England, the proportion of the population living in nonurban areas declining from a little over 35 percent in 1951 to not much more than 20 percent twenty years later.

Although approximately three-quarters of the land surface is used for agriculture, very few people are employed in the agricultural industry. There has been a persistent drift from land work since industrialization in the eighteenth and nineteenth centuries, a trend that continues. More than 700,000 people were employed in agriculture, forestry, and fishing in 1961. By 1990, the figure was below 300,000 and continues to decline. Increased efficiency and greater mechanization have in part facilitated this development. (Britain has one of the heaviest tractor densities in the world.) There are more than 250,000 farm holdings in Britain, with three-fifths of the full-time farms being devoted mainly to dairying or beef cattle and sheep. Farms devoted to arable crops are predominant in the eastern

TABLE 1.2   Urban concentration in the United Kingdom, 1991

Area	Population (thousands)
Greater London	7,651
West Midlands[1]	2,296
Greater Manchester	2,277
West Yorkshire[2]	1,446
Tyneside[3]	886
Liverpool	838
Glasgow	663
Sheffield	633
Nottingham	614
Bristol	523

[1] Includes Birmingham, the nation's second largest city
[2] Includes Leeds and Bradford
[3] Includes Newcastle upon Tyne
SOURCE: *Social Trends 29* (National Statistics, 1999), p. 32.

part of England. Sheep and cattle rearing is a feature of the hills and moorland areas of Scotland, Wales, and northern and southwestern England.

Although Britain exports agrochemicals, agricultural equipment, and some agricultural produce and food products, it nonetheless has to import a substantial portion of its food supply.[1] Indeed, Britain is heavily dependent on imports of raw materials. Compared with other large industrialized (and some developing) nations, Britain is notably lacking in natural resources. The exception is energy resources: It is a major world producer of oil and natural gas. However, it is largely dependent on other nations either wholly or in part for products such as cotton, rubber, lead, tin, phosphates, rice, corn, silk, coffee, and tobacco. The list is by no means exhaustive. The United States, by contrast, is self-sufficient in most of these products, with surplus supply in several cases. Among other things, the United States is the world's largest producer, and consumer, of lead. France, Germany, Canada, Japan, and India also are more self-sufficient than Britain. This lack of raw materials is important not only for an understanding of contemporary Britain but also in providing a partial explanation of Britain's internationalist and imperialist history.

LINGUISTIC AND RACIAL DIFFERENCES

The population is predominantly English in birth as well as residence. It also is predominantly white and English-speaking. It is not, however, totally homogeneous. Not only is there a division in Britain between the English, the Scots, and the Welsh; there is also a division in Scotland between those who do and do not speak Gaelic, and in Wales between those who do and do not speak Welsh. In both cases, those who speak the traditional native languages are in a small minority. In Wales, only about one in five inhabitants can speak Welsh. Only about 80,000 Scots are believed to speak the indigenous Scots Gaelic, most of them concentrated in the Scottish highlands and islands. Looking beyond Britain to Northern Ireland, a few families in the province still speak the Irish form of Gaelic. However, as we shall see in Chapter 10, the absence of homogeneity in the province extends far beyond linguistic differences.

The influx of immigrants into Britain, especially in the 1950s and early 1960s (numbers have been limited since the passage of the Commonwealth Immigrants Act of 1962), also has added to the diversity of the population and to linguistic differences. Immigration has resulted in a significant increase in the number of nonwhite citizens, though they constitute a small proportion of the population. The number of nonwhite people in Britain is now just over 3.3 million—up from more than 1 million in 1968—with the largest single nonwhite community being the Indian (see Table 1.3). Of the ethnic minority population, just over half is U.K.-born. The nonwhite community constitutes 6 percent of the total household population. It is, though, relatively heavily concentrated—a factor often claimed to exacerbate racial tension—in a number of urban areas, notably London, Leicester, Birmingham, Bradford, and various towns in the West Midlands and Yorkshire.

The United States has experienced analogous problems of concentration but has a much larger nonwhite population, African Americans accounting for more than 12 percent of the population. (There are also more than 7 million other nonwhite Americans.) There is also another significant difference. The African American population is as indigenous as the white. (Native Americans now account for well under 1 percent of the population.) As such, it is unusual for a black American to be asked, "Where do you come from?"—meaning, "What is your country of origin?"—whereas such a question is often asked of nonwhite Britons. The United States also has a far greater ethnic mix than the United Kingdom. The combined noun is common in discussions of that mix (German Americans, Polish Americans); there is no equivalent use in the United Kingdom.

TABLE 1.3 Minority ethnic groups, 1996

Ethnic Group	Estimated Population (thousands)
Black Caribbean	477
Black African	281
Other Black	117
Indian	877
Pakistani	579
Bangladeshi	183
Chinese	126
Other Asian	161
Other ethnic minorities	506
Total:	3,307

SOURCE: *Social Trends 27* (National Statistics, 1997), p. 31.

RELIGION

Britain, like the United States, is a predominantly Protestant country. There the similarity largely ends. Britain has an established church, the United States does not. There is no separation of church and state in the United Kingdom. Religious assemblies are held in schools, mangers are displayed on public land at Christmas, and various official occasions—such as the enthronement of a new monarch—are held in church. Disputes over prayers in school occur but are unrelated to the principle of whether or not prayers should be held: The dispute is over whether they have to be predominantly Christian. (Some schools have a majority of non-Christian pupils.) Such a link between church and state says little, however, about religious dedication. Few Britons are regular church-goers; according to a 1997 survey, only 10 percent of men and 15 percent of women attend a place of worship once a week or more; almost two-thirds (63 percent) of men never or practically never attend. (The proportion of women was 48 percent.)[2] In a 1995 Gallup poll, over half of those questioned (54 percent) said religion was "not very important" in their life.[3] In the United States, church attendance is widely practiced. "Less than a tenth of the English people are zealous Christians. . . . Between 40 percent and 50 percent of Americans are in church on a typical Sunday. Nearly two-thirds of Americans say a strong religious commitment is 'absolutely essential' or 'very important.'"[4]

The Anglican Church of England is "by law established" the official church in England. (The Presbyterian Church of Scotland is the established church there.) As such, it is variously involved in the affairs of state. The monarch is the supreme governor (temporal head) of the church, and archbishops, bishops, and deans are appointed by the queen on the advice of the prime minister. The coronation of a new monarch is conducted by the senior churchman in the Anglican faith (the archbishop of Canterbury), and services of national celebration, or grief, are conducted in one of the principal Anglican churches, usually Westminster Abbey or St. Paul's Cathedral in London. The monarch is required by statute to be a member of the Church of England and must promise to uphold the faith. The senior figures in the church—two archbishops and 24 bishops—sit in the House of Lords. Various measures affecting the governing principles of the church require parliamentary approval.

A broad Protestant church, the Church of England was founded by King Henry VIII in the sixteenth century following his break with the Roman Catholic church.[5] It comprises two provinces: Canterbury, headed by the archbishop of Canterbury (titled primate of all England), with 30 dioceses, and York, headed by the archbishop of York (primate of England), with 14 dioceses. Within the dioceses, there are more than 13,000 parishes. Though just over half of the population claim to be Anglicans, fewer than 2 million are actually members of the church. The membership is lower than that of the Roman Catholic church and—in common with most, though not all, Christian churches—is declining (Table 1.4). It is set to decline further. In recent years the church has faced a schism on the issue of women priests. In 1992, the General Synod (the central governing body, comprising bishops, clergy and

TABLE 1.4   Church membership in the United Kingdom, 1970–1995

	Membership (millions)	
	1970	**1995**
Trinitarian Churches		
Church of England	3.0	1.8
Presbyterian	1.8	1.1
Methodist	0.7	0.4
Baptist	0.3	0.2
Other Protestant churches	0.5	0.6
Roman Catholic	2.7	1.9
Orthodox	0.2	0.3
Total	9.2	6.4*
Nontrinitarian Churches		
Mormons	0.1	0.2
Jehovah's Witnesses	0.1	0.1
Other nontrinitarian	0.1	0.2
Total	0.3	0.5
Other Religions		
Muslims	0.1	0.6
Sikhs	0.1	0.4
Hindus	0.1	0.2
Jews	0.1	0.1
Others	0.0	0.1
Total	0.4	1.3*

* Totals rounded
SOURCE: *Social Trends 29* (National Statistics, 1999), p. 220.

lay members) voted to admit women to the priesthood, a move bitterly opposed by traditionalists, some of whom—clergy included—left the church. A further split took place over the issue of whether known homosexuals could be ordained.

The Roman Catholic church, the "out" and often legally-discriminated-against church for most of the period since the Reformation in the sixteenth century, now enjoys the same freedoms as other religions. It is divided into seven provinces in Britain, each headed by an archbishop; the premier archbishop is the archbishop of Westminster. There are 30 episcopal dioceses, and 6 more in Northern Ireland. The church places particular emphasis on religious education as well as devotion, though the proportion of church members who attend services on a typical Sunday is not much different from the proportion of Anglican church members. As with the Church of England, membership is declining, as is regular attendance at church.

Membership of other trinitarian churches (those believing in the union of the Holy Trinity under one Godhead) also has fallen in recent years. Increases have come in membership of the nontrinitarian churches and, more significantly, in the Sikh and Muslim religions. Both the Jewish and Muslim faiths are large communities by European standards. The Jewish community in Britain—about 400,000, with about one-quarter constituting adult members of the faith—is the second largest in Europe. Most are Orthodox Jews, with about 20 percent being members of the Reform or Liberal and Progressive movements. There are about three hundred Jewish congregations in the country. Muslims are served by over a thousand mosques and prayer centers. The Islamic Cultural Center (and London Central Mosque) on the edge of London's Regent's Park constitutes the most important Muslim institution in the Western world.

Though religion remains politically and socially central to the life of Northern Ireland, its importance in Britain has declined throughout the twentieth century. In significance, it has been displaced by class.

CLASS

The United States does not have a feudal history. The significance of this fact was well described by Louis Hartz in his incisive work on the Lockean basis of U.S. society.[6] Britain, by contrast, does have a feudal past. Furthermore, unlike some of its European neighbors, it has witnessed no revolutionary break with past experience. As a result, the class patterns of a capitalist society have been superimposed on the hierarchical social structure of a departing feudal society.

Status derives from the tendency of people to accord positive and negative values to human attributes and to distribute respect accordingly. In feudal society, a superior status was accorded to the landowning aristocracy and gentry. They were deemed to have breeding and to be the best people to govern the land. They were deferred to as a socially superior body. It was a status that was passed on by inheritance, not one that could be acquired by merit or work.

Whereas status is essentially the product of a social system, class is the product of the economic.[7] Defining the concept of class is not an easy task. Marx distinguished two classes, bourgeois and proletarian, based on the ownership of the means of production. This is not a particularly useful definition, given the significant distinction between ownership and control.

The problem is compounded by the fact that there is a difference between attempts at objective measurement and subjective self-assessment. In other words, how social scientists measure class—and there are an increasing number of measures used—and how others perceive it (particularly in terms of self-ascription) often are far from congruent. Though there are now several definitions of class, the most used is that of groups formed on the basis of occupational difference.

Britain has generally been seen as having two classes, the middle and the working; as A. H. Halsey has observed, it is a characteristically British distinction.[8] Within each of the two classes, there are further divisions. Table 1.5 provides a simple delineation of them.

Class grew out of industrialization and the development of a capitalist economy. It did not displace status; it usurped it. In the nineteenth century, the upper

TABLE 1.5 Social classes in Britain

Class	Market Research Designation	Encompassing
Middle class		
Upper-middle	A	Higher managerial and professional
Middle	B	Lower managerial and administrative
Lower-middle	C1	Skilled or supervisory nonmanual, lower nonmanual
Working class		
Upper-working	C2	Skilled manual
Working	D	Unskilled manual
	E	Residual, pensioners

class comprised the traditional landed aristocracy, but it was an aristocracy that had absorbed largely, if not wholly, the new men of wealth who had made their money from trade and industry. These new men were drawn into this class until, eventually, they overwhelmed it.[9]

This combination of class and status was carried into the twentieth century. In recent decades, however, it has been weakened. Some of the features of a status society, such as peerages, can be passed from father to son: The inheritance is founded in law. Class can be inherited but it is an inheritance based on the market, which is less predictable than the law. Recent years have witnessed a growing social mobility. The children of many working-class parents have been upwardly mobile socially. The children of some middle-class parents have taken up working-class occupations. Writes Halsey, "Men and women, moving and marrying between different occupational levels, both over the generations and also within their own working lives or careers, have become an increasingly common feature of British social life in the past half century."[10]

The general pattern of change has been one of upward mobility. Greater mobility and affluence have eroded the claims to status. Mobility deprives one of claims to breeding. Acceptance of the principle of meritocracy is discordant with claims of inherited worth. Status remains important but it is no longer the central feature of British society that it was in preceding centuries.

The importance of class was highlighted by the survey conducted three decades ago by Butler and Stokes. They asked respondents to name the main social classes and the class to which they would ascribe themselves. They found that "virtually everyone accepted the conventional class dichotomy between middle and working class"[11] with 77 percent spontaneously ascribing themselves to one or the other. Though increased social mobility and changes in the occupational profile of the nation appear to have reduced the significance (or, perhaps more accurately, the measurability) of class, most citizens continue to consider themselves members of a particular class. Surveys in 1987 and 1989 found only 3 percent of respondents giving a "don't know" answer when asked to identify the social class they belonged to,[12] and, as in the Butler and Stokes survey of twenty years before, most identified themselves with the class of their parents (Table

1.6). Insofar as there is a difference between the class of self and parents, the figures in Table 1.6 reinforce the thesis of upward mobility.

Awareness of class also remains a feature of contemporary society. Indeed, recent survey data suggest that, if anything, that awareness is increasing, not diminishing. In a 1981 Gallup poll, 66 percent of those questioned thought that there was a "class struggle" taking place in Britain. In 1986 the portion giving that answer was 70 percent. In 1995 it had increased to 81 percent.[13] Another Gallup poll at the end of 1996 found that 72 percent of respondents thought that people were "very" or "quite" aware of social differences in Britain today—compared to 63 percent giving those responses in 1982—and 93 percent thought that a person's social class affected to some degree "their opportunities in Britain today" (Table 1.7), compared to 86 percent expressing that view in 1982.[14] Only 4 percent of respondents in 1996 said that social class did not affect a person's opportunities.

Class remains important in Britain. The contours of class have changed as occupational opportunities have changed. A report commissioned by the Office of National Statistics and published in 1997 recommended that the number of occupational groups—identified in Table 1.5—be expanded from five to eight. The intention was to recognize an "underclass" of people who had never worked or were long-term unemployed, as well as to create a new category for the self-employed. According to the leader of the review, "John Major [prime minister 1990–97] liked to talk about a classless society, but if anything occupational class has become more significant as we learn to live with the flexible labor market."[15] The different categories still relate to the broad distinction between middle and working class, the first five of the eight new proposed categories comprising professional, associate professional, intermediate (essentially other white-collar occupations), the self-employed, and "other supervisors," and the other three, those engaged in routine manual work (e.g., assembly line worker), elementary occupations (e.g., fast-food waiter) and those with no work at all.

Though measured principally in terms of occupation, class also connotes significant differences in lifestyles.[16] A whole range of interests and pursuits is associated with each particular class. The middle class, bolstered traditionally by higher incomes, have been able to afford their own homes—usually semi-detached or

TABLE 1.6   Social class by self-ascription, 1989

If you had to make a choice, would you call yourself middle class or working class?

	Self (%)	Parents (%)
Middle class	30	21
Working class	67	75
Don't know	3	4

SOURCE: E. Jacobs and R. Worcester, *We British* (Weidenfeld & Nicolson, 1990), pp. 138–139.

TABLE 1.7   Impact of social class, 1982–1996

To what extent do you think a person's social class affects his or her opportunities in Britain today—a lot, a little, or not at all?

	April 1982 (%)	December 1996 (%)
A lot	51	60
A little	35	33
Not at all	10	4
Don't know	4	4

Totals may exceed 100% due to rounding.
SOURCE: *Gallup Political and Economic Index*, January 1997, p. 26.

detached houses—and to take holidays in exotic climes. They have encouraged children to do well educationally and to go to university. They have pursued a range of leisure interests such as golf, tennis, squash, and skiing. They belong to country clubs and chambers of commerce. They are more likely than working-class families to be theater-goers and to be joiners of civic organizations and pressure groups. Working-class families traditionally have lived in often rented row houses; taken holidays—when they can afford them—at seaside resorts in the United Kingdom and, more recently, in Spain and the Mediterrean islands; been less able to provide a supportive environment for children to pursue education to degree level; and been more likely than the middle class to pursue interests such as football and snooker and more inclined to spend more time drinking in the local public house, or "pub." These are crude generalizations, but they point to the very real differences of lifestyles that are essentially ingrained and that often remain unaffected by significant changes in income.

The importance of class is political as well as social. For most of the twentieth century, there has been a significant relationship between class and politics. The Labour party has attracted largely but not wholly the support of the working class, and the Conservative party that of the middle class. The significance of the class–party nexus will be explored in more detail later. There is recent evidence of a decline in class identification and in the correlation between class and party. Such decline, though, has been relative. Class remains a feature of British society. Most Britons continue to ascribe themselves to a particular class. Politicians still employ the concept of class (if only now to decry it) and sociologists would be lost without it.

EDUCATION

Education in Britain is best seen in pyramidal terms. All children receive a primary and secondary school education. Thereafter, only a minority proceed to institutions of higher education. For children receiving education at private schools, the structure is less pyramidal: A greater proportion of those educated at private schools proceed to university than those attending state schools. After entering primary school at the age of 5, children in England receive a common education until the age of 11, when they enter secondary schools. In the two decades following the passage of the 1944 Education Act, secondary schools were divided into grammar and secondary modern schools. The former were essentially academic institutions, oriented to scholastic skills, with a large proportion of pupils achieving university entrance. The latter taught more practical skills, some pupils going on to a technical college and a very few achieving admission to university. Selection for entry to grammar schools was made by examination taken at age 11. Labour politicians came to view the bifurcation of grammar and secondary modern schools as socially divisive, with those attending secondary modern schools being unable to shake off the perception of being failures and unable to achieve the occupational opportunities of grammar school pupils. Following the return of a Labour government in 1964, a new scheme of education was introduced, with selection and the dual school system being replaced by a nonselective, all-encompassing system of comprehensive education. Comprehensive schools were introduced over the next twenty years, under both Conservative and Labour governments. In 1971, 38 percent of secondary schoolchildren in England attended comprehensive schools; by 1990, the proportion had reached 92 percent. In Wales and Scotland, it was 99 percent and 100 percent, respectively.

From the mid-1980s onward, Conservative governments introduced other changes, largely designed to ensure that basic subjects were not ignored and that parents had a greater influence over their children's schools. The reforms included the introduction of a national curriculum, with three core subjects (English, science, and mathematics) and seven foundation subjects (history, geography, technology, art, physical education, music, and a modern foreign language), each with attainment targets and assessment arrangements. Greater powers were also given to school governors. Funding remained publicly provided, but school governing bodies were given power to determine the spending priorities for most of their budget. Also, a school could seek to take full control of its own budget and admissions policy through opting out of the existing framework of control. Many of these changes—especially the power for schools to opt out—proved contentious, the Conservatives seeing them as means of raising educational standards and critics claiming they were attempts to restore some of the features of the system that existed in the 1950s. When a new Labour government was elected in 1997, some changes were made to the status of those schools that had opted out, but otherwise most of the changes introduced in recent years were kept in place.

Although secondary education is compulsory, parents are not required to send their children to state schools but can choose instead to send them to private schools. Private schools tend to stress academic achievement and concentrate on developing the ability to pass examinations and on building self-confidence. Believing that their children will receive a better and more disciplined education, with a greater prospect of university entry than from a state school, many parents who can afford it send their children to such private institutions, known (confusingly) as "public schools." Fees at such schools vary. The more prestigious, such as Eton, Harrow, and Winchester, can afford to charge annual fees in excess of £14,000 ($22,400),[17] whereas some less-prestigious day schools may charge less than £4,000 ($6,400). About 7 percent of children attend private schools, though more than one-quarter of entrants to the older universities are drawn from such schools.

From secondary school, students may proceed to institutions of further and higher education. *Further education* allows students to pursue especially work-related or vocational courses, or to study for qualifications not already gained in secondary school. Of students who proceed to study beyond secondary school, most do so in colleges of further education. *Higher education* comprises primarily the university sector. Recent years have seen both a change in the structure of higher education and an increase in the proportion of those going on to study beyond secondary school. Until 1992, institutions of higher education were divided into universities and polytechnics. The former were more academic, whereas the latter—first established in 1967—were more vocationally oriented, often providing "sandwich" courses (part study, part practical job experience) for their students. In 1992, the formal dividing line, known as the binary line, between universities and polytechnics was abolished, allowing polytechnics to acquire university titles, and a common funding agency was established. Even with the addition of the polytechnics to the ranks of the universities, the number of universities remains small by U.S. standards: just under a hundred.

The sector of higher education, though, is growing. At the turn of the century, England had only seven universities, Scotland had four, and Wales had one. Relatively few were founded in the first few decades of the century. Recent decades have seen a significant expansion. Of the 46 universities that existed before 1992, 28 were founded after 1945. As we have seen, polytechnics were first created in 1967. By the time the binary line was abolished, there were 30. (The 1960s also saw the creation of the "open university," a nonresidential university requiring no formal academic qualifications for admission and offering tuition by correspondence and through special radio and television programs.) By comparison with the United States, the number studying beyond secondary school is small. Though a majority of 18-year-olds are now in some form of further education or training, only a minority go to university. By comparison with the past, though, the figure has grown rapidly. The expansion in recent years has been marked, especially in higher education. At the end of the 1980s, 1 in 6 young people went on to higher education. By 1996, the figure was 1 in 3.

Within universities there is something of a hierarchy. The oldest universities, led by Oxford and Cambridge, have traditionally been viewed as the most prestigious, and again there is a social element to the prestige. Students from leading private schools will try to get a place at Oxford or Cambridge (commonly described collectively as "Oxbridge"), as will the more academically gifted pupils from state schools. Universities founded in the nineteenth century and first half of the twentieth are commonly referred to as "redbrick" universities (after the color of the brickwork), and universities founded in the latter half of the century are frequently dubbed "new universities." The new universities are

TABLE 1.8   Participation rates in higher education by social class

	%		
	1991–92	**1994–95**	**1997–98**
Professional	55	78	80
Intermediate	36	45	49
Skilled nonmanual	22	31	32
Skilled manual	11	18	19
Partly skilled	12	17	18
Unskilled	6	11	14

The number of home domiciled entrants aged under 21 to full-time undergraduate courses expressed as a proportion of the averaged 18- to 19-year-old population.
SOURCE: *Social Trends 29* (National Statistics, 1999), p. 61.

distinguished from the former polytechnics that have achieved university status, the latter being referred to by various names, the most common simply being "the ex-polys." This hierachy has its parallel in the United States, the Ivy League universities constituting the equivalent of Oxbridge, though the United Kingdom lacks the significant divide that exists in the United States between private and state universities.

A university education continues to provide occupational advantage. More than 80 percent of graduates have ended up in the professional and managerial classes. They constitute fewer than one-third of those in these classes, but—as Table 1.8 shows—it is these classes that will provide proportionally more children than any other for university entry. The likelihood that a person will go to university, especially the older (nonpolytechnic) universities, remains strongly linked to social class. "Roughly speaking, the lower the socioeconomic group of someone's father, the more likely it is that his or her full-time education ended in school, rather than college or university."[18]

MARRIAGE AND FAMILY

Although much emphasis is placed on the individual, the family is still the most important social unit in Britain. There remains strong attachment to the ideal of marriage and having children. Despite a high divorce rate, marriage—and remarriage—remains popular. As Jowell, Witherspoon, and Brook have noted in their survey of British social attitudes, "In their attitude towards marriage and other family matters, the British emerge as highly and consistently conventional."[19]

Nonetheless, there have been important changes in recent years. There has been some variation in the number of people getting married and in the number getting divorced. The number of marriages has declined consistently and markedly in the past three decades. There were 400,000 first marriages in 1970. In 1995 the number was 192,000. Even so, Britain still has the third-highest marriage rate in the European Union, after Denmark and Portugal. Divorce rates, expressed as a proportion of the married population, more than doubled in the period from 1971 to

1991 (rising from 5.9 per 1,000 married population in 1971 to just over 13.5 per 1,000 in 1991), but then saw a small decline (to just over 13 per 1,000 married population in 1995). Despite the slight dip in the divorce rate in the 1990s, the United Kingdom has the highest divorce rate in the European Union. Even so, the divorce rate in the United Kingdom remains well below that of the United States.[20]

Households also have been getting smaller. In 1971, 18 percent of households in Britain comprised one person, and 35 percent of households comprised a couple with dependent children. The same percentage comprised couples with no children or nondependent children. By 1995–96, the percentage of one-person households had increased to 28 percent. The percentage of households comprising couples with dependent children had fallen to 23 percent. In 1961, the average household size was 3.1 people. By 1971, the number had fallen to 2.9 and by 1995–96 it was 2.4.[21]

The decrease in the number of families with children reflects a fall in the birthrate, a feature common to all EU countries. The increase in the number of one-person households is in part explicable by the increase in the size of the elderly population. In 1971, 12 percent of households comprised one person of pensionable age, compared with 6 percent under pensionable age. By 1995–96, the largest number of one-person households was still accounted for by people of pensionable age, but the gap was not so great: 15 percent of households comprised one person of pensionable age but 13 percent comprised an individual under pensionable age.[22] The largest increase in the period was of men under pensionable age.

There also has been a change within the nature of family groupings, recent years seeing a marked increase in the number of unmarried couples living together. In 1984, one in ten births registered were of children born to unmarried couples. By 1996–97, the proportion had increased to one in three.[23]

Within these trends, there also are some variations correlated to region and class. In terms of births outside marriage, the percentage is greater in the northern regions of England (north, northwest, Yorkshire) than in southern regions. There is some correlation between household size and socioeconomic grouping. In 1989–90, one in three households headed by someone in the professions or management had a child age 15 or under. For those headed by semi-skilled or unskilled workers, the proportion was one in four.[24]

The traditional attachment to marriage remains a feature of British society, even if a substantial proportion of those marriages fail. The attachment to creating a family unit appears even stronger, with the number of couples cohabiting increasing. In 1996–97, there was the first fall in thirty years in the number of families headed by a single parent.

EMPLOYMENT

Britain was the first major nation to experience industrialization. Most of the population in the nineteenth century moved from the land to find jobs in manufacturing industries in the towns and cities. The north of England in particular witnessed the growth of major industrial conurbations. "Mill towns" became common features. So, too, did mining communities. Most of the economically active population came to be employed in primary industries and manufacturing. In the twentieth century, especially in the period since 1945, more and more workers have moved into service industries. In 1955, 42 percent of those in employment had jobs in manufacturing. By 1997, the figure was 17 percent.

The growth of service industries has been particularly marked in London and the southeast, where almost 75 percent of employees are now in the service sector. There has been a corresponding decline in employment in manufacturing, especially in the north. The closure of local factories, mills, and coal mines has been met in some cases by diversification and attracting new firms, but otherwise by migration and higher levels of unemployment than elsewhere. Today, Britain can be described as having a predominantly service economy (Table 1.9) with the southeast of England enjoying a preeminent position in that economy. That preeminence is now consolidated by British membership in the European Union and the increased trade with EU countries. The southeast of England forms part of a "golden triangle" within the Union, with access to the continent not enjoyed by more distant parts of the United Kingdom.

Within employment, recent years have seen a growth in the number of female workers and in the number of self-employed. In all categories other than service industries, male employees outnumber females. The extractive industries have been traditionally male preserves. In the service industries, more than half the workers are women. There have also been some significant changes in the type of employment on offer. Part-time jobs are now a significant feature of the British economy. In 1997, 25 percent of those in employment worked part-time. This type of employment is marked among female employees: Almost half of the females in employment in 1996 worked part-time, compared to less than 10 percent of males in employment.[25] Part-time employment is marked in certain sectors, most notably distribution. Self-employment is highest in craft and related industries (accounting for 28 percent of those in the sector), followed by managers and administrators (24 percent).[26] The self-employed also constitute one of the categories most vulnerable to recessions in economic

TABLE 1.9 Employment by main sector, 1991–1997

	Number in Employment (thousands) % in parentheses	
	1991	**1997**
Service industries	16,199 (74.0)	17,263 (75.7)
Manufacturing industries	4,096 (18.7)	4,111 (18.0)
Mining, energy, and water supply	344 (1.6)	251 (1.1)
Other industries	1,265 (5.8)	1,166 (5.1)

SOURCE: *Britain 1998: An Official Handbook* (National Statistics, 1998), p. 171.

performance. The early 1990s witnessed a record number of businesses, particularly among the self-employed, go bankrupt.

Unemployment increased in the early 1980s—producing the worst unemployment figures of the seven major countries of the Organisation for Economic Cooperation and Development (OECD)—and peaked in 1986, when just over 3 million people—11 percent of the work force—were out of work. With economic recovery, unemployment rates fell and were below 6 percent by 1990. Recession then pushed the numbers up again and they reached a peak in 1993; since then the figures have fallen. In August 1996, claimant unemployment totalled 2.1 million, 7.5 percent of the workforce. Within the United Kingdom, the highest unemployment rate remains that of Northern Ireland, where the percentage of people unemployed is consistently well above 10 percent. In 1992 the figure stood at 14 percent and in 1996 at 11.3 percent. Most West European countries now have higher rates of unemployment than the United Kingdom.

PERSONAL WEALTH AND TAXATION

As we have seen, the country has witnessed some notable shifts in social behavior as well as in patterns of employment. There has been less significant change in the distribution of wealth.

The distribution of marketable wealth is skewed in favor of a minority. Marketable wealth comprises stocks and shares, cash, bank deposits, consumer durables, buildings, trade assets, land, and dwellings net of mortgage debt. In 1976, the total marketable wealth of the country was estimated to be £280 billion ($448 billion) and in 1995 it was estimated at £2,033 billion ($3,253 billion) (Table 1.10). The most wealthy 10 percent of the population own half of the marketable wealth; the most wealthy 25 percent of the population own over 70 percent of the wealth. The least wealthy half of the population owns under 10 percent of the country's marketable wealth.

TABLE 1.10   Distribution of marketable wealth, 1976–1995

Percentage of Population	Percentage of Marketable Wealth Owned		
	1976	1986	1995
1	21	18	19
5	38	36	38
10	50	50	50
25	71	73	73
50	92	90	92

SOURCE: *Social Trends 29* (National Statistics, 1999), p. 100.

When occupational and state pension rights are added to marketable wealth, there is a change in the pattern of distribution. The proportion of this wealth owned by 1 percent of the population has declined. Most of this wealth continues to reside in the hands of the most wealthy half of the population, but one-fifth of it is owned by the least wealthy half. Most wealth clearly remains in the hands of a minority, more than 70 percent being owned by the most wealthy 25 percent of the population.

Taxation is progressive, though the various rates have been reduced to two: a basic rate of 22 percent (with a lower rate of 10 percent for the lower–paid) and a top rate of 40 percent. (At one stage there was a maximum rate of 83 percent.) The reduction—with a shift of emphasis from direct to indirect taxation—also has resulted in income tax constituting a smaller proportion of the gross domestic product (GDP): from 11.2 percent in 1979 to 10.3 percent at the beginning of the 1990s. Despite the reduction in the number and level of rates, the proportion of tax paid by the highest 5 percent of taxpayers has increased, from approximately one-quarter in 1979 to more than 30 percent in 1991.

In terms of earned income, there are some notable, but predictable, differences in terms of family type. Single people with children are disproportionately to be found in the bottom income quintile, whereas the position is reversed with a couple with dependent children. At the beginning of the 1980s, retired people were also more likely to figure disproportionately in the bottom fifth (especially couples), whereas the position was reversed in the case of a single person without children. However, these disparities—that is, as far as pensioners and single people are concerned—were far less pronounced in the mid 1990s.[27]

CONCLUSION

Britain constitutes a small and crowded island with relatively few natural resources, with wealth and population heavily concentrated in the southeast of England. It is a largely secular society and one in which class remains important. These features distinguish it from the United States, which shares none of them. Though some of these features are shared with other European countries, in combination they render Britain distinct from its neighbors.

Compared with the United States and most European countries, Britain is notable for the absence—certainly since the seventeenth century—of invasion or revolution. Continuity in both institutions and many social traditions is a feature that underpins many of the structures and political relationships that form the basis of discussion in later chapters. Nonetheless, some change has taken place. That is apparent from the brief description offered in this chapter. We have touched upon some of the social changes that have occurred. We will later draw out the extent of political change. Some of that change has been significant and dramatic, especially in recent decades. Observing change can nonetheless obscure the extent of continuity. This volume is designed to ignore neither. It seeks to explain both. Hence our theme of the two C's: continuity and change.

NOTES

[1] In 1996, food, feed, and beverages accounted for about 10 percent of the nation's imports by value. Central Office of Information, *Britain 1997: An Official Handbook* (The Stationery Office, 1997), p. 305.

[2] *Social Trends 29* (The Stationery Office, 1999), p. 220.

[3] *Gallup Political and Economic Index,* August 1996, p. 21.

[4] "Bagehot: The Worst of Worlds," *The Economist,* December 26, 1992, p. 30.

[5] Henry VIII was excommunicated by the pope in 1533, following the crowning of Anne Boleyn as queen, the pope having refused to annul Henry's previous marriage to Catherine of Aragon. Parliament responded with various acts establishing Henry's position as head of the church. By the Act of Supremacy of 1534, the king was recognized as "the only supreme head of the Church of England, called Anglicana Ecclesia."

[6] L. Hartz, *The Liberal Tradition in America* (Harcourt, Brace & World, 1955).

[7] See A. H. Halsey, *Change in British Society,* 2nd ed. (Oxford University Press, 1981). This section draws heavily on this work.

[8] Ibid.

[9] Ibid., p. 47.

[10] Ibid., pp. 53–54.

[11] D. Butler and D. Stokes, *Political Change in Britain,* 2nd ed. (Macmillan, 1974), p. 69.

[12] R. Jowell, S. Witherspoon, and L. Brook, *British Social Attitudes: The Fifth Report, 1988–1989* (Gower, 1988), p. 227; E. Jacobs and R. Worcester, *We British* (Weidenfeld & Nicolson, 1990), pp. 138–139.

[13] Gallup, *Report 423,* November 1995.

[14] *Gallup Political and Economic Index,* January 1997, p. 26.

[15] "Class tightens its grip on Britain," *The Times,* 15 December 1997.

[16] See A. Adonis and S. Pollard, *A Class Act: The Myth of Britain's Classless Society* (Hamish Hamilton, 1997).

[17] In 1999, for example, the fees at Eton were £4,932 per term. There are three terms a year (though, confusingly, each term is known as a "half"!).

[18] J. Statham and D. MacKinnon, with H. Cathcart, *The Education Fact File* (Hodder & Stoughton, 1989), p. 160.

[19] R. Jowell, S. Witherspoon, and L. Brook, *British Social Attitudes: The 1987 Report* (Gower, 1987), p. 140.

[20] In 1988, the divorce rate in the United States was almost two-thirds higher than in the United Kingdom. The disparity was greatest among the under-25 age group. The duration of marriages ending in divorce also was shorter in the United States than in the United Kingdom. *Population Trends, Autumn 1991* (Her Majesty's Stationery Office, 1991), p. 2.

[21] *Social Trends 27* (The Stationery Office, 1997), p. 40.

[22] Ibid.

[23] "Fall in number of lone parents and divorces," *The Daily Telegraph,* 29 January 1998.

[24] *Social Trends 22* (Her Majesty's Stationery Office, 1992), p. 41.

[25] *Social Trends 27* (The Stationery Office, 1997), p. 76.

[26] *Britain 1998: An Official Handbook* (The Stationery Office, 1998), p. 170.

[27] *Social Trends 27* (The Stationery Office, 1997), p. 99.

Chapter 2

The Political Culture

Political culture is a vague, abstract concept that has been subject to various definitions.[1] In its simplest form, it may be described as denoting the emotional and attitudinal environment within which a political system operates.[2] If we are to understand how a political system is formed and operates, we have to understand the environment that produced and nurtures it.

The focus of this chapter is the political culture of Britain and the means through which individuals are socialized into that culture. As I shall seek to show, that culture cannot be divorced from the constraints of history and of physical and spatial resources. Each has had a significant impact on the other. The collection of emotions and attitudes that form the political culture has served to shape actions and hence affect the nation's history. Conversely, those actions, as well as the country's geographic location and limited resources, have had consequences that have affected elite and mass attitudes.

A number of problems have to be borne in mind. There is the danger especially of tautology and, as may be inferred from the preceding paragraph, the "chicken and egg" problem—which came first?—in attempting to discern the cause-and-effect relationships among culture, history, and resources. The existence of a stable political culture in Britain has been ascribed by some to the effectiveness of government in being able to implement programs of public policy. But what has enabled government to be effective? Has it been a distinctive political culture, citizens accepting the legitimacy of government to act in the way that it does? If so, what explains the existence of such a culture? Is not a partial explanation the effectiveness of government? The problem is an acute one in Britain given the absence of any clear point of departure. Where do English, Scottish, and Welsh history begin? At what point is a political culture discernible? The basic conundrum is insoluble. It is important, though, to bear it in mind, with an awareness of it informing our study.

What, then, are the basic components of the British political culture? And by what process are the values and attitudes that form that culture imbued by Britons?

POLITICAL SOCIALIZATION

The various values and beliefs that coalesce to create, maintain, and variously modify the political culture are not generated in a vacuum; they are acquired through a process of socialization. In that process, the most important influences usually are family, education, occupation, geographic location, and to a lesser extent, the mass media. For illustrative purposes, we shall consider their impact in shaping class and partisanship, before considering the basic underlying values that form the political culture.

Family

It is primarily from parents that children acquire particular values and habits. It is largely the parents who shape the child's view of society, including one's status in that society. It is also parents who significantly influence political perceptions and partisan support.

Perceptions of social class are derived not only from objective position but also often from inherited class orientations. Most children, as we have seen (Table 1.6) ascribe themselves to the same social class as their parents. The self-ascription is important and does not always correlate with objective assessments derived from socioeconomic conditions. Jacobs and Worcester also found a relationship between those who were upwardly mobile and those who believed their parents were upwardly mobile. Their survey found that "46% of those who described themselves as upwardly mobile middle-class described their parents in the same terms and so did 44% of those who called themselves upwardly mobile working-class."[3] As they note, with possibly a greater degree of insight than they realize, the claim to upward mobility may be an inherited characteristic.

Political habits and values are passed from parent to child. Children tend to inherit their parents' interest in politics (or, as appropriate, lack of it) and their partisan preferences. The influence is strongest when both parents share the same preference and that preference is known to the child.[4] There is evidence of decline in the class-party nexus,[5] but parents' preferences remain an important influence on partisan preference.

The influence of parents on partisanship is relevant for our study in later chapters. Of more immediate relevance for the political culture is the wider impact of parents: the fact that, whatever divergent influences may serve to modify or undermine particular values, it is the mother and father who remain the first and foremost points of reference in defining the political and social environment.

Education

Formal education is important in political socialization, less for its effect on partisan support (family remains the predominant influence) than for helping shape awareness of the political system and explicitly or, more often, implicitly the values that underpin it. In their classic but now dated study of the civic culture, Almond and Verba found that there were differences in attitude toward government between those with different levels of education, and between those who had received some formal education and those who had received none. The more extensive the education, up to university level, the greater the perceived significance of government action.[6] Nonetheless, the overwhelming majority of those with some formal education, primary or above, considered that national government had some effect.

It would thus seem plausible to hypothesize that the increase in educational provision in postwar years, and in the raising of the school-leaving age, will have raised political awareness and perceptions of political efficacy. Indeed, expanded educational opportunities and the development of the broadcast media have been identified as generating greater involvement in civic activity, a process that Inglehart has termed *cognitive mobilization.*[7] The disparity in the levels of education continues to correlate with levels of political activity. One *British Social Attitudes* survey found that those with educational qualifications, and graduates in particular, were more confident in their ability to understand politics and more inclined to participate in political activity than those without such qualifications; they also were more likely to be liberal in their moral values.[8]

A further study not surprisingly found a relationship between the study of politics by students and greater political awareness and ideological sophistication.[9] Data from the British General Election study for 1992 also reveal a relationship between education and knowledge of the legislature, though finding no relationship between knowledge and support for the institution.[10]

Types of education may also serve to reinforce values and behavior. Public schools tend to reinforce middle- and upper-middle–class norms and expectations. Conservative members of Parliament, for example, have been drawn disproportionately from public schools and the universities of Oxford and Cambridge. At such schools, leading public figures frequently are invited to speak and pupils are encouraged to engage in activities appropriate for later public service (for example, taking part in school debates), an environment maintained at Oxford and Cambridge. No such environment or traditions are normally provided in state comprehensive schools. In most cases, the school environment tends to reinforce the influence of the home background.

Occupation

Occupation and class, as we have seen (Chapter 1), are closely related. The former usually is employed as the primary criterion for determining the latter. Both are important in the context of political socialization. The nature of the occupation can affect values and perceptions of society. Having a poorly paid, mundane, and personally unrewarding job or, indeed, having no job at all is likely to invoke a greater sense of alienation than pursuing a well-paid and satisfying position. It would seem plausible to assume a broad correlation between these two positions and class, with those in the working class more likely to have more mundane, less-well-paid jobs and the middle class to have better-paid and probably more varied jobs. There also appears to be a broad correlation with perceptions of political efficacy. Those in the working class are more likely than those in the middle class to consider that governments are not particularly able to change things.[11]

There also is a significant, and much charted, relationship between class and partisan support: The middle class has traditionally preferred the Conservative party and the working class the Labour party. The relationship is not exact and is declining, but—as we shall see in later chapters—remains important. The relationship is not that surprising, given that those in the middle class are more likely to occupy better-paid jobs and consequently able to pursue a preferred lifestyle than those in working-class positions; hence, as the "haves" in society, they are more likely to prefer the party that is more oriented to maintaining the status quo. The "have-nots" are more likely to support a party favoring a change to the existing system. This hypothesis has largely been borne out by the empirical evidence,[12] though the relationship—as we shall see—is no longer as strong as it once was.

The nature of particular jobs also may influence other values. Those who are employed as part of a large factory work force are more likely to imbue values of social and political solidarity than those who occupy isolated positions, with little contact with fellow workers. Those employed in the armed services are taught the importance of discipline. Those employed in the private sector are more likely to acquire an attachment to private enterprise than those employed in the public sector.

In many, if not most, cases the experience of occupation serves to reinforce values acquired through family, children seeing themselves occupying the same social stratum as their parents and taking up jobs that maintain them in that same social stratum. Again, though, as we have noted, there is some change, with a degree of class mobility, especially upward mobility.

Location

Location also can be important in the process of political socialization. Living in an area of expensive detached houses can serve to reinforce one's sense of being middle-class. The area provides a social milieu that reinforces that awareness. Conversely, living in an area of terraced public accommodation can reinforce one's identification with the working class. Within such areas, there is often a particular lifestyle.

The independent influence of location is borne out when correlated with partisan support. As Miller found: "At a minimum, the class characteristics of the social environment have more effect on constituency partisanship than class differences themselves, perhaps much more. The partisanship of individuals is influenced more by where they live than what they do."[13] As we shall see in Chapter 5, there also is a correlation between party support and urban and rural locations and between party and region.

The values that may be reinforced or shaped by location are not confined to political partisanship and class. People living in small, self-sufficient rural communities are likely to have different values than those confined to overcrowded and largely transient urban areas. Those who live in small, tightly-knit communities for decades are more likely to have a different view of life than those who lead a peripatetic existence. Britain, as we have seen, occupies a relatively small land mass but nonetheless exhibits a number of significant regional variations.

Mass Media

The mass media of communication—principally television, radio, and newspapers—also are important agents of socialization. They constitute the most-used sources for acquiring knowledge of what is going on in society. As in the United States, television in Britain constitutes the most-used source.[14] Perceptions of the reliability of the different media also are similar in both countries: One survey of Americans in the 1980s found that, given conflicting reports from different media, 53 percent of respondents would consider television the most believable; a similar survey in the United Kingdom found 57 percent giving the same response.[15]

The media can serve, deliberately or otherwise, to reinforce, and possibly even change, values. Reinforcement is more likely given evidence that readers and viewers are likely to engage in a process of selective retention, selecting those items that reinforce existing beliefs (see Chapter 14). That reinforcement also can take the form of bolstering the legitimacy of existing institutions and processes. As we shall see, media exposure also can serve to have a "magnetizing" effect on partisan preferences. Most newspaper readers choose a paper whose partisan stance is in line with their own partisanship or, for young people, with that of their parents. Butler and Stokes, in their seminal but now dated study, found that when the children absorbed and accepted the preferences of their parents, they continued to read the same newspaper.[16]

These media are also complemented now by the Internet. Newspapers can be accessed on line. The BBC has an award-winning web site. Many other organizations, as well as individuals, can disseminate material via the Internet. The effect of this particular mode of communication on socialization is not yet clear. It opens up a far greater range of sources of information and comment than could previously by accessed by the average citizen.

A Complex Mix

The process of socialization is a complex and continuous one. The influences just outlined are the most important, but they are not the only influences, nor are they mutually exclusive. Usually the reverse: They clearly interact and, more often than not, will reinforce one another. Parents remain the most important influence. Parental influence usually will be reinforced by the choice of newspaper and often by the choice of school and job. However, the influences are not always reinforcing: Social mobility, marriage into a family with different values, and exposure to certain programs or stories in the media may challenge received parental wisdom. Parental values may conflict with prevailing social norms: the belief in arranged marriages in traditional Indian families, for example, in a society where the belief in free choice for individuals prevails. Nor are the influences themselves necessarily static. Educational opportunities have changed during the twentieth century, economic conditions have changed, and the mass media have developed, with the broadcast media assuming a new and central significance. And, in more recent years, more and more people are making greater use of the Internet for recreation and for acquiring information.

The importance of various of these changes, especially for partisan support, will be touched upon later in this volume. However, the changes we have mentioned are relative. In terms of the basic values being transmitted, the most significant feature is not change but continuity. There are differences in social and political values. We have illustrated the media of socialization in terms particularly of structuring social class and partisanship. There is, though, some convergence on a number of basic values. It is that convergence that provides the essential British political culture. In identifying the media of socialization, we have not identified those basic values. To know the media through which values and beliefs that coalesce to form the political culture are transmitted is useful, but does not serve to identify the culture itself.

THE POLITICAL CULTURE

In his work on political oppositions in Western democracies, Robert Dahl observed that patterns of opposition may have something to do with widely shared cultural premises. He noted that four kinds of culturally derived orientations toward politics seem to have a bearing on the pattern of opposition.[17] Those four orientations can usefully be employed not only to help one understand and explain attitudes toward political opposition in Britain but also to identify the fundamental characteristics of the political culture. They enable one to draw out the distinctive features of that culture and to consider the impact of both history and resources. Those four orientations, listed not in the order provided by Dahl but in the order I believe to be most significant to an understanding of the British political culture, are toward (1) problem solving, (2) the political system, (3) cooperation and individuality, and (4) other people.

Orientation toward Problem Solving

Giovanni Sartori has distinguished two approaches to problem solving: the empirical and the rational.[18] The empirical approach is concerned with what is and what can be seen and touched, proceeding on the basis of testing and retesting and largely rejecting dogma and abstract or coherent grand designs for change. The rationalist approach, by contrast, is concerned with abstraction rather than facts, stressing the need for deductive consistency and tending to be dogmatic and definitive. According to Dahl, "While the empirical approach takes the attitude that if a program does not work in practice there must be something wrong about the theory, the rationalist will retort that what is true in theory must also be true in practice—that it is the practice, not the theory, that is wrong."[19]

France has been identified as employing a rationalist approach. Germany and Italy, to some extent, also tend to find such an approach useful. Britain and the United States, by contrast, are seen as the exemplars of an empirical approach. Indeed, it is my contention that this approach is *most* marked in the British case and that it constitutes the most significant aspect of British political culture.

Although oriented more toward an empirical approach, the United States has exhibited some elements of the rationalist. The framers of the U.S. Constitution, although tempered by experience and (according to Charles Beard) self-interest, were informed by values articulated by the English philosopher John Locke and sought to impose a political framework in line with a Lockean conception of society.[20] Those values, expressed succinctly in the second paragraph of the Declaration of Rights (encompassing inalienable rights such as life, liberty, and the pursuit of happiness), and that conception of society have permeated the American consciousness, so much so that they have largely gone unstated. They have been so pervasive and so self-evident that there has been little point in articulating them.[21] Hence, the United States might be described as being oriented toward a mix of the empirical and the rationalist, albeit with the former being clearly the more dominant of the two.

Britain, by contrast, has a distinct orientation toward the empirical approach. Even the political system, however strong the attachment to it, tends to be justified in pragmatic terms. Democracy, having been implemented in largely pragmatic fashion, has been lauded on the grounds that "it works." The point has been well put by Vivien Hart in comparing U.S. and British approaches: "In America the emphasis has been on what democracy is and *should* be, while Britain has been characterized by a more pragmatic and less urgent emphasis on what democracy is and *can* be."[22] Empiricism seems appropriate to the English consciousness. Instinct, trial and error, and incremental change are the essence of the English approach to problem solving.

Such an orientation to problem solving has been a distinctive feature of English political culture for many centuries, discernible, I would suggest, since at least the thirteenth century. It is an approach that has informed political actions and hence the political history of the country. An empirical orientation in turn has been reinforced by the experience of history—it is the approach that has always been employed, and no external constraints have managed to force themselves on the nation to generate conditions in which a rationalist approach would be possible. In the wake of the War of Independence, Americans were able to sit down and generate a political system from first principles. Invasions by foreign powers and liberations from foreign powers have put other states in similar positions. England, by contrast, never has been faced with or sought such an opportunity. The closest it came was during the Protectorate of Oliver Cromwell in the seventeenth century. When that failed, the country resorted as far as possible to the conditions prevailing prior to its creation. English history is scattered with philosophers generating theories that have failed to find congenial soil in the nation's consciousness. Ideologies have been either discarded or else molded to fit with the experience of history. Prevailing theories, once they no longer seem appropriate, have been dispensed with. The act of dispensing with them has not always met with common assent nor has it always been smooth—the English historical landscape is scattered with periods of violence and upheaval—but once the dispensing process is achieved, it has largely been accepted. Hankering after the old order is congenial to some minds, but seeking to revert by force or civil unrest to the *status quo ante* is not. In the English perception, empiricism is both a descriptive and a prescriptive term. To the Briton, it is both what is and what he or she believes always has been.

Orientation toward the Political System

Orientation toward the political system may be classified as allegiant when attitudes, feelings, and evaluations are favorable to the political system; apathetic or detached when feelings and evaluations are neutral; and alienated when such feelings and evaluations are unfavorable.[23] Italy and France have been cited as examples of political cultures that generate alienation and a large measure of apathy. The former West Germany has been put forward as having a culture that generated detachment. In contrast, Britain and the United States are among those countries cited as exhibiting a strong allegiant orientation.[24]

Almond and Verba found that evaluation of the political system in Britain was the product of a mix of participant and deferential orientations. A participant orientation developed in Britain (citizens being oriented to the input as well as the output side of the political system, believing that they enjoyed access to it), but it was one adapted to the existing deference to the independent authority of government. The participant orientation did not displace the deferential;[25] deference remained important.

The participant orientation finds expression in citizens' beliefs that they can influence government at both national and local levels. Although Almond and Verba found few people in their survey who actually sought to exert such influence, the proportion who believed they *could* do so was significant. Of British respondents, approximately three out of five believed they could influence government. (Only the United States managed to produce a higher proportion.) The proportion believing they had no influence was only one in five. A 1974 survey by Barnes and Kaase showed that high levels of political efficacy remained in the 1970s,[26] and evidence from the 1985 and 1987 *British Social*

Attitudes surveys suggested continuing high levels in the 1980s.[27] Nowadays there is evidence that citizens do seek to influence government. Survey data show that Britons are more likely to engage in political participation than citizens of other European nations. Participation has increased in European countries since the 1950s, with the greatest increase taking place in Britain. With participation defined as engaging in some form of political participation beyond voting, 77 percent of those questioned in Britain in 1990 had engaged in such participation. Other high percentages were recorded by Sweden (74 percent) and Norway (68 percent). Among Britain's West European neighbors, the percentages were generally between 50 and 60 percent. At the bottom end of the scale, the figure for Finland was 38 percent and for Spain 32 percent.[28] Furthermore, the form of participation in Britain is of peaceful activity within the established political framework. In the MORI *State of the Nation* poll in 1995, 55 percent of those questioned had signed a petition in the preceding two or three years; only 7 percent had taken part in a demonstration, picket, march or sit-in.[29]

Deference remains important, but it is contingent and is more marked in terms of respect for law and those who operate above the political fray. Deference to authority has found expression in a number of ways. It can be shown in the extent to which Britons trust the state and the extent to which they comply voluntarily with laws passed by Parliament. Recent survey data show that a willingness to trust the state is more marked in Britain than it is in other Western European nations and more marked than in the USA (Table 2.1). As can be seen from Table 2.1, only in Britain is an absolute majority of those questioned prepared to trust the state. Criminal acts tend to be antisocial rather than conscious acts against the state.[30] Recent decades have seen relatively little overt opposition, at least in Britain (as distinct from the United Kingdom), to the parliamentary form of government that exists. Some may want to modify its form— sometimes radically—and many at times may want to change the politicians who operate it, but they do not challenge the principle that underpins it, nor

TABLE 2.1   Trust in the state, 1998

Q. Would you say you basically trust the state or not?

	Yes %	No %	Don't know %
Great Britain	57	32	11
Germany	41	41	18
United States	40	56	4
Spain	38	42	20
Italy	35	51	14
France	33	59	8

SOURCE: Pew Research Center for the People and the Press, reported in *British Public Opinion*, Vol. XXI (3), April 1998, p. 2.

do they seek to change its form through unlawful or violent means. When government authority has been challenged, citizens have expressed themselves in favor of maintaining that authority.

Such deference has been seen as allied with a social deference, citizens according certain skills of government to those drawn from a particular group. Walter Bagehot, in his classic work *The English Constitution*, identified England as a "deferential nation," one that had a structure of its own. "Certain persons," he wrote, "are by common consent agreed to be wiser than others, and their opinion is, by consent, to rank for much more than its numerical value."[31] Such deference, though in diluted form, survived into the era of mass suffrage and the democratic ideal. It has been seen as a lingering feature of twentieth-century Britain and has been variously offered as a partial explanation of the continuing success of the Conservative party and its socially atypical leadership.[32]

Such deference, though, has been contingent rather than certain. It has been built on a reciprocity between governors and governed. The populace has deferred to the independent authority of government and to those who occupy government in return for the satisfaction of expectations. Those expectations have covered the substance of policies as well as the form and practices of government. If the governing regime fails to satisfy expectations, either in terms of policy or conduct, then deference is withdrawn, as the incumbent party of government has variously found to its cost, most recently in the general election of 1997.

Conversely, those to whom citizens accord deference have been characterized as having a sense of duty and as recognizing their responsibility to others. A stress on responsibilities as well as rights has been seen as a significant characteristic of the British political elite, and has been associated with a particular and often predominant tradition within the party that dominated government for most of the past century, the Conservative party (Chapter 6). If that responsibility has not been exercised, then popular support has been withdrawn.

The greater the perception of public service, exercised impartially, the greater the level of public trust. Confidence traditionally has been—and remains—high in the armed services and the police force, with levels of confidence exceeding those in other Western countries.[33] In 1998, for example, 88 percent of Britons questioned in a *British—and European—Social Attitudes* survey expressed pride in the armed forces, a figure not matched in the other countries included in the survey.[34] Figures for politicians and bureaucrats tend to be more mixed. People tend to trust the state but, perhaps perversely, not those employed or elected to run its machinery. Politicians are generally not well-regarded and, historically, never have been. The institutions in which they serve attract mixed notices. In the 1995 Gallup poll, less than a quarter of those questioned expressed a great deal or quite a lot of confidence in Parliament. Given that deference is contingent, not certain, this figure is not that surprising. At the time the government, which is drawn from and remains within Parliament, was experiencing unprecedented levels of unpopularity, and there were significant demands for constitutional change. Yet in a MORI poll the same year, the percentage of citizens expressing satisfaction with the way Parliament works slightly exceeded those expressing dissatisfaction.[35] And within three years of that poll, the proportion of those believing the system of governing Britain "could be improved in small ways but generally works well" had almost doubled.[36] The proportion believing Parliament worked well had also increased.

Orientation toward Cooperation and Individuality

Some cultures emphasize the values of cooperating with others, conciliating opposing views, and being prepared to compromise and submerge personal ideas in a broader and more popularly acceptable solution. Others, by contrast, stress the virtues of maintaining the distinctiveness, ideas, and integrity of the group or the individual, such virtues being considered superior to those of compromise and cooperation.[37]

Various countries and regions have been cited as exhibiting a noncooperative orientation, with the maintenance of group and individual integrity being stressed in both the general culture and political life. Dahl, for example, cited France and Italy.[38] Highly visible contemporary examples include large parts of the Middle East, the Balkans, and, indeed, one part of the United Kingdom: Northern Ireland. Northern Ireland stands out as an atypical part of the United Kingdom. Britain, along with the United States, is among those countries in which the political culture emphasizes the virtues of compromise and conciliation, without threatening personal integrity. The Anglo-American perception was well expressed by Edmund Burke in 1775. "All government, indeed every human benefit and enjoyment, every virtue, and every prudent act," he declared, "is founded on compromise and barter."[39]

Given the relatively weak emphasis on what should be, as opposed to what can be, we would suggest that this orientation is more marked in Britain than in the United States. In Britain, there is an almost instinctive distaste for conflict, both in personal relationships and in political life. An adversarial relationship between political parties has tended to mask a general acceptance of the rules of the game under which that relationship operates. At an elite level, partisanship influences the stance taken on the rules of the game, but the rules are generally accepted[40] and, indeed, the basic rules of parliamentary procedure have been notable for remaining in place despite the capacity of government, secure in a parliamentary majority, to seek to change them.[41] The relationship between bureaucrats and representatives of organized interests has been characterized as one of accommodation.[42] Though industrial relations often have been marked by an adversarial relationship, resolving disputes through bargaining has generally formed part of the culture of industrial life. There is almost a penchant for resolving disputes by discussion, by sitting around a table and ironing out differences. It is an orientation compatible with the others we have identified and is congenial to a society that stresses the responsibilities as well as the rights of the citizen. It is a predominant orientation: There are certainly exceptions, not least—as we have mentioned—in a particular part of the United Kingdom, namely Northern Ireland, but even there negotiations appeared to bear some fruit in 1998 (see Chapter 10). It is an orientation that remains a feature of British society, one that constitutes for many Britons a source of pride.

Orientation toward Other People

A belief that one can have confidence in others has been put forward as a culturally rooted phenomenon, with potentially important implications for political life. Research in the 1950s by Morris Rosenberg found that "faith in people" was related to democratic and internationalist values and attitudes.[43] In their study, Almond and Verba found that Americans and Britons "tend to be consistently more positive about the safety and responsiveness of the human environment."[44] The Germans and the Italians, by contrast, were found to be more negative, and the Mexicans inconsistent.

Surveys in recent years have shown that Britons retain a fairly positive view of themselves. A 1985 Gallup poll found that they regarded themselves as friendly, polite, hard-working, fun-loving, and with a sense of humor.[45] Eighty percent declared themselves to be very or quite proud of being British; the proportion was fairly well spread throughout different groups in society. Only 4% were not at all proud to be British. The *British—and European—Social Attitudes* survey in 1998 of four European countries found that the highest level of national pride was to be found in Britain (Table 2.2). "Not surprisingly, national pride is related to attachment to one's country. In general, those who feel 'close' to their country display higher levels of national pride than those who do not feel as close."[46]

Various surveys have found that Britons tend to regard other Britons as fairly trustworthy,[47] though trust in one's own nationality tends to be a feature of most countries of western Europe.[48] There are, though, some differences in levels of trust in other nationalities, though again a similar feature exists in other European countries. Britons tend to be more trusting of northern Europeans (Scandinavians, Germans, and Dutch) and Americans than of southern Europeans (Spanish, Italians, and Greeks).[49] Britain's old historical enemy, the French, fall into the latter category. There are strong emotional ties to old Commonwealth countries such as Canada, New Zealand, and Australia. The positive orientation toward the United States and a number of Commonwealth countries is hardly surprising, partly for reasons of history and partly for reasons of language. Britons have tended to look toward the English-speaking world rather

TABLE 2.2   Levels of national pride, 1998

Mean scores on national pride scale				
Britain	Spain	Sweden	Eastern Germany	Western Germany
20.6	20.4	19.8	17.9	17.2

SOURCE: *British—and European—Social Attitudes* (Ashgate, 1998), p. 8.

than to countries whose languages they have been reluctant to learn. The English and the Scots, as Anthony King has observed, have tended not to think like Europeans nor to think of themselves as Europeans.[50] This is relevant for understanding both the British political culture and the difficulties of Britain in adjusting to membership in the European Union. As we shall see (Chapter 9), the United Kingdom has at times looked more like a semidetached member of that union than a fully integrated one.

Britons thus tend to have faith in themselves and a relatively discriminating faith in others. This is an important component of the political culture, though not one that renders Britain distinctive. It is the combination of orientations that renders the country distinct from the United States and from its European allies.

A DECLINING CIVIC CULTURE?

The political culture of Britain may then be characterized, in broad terms, as having the four orientations identified: empirical in terms of problem solving and change, allegiant in terms of the political system, cooperative in making decisions, and trusting in relation to fellow citizens and allies. These, it is important to stress, are generalizations. There are various subcultures that deviate from these orientations and some that do not share them all. Nor is the list of orientations exhaustive. There is a richness of cultural diversity not encompassed by these four principal orientations. A more detailed study would differentiate the political cultures of England, Scotland, and Wales. Furthermore, it is important to stress that it is the British political culture under discussion. As we shall see in Chapter 10, the political culture of Northern Ireland is distinctive. What is important for our purposes, though, is that the four orientations remain the orientations of *most* Britons, at both the mass and the elite levels.

The strength of the culture may be said to lie in the convergence of these orientations—that is, they are compatible with and reinforce one another, and similarly are compatible with and are reinforced by the experience of history. The stress on cooperation and compromise, an emphasis compatible with an empirical approach to change, has facilitated the integration of groups and individuals into the political system. Such integration may be seen as reinforcing an allegiant rather than a neutral or alienated orientation to the political system. History has been kind: The country has staved off invasion by its enemies, and the resources have usually been available for government to make and meet commitments in response to changing demands and expectations. As a result, it has been possible to interpret the experience of history as justifying or reinforcing an attachment to empirical problem solving and to the virtues of cooperation and trust. The interplay of these variables generated what Almond and Verba characterized as "the civic culture," "a pluralistic culture based on communication and persuasion, a culture of consensus and diversity, a culture that permitted change but moderated it."[51]

What of the contemporary civic culture? There are two conflicting analyses. One is that the civic culture is in decline. The other is that there has been no fundamental decline in the culture, but rather a misperception of that culture.

The argument that the civic culture is in decline has gained ground over the past twenty years. It was articulated especially by a distinguished American observer of British politics, Samuel Beer, in the 1980s and has been taken up since by a number of groups commited to constitutional reform. On the basis of survey evidence, Beer concluded in 1982 that "it is no exaggeration to speak of a decline in the civic culture as a 'collapse.'"[52] The orientations of the culture—the positive orientation toward institutions and cooperation—were diminishing, reflected in a conflict between elite and popular behavior. For Beer, as for constitutional reformers in the early 1990s, a dysfunctional constitutional system was both cause and effect of this decline. Old institutions have been unable to meet expectations and to harness popular support. As institutions fail to meet those expectations, so trust in the effectiveness and equity of government diminishes. The greater the lack of trust, the greater the lack of cooperation, and hence the more government has to centralize power in order to meet its policy goals.

Empirical support for this thesis is found in a decline in voter turnout, a belief that the system of government is in need of change, and in the perceived centralization of government during the years that Margaret Thatcher was prime minister (1979–90). Since the 1950s, the membership of political parties has declined and voter turnout has fallen, as has the percentage of the population voting for the two main parties. Single-party governments have been elected on smaller percentages of the poll than before, sometimes no more, and on occasion even less, than 40 percent. In 1997, the Labour party won a stunning victory in the general election with a smaller percentage of the votes than the Conservative party achieved in 1992, when it won a narrow parliamentary victory. The explanation for this disparity is to be found in the number of voters who stayed at home in 1997. In 1973, 49 percent of those questioned in one survey thought the system of government needed "a great deal" of improvement or could be "improved quite a lot." In 1991 the figure had increased to 63 percent and in 1995 it was 75 percent. The years of Thatcher government were seen by many commentators as demonstrating an increased concentration of power in the prime-ministership, Parliament and organized interests being kept at bay, and decisions being taken by the prime minister and a few key advisers. The existing system, according to the constitutional reform body, Charter '88—founded, as its name implies, in 1988—was locked into a spiral of decline. The civic culture, on this argument, could be restored only through a new constitutional settlement, with existing structures swept away and replaced by a political system that engages the participatory energies of citizens.[53] Even if more people were taking part in political activity, that activity could be argued to be the product of an unresponsive political system. Pressure for constitutional reform became marked as the 1990s progressed. With the election in 1997 of a Labour government committed to a program of constitutional reform, proponents of the "decline" thesis saw their argument as being vindicated and that the reforms to be implemented by the new government would help reverse the decline.

The counter argument is that what has changed radically over the past twenty years or so is not the political culture itself, but perceptions of that culture. Analyses of the political culture have swung, pendulum fashion, from one extreme to the other. At times of apparent stability, contentment, and political success, there has been a tendency to see the political culture in idealized terms, to hold it aloft as a culture to be admired, even envied. Although Almond and Verba drew attention to some of the inconsistencies and problems inherent in the civic culture, it was nonetheless difficult not to ascribe positive connotations to that culture.

At times of economic difficulty, there is a tendency to see it in a different light. Popular discontent with government starts to shade into discontent with the system of government itself. We have already seen that a critical attitude toward the system of government was marked in the mid 1990s. Evidence of discontent can then be read as suggesting a decline in the civic culture, a decline that can be reversed only by radical change to existing structures and relationships.

Concentration on immediate difficulties and on shifts, sometimes small shifts, in popular opinions and attitudes are—on this counter-argument—given undue attention, masking the fact that the essential orientations of the culture remain strong. Far from having participation decline, the cognitive mobilization identified by Inglehart has resulted, as we have already seen, in a population far more active than before. A massive growth in the number of organized groups has offered citizens new outlets for participation. And survey data, rather than proving the thesis of decline, can be utilized to demonstrate the continuing strength of that culture. At the end of the 1980s, eight out of every ten citizens, according to one *British Social Attitudes* survey, believed the democratic system worked well and needed little or no change.[54] A similarly large number continue to think that Britain is an open society[55] and, as we have seen, the proportion believing the system of government is in need of a lot or a great deal of change has actually declined in the period between 1995 and 1998. Discontent peaked in 1995, declined in 1997, and declined further in 1998. What this suggests is not some fundamental decline in the civic culture, but rather that attitudes toward the system of government fluctuate according to the popularity of the incumbent regime. The figures for trust in the state would suggest— along with the continuing orientation to obeying rules—an underlying strength in the civic culture. The widespread public grief witnessed following the death in a car accident of the popular Diana, Princess of Wales, in August 1997 was seen by some commentators as marking a significant shift in popular attitudes and sentiments in Britain. It could be argued that it did not mark a change, but rather that the event served as a catalyst for an expression of the cooperative orientation that characterizes the culture, especially at times of stress.

These competing analyses are basic to any study of contemporary British politics. They represent the two elements of change and continuity; the "decline" proponents identifying significant change in the civic culture, and the opponents of the decline thesis emphasizing continuity. They underpin, respectively, calls for—and a rejection of—a new constitutional settlement for the United Kingdom. We will variously have cause to refer to them in later chapters, not least in a new era of British politics following the election of a government in 1997 committed to constitutional change. The contending theses will form the basis of the concluding chapter, which will address the question, "Which is the most plausible analysis?"

NOTES

[1] See D. Kavanagh, *Political Culture* (Macmillan, 1972), pp. 10–11.

[2] Ibid., p. 10.

[3] E. Jacobs and R. Worcester, *We British* (Weidenfeld & Nicolson, 1990), pp. 143–144.

[4] See especially M. Franklin, *The Decline in Class Voting in Britain* (Oxford University Press, 1985), pp. 69–71, 78–79.

[5] R. Rose and I. McAllister, *Voters Begin to Choose* (Sage, 1986), pp. 104–106.

[6] G. Almond and S. Verba, *The Civic Culture* (Princeton University Press, 1963), pp. 86–87.

[7] R. Inglehart, *The Silent Revolution* (Princeton University Press, 1977).

[8] R. Jowell, S. Witherspoon, and L. Brook, *British Social Attitudes: The 1987 Report* (Gower, 1987), p. 65.

[9] D. Denver and G. Hands, "The Effects of 'A' Level Politics: Literacy, not Indoctrination," *Social Studies Review, 4* (1), 1988, p. 40.

[10] J. R. Baker, L. L. M. Bennett, S. E. Bennett, and R. S. Flickinger, "Citizens' Knowledge and Perceptions of Legislatures in Canada, Britain and the United States," *The Journal of Legislative Studies, 2* (2), 1996, pp. 44-62.

[11] R. Jowell and S. Witherspoon, *British Social Attitudes: The 1985 Report* (Gower, 1985), p. 18. See also R. Jowell, S. Witherspoon, and L. Brook, *British Social Attitudes: Special International Report* (Gower, 1989), pp. 132–133.

[12] R. J. Johnston, C. J. Pattie, and J. G. Allsopp, *A Nation Dividing?* (Longman, 1988), p. 49.

[13] W. L. Miller, *Electoral Dynamics* (Macmillan, 1977). See also Johnston, Pattie, and Allsopp, pp. 61–63.

[14] Jowell and Witherspoon (1985), p. 46.

[15] Ibid., p. 47.

[16] D. Butler and D. Stokes, *Political Change in Britain* (Penguin, 1971), pp. 281–300.

[17] R. A. Dahl (ed.), *Political Opposition in Western Democracies* (Yale University Press, 1966), p. 353.

[18] G. Sartori, *Democratic Theory* (Wayne State University Press, 1962), p. 233, cited in Dahl, p. 354.

[19] Dahl, p. 355.

[20] L. Hartz, *The Liberal Tradition in America* (Harcourt, Brace & World, 1955). For the analysis by Charles Beard, see C. Beard, *An Economic Interpretation of the Constitution* (Macmillan, 1913).

[21] Indeed, they have been so pervasive that Americans will not necessarily accept that there is such a pervasive consciousness. It can only be appreciated by being outside it.

[22] V. Hart, *Distrust and Democracy* (Cambridge University Press, 1978), pp. 202–203.

[23] Dahl, p. 353.

[24] Almond and Verba, Ch. 14.

[25] Ibid., pp. 455–456.

[26] Reproduced in D. P. Conradt, "Changing German Political Culture," in G. Almond and S. Verba (eds.), *The Civic Culture Revisited* (Little, Brown, 1980), p. 232.

[27] Jowell and Witherspoon (1985), p. 12; Jowell, Witherspoon, and Brook (1987), p. 58.

[28] M. Kasse and K. Newton, *Beliefs in Government* (Oxford University Press, 1995), Table 3.4, p. 51.

[29] MORI, *State of the Nation 1995* (MORI, 1995), p. 12.

[30] See R. N. Berki, *Security and Society* (Dent, 1986). Even though people trust the state, the concept of the state is not that well entrenched in English consciousness. It is, though, important to stress *English* consciousness: As we shall see in Chapter 9, a proportion of the citizenry in Scotland and Wales have variously expressed resentment toward what is seen as an "English" state, and in Northern Ireland some inhabitants have engaged in explicit and violent antistate activity.

[31] W. Bagehot, *The English Constitution* (first published 1867; Fontana, 1963 edition).

[32] See, e.g., R. McKenzie and A. Silver, *Angels in Marble* (Heinemann, 1968); and P. Norton (ed), *The Conservative Party* (Harvester Wheatsheaf/Prentice-Hall, 1996), introduction.

[33] Webb and Wybrow, pp. 103–104; *Eurobarometer, No. 33,* June 1990, Table 14.

[34] *British—and European—Social Attitudes* (Ashgate, 1988), p. 9.

[35] MORI, *State of the Nation 1995* (MORI, 1995).

[36] *British Public Opinion,* Vol. XXI (3), April 1998, p. 2.

[37] Dahl, p. 354.

[38] Ibid.

[39] Speech on conciliation with the American Colonies, March 22, 1775.

[40] See D. D. Searing, "Rules of the Game in Britain: Can the Politicians be Trusted?" *American Political Science Review, 76,* 1982, pp. 239-58.

[41] See P. Norton, "Parliamentary Procedure," in D. Butler et al. (eds.), *The Law, Politics and the Constitution* (Oxford University Press, 1999).

[42] J. Richardson (ed.), *Policy Styles in Western Europe* (George Allen & Unwin, 1982).

[43] M. Rosenberg, "Misanthropy and Political Ideology," *American Sociological Review, 21,* pp. 690-695; and "Misanthropy and Attitudes towards International Affairs," *Journal of Conflict Resolution, 1,* 1957, pp. 340-345, cited in Almond and Verba, p. 266.

[44] Almond and Verba, p. 268.

[45] G. Heald and R. J. Wybrow, *The Gallup Survey of Britain* (Croom Helm, 1986), p. 277.

[46] *British—and European—Social Attitudes* (Ashgate, 1998), pp. 8-9.

[47] *Eurobarometer, No. 33,* June 1990, Table 14.

[48] N. Webb and R. Wybrow, pp. 103-104; *Eurobarometer, No. 33,* June 1990, Table 14.

[49] N. Webb and R. Wybrow, *The Gallup Report* (Sphere Books, 1981), pp. 103-104; *Eurobarometer, No. 33,* June 1990, Table 14.

[50] A. King, *Britain Says Yes* (American Enterprise Institute, 1977), p. 6. See also L. Barzini, *The Impossible Europeans* (Weidenfeld & Nicolson, 1983).

[51] Almond and Verba, p. 8.

[52] S. H. Beer, *Britain Against Itself* (Faber, 1982), p. 119.

[53] See especially D. Marquand, *The Unprincipled Society* (Fontana, 1988).

[54] R. Jowell, S. Witherspoon, and L. Brook, *British Social Attitudes: Special International Report* (Gower, 1989), p. 133.

[55] *The Guardian,* November 20, 1991, reporting the findings of the Eighth Report of the British Social Attitudes Survey.

Chapter 3

Past and Present

Historical Perspective and Contemporary Problems

A number of introductory texts on British politics do not have chapters devoted specifically to political history. The omission is a surprising one. When the proposal for this book was under consideration by the publishers, a number of American professors were asked for their comments. One responded with this advice: "Make sure you incorporate as much historical detail as possible. American students don't know much about British history." The need for historical detail, however, is not confined to Americans interested in the subject; it encompasses all those who seek to make some sense of the institutions and complex relationships that form the British polity.

The country has witnessed continuous and sometimes dramatic change. In the past three hundred years alone, the nation has experienced industrialization, the advent of democracy, and the introduction and growth of the welfare state—yet the changes have been built upon and have adapted that which already existed. The body politic may have undergone radical surgery and it may have aged considerably, but it has continued to endure.

What, then, are the significant features of British history that help us understand the contemporary political system and the political culture? Limitations of space preclude a lengthy dissertation on what is a vast subject. That vastness is apparent when put in comparative perspective. The Magna Carta, for instance, was signed more than two centuries before Christopher Columbus set sail. A parliament was summoned more than five hundred years before the United States Congress first assembled. And a U.S. president, unlike a British monarch, cannot trace his forebears in office back more than a thousand years. Nonetheless, it is possible to provide a brief but structured sketch that furthers our understanding of contemporary British politics. This can be done under three headings: the emergence of parliamentary government, the development of the welfare state and managed economy, and the politics of Thatcher and Blair.

HISTORICAL PERSPECTIVE

The Emergence of Parliamentary Government

One of the essential features of the British constitution is a parliamentary government under a limited, or symbolic, monarchy. The formal elements of this type of government will be more fully outlined in the next chapter. For the moment, what concerns us is that this government is the product of change extending over several centuries, coming to fruition only in the past century. Its development sometimes has been characterized as being evolutionary, but in practice it is the outgrowth of piecemeal change.

Let us begin in the thirteenth century. Traditionally, the sovereign power in England resided in the monarch. Nonetheless, the king was expected to consult with his tenants-in-chief (the leading churchmen and the barons) in order to discover and declare the law and to have their counsel before any levies of extraordinary taxation were made. This expectation was to find documented expression in the Great Charter (*Magna Carta*) of 1215, by which the king recognized it as a right of his subjects "to have the Common Council of the Kingdom" for the assessment of extraordinary aids—that is, taxation. Such consultation was undertaken through a Great Council, from which evolved what was to be recognized as a *parlement* or Parliament. The Great Council itself was the precursor of the House of Lords. The House of Commons evolved from the summoning to council, in the latter half of the thirteenth century on a sporadic basis, of knights and burgesses as representatives of the counties and towns. At various times in the fourteenth century the Commons deliberated separately from the Lords, and there developed a formal separation of the two bodies.

During the period of the Tudor monarchs in the sixteenth century, Parliament acquired enhanced status. It was generally supportive of the monarch but became more powerful because the monarchs depended upon it for that support, especially during the reign of Elizabeth I. The relationship between Crown and Parliament under the subsequent Stuart dynasty was one of conflict. The early Stuart kings—James I and Charles I—sought to assert the doctrine of the divine right of kings and to deny many of the privileges acquired or asserted by Parliament. This conflict was to lead to the civil war and the beheading of Charles I in 1649. With the abolition of the monarchy came a brief period of rule by a Council of State elected by what was termed the Rump Parliament. (Some attempts were actually made to formulate what amounted to a written constitution, but they came to nothing.)[1] Rule by the Council of State was succeeded by Oliver Cromwell's unsuccessful military dictatorship, and in 1660 Charles's eldest son returned to assume the throne as Charles II. The period between 1642 and 1660 proved an aberration in British history. The Restoration witnessed an attempt to return, unconditionally, to the country's position as it was at the beginning of 1642.[2] Through this attempt, the Restoration lent itself to a repetition of the earlier struggle between king and Commons. Relations between the two gradually deteriorated during the reign of Charles II and became severe in the reign of his successor, James II. James sought to reassert the divine right of kings, and Parliament combined against him. In 1688 James fled the country. At the invitation of Parliament, the throne was taken by William and Mary of Orange, James's son-in-law and daughter. The new occupants of the throne owed their position to Parliament, and the new relationship between them was asserted by statute in the Bill of Rights. Although the Bill of Rights was important for enumerating various "Liberties of this Kingdom" (some of which were to be similarly expressed during the following century in the Bill of Rights embodied in the United States Constitution),[3] its essential purpose was to assert the position of Parliament in relation to the Crown. The raising of taxes or the dispensing of laws without the assent of Parliament was declared to be illegal. The monarch was expected to govern, but to do so only with the consent of Parliament. The Act of Settlement of 1701, which determined the succession to the throne, affirmed that the laws of England "are the Birthright of the People thereof and all the Kings and Queens who shall ascend the Throne of this Realm ought to administer the Government of the same according to the said Laws and all their Officers and Ministers ought to serve them respectively according to the same."

The monarch thus became formally dependent on Parliament for consent to the raising of taxes and for the passage of legislation. In practice, he or she became increasingly dependent also on ministers for advice. The importance of ministers grew, especially in the eighteenth century. The Hanoverian kings were not uninterested in political life, but they had difficulty comprehending the complexities of domestic and foreign affairs. According to the historian J. H. Plumb, both George I and George II were "crassly stupid" and "incapable, totally incapable, of forming a policy."[4] During the period of their reigns, the leading body of the king's ministers, generally known as the cabinet, began to meet without the king being present.[5] The period also witnessed the emergence of a minister who was to become popularly known as the prime minister. (Not until the twentieth century, though, was the office of prime minister to be mentioned in a statute.) The relationship among Crown, ministers, and Parliament in the century was one in which the king relied on his ministers to help formulate policy. Those ministers were chosen by the king on the basis of his personal confidence in them, and they remained responsible to him. They also were responsible to Parliament in order to achieve their ends, a fact recognized by both the king and his ministers. Nonetheless, parliamentary support was not difficult to obtain; the king and his ministers had sufficient patronage and position usually to ensure such support. A ministry that enjoyed royal confidence could generally take the House of Lords for granted, and provided it did not prove incompetent or seek to impose excessive taxation, "its position was unassailable in the Commons."[6] The position was to change significantly in the nineteenth century.

Britain underwent what has been popularly referred to as an industrial revolution from the middle of the eighteenth century to the middle of the nineteenth. Seymour Martin Lipset has characterized the United States as the "first new nation," but Britain has been described as "the first industrial nation."[7] Industry became more mechanized, improvements took place in agricultural production techniques, and there were improvements in transport and the organization of trade and banking. There was a notable growth in the size of cities, particularly in the early part of the nineteenth century. Men of industry and commerce began to emerge as men of some wealth. In 1813 Robert Owen referred to the "working class," a term brought into common speech by Lord Brougham.[8] By the 1830s, a non-landed middle class, artisans, and an industrial work force were important constituents of the country's population.

Parliament remained dominated by the aristocracy and by the landed gentry. Representation in the House of Commons was heavily weighted in favor of the rural counties. Some parliamentary constituencies had only a handful of electors: Known as "rotten boroughs," these areas were often in the pocket of an aristocrat or local landowner.[9] Pressure for some parliamentary reform, with a redistribution of seats and a widening of the franchise, began to develop. It was argued that a Parliament full of men of wealth and property was unlikely to view industry, trade, and agriculture from the point of view of the laboring classes. Rotten boroughs were criticized as being used by the ministry to help maintain a majority. Unrest in a number of areas, both agricultural and industrial, and the French Revolution of 1830 (a spur to radical action) increased the pressure for change. One political group in particular, the Whigs, who had been the "outs" in politics for the 25 years prior to 1830, began to see the need for some response to this pressure. The concession of some parliamentary reform was seen as necessary in order to prevent worse happenings. The result, following the return of the Whigs to power, was to be the Reform Act of 1832.

The Reform Act, introduced, ironically, by the most aristocratic government of the century, reorganized parliamentary constituencies and extended the franchise. The electorate increased in size from a little under 500,000 to 813,000 electors.[10] Much remained the same as before—the new electorate constituted but one-thirtieth of the population, 31 boroughs still had fewer than 300 electors in each, voting remained by open ballot (secret ballots were considered rather un-English), and the aristocracy still held great sway politically. But the act precipitated important changes both within and outside the House of Commons.

The redistribution of seats and the extension of the franchise helped loosen the grip of the aristocracy and of ministers on the House of Commons. The size of the new electorate encouraged the embryonic development of political organizations. Members of Parliament (MPs) became less dependent on aristocratic patrons without acquiring too great a dependence on the growing party organizations. The result was to be a House of Commons with a greater legitimacy in the eyes of MPs and electors and with an ability to assert itself in its relationship with government. There was relatively little legislation—the domain of public policy was not great[11]—but what there was, the House proved willing to amend or reject. The House on occasion forced individual ministers to resign and sometimes even the whole government. In his classic work on the constitution, Walter Bagehot attached much importance to this "elective function"; the House of Commons, he declared, was "a real choosing body: it elects the people it likes. And it dismisses whom it likes too."[12] Debates in the House counted for something and, with the exception of the period from 1841 to 1846, party cohesion was almost unknown. The House of Commons did not itself govern, but government was carried on within the confines of its guidance and approval.

The period after 1832 also witnessed important changes in the relationships within and among the different elements of Crown, government, and Parliament. The monarch retained the formal prerogative power to appoint the prime minister, but the changed political circumstances essentially dictated that the person chosen should be able to command a majority in the House of Commons. Royal favor ceased to be an essential condition for forming the government. Within Parliament, the relationship between the two houses also changed. Members of the House of Lords sat by virtue of birth, holding hereditary peerages. The acceptance of the Commons as the "representative" chamber undermined the authority of the peers to challenge or negate the wishes of the other house. After the 1830s, the Lords tended to be somewhat restrained in their attacks on government measures. "This," as Mackintosh noted, "followed from the view that while a ministry retained the confidence of the elected representatives it was entitled to remain in office. The peers on the whole accepted these assumptions, though many found the explicit recognition of the situation hard to bear."[13] The remaining authority of the House of Lords was in practice to be removed in consequence of the 1867 Reform Act, though not until the twentieth century was the House forced formally to accept its diminished status.

Whereas the 1832 act helped ensure the dominance of the House of Commons within the formal political process, the passage of the Reform Act of 1867 began a process of the transfer of power from Parliament to ministers. The act itself was the product of demands for change because of the limited impact of the 1832 act and because of more immediate political considerations.[14] Its effect was to increase the size of the electorate from 1,358,000 to 2,477,000. (The number had grown since 1832 because of increased wealth and population.) Other significant measures followed in its wake. Secret voting was introduced by the Ballot Act of 1872. Other acts sought to prohibit as far as possible corrupt practices and limited the amount of money a candidate could spend on election expenses. Single-member districts (known in Britain as constituencies) of roughly equal electoral size were prescribed as the norm.[15] The 1884 Representation of the People Act extended the franchise to householders and tenants and to all those who occupied land or tenements with an annual value of not less than ten pounds. The effect of the act was to bring into being an electorate in which working men were in a majority. The consequence of these developments was to be party government.

The size of the new electorate meant that the voters could be reached only through some well-developed organization, and the result was to be the growth of organized and mass-membership political parties. The Conservative National

Union and the National Liberal Federation were formed to facilitate and encourage the support of the new electors. However, contact with the voters was insufficient in itself to entice their support. Not only had a large section of the population been enfranchised, but also it was a notably different electorate from that which had existed previously. The new class of electors had different and greater demands than those of the existing middle-class electors. If the votes of working men were to be obtained, the parties had to offer them something. And the parties could fulfill their promises only if they presented a uniform program to the electorate and achieved a cohesive majority in the House of Commons to carry through that program. What this was to produce was a shift of power away from the House of Commons to the cabinet and the electorate, with political parties serving as the conduit for this transfer.

The electorate proved too large and too politically unsophisticated to evaluate the merits of an individual MP's behavior. Political parties provided the labels with which electors could identify, and elections became gladiatorial contests between parties rather than between individual candidates. The all-or-nothing spoils of an election victory and the method of election encouraged (if not always produced) a contest between two major parties.[16] And having voted for party candidates, the electors expected the members returned to Parliament to support the program offered by their leaders at the election. Party cohesion soon became a feature of parliamentary life.[17] The House of Commons in effect lost two of the most important functions ascribed to it by Bagehot, those of legislation and of choosing the government: The former passed to the cabinet and the latter to the electorate. The cabinet constituted the leaders of the party enjoying a parliamentary majority. It assumed the initiative for the formulation and introduction of measures of national policy and became increasingly reluctant to be overruled by the House. The growth in the number and complexity of bills further limited the influence of the individual MP. Increasingly, his role became one of supporting his leaders. The cabinet previously had rested its authority on the support of the House; now it derived its authority from the electors. As Mackintosh states, "The task of the House of Commons became one of supporting the Cabinet chosen at the polls and passing its legislation. By the 1900s, the Cabinet dominated British government."[18]

Further modifications and addenda took place in the first half of the twentieth century. The House of Lords was forced by statute in 1911 to accept its diminished status. The franchise was variously extended, most notably to half the population previously excluded because of their sex. (The first female MP to take her seat in the House of Commons did so in 1919.) The monarch's political influence further receded. The growth and increasing economic weight of groups generated more extensive and complex demands of government. And the size of government grew as its responsibility expanded.

Basically, though, the essential features of the political system were those established in the preceding century. The responsibility for making public policy rested with the government, a government derived from and resting its support upon a political party. That same party's majority in the House of Commons ensured that the government's measures were approved. Formal and political constraints limited the effect of any opposition from the House of Lords. The monarch gave formal assent to any legislative measure approved by the two houses. Thus, within the formal framework of deciding public policy, the government was dominant. The role of Parliament became largely but not wholly one of legitimating the measures put before it. For the monarch, that became the exclusive role (that is, in respect of legislation). Government, as we shall see, operated within a political environment that imposed important constraints, but the limitations imposed formerly by Parliament and the monarch were largely eroded. Britain retained a parliamentary form of government, but what that meant was not government by Parliament but government through Parliament.

The Welfare State and the Managed Economy

To comprehend some of the problems faced by contemporary British government, it is necessary to know not only the structure and relationships of the political system but also the popular expectations and the burden of responsibilities borne by government. Those expectations and responsibilities have not been static. Just as the governmental structure has been modified in response to political demands, so the responsibilities of government have grown as greater social and economic demands have been made of it.

Toward the end of the nineteenth century and more so in the twentieth, the responsibilities of government expanded. In part this expansion was attributable to the growth of the empire. (As prime minister in the 1870s, Benjamin Disraeli had played the "imperial card," the British empire expanding rapidly: By 1900 it covered virtually a quarter of the globe.) It was also attributable to the increasing demands and expectations of the newly enfranchised working population. Government began to conceive its duties as extending beyond those of maintaining law and order and of defending the realm. The statute book began to expand, with the addition of measures of social reform. Various such measures were enacted prior to 1867, though the most notable were to be enacted in the remaining decades of the century. They included measures to limit working hours for women and children, to improve housing and public health, to make education for children compulsory, to provide for the safety of workers (including the payment of compensation by employers in the event of accidents at work), and even to extend the right to strike.[19] Such measures, exploited for electoral advantage, were within the capabilities of the government to provide. They did not create too great an economic burden; they were not themselves economic measures.

The growth of expectations and the greater willingness of government to intervene in areas previously considered inviolate was to be continued and become more marked in the twentieth century. The general election of 1906 was something of a watershed in British politics. It was the first election to be fought essentially on national issues and it witnessed the return not only of a reforming Liberal government but also, and in some respects more significantly, of 27 Labour MPs. The Labour party had been created for the purpose of ensuring working-class representation in Parliament, and from 1906 onward class became a significant influence in voting behavior. The nature of electoral conflict changed as the Labour party succeeded the Liberal as the main opposition party to the Conservatives. The franchise was further extended, notably in 1918 and 1928, and new expectations were generated by the experience of the two world wars.

During the First World War (1914–1918), socialists within the Labour party argued the case for the conscription of wealth (public ownership) to accompany the conscription of labor (the drafting of men into the armed forces). Politicians fueled rather than played down the belief that Britain should become, in the words of one politician, "a land fit for heroes" once "the war to end all wars" was won—in other words, that provision should be made for those who had fought for king and country. The period of the Second World War (1939–1945) witnessed a significant shift of attitudes by a sizable fraction of the electorate. One informed estimate was that by December 1942, about two out of five people had changed their political outlook since the beginning of the war.[20] Opinion was moving toward the left of the political spectrum. There was a reaction against (Conservative) government unpreparedness for war in the 1930s and against those who had not done more to solve the nation's problems during the depression. There was support for calls for equality of sacrifice. There was some degree of goodwill toward the Soviet Union as a wartime ally. There was also, very importantly, the enhanced position of the Labour party. It had entered into coalition in 1940 (its leader, Clement Attlee, became deputy prime minister to Churchill) and had demonstrated its claim to be a capable partner in government. As the 1940s progressed, there developed a notable movement, including within the Conservative party, for a greater degree of social and economic intervention by government. This was to find some authoritative expression during the war years themselves and especially in the years after 1945, when a general election resulted in the return of the first Labour government with a clear working majority in the House of Commons. The 1940s and the 1950s were to produce what Samuel Beer has referred to as the welfare state and the managed economy, or what some commentators have referred to as the period of the social democratic consensus.

The welfare state and the managed economy did not suddenly emerge full-blown in this period. The preceding decades had not witnessed governments unresponsive to electoral expectations and the nation's problems. The Liberal government before the First World War had made the first tentative steps in the introduction of old-age pensions (1908) and national health and unemployment insurance (1911). The interwar years had seen the introduction of a number of significant measures of social reform, especially those associated with a Conservative, Neville Chamberlain, as minister of health. He proposed to the cabinet

25 measures and secured the enactment of 21 of them. These included unemployment insurance, public health and housing, and the extension of old-age pensions. Much of this legislation, as one biographer noted, "has an important place in the development of the Welfare State."[21] The Conservative government also began to engage in certain measures of economic management. It embarked on a protectionist policy and, in return for the grant of a tariff to an industry, demanded that its major producers reorganize themselves. Such producers were encouraged to reduce capacity and maintain prices. The gold standard was abandoned, the pound was devalued, and interest rates were lowered. The government even proved willing to take certain industries into public ownership: broadcasting, overseas airways, and the electricity-generating industry. By indulging in such policies, Beer has contended, government was beginning to move in the direction of a managed economy.[22] The movement, though, was modest. Government adhered to the prevailing orthodoxy that balanced budgets were necessary and desirable and that deficit financing was neither. Ministers showed little desire to emulate the extensive public works programs implemented in the United States by Franklin Roosevelt during the period of the first New Deal. (Indeed, Conservative leader Stanley Baldwin commented at one point that the United States Constitution had broken down and was giving way to dictatorship.)[23] Britain and the United States were similar, though, in that both were to be brought out of the depression of the 1930s not by government economic policies but by rearmament and the Second World War.

Two major documents published in the war years provided the planks for the final emergence of the welfare state and managed economy. These were the Report on Social Insurance and Allied Services by Sir William Beveridge (the so-called Beveridge Report), published in November 1942, and the White Paper on Full Employment, published in 1944. The former proposed a comprehensive scheme of social security, one to provide "social insurance against interruption and destruction of earning power and for special expenditure arising at birth, marriage or death."[24] The latter was significant because of its opening pledge: "The Government accepts as one of their primary aims and responsibilities the maintenance of a high and stable level of employment after the war." There was also one particularly significant measure of social reform enacted during wartime: the 1944 Education Act, pioneered by R. A. Butler. It provided for the division among primary, secondary, and higher education—and, within secondary education, between secondary modern and grammar schools—that was to form the basis of the educational system for almost a generation.

The welfare state was brought to fruition by the passage of the 1945 Family Allowance Act, the 1946 National Insurance Act, the 1948 National Assistance Act, and by the establishment of the National Health Service (NHS) in 1948, entailing the nationalization of hospitals and the provision of free medical treatment. The principle enunciated by the Beveridge Report was largely put into practice. National insurance ensured a certain level of benefit in the event of unemployment or sickness. For those who required special help there was "national assistance," the provision of noncontributory benefits dispensed on the basis of means-testing. There were family allowances for those with children. The state now provided something of a protective safety net from the cradle to the grave. It was still possible to pay for private treatment in the health service, but for most people it was a case of having treatment "on the national health." The NHS became a feature of some pride at home and of considerable interest abroad.

Acceptance and usage of techniques pioneered by the economist John Maynard Keynes ushered in the managed economy. Government accepted responsibility for keeping aggregate monetary demand at a level sufficient to ensure full employment or what was considered as far as possible to constitute full employment (an unemployment rate of 1 percent or 2 percent was considered acceptable), and the annual budget was to be used as the main instrument of economic policy. The Labour government proved unwilling to pursue a more overtly socialist approach; physical controls acquired during wartime were eventually discarded and those industries that were nationalized, such as steel, the mines, and the railways, were basically essential and loss-making concerns. Government was prepared to pursue a managed rather than a controlled economy.

The Conservative party was returned to office in 1951 and was to remain there until 1964. It accepted, or appeared to accept, both the welfare state and Keynesian models of demand management. Indeed, it gave the impression of making a success of both. As heir to the Disraelian belief in elevating the condition of the people and as a party seeking to enhance its image among working-class voters, the Conservative party could claim both a principled and a practical motive for maintaining the innovations of its predecessor. At the same time, it was reluctant to pursue policies that would increase the tax burden on the public sector of the economy. Good fortune was with the government: World economic conditions improved and heralded a period of sustained growth in industrial output and trade. Government revenue was such that not only was it possible to sustain and indeed expand expenditure on the National Health Service, but it was also possible to do so without substantial increases in taxation. Indeed, reductions rather than increases in tax rates were a feature of the period. There was an extensive and successful house-building program. Economic prosperity allowed government to maintain peace with the labor unions by allowing high wage settlements. It was also possible finally to abandon many of the controls maintained since wartime. Government was able to claim to have maintained full employment, an expanding economy, stable prices, and a strong pound. Despite the agonies of withdrawing from the imperial period of empire and various undulations in economic performance, the 1950s was seen more than anything as "an age of affluence."[25] In July 1957 Prime Minister Harold Macmillan was able to declare that, for most of the people, "You've never had it so good."

The 1960s witnessed a downturn in economic performance and a growing realization that, in comparative terms, Britain was faring less well than many of her continental neighbors. The Conservative government of Harold Macmillan responded with various novel proposals, including indicative economic planning and an application to join the European Economic Community. The succeeding Labour government of Harold Wilson, returned to office in 1964, sought a more comprehensive method of national economic planning as part of its grand design of modernization. Inflation and unemployment became more visible problems.

Despite the economic problems and some unrelated political problems of the 1960s, the country remained a relatively prosperous one. Living conditions continued to improve. The rise in wages exceeded the rise in inflation. Where economic conditions impinged on the ability to maintain the welfare state, it was essentially at the margin: Government imposed nominal charges for medicines obtained on NHS prescriptions. Parties tended to argue more about means rather than ends. The consensus that developed in the 1950s remained intact.

The Politics of Thatcher and Blair

The first attempt to break away from that consensus was made by the Conservative government of Edward Heath, which was returned to office in 1970. There was an emphasis on the withdrawal of government from economic activity and an attempt, ultimately unsuccessful, to curb trade union power. The aim was to force British industry to be more competitive. This goal also provided some of the motivation for British membership in the European Community, which Heath achieved in 1972. (Britain became a member of the Community on January 1, 1973.) However, the government's measures failed to stem a rise in inflation, and when unemployment reached record levels, the government embarked on a new interventionist policy, including the imposition of a pay and prices policy. The government lost office in 1974.

The return of another Conservative government five years later saw a more determined effort by Heath's successor as party leader, Margaret Thatcher, to achieve a free-market economy and to move away from, indeed dismantle, the postwar consensus. The Thatcher government heralded a break with its predecessors both in terms of style and substance. The prime minister in particular adopted a combative style of government in pursuit of her goal: a rolling back of the frontiers of the state. Government intervention was seen as economically harmful, stifling initiative and the creative forces of the market. "The public had to be persuaded to lower its expectations of, and dependence on, the state; the social democratic consensus had to be replaced by a new neoliberal consensus."[26] Various policies were pursued in an attempt to achieve this goal.

The Thatcher government was to make a notable difference to British economic and political life. The change was not as great as Margaret Thatcher wanted. Politically, despite periods of tremendous strength during her eleven and a half years as prime minister, Thatcher was never able to mold a party and a cabinet completely committed to her neoliberal philosophy (see Chapter 6). Many of the government's policies were not as radical as she wanted. Subsidies to public-sector industries were maintained. Mechanisms for controlling the money supply were less than adequate to the task. When the economy went into recession, the Conservative government under Thatcher's successor opted for budget deficits and a shift of emphasis from fighting inflation to pursuing growth.

There was no social revolution that could have resulted in established social position being displaced by a new meritocracy, nor was there a paradigmatic shift of attitudes. A survey by the *Economist* in 1992 found little change, compared with the position twenty years before, in the dominant position of public (i.e. private) school and Oxbridge graduates in the top posts in business, the arts, and the professions. In some areas, a number of people had made it to the top from humble backgrounds, including Prime Minister John Major. "But change has not just been slow. It has been almost non-existent."[27]

There was similarly little move toward values espoused by Margaret Thatcher. Ten years after Mrs. Thatcher came to power, a survey of popular attitudes found that, asked to choose between a Thatcherite and a "socialist" society, respondents opted for the Thatcherite model on only two out of five dimensions, and then only by slender majorities. Indeed, over the decade, opinion on some issues had moved away from a Thatcherite position: Asked to choose between cutting taxes and extending public services, opinion in 1979 was equally divided; ten years later, those favoring extending services outnumbered tax cutters by a margin of seven to one.[28] Where Margaret Thatcher carried, and sometimes increased, support was on issues on which she already had prevailing public support when she entered office.

Yet the Thatcher era did witness major changes, some of the most significant being continued or sustained by her successors. In terms of substantive changes, the most significant was the reduction in the size of the public sector. Various utilities and companies previously taken into public ownership were privatized (that is, sold back to the private sector), a policy also pursued by the government of Thatcher's successor, John Major. In the period of Conservative government from 1979 to 1997, almost fifty major companies were privatized, including the telephone, gas, water, steel, coal, and electricity utilities. Among them, the companies employed almost one million workers. By 1996 there were only seven major nationalized industries remaining. These were run by management boards, with government expecting them to be run as commercial enterprises. The size of the public sector thus contracted.

The emphasis on a market economy also led to reductions in income tax (to the basic rates detailed in Chapter 1); to curbs on trade union power; to the ensuring of wider private ownership (not only of shares but also of housing); to the introduction of a greater market orientation for bodies remaining in the public sector, including local government and the national health service; and to greater autonomy in policy making by government. Organized economic interests that previously had been effectively co-opted in economic policy making were kept at arm's length. By the end of Margaret Thatcher's tenure of office in 1990, the nature of government and of public debate and the division between public and private sectors had changed significantly. Political parties were forced to work on the basis of a new political agenda.

Her successor as Conservative prime minister, John Major, continued a number of her innovative policies, including those on privatization, but sought neither to emulate her style nor to pursue her particular vision of future society. Rather, he consolidated the changes of the Thatcher era. The biggest impact of the Thatcher government was remarkably not so much on Thatcher's Conservative successor as prime minister, but rather upon her successor but two—Labour prime minister Tony Blair, elected to office in 1997.

Richard Rose, in a seminal work entitled *Do Parties Make a Difference?* argued that political parties make some difference in British politics, but not as much as is commonly believed, and not as much as suggested by the "adversary politics" approach.[29] The latter contends that one party elected to office reverses the policies of the party previously in government and so one has almost a Ping-Pong effect in policy terms. Rose argues that British politics is characterized instead by a rolling consensus, one party making some difference, the opposition party then adapting to the changes made and, when it comes to office, accepting those changes and making some change of its own. The government of Tony Blair appeared to validate Rose's thesis. The prime minister adopted a high profile style of leadership not dissimilar to Margaret Thatcher's. He emphasized the importance of private enterprise and of the market. The government made no attempt to bring back into public ownership the firms privatized during the period of Conservative government. Rather, it moved to allow greater freedom of commercial enterprise to some organizations still in the public sector, such as the Post Office. There were some changes to the law governing industrial relations, but none that undermined fundamentally the changes made by the Conservative government. Rates of income tax remained the same or, in the case of the standard rate, were lowered; the government also implemented an election pledge to stick to the Conservative spending plans it had inherited for the first two years of government. In other sectors, the government also failed to reverse Conservative changes, indeed in some cases appeared willing to build on them. Where it did make a change of its own was in introducing a program of constitutional change. And vindicating the Rose thesis was the Conservative response to that change. Though the Conservative opposition voted against the measures of constitutional change introduced by the Blair government, the new leader of the Conservative party, William Hague, announced that a future Conservative government would not seek simply to reverse them.

By the end of the 1990s, the political and economic landscape of Britain was thus very different from that of fifty years before. Much was still the same. Most traditional structures remained in place, as did many popular attitudes: the popular attachment to the National Health Service, for instance, remained strong. Government spending as a proportion of the gross domestic product (GDP) continued to grow. Continuity in many areas was marked, but so too was change. The economy was now a service economy with a greater emphasis on efficiency and global competition. Major utilities were operating in the private sector. Trade unions were no longer the significant political players they once had been. And political structures began to change following the election of a Labour government in 1997.

BRITISH ECONOMIC DECLINE?

In the 1950s and 1960s, Britain, as we have noted, experienced economic growth, but the rate of growth failed to keep pace with other western industrialized nations. Only in the 1960s, with economic downturn, was there a growing awareness of the relative position and the implications. Since then, there has been a fierce debate surrounding Britain's "decline" as a major force in the world economy. The concept of decline has to be treated with some caution. At times, the British economy has prospered, the country outstripping its principal rivals on several economic indicators. The economy appeared in a strong position in the latter half of the 1990s, and the United Kingdom remains a major nation in world economic terms. However, according to advocates of the thesis of decline, there is an underlying trend, one that characterized the latter half of the twentieth century (and, in some analyses, the first half as well), of the U.K. declining economically relative to other competitor nations. The nation has generally been outstripped by its competitors in terms of output and standard of living. Over the past fifty years, the annual increase in the GDP has usually lagged behind that of Organisation for Economic Development and Cooperation (OECD) countries. Britain's share of international trade in manufactures has fallen more or less continuously over the same period.[30]

In the debate about Britain's economic decline, several diagnoses have been offered. They can be grouped under three, albeit not mutually exclusive, heads: economic, sociological, and structural.

Economic Explanations

Three explanations can be subsumed under this particular head: the legacy of the empire, a resistance to modernize and invest, and the post-war consensus.

Some economists have laid the blame for economic failure at least partially on the emphasis given by successive governments to maintaining a balance of payments surplus in order to fund overseas military commitments and foreign investments, a policy pursued at the expense of economic growth.[31] A consequence of the empire has been that Britain has tended to retain a number of overseas commitments beyond what many regard as being within its financial capacity to do so. Despite a reduction in overseas commitments, the United Kingdom retains interests beyond those of the North Atlantic alliance, resulting in various occasions in the committal of troops: most notably in the Falkland Islands in 1982, but also in the Gulf War in 1991, in Bosnia in 1992, and in Kosovo and East Timor in 1999.

Another economic explanation for poor economic performance is a failure to modernize. There is a popular view that the Second World War was, for Britain, a military success but an economic disaster. The country was left in serious debt, primarily to the United States,[32] and with a large portion of its industrial plant still intact. There was neither the capacity nor the incentive to start afresh; a number of other countries had no option but to begin anew, both politically and economically. Britain continued to produce in markets with low skill requirements. Companies and financial institutions remained—and remain—more interested in profits than in long-term investment. Britain has thus been unable to keep pace with the development of new, science-based industries.[33]

The third explanation is that economic policies pursued by postwar governments created a dependency culture as well as maintained, indeed strengthened, vested interests and restrictive practices. Attempts by government to ensure industrial harmony proved expensive to the nation's capacity to compete. Industry was dogged by practices designed to maintain wage levels and employment even if those practices were manifestly inefficient and made the firm uncompetitive in international markets. Under this analysis, government has often not been part of the solution but rather part of the problem.

All three explanations remain current. Despite diversification and inward investment, with many new Japanese car plants and high-technology industries, there remains some attachment to established industries and Britain's status as a military power. When attempts were made, following the collapse of the Iron Curtain, to reap the "peace dividend" by reducing the size of Britain's armed services, there was sustained opposition from many politicians who believed the cuts threatened Britain's capacity to maintain its global influence. Profit-maximizing continues to characterize the approach of major companies and city institutions. British companies lag behind foreign competitors in terms of skills training and investment in research and development.

Sociological Explanations

Some explanations of decline have been primarily sociological. As we have seen in Chapter 1, class did not displace status in British society. Preindustrial aristocratic attitudes were carried over into an industrial age. These attitudes included looking down on the pursuit of "trade" as somewhat socially inferior. Low priority was given to industry and science and, so this analysis goes, a tendency grew for those with wealth to favor professions such as the law.[34] Such attitudes are less pronounced but still apparent today. An allied perception, still pronounced, is that breeding—meaning principally status by inheritance—and a good general education constitute the basis for positions of eminence. The top positions in business and elsewhere are, as was found in the 1992 survey already mentioned, still likely to be held by men (rarely women) with a public school and Oxbridge education—or, indeed, no university education. Whereas nine out of every ten senior managers in the United States and Japan will be graduates, often with specialist degrees, the proportion in the United Kingdom is only about one in four. Top management has thus often been notable for having no particular training for the task, the "old school tie" proving more valuable than a particular degree for advancing up the career ladder.

Some blame for sluggish economic performance also has been imputed to the egalitarianism of the labor movement, which harbors dislike of profits, risk taking, and management.[35] "There have been constant complaints of poor motivation of the labor force and lack of readiness to co-operate in changes of organization, equipment and productive methods (or, put differently, bloody-mindedness and militancy). Nor are such complaints new."[36] Unlike the case in the United States, there is no culture in the United Kingdom that favors ambition among blue-collar workers to achieve a junior managerial post and then a post above that. In some industries, it is not just management positions that traditionally have been seen as having passed from father to son, but the manual jobs as well.

In short, bringing the two sociological explanations together, the attitudes of both the social elite and the labor movement—generating an "us" and "them" mentality in industrial relations—have hindered economic growth.[37] Both sides have been content to maintain that relationship, with attempts to break it down coming from outside, from government legislation, or from the influx of working practices of those, such as the Japanese, responsible for establishing new factories on U.K. sites.

Structural Explanations

Structural explanations, like the economic, can be subsumed under three heads: adversary politics, centralization, and pluralist stagnation.

The adversary politics thesis is one that we have already touched on. It was developed in the 1970s and achieved renewed prominence in the 1990s. It contends that attempts to generate long-term solutions to problems are thwarted by a system that encourages an adversary relationship between the two main political parties, with those parties vying with one another for the all-or-nothing spoils of a general election victory.[38] Investors and managers are unable to plan ahead because they are uncertain as to what a future government may do. A party in opoposition will say that it will reverse a policy brought forward by government: In the event it may not do so, but its threat to do so leaves markets uncertain. Furthermore, an adversary relationship has meant that government, despite large parliamentary majorities, has been unable to mobilize a consensus in support of its policies. For those who advance this thesis, the political system does not offer the means of resolving the nation's problems; rather the way the system is structured is seen as part—a very central part—of the problem.

The thesis of centralization dovetails to some extent with that of adversary politics. As government responsibilities in the twentieth century have expanded, so government power has become increasingly centralized. The problem, according to a number of observers, was exacerbated by the election in 1979 of a Conservative government under Margaret Thatcher. To implement the goal of a free-market economy, the government had to strengthen its own powers, creating what Andrew Gamble termed "the Strong State."[39] Many commentators see that concentration of power maintained under the premiership of Tony Blair. Although some power is being devolved to elected assemblies in Scotland and Wales, power over central economic and political issues remains firmly entrenched in Downing Street.

A centralization of power is seen as part of a vicious circle. The government, by virtue of a political system that allows it largely unfettered lawmaking power (through a parliamentary majority), is able to extend its formal powers. However, the adversarial nature of that same system militates against its mobilizing the support of disparate groups—and the population generally—to tackle economic problems. Consequently, to tackle these problems, the government takes more powers. The more powers it takes, the more distant it becomes from those groups it needs to mobilize; hence a government with strong legal powers vested by Parliament but an increasingly limited capacity to mobilize support. This line of argument was especially prominent during the years of Thatcher government, from 1979 to 1990.

The thesis of pluralist stagnation asserts that the problem lies with the growth of groups in Britain, each group pursuing its own interests and bringing pressure to bear on government to provide resources or pursue policies to the benefit of its members. Government for its part has been unwilling to pursue policies that would arouse opposition from well-entrenched groups, resulting in inertia.[40] The problem has been exacerbated by the growth in the number of organized groups. Because there are so many, self-restraint would bring no discernible benefit to any particular group. As a result, even though recognizing the need for restraint, a group is tempted to maintain or increase existing demands. Other groups then compete by raising their demands. Government is then overwhelmed by the multiplicity of self-serving demands.

These various explanations have vied with one another and have variously influenced government policy. As we have seen, the Thatcher government pursued policies designed to limit trade union influence, to keep interest groups at arm's length, and to create a free market. According to critics, what the government did was to exacerbate the problem by destroying the nation's manufacturing base *and* to exacerbate the adversary nature of British politics. The Labour government of Tony Blair has sought to be more inclusive in policy making, while maintaining many of the changes made by his Conservative predecessors. Power, however, remains concentrated in the hands of the prime minister and senior ministers.

These competing theses also have relevance for our later analyis of the political system. The pursuit of particular economic policies and the structure of the political system constitute two principal, and competing, explanations for the decline in support for the two main political parties in recent years (Chapter 6). Pluralist stagnation, and the attempts by government to break out of a cycle of stagnation, are important for explaining the activity of pressure groups in recent decades (Chapter 7). Structural—and sociological—analyses underpin current debate on government and the civil service (Chapter 8) and, most important of all, the combination of adversary politics and centralization have been at the heart of demands for new constitutional arrangements in the United Kingdom. The debate about those constitutional arrangements features throughout subsequent chapters and forms the basis of our concluding chapter. The United Kingdom is witnessing some constitutional change, but is that change based on an accurate analysis of the problem?

NOTES

[1] See A. H. Dodd, *The Growth of Responsible Government* (Routledge & Kegan Paul, 1956), pp. 43–44.

[2] B. Kemp, *King and Commons 1600–1832* (Macmillan, 1957), p. 3.

[3] Its provisions included, for example, "That excessive Baile ought not to be required nor excessive Fines imposed nor cruell and unusuall Punishments inflicted." Compare this with the Eighth Amendment to the United States Constitution, which prescribes that "Excessive bail shall not be required, nor excessive fines imposed, nor cruel and unusual punishments inflicted."

[4] J. H. Plumb, *England in the Eighteenth Century* (Penguin, 1950), p. 5.

[5] J. Mackintosh, *The British Cabinet,* 3rd ed. (Stevens, 1977), pp. 50–51.

[6] Ibid., p. 64.

[7] S. M. Lipset, *The First New Nation* (Heinemann, 1964); P. Mathias, *The First Industrial Nation* (Methuen, 1969).

[8] Sir L. Woodward, *The Age of Reform 1815–1870,* 2nd ed. (Oxford University Press, 1962), p. 3.

[9] A table compiled in 1815 revealed that 144 peers, along with 123 commoners, controlled 471 seats (more than two-thirds of the total number) in the House of Commons. M. Ostrogorski, *Democracy and the Organisation of Political Parties,Vol. 1: England* (Macmillan, 1902), p. 20.

[10] J. B. Conacher (ed.), *The Emergence of British Parliamentary Democracy in the Nineteenth Century* (Wiley, 1971), p. 10. Different authors cite different figures.

[11] Most measures placed before Parliament were usually small measures affecting private interests, for example giving the power necessary to enclose land or build a new railway line.

[12] W. Bagehot, *The English Constitution* (first published 1867; Fontana ed., 1963), p. 150.

[13] Mackintosh, p. 113.

[14] See Conacher, pp. 68–69, for a summary.

[15] See H. J. Hanham, *Elections and Party Management,* 3rd ed. (Harvester Press, 1978), p. xii.

[16] Similarly, in the United States the all-or-nothing spoils of presidential victory have encouraged two rather than many parties.

[17] A. L. Lowell, *The Government of England*, Vol. 2 (Macmillan, 1924), pp. 76–78.

[18] Mackintosh, p. 174.

[19] Reforms were introduced by Conservative as well as Liberal governments. On the Conservative reforms, see P. Norton (ed), *The Conservative Party* (Prentice Hall/Harvester Wheatsheaf, 1996), p. 29.

[20] P. Addison, *The Road to 1945* (Quartet, 1977), p. 127.

[21] I. Macleod, *Neville Chamberlain* (Muller, 1961), p. 123.

[22] S. H. Beer, *Modern British Politics* (Faber, 1969 ed.), pp. 278-287.

[23] Addison, p. 29.

[24] *Social Insurance and Allied Services—Report by Sir William Beveridge*, Cmnd. 6404 (Her Majesty's Stationery Office, 1942), para. 17, p. 9.

[25] Based on the title of Vernon Bogdanor and Robert Skidelsky (eds.), *The Age of Affluence 1951-1964* (Macmillan, 1970).

[26] I. Crewe, "The Thatcher Legacy," in A. King (ed.), *Britain at the Polls 1992* (Chatham House, 1993), p. 18.

[27] "The Ascent of British Man," *Economist,* December 19, 1992, p. 21.

[28] Crewe, pp. 19-22. See also P. Norton, "The Conservative Party from Thatcher to Major," in A. King (ed.), *Britain at the Polls 1992* (Chatham House, 1993), pp. 32-33.

[29] R. Rose, *Do Parties Make a Difference?* 2nd ed. (Macmillan, 1984). The "adversary politics" is discussed in the next section.

[30] A. Cairncross, *The British Economy Since 1945,* 2nd ed. (Blackwell, 1995), pp. 16-19.

[31] See, for example, A. W. Manser, *Britain in Balance* (Penguin, 1973).

[32] This fact is resented by part of the political elite in Britain. This was reinforced in 1945 by the terms of the loan to Britain by the United States. Some Conservative members of Parliament saw the terms as part of an attempt to open up world markets to the benefit of the United States, and some Labour members feared that it would, in the words of one of them, hitch the nation "to the American bandwagon." Further resentment was caused by the active opposition of the U.S. government to Britain's attempt to occupy the Suez Canal zone by force in 1956.

[33] W. Grant, *The Politics of Economic Policy* (Harvester Wheatsheaf, 1993), pp. 16-17, 20.

[34] See, e.g., M. Postan, *An Economic History of Western Europe 1945-64* (Methuen, 1967).

[35] See, eg., K. Joseph, *Stranded on the Middle Ground* (Centre for Policy Studies, 1976).

[36] Cairncross, p. 26.

[37] See Cairncross, pp. 26-27.

[38] See especially S. E. Finer (ed.), *Adversary Politics and Electoral Reform* (Wigram, 1975); D. Coombes, *Representative Government and Economic Power* (Heinemann, 1982); and A. M. Gamble and S. A. Walkland, *The British Party System and Economic Policy 1945-1983* (Oxford University Press, 1984).

[39] A. Gamble, *The Free Economy and the Strong State* (Macmillan, 1988).

[40] See I. Gilmour, *The Body Politic,* rev. ed. (Hutchinson, 1971); and J. E. S. Hayward, *Political Inertia* (University of Hull Press, 1975).

PART II

The Political Environment

CHAPTER 4

The Uncodified Constitution

A constitution may be defined as the body of laws, customs, and conventions that define the composition and powers of organs of the state and that regulate the relations of the various state organs to one another and to the private citizen.[1]

The United States has a constitution; so does the United Kingdom. Expressed in purely formal terms (Table 4.1) there is very little similarity between them. Indeed, the differences are such that to the student weaned on a study of the U.S. Constitution, the British Constitution is nearly incomprehensible. Even to the student of British politics it is not well understood. Nonetheless, the differences should not be emphasized to the exclusion of certain common features. Both Constitutions are strong in that they reflect their respective political cultures.

The U.S. Constitution is considered by Americans to embody the principles of a higher law, to constitute "in fact imperfect man's most perfect rendering of what Blackstone saluted as 'the eternal immutable laws of good and evil, to which the creator himself in all his dispensations conforms: and which he has enabled human reason to discover, so far as they are necessary for the conduct of human actions.'"[2] As the embodiment of a higher law, it thus not only needs to be distinguished from ordinary law, but also needs to be protected from the passing whims of politicians—hence the introduction of extraordinary procedures for its amendment.

By contrast, the British Constitution has been admired by Britons for reflecting the wisdom of past generations, as the product of experience—in short, a constitution that stipulates what should be on the basis of what has proved to work, rather than on abstract first principles. The empirical orientation to change that underpins such a constitution also favors flexibility in amendment: As conditions change, so some amendment may be necessary. Formal extraordinary procedures for its amendment have not been found necessary.

TABLE 4.1 U.S. and British constitutions

Characteristics	Constitutions	
	United States	**United Kingdom**
Form of expression	Written	Part written but uncodified
Date and manner of formulation	1787 by a constitutional convention.	No one date of formulation, no precise manner of formulation
Means of formal amendment	By two-thirds majorities in both houses of Congress and by ratification of three-quarters of the states, or by conventions	No extraordinary provisions for amendment
Location of its provisions	The written document (also judicial decisions, custom usage, works of authority)	Statute law, common law conventions, works of authority
Bodies responsible for interpretation of its provisions	The judiciary primarily (can be overridden by constitutional amendment)	The judiciary (statute and common law), scholars, politicians (conventions)
Main provisions	Document as "supreme law," judicial review, separation and overlap of powers, federal system, bill of rights, republican form of government	Parliamentary sovereignty, "rule of law," unitary (union) state, parliamentary government under a constitutional monarchy
Public promulgation of its provisions (in textbooks, etc.)	Extensive	Infrequent

The differences in political culture have thus produced somewhat different constitutions, but the attachment to them is similar in the two countries. Also, as we shall see, there are certain similarities in sources and in the means of interpretation. The similarities are also somewhat greater as a result of constitutional changes in the United Kingdom in recent years. Indeed, we can distinguish between what may be termed the "traditional"—or Westminster—Constitution and what may, with some justice, be characterized as a modified Westminster Constitution that is developing in the United Kingdom. Let us consider first the essential features of the traditional constitution.

FORMS OF EXPRESSION

New nations from the eighteenth century onward have found it both necessary and useful to codify their constitutions. At the time that the founding fathers promulgated the U.S. Constitution in Philadelphia, a written constitution was exceptional. Today it is the norm. Having lacked the opportunity to create a new constitutional framework afresh from first principles, Britain now stands out as one of the few nations lacking such a document.

The absence of a written constitution similar to that of the United States and other nations has led to the British Constitution being described as unwritten, but such a description is misleading. As we shall see, various elements of the Constitution find expression in formal, written enactments. What distinguishes the British Constitution from others is not that it is unwritten, but rather that it is part written and uncodified. The lack of codification is of special importance. It makes it difficult to identify clearly and authoritatively what constitute the provisions of the Constitution. As Madgwick and Woodhouse have noted, "it is easier to say what the British constitution is not than to say what it is."[3] Nonetheless, certain principles clearly are at the heart of the Constitution, parliamentary sovereignty being the prime example, but there are many provisions, be they expressed through statute law or the writings of constitutional experts, that are of constitutional significance but on which there is no clear agreement that they are core provisions of the British Constitution. It is this lack of codified certainty that makes a study of the constitution so fraught with difficulty.

SOURCES

Because one cannot have recourse to one simple authoritative document to discover the provisions of the British Constitution, one has instead to research four separate sources: statute law, common law, conventions, and works of authority. Such sources are also relevant in analyses of the U.S. Constitution. Congress may pass measures of constitutional significance, such as certain stipulations of electoral law or the War Powers Act. Provisions of the Constitution are developed and molded by judicial decisions. In seeking to interpret the Constitution, the courts may have recourse to works by constitutional experts. The difference between the two countries is that in Britain such sources are primary sources, and in the United States the primary source is the written document.

Of the four sources, statute law is perhaps the best understood and, nowadays, the most extensive. It provides the main source for the part-written element of the British Constitution. It comprises acts of Parliament and subordinate legislation made under the authority of the parent act. Many acts of Parliament that have been passed clearly merit the title of constitutional law. Acts that define the powers of the various state organs (for example, the 1911 and 1949 Parliament Acts) and acts that define the relationship between Crown and Parliament (notably the Bill of Rights of 1689), between the component elements of the nation (the Act of Union with Scotland of 1707, for example, and the Scotland Act 1998), between the United Kingdom and the European Union (the 1972 European Communities Act and subsequent amending acts), and between the state and the individual (as with the Habeas Corpus Act of 1679 and the Human Rights Act 1998) clearly constitute important provisions of the Constitution. They are published in authoritative, written form and, as acts of

Parliament, are interpreted by the courts. This is the most important of the four sources both in quantitative and qualitative terms. It has increasingly displaced common law as the most extensive form of law in Britain and it is the most definitive of the four. It takes precedence over any conflicting common law and is superior to the conventions of the Constitution and to works of authority. Its precedence derives from the concept of parliamentary sovereignty. It has, as we shall see, also made possible the introduction of what amounts in effect to a "higher law" in the form of certain international treaties.

Common law constitutes legal principles developed by the courts and rules and customs of ancient lineage that are so well established that they have been upheld as law by the courts in cases decided before them. Once a court has upheld a provision as being part of common law, it creates a precedent to be followed by other courts. In past centuries, when few statutes were enacted, common law constituted the main body of English law; today, it has been largely but certainly not wholly displaced by statute law. Certain principles derived from common law remain fundamental to the Constitution, and these include the principle of parliamentary sovereignty.

Under the heading of common law comes also prerogative powers—the powers and privileges recognized by common law as belonging to the Crown. Although many prerogative powers have been displaced by statute, many matters at the heart of government are still determined under the authority of the prerogative. These include the appointment of ministers, the making of treaties, the power of pardon, the dispensing of honors, and the declaration of war. By convention, such powers are normally exercised formally by the monarch on the advice of ministers (the ministers, in practice, make the decisions). There is no formal requirement that Parliament assent to such decisions. This is in stark contrast to the position in the United States, where Congress alone has the formal power to declare war and the Senate's consent is necessary for the ratification of treaties and the appointment of federal public officers. (In practice, the differences are not that great: "presidential wars" have been waged without a congressional declaration of war, and in Britain a government taking military action abroad will seek the consent of Parliament.) In 1972 the Treaty of Accession to the European Community was signed under prerogative powers. In 1982 a naval task force was dispatched to the Falkland Islands under the same authority. Although diminishing in number, prerogative powers clearly remain of great importance.

Generally included under the generic heading of common law is the judicial interpretation of statute law. Unlike those in the United States, British courts have, under the traditional constitution, no power to hold a measure unconstitutional. They are limited to the interpretation of provisions of acts of Parliament. Even in exercising their power of interpretation, they are limited by rules of interpretation and by precedent. (The exception is the House of Lords, the highest domestic court of appeal, which is not now bound by its previous decisions.) Nonetheless, judges retain the power to distinguish cases, and by their interpretation they can develop a substantial body of case law. In interpreting acts of Parliament, they traditionally have assumed Parliament to have meant what, on the face of it, the words of an act appear to mean. However, following a decision of the House of Lords (in its judicial capacity) in 1992, it is now possible for courts, where they consider it necessary, to look at the proceedings of Parliament in order to determine what Parliament really meant. The courts have also assumed a new role as a consequence of British membership in the European Union—changing fundamentally the traditional constitution—but this role, as we shall see, derives from the provisions of an act of Parliament.

The third and least tangible source of the Constitution is that of convention. Conventions of the British Constitution are most aptly described as rules of behavior that are considered binding by and upon those who are responsible for making the Constitution work, but rules that are not enforced by the courts or by the presiding officers in either house of Parliament.[4] They derive their strength from the realization that not to abide by them would make for an unworkable Constitution. They are, so to speak, the oil in the formal machinery of the Constitution. They help fill the gap between the constitutional formality and the political reality. For example, ministers are responsible formally to the monarch. Because of the political changes wrought in the nineteenth century, they are by convention responsible now also to Parliament. By convention, the government of the day resigns or requests a dissolution of Parliament if a motion of no confidence is carried against it in the House of Commons. By convention, the monarch gives the Royal Assent to all legislative measures approved by Parliament. The last time a monarch refused assent was in 1707, when Queen Anne vetoed a Scottish Militia Bill. Queen Victoria in the nineteenth century contemplated refusing her assent to a measure, but wiser counsels prevailed.

No formal, authoritative documents establish these rules, and they find no embodiment in statute law. The courts may recognize them but have no power to enforce them. They are complied with because of the recognition of what would happen if they were not complied with. For the queen to refuse her assent to a measure passed by the two houses of Parliament would draw her into the realms of political controversy, hence jeopardizing the claim of the monarch to be "above politics." A government that sought to remain in office after losing a vote of confidence in the House of Commons would find its position politically untenable: It would lack the political authority to govern. For ministers to ignore Parliament completely would prove equally untenable.

Some conventions may be described as being stronger than others. Some on occasion are breached, whereas others are adhered to without exception. On three occasions in the past century, the convention of collective ministerial responsibility has been suspended temporarily by the prime minister of the day. In contrast, no government has sought to remain in office after losing a parliamentary vote of confidence. The point at which a useful and necessary practice is accorded the status of a constitutional convention is not clear. Once a practice has become well established in terms of the relationship within or between different organs of the state, finding recognition in works of authority and by those involved in its operation, then it may be said to have reached the status of a convention. At any one time, though, a number of relationships may be said to be in a constitutional haze. Is it a convention of the Constitution that the government of the day must consult with interested bodies before formulating a legislative measure for presentation to Parliament? A noted constitutional lawyer, Sir Ivor Jennings, once argued that it was.[5] Prime Minister Harold Wilson appeared to give some credence to this view in 1966 when he said in the House of Commons that it was the *duty* of the government to consult with the Trades Union Congress and the Confederation of British Industry.[6] Few other authorities have supported Jennings's assertion and it has not found acceptance by most practitioners of government. Governments often do engage in such consultation, but it is not a convention of the Constitution that they do so.

The fourth and final source of the Constitution is that of works of authority. These have persuasive authority only. What constitutes a "work of authority" is rarely defined. Various early works are accorded particular standing by virtue of the absence of statutes or other written sources covering a particular area. The statements of their writers are presumed to be evidence of judicial decisions that have been lost and are therefore accepted if not contrary to reason.[7] Among the most important early sources are Fitzherbert's *Abridgment* (1516) and Coke's *Institutes of the Law of England* (1628–1644). More recent works have been called into aid on those occasions when jurists and others have sought to delineate features of the contemporary Constitution; this has been the case especially in determining the existence or otherwise of conventions. Given that conventions are prescribed neither by statute nor by judicial interpretation, one must study instead scholarly interpretations of political behavior and practice. Especially important authoritative works in the nineteenth century were those by John Austin and A. V. Dicey. Important names in the twentieth century included constitutional lawyers Sir Ivor Jennings, Sir Kenneth Wheare, O. Hood Phillips, and E. C. S. Wade.[8]

Given the disparate sources of the British Constitution and the fact that important relationships within and between organs of the state are not laid down in any one formal or binding document, it is not surprising that one must have recourse to books by constitutional scholars to discover the extent and nature of those relationships. Works of authority tend to be consulted more frequently in the field of constitutional law than in any other branch of English law.

MEANS OF AMENDMENT

Given the disparate primary sources of the British Constitution and the difficulty in determining where the Constitution begins and ends, it is perhaps not surprising that there are no extraordinary procedures for its amendment. Statute and common law of constitutional significance are subject to amendment by the same process as that employed for other legislative enactments. Conventions can be modified by changes in behavior or by reinterpretations of the significance of certain behavior. Works of authority can be rewritten or subjected to different interpretations in the same way as can other texts.

Much the same can be said about constitutionally significant statute law, judicial decisions, and works of authority in the United States. Even the provisions of the formal document, the U.S. Constitution, may be amended by judicial decisions and custom usage. The difference between the two countries is that the formal wording of the U.S. Constitution can be amended only by an extraordinary process, that is, one that goes beyond the provisions employed for amending the ordinary law. (Because of the extraordinary procedures necessary for amendment, the provisions of the Constitution are commonly referred to as "entrenched.") No such formal amending procedures exist in Britain, where there is no formal document.

INTERPRETATION

As may be surmised from the foregoing, there is no single body endowed with responsibility for interpreting the provisions of the Constitution. As in the United States, statute and common law are subject to judicial interpretation, but there is no power of judicial review, at least not as the term is understood in the United States. The courts can influence and to some extent mold certain provisions through their interpretation of statute and common law. Indeed, their use of common law has been of special importance in outlining and protecting certain rights of the individual. However, at the end of the day, they are subject to the wishes of Parliament. Judicial interpretation of statute law can, under the traditional constitution, be overridden by a new act of Parliament.

Identification and interpretation of conventions have little to do with the courts. Conventions arise as a result of changes in the relationships within and between different organs of the state. Their delineation rests with scholars, and their enforcement rests with those at whom they are aimed.

The Constitution, in short, is subject to interpretation by different bodies, the most prominent being politicians, judges, and scholars. The same can be said of the U.S. Constitution, but in Britain there is no body that stands in a position analogous to that of the U.S. Supreme Court. This is an important difference, reflecting the differences in political culture. The Lockean basis of constitutional interpretation in the United States—a higher law cognizable by independent, rational magistrates operating free of outside interests[9]—finds no parallel in Britain.

MAIN PROVISIONS

The central provisions of the traditional, or Westminster, British Constitution are listed in Table 4.1: parliamentary sovereignty, the rule of law, a unitary (as opposed to a federal) system, and what I have termed "parliamentary government under a constitutional monarchy." The notable characteristic of this constitution is that it facilitated strong government in the United Kingdom. Under it, power has been concentrated both politically (Whitehall as the center of the executive) and geographically (Whitehall being at the center of the nation's capital). The constitution derived from the Glorious Revolution of 1688–89 and events subsequent to that, especially—as we shall see—in the nineteenth century. Formally, the Westminster Constitution still exists—the four components remain in place—but it has changed dramatically in the last three decades. What the United Kingdom now has, insofar as it can be characterized, is a modified Westminster Constitution. It no longer facilitates, to the extent that it did in the period from the late nineteenth century to the 1970s, strong, central government. The reasons for this change are to be found in two developments. The first is British membership in the European Community, now the European Union. Membership has added a new dimension to the British constitution (see later, Table 4.2) and forms, in effect, a fifth central component. The second development comprises various constitutional changes introduced by the Labour government of Tony Blair (see later, Table 4.3). Foremost among these is devolution—the devolving of powers to elected assemblies in Scotland, Wales, and Northern Ireland—and the passage of a Human Rights Act. None destroys, at least not formally, any of the existing core components of the Constitution, but they serve variously to weaken or strengthen them.

Parliamentary Sovereignty

Parliamentary sovereignty was identified by the great nineteenth century constitutional lawyer, A. V. Dicey, as one of the twin pillars of the British Constitution.[10] (The other was the rule of law.) Dicey also offered the most succinct definition of parliamentary sovereignty, one that has been highly influential ever since. Parliamentary sovereignty, he wrote, means that Parliament has "the right to make or unmake any law whatever; and, further, that no person or body is recognized by the law of England as having a right to override or set aside the legislation of Parliament."[11] An act passed by Parliament will be enforced by the courts, the courts recognizing no body other than Parliament as having authority to override such an act. Parliament itself can substitute an act for an earlier one. One of the precepts derived from the principle is that Parliament is not bound by its predecessors. Once Parliament has passed an act, it becomes the law of the land. It is not open to challenge before the courts on the grounds of being unconstitutional.

Although Dicey claimed more ancient lineage for it, the principle of parliamentary sovereignty became established as a judicial rule in consequence of the Glorious Revolution of 1688 and subsequent Bill of Rights, which established the relationship between the Crown and Parliament (see Chapter 3). It was the product of an alliance between Parliament and common lawyers and of the intimidation of judges by the House of Commons. Assertion of the principle served to do away with the monarch's previously claimed powers to suspend or dispense with acts of Parliament and it served to deny judges the power to strike down measures. It came to occupy a unique place in constitutional law. The principle finds no expression in statute or any other formal enactment. It exists in common law but enjoys a special status beyond that enjoyed by other principles of common law. Its underpinnings are not only legal but also political and historical. Judicial obedience to it constitutes what H. W. R. Wade referred to as "the ultimate political fact upon which the whole system of legislation hangs."[12] No statute can confer the power of parliamentary sovereignty, for that would be to confer the very power being acted upon. It is therefore considered to be unique. As Hood Phillips states, "It may indeed be called the one fundamental law of the British Constitution."[13]

However, as we shall see, this "one fundamental law" is challenged, in effect, by the consequences of British membership of the European Union (EU) and by devolution. The use of referendums—to approve, for example, devolution in Scotland, Wales, and Northern Ireland—has also been argued to limit parliamentary sovereignty: Though the results of the referendums are advisory, it would appear perverse for Parliament to then go against them. The doctrine remains extant—Acts of Parliament remain omnicompetent—but the capacity of Parliament to make or unmake any law whatsoever, with no body other than Parliament being able to set aside that law, is now limited.

The Rule of Law

The second pillar identified by Dicey was that of "the rule of law." Few students of the Constitution would deny the importance of the tenet. However, it is a concept that has labored under two limitations. One limitation has been that there is no agreed definition of the term. Dicey himself argued that it comprised "at least three distinct though kindred conceptions": "that no man is punishable or can be lawfully made to suffer in body or goods except for a distinct breach of law established in the ordinary legal manner before the ordinary courts of the land"; that "no man is above the law [and] every man, whatever be his rank or condition, is subject to the ordinary law of the realm and amenable to the jurisdiction of the ordinary tribunals"; and that "the general principles of the constitution [are] the result of judicial decisions determining the rights of private persons in particular cases brought before the courts." These three conceptions have been subject to various criticisms: among them, that many discretionary powers are vested in officials and public bodies, that many officials and bodies have immunities that the ordinary citizen does not have, and that certain rights have been modified by or enacted in statute. Furthermore, it is not clear why Dicey's third conception should be considered "kindred" to the other two. Some students of the Constitution find Dicey's analysis useful, and others tend to be dismissive; even Dicey later revised his own definition.

The rule of law, then, stands as a central element of the British Constitution, but no one is sure precisely what it means. It remains "one of the most elusive of all political concepts."[14] Some writers, especially in recent years, have tended to accord it a wide definition, encompassing substantive rights. On their argument, the rule of law cannot be said to exist unless basic human rights are protected. Others have adopted a narrow and more long-standing definition, contending that the concept entails certain procedural (or "due process") rights, that government must be subject to the law, and that the judiciary must be independent. The problem is one of determining what those rights are, how they are to be protected, and how the independence of the judiciary is to be maintained.

The second limitation is that the rule of law is not logically compatible with that of parliamentary sovereignty. Parliament could, if it so wished, confer arbitrary powers upon government. It could fetter the independence of the judiciary. It could limit or remove altogether certain rights presumed to exist at common law. The rule of law, in short, could be threatened or even dispensed with by parliamentary enactment. Dicey himself recognized this problem and sought to resolve it. He argued, in essence, that the rule of law prevented government from exercising arbitrary powers. If government wanted such powers, it could obtain them only through Parliament (Parliament itself has never sought to exercise executive powers) and the granting of them could take place only after deliberation and approval by the triumvirate of monarch, Lords, and Commons.[15]

Such an argument serves to explain potential impediments to a government intent on acquiring arbitrary powers. It does not deny the truth of the assertion that Parliament could, if it wished, confer such powers upon government. Critics of the Westminster Constitution have variously sought to provide some means of protecting rights from a powerful executive. For many years they advocated an entrenched Bill of Rights or, at least, the incorporation into British law of the European Convention on Human Rights (see Chapter 14). With the return of a Labour government in 1997, they achieved the latter. The Human Rights Act 1998 brought the provisions of the Convention into British law. Parliamentary sovereignty remains in place—the courts are not empowered to strike down laws that contravene the Convention, and Parliament could repeal or amend the 1998 Act. But the Act creates a legal environment that makes it difficult for Parliament and government to consider overriding its provisions, or not to act when the courts declare a measure in breach of the Convention.

Unitary (or Union) State

The third feature of the Constitution that I have listed—that the United Kingdom is a unitary state—is a less difficult one to comprehend. The United States is a federal nation. The power vested in the federal government is that delegated in the U.S. Constitution: All other powers not delegated rest with the states or the people. The U.S. Congress cannot abolish the states nor legislate to remove those powers. In the United Kingdom, Parliament exercises legal sovereignty. It can create regional and local units of government and confer powers and responsibilities on them. It can also remove those units of government and their powers.

The unitary nation is that of the United Kingdom of Great Britain and Northern Ireland. Wales was integrated with England in 1536 by act of Parliament (the Laws in Wales Act), and Scotland and England were incorporated in 1707 by the Treaty of Union and by the Act of Union with Scotland. Ireland entered into legislative union in 1801. Following an armed uprising, the emergence of the Irish Free State was recognized in 1922 and given the status of a self-governing dominion. (The Irish Constitution of 1937 declared the country to be a sovereign independent state, a position recognized by the Westminster Parliament in 1949.) Excluded from the Irish Free State were the northern six counties of Ireland, forming part of the traditional region of Ulster. The Protestant majority in Ulster wished to remain part of the United Kingdom, and the province of Northern Ireland has so remained.

Though power remains centralized, the different parts of the United Kingdom have retained their national identities and, in the case of Scotland, retained a legal and educational system different from that of the rest of the United Kingdom. It is because of these distinct identities that the United Kingdom has sometimes been characterized as a union state, several countries coming together in one union. Recent years have seen a greater emphasis on this element, with some political powers now being devolved to elected assemblies in Scotland, Wales, and Northern Ireland (Chapter 10). (There is also some pressure for powers to be devolved to elected regional assemblies in England or to an English parliament.) Again, parliamentary sovereignty remains in place—Parliament can repeal or amend the acts setting up the elected assemblies (as it did with an earlier act creating a parliament in Northern Ireland)—but political pressures may make it difficult to change the arrangements. Some commentators also have argued that the basis on which a Northern Ireland parliament and related bodies were created in 1998, involving agreement and cooperation with another country (the Republic of Ireland), makes it difficult for Parliament unilaterally to alter the arrangements.

Parliamentary Government under a Constitutional Monarchy

The fourth element of the Constitution is one that I have described as a parliamentary government under a constitutional monarchy. It is this element that is especially important in terms of the current relationships among the different organs of the state and the one in which conventions of the Constitution are predominant. It constitutes an assembly of different relationships and powers, the product of traditional institutions being adapted to meet changing circumstances. The developments producing this form of government were sketched in Chapter 3. The result, as we have seen, was parliamentary government in the sense of government *through* Parliament rather than government *by* Parliament, with a largely ceremonial head of state. The essentials of this form of government may be outlined as follows.

In the relationship among government, Parliament, and the monarch, the government dominates. Although lacking formal powers, the cabinet is recognized by convention as being at the heart of government. It is responsible for the final determination of policy to be submitted to Parliament, for the supreme control of the national executive in accordance with the policy prescribed by Parliament, and for continuous coordination and delimitation of the interests of the several departments of state.[16] It is presided over by the prime minister. The prime minister is appointed by the monarch. By convention, the monarch summons the leader of the party with a majority of seats in the House of Commons. (In the event of a party having no overall majority, the monarch summons whomever he or she believes may be able to form an administration.) The prime minister then selects the members of his or her cabinet and other government ministers and submits their names to the monarch who, by convention, does not deny the prime minister's choice. By convention, ministers are drawn from Parliament and, again by convention, predominantly from the elected house, the House of Commons. Although the government no longer is chosen by the Commons, it nonetheless is elected through the House of Commons: There is no separate election of the executive. There is a separation and overlap of powers between the government and the House of Commons in Britain but no equivalent separation of personnel. Government ministers are drawn from, and remain within, Parliament.

Legally, ministers are responsible to the monarch. Politically, they are responsible for their policies and actions to Parliament. Ministers are responsible to Parliament through the convention of individual ministerial responsibility, which assigns to them control of their departments, for which they are answerable to Parliament. The cabinet is similarly responsible to Parliament through the convention of collective ministerial responsibility. This convention, one scholar writes, "implies that all cabinet ministers assume responsibility for cabinet decisions and actions taken to implement those decisions."[17] It also has begotten two other conventions. It is a corollary of collective responsibility that any minister who disagrees publicly with a cabinet decision should resign and that a government defeat in the House of Commons on a vote of confidence necessitates either the resignation of the government or a request for a dissolution of Parliament. (There is no convention as to which of these alternatives the government should select.) Party cohesion ensures that the cabinet usually enjoys a parliamentary majority, but political parties remain largely unknown to the Constitution.

The cabinet approves government bills to be presented to Parliament. (In drawing up measures, it is aided primarily by its officials—that is, civil servants—and will frequently consult with interested bodies: Such consultation, though, enjoys no formal recognition in constitutional terms.) Within Parliament, the most important house is the Commons. It is expected to submit bills to sustained scrutiny and debate before giving its assent to them (or not giving its assent to them, but the influence of party usually precludes such an outcome). Formally, the Commons is free to pass or reject bills as it wishes. The House of Lords is more constrained (see Chapter 3); it was forced to accept a restricted role under the terms of the 1911 and 1949 Parliament Acts. Under the provisions of the 1911 act (a measure to which the Lords acquiesced under threat of being swamped with a mass of new Liberal pro-reform peers), the Lords could delay passage of non-money bills for only two successive sessions, such bills being enacted if passed by the Commons again in the succeeding session. Money bills, those certified as such by the speaker of the House of Commons, were to receive the Royal Assent one month after leaving the Commons, whether assented to by the House of Lords or not. The only significant power of veto retained was that over bills to prolong the life of a Parliament. (The delaying power over non-money bills was reduced by a further session under the terms of the 1949 Parliament Act, itself passed under the provisions of the 1911 act.) There is an agreement among the parties in the House, dating from the Parliament of 1945–50, that a bill promised in a government's election manifesto—and by extension, the government's legislative program—should be given an unopposed second reading (see Chapter 12). Though the House of Lords may amend a government bill, it does not reject it. In 1999, an act was passed changing the composition of the House of Lords (see Chapter 12), though not its powers.

Once a bill has received the assent of both houses, it goes to the monarch for the Royal Assent. By convention, this assent is always forthcoming. As was already mentioned, not since Queen Anne's reign has a monarch refused assent. Queen Victoria contemplated such refusal but was persuaded otherwise. By convention, the queen exercises her powers on the advice of her ministers. In certain extreme circumstances, Her Majesty may find herself in a position in which she is called on to use her discretion in making a political decision. Such cases are rare, though the queen would probably prefer them to be nonexistent. The strength and the value of the contemporary monarchy derives from being above and avoiding political decisions.

The moment a bill receives the Royal Assent it becomes an act of Parliament. It is then enforced and upheld by the agencies of the state. The development of a form of representative democracy in the nineteenth century led Dicey to distinguish between legal sovereignty, which continued to reside with the triumvirate of the monarch, Lords, and Commons, and political sovereignty, which he deemed to rest with the electorate. This somewhat clumsy distinction has a certain utility. The electorate may have the power to choose the members of the House of Commons, but the will of the electorate is not something formally recognized by the courts. The courts recognize and will enforce only acts of Parliament.

Under the provisions of the 1911 Parliament Act, the maximum life of a Parliament is five years. (Previously, the period was seven years.) Within that period, the prime minister is free to recommend to the monarch a dissolution—in effect, to call a general election. Unlike the United States, Britain has no fixed-term elections at a national level. The ability of a prime minister effectively to call a general election has been regarded by some writers as the most important weapon in ensuring parliamentary support. The prime minister can threaten to recommend a dissolution if he or she does not receive the necessary support to get a measure through. Such a threat may constitute a bluff in that the prime minister is unlikely to want to run the risk of losing office, but nonetheless it has proved a potent influence in determining parliamentary behavior. It would be exceptional, albeit not unknown, for MPs of the government party to vote against their own side on a vote of confidence. No government in the twentieth century has lost a vote of confidence as a result of dissent by its own supporters[18]—hence the dominance of government.

In summary, then, the fourth element of the Constitution—parliamentary government under a constitutional monarchy—may be seen to comprise different relationships and powers, which are the product of traditional institutions being adapted to meet changing circumstances and are prescribed by a variety of measures of statute and common law and by convention. The working of the various relationships within the framework established by law and convention is made possible by the operation of bodies not widely recognized by the Constitution, namely political parties. To understand contemporary British politics, one has to understand this framework.

THE CHANGING CONSTITUTION

To understand British politics fully, one also has to go beyond this framework. This brings us to two periods, or waves, of major constitutional change in the United Kingdom They can be characterized as waves of change because they continue to flow, almost tide-like, over a period of time. The first wave of change has been membership of the European Community—now the European Union—and the changes brought about by amendments to the treaties creating the Community. The second wave has comprised the various changes to the constitutional framework introduced since 1997 by the Labour government under Prime Minister Tony Blair.

European Union Membership

What now constitutes in effect the fifth core element of the British Constitution is something for which there is no parallel in North America: that is, membership in a supranational body.[19] The United Kingdom became a member of what was then the European Community (EC) on January 1, 1973. Under the Treaty on European Union (the Maastricht Treaty) in 1993, the EC became one of three pillars in a new European Union (EU). The effect of membership in the EC, now the EU, has been to add a new dimension to the formulation, approval, and enforcement of measures of public policy.

By virtue of membership, decision-making competence in a number of sectors has passed from the British government to the principal executive institutions of the EU: the Council of Ministers, comprising the relevant ministers drawn from the member states, and the Commission, the permanent bureaucracy headed by a College of Commissioners. (The commissioners are nominated by, but required to be independent of, the member states.) The council is the ultimate decision-making body; the Commission alone has the power to propose legislation.

British ministers thus form part of a wider, collective decision-making body. Under the terms of the international treaties creating the bodies, the council and Commission can issue different forms of legislation (see Chapter 9). Under the terms of the European Communities Act of 1972, which provides the legal basis necessary for membership, the force of law is given in the United Kingdom to European regulations. Such legislation has immediate and general applicability. The assent of Parliament is not required: It has, in effect, been given in advance under the provisions of the 1972 act. In the event of any conflict between domestic (known as municipal) law and European law, the latter is to prevail. Disputes concerning European law are to be treated by British courts as matters of law, and cases that reach the highest domestic court of appeal—the House of Lords—must, under the provisions of the Treaty of Rome, be referred to the European Court of Justice for a definitive ruling. Requests also may be made from lower courts to the Court of Justice for a ruling on the meaning and interpretation of the treaties.

TABLE 4.2   Constitutional implications of membership in the European Community

The European Communities Act 1972:

[1] Gave the force of law in the United Kingdom to existing and to *future* European legislation.

[Thus when law is made within the institutions of the European Community, the assent of Parliament is not required: Parliament has given its assent in advance under the terms of the 1972 Act.]

[2] Gave European law precedence over United Kingdom law.

[3] Gave the power to determine disputes to the courts.

[Thus the courts are the final arbiters of the provisions of the European treaties. The ultimate arbiter is the European Court of Justice.]

Membership has thus had profound constitutional implications for the United Kingdom. These implications are even more pronounced now as a result of the implementation of a new treaty, popularly known as the Single European Act, which came into force on July 1, 1987. (As an amendment to the original treaties, it required parliamentary approval, and this was given under the provisions of the European Communities [Amendment] Act of 1986.) The effect of the treaty was to change the power relationship *between* the institutions of the Community and the member states, and *within* the Community among the different institutions. The treaty extended the provision for qualified majority voting (QMV) in the Council of Ministers: This means one or more ministers can be outvoted by the ministers from the other countries. (Each minister enjoys a stipulated number of votes, depending on the size of the country, with 62 votes out of 87 being necessary to approve a proposal.) A measure thus can be opposed by the British government and Parliament and yet, if it achieves the necessary number of votes in the council, be enforced as law in the United Kingdom. The treaty also accorded a stronger role to the directly-elected European Parliament; it now is more directly involved in the discussion and amendment of council proposals and, in certain circumstances, can fulfill a significant blocking role. Its powers have been further strengthened under the Maastricht and Amsterdam Treaties (see Chapter 9). The Maastricht Treaty brought into being the European Union, of which the European Community constitutes one pillar.

Membership in the EU has been added on and, as far as possible, integrated with the existing provisions of the Westminster Constitution. The "fit," as we have already had cause to note, has not necessarily been complete. The British government retains its autonomy in several significant sectors of public policy, though the number is diminishing. There is a capacity for tension between the established national institutions and those grafted on at a supranational level. Various provisions of statute law—the European Communities Act of 1972 and the subsequent amending Acts—may be seen as constituting a Trojan horse, allowing the introduction of a new layer to the British Constitution. Existing institutions and procedures have not yet become fully accommodated to this new dimension.

The most fundamental lack of "fit" exists in relation to the doctrine of parliamentary sovereignty. The doctrine has been undermined, especially as a result of a rulings by the European Court of Justice and by the House of Lords—notably in the 1994 case of *Ex Parte EOC,* in which the House of Lords held provisions of an Act of Parliament to be incompatible with EC law—but remains intact in that Parliament retains the power to repeal the original European Communities Act of 1972. For Parliament to repeal the act would be to breach the nation's treaty obligations, under which membership is in perpetuity, but the British courts would, under the doctrine of parliamentary sovereignty, enforce the act of repeal. However, repeal is not regarded as likely and the longer the period of membership in the EU the more likely the prospect of the doctrine falling away, the provisions of the European treaties forming some form of "written" constitution for the United Kingdom.

Constitutional Reform under a Labour Government

Constitutional changes introduced under the Labour government elected in 1997 have further served to modify the contours of the British Constitution. Some of these changes we have touched upon already. They are summarized in Table 4.3. Some have had a limited impact on the basic features of the traditional, Westminster Constitution; others have had a significant impact.

TABLE 4.3   *Constitutional changes introduced by the Labour government 1997–2000*

Referendums
   Use of referendums in Scotland (1997), Wales (1997), and Northern Ireland (1998) to approve the creation of elected assemblies, and in London (1988) to approve the establishment of an elected mayor and authority. Promised referendum on a new electoral system for parliamentary elections and in the event of the government recommending that the U.K. joins a single European currency.

Devolution
   Creation of elected assemblies in Scotland, Wales, and Northern Ireland, and of an elected mayor and authority in London.

Human Rights
   Passage of an act—the Human Rights Act 1998—to incorporate the provisions of the European Convention on Human Rights into British law.

Electoral Systems
   Introduction of systems of proportional representation, of different sorts, for elections to the European Parliament, the Scottish Parliament, the Welsh Assembly, the Northern Ireland Assembly, and the London Authority.

Freedom of Information
   Introduction of a Freedom of Information Bill 2000, covering not only government departments but also a range of bodies fulfilling public functions.

The House of Lords
   Passage of an act—the House of Lords Act 1999—removing most hereditary peers from membership of the House of Lords.

The doctrine of parliamentary sovereignty has, as we have seen, been challenged by the consequences of membership in the European Union. It has also been challenged—albeit, at least formally, to a lesser extent—by the incorporation of the European Convention on Human Rights into British law. The Convention is an international treaty that seeks to protect basic human rights. (Among its provisions: a right to life, liberty, and respect for private and family life, and freedom from torture and discrimination.) It was ratified by the United Kingdom in 1951 but never incorporated into British law. In 1965 British citizens were given the right to petition the European Court on Human Rights if their rights were infringed. If the United Kingdom lost a case in the Court, the government brought forward legislation to bring United Kingdom law into line with the judgement of the Court. However, it was not legally obliged to do so. Cases brought before the European Court also usually took several years to resolve. In 1998, the Labour government achieved passage of an act incorporating the Convention into British law. The act maintains the doctrine of parliamentary sovereignty. The courts cannot strike a British law as being contrary to the provisions of the Convention. All they can do is issue a certificate of incompatability, declaring a provision to be in breach of the Convention. It is then up to Parliament as to whether or not it changes the law to bring it into line with the provisions of the Convention. In practice, whenever the courts declare a provision of British law in breach of the Convention, the Government will bring legislation forward, or take appropriate action, to bring it into line with the decision of the courts. Thus, although formally the doctrine of parliamentary sovereignty remains intact, in practice it is being undermined: the courts will, in effect, be deciding whether a provision of British law is in conflict with some higher law and should be set aside. Parliament retains the power to amend or repeal the Human Rights Act, but it is unlikely to exercise that power. The longer the Act remains in force then, as with the European Communities Act, the greater the prospect of the doctrine of parliamentary sovereignty falling away.

The effect of the Human Rights Act has been to undermine one pillar of the Constitution while strengthening another: that of the rule of law. As we have noted, under the traditional Constitution the rule of law is logically subordinate to the doctrine of parliamentary sovereignty. The enactment of the Human Rights Act gives a greater protection to the second pillar, though not formally destroying the first pillar. The rights of citizens have also been extended by proposals for freedom of information legislation, though the proposals introduced by the government in 2000 were criticized by human rights groups for not being radical. The effect of membership of the EU and the passage of the Human Rights Act has been to create a major new judicial dimension to the British Constitution, giving the citizen far greater opportunities than ever before to pursue through the courts claims against the government or another public body.

The unitary state remains formally intact but has been modified in practice by the creation of elected assemblies in different parts of the United Kingdom. Ultimate power to modify the powers of these assemblies and, indeed, to abolish them, remains with Parliament. That is the formal constitutional position.

The political reality is that it is virtually impossible for Parliament to abolish the new assemblies that are now in operation in Scotland and Wales (see Chapter 10). The Scottish parliament, in particular, has been vested with a wide range of legislative and executive powers, including a power to vary the standard rate of income tax. So long as the new assemblies remain in place, the United Kingdom has an unusual constitutional structure, with elected assemblies in different parts of the kingdom but not in the part in which the vast majority of Britons live: that is, England. The United Kingdom thus has what has been termed assymetrical devolution: a United Kingdom Parliament and elected assemblies in Scotland, Wales, and Northern Ireland, but not in England. Formally, it remains a unitary state but with power dispersed in a skewed manner.

Parliamentary government is challenged by the use of referendums. Again, the formality is retained in that referendums are advisory only. Parliament is the body that deliberates and ultimately decides. However, referendums represent, in practice, particular issues being handed over for determination by the electorate. Though a referendum is formally advisory rather than binding, it would be perverse for Parliament to authorize a referendum and then legislate contrary to the outcome of the referendum. Referendums have been a notable feature of the period since the election of a Labour government in 1997, with more promised. The use of forms of proportional representation (PR) for elections to the different assemblies, as well as for the election of the mayor of London, also has potential implications for this feature of the traditional constitution. The use of PR systems for other elected bodies may add pressure for the use of PR in elections to the House of Commons: Its use would, according to critics, undermine the accountability of the present parliamentary system (see Chapter 5). The removal of most hereditary peers from the House of Lords, under the provisions of the 1999 House of Lords Act, does not formally affect the basic relationships of the traditional Constitution, but any second stage reform—the removal of hereditary peers constituting a first stage—may involve a change in form and powers, with important consequences for the relationship between the two chambers of Parliament. Parliamentary government under a constitutional monarchy thus remains a central feature of the Constitution, but one that, like other features, is being modified and may be under further threat in the future.

CONCLUSION

The shifting and complex web of relationships and powers that forms the British Constitution is not an easily discernible one. Some powers and relationships recognizably fall within the rubric of the Constitution. Others are less easy to classify. Sometimes a feature of the Constitution is discerned as such only at the time when it has just ceased to have much relevance. Walter Bagehot's *The English Constitution,* published in 1867, constituted a classic description of a Constitution that had not previously been so well sketched, yet a Constitution that was to undergo significant modifications as a result of the passage that very same year of the Second Reform Act. Bagehot's work continued to be regarded as an authoritative work long after the Constitution had undergone fundamental change. A description of the Westminster Constitution penned in 1970 would be in need of significant amendment within two years, as would a description penned just before the general election of 1997.

Grasping the essentials of the Constitution at any given moment is clearly a demanding and confusing task. Dicey claimed that, as a result of his work, the constitution no longer appeared as a "sort of maze." According to one recent critic, "it stills feel like a maze when you seek to leave it."[20] It is confusing even to those charged with its interpretation and to those who seek to make it work. To the student of the subject, the British Constitution appears complex, confusing, ill-defined, and in many respects amorphous. Such a reaction is both natural and understandable: The Constitution does exhibit those very characteristics.

At the heart of the difficulty of delineating clearly the essential features of the Constitution is its ever-changing nature. Statute law, as we have seen in the case of membership in the European Union and devolution, can introduce new bodies of government. Constitutional norms serve to influence and mold political behavior. Conversely, political behavior helps influence the contours of the Constitution. As we have seen, such changes are made possible by the assimilating influence of conventions. "The conventions of the constitution," as LeMay observed, "have meaning only when they are looked at against a background of continuous political change. It is very difficult to say with certainty what they were at any particular moment. Above all, they cannot be understood 'with the politics left out.'"[21]

The Constitution has proved adaptable to changing political conditions. That adaptation, though, has not been smooth or seamless. The Westminster Constitution encountered criticism and was on the agenda of political debate from the 1970s onwards. There were calls for a radical overhaul, some reform bodies arguing for a new constitutional settlement to replace that of 1688–89. In the event, the Labour government elected in 1997 embarked on a program of constitutional reform (Table 4.3), though one that fell short of replacing the Westminster Constitution with a new one. What we have, in effect, is a modified Westminster Constitution. Some critics would argue that the changes have gone too far, and that what the United Kingdom has is a fairly shapeless Constitution. Others—advocates of a new Constitution—argue that it has not gone far enough.

NOTES

[1] O. Hood Phillips, *Constitutional and Administrative Law,* 6th ed. (Sweet & Maxwell, 1978), p. 5.

[2] C. Rossiter, prefatory note to E. S. Corwin, *The "Higher Law" Background of American Constitutional Law* (Cornell University Press, 1979 ed.), p. vi.

[3] P. Madgwick and D. Woodhouse, *The Law and Politics of the Constitution* (Harvester Wheatsheaf, 1995), p. 11.

[4] See G. Marshall and G. Moodie, *Some Problems of the Constitution,* 4th rev. ed. (Hutchinson, 1967), p. 26.

[5] I. Jennings, *The Law and the Constitution,* 5th ed. (University of London Press, 1959), p. 102.

[6] A. H. Hanson and M. Walles, *Governing Britain,* rev. ed. (Fontana, 1975), p. 156.

[7] Phillips, p. 25.

[8] P. Norton, *The Constitution in Flux* (Basil Blackwell, 1982), p. 9.

[9] See L. Hartz, *The Liberal Tradition in America* (Harcourt, Brace and World, 1955), p. 9.

[10] A. V. Dicey, *An Introduction to the Study of the Law of the Constitution,* 10th ed. (first published 1885; Macmillan, 1959).

[11] Ibid., pp. 39-40.

[12] H. W. R. Wade, "The Basis of Legal Sovereignty," *Common Law Journal,* 1955, cited by E. C. S. Wade in his introduction to the 10th ed. of Dicey, p. lvi.

[13] Phillips, p. 46.

[14] "The Rule of Law in Britain Today," *Constitutional Reform Centre: Politics Briefing No. 6* (Constitutional Reform Centre, 1989), p. 1.

[15] See Norton, pp. 16-17.

[16] As listed by *The Report of the Machinery of Government Committee* (His Majesty's Stationery Office, 1918).

[17] S. A. de Smith, *Constitutional and Administrative Law* (Penguin, 1971), p. 176.

[18] The government of Neville Chamberlain effectively fell in 1940 because of dissent by its own backbenchers, though it retained a majority in the parliamentary vote that took place. The government, in effect, got the message without having to be defeated formally. On three occasions in this century, government has actually lost a vote of confidence—in 1924 (twice) and 1979—but in each instance the government party did not enjoy an overall parliamentary majority.

[19] In a North American context, the closest equivalent is the North American Free Trade Agreement (NAFTA), but that does not have the governmental element of the EU.

[20] A. Barnett, *This Time: Our Constitutional Revolution* (Vintage, 1997), p. 281.

[21] G. LeMay, *The Victorian Constitution* (Duckworth, 1979), p. 21.

Chapter 5

The Electoral System
Campaigns, Voting, and Voters

In the United States, citizens are presented with the opportunity to go to the polls at frequent and fixed intervals to elect at national, state, and local levels a host of legislators, executive heads, councilpersons, officials, and even, in some states, judges. Before polling day, the citizen is faced with a lengthy election campaign: There are primary campaigns, the primary elections, the general election campaign, and the general election itself. The presidential election campaign lasts for nearly a year; with all the preplanning, advance publicity, and fund-raising, it lasts for much longer. Given the short interval between elections, campaigns for the U.S. House of Representatives are virtually continuous. Candidates spend much of their time raising funds to fight the next election. In financial terms, elections are big business. Once in the polling booth, the voter is faced with a daunting array of candidates: Given the number of offices to be filled and the number of people seeking to fill them, the number of names may be a three-figure one. Voting and its subsequent tabulation are much eased by the use of voting machines. With more than one office usually to be filled in an election, voters can—and do—split their tickets between parties. Once elected, there is a gap of over two months before officeholders take up their posts.

How do such characteristics compare with elections in the United Kingdom? For most of the past century, the two electoral systems have been marked by their differences rather than by their similarities. In the United Kingdom, a citizen may have the opportunity to vote in the election of a national body only once every five years. That election is for the House of Commons and the House of Commons alone. As we shall see (Chapter 12) the members of the House of Lords are not elected. There is no separate election of the executive: The leader of the party with a majority of seats in the House of Commons is invited to form a government. (The choice of party leaders is a matter for the parties themselves.) The date of an election is not known until approximately four weeks before the event, when the prime minister recommends to the queen a dissolution of Parliament. Although there is much anticipatory planning, the election campaign proper extends over approximately three weeks. There are no primaries: Candidate selection is an internal matter for the parties. The campaign is fought on a national, and party, basis. Funding and organization in the constituencies as well as nationally is undertaken by the established parties, not by individual candidates or campaign organizations created by the candidates. The amount of money spent on electioneering during this period, at least at constituency level, is strictly limited by law. On polling day the elector is faced with a small ballot slip on which are printed the names usually of about five or six candidates. (Six or more candidates standing in any one constituency would be unusual.) The voter places a cross next to the name of only one of them. With each elector having only one vote to cast for only one candidate, there is no such thing as ticket splitting. At the close of polling, the votes are collected in one central area in each constituency and counted by hand. A sufficient number of results is usually announced within a few hours of the close of the polls to know which party has won the election. If the party in office has lost, the prime minister goes to Buckingham Palace to tender his or her resignation. The leader of the party newly returned with a majority of seats is then summoned. The new cabinet and other ministerial appointments are announced within a matter of days, sometimes within a matter of hours. Within a month of an election being called, Britain may find itself with a new government.

These features of the British system remain in place. However, there have been changes in recent years that mean that, in quantitative terms, there are features of elections in Britain that now bring Britain closer to the American experience. However, those very same changes have meant that, in qualitative terms, the differences between the two systems are even more pronounced. In quantitative terms, there are now more elections in the United Kingdom. Until 1979, voters in Britain were able to vote for members of local councils and for members of the House of Commons. In 1979, direct elections to the European Parliament were introduced, giving British voters the opportunity to elect British Members of the European Parliament (MEPs). In 1998, Parliament in Britain approved legislation setting up elected assemblies in Scotland, Wales, Northern Ireland, and London. In all these places, electors have acquired the right to elect members of bodies that exist between local and national level. A voter in Scotland, for example, is thus now entitled to vote in elections to a local council, the Scottish Parliament, the House of Commons, and the European Parliament. The extension in the number of elections is thus substantial, relative to past experience, but is still limited. Voters in England, other than in London, have no intermediate layer of government to elect. The qualitative change is in terms of the type of voting systems employed. For local elections and elections to the House of Commons, the system employed is the same as that in the United States: the first-past-the-post system, the candidate with a plurality of votes being declared elected. However, for elections to other bodies, different systems of proportional representation have been introduced. A form of additional member system

(AMS) has been introduced in Scotland and Wales. The regional list system is employed for elections to the European Parliament (except in Northern Ireland, where the single transferable vote system is used). And a system known as the supplementary vote (SV) is used for the election of a London mayor. Voters in the United Kingdom are now thus called upon to (1) vote more often than before and to (2) do so using different voting systems. In the former case, they are coming closer to the experience of U.S. voters. In the latter, they are moving further away.

In this chapter, the focus is national elections. That means elections to the House of Commons. It is these elections that determine which party forms the government of the United Kingdom. Elections to the Scottish, Welsh, Northern Ireland, and London assemblies will be discussed in Chapter 10 and elections to the European Parliament in Chapter 9. Given that our focus here *is* national elections, the American and British systems remain notable for their differences.

The essential characteristics of national elections in the United States and the United Kingdom are contrasted in Table 5.1. Let us consider in a little more detail some of the main features of national elections in Britain and of electoral behavior before proceeding to a consideration of the current controversy surrounding the electoral system.

THE ELECTORAL STRUCTURE

Electors

As we have seen (Chapter 3), the franchise was variously extended in the nineteenth century. The basis on which the vote was given was that of property. Not until 1918 was universal manhood suffrage introduced on the basis of (six months') residence. In the same year, women age 30 and over, if already local government electors or married to such electors, were given a vote in general elections. The vote was extended to all women aged 21 and over in 1928. It was extended to 18- to 20-year-olds in 1969. The various extensions of the franchise during the course of the twentieth century, much more radical in numerical terms than the various extensions of the previous century, and the growth in population have resulted in the electorate growing from 6,730,935 in 1900 to 43,784,659 in 1997. The 1949 Representation of the People Act, which abolished plural voting, effectively brought to final fruition the principle of "one person, one vote."[1] The only people excluded from the franchise are members of the House of Lords (given that they have their own house), imprisoned criminals, those of unsound mind, people convicted of certain election offenses, and aliens.

To exercise one's right to vote, it is necessary to be on the electoral register, which is compiled annually. Each year every household receives an electoral registration form. The head of the household is required to complete it and to list all those who are resident in the dwelling on a particular date—October 10 in Great Britain and September 15 in Northern Ireland—and are eligible for

TABLE 5.1   United States and United Kingdom national elections

Characteristics	United States	United Kingdom
Bodies elected	President and vice president Senate House of Representatives	House of Commons

Constituencies	President: national
	Senate: state
	House: single-member
	    districts (435)
		Single-member districts
		    (constituencies) (659)

Terms of Office	President: 4 years (two-term
	    maximum)
	Senate: 6 years (one-third
	    elected every 2 years)
	Representative: 2 years (limits to
	    seeking reelection by senators or
	    representatives vary by state)
		Maximum of 5 years
		    (no limit to seeking
		    reelection)

Eligibility for
    candidature
	President: native-born citizen, age
	    35 or over, 14 years resident in U.S.
	Senator: age 30 or over, 9 years a
	    citizen, inhabitant of state
	Representative: age 25 or over, 7
	    years a citizen, inhabitant of state
		Citizen age 21 or over
		    (certain exceptions)

Fixed-term or
    irregular
    elections
	Fixed term	Irregular (but must not go
		    beyond 5-year intervals)

Mode of election	Plurality vote for Senate and House,
	    popular vote and electoral college
	    for president
		Plurality vote

Date of election
    determined by
	Acts of Congress	Recommendation of
		    prime minister to monarch
		    (within 5-year limit and
		    subject to certain
		    qualifications)

Franchise	Citizens age 18 and over
	    (certain exceptions)
		Citizens age 18 and over
		    (certain exceptions)

Registration
    procedures
	Varies by state:
	    historically, required to
	    register in person
		Head of household by
		    law completes annual
		    registration form,
		    submitted by mail

Turnout at
    elections
	Less than 60% post-1968
	    (40% or less in midterm elections)
		Regularly over 70%

inclusion, including those who will attain the age of 18 years during the period that the new register comes into effect. These forms are returned by mail to the registration officer for the constituency. About a third of households fail to respond and have to chased up by mail and, if that fails, in person.[2] Once the register is compiled, it is open for inspection; it takes effect the following February, and is in force for one year. Electors who move to another constituency during the course of the year are entitled to apply to vote by post in the constituency in which they are registered.

Compared with registration procedures adopted previously in most U.S. states,[3] the British practice is efficient and effective. Completing the registration forms is a legal requirement. Supplementary registers are published every month to allow registration officers to include people wrongly omitted. Even so, it has been estimated that anywhere between 5 and 10 percent of adults fail to register. Some voters fill in registration forms incorrectly or, for a variety of reasons, fail to complete them.[4] There is no procedure analogous to the U.S. practice of registering as a Republican, Democrat, or Independent; given the absence of primary elections in Britain, there is no logical reason that one should exist.

Constituencies

The United Kingdom is divided into single-member constituencies. There are currently 659, though the number can and does vary. From 1974 until 1983, for example, there were 635, and at one time earlier in the twentieth century (when the whole of Ireland was still part of the United Kingdom) there were over 700.

The drawing of boundaries is the responsibility of bodies known as boundary commissions: There is a commission each for England, Scotland, Wales, and Northern Ireland.[5] Each commission is chaired by the speaker of the House of Commons (a nonparty figure who, in practice, never participates) and each has a judge as deputy chairman. Assistant commissioners, usually lawyers, are appointed to supervise local inquiries, and the staff of the commissions includes the country's main officials dealing with population and geographic surveys.

In redrawing boundaries the commissions are guided by rules laid down by act of Parliament. They are supposed to ensure that constituencies are as equal as possible in the size of their electorates. However, they are permitted to deviate from this equality if special geographic considerations (for example, the size, shape, and accessibility of a constituency) appear to render such a deviation desirable. Other rules further complicate the position. The commissioners are enjoined not to cross local authority boundaries in creating parliamentary constituencies. They also have to work within the context of regional disparities. Scotland, with a large land area but relatively small population, has a greater number of constituencies allocated to it than its population strictly allows, and the same applies to Wales. Hence, the electoral quota (the national electorate divided by the number of seats) is greater in England than in Scotland or Wales.

The frequency of reviews has varied. Under legislation passed in 1992, there must now be a review every eight to twelve years (previously it was every ten to fifteen years) though a commission may issue an interim report. Before making their recommendations, the commissioners consider submissions from interested bodies, primarily the local political parties. If a proposed change has the support of the local parties, it is usual for the commissioners to accept it. Once they have completed their work, their recommendations are presented to a government minister, the home secretary, who is then required to lay them before the House of Commons for approval. They are rarely free of criticism. Boundary reviews in 1948 and 1955 were the subject of protests, and in 1969 the Labour home secretary advised his supporters in the House to vote against the commission's recommendations, which they did. As a result, the 1970 general election was fought on the basis of the old boundaries. The commission's recommendations were implemented in the new Parliament. The next review by the commission was completed in 1982 and challenged unsuccessfully in the courts by the Labour party. The most recent review was completed in 1995 and accepted without challenge, the 1997 general election taking place on the basis of the revised boundaries.

A combination of population shifts (about three-quarters of a million people move every year in Britain), the disparity among constituency electorates recommended by the commissioners in favor of other criteria (maintaining local government boundaries and the like), the lapse of time between reviews, and the disparity in the number of seats allocated to the different countries in the United Kingdom has meant that marked differences often exist among the sizes of electorates. For example, before the boundary revisions made in 1983, 39 percent of seats deviated from the electoral quota by +/− 20 percent. Even after the revisions, 5 percent of the seats still deviated from the quota by the same margin. By 1990, one seat—Milton Keynes—had an electorate of 107,000. The Boundary Commission took the unusual step of issuing an interim report recommending the creation of a new seat to deal with the situation. As a result, the number of seats increased in the 1992 general election from 650 to 651. As a consequence of the boundary changes approved in 1995, the number of seats increased, with effect from the 1997 election, to 659. The number is expected to be reduced when the next review is completed, the government having indicated in 1998 that it would ask the boundary commissioners to bring the electoral quota in Scotland into line with that in England, a consequence of Scotland acquiring its own parliament.

Campaigns

An election campaign extends formally over a period of three to four weeks, though if a Parliament goes beyond four years in duration there is a tendency for parties to start campaigning de facto in anticipation of an election being called. Both the 1992 and 1997 elections took place at the end of Parliaments that had lasted five years and both were preceded by what were, in effect, lengthy campaigns by the main parties. However, the formal campaign gets under way only after Parliament has been dissolved and candidates formally nominated. For U.S. politicians, there are essentially four stages in an election campaign: profile raising, fund-raising, the primary campaign, and the general election. For British politicians, only the first and the last stages apply. Incumbents and challengers in Britain do not have to contest primary campaigns, and fund-raising is the task of the local party organizations. Activity in the constituency—and, for the incumbent, in the House of Commons—is important for gaining visibility with electors. However, only in the event of a formal election campaign are the resources of the local party mobilized on an extensive scale.

In British elections, unlike those in the United States, the personalities of candidates (except for national leaders) and their personal wealth play only a marginal role. There is some evidence that incumbency can make some difference, affecting the outcome in tight contests,[6] but the impact of the candidate is usually overwhelmed by the impact of party. The campaign is fought in practice on a national level between the two main parties, the candidates and the local campaigns serving to reinforce the national campaigns of their leaders. Candidates are selected locally by the parties, and the parties provide the finance and the organization for the campaign.

Election expenses in each constituency are limited by statute and have been since 1883. Expenditure is permitted only where authorized by the candidate, the candidate's election agent, or a person authorized in writing by the agent. The maximum permitted expenditure is calculated on the basis of a fixed sum plus a limited amount based on the number of electors: in 1997, £4,965 ($8,193) plus 5.6 pence per voter in each county (predominantly rural) constituency and £4,965 plus 4.2p per voter in borough (urban, and smaller in area) constituencies. Certain types of expenditure are illegal (for example, paying an elector to exhibit a poster or paying for voters to be taken to and from the polling booths), and separate committees to promote a candidate are not permitted. Even with the modest expenditure that is permitted, most candidates fail to spend the maximum allowed.[7] Some devices for keeping costs low are employed and these can, where required, provide up to an extra 20 percent of expenditure:[8] A popular ploy is to purchase stationery in advance and then resell it cheaply to the candidate as secondhand stock. In 1997, telephone canvassing was variously employed "although its costs seldom appeared in expense returns."[9] Few candidates, though, are prepared to run too many risks for fear of having their elections challenged and declared void: Expenses have to be declared and opponents keep a wary eye open for any infringements of election law. There is, in any event, a major practical constraint: The parties have difficulty raising sufficient money to fight campaigns.

Each candidate is permitted one postage-free mailing of one piece of election literature. Other literature is distributed by unpaid party activists. The main item of literature is the candidate's election address. This will usually incorporate a summary of the main points of the party's national election manifesto. Candidates have traditionally spent a good part of their time making speeches throughout the constituency, not infrequently at thinly attended meetings, and canvassing door to door where possible. Attendance at meetings is nowadays so thin that candidates organize few if any meetings, preferring instead to attend meetings for all candidates organized by local bodies, such as churches, and to get out on the streets canvassing. The candidate will be aided by volunteers who help in the campaign office—much use being made nowadays of computer-generated labels and literature—and who do doorstep canvassing to try to determine where supporters live. On election day they will keep a running tab on who has voted in order to ensure that support is maximized. The Labour party made particular use of computers for recording and analyzing support in the 1997 election. Indeed, in that election there was something of a shift, at least in the Labour party, from a labor-intensive to a technology-intensive campaign.

The main focus of the campaign is national. The party leaders make regular and well-publicized appearances throughout the country, ensuring that the national press and television reporters follow in their wake, as well as hold daily press conferences. The press conferences are usually held early in the morning in an attempt to set the day's political agenda. The national party organizations also increasingly make use of press advertising. As long as expenditure cannot be said to apply in support of specific candidates, national party campaigns do not fall foul of the election finance restrictions. During and in the run-up to the 1997 election campaign, the Conservative, Labour, and Liberal Democratic parties spent more than £33 million ($52.8 million) centrally.[10] The largest single item of expenditure was advertising. The parties also enjoyed the benefit of free but limited television time. Paid political advertising on television is not allowed: Each party is allocated a set number of ten-minute party election broadcasts that are transmitted on all television channels. These broadcasts, though, "lack credibility and quickly lose viewers,"[11] the parties relying instead on television news coverage to try to shape the agenda and get their message over to viewers.

The basis of the parties' appeal to the country is the election manifestos that they issue. In recent elections these have become increasingly lengthy and specific documents, detailing the intended policies and measures to be pursued by a party if returned to office. They constitute a topic of some controversy. It has been argued that very few electors actually read them—though available for sale at bookshops, the manifesto of a party will be purchased by fewer than 1 in every 200 voters[12]—and that many of the commitments made do not enjoy widespread support among voters, even among those voting for the parties that issued them.[13] They also are viewed as hostages for the future, parties in office being open to attack when promises are not fulfilled, even if conditions no longer make the proposal viable. In practice, they constitute something of a guide to interested bodies and provide a framework for the main items of legislation introduced by an incoming government in the first session or two of a new Parliament: Most manifesto promises are usually implemented.[14] A more relevant criticism is that manifesto promises may not address themselves to the country's real problems. Some would argue that, by virtue of the manner of their compilation and their utilization as a means furthering the adversary relationship between the parties, manifestos add to those problems rather than offering solutions.[15]

Candidates

Any citizen age 21 years or over is eligible to be a candidate for election to the House of Commons. There are certain limited exceptions. Precluded from serving in the House of Commons are those who are disqualified from voting, as well as policemen, civil servants, judges, members of the boards of nationalized industries, undischarged bankrupts, members of the armed services, and clergy of the Churches of England, Scotland, Ireland, and the Roman Catholic Church. The exclusion of public servants has an acceptable rationale to reinforce it; they are free to resign their positions should they wish to stand for election. The exclusion of certain clergy is less easy to justify (a relic of the time when religious disputes were at the heart of national affairs), as is the exclusion of 18- to 20-year-olds: When the voting age was lowered in 1969, the age of eligibility for candidature was not.[16] To be a candidate one has to obtain the signature of ten electors in the constituency and—a practice unknown in the United States—submit a deposit of £500 ($800), returnable in the event of receiving 5 percent of the votes cast. (From 1918 to 1985 the deposit was £150, returnable in the event of receiving one-eighth of the votes cast.) Unlike in the United States, there are no residence requirements: Hence, parties enjoy a wider range of choice in the selection of candidates.

In practice, candidates are party candidates. As a result of a change in the law in 1969, this fact is now more formally recognized: Candidates are permitted to include their party designation on the ballot paper. Though in some recent general elections there have been examples of locally popular candidates holding their marginal seats against the national swing (even in some instances increasing their majorities) and, as we have noted, recent research has suggested that the "personal vote" achieved by candidates may be higher than was previously assumed, party remains the primary and almost exclusive influence on voting behavior. Since 1950, only four MPs have been elected in Britain (excluding Northern Ireland) without the support of a major party, and those four were all incumbent party members who had broken with their parties. In 1997, one Independent candidate was elected, but he was fighting for a seat in which both the Labour and Liberal Democratic candidates had stood down in his favor.

All constituencies in Great Britain are contested usually by Conservative, Labour and, nowadays, Liberal Democratic candidates. (The exception in 1997 was the seat in which the Independent was elected, where the contest was between the Independent candidate and the incumbent Conservative.) The top three places in each constituency in England will normally be taken by candidates from these three main parties. In the other parts of the United Kingdom, the picture is more complicated.

In Scotland, the Scottish National Party (SNP) is a significant electoral force. Its parliamentary representation has fluctuated. In October 1974 it won 11 seats, but only 2 in the following Parliament. In 1997, it won 6 of the 72 seats in Scotland. However, it has established itself as the main challenger to the Labour party, which is the dominant party in Scotland. In 1997, the SNP won 22 percent of the votes cast in Scotland, ahead of both the Conservatives (17.5 percent) and the Liberal Democrats (13 percent). In 1999, it consolidated its position as the second largest party, winning 35 seats in the new 129-member Scottish parliament, against 56 won by Labour (see Chapter 10). The same year it also won two seats in the European Parliament (Chapter 9).

In Wales, the nationalist party is Plaid Cymru (the Party of Wales) which, between 1974 and 1997, has won between 2 and 4 seats in the province. In 1997, it held 4 of the 40 seats in Wales, putting it ahead of the Liberal Democrats, who won 2, and the Conservatives, who won none at all. (All the remaining seats—34—were won by Labour.) In the elections to the new Welsh assembly in 1999, the party won 17 seats, a number in excess of the combined total won by the Conservatives and the Liberal Democrats (see Chapter 10). Like the SNP, it also holds two seats in the European Parliament. In Northern Ireland, the principal parties are specific to the province, comprising two main Unionist parties (the Ulster Unionists and the Democratic Unionists) and two nationalist parties (the Social Democratic and Labour Party and Sinn Fein, the latter being the political wing of the Provisional IRA). All four parties won seats in the province in 1997, with the Unionists dominating: Of the 18 seats, the Ulster Unionists won 10, the Democratic Unionists 2 and a United Kingdom Unionist 1. Three SDLP MPs were elected, as were two Sinn Fein candidates, though the latter refused to take their seats. There is also a nonsectarian Alliance party in the province. All the parties received representation in the new Northern Ireland Assembly, elected in 1998 (Chapter 10). Traditionally, the main British parties have steered clear of campaigning in the province. The Ulster Unionists used to be part of the Conservative party but severed their links following the introduction of direct rule in the province in 1972. More recently, the Conservative party has sought to get organized in the province, fielding candidates in a number of seats in 1992 and 1997, but it has had little appreciable impact.

The election of candidates representing regionally based parties has meant that there are ten parties represented in the House of Commons. Of the three main parties, the Labour party is strongest in northern England, Scotland, and Wales. The Conservative party is strongest in southern England (and, following the 1997 election, has no seats in Scotland and Wales). And the Liberal Democrat party traditionally is strongest in what is known as the "Celtic fringe" of southwest England, Scotland, and Wales, though it has also picked up some seats in the south of England at the expense of the Conservatives and some urban seats at the expense of Labour.

Other parties also ostensibly are keen to be represented in the House of Commons. Recent decades have seen a growth in the number of candidates contesting seats. The 1951 general election was fought by 1,376 candidates, that of 1983 by 2,579, an average of 4 per seat. It was in order to deter supposedly frivolous candidates that the deposit for candidature was raised to £500 in 1985, but the deterrent effect was short-lived and modest. In 1987, the number of candidates was not much fewer than in 1983: a total of 2,325. In 1992, the figure was 2,948 and in 1997 it reached a record 3,724 candidates (5.6 candidates per constituency). The increase is the result principally of fringe candidates supplemented by candidates from well-organized minor parties. In the 1992 election, there were 256 candidates of the Green party (up from 133 in 1987) and no less than 309 candidates standing for a new, eccentric pseudo-scientific and quasi-religious party, the Natural Law party. In the 1997 election, a Referendum party—founded by multimillionaire businessman Sir James Goldsmith to press for a referendum on the issue of European integration—fielded 547 candidates and won more than 800,000 votes. It was the only party—other

TABLE 5.2   General election results, 1945–1992

General Election (Winning Party in Capital Letters)	Votes Cast[1]		Seats Won[2]	
July 1945				
LABOUR	11,995,152	(47.8)	393	(61.4)
Conservative	9,988,306	(39.8)	213	(33.3)
Liberal	2,248,226	(9.0)	12	(1.9)
Others	854,294	(2.8)	22	(3.4)
Turnout: 72.7%	25,085,978	(99.4%)	640	(100.0%)
February 1950				
LABOUR	13,266,592	(46.1)	315	(50.4)
Conservative	12,502,567	(43.5)	298	(47.7)
Liberal	2,621,548	(9.1)	9	(1.4)
Others	381,964	(1.3)	3	(0.5)
Turnout: 84.0%	28,772,671	(100.0%)	625	(100.0%)
October 1951				
CONSERVATIVE	13,717,538	(48.0)	321	(51.4)
Labour	13,948,605	(48.8)	295	(47.2)
Liberal	730,556	(2.5)	6	(1.0)
Others	198,969	(0.7)	3	(0.5)
Turnout: 82.5%	28,595,668	(100.0%)	625	(100.1%)
May 1955				
CONSERVATIVE	13,286,569	(49.7)	344	(54.6)
Labour	12,404,970	(46.4)	277	(44.0)
Liberal	722,405	(2.7)	6	(0.9)
Others	346,554	(1.2)	3	(0.5)
Turnout: 76.7%	26,760,498	(100.0%)	630	(100.0%)
October 1959				
CONSERVATIVE	13,749,830	(49.4)	365	(57.9)
Labour	12,215,538	(43.8)	258	(40.9)
Liberal	1,638,571	(5.9)	6	(0.9)
Others	142,670	(0.8)	1	(0.2)
Turnout: 78.8%	27,746,609	(99.9%)	630	(99.9%)
October 1964				
LABOUR	12,205,814	(44.1)	317	(50.3)
Conservative	12,001,396	(43.4)	304	(48.2)
Liberal	3,092,878	(11.2)	9	(1.4)
Others	347,905	(1.3)	0	(0.0)
Turnout: 77.1%	27,647,993	(100.0%)	630	(99.9%)
March 1966				
LABOUR	13,064,951	(47.9)	363	(57.6)
Conservative	11,418,433	(41.9)	253	(40.2)
Liberal	2,327,533	(8.5)	12	(1.9)
Others	422,226	(1.2)	2	(0.3)
Turnout: 75.8%	27,233,143	(99.5%)	630	(100.0%)

(continued)

TABLE 5.2   (continued)

General Election (Winning Party in Capital Letters)	Votes Cast[1]		Seats Won[2]	
June 1970				
CONSERVATIVE	13,145,123	(46.4)	330	(52.4)
Labour	12,179,341	(43.0)	287	(45.6)
Liberal	2,117,035	(7.5)	6	(0.9)
Others	903,299	(3.2)	7	(1.1)
Turnout: 72.0%	28,344,798	(100.1%)	630	(100.0%)
February 1974				
LABOUR	11,639,243	(37.1)	301	(47.4)
Conservative	11,868,906	(37.9)	297	(46.8)
Liberal	6,063,470	(19.3)	14	(2.2)
Others (Great Britain)	1,044,061	(3.4)	11	(1.7)
Others (Northern Ireland)[3]	717,986	(2.3)	12	(1.9)
Turnout: 78.7%	31,333,666	(100.0%)	635	(100.0%)
October 1974				
LABOUR	11,457,079	(39.2)	319	(50.2)
Conservative	10,464,817	(35.8)	277	(43.6)
Liberal	5,346,754	(18.3)	13	(2.0)
Scottish National Party	839,617	(2.9)	11	(1.7)
Plaid Cymru	166,321	(0.6)	3	(0.5)
Others (Great Britain)	212,496	(0.8)	0	(0.0)
Others (Northern Ireland)	702,904	(2.4)	12	(1.9)
Turnout: 72.8%	29,189,178	(100.0%)	635	(99.9%)
May 1979				
CONSERVATIVE	13,697,690	(43.9)	339	(53.4)
Labour	11,532,148	(36.9)	269	(42.4)
Liberal	4,313,811	(13.8)	11	(1.7)
Scottish National Party	504,259	(1.6)	2	(0.3)
Plaid Cymru	132,544	(0.4)	2	(0.3)
Others (Great Britain)	343,674	(1.2)	0	(0.0)
Others (Northern Ireland)	695,889	(2.2)	12	(1.9)
Turnout: 76.0%	31,184,015	(100.0%)	635	(100.0%)
June 1983				
CONSERVATIVE	13,012,602	(42.4)	397	(61.1)
Labour	8,457,124	(27.6)	209	(32.1)
SDP/Liberal Alliance	7,780,577	(25.4)	23	(3.5)
Scottish National Party	331,975	(1.1)	2	(0.3)
Plaid Cymru	125,309	(0.4)	2	(0.3)
Others (Great Britain)	198,834	(0.6)	0	(0.0)
Others (Northern Ireland)	764,474	(2.5)	17	(2.6)
Turnout: 72.7%	30,670,895	(100.0%)	650	(99.9%)

TABLE 5.2   (continued)

General Election (Winning Party in Capital Letters)	Votes Cast[1]		Seats Won[2]	
June 1987				
CONSERVATIVE	13,760,525	(42.3)	376	(57.8)
Labour	10,029,944	(30.8)	292	(35.2)
SDP/Liberal Alliance	7,341,152	(22.6)	22	(3.4)
Scottish National Party	416,873	(1.3)	3	(0.5)
Plaid Cymru	123,589	(0.4)	3	(0.5)
Others (Great Britain)	127,329	(0.4)	0	(0.0)
Others (Northern Ireland)	730,152	(2.2)	17	(2.6)
Turnout: 75.3%	32,529,564	(100.0%)	650	(100.0%)
April 1992				
CONSERVATIVE	14,092,235	(41.9)	336	(51.6)
Labour	11,559,735	(34.4)	271	(41.6)
Liberal Democrat	5,999,384	(17.8)	20	(3.1)
Scottish National Party	629,555	(1.9)	3	(0.5)
Plaid Cymru	154,390	(0.5)	4	(0.6)
Others (Great Britain)	445,612	(1.3)	0	(0.0)
Others (Northern Ireland)	731,782	(2.2)	17	(2.6)
Turnout: 77.7%	33,612,693	(100.0%)	651	(100.0%)
May 1997				
LABOUR	13,518,167	(43.2)	419	(63.6)
Conservative	9,600,943	(30.7)	165	(25.0)
Liberal Democrat	5,242,947	(16.8)	46	(7.0)
Scottish National	621,550	(2.0)	6	(0.9)
Plaid Cymru	161,030	(0.5)	4	(0.6)
Others (Great Britain)[4]	1,362,661	(4.3)	1	(0.2)
Others (Northern Ireland)	790,762	(2.5)	18	(2.7)
Turnout 71.5%	31,298,060	(100.0%)	659	(100.0%)

[1] Percentages do not always add up to 100 because of rounding.
[2] The Speaker, where seeking reelection, is included with original party.
[3] Prior to 1974, Ulster Unionists were affiliated with the Conservative party. Thereafter they sat as a separate parliamentary party.
[4] Includes the Referendum party, which won 811,827 votes.

than the three principal parties—to contest a majority of the seats. The Natural Law party remained in the field, with 196 candidates. The UK Independence party, favoring British withdrawal from the European Union, put up 194 candidates. Altogether, a total of 169 different labels were used in the 1997 election. Some 43 parties put up two or more candidates, with 17 putting up 20 or more. Those putting up 20 or more candidates included a single-issue group—the Pro-Life Alliance—and two colorful groups on the fringe of British politics that have attracted a small band of supporters, the Rainbow Dream

Ticket party (29 candidates) and the Monster Raving Loony party (24 candidates). They made little impact. Apart from the Referendum party, the only minor party to achieve a six-figure vote was the UK Independence party, with a total of 105,722 votes—an average of 545 votes in each seat in contested. No candidate of any fringe party won even as much as 10% of the votes cast. The experience of the fringe candidates in the seats shown in Table 5.3 is typical of how they fared.

Candidate Selection

Candidate selection is undertaken locally, though with the national party organizations exercising some degree of control. In Britain, unlike in the United States, there are no primary elections and the selection of a candidate is in practice determined by the party activists. Where a seat is a "safe" seat for a party, this selection is usually tantamount to election.

In the Conservative party, aspiring candidates have to be on the party's Candidates List maintained by the party's national headquarters. (Local parties may

TABLE 5.3 Selected constituency results, 1997

Blaneau Gwent		
Electorate: 54,800		
L. T. Smith (Labour)	31,493	(79.5%)
Mrs. G. Layton (Liberal Democrat)	3,458	(8.7%)
Mrs. M. Williams (Conservative)	2,607	(6.6%)
J. Criddle (Plaid Cymru)	2,072	(5.2%)
LABOUR MAJORITY	28,035	(70.7%)
Total vote: 39,630		
Turnout: 78.13%		

In the heart of the traditional mining area of Wales, an area of particular Labour strength and Conservative weakness (the Conservative being pushed into third place in this election), Blaneau Gwent was Labour's safest seat in Wales in 1997 and the fourth safest in Britain.

Huntingdon		
Electorate: 76,094		
J. Major (Conservative)	31,501	(55.3%)
J. Reece (Labour)	13,361	(23.5%)
M. Owen (Liberal Democrat)	8,390	(14.7%)
D. Bellamy (Referendum)	3,114	(5.5%)
C. Coyne (UK Independence)	331	(0.6%)
Ms. V. Hufford (Christian Democrat)	177	(0.3%)
D. Robertson (Independent)	89	(0.2%)
CONSERVATIVE MAJORITY	18,140	(31.8%)
Total vote: 56,963		
Turnout: 74.9%		

Huntingdon, in the east of England, is the safest Conservative seat in the country, expressed both in terms of the size of the majority and as a percentage of the vote achieved by the winning candidate. The seat is held by John Major, who at the time of the election was prime minister.

TABLE 5.3   (continued)

Enfield Southgate

Electorate: 65,796		
S. Twigg (Labour)	20,570	(44.2%)
M. Portillo (Conservative)	19,137	(41.1%)
J. Browne (Liberal Democrat)	4,966	(10.7%)
N. Luard (Referendum)	1,342	(2.9%)
A. Storkey (Christian Democrat)	289	(0.6%)
A. Malakouna (Male Voice of the People)	229	(0.5%)
LABOUR MAJORITY	1,433	(3.1%)
Total vote: 46,533		
Turnout: 70.7%		

A seat in north London, previously regarded as a safe Conservative seat, it provided one of the Labour party's spectacular wins in the 1997 election, the Labour candidate ousting Cabinet minister Michael Portillo. In the 1992 election, Portillo had won 28,390 votes (57.9% of the votes) to the Labour candidate's 12,845 (26.2%).

Inverness East, Nairn, and Lochabar

Electorate: 65,701		
D. Stewart (Labour)	16,187	(33.9%)
F. S. Ewing (Scottish National Party)	13,848	(29.0%)
S. H. Gallagher (Liberal Democrat)	8,364	(17.5%)
Mrs. M. E. Scanlon (Conservative)	8,355	(17.5%)
Ms. W. Wall (Referendum)	436	(0.9%)
M. Falconer (Green)	354	(0.7%)
D. Hart (Christian Unity)	224	(0.5%)
LABOUR MAJORITY	2,339	(4.9%)
Total vote: 47,768		
Turnout: 72.7%		

A large rural constituency in the north of Scotland, the seat was previously held by a Liberal Democrat. It is a classic example of where a split between several challengers can result in a candidate winning with only one-third of the votes cast. In 1992, with the top four candidates getting almost the same number of votes, a Liberal Democrat held the seat with 26.7% of the vote.

choose someone not on the list, but that candidate must then be approved by the party nationally.) Achieving a place on the list was previously done through an interview with the party vice-chairman and the national committee responsible for candidates. In recent years, the procedure has been extended and more professional methods of selection employed. Aspiring candidates are first interviewed by a three-person panel, then by the party vice-chairman responsible for candidates and, if deemed suitable, then required to attend a vigorous weekend selection process in which they are put through a series of exercises (for example, taking part in debates, writing and discussing essays). About half of those taking part make it through to the Candidates List. About three or four such weekends are held each year, each attended by about 48 aspiring candidates. These procedures have been variously criticized—producing "clones" according to one party deputy chairman[17]—and, following the 1997 election, it was announced that those on the existing list were being removed and that the party was starting from scratch in compiling a new list.

A local Conservative association seeking a candidate will invite applicants and will be sent the names of those on the Candidates List wishing to be considered for the seat. In a safe Conservative seat, the number of applicants will usually run into the hundreds. The association will appoint a selection committee, usually comprising the association officers and representatives from its different branches and associated groups, to draw up a short list and then recommend three or more names to the executive council, the main decision-making body of the association. The council may then recommend one name for approval to a general meeting of the association or it may put forward more than one name and leave it to the general meeting to decide.

Traditionally, Conservative selection committees have been less concerned with the political views of applicants than have Labour committees.[18] Selection committees have tended to be influenced by an applicant's knowledge of the constituency (and willingness to live in it if selected), his or her stature and delivery of speech, and whether or not he or she has the makings of a good constituency member or, in some cases, a national figure. On occasion, more esoteric considerations may apply.)[19] Other influences can include, in some areas, religion and quite often age and sex: Local parties are reluctant to adopt women candidates (the folklore being that women voters dislike voting for them) and anyone under 30 or over 50 years of age. There also is a tendency to prefer married men (single men over 30 are considered somewhat suspect), and wives are often asked to appear before selection committees. Because wives are looked on as surrogates for their husbands while the latter are at Westminster, their attitudes to constituency work are considered important. In recent years, the party nationally has been urging local associations to adopt more female candidates. In 1992 it also signaled a desire for a broader age range. The appeals for more female candidates had little impact. In 1987, the party fielded 46 female candidates, in 1992 the figure was 59 and in 1997 it was 66. Of the 66 candidates in 1997, 13 were elected. In 1997, the party also fielded 10 candidates from black or Asian backgrounds:[20] None was successful, the party's only Asian MP losing his seat. Excluding those who had been MPs previously, the ages of the new Conservative intake in 1997—a small number given the party's election disaster—ranged from 30 to 49.[21]

It is rare for local Conservative parties to oust sitting MPs—they are normally automatically re-adopted as candidates. Occasionally, an MP has been quietly persuaded—sometimes not so quietly—to stand down because of some personal problem (drink or divorce), though rarely on policy grounds. In the 1992–97 Parliament, three were deselected, two for reasons related to their personal life and the third because of public disloyalty to the prime minister; two more retired under threat of deselection. Compared with previous Parliaments, the number was high.

Although the Labour candidates selected are increasingly similar in background to Conservative candidates, the selection procedure in the Labour party differs from that of the Conservatives. It also has undergone a number of recent changes. A local Labour party will seek a candidate by inviting nominations. Nominations may be made by local ward committees, party groups such as the women's section, and affiliated organizations, principally trade unions. (An aspiring candidate can approach such groups to solicit a nomination.) Once nominations are received, the executive committee, responsible for the day-to-day running of the party, will draw up a short list. Until 1989, the selection had been made by the General Management Committee, comprising representatives from the different ward committees and affiliated organizations. From 1989 until 1993, the selection was made by an electoral college in which at least 60 percent of the votes were allocated to local party members and up to 40 percent to affiliated organizations. In 1993 the party conference voted to approve selection on the basis of one member, one vote (OMOV). The conference also voted to introduce all-women shortlists in 50 percent of the most winnable seats and 50 percent of those where Labour MPs were retiring. This policy was in place until 1996, when an industrial tribunal held it to be unlawful. The policy nonetheless resulted in a record number of women being selected as women candidates.

The successful candidate has to be endorsed by the party's National Executive Committee (NEC). The NEC has also acquired more direct powers to influence outcomes in certain cases. It now has the power to determine the shortlist for candidates in by-elections (a power acquired following some highly controversial choices as candidates by local parties) and in seats where the incumbents retire after an election has been called. Seven Labour MPs announced their retirement following the calling of the general election in 1997, the NEC providing the shortlists from which the local parties chose their replacements. On occasion, the NEC has also used its power to refuse endorsement to candidates and to block attempts by local parties to replace incumbent MPs.

Candidate selection was a controversial issue in the 1980s, leftwing activists persuading the party conference in 1981 to change the party rules in order to make it easier for local activists to oust sitting Labour MPs. By 1986, a total of 14 MPs had been deselected. The changes in the method of local selection from 1989 onward were designed to limit the influence of leftwing activists. In the 1987–92 Parliament, only two Labour MPs were deselected, and in the 1992–97 Parliament, only one. (A number of others failed to be selected after their seats disappeared or were radically altered in the review of constituency boundaries.) In 1998, the party NEC approved changes that provide for automatic reselection of sitting MPs, unless opponents can trigger and win a ballot requiring a reselection contest. It also approved the introduction of an approved candidates' list, similar to the practice of the Conservatives. In addition, it agreed that local parties should in future be sent reports on their MPs' parliamentary performance. According to party leaders, this was in order that local parties could decide if any action should be taken against MPs who were not applying themselves to their parliamentary duties. In the eyes of leftwing Labour MPs, it was a means of using local parties to discipline them if their voting records revealed they were disloyal to the leadership.

The principle of local selection is also a feature of the other national parties in Britain with parliamentary representation. However, there is a difference in that whereas Conservative and Labour local parties usually have to choose from many eager applicants, other parties often have difficulty in recruiting candidates. At the 1989 Liberal Democrat conference, an appeal was made for activists to offer themselves as candidates. Consequently, there is often a willingness by the national leadership to accept whomever the local party has managed to recruit.

The candidates selected by the major parties tend to be middle class, middle aged, male, and white. Female and nonwhite candidates are exceptional, but not as exceptional as they used to be. In the 1997 election, a record number of women were elected to the House of Commons—120 (18 percent of the House), double the number elected in 1992—as were 9 black and Asian MPs, compared with 6 in 1992, 4 in 1987, and none before 1987. The successful candidates more than the unsuccessful ones tend to be middle-aged, university educated (and, in the case of Conservative MPs, products of public schools), and drawn from business and the professions (see Chapter 12). In postwar years, there has been a tendency for MPs to be even more middle-class than previously.[22] Recent decades also have seen the emergence of more career-oriented MPs, devoted to politics and a lifetime of service in the House of Commons.[23]

Elections

In each of the 659 single-member constituencies, the method of election employed is the plurality or "first-past-the-post" method, with the candidate who wins the largest single number of votes—even though it may not be an absolute majority—being declared the winner. It is the same method as that employed in the Senate and House elections in the United States. However, whereas most contests in the United States are straight fights between Democrats and Republican candidates, thus producing a victor with more than 50 percent of the votes cast, the three- or four-way fights that are now common for U.K. seats can result in the winning candidate achieving way below 50 percent of the vote. Indeed, in hotly contested four-way fights it is actually possible to win with less than 30 percent of the vote, as happened in the constituency of Inverness, Nairn, and Lochabar in the 1992 election, when the victorious candidate won with 26.7 percent of the vote. (The winning candidate in 1997 won with just under 34 percent of the vote: see Table 5.3.) The result in the constituency was exceptional, though not unique.

Most seats are usually considered safe seats for one or the other of the two main parties—that is, the winning candidate has achieved a margin that constitutes 10 percent or more of the total poll—with the election battle taking place, in effect, in the minority of seats that are considered "marginals." In the 1980s and early 1990s, more than 70 percent of seats fell in the category of safe seats. Some were deemed to be very safe. In the 1992 election, for instance, more than 150 seats were held by Conservative or Labour candidates with margins that represented 30 percent or more of the poll (77 Conservative, 85

Labour). In 1992, fewer than 170 seats were classed as marginal: 92 Conservative, 60 Labour, and 11 Liberal Democrat and 6 other marginal seats. However, the 1997 general election saw such a stunning victory for the Labour party that more than 70 "safe" Conservative seats—in addition to the Conservative marginal seats—were lost. Table 5.3 shows the result in a seat—Enfield Southgate—previously classified as a very safe Conservative seat. In the 1992 election, the Conservative candidate won with a majority representing 31.7 percent of the poll. In 1997, the Labour candidate topped the poll, achieving a majority of 1,433 over the incumbent Conservative. The effect of the 1997 election was to change perceptions of safe and marginal seats. Seats held by Conservatives in such a disastrous year for the party were assumed to be safe—regardless of the majority—while many seats won by Labour candidates with majorities representing more than 10 percent of the poll were not assumed necessarily to be safe, especially where the seat had previously been a "safe" Conservative seat.

The electoral system, as we shall see, has facilitated the return of governments enjoying an overall majority of seats in the House of Commons. In all but one of the general elections since (and including) 1945, one party has won an absolute majority of seats. The Labour party has achieved an overall majority in six elections, on three occasions by slim margins (in 1950, 1964, and October 1974). The party also formed the government following the February 1974 election, in which it won more seats than any other party but did not obtain an overall majority (see Table 5.4). Its best result was in 1997, winning 418 seats in the 659-member House. Conservatives have won overall majorities by clear margins in eight elections since 1945, four of them consecutively in the period after 1979.

TABLE 5.4 Parliamentary majorities, 1945–1997

Parliament	Party Returned to Office	Overall Majority*
1945–1950	Labour	146
1950–1951	Labour	5
1951–1955	Conservative	17
1955–1959	Conservative	60
1959–1964	Conservative	100
1964–1966	Labour	4
1966–1970	Labour	98
1970–1974	Conservative	30
1974–	Labour	−33
1974–1979	Labour	3
1979–1983	Conservative	43
1983–1987	Conservative	144
1987–1992	Conservative	101
1992–1997	Conservative	21
1997–	Labour	179

* Overall majority following general election. The speaker, where seeking reelection, is included in the original party. A negative number indicates that a minority government was returned to office.

VOTING BEHAVIOR

Recent decades have seen some significant shifts in the nature and pattern of electoral support for British political parties. In the quarter century after the Second World War, Britain displayed the characteristics of a stable two-party system.[24] During that period:

1. There was a high turnout of electors.
2. Of those who voted, virtually all voted for either the Conservative or the Labour party.
3. The most significant predictor of party voting was class.
4. The class base of voting produced stable blocks of voting support, with changes in government being determined by small shifts of voting support from one party to another.

The first two generalizations are borne out by the data in Table 5.2. In every general election held from 1950 to 1966 inclusively, more than three-quarters of those on the electoral register turned out to vote and, of those who did so, 87 percent or more voted for either the Conservative or Labour candidates. In the 1950 election, turnout reached 84 percent. In the election of the following year, almost 97 percent of those who voted cast their ballots for one of the two main parties.

The third generalization is drawn from survey data, which demonstrate the close relationship of class and party in this period. In the general elections held in the 1950s, 70 percent or more of middle-class voters cast their votes for the Conservative party. In the 1960s, 60 percent or more of working-class voters cast their votes for the Labour party.[25] Party support was most marked at the two extremes of the social scale. In 1951, 90 percent of the upper-middle class voted Conservative. In 1966, 72 percent of the "very poor" voted Labour.[26] Class was not an exclusive predictor of voting behavior, nor was the relationship between class and party symmetrical: The middle class was more Conservative than the working class was Labour. One-third of working-class voters regularly voted Conservative. Nonetheless, class remained the most important predictor of how an elector might vote—so much so that one writer, Peter Pulzer, was to declare in 1967 that "class is the basis of British party politics: all else is embellishment and detail."[27]

The class basis of electoral behavior provided each party with a substantial base of support. Small shifts in support could turn one party out of government at an election and replace it with another, but the period of the 1950s in particular did not witness major shifts in voting intentions between elections. This was reflected in by-election results. In the period from 1945 to 1959, there were 168 by-elections: Only ten of them resulted in losses by the incumbent party. Stability seemed a feature of the two-party system.

The period since the end of the 1960s has produced a very different picture. Turnout since 1966 has been more variable. In the four general elections held from 1950 to 1959, the average turnout was just over 80 percent. In the elections from 1964 onward, the average has been 5 percent lower, with turnout in four falling below 73 percent. In the seven elections since, and including, February 1974, the percentage of voters casting their ballots for the Conservative or Labour parties reached 80 percent in only one election, that of 1979 (Table 5.5). In the remaining six elections, the percentage has averaged 74 percent. This is approximately 20 percent lower than the average achieved in the four elections from 1950 to 1959. The 1983 general election marked the low point in terms of the combination of turnout and two-party support; 1997 marked the low point in terms of turnout.

The explanation for this change generally has been ascribed to a decline in the class–party nexus. The two main parties can no longer rely on their "natural" class support. The relative decline in this support is borne out by survey data from recent general elections (Table 5.6). The figures in Table 5.6 show the extent to which Labour could not rely on its traditional class support in the 1992 election—not even mustering the support of a majority of working-class voters—and the failure of the Conservatives to hold on to their traditional middle-class support in 1997. The figures for the two elections reveal the remarkable volatility in voting behavior. Labour made remarkable gains in 1997 but the improvement took place across all social classes.[28] Although social class continues to structure party choice, it is no longer the predictor of party choice that it once was.

Also of declining significance have been the variables of gender, age, and religion. Traditionally, women have been somewhat more likely to vote Conservative than men. In most postwar elections, more men have voted Labour than have voted Conservative, whereas more women have voted Conservative than voted Labour. However, the bias was a slight one. According to Gallup, the bias disappeared in 1983 and according to MORI it disappeared in 1987. There was a slight bias in 1992 but again it disappeared in 1997 (Table 5.7). Gender cannot be drawn upon as a reliable predictor of voting behavior.

TABLE 5.5   Turnout and two-party voting, 1959–1997

General Election	Percentage Turnout	Of Those Voting,% Voting Con. or Lab.
1959	78.8	93.2
1964	77.1	87.5
1966	75.8	89.8
1970	72.0	89.4
1974 (Feb.)	78.7	75.0
1974 (Oct.)	72.8	75.0
1979	76.0	80.8
1983	72.7	70.0
1987	75.3	73.0
1992	77.7	76.3
1997	71.5	73.9

TABLE 5.6 Vote by social class, 1997

Party	Professional and Managerial (AB) %		Office and Clerical (C1) %		Skilled Manual (C2) %		Semiskilled, Unskilled, Residual (DE) %	
Conservative	42	(57)*	26	(41)	25	(38)	21	(37)
Labour	31	(20)	47	(33)	54	(41)	61	(47)
Liberal Democrat	21	(21)	19	(14)	14	(18)	13	(15)

* 1992 percentages in parentheses.
SOURCE: NOP/BBC exit polls; J. Curtice, "Anatomy of a Landslide," *Politics Review*, 7 (1), 1997.

Age also shows some variation, but again, as a predictor of voting behavior, is of limited utility. The older the voter, the greater the likelihood of voting Conservative (Table 5.8). As is apparent from the data in Table 5.8, there is no clear pattern of support among the different age groups. Labour in 1992 attracted more support from those in the 25–44 age range than it did from voters aged 45 and over, but it attracted less support from first-time voters than it did from those in the 25–34 range. It is possible that this reflects a generational cohort change; Butler and Stokes found in their survey that it is not age as such that influences voting behavior but rather the period at which one becomes politically aware. Once one has built up a pattern of voting for a particular party, one is less likely to change. Though Labour made sharp gains across all age groups in 1997, the most dramatic improvement was among first-time voters. As is apparent from both Tables 5.7 and Table 5.8, gender and age have no relevance in explaining support for the Liberal Democrats.

Religion, once an important variable in explaining voting behavior, is no longer the force it was. It was a significant influence in the nineteenth century, but declined rapidly in the twentieth as class became more important. Butler and Stokes found the relationship between religion and party of declining relevance with each generation. In some areas where religious loyalties remain strong, such loyalties can still alter the pattern of class voting. An obvious example is Northern Ireland (see Chapter 10), though mainland examples can be

TABLE 5.7 Party support by gender, 1992–1997

	1992		1997	
	M %	W %	M %	W %
Conservative	41	44	31	32
Labour	37	34	44	44
Liberal Democrat	18	18	17	17

SOURCE: MORI 1992, BBC/NOP 1997.

TABLE 5.8   *Party support by age, 1997*

	Age				
	18–24 %	25–34 %	35–44 %	45–64 %	65+ %
Conservative	22 (38)*	25 (37)	26 (38)	29 (46)	36 (49)
Labour	56 (35)	50 (41)	53 (38)	44 (35)	44 (33)
Liberal Democrat	13 (22)	17 (16)	12 (21)	18 (19)	12 (14)

* 1992 percentages in parentheses.
SOURCE: Gallup.

found in certain cities, notably Glasgow and Liverpool. In such cities, there is a sizable Irish Catholic vote, and that swells the Labour vote in elections.[29] Liberal Democrats also tend to maintain support in areas of traditional strength of nonconformist religions. Overall, though, the impact of religion is marginal and that marginality is reflected in the fact that it no longer figures in analyses of general elections.

Class, then, is of declining relevance as a predictor of voting behavior, and it has not been displaced by the other variables we have identified. The waning of the class–party nexus would appear to explain a greater volatility in voting intentions. Though the Conservative party won four consecutive general elections from 1979 onward, each time with roughly the same share of the national poll, this did not reflect a stability in support among the electorate. Opinion polls showed some marked swings in opinion in between elections and the Conservative party had difficulty winning seats in by-elections: indeed, during the prime ministership of John Major (1990–97), the party failed to hold on to any of the seats it was defending in by-elections. In late 1992 the party suffered a major loss of support in the polls and in 1997 suffered its worst defeat this century. The extent of the massive swing of support from the Conservatives to Labour is apparent from the preceding tables. The extent of change is apparent if one compares the results of the general election of 1983 with those of 1997 (Table 5.2).

Electoral behavior has thus changed significantly. The class–party nexus has waned, though not disappeared. Both main parties have substantial bodies of committed supporters, but not to the same extent as before. Voters do not identify with parties to the same degree as in earlier decades.[30] The Conservative and Labour parties still dominate in the parliamentary arena, but in combination no longer enjoy the monopoly they once enjoyed.

Explanations of Voting Behavior

Is it possible, then, to provide any clear explanation of contemporary voting behavior? The analysis of electoral behavior has been a significant feature of British political science in recent years. Several, often competing, models of electoral behavior have been constructed. The class-based model held sway in postwar decades but has declined in significance since.

The different explanations can be grouped under two headings. There are those explanations that derive from the voter as part of a wider and usually enduring body, and those that derive from the voter as a free-thinking individual. The former encompasses class, consumption, and location and can help explain consistent patterns of party support. The latter encompass issues and performance evaluation and can help explain volatility in voting behavior.

Class.   The class–party nexus, as we have seen, declined in the 1970s and 1980s. Class became a less useful predictor of voting behavior, apparently because of changing social patterns—rendering class itself less relevant—and because of class dealignment, or those within a class being less likely to vote for their "natural" class party. Class, nonetheless, has not ceased to be relevant. As can be seen from Table 5.6, those at the top end of the social scale are more likely to vote Conservative than Labour, those at the other end are more likely to vote Labour than Conservative. However, the figures in the table also show now the limitations of trying to predict voting on the basis of class. In 1992, Labour received less than 50 percent of the votes of those in social classes DE. In 1997, the Conservatives failed to carry an absolute majority of those in classes AB. Among white-collar workers, the Conservatives had an 8 percent advantage in 1992. In 1997, that had switched to a 21 percent advantage to Labour.

Some students of electoral behavior sought in the 1980s to demonstrate that class remained of greater utility than critics claimed. They did so through a redefinition of class. Instead of relying on the occupation of the heads of households, they utilized more sophisticated criteria. Heath, Curtice, and Jowell, for example, took into account authority at work and those who were self-employed.[31] The problem with these new variables was that those with the greatest predictive value covered but a small proportion of the population. In the analysis of Heath and his associates, only about one in three voters were in categories where as many as half of the voters supported one party.[32] The explanatory value of this approach was thus extremely limited.

Another analysis, published early in the 1990s, suggested the continuing relevance of class polarization, but only in a particular part of the country. Political geographers Johnston and Pattie argued that class divisions had persisted in the north of England but declined substantially in the south.[33] Thus, even on the basis of the more recent analyses that seek to utilize the concept, class has some continuing relevance, but not to the same extent as before. It is necessary to identify other influences that have become more salient. That is emphasized especially by the findings from the most recent general elections.

Consumption.   One of the more controversial theses in the 1980s was that first advanced in 1979 by Patrick Dunleavy.[34] He contended that not only has there been a class dealignment but also that there has been a realignment: The cleavage based on production has been replaced by one based on consumption. In other words, class voting—derived from one's stance in relation to the means of production—has been replaced by voting based on public and private consumption. Those who rely on services provided by the state (housing, education, health, transport) are most likely to vote Labour; those who rely on services provided by the private sector are most likely to vote Conservative. The greater the degree of private-sector consumption, the greater the likelihood of voting Conservative. Thus, home-owning households with two cars were 4.39 times more likely to vote Conservative than those with no car who rent their homes from the local authority.

The problem with this particular analysis is the same as that with the redefinition of class: The ideal type (home-owning, car-owning, privately educated, buying private health care) is relatively small. One test of the consumption cleavage thesis found that it did not explain anything that could not be explained through existing approaches.[35]

Location.   Various studies have demonstrated the independent influence of location in voting behavior. A middle-class voter in an urban area is more likely to vote Labour than is a middle-class voter in a rural area. A trade unionist in a rural area is more likely to vote Conservative than is a trade unionist in an urban area. One explanation for this phenomenon is the process of socialization. Living for a long period of time in a particular locality, one begins to absorb the predominant values of that community.

Recent decades have witnessed a marked north–south polarization and an urban–rural polarization in party support. Research by Curtice and Steed found that the spatial divisions began to emerge after 1955. "A North-South cleavage began to emerge in the 1955–59 swing while the urban-rural cleavage became clearly more evident in the 1959–64 swing."[36] Conservative support has become more pronounced in the south of England, whereas Labour support has increased in the north and Scotland.

In each of the elections between and including 1979 and 1992, the Conservative party was carried to victory largely on the votes of the electorate in the southern half of England, below a line drawn from the River Severn to the Wash (see Map 5.1). Labour, despite the challenge of the Scottish National Party and a slight swing to the Conservatives in the 1992 election, achieved a notable predominance in Scotland. The divide was exacerbated in the 1997 general election. In the general election of 1959, the Conservatives won 31 seats in Scotland and Labour won 38. In 1997, the Conservatives won no seats at all in Scotland; Labour won 56. A similar predominance has been achieved by Labour in Wales: in 1997 it won 34 seats, the Conservatives won none at all. In contrast, the Conservatives have tended to dominate in southern England. This dominance was pronounced in the 1980s and early 1990s. Labour made significant inroads into Conservative strength in the south in the 1997 election (see Map 5.1) but the base of Conservative strength remained in the south. In the southeast, excluding Greater London, the Conservatives won 73 seats to Labour's 36.

The urban–rural divide has been equally pronounced. Conservative support in the larger cities has been declining for 30 years. By 1983, the number of seats it was winning in the larger cities was half that achieved in 1959. The

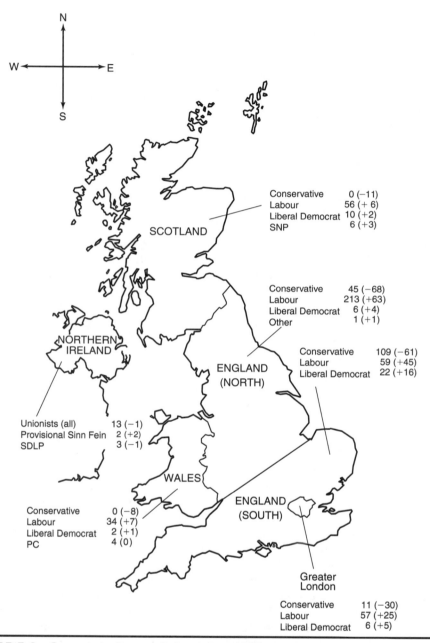

MAP 5.1 *General election results by region, 1997*

Note: Net gains and losses are shown in parentheses. Because of changes in constituency boundaries and in the number of seats, the losses and gains are derived in some cases from assumptions as to which party was notionally the incumbent party.
Source: D. Butler and D. Kavanaugh (eds.), *The British General Election of 1997* (Macmillan, 1997), Appendix 1.

position became more pronounced in subsequent elections. In 1959, in the three large cities of Glasgow, Liverpool, and Manchester, the Conservatives won 15 seats. In 1983, they won just 1, and in 1987, 1992, and 1997, none at all. In the 1997 general election, the Conservative party was essentially eliminated as an "urban" party.

The explanations for the spatial polarization are to be found in mobility and economic change. The north of England has continued to rely on many old traditional industries, characterized by mass unionized work forces and relatively little mobility. It has thus retained an environment conducive to established class politics, as identified by Johnston and Pattie. Economic decline in recent decades has hit the traditional manufacturing industries hardest, producing high unemployment. The area has thus been the one area in which Labour has been able to maintain a strong base. The south has been characterized by a growing service industry, less tied to traditional trade unionism than the north, and by greater mobility in the work force. A similar development has characterized urban and suburban areas, inner cities being characterized often by economic decline, with the more prosperous white-collar workers moving to the suburbs. Other influences appear to have been at work in Scotland and Wales, where the Conservatives seem to have suffered from perceptions of being an English party. There is thus a correlation between location and party support, with location being both an independent as well as a dependent variable in explaining that support. However, location can only offer a partial explanation. It cannot serve to explain Labour support in rural areas, nor can it serve to explain the dramatic swing in support to the Labour party in 1997, which occurred—albeit with some limited variations—across all parts of Great Britain.

Issues.   As class was perceived to have declined as a determinant of voting behavior, various analysts asserted the increasing significance of issue-based voting. The most sophisticated analysis has been that offered by Mark Franklin in *The Decline of Class Voting in Britain.*[37] He charts the decline in class-voting since 1964, which he contends is a consequence of changing social structures and a reduced appeal of the Labour party to its traditional class groups. "The decline in the class basis of voting amounts to a weakening of constraints on volatility and self-expression and the consequence was to open the way to choice between parties on the basis of issue preferences."[38] As the constraint of class has declined, so attitudes—reevaluated in the light of changing conditions—have played a greater role in shaping voting choice. Voters have been more willing to vote on the basis of issue preference and that has generated greater volatility in electoral behavior. In the 1983 and 1987 elections—especially the former—the issue of defense was an electoral plus for the Conservatives. In the 1992 election, with the end of the cold war, defense did not figure prominently in voters' evaluations. Instead, salient issues were those of health care, unemployment, replacing the poll tax, education, and housing (all electoral pluses for Labour) along with management of the economy, taxation, law and order, and—at the bottom end of the scale in voters' ranking of importance—

Europe and Northern Ireland (electoral pluses for the Conservatives).[39] Preferences thus vary and can change over time. Issue voting, as Franklin recognized, makes for uncertainty in electoral outcomes.

The issue-voting approach has been the subject of both challenge and defense.[40] It contributes an important, but not the only, part of the jigsaw for explaining electoral behavior. Were issue-voting the sole determinant of electoral behavior in Britain, survey data suggest that Labour would have won the general election in 1992. "Sixty-three percent of those who considered unemployment important favored Labour's ability to handle it, yet only 47 percent of them actually voted Labour."[41] Similar disparities were found on other issues. Other explanations thus have to be sought.

Performance Evaluation.   Class, however important as a variable in shaping voting behavior, has never been an exclusive influence. If it were, elections would have demonstrated a more consistent outcome. Other variables served to make the difference between success and failure in general elections. Various studies have reinforced the accepted wisdom that evaluation of performance in office has been crucial. With the decline in the class–party link, this instrumental variable becomes more important.

Evaluation takes different forms. Voters may evaluate a party in terms of retrospective and prospective performance, in other words, judging parties according to how they have performed in office or according to how they think they will perform in office. The evaluation may also be subjective or objective, that is, judging parties on the basis of what the voter thinks of the performance in office or on the basis of what the parties have actually delivered.

These distinctions were developed by Paul Whiteley in the 1980s. Utilizing data drawn from the 1979 Election Study, he concluded that subjective judgements were better predictors of voting behavior than objective factors, and that of retrospective and prospective evaluations, the former were more significant than the latter for explaining support—and the decline in that support—for the Labour party.[42] Though critics have questioned his thesis, doubting the extent to which Labour suffered in later elections from retrospective evaluation, there is substantial evidence to support the utility of performance evaluation.

Evaluation of performance emerges as a highly plausible explanation of both the Conservative victory in 1992 and the massive Labour victory in 1997. In terms of objective, retrospective evaluation, it could be argued that the Conservatives should have lost heavily in 1992. The election took place during the longest recession since the 1930s. Similarly, on the same criteria, the Conservatives should have won in 1997, when the economy was strong, with inflation and interest rates at low levels. However, voters judged the Conservatives in 1992 on a more subjective and prospective basis:

> In April 1992, notwithstanding objective economic conditions, most voters did not hold the Major government responsible for the length and depth of the recession, and many believed that their own economic

circumstances were most likely to improve if the Conservatives continued in office.[43]

In 1997, the Conservatives were seen by electors as having destroyed their claim to be competent in handling the economic affairs of the nation. The withdrawal from the European exchange rate mechanism in September 1992 triggered a collapse in support from which the party never recovered. Other activities of government and of individual politicians reinforced the negative perception of the party's performance in office, resulting in the party's disastrous performance in the general election.[44]

These individual-level analyses are important for helping make sense of the growing volatility in electoral behavior. Recent decades have seen a growing electoral volatility in Britain, though no greater than the volatility in other West European countries. However, the 1997 election was remarkable for the extent of change, exhibiting a volatility unusual by European standards.[45]

However, none of these approaches is sufficient to provide an exclusive explanation of voting behavior. Class and location may enable one to predict that the owners of a mansion in a rural county in the south of England are likely to vote Conservative, but they do not help predict or explain why some mansion owners do not vote Conservative or why, in 1997, many of them switched to vote Labour. Given a party's variable performance in office, performance evaluation does not help explain why millions of voters continue to vote for the same party, election after election. In 1997, the Conservative party went down to a massive defeat, yet still garnered 9.6 million votes.

Most of the explanations we have considered serve to explain some degree of behavioral change. In the 1980s, Rose and McAllister found that about 80 percent of voting variance could be explained by five influences: pre-adult socialization, socioeconomic interests (class), political principles, current performance of parties, and party identification.[46] What is significant about this finding is, first, the number of variables and, second, the fact that—despite that number—20 percent of the variance remains unexplained. Elections in Britain, to quote Rose and McAllister, have become more open. That feature has become even more marked since their study was completed. As elections have become more open, the study of them has become more extensive and increasingly sophisticated.

THE CURRENT DEBATE

Electoral behavior, then, has been the subject of extensive academic analysis. That behavior occurs within the context of a particular electoral system, and in recent years that system itself has been the subject of public debate. The debate became prominent in the latter half of the 1970s and has reemerged since the end of the1980s as part of a wider discussion about Britain's constitutional arrangements. In 1997, a party was elected to government that was committed to holding a referendum on the electoral system. The electoral system, according to its critics, is a dysfunctional one, in need of replacement. The view is not one that enjoys universal support.

A Dysfunctional Electoral System?

Critics of Britain's first-past-the-post electoral system have grown in recent decades. They have leveled three principal objections.

The first is that it does not deliver the political goods so frequently claimed for it. The traditional strength of the system is argued to be that it facilitates the return of a single party to government, secure in a majority of seats in the House of Commons. In the February 1974 general election, no one party gained an overall majority. In the following Parliament, elected in October 1974, Labour was returned with a minute overall majority, and two years later slipped into minority status in the House. It survived in government for a year (1977–78) as a result of a pact with the parliamentary Liberal Party. In the Parliament elected in 1992, the government's majority fell as a result of by-election losses and defections, and by the end of the Parliament, the government was in a minority in the House. Given the increasing volatility of the election, and the increase in the number of third parties, critics argue that the chances of a hung Parliament— no one party enjoying an overall majority of seats—are greater than before.[47] The volatility may result in a massive majority for a party—as happened in 1983 and 1997—but equally it may result in no one party having an absolute majority and being able to form a government. The claimed "stability" of the existing system is thus not what it was.

The second and most powerful argument deployed by critics is that the existing system is unfair. There are four potential victims of this unfairness. The first is the voter. As can be seen from Table 5.2, the electoral system does not produce a precise correlation between the percentage of votes cast for a party and the percentage of seats the party wins in the House of Commons. One party gets into government, even though it has failed to win a majority of the votes cast. (Not since 1935 has a party been elected to office with more than 50 percent of the votes cast.) Thus, it is claimed, voters do not get the results they want. The second victim is a particular category of voter: those voting for candidates who lose. Only the votes cast for the winning candidate count. Those cast for losing candidates are termed "wasted votes": they have not had an effect on the outcome. Thus, for example, what is the point voting Conservative or Liberal Democrat in the constituency of Blaneau Gwent (Table 5.3)? The votes cast for the Conservative and Liberal Democrat candidates are wasted. The third potential victim is one of the major parties. Because of the distribution of party support in constituencies, it is possible for one party to gain more votes than the other party, yet win fewer seats.[48] A similar phenomenon is apparent in the United States, where it is possible for a candidate for the presidency to win more popular votes than the other main candidate, yet end up with fewer votes in the Electoral College. Whereas the U.S. has not had a president elected this century who came second in terms of popular votes, Britain has twice had parties who came second in the poll taking up the reins of government. As can be seen from Table 5.2, the Labour party gained more votes than the Conservatives in the 1951 general election, but the Conservatives won a majority of seats and formed the government. The situation was reversed in February 1974, when the Conservatives won more votes than Labour, but fewer seats. Labour went on to form the government. The fourth victim of unfairness is the Liberal Democratic party. As the third party, it has tended to suffer from its support being fairly consistently spread around the country. It is possible to win 20 percent of votes in most seats and not win any seats at all. The situation has not been quite that bad for the party, but it has not been that far from it. The disparity between the percentages of votes won and the seats in the House of Commons can be seen in Table 5.2. In 1983, the Liberal/Social Democratic Alliance won just over 25 percent of the votes cast—only 2 percent behind the Labour party—but got only 3.5 percent of the seats: Labour gained 32 percent of the seats. Even in 1997, with its best performance in terms of the number of seats won for sixty years, the Liberal Democrats garnered 16.8 percent of the votes cast but held only 7 percent of the seats in the House of Commons.

The third criticism of the electoral system is that it encourages adversarial politics in Britain, with consequent negative consequences for the nation's economic performance. The "adversary politics" thesis, first developed following the 1974 elections by a number of academics led by S. E. Finer[49] (see Chapter 3), is that the electoral system has encouraged a polarized contest between two parties for the winner-take-all spoils of a general election. One party is returned to office with an overall majority and implements its manifesto program, a program neither known nor supported by most electors and one drawn up on the basis more of party dogma than of a dispassionate and well-informed analysis of Britain's problems. If the other party then wins at a subsequent election, it implements its own distinctive program. There has thus been the potential for public policy to lurch from one position to another, the policy pursued by government never quite matching the wishes of the electoral center. The results, in short, have been unrepresentative governments—pursuing policies more politically extreme than those favored by the more centrist electorate—and policy discontinuity. Policy discontinuity has frustrated industrialists and investors who wished to engage in forward planning: They could not anticipate stability in government programs. Adversary politics and changes in government may make for "exciting politics," but they produce "low-credibility Government strategies, whichever party is in power."[50]

Indeed, the conditions created by the electoral system have been seen as being at the heart of Britain's problems. To win an election, a party makes extravagant promises, doing so to outbid the other party. In office, it finds it can no longer raise the resources to meet those promises. It therefore has to change tack, further adding to confusion in governmental policy making. However, it also has to act in a way that does not jeopardize its chance of winning the next election. Hence it is reluctant to take the unpopular measures deemed by some to be necessary to tackle Britain's long-term problems. Even when, as in the

1980s, a government gained reelection, the adversary relationship militates against its being able to mobilize popular support in order to achieve its goals. The response of the Conservative government, according to critics, was to strengthen its own power, thus further reducing its capacity to mobilize necessary, and voluntary, support. The result, in short, has been a vicious circle.[51]

The solution to the problem, or at least a partial one, was perceived by these critics as the introduction of a new electoral system, one that introduced a method of proportional representation (PR). Proportional representation, it was argued, would be fairer than the existing electoral system, ensuring that a party received the share of parliamentary seats equivalent to its national vote. Furthermore, given existing voting behavior, it would deprive any one party of an overall majority of seats. Forming a government with an overall parliamentary majority would thus necessitate a coalition. This would likely involve one of the main parties having "to co-operate with a party or parties taking a more central stance," hence leading to greater moderation in policy.[52] Given that such a coalition would enjoy the support of more than 50 percent of electors and that the turnover of seats under PR is small, the coalition would likely remain in office for the foreseeable future and hence be in a position to ensure a degree of policy continuity. The overall effect of PR would thus be to put an end to the worst features of adversary politics and its unfortunate consequences.

An Effective Electoral System?

Supporters of the electoral system tended to remain quiet in the 1980s and early 1990s, largely on the basis that—under a Conservative Government—there was not going to be any change in the system. However, as critics of the system became more vocal, and began to attract some support among Labour politicians, supporters of first-past-the-post began to engage in debate.

The principal justifications advanced for the existing electoral system have been fourfold. First, the system is coherent. The electoral system facilitates the return of a single party to government. Political power thus resides in one body (the party in government) and the rest of the political system revolves around that one central political fact. People understand how the system works—the system is perceptible—and know who is responsible for decisions that are made. Second, and crucial to the defense of the existing arrangements, the electoral system helps ensure that the government is accountable. Electors know whom to hold accountable for decisions that are made and can remove them from office. There is one body—the party in government—that is responsible for making domestic public policy. That body cannot blame anyone else if electors find policy unpalatable. The distinguished political philosopher Sir Karl Popper argued that the most important attribute of an electoral system was not the ease by which a government could be elected, but rather the ease by which it could be removed.[53] If electors do not like what government is doing, they can sweep it out of office at the next election. Members of the government know that they are not going to be able to engage in post-election bargaining with other parties to stay in power. Thus, in Popper's words, election day constitutes "Judgement Day." Third, the system is responsive. Because a government knows it may be swept out at the next election, it is responsive to public reaction to its policies. When the Conservative government under Margaret Thatcher introduced a new local tax (the community charge, popularly dubbed the poll tax) in place of the existing local tax, it proved widely unpopular, generating demonstrations and even riots. Recognizing that it could lose the next election as a result, the party in government got rid of the tax, in the process getting rid of the party leader, who was committed to maintaining the tax. Fourth, it is effective. The electoral system enables a single party to be returned to office and that party is then able to implement the program that it placed before voters during the election. Governments have a high success rate in implementing the commitments embodied in their party manifestos.[54] There may be some modification during the lifetime of the Parliament, but overall they implement what they have promised to implement. If electors then disapprove, they can turn out the government at the next election.

Defenders of the first-past-the-post system also challenge the basis of the claims for a new electoral system. The argument is "fairness" is contested.[55] The existing system may place disproportionate political power in the largest single party but that, it is argued, is fairer than placing disproportionate political power in the hands of the smallest or one of the smallest political parties, which would be the case under a more proportional system, a third party holding the balance of power. Ensuring a party with 15 percent of the votes had 15 percent of the seats could produce a highly unfair distribution of political power since the party holding 15 percent of the seats could, by holding the balance of power, exercise more than 15 percent of the negotiating power in the House of Commons. A more proportional system, it is argued, would also be unfair in that it would likely result in the choice of government resting not with electors exercising their judgement in the polling booths, but with party leaders engaging in post-election bargaining. The result of post-election bargaining could be a coalition for which not one elector has definitively voted.

The adversary politics thesis developed by the reformers has also been challenged. Two mutually exclusive arguments are deployed against it. One line of argument accepts the notion of an adversary relationship between the parties but considers this a beneficial rather than a harmful process: It offers a clear choice to the electorate and it results in one party with a mandate from the people getting on with the job of governing. Proportional representation, it is feared, would facilitate a blurring of choice and prevent a party from being returned with a mandate clearly approved by the people.

The other argument deployed against the adversary politics thesis calls into doubt the relevance of the notion itself. The rhetoric of adversary politics, it is argued, hides a more consensual substance. In terms of government legislation, empirical research has indicated that a consensual model is indeed more applicable.[56] In this view, parties are seen as being not quite as central to formulation of public policy as both reformers and the politicians themselves believe. The external demands on government are such that it can often act only as arbiter between competing demands and respond, under guidance from civil servants, to international events and trends over which it has no direct influence. Whichever party is in power makes some, but not a great deal, of difference. This particular argument received reinforcement by a study undertaken by Richard Rose early in the 1990s. He examined the relationship between electoral systems and economic performance in 21 advanced industrial nations and found that there was no consistent link. "Differences in economic performance," he wrote, "cannot be explained by differences in electoral systems."[57] His conclusion undermined a central tenet of the reformers' case.

For defenders of the first-past-the-post system, the alternatives threaten to undermine the advantages of the existing system, offering no tangible benefits in their place and threatening to undermine the stability and effectiveness of the political system.

A New Electoral System?

Supporters of electoral reform made much of the running in debate in the 1980s and 1990s. They also grew in number. The Liberal Democrats were long-standing supporters of reform. A growing body of Labour supporters also came round to their point of view. An umbrella reform movement, Charter '88, was formed in 1988, and included in its manifesto the introduction of a new electoral system. Labour leader Neil Kinnock set up a commission to consider electoral reform (the Plant Commission, which recommended the supplementary vote, a variant of the alternative vote). His successor as Labour leader, John Smith, committed the party to supporting a referendum on electoral reform. His successor, Tony Blair, maintained that commitment. The Labour manifesto in the 1997 general election declared: "We are committed to a referendum on the voting system for the House of Commons. An independent Commission on voting systems will be appointed early to recommend a proportional alternative to the first-past-the-post system."[58] Shortly after the party was returned to power, Prime Minister Tony Blair appointed a commission under a leading Liberal Democrat (and ex-Labour cabinet minister), Lord Jenkins of Hillhead, to propose an alternative to the existing system.

The various alternative systems on offer are listed in Box 5.1. The Liberal Democrats have favored the use of the Single Transferable Vote (STV). Support for the Additional Member System has been more pronounced among Labour politicians. Some Labour MPs have tended to support the Alternative Vote or Supplementary Vote because it can be utilized within existing constituencies, and thus is the least disruptive. As we noted in the introduction to the chapter, most of the systems have now been used for elections to various positions in the United Kingdom, but there is no agreement that any one of them should be employed for elections to the House of Commons. Though a regional list system has been introduced for elections to the European Parliament, there are no advocates of its use for elections to the House of Commons, principally because it destroys

Box 5.1   Alternative Electoral Systems

List System

Electors vote for lists of candidates put forward by the parties and seats are allocated on the basis of the percentage of the votes won by each party. Under "closed" list systems, electors cannot influence the rank ordering of candidates; under "open list" systems they can (though in practice they rarely do). The system can be organized on a regional or national basis. A regional list system has been adopted in Britain for the election of Members of the European Parliament.

Single Transferable Vote (STV)

Under this system, there are multi-member constituencies, with each elector able to indicate a preference on the ballot paper, putting the number 1 beside the name of the candidate most preferred, 2 against the name of the elector's second choice, and so on. A quota is established by the formula of dividing the number of valid ballots cast by the number of seats, plus one: to the resulting figure, one is added. Thus in a five-member constituency in which 120,000 ballots are cast, the formula would be

$$\frac{120,000}{5 + 1} + 1$$

Hence the quota (the number of ballots required to elect one member) would be 20,001. Any candidate receiving this number of votes is declared elected. The second preferences of any of the candidate's surplus votes, plus those of the candidate at the bottom of the poll, are then redistributed, and so on until the necessary number of candidates reach the quota. The STV system has been employed in the United Kingdom for the elections of the three Members of the European Parliament returned from Northern Ireland.

Additional Member System (AMS)

Under this system, single-member constituencies are retained, with the first-past-the-post method of election retained in each. Additional seats are then allocated to parties on a regional basis, usually with a threshold requirement (a party has to obtain a specified percentage—say 5 percent—of the vote in any area of allocation in order to obtain additional seats). Additional seats go to the parties on the basis of the proportion of votes received in the region. The additional member system is being employed in the United Kingdom for elections to the Scottish parliament and the Welsh Assembly (See chapter 9).

(continued)

BOX 5.1 (CONTINUED)

Alternative Vote (AV)

This is not a proportional system. It retains the single member constituency. Voters list their preferences against candidates names. If a candidate receives an absolute majority of the votes cast, then he or she is declared elected. If no candidate receives an absolute majority, the candidate with the least number of votes is eliminated and the second preferences of that candidate are then redistributed; the process continues until a candidate has an absolute majority.

Supplementary Vote (SV)

This is a variant of the Alternative Vote. A single member constituency is retained but each voter has only two votes—a principal and a supplementary vote. If one candidate achieves an absolute majority of the principal votes cast, then the candidate is declared elected. If no candidate achieves an absolute majority, all the candidates other than the top two are eliminated and the second preferences of the eliminated candidates are then redistributed. If the second vote is for an eliminated candidate, it is discarded.

Alternative Vote Plus (AV Plus)

This utilizes the Alternative Vote in individual constituencies but then provides for a "top up" of members from a list system. The number of members elected under a list system can be used to correct for the disproportionality that can result from the use of the Alternative Vote.

the need for constituencies and can allow for a concentration of power in the hands of party leaders in selecting and ranking candidates. The STV system cannot necessarily produce strict proportionality: it has been categorized as "contingently proportional."[59] The Additional Member System can deliver proportionality, though that depends on the proportion of additional members (a 50-50 split between constituency members and additional members delivers proportionality) and on voters not splitting their votes between the constituency and the list. Critics also claim that it will result in two tiers of MPs, those elected by constituencies having to carry a massive and unnecessary burden of constituency work. They point now to the experience of the Scottish Parliament, elected by such a system, which has experienced clashes between constituency-elected members and list members over who represents people in a certain area.[60] The Alternative and Supplementary Vote are attacked because they are not proportional systems.

One variant that came on the agenda of debate in 1998 was termed "AV Plus" or "AV Top Up." This entailed utilizing the Alternative Vote—thus allowing constituencies to be retained, with a direct link between electors and a particular MP—but with additional Members being created to provide for some element of proportionality. This was seen as an attempt to square a circle, introducing a greater element of proportionality without losing the constituency link. Critics noted that had the AV system been used in 1997, the results would have been more disproportional than they were under the first-past-the-post system, and that seeking to introduce such a skewed system and then introducing an extra element to overcome the very defect that had been introduced was to employ rather warped and tortuous logic.

The Jenkins Commission reported in October 1998 and recommended "AV Plus," though with the bulk of MPs being elected by constituencies.[61] By introducing the "top-up" element, the system was designed to be more proportional than the existing one. By recommending that most MPs be elected by constituencies (rather than a 50-50 split between constituency and "top-up" members), the potential of a single party being elected to government was retained. The report was immediately attacked by supporters of the existing electoral system[62] and by some supporters of reform who favored other PR systems. Supporters of the existing system argued that it went too far: It was calculated that under this system most elections since 1945 would have produced "hung" Parliaments (i.e., no one party winning an overall majority). They also pointed out that no other country employed AV Plus. Supporters of other PR systems argued that it did not go far enough, since it did not provide for strict proportionality. The government was noncommittal on when the Commission's recommendation would be put to a referendum and it became increasingly clear that it would not be before the next general election. Various leading members of the cabinet were known to be opposed to the proposal and the prime minister did not appear enthusiastic to pursue it.

Opinion polls suggest that electoral reform elicits far less support than other items of constitutional reform. Support for change is broad but not particularly deep.[63] In the 1991 MORI State of the Nation Poll, 50 percent of those questioned favored a move to a PR system but only 23 percent "strongly" supported change; 23 percent of those questioned opposed change. In 1995, 46 percent favored change, only 18 percent doing so strongly; 21 percent opposed change. More than one in three of those questioned either did not support or oppose PR or did not have an opinion. In both 1991 and 1995, only 5 percent of those questioned claimed to know a "great deal" about proportional representation. (In 1995, 11 percent said they had never heard of it.)[64] Opponents of change anticipate more support for the existing system once a specified alternative is on offer. The Liberal Democrats support a new system, the Conservatives oppose it, and the Labour party is divided on the issue. The outcome of any referendum is not certain.

NOTES

1 Until then, some voters had two votes. There were twelve University seats, with the Members being elected by graduates. A graduate thus had a constituency vote and a University vote. The seats were abolished by the 1949 Act.

[2] R. Blackburn, *The Electoral System in Britain* (Macmillan, 1995), p. 85.

[3] F. F. Piven and R. A. Cloward, *Why Americans Don't Vote* (Pantheon, 1989); D. McSweeney and J. Zvesper, *American Political Parties* (Routledge, 1991), pp. 146–147.

[4] See Blackburn, pp. 84–86. Some people have no interest in voting, some may fail to register if there is no election in the offing, and in 1990 a notable decline in registration was attributed to people wanting to avoid paying the "poll tax" (see Chapter 9).

[5] See Blackburn, pp. 118–142 and R. McLeod, "Reviewing the Situation," *The House Magazine*, 571, November 16, 1992, p. 10.

[6] See P. Norton and D. M. Wood, *Back from Westminster* (University Press of Kentucky, 1993).

[7] See D. Butler and D. Kavanagh, *The British General Election of 1997* (Macmillan, 1997), p. 223.

[8] M. Pinto-Duschinsky, *British Political Finance 1830–1980* (American Enterprise Institute, 1981), p. 249.

[9] Butler and Kavanagh, p. 212.

[10] Butler and Kavanagh, pp. 241–242.

[11] D. Kavanagh, *Election Campaigning* (Blackwell, 1995), p. 41.

[12] According to the figures in Blackburn, p. 287, fewer than 200,000 copies of each party manifesto were printed and sold in 1992.

[13] See S. E. Finer, *The Changing British Party System, 1945–79* (American Enterprise Institute, 1980), pp. 125–126.

[14] R. I. Hofferbert and I. Budge, "The Party Mandate and the Westminster Model: Election Programmes and Government Spending in Britain, 1945–85," *British Journal of Political Science*, 22, 1992, pp. 151–182.

[15] For a thorough discussion, see D. Kavanagh, "The Politics of Manifestos," *Parliamentary Affairs,* 34 (1), 1981, pp. 7–27.

[16] P. Norton, "The Qualifying Age for Candidature in British Elections," *Public Law*, 1980, pp. 55–73.

[17] B. Criddle, "MPs and Candidates," in Butler and Kavanagh, p. 195.

[18] See M. Rush, *The Selection of Parliamentary Candidates* (Longman, 1969) for the period of the 1950s and 1960s. No changes were reported in M. Rush, "The 'Selectorate' Revisited: Selecting Parliamentary Candidates in the 1980s," *Teaching Politics*, 15 (1), 1986, pp. 99–113.

[19] When this author served on a selection committee many years ago, one question asked during the short-listing process was "Can't we interview him? He has a nice name." The response: a polite "no."

[20] B. Criddle, "MPs and Candidates," in Butler and Kavanagh, p. 197.

[21] When those who had been MPs before are included, the age range achieves a slightly broader spread. The oldest (Alan Clark) was actually age 69, having previously been an MP from 1974 to 1992.

[22] C. Mellors, *The British MP* (Saxon House, 1978); and M. Rush, "The Members of Parliament," in M. Ryle; P. G. Richards (eds.), *The Commons under Scrutiny* (Routledge, 1988), pp. 26–27; B. Criddle, "MPs and Candidates", in Butler and Kavanagh, pp. 204–206.

[23] A. King, "The Rise of the Career Politician in Britain—and Its Consequences," *British Journal of Political Science,* 2 (3), 1981, pp. 249–285; P. Riddell, *Honest Opportunism* (Hamish Hamilton, 1993).

[24] See G. Sartori, *Parties and Party Systems: A Framework for Analysis* (Cambridge University Press, 1976), pp. 158–189; P. Norton, "Britain: Still a Two-Party System?" in S. Bartolini and P. Mair, *Party Politics in Contemporary Western Europe* (Frank Cass, 1984), pp. 27–45.

[25] B. Sarlvik and I. Crewe, *Decade of Dealignment* (Cambridge University Press, 1983), p. 87.

[26] The Gallup Poll, "Voting Behaviour in Britain," in R. Rose (ed.), *Studies in British Politics,* 3rd ed. (Macmillan, 1976), p. 206.

27 P. Pulzer, *Political Representation and Elections in Britain* (Macmillan, 1967), p. 98.

28 See J. Curtice, "Anatomy of a Landslide," *Politics Review,* 7 (1), 1997, pp. 2–8.

29 R. Rose, *The Problem of Party Government* (Penguin, 1976), p. 43.

30 See Sarlvik and Crewe, pp. 334–336.

31 A. Heath, R. Jowell, and J. Curtice, *How Britain Votes* (Pergamon, 1985), pp. 22ff.

32 R. Rose and I. McAllister, *Voters Begin to Choose* (Sage, 1986), p. 46.

33 R. Johnston and C. J. Pattie, "Class Dealignment and the Regional Polarisation of Voting Patterns in Great Britain, 1964–1987," *Political Geography,* 11 (1), 1992, pp. 73–86.

34 P. Dunleavy, "The Urban Basis of Political Alignment: Social Class, Domestic Property Ownership and State Intervention in Consumption Processes," *British Journal of Political Science,* 9, 1979, pp. 409–444.

35 M. Franklin and E. Page, "A Critique of the Consumption Cleavage Approach in British Voting Studies," *Political Studies,* 32, 1984, pp. 521–536.

36 J. Curtice and M. Steed, "Electoral Choice and the Production of Government," *British Journal of Political Science,* 12, 1982, p. 256

37 M. Franklin, *The Decline of Class Voting in Britain* (Oxford University Press, 1985).

38 Franklin, p. 176.

39 Derived from the findings of a MORI poll. See "Issues of Influence," *The Times,* April 11, 1992.

40 See Rose and McAllister, p. 147; and R. J. Johnston, C. J. Pattie, and J. G. Allsop, *A Nation Dividing?* (Longman, 1988), p. 59.

41 D. Sanders, "Why the Conservative Party Won—Again," in A. King (ed.), *Britain at the Polls 1992* (Chatham House, 1993), p. 195.

42 P. Whiteley, *The Labour Party in Crisis* (Methuen, 1983), p. 106.

43 D. Sanders, "The New Electoral Battleground" in A. King (ed), *New Labour Triumphs: Britain at the Polls* (Chatham House, 1997), p. 224.

44 See D. Denver, "The Government That Could Do No Right" and P. Norton, "The Conservative Party: 'In Office but Not in Power' " in King, *New Labour Triumphs.*

45 See Sanders, "The New Electoral Battleground," pp. 222–223.

46 Rose and McAllister, pp. 128–133.

47 J. Curtice and M. Steed, "Electoral Choice and the Production of Government," *British Journal of Political Science,* 12 (2), 1982, pp. 249–298.

48 For example, Party A could win two marginal seats by the barest of margins while Party B won one seat with an overwhelming majority; the aggregate vote for Party B in the three seats could well exceed that of Party A, but Party A has won twice as many seats. Similarly a candidate for the U.S. presidency could carry two large states by tiny margins and his opponent carry another large state by a massive majority, the aggregate number of votes being greater for the opponent, yet the candidate carrying the two states winning more Electoral College votes.

49 S. E. Finer (ed.), *Adversary Politics and Electoral Reform* (Wigram, 1975), pp. 30–31

50 M. Shanks, *Planning and Politics* (Political and Economic Planning, 1977), p. 92.

51 See the comments of P. Jay, "Englanditis," in R. E. Tyrell, Jr. (ed.), *The Future That Doesn't Work* (Doubleday, 1977), p. 181; and S. E. Brittan, *The Economic Consequences of Democracy* (Temple Smith, 1977).

52 Finer, pp. 30–31.

53 Sir K. Popper, " 'The Open Society and Its Enemies' Revisited," *Economist,* April 23, 1988.

54 R. Rose, *Do Parties Make a Difference?* 2nd ed. (Macmillan, 1984), pp. 64–67; R. I. Hofferbert and I. Budge, "The Party Mandate and the Westminster Model: Election Programmes and Government Spending in Britain, 1945–85," *British Journal of Political Science,* 22 (2), 1992, pp. 151–182.

[55] See P. Norton, "The Case for First-Past-The-Post," *Representation,* 34 (2), 1997, pp. 84–88.

[56] Rose, *Do Parties Make a Difference?*

[57] R. Rose, *What Are the Economic Consequences of PR?* (Electoral Reform Society, 1992), p. 17.

[58] Labour Party, *New Labour: Because Britain Deserves Better* (Labour Party, 1997), p. 33.

[59] P. Dunleavy, H. Margetts, B. O'Duffy, and S. Weir, *Making Votes Count* (University of Essex, 1997), p. 28.

[60] In November 1999 an investigation was ordered by the presiding officer after a clash between some constituency members and some elected from the party list as to who represented the people in a certain area.

[61] *The Report of the Independent Commission on the Voting System* (The Stationery Office, 1998).

[62] See, e.g., P. Norton, *Power to the People* (Conservative Policy Forum, 1998).

[63] MORI, *State of the Nation 1995* (MORI, 1995), p. 10.

[64] *State of the Nation* 1995, p. 9.

Chapter 6

Political Parties
More or Less Than a Two-Party System?

In the United States, political parties provide some measure of choice among candidates at election time. They offer a reference point for many electors. They do little else. U.S. parties remain weak bodies, characterized by faction rather than party.[1] Ideological and structural factors militate against them developing as coherent and programmatic bodies. They operate within a broad ideological consensus,[2] rendering differences between parties that are often largely differences of degree rather than kind. Elections, consequently, are often fought on the basis of trust, personality, or particular issues rather than competing programs. Even if the parties were geared to presenting coherent and competing programs, the structure of the U.S. political system would work against such a program being carried through successfully: A party would need to be cohesive, it would need to capture the White House, and it would need to achieve the return of a majority of its supporters in both houses as well as overcome internal procedural constraints within Congress. The occasions when the conditions of programmatic coherence, party unity, and control of executive and legislative branches have been present—as during the period of the first New Deal and the Great Society program—are notable for their rarity—and their brevity. It has proved impossible to sustain strong party government in the United States.

Britain lacks those features that have facilitated a weak party system in the United States. A unitary and parliamentary form of government has favored the development of centralized and cohesive parties geared to offering a programmatic choice to the electors and to carrying out that program once the all-or-nothing spoils of a general election have been gained. The executive dominance of the House of Commons ensures legislative approval of the party program: The doctrine of parliamentary sovereignty puts the program's implementation beyond challenge by the courts. It is, in short, the very model of a strong party government. It is a model that has been variously admired. It has variously found

123

favor with U.S. scholars because of its apparent ability to ensure the realization of social reform.[3] It appeared to influence the report of the Committee on the Constitutional System in 1987, which recommended that members of Congress be permitted to sit in the Cabinet.[4] It is held up as an antidote to the brokered politics of the United States.

To stress the differences of the two systems is both important and necessary. However, it runs the risk of obscuring some important similarities. U.S. parties may be weak and British parties strong by comparison, but both the United States and Britain are notable for having systems dominated by two parties. The Republican and Democratic parties are dominant in U.S. elections, the Conservative and Labour parties (albeit to a lesser extent) dominate in British elections. There are also *some* similarities between the parties themselves. The Republican party in the United States and the Conservative party in Britain are essentially right-of-center parties that tend to attract support from similar constituencies, notably the middle class. In the 1980s, there was a notable empathy between President Ronald Reagan and Prime Minister Margaret Thatcher as well as between their successors, George Bush and John Major. During the 1992 presidential election campaign, there was some contact and cooperation between the Republican campaign team and Conservative party headquarters. The Democratic party and the Labour party are more left-of-center parties appealing to blue-collar workers. In the 1960s, Labour leader Harold Wilson is reputed to have wanted to model himself on John Kennedy and his party on the Democratic party. The new Labour Prime Minister in 1997, Tony Blair, developed an affinity with President Clinton; both tried, with some success, to make their parties more attractive to a wider social spectrum, Blair to "middle England" and Clinton to "middle America." In recent decades, parties in both countries have witnessed similar but not identical falls in support and partisan identification among electors. These, though, are broad generalizations and should not be pushed too far. The correlation between U.S. and U.K. parties is far from exact, and those parties operate in political systems that are notable for their very sharp differences.

It is important first to consider the growth and the nature of the two main political parties. In their origin and growth, they are distinctly British and can be understood only within the context of British history and political culture.

THE PARTIES IN BRITAIN

The first principle of party, according to Edmund Burke in the eighteenth century, was "to put men who hold their opinions into such a condition as may enable them to carry their common plans into execution." At the time that he was writing, that "condition" meant gaining the confidence of the king. With the widening of the franchise in the nineteenth century, it came instead to depend on the confidence of the electors. As bodies that seek electoral success in order to form the government, political parties may be said to have developed in Britain following the Reform Act of 1832; as bodies seeking that success in order to fulfill a particular program—a stage arguably never reached by U.S. parties—they are more especially the product of the Reform Act of 1867.

The need for electoral support after 1832 and the difficulty of establishing direct personal contact with the enlarged electorate encouraged the development of embryonic political *organization*: Political clubs were formed, election funds were established, registration societies—to ensure that supporters were registered to vote—were brought into being, and in some parts of the country (notably Lancashire) constituency associations were formed. Nonetheless, as we have seen (Chapter 3), the differences between pre- and post-1832 days were not as marked as some might have supposed: The aristocracy remained politically eminent, voting was still by open ballot, and corrupt practices were still common. All this was to change as a result of the Reform Act of 1867 and the reforming measures of the next 18 years. The electorate was now of such a size (2.5 million: see Chapter 3) and of such a nature that highly organized political parties became necessary both for facilitating contact and for aggregating the interests of voters through some form of party platform. Bribery and other corrupt practices, as well as the open ballot, were formally done away with by statute, though the size of the electorate alone did much to remove bribery as an effective weapon of influence. Organized corruption, as Richard Crossman observed, was gradually replaced by party organization,[5] and the two main parties of the day, to employ Maurice Duverger's terminology, were developed from cadres into mass-membership parties. The Liberal party created the National Liberal Federation to widen its appeal to the newly enfranchised voter. The Conservative party created the Conservative National Union in 1867 and Conservative Central Office in 1870, the latter to provide professional support to the voluntary wing of the party. Highly organized, mass-membership political parties became a feature of British political life.

In the latter half of the nineteenth century the two dominant parties were the Conservatives and the Liberals.[6] Both adhered to a hierarchical conception of party structure and both had parliamentary parties that predated the creation of the extraparliamentary parties. The voluntary organizations were created primarily to mobilize support for the parliamentary leaders: They were not expected to formulate policies or to give instructions. The conventions of the Constitution also facilitated this form of "top-down" leadership within the parties. Although both parties began to appeal to the country on the basis of particular platforms, the notion of "the manifesto" was not well developed. The party leaders were expected to make an appeal to the country and, if elected, were expected to proceed with the task of governing.

Such approaches were to be modified in the twentieth century. One important influence was the development of the Labour party. It was created to achieve the return to Parliament of representatives of the working classes and it adhered to the concept of intraparty democracy. Implementation of the party's election manifesto became the touchstone by which party activists could determine whether party leaders were adhering to the party's program. The party's internal norms were not altogether compatible with those of the Constitution.

The party favored the election of party leaders, which in government would mean the members of the cabinet, whereas the Constitution conferred such power on the prime minister. Under the leadership of Ramsay MacDonald, the first Labour prime minister, this conflict was resolved largely in favor of the Constitution. Nonetheless, tension between a "top-down" form of political leadership, in which the party defers to the guidance given by its leaders, and a "bottom-up" form, in which leaders are bound by decisions taken by party members, has been a recurrent feature of Labour party politics.

The Labour party displaced the Liberal party as one of the two main parties in Britain in the 1920s. In 1922 it was recognized as the main opposition party in Parliament. During the twentieth century, the Conservative party has tended to be the governing party, with the Labour party as the challenger. The Conservatives dominated the inter-war years, between 1918 and 1939, and then, in the 50 years following the end of the Second World War, held office for 33 of them. As we saw in Chapter 5 (Table 5.4), the Labour party has been returned to office with substantial majorities on only three occasions (1945, 1966, and 1997). However, although the century has been characterized as the Conservative Century,[7] the last election of the century saw a remarkable change of party fortunes, Labour winning with a stunning majority and the Conservatives suffering one of their worst defeats. The end of the century also saw a notable increase in the parliamentary representation of the principal third party, the Liberal Democratic party, successor to the Liberal party, as well as some successes for other third parties in elections to other bodies, notably the European Parliament and the new assemblies in the different parts of the United Kingdom. The increasing volatility of the British electorate (Chapter 5), and the use in 1999 of new electoral systems for elections to parliamentary bodies other than the House of Commons, have meant that the fortunes of the parties have become less predictable than before.

The Conservative Party

Although British Conservatism can be traced back several centuries, indeed to Hooker in the sixteenth century, the emergence of a political party with the name Conservative took place in the fourth decade of the nineteenth century. The name Conservative was first used by an anonymous writer in 1830, and the term was in common usage by 1832. The party set up an election fund in 1835.[8] It was the successor to the Tory party, the party of the landowning gentry, which had largely disintegrated under the leadership of the duke of Wellington in the 1820s. The new party inherited both the base of Tory support and the party's central tenets.[9] Foremost among these was a belief in the organic nature of society. Society was seen as a historical product, a thing of slow and natural growth, an organic entity with unity and character. Concomitantly, the party inherited from the philosophy of Edmund Burke a belief in gradual change: Society was evolutionary, not static. Change, though, had to be evolutionary, not revolutionary. It had to improve, not destroy. Change had to take place without doing violence to the existing fabric of society. The party was committed to the defense of existing and worthwhile institutions: It stood for the defense of Constitution, Crown, and Church. If there was to be reform it should be to save the Constitution, not to subvert it. It was a corollary of such beliefs that the party adhered to an ordered society, one in which law, order, and authority were upheld. It stood for the defense of property. Private property, as Burke contended, was a bulwark against tyranny: Without private property, the overpowerful state could not be resisted. One could identify the party as adhering also to limited but not necessarily weak government. Government was perceived as having but a limited role to play in society, primarily that of defending the realm, but if strong government was on occasion necessary to maintain the king's government, then so be it. In short, then, the party stood basically for the existing order of things but was prepared to admit the need for occasional change, change not for the sake of change but in order to preserve.

The party's base of support initially was a restricted one. It was essentially a party of the landed interest. It had no national appeal and for the middle years of the century was very much the "out" party in politics. It was transformed into a national party by Benjamin Disraeli. He had to devise an appeal that made the party relevant to the problems of the day. This he did: To the corpus of Conservative beliefs he added adherence to the notion of One Nation—that is, One Nation at Home and One Nation Abroad. Domestically, this meant that the party would not divide the nation in the interests of one class but would look after the interests of all classes. The party would balance social forces and establish common goals. Internationally, it meant the development and maintenance of the empire. This concept identified the party with the achievements of the nation; it provided an inspiring theme to unite in patriotic harmony all Englishmen, if not all Britons. As part of the theme of One Nation, Disraeli was to demonstrate concern for the welfare of the people—much of the social reform legislation of the latter half of the century was Conservative-inspired—while stressing the imperative of maintaining institutions and social stability. Coupled with this national appeal was the development of the party as a mass-membership organization, one that ensured that the party's message reached the new electors. By the time of Disraeli's death in 1881, the Conservative party had laid claim to be a national party, one of responsibility and government. For the last quarter of the century and for much of the twentieth, the party was to dominate British politics.[10]

As the party developed to acquire its national status, so it acquired new support. It obtained the support of a substantial fraction of working-class voters, in large part because industrialists and mill owners—the employers of the workers—were associated with the Liberal party. It acquired defectors from the ranks of the Liberals, notably the Liberal Unionists, toward the end of the nineteenth century. The influx of Liberals tended to move it more in the direction of a capitalist party, supporting the making of money by individual enterprise rather than looking down on it as a slightly degrading pursuit. By the twentieth century the Conservative party was cohesive but constituted a coalescence of different strands of thought.

Within British Conservatism, there are two main strands: the "Tory" and the "Whig," each of which may be further subdivided.[11] The Tory strand of thought places emphasis on social discipline, on authority, on continuity, and on ensuring that change does not do violence to the essential fabric of society; it tends to adhere strongly to the Disraelian concept of One Nation. The Whig strain is more concerned with future goals and places emphasis on the creation of wealth and the most efficient form of economic organization. It is thus more concerned with economics, whereas the Tory strain is more concerned with morals. Within the party, there is the potential for tension between continuity and change, between those favoring change in more radical or rapid form and those favoring moderation, and also between the Tory emphasis on social unity and the Whig neoliberal element, which stresses creative tension and competitive struggle.[12] On occasion, such tension has been realized: in the 1840s and again in the first decade of the twentieth century on the issue of tariff reform (the liberal strain within the party favoring free trade, the Tory element favoring the erection of tariff barriers to protect British industry), in the 1970s and 1980s on the issue of economic policy, and in the 1990s on the issue of European integration. Such occasions, though, have been the exception rather than the rule. Cohesiveness has been a distinguishing feature of the party for most of its history.

The cohesiveness of the Conservative party may be attributed largely to the fact that, unlike the Labour party, it is a party of tendencies rather than of factions[13]—that is, it lacks permanent factions organized to promote a specific set of beliefs. Rather, it comprises a set of differing but not mutually exclusive stands of thought that are not aligned in consistent opposition to one another. On some issues there may be dissent within the party, but the composition of the dissenting body changes from issue to issue, almost like a chemical reaction. One may be a Tory on one issue and something of a Whig on another. In consequence, a party member may disagree with the party on one issue but agree with it on other issues. This is in contrast to the Labour party, which throughout its history has tended to be divided on a factional basis, with a clear divide between left and right wings of the party.

The Conservative party traditionally has been led by leaders drawn more from the Tory than the Whig strain within the party. The postwar leaders up to 1965—Winston Churchill, Sir Anthony Eden, Harold Macmillan, and Sir Alec Douglas-Home (see Table 6.1)—were men essentially in the Tory paternalist mold, more concerned with social harmony and order than with the intricacies of economic management. In the 1960s the party's fortunes took a turn for the worse. The economy began to falter, and the party suffered a bitter, public battle for the party leadership in 1963. It seemed unable to offer a young and dynamic leadership to match that which the Labour party was providing. Macmillan had married into the family of the duke of Devonshire and was often photographed on the Scottish moors shooting grouse. Sir Alec Douglas-Home was able to assume the office of prime minister only after renouncing his title as the 14th Earl of Home. (The prime minister, by convention, sits in the Commons, not the House of Lords.) The party seemed to be out of touch with the tenor of the times, and in 1964 it lost the general election.

TABLE 6.1 Conservative party leaders since 1945

(1940)–55	Winston Churchill	[prime minister 1940–45, 1951–55]
1955–57	Sir Anthony Eden	[prime minister 1955–57]
1957–63	Harold Macmillan	[prime minister 1957–63]
1963–65	Sir Alec Douglas-Home	[prime minister 1963–64]
1965–75	Edward Heath	[prime minister 1970–74]
1975–90	Margaret Thatcher	[prime minister 1979–90]
1990–97	John Major	[prime minister 1990–97]
1997–	William Hague	

In July 1965, Douglas-Home resigned the party leadership. Previously the leader had not been elected but had been allowed to "emerge" following private consultations within the party hierarchy. Following the struggle for the leadership in 1963, rules for the election of the leader were adopted in 1964 and first employed in 1965. The electorate was the parliamentary party, and the MPs chose as leader Edward Heath, in preference to former Chancellor of the Exchequer Reginald Maudling. Maudling was in the traditional Tory mold, though lacking the aristocratic background of previous leaders. Heath was seen by his supporters as a neoliberal and as capable of challenging the Labour party under the leadership of Harold Wilson. Both Heath and Wilson came from relatively humble origins, were of similar age, and stressed the need for economic efficiency.

The first four years of Heath's leadership were inauspicious ones, but in 1970 he led his party to a largely unexpected election victory. As prime minister he pursued what appeared to be a free-market economic policy. The aim was to force British industry to be more efficient. This goal also provided part of the motivation for British membership in the European Community, which Heath achieved in 1972 (see Chapter 9). However, the government's economic policy failed to produce the desired results. Unemployment and inflation spiraled, and in 1972 Heath dramatically undertook U-turns in industrial and economic policies: Public money was made available to help regional development and a statutory pay-and-prices policy was introduced.[14] The government's strategy was dashed by a world energy crisis and by opposition at home from trade unions. Heath called an election in February 1974 and, although the Conservatives got more votes than Labour, they got fewer seats. After seeking unsuccessfully to arrange a deal with the parliamentary Liberal party, Heath resigned. A minority Labour government took office. In October, another general election gave Labour more seats and a small overall majority.

Heath's U-turns had not been popular with a section of the Conservative party, especially neoliberals who saw them as an abandonment of their cherished free-market doctrine. Heath's unpopularity spread following the loss of the two 1974 elections and various calls were made for him to resign or offer himself for reelection. Pressure within the parliamentary party resulted in Heath agreeing to new rules providing for the annual election of the leader. Heath immediately offered himself for reelection. The election was held in February 1975. Heath was confident of victory. His main challenger was Margaret

Thatcher, a little-known figure who had served in his Cabinet as education minister. She espoused the rhetoric of the neoliberal wing of the party and offered a new style of leadership. Her campaign was well-organized, whereas Heath's was marred by overconfidence. In the first ballot, Thatcher got 130 votes to Heath's 119. (A third candidate got 16 votes.) Heath promptly resigned the leadership and in a second ballot—in which new challengers were able to stand—Thatcher easily beat her other rivals. The Conservative party had acquired its first female leader, one who was more clearly identified with the neoliberal wing of the party than any of her male predecessors.

Thatcher led the party in opposition until 1979, when the Labour government—by that time in a minority in the House of Commons—was defeated in a vote of confidence. A general election ensued, in which the Conservatives capitalized on the unpopularity of the government, its tax policies, and its links with the unions. Margaret Thatcher led her party to victory and she entered Downing Street as Britain's first female prime minister. She was to remain in Downing Street longer than any other prime minister of the twentieth century, a total of 11 years and six months. Her premiership went through three distinct periods.

The first period was one of bitter conflict. Under her leadership, the government embarked on a rigorous policy of controlling the money supply, reducing direct taxation, and limiting public expenditure in order to combat inflation. The policy ran into trouble. Techniques for controlling the money supply proved inadequate for the purpose. Attempts to reduce public spending proved unpopular in the country and with sections of the Conservative party. The Tory wing proved especially uneasy about the effects the policy was having. Thatcher dismissed her party critics as "wets."[15] (Her supporters were then dubbed "dries," though becoming more frequently known by the eponymous title of "Thatcherites.") However, some of those critics were in the Cabinet and, despite the dismissal of various "wets" from the Cabinet between 1981 and 1983, the prime minister failed to persuade her own government to adopt more stringent measures. Subsidies to nationalized industries were continued. Trade union reforms were radical, but not as radical as the prime minister wanted.

The effects of government economic policy at a time of recession, and splits within the party, resulted in government unpopularity. The party trailed in the opinion polls. At one point in 1981, following the formation of the Social Democratic party, the Conservative party was actually third in the polls. Within the parliamentary party, there were threats of a candidate running against Thatcher for the party leadership. The threat was never carried out but it served to emphasize the leader's political vulnerability.

The second period was that of domination by the leader. It began in 1982. The government's response to the Argentinian invasion of the Falkland Islands—dispatching a military task force to expel the invaders—restored it to popular favor. Following the successful recapture of the islands, the Conservative lead in the opinion polls held until the 1983 general election, sustained by some change in economic indicators (inflation and interest rates both fell) and by disarray within the Labour party. The Falklands campaign also transformed the image of the prime minister. Prior to the campaign, the percentage of electors satisfied with her leadership was less than 30 percent; afterward, it was nearly 60 percent.[16] In the 1983 election, the party was swept back to office with the largest majority achieved by any Conservative government since 1935.

Thatcher's ascendancy was maintained in the new Parliament. The government faced down a prolonged national miners' strike; after 11 months of bitter conflict, the strike collapsed. It undertook an extensive program of privatization, a range of public utilities and companies being sold off to the private sector. Some sales, such as those of British Petroleum (BP), proved particularly popular. The proportion of the population owning shares quoted on the stock exchange doubled. Economic conditions improved: Unemployment peaked in 1986 and began to drop; inflation continued its downward trend. Economic improvement generated greater optimism for the future.

During this period, the government suffered a number of setbacks, including a major dispute between senior ministers in 1986, when two clashed over the most appropriate rescue package for Britain's only remaining, and ailing, helicopter company (Westland). The clash resulted in the resignation of both ministers, and generated complaints of a directionless cabinet and of a cover-up over the leaking of certain documents.[17] Dubbed the Westland affair, it dented the government's popularity, but the unpopularity proved short-lived. The government recovered and was in a sufficiently strong position for Thatcher to lead it to election victory again in 1987. In so doing she achieved an event unprecedented in the history of mass politics in Britain: She was the first leader to take her party to victory in three consecutive elections. The party was returned to office with an overall parliamentary majority of 101. Margaret Thatcher was at the zenith of her power.

The third period was one of conflict and fall.[18] In the new Parliament, the government embarked on a number of radical legislative measures. These included the replacement of the domestic rates, a local property tax paid annually, with a community charge based not on property but on the number of residents. Popularly dubbed the "poll tax," it was the most unpopular of several unpopular measures. Economic indicators also began to worsen. In 1989, inflation began to rise and Thatcher got into what became a public dispute with her chancellor of the exchequer, Nigel Lawson, over economic policy. In October 1989, he resigned. The party also witnessed internal rifts over the issue of European union. In 1988, Thatcher delivered a speech putting the case against further moves toward political and economic union. The speech generated a clash between opponents (Euroskeptics) and supporters (Euro-enthusiasts) of such union. The clash meant that the party faced the European Parliament elections in June 1989 in disarray. In those elections the party lost 13 of its 45 seats, all to Labour candidates. It was the first time Margaret Thatcher had led her party to an electoral defeat.

Thatcher's stance on Europe propelled one Euro-enthusiast in the parliamentary party to challenge her in 1989 for the party leadership. Sir Anthony Meyer, a 69-year-old backbencher with no ministerial experience, knew he had no chance of winning, but was keen to allow dissidents to make their opposition clear. In the December 5 ballot, 314 Conservative MPs (84 percent of the parliamentary party) voted for Thatcher, 33 (9 percent) voted for Meyer, and 27 (7 percent) spoiled their ballots or abstained from voting. Sixty MPs had withheld their support from the leader. A number of those who voted for her had written privately to her urging her to moderate her stance, especially on the issue of Europe, if she wanted their support on future occasions. The result was a political embarrassment for Thatcher. A shot had been fired across her bow. At that stage, it was no more than that. Initially, the prime minister appeared to be adopting a conciliatory stance in response to the ballot, but that stance was short-lived.

In the spring of 1990, the introduction of the poll tax in England and Wales resulted in a significant level of nonpayment and demonstrations, some of them violent; London witnessed its worst riot in recent history. Labour led the Conservatives in the opinion polls by more than 20 points. Some Conservative MPs pressed for a reform, or even abolition, of the tax. Thatcher made clear she was committed to it. In the fall, she reiterated her opposition to further European union: "No, no, no," she thundered in the House of Commons. Those words precipitated the resignation of a senior cabinet minister, Sir Geoffrey Howe. His resignation speech, delivered on November 13, offered a stunning indictment of the prime minister's leadership. The following day, Michael Heseltine—a former cabinet minister, out of office since the Westland affair—announced he would challenge Thatcher for the party leadership.

The first ballot in the leadership contest was held on Tuesday, November 20. Heseltine's campaign was effectively run by a team of supporters. Thatcher's campaign was not dissimilar to Heath's in 1975: badly run and overconfident. The prime minister herself was in Paris at a European summit the day of the poll. Her campaign managers misjudged the mood on the back benches. They expected her to get the votes necessary for a clear victory. Under the 1975 rules, to win in the first ballot a candidate had to win an absolute majority and a majority that constituted 15 percent of those eligible to vote. With 372 Conservative MPs, that meant Thatcher required a 56-vote majority over Heseltine. In the event, she fell 4 votes short. She got 204 votes, Heseltine 152, and 16 MPs abstained. Under the rules, a second ballot was necessary. Thatcher declared her intention to contest that ballot. However, after consulting members of her Cabinet, she decided against doing so. In so deciding, she brought her leadership of the Conservative party—and hence her premiership—to an end.

In the second ballot, two new challengers emerged to contest the leadership against Heseltine: Foreign Secretary Douglas Hurd and Chancellor of the Exchequer John Major. Major was 48 and was little known outside Westminster. Unlike Hurd and Heseltine, he had no extensive past political history that could be used against him and no obvious commitment to any particular ideological tendency within the party. He attracted support very quickly within the parliamentary party, and a highly effective campaign team was put together. His campaign overshadowed the others. In the ballot, held on November 27, Major led the field: He got 185 votes, Heseltine 131, and Hurd 56. Under the rules, an absolute majority alone was necessary on the second ballot. If an absolute majority was not achieved, a third ballot had to be held. Major was 2 votes short of an absolute majority, but as it was obvious he would achieve those votes in a third ballot, the two other candidates immediately conceded defeat and the third ballot was abandoned. John

Major was the new party leader and the following day he was summoned to Buckingham Palace to become prime minister. He was to serve as prime minister for seven years. There were two distinct periods to his leadership.

The first period was one of recovery. Major brought in a new leadership style as prime minister. Unlike his predecessor, he did not adopt a confrontational stance, either in the cabinet or on the public platform. He preferred private, face-to-face meetings to the public arena. It was an approach that proved politically effective. He was more popular than his party. Despite the country slipping deeper into recession, survey data showed that electors blamed global economic conditions and his predecessor rather than John Major. Though the Conservatives trailed Labour in the opinion polls for most of 1991 and early in 1992, Major nonetheless led the Conservatives to victory in a general election on April 9, 1992. His government had the appearance of newness—unlike the old Thatcher government—and electors' unwillingness to trust Labour outweighed their dislike of the government's handling of a range of issues. The Conservatives were returned to office with a reduced parliamentary majority (of 21), but a majority nonetheless.

The second period was one of dramatic decline and internal party warfare. The election victory proved to be the one bright spot for the Conservatives. In 1992, the party again split badly on the issue of Europe (see Chapter 9), and a pound sterling crisis in September forced the government to withdraw from the European exchange-rate mechanism. In the three months prior to Britain's withdrawal, the Conservatives trailed Labour in the opinion polls by an average of just over 2 percent: In the three months following it, they trailed by almost 18 percent and never really recovered during the rest of the Parliament. "Confidence in John Major, the government's overall record and the future of the economy collapsed in tandem."[19] The party had lost its claim to be the party of economic competence. In May 1993, the prime minister dismissed the much-criticized chancellor of the exchequer, Norman Lamont. In his resignation speech in the House of Commons, Lamont savaged the government, claiming it was in office but not in power. Two months later, John Major was the most unpopular prime minister since opinion polling began, and the party slumped to third place in the opinion polls, behind Labour and the Liberal Democrats. The party continued to court unpopularity as its MPs squabbled over the issue of European integration—Major himself criticizing some members of his own cabinet—and was hit by claims of financial and sexual impropriety leveled against various ministers and backbenchers.[20] Major's leadership became an increasing topic of debate, with various claims that he would be challenged for it. In the summer of 1995, he decided to take on his critics. He resigned the party leadership, offered himself as a candidate and dared his critics to stand against him. A member of his own cabinet, John Redwood, resigned in order to contest the leadership. Though Major won—by 218 votes to 89, with 8 abstentions and 12 spoiled ballot papers—more than a hundred MPs, a third of the party, failed to back him.[21] Major's reelection failed to stem the party in-fighting. The party continued to be hit with allegations of private misconduct by MPs and with clashes over the issue of European integration.

Major delayed a general election as long as possible, trying to hold together a parliamentary party as the government's overall majority disappeared, a consequence of by-election losses and defections: During Major's leadership, the party failed to hold on to any of the seats it defended in by-elections (in the 1992–97 Parliament, it defended eight seats and lost them all), and four Conservative MPs defected to other parties. On March 17, 1997, Major announced that the election would be held on May 1. The party entered the campaign trailing Labour by more than 20 points in the opinion polls. The party—previously seen by electors as united and competent in handling the nation's economy—was now viewed by them as "sleazy," divided, and not competent in handling the economic affairs of the nation.[22] The divisions within the party marked the opening of the campaign—especially on the issue of a single European currency—as did media concentration on a campaign in a constituency being defended by a Conservative accused of accepting cash for tabling parliamentary questions.

The result of the 1997 election was a disaster for the party: It lost just over half of the seats it was defending. It was reduced to 165 members in a 659-member House. Labour achieved an overall majority that was bigger than the size of the Conservative parliamentary party. Seven members of the cabinet were among the casualties. (One high-profile defeat was of the defence secretary, Michael Portillo, in Enfield Southgate: see Table 5.3). Taking the party's share of the vote together with the number of seats it won, it was the party's worst defeat of the twentieth century.

Once the results of the election were known, Major resigned as prime minister. Rather than spend a lengthy period as leader of the opposition, he immediately announced his resignation as party leader. Five former cabinet ministers contested the leadership. Two did badly in the first ballot and dropped out. In the second ballot, former Chancellor Kenneth Clarke got 64 votes, former Welsh Secretary William Hague got 62 and John Redwood, who challenged Major in 1995, got 38. Clarke—a noted supporter of European integration—was the candidate of the party left, Hague was seen as the candidate of the party center and center-right, and Redwood represented the Euro-skeptic right. Under the party's rules, Redwood was eliminated from the contest. In the third ballot, Hague won with 92 votes to 70 for Clarke. Hague was carried to victory by the votes of party loyalists and Euro-skeptics.[23] Like John Major, his support was broad but not deep.

The Conservative party has been notable in recent decades for having leaders who do not conform to stereotypes of party leaders (a female leader followed by a lower-middle-class leader who never went to university) and Hague was the least stereotypical of the candidates in 1997. He was 36 years of age. He had first come to national attention when, as a 15-year-old schoolboy, he had addressed the party conference. He had entered Parliament in 1989—still in his twenties—and become the youngest member of the cabinet in 1995 at the age of 34. As soon as he was elected leader, he immediately set about reforming the party. He instituted a radical change in the structure and organization of the party. He introduced a new method of electing the party leader, involving the membership of the party. He apologized for various past mistakes the party had made. He began a campaign of "Listening to Britain," all in an attempt to dispel the perception that the party had been arrogant in power. Recognizing that the electors were not likely to be that interested in the Conservative party for some time, nor to forgive it for some time either, Hague was willing to invest energy in reforming the party in readiness for a serious challenge for power in subsequent elections. Given the small size of the parliamentary party, and the widespread feeling among commentators that it would take at least two elections for the Conservatives to stand any chance of again forming a government, it was an uphill struggle. Although Hague proved a particularly effective performer in the House of Commons, and the party achieved a remarkable success in the 1999 elections to the European Parliament—emerging, ahead of Labour, with the largest number of seats—the party continued to trail badly behind in the opinion polls. It rarely achieved more than 30 percent support. Its fortunes appeared to improve in September 2000 when popular protests over fuel prices dented the government's popularity. For the first time in eight years, the Conservatives overtook Labour in the polls. The challenge facing the party was trying to sustain a level of support that had eluded it throughout the 1990s.

Party Organization.   Until 1998, the party had three distinct elements. One was the parliamentary party. This stood as an essentially autonomous body within the party. Another was the professional organization, comprising full-time professionals who existed to service the rest of the party. Most were employed in the party's Central Office, though some were employed at a regional level. The third element was the voluntary wing of the party, comprising party members throughout the country. The voluntary wing was organized through the National Union of Conservative and Unionists Associations. As we have already noted, both the Central Office and the National Union were created as a response to the new political situation brought about by the Reform Act of 1867. The National Union brought together the essential components of the party: the constituency parties. Each constituency party elected its own officers, had its own branches, and enjoyed a large measure of autonomy in selecting parliamentary candidates. Each local party engaged in fund-raising and social activities as well as candidate selection and campaigning during elections. Each local party also undertook membership recruitment. Members were recruited on a dues-paying basis (though there was no fixed membership fee) and membership was of the local constituency party. Legally, there was no national Conservative party that one could join, the party comprising an amalgam of the local parties.

At the head of the party was the leader, in whom was vested enormous power. The leader was the fount of all policy, and chose the chairman and other leading officers of the party organization as well as the members of the front bench in the House of Commons. The annual party conference and other bodies within the party had advisory roles only. The leader was not all-powerful, in that there was a mutual dependence of the leader and led on one another—the leader had to carry the party in order to ensure that the leader's goals were met—and the position of the leader was sometimes under threat.[24] Even so, the leader was a powerful figure and recognized as such: The party looked to the leader to lead.

The party organization was variously reformed. There were significant changes following the party's loss of power in 1945. New bodies, such as the Conservative Political Centre (to encourage two-way discussion between members and party leaders), were formed, the party's youth wing was reorganized as the Young Conservatives, and a major—and successful—membership drive was undertaken. Even so, the basic structure of the party remained intact. This was to change following the election of William Hague as party leader in 1997.

When Hague took over the leadership in 1997, the Conservative party faced a situation where it had (by historical standards) a small parliamentary party, a declining party membership (some constituency parties virtually existed in name only) and difficulty in raising funds to maintain the level of activities normally undertaken by Central Office. To meet what was seen as a critical situation for the party, Hague immediately undertook to overhaul party organization. He proposed a new party structure as well as new rules for electing the party leader, and put his proposals—and his leadership—to a vote of party members, obtaining an overwhelming majority from those who voted. The new party structure took effect in 1998.

Under the new structure, the three elements of the party are integrated into one. At the head of the party organization is a governing board, with most of its members elected, drawn from each part of the party. Below the board are new regional and area structures (though for financial reasons the regional structure may not become fully operational). In addition to the annual party conference, there is now a national Conservative convention, which meets twice a year to act as a link between the party leadership and members. The essential components of the organization remain the constituency parties. Each local party now has a chair, plus one deputy chair responsible for political activity and campaigning and another responsible for finance and membership.

Among other changes, the party now has a national membership (and a national minimum subscription): Members join "the" Conservative party. The national membership—producing, for the first time, a centrally-held list of members—also makes possible one other major change: the involvement of the party members—and not just MPs—in the election of the party leader. A leadership contest can only be triggered by MPs, with MPs balloting to narrow the field to two candidates, but, in the final ballot, the choice rests with party members, voting on the basis of one member, one vote (OMOV). For the Conservative party, this change represents a massive shift from past practice.

Though the party still places great emphasis on the role of the leader, and the leader still exercises many of the traditional powers of the leader (including the selection of the party chairman—who chairs the new governing board—and front benchers), there is a far greater emphasis on the party membership. By 1997, the membership—which in the early 1950s claimed to be almost 3 million—was small (according to some calculations, 750,000, and according to others, around or below 500,000) and aging; according to one survey early in the 1990s, the average age of members was 61.[25] William Hague set a membership target of one million members for the new millennium. Following the creation of the new party structure, there was some evidence of an increase in membership, but the initial increase was modest. By mid-2000, the membership was reported to be no more than 350,000.

Party Funding.   Of the political parties, the Conservative has historically been the best financed. In recent years, its income has tended to be between £10 million and £15 million a year, increasing—sometimes doubling—in an election year. Its income derives from four sources: constituency associations, companies, individuals, and the sale of services. Annual income from the constituency parties—which raise funds through holding dinners, coffee mornings, other money-raising events, and appeals for funds—has tended to account for about 10–20 percent of the party's national income, though in the 1990s the proportion fell to below 10 percent (in 1993-95, it fell below 6 percent), reflecting in part the party's declining membership.[26] The party has traditionally been seen as the one most sympathetic to the interests of business, and a number of large companies have given the party a proportion of their profits each year. Income from companies has tended to account for over half of the party's annual income. Between 1979 and 1992, 12 companies each donated £500,000 ($800,000) or more to the party. However, taking all the companies who donate, the average donation per company is small. In the 1990s the number of companies making donations declined and, of those still giving, the donation was frequently reduced.[27] The third source of income is also, proportionally, becoming the most important: that from individuals. The party attracts income from wealthy supporters including, at times, supporters living abroad. One benefactor revealed in 1991 was a Greek shipping tycoon, who gave £2 million ($3.2 million). The controversy generated by overseas donors was such that, upon becoming leader, William Hague decided that the party would not accept such donations. Individual donations also include the money generated by national mailshots. The party variously makes appeals direct to supporters, especially during election campaigns. The fourth and final source of income is that derived from the sale of services, such as literature and hiring out stalls at party conferences. This now accounts for about 10–20 percent of the party's income.

Outside of election years, party income is spent on routine administration, salaries, and maintenance of the services the party provides to local associations. In election years, the party regularly outspends its opponents, though the gap between the two main parties is narrowing (Table 6.2). In the 1987 election, the party spent £9 million ($14.4m) against the Labour party's £4.7 million ($7.5m). In 1992, it spent £11.2 million ($17.9m) against the Labour party's £10.6 million ($17.5m).[28] For the 1997 election, the Conservative party spent £28.3 million ($45.4m) against £26 million ($41.6) spent by the Labour party.[29] During the election campaign, the Conservatives spent £13.2 million ($21.2m) on advertising and Labour spent £7.4 million ($11.8).[30]

The party has had difficulty in recent years in raising funds to meet all its organizational commitments. Even with various attempts at streamlining since the 1970s, costs have continued to exceed income. During the 1980s and early

TABLE 6.2   Party spending on election campaigns

	Spending (in £ million)					
	1964	1979	1983	1987	1992	1997
Conservative	1.23	2.3	3.8	9.0	11.2	28.3
Labour	0.5	1.6	2.3	4.7	10.6	26.0
Liberal/Liberal Democrat	*	0.2	1.9	1.75	1.8	3.2

* Not known
SOURCE: M. Pinto-Duschinsky, "Problems arise calculating the price of democracy," *The Times*, April 14,1998.

1990s, the party ran up a sizable deficit, which by 1993 had reached £19 million ($30.4m). A combination of energetic fundraising and a significant reduction in staff and activities brought the party back into balance in 1997.[31] However, in the wake of the 1997 election, financial problems reemerged. The party had a deficit believed to be in the region of £4 million ($6.4m) and it was not attracting the money from donors and fund-raising appeals that it had when in government. The party's bankers were reportedly refusing to extend the party's overdraft. The new party leader, William Hague, brought in one of the party's new MPs—a former chief executive of one of the nation's biggest supermarket chains—to serve as chief executive and streamline the party organization. The leader also brought in a new treasurer, Michael Ashcroft, a multimillionaire, who attracted controversy because of his overseas business links (especially in Belize) and because of the extent to which he contributed his own money to the party; there were fears expressed that the party might become too dependent on him. For the Conservative party, the new period in opposition was one of reorganization and retrenchment. For most of the twentieth century, the party was in power and was a well financed organization. By the end of the century, its dilemma was that it was neither.

The Labour Party

The Labour Party is best described as a coalition of disparate interests. It was formed, in effect, on February 27, 1900, at a conference comprising representatives of the socialist Independent Labour party (the ILP), the Marxist Social Democratic Federation (the SDF), the Fabian Society (which believed in socialism by gradual means), and 65 trade unions. It called for "establishing a distinct Labour Group in Parliament, who shall have their own whips and agree upon policy, which must embrace a readiness to cooperate with any party which for the time being may be engaged in promoting legislation in the direct interest of labour, and be equally ready to associate themselves with any party in opposing measures having an opposite tendency." The conference refused to accept an SDF motion linking it with socialism and the class war, and the SDF subsequently withdrew from the movement. An executive committee, the Labour Representation Committee, was set up, consisting of representatives from the different organizations, the trade union representatives being in the majority. There was thus witnessed, in Carl Brand's words, "an alliance between socialism and trade unionism"; he added, "It was done in characteristically British fashion: with scant regard for theory, the best tool possible under the circumstances was fashioned. In spite of the fact that for two decades the drive had come from the socialists, they did not insist upon their name or programme."[32] In the general election of 1906, 29 Labour MPs were elected and the Labour Representation Committee thereupon changed its name to the Labour party. The Labour party had established itself on the British political scene.

The next major event in the party's history was the adoption of a new Constitution in 1918. There was a strong socialist element within the party, notably represented by the ILP, and the First World War had appeared to make socialist principles more relevant than they had been previously. It has also been argued that adopting a socialist program served a functional purpose in differentiating the party from the Liberals.[33] In any event, the party adopted what has been termed a Socialist Commitment and, in clause four of its new Constitution, committed itself to the common ownership of the means of production. (The words "distribution and exchange" were added in 1928.) At its subsequent conference it adopted a program, *Labour and the New Social Order*, incorporating four principles: the enforcement of a national minimum (in effect, a commitment to full employment and a national minimum wage); the democratic control of industry, essentially through public ownership; a revolution in national finance (financing of social services through greater taxation of high incomes); and surplus wealth for the common good, using the balance of the nation's wealth to expand opportunities in education and culture. The program was to form the basis of party policy for more than 30 years.[34] At the same time, however, the party amended its own procedures in a way that weakened the socialist element within its ranks: The trade unions, on whom the party depended for financial support, were given greater influence through the decision to elect members of the party's national executive committee at the party conference, where the unions dominated; and the ILP was weakened by the decision to allow individuals to join the Labour party directly. Previously, membership was indirect, through membership of affiliated organizations, and the ILP had been the main recruiting agent for political activists. Socialists within the party were to become increasingly wary of the attitude adopted toward the party's program by those who dominated the party leadership.

At the 1918 general election 63 Labour MPs were returned. In 1922 the number rose to 142, making the party the second largest in the House of Commons. In the 1923 general election the Conservatives lost their overall majority and Labour, with Liberal acquiescence, formed a short-lived minority government under the leadership of Ramsay MacDonald. Given the political constraints, the government achieved little—its main domestic success was the passage of a housing bill—and lasted less than ten months. A second minority Labour government was formed following the 1929 general election. Its domestic program was largely crippled either by the Liberals in the Commons or the Conservatives in the Lords. In response to the depression, it sought international loans, but these were dependent on financial cutbacks at home. The cabinet was divided on the issue and MacDonald tendered the government's resignation, subsequently accepting the king's invitation to form a coalition, or "National," government incorporating Conservative and Liberal MPs. The new government, though led by MacDonald, was dominated by the Conservatives. Within the Labour party, MacDonald's action was seen as a betrayal of the party's cause and only a handful of Labour MPs followed him into the new government. The majority of the parliamentary party, along with the trade unions, disavowed his action, and he and his supporters were subsequently expelled from the party. The National government, with MacDonald and his supporters standing as National Labour candidates, won a landslide victory in a quickly called general election. The Labour party achieved the return of only 52 MPs and, though the number increased to 154 in the 1935 general election, spent the 1930s in a political wilderness.

The Second World War, as we have seen (Chapter 3), had a significant impact on the fortunes and the appeal of the party. There had been a shift in popular attitudes, conducive to some form of social welfare program, and the party had proved itself a responsible partner of government in the wartime coalition. In 1945 it was returned with a large overall majority. In office, it implemented its election manifesto *Let Us Face the Future*, bringing into public ownership various public utilities and introducing a comprehensive social security system and national health service. Much of its program was soon implemented, perhaps too soon. By the end of the Parliament, the party had begun to lose its impetus and there were growing doubts as to the direction in which it should be going. In the general election of 1950 "Labour's campaign looked as much to the past as to the future"[35] and it was returned with a bare overall majority; in the general election called the following year it lost that majority altogether (despite receiving more votes than any other party), the Conservatives being returned to office.

The 1950s proved to be a period of bitter dispute within the party. The left wing within the party continued to press for greater control of the economy and the taking into public ownership of important industries: It remained committed to Clause 4 of the party's constitution. Revisionists within the party, influenced by Anthony Crosland and his 1956 seminal work, *The Future of Socialism*, argued that public ownership was no longer necessary because of the absence of large-scale unemployment and primary poverty. Rather, they argued, one should accept the mixed economy and seek instead the goal of equality—equality of opportunity, especially in the sphere of education. Such a goal was possible in an affluent managerial society. Public ownership was seen as largely irrelevant. The dispute between the two sides culminated at the turn of the decade, when party leader Hugh Gaitskell sought to remove Clause 4 from the party constitution. The major unions swung against him at the party conference and he was forced to back down. "Clause IV was retained, though, as a face saver, supplemented by an additional, fuller (and rapidly forgotten) statement of principles."[36] Gaitskell then turned his attention to the issue of the British nuclear deterrent, vigorously opposing attempts to commit the party to a policy of unilateral nuclear disarmament, and in so doing faced another serious internal party dispute.

Conservative unpopularity in the early 1960s and the election of Harold Wilson as party leader in 1963 following the sudden death of Gaitskell helped restore unity to the Labour party as it sensed electoral victory. The party was returned to office in 1964. However, its periods of office from 1964 to 1970 and later from 1974 to 1979 were not successful ones. The attempt at a national plan in the first Wilson government was effectively stillborn, and both periods of government witnessed generally orthodox attempts to respond to economic crises. The period of Labour government from 1974 onward, in particular, appeared to lack any clear direction, being pushed in different directions by international pressures and the domestic problems associated with trying to stay in office while lacking an overall parliamentary majority. The period witnessed a growing tension within the party between those who adhered to a gradual approach to the achievement of socialists' goals, recognizing the constraint imposed by prevailing conditions, and those on the left who pressed for more immediate action and the taking into public ownership of key industries such as the banks. This tension effectively emerged onto the political stage as open and violent political warfare following the election defeat of 1979. It was not only to take the form of a policy dispute but also to be fought largely and ostensibly on the question of the party's constitution.

The Left within the Labour party argued that the social democratic consensus policies of the 1950s had been tried and had failed. What was needed was a socialist economic policy, one not seriously tried before by a Labour government. The Left sought to increase its influence within the party by arguing for (1) the election of the party leader by a wider franchise than the parliamentary Labour party (the Left was much stronger within constituency parties than it was in the parliamentary party); (2) the compulsory reselection of MPs—that is, for MPs to be subject to a full reselection process by local parties during the lifetime of a Parliament rather than the usual process of automatic readoption when an election was called; and (3) the vesting of the responsibility for writing the election manifesto in the party's National Executive Committee (the NEC), where the Left was strong, rather than jointly by the NEC and the parliamentary leadership. At the party's 1980 conference the Left was successful in achieving two of these three objectives: the widening of the franchise for electing the leader, and MPs being subject to compulsory reselection procedures. At a special conference in January 1981 the party adopted a formula for the election of the leader by an electoral college, the trade unions to have 40 percent of the votes, constituency parties 30 percent, and the parliamentary Labour party 30 percent. (This new method was employed for the first time in 1983 following the resignation of party leader Michael Foot.)

For a number of politicians on the right of the party, already bitterly opposed to the party's policy to withdraw from the European Community, the constitutional changes constituted the final straw. They responded by creating a Council for Social Democracy and then, in March 1981, broke away from the party completely, forming a new party, the Social Democratic party (the SDP). Others in sympathy with their views remained within the Labour party to fight the battle there.

The next two years proved politically disastrous for the Labor party. In the fall of 1981, there was a bitterly fought contest for the party deputy leadership between the incumbent, Denis Healey, and the candidate of the Left, Tony Benn. Healey won by a tiny margin. More and more Labour MPs defected to join the SDP. The party entered the 1983 general election campaign with a manifesto that called for withdrawal from the European Community, a non-nuclear defense program, a "massive" rise in public expenditure, a wealth tax, and the return to public ownership of assets privatized by the Conservatives. The manifesto was described by one of the party's own leading figures as "the longest suicide note in history." The party faced both a Conservative government buoyed by the success of the 1982 Falklands campaign and the SDP, which was drawing away some of Labour's traditional supporters. The party had a disastrous campaign, with a leader (Michael Foot) whom the media refused to take seriously as a potential prime minister. On election day, Labour suffered its worst result since 1918 in terms of the percentage of the vote obtained. It got 28 percent of the votes cast, only marginally ahead of the share obtained by the alliance of Liberal and Social Democratic parties.

In the wake of the election defeat, Foot resigned the leadership and was succeeded by Neil Kinnock, a 41-year-old Welshman with no ministerial experience. Despite occasional effective speeches on the conference platform, Kinnock did not shine in the House of Commons and was no match for Margaret Thatcher. He did, however, achieve greater control than his predecessor over the party organization and began to mold it into a more effective body for fighting elections. His performance in the 1987 general election was recognized as highly professional—according to a Gallup poll, 43 percent of those questioned thought he had campaigned impressively, against 20 percent so rating Thatcher—and Labour mounted a more polished campaign than the Conservatives. The party's manifesto, however, remained an electoral liability, its defense policy in particular being exploited by its opponents. (It had committed itself to replacing nuclear defense with a conventional force.) In an exit poll on election day, 52 percent of those questioned said the party's defense policy had made them "less likely" to vote Labour. The party made some gains, especially in Scotland, but was still relegated to the political wasteland of opposition.

Immediately after the election, the party established seven policy groups to review policy. In 1988, the groups produced a broad review of policy and the following year produced specific policy recommendations. The recommendations shifted the party away from the policies that had proved an electoral liability. On defense, for example, it moved the party toward multilateral nuclear disarmament. Neil Kinnock was able to use his control of the party's National Executive Committee and an increasing body of support within the party to achieve endorsement by the party conference of the recommendations.

The party's new policy was embodied in a policy document, *Meet the Challenge, Make the Change* (1989), and in two subsequent documents, *Looking to the Future* (1990) and *Opportunity Britain* (1991). "Overall, two major themes emerged. . . . First, intraparty political debate over the extent of public and private ownership was outdated; and second, the quality of public service should be improved by putting the needs of the user before those of the producer."[37] The review established a new paradigm for the party, aided in the defense sector by the collapse of the Iron Curtain and the end of the Cold War. By 1990, Labour began to appear as a moderate and credible alternative to the increasingly unpopular Thatcher government.

Labour achieved a large lead in the opinion polls early in 1990. That lead receded later in the year and briefly disappeared altogether following the replacement of Margaret Thatcher with John Major as prime minister, and in the wake of the 1991 Gulf War. The party reestablished a lead in the polls later in 1991, which it retained into 1992 and the election campaign in March and April. However, the lead was not as large as might have been expected given the severity of the recession and, against general expectations that Labour would win more seats than the Conservatives, Labour failed to pull off an election victory. Though losing seats, the Conservatives held on to an overall majority in the House of Commons. Despite it being preferred over the Conservatives on most social issues, Labour had failed to shake off a lingering public distrust in its competence to handle the economy and in the qualities of its leader. Most voters believed the Conservatives were better able to handle the economy than Labour, that a Labour government would increase taxes, and that John Major was better qualified to be prime minister than Neil Kinnock.[38]

In the wake of the election defeat, Neil Kinnock resigned the leadership. In July, he was succeeded by a 53-year-old Scot, John Smith, who won the leadership contest decisively: He got 91 percent of the votes (winning easily in each of the three parts of the electoral college), his challenger, Bryan Gould, the candidate of the Left, picking up the remaining 9 percent. Smith was seen as a solid performer and got off to a good start, but thereafter failed to shine. Conservative unpopularity, however, ensured Labour maintained a strong lead in the opinion polls. Smith's leadership was short. On May 12, 1994, he suffered a massive and fatal heart attack. The leadership was then contested by three candidates: Tony Blair, John Prescott, and Margaret Beckett. Blair was 41 years of age, a lawyer by training, and represented a new, right-wing modernizing element in the party. "After eleven years in opposition, and after the success of both Bill Clinton and the Australian Labour party, Blair had developed into a convinced modernizer believing that only a moderate, left-of-center, pro-European party, independent of the trade unions, would be elected to office."[39] Prescott and Beckett were both on the party's left wing and in parliamentary terms were long-serving Members. (Prescott had been elected to Parliament in 1970 and Beckett was first elected in 1974, whereas Blair was elected to the House in 1983.) Blair won a comfortable—but not overwhelming—victory, carrying each section of the electoral college (each now having equal weight in the contest, with the principle of one member, one vote being applied in each): He achieved just over 60 percent of the votes in the parliamentary section and just over 50 percent in each of the other two sections. Prescott was elected deputy leader.

Once elected as leader, Blair immediately set about creating what he termed—and what was to become in common parlance—"New Labour." One of his first acts was to get the party to jettison Clause 4 of the party constitution

TABLE 6.3   Labour party leaders since 1945

(1935)–55	Clement Attlee	[prime minister 1945–51]
1955–63	Hugh Gaitskell	
1963–76	Harold Wilson	[prime minister 1964–70, 1974–76]
1976–80	James Callaghan	[prime minister 1976–79]
1980–83	Michael Foot	
1983–92	Neil Kinnock	
1992–94	John Smith	
1994–	Tony Blair	[prime minister 1997–]

and replace it with a new clause entitled *"Labour's Aims and Values."* The change was approved by a special party conference in 1995. The new clause defined Labour as a "democratic socialist party" and committed the party to common endeavors and to work for a dynamic economy (joining the enterprise of the market with the forces of partnership and cooperation), a just society, an open democracy, and a healthy environment. The new clause is reproduced in Figure 6.1. Blair also committed the party to five principal and specific aims if returned to office: cutting class sizes in junior schools, speeding up punishments for young offenders, cutting the waiting lists of those waiting for hospital treatment, taking 250,000 young people off welfare benefits (using a "windfall" levy on profits of utilities that had been returned to the private sector), and setting tough rules on government borrowing and spending. In addition, a commitment was made to stick to Conservative spending plans during the first two years of a Labour government. In addition, there were to be no increases in the basic and top rates of income tax. "Moderation and caution were the essence of New Labour's appeal to the voters."[40]

This new moderate message was accompanied by a continuing utilizing of new campaign techniques. The party threw off its old image as an old-fashioned organization and embraced new technology. It utilized the Internet to disseminate information; a "cyber cafe" was created at the party conference. It used telephone canvassing on an extensive basis. Focus groups were used to test reaction to policies. Key seats and key groups of voters—especially middle-income families—were targeted for special treatment. "New Labour" came across as a new party both in terms of what it stood for and in terms of how it was organized. It increasingly attracted back supporters who had defected in the 1980s to the Social Democratic party. It made inroads into traditional areas of Conservative strength and entered the 1997 election campaign with a massive lead in the opinion polls. That lead was translated into victory at the polls.

Labour was elected in 1997 with an overall majority of 179 in the House of Commons. As we have seen in Chapter 5 (Table 5.4), it was the largest majority achieved by a postwar government. The government set about implementing its election promises. At the forefront of these was its pledge to introduce constitutional change. As we have seen in Chapter 4, these promises encompassed, among other things, elected assemblies in Scotland and Wales, an elected mayor and authority for Greater London, the incorporation of the European Convention

---

Clause 4: Labour's Aims and Values

1. The Labour Party is a democratic socialist party. It believes that by the strength of our common endeavour we achieve more than we achieve alone, so as to create for each of us the means to realise our true potential and for all of us a community in which power, wealth and opportunity are in the hands of the many not the few, where the rights we enjoy reflect the duties we owe, and where we live together, freely, in a spirit of solidarity, tolerance and respect.

2. To these ends we work for:
   A dynamic economy serving the public interest, in which the enterprise of the market and the rigour of competition are joined with the forces of partnership and co-operation to produce the wealth the nation needs and the opportunity for all to work and prosper, with a thriving private sector and high quality public services, where those undertakings essential to the common good are either owned by the public or accountable to them;
   A just society, which judges its strengths by the condition of the weak as much as the strong, provides security against fear, and justice at work; which nurtures families, promotes equality of opportunity and delivers people from the tyranny of poverty, prejudice and the abuse of power;
   An open democracy, in which the government is held to account by the people; decisions are taken as far as practicable by the community they effect; and where fundamental human rights are guaranteed;
   A healthy environment, which we protect, enhance and hold in trust for future generations.

3. Labour is committed to the defence and security of the British people, and to co-operating in European institutions, the United Nations, the Commonwealth and other international bodies to secure peace, freedom, democracy, economic security and environmental protection for all.

4. Labour will work in pursuit of these aims with trade unions, co-operative societies and other affiliated organisations, consumer groups and other representative bodies.

5. On the basis of these principles, Labour seeks the trust of the people to govern.

FIGURE 6.1 New Clause 4 of the Labour party constitution

on Human Rights into British law, and the removal of (most) hereditary peers from the House of Lords. There were also several measures passed covering education and law and order and another to introduce a national minimum wage.

Tony Blair also strengthened his hold on the party organization. The new methods of election to the European Parliament were seen as being used by the leadership to remove left-wing incumbents. The party conference was given a new format to squeeze out motions that challenged government policy. Stricter discipline was imposed in the parliamentary party, MPs being given instructions on how to vote and what to do via pagers. It was also decided to send to local parties each year a report on the activity of the local MP. At government level, the prime minister appointed in 1998 a new minister for the cabinet office—dubbed by the media as "the enforcer"—to ensure that departments carried out government policy. All such activity led various commentators to assert—as they had variously done under the prime ministership of Margaret Thatcher—the "presidentialization" of British politics.

The Blair government encountered various embarrassments in its first years of office. It failed to live up to its own expectations in elections held in 1999.

Though emerging as the largest single party in elections to the new Scottish parliament, it failed to win an absolute majority of seats; it was forced to enter into coalition with the Liberal Democrats. It came in second to the Conservatives in elections to the European Parliament, winning only 29 seats (the Conservatives won 36), compared with the 45 it had won in the previous elections to the Parliament. The following year, its support in the opinion polls fell when demonstrations against rises in fuel taxes drew popular support. Up until that point, it had led the Conservatives in the opinion polls by a wide margin. It nonetheless continued to enjoy a massive majority in the House of Commons and, even with the drop in the polls, it looked likely to emerge as the largest single party in the next election or, as many commentators expected, a clear winner. Born in 1900, the party was ending the century as the dominant force in British politics.

Party Organization.   Formally, the party stresses the concept of intraparty democracy. Historically, the two most important bodies in the party, according to the party's constitution, have been—and remain—the party conference and the National Executive Committee (NEC). The party conference, which meets each year in the autumn, is formally responsible for determining the party program. A proposal that receives two-thirds or more of the votes cast at conference is adopted as part of the program. Between conferences, the body responsible for party organization and policy discussion is the party's National Executive Committee (NEC), which will normally bring policy documents forward for approval by the conference.

In practice, the reality of power in the party is much more complicated. This is partly a product of the fact that the party's program is not the same as its election manifesto. Under the party's constitution, the NEC in conjunction with the leaders of the parliamentary party decide which items of the program are to be included in the manifesto. Sometimes, as in 1983, the program and the manifesto have been synonymous, but in practice this has not always been the case. On occasion, the party leader has prevented certain parts of the program being included or has exercised a predominant influence in determining the content of the party manifesto. Furthermore, when it comes to implementing the program, some latitude is given to the parliamentary leadership, which is expected to give effect to the party's principles "as far as may be practicable." When in office, Labour leaders have sometimes not found it "practicable" to implement party commitments, giving rise to conflict between organs of the party, such as the NEC and the leadership.

The picture is further complicated by changes brought about in the 1980s and 1990s. Some of these changes are formal and the others the product of a shift of power in the party. During Neil Kinnock's leadership, changes in the membership of the NEC meant it became a body largely supportive of the leadership. At the same time, the power of the NEC in relation to local parties was increased while its powers of policy making were, in effect, decreased. The Committee was given power to impose short-lists of parliamentary candidates in certain circumstances (in by-elections and during general election campaigns when the incumbent announced retirement after the election was announced), thus enabling the leadership, through the NEC, to block the candidature of left-wing candidates and to enable candidates favored by the leadership to be short-listed. At the same time, policy making power shifted to a Joint Policy Committee, comprising members drawn in equal numbers from the NEC and the shadow cabinet (with additional members drawn from the party in local government and in the European parliament); policy commissions were established to report to it.

Changes in the nature and composition of the NEC have also been matched by changes to the party conference. At the conference, voting has historically been based on an organization's membership, not on the individual votes of those present. Thus the trade unions, with large affiliated memberships, have cast the most votes. In the 1950s, the unions' so-called block vote used to be cast regularly in support of the party leadership but became less predictable from the early 1960s onward. Under the leadership of Neil Kinnock, the unions generally supported his attempts to moderate the party in policy terms but were wary of attempts to reform their own role in party activities. Moves by Kinnock to reduce union influence at conference and in candidate selection in constituencies ran into some union criticism. "No say, no pay" was how one union leader responded to attempts to reform the block vote. At the 1992 conference, it was agreed to cut the union voting strength at conference from 87 percent to 70 percent. John Smith sought to limit the collective impact of the unions even further, again encountering opposition. A further reduction in the union vote was achieved under Blair's leadership. At the 1995 conference, the union's voting strength was reduced to 50 percent.

Traditionally, Labour conferences have differed from Conservative conferences in that the latter are advisory and often stage-managed affairs. Labour conferences have often been lively and unpredictable. Recent years have witnessed something of a convergence in that Labour conferences are more geared to the media and Conservative conferences have occasionally proved difficult to manage. Indeed, under Blair's leadership Labour conferences have been molded for the purposes of media presentation. In 1998, the party leadership ran into criticism from some party members for holding some sessions in private, for not publishing all the motions submitted for the conference (not all of which were supportive of the leadership), and for taking control of what would be debated.

The transformation of the party from an apparently old-fashioned, left-wing, union-dominated party to a modern, centrist party free of union control has also been reflected in changes in its membership. The party has a large, indirect membership deriving from trade unions and other affiliated organizations. Members of unions pay, as part of their union subscription, a "political levy" (unless they explicitly opt out of so doing) and thus become affiliated members of the party. This affiliated membership provides the party with most of its income as well as a large paper membership. The party has almost 5 million affiliated members. This affiliated membership has dwarfed the number of individuals who have joined the party directly, thus allowing the unions to dominate both the party conference and local parties. The direct membership of the party has traditionally been much lower than that of the Conservative party. Even in the early 1990s, the Labour party had fewer direct members than the Conservative party. Direct membership showed a slight increase in 1990 but then declined, and by the time of the 1992 conference was down to 261,000, still lower than the membership of the Conservative party. All this changed in the succeeding five years. Membership increased under Blair's leadership and by 1997—the year of Labour's triumph at the polls—topped the 400,000 mark, outstripping the declining membership of the Conservative party. By the 1997 election, the Labour party had been revitalized as a political party, with a reformed party organization, a highly efficient campaign organization, and active and supportive local parties.

Party Funding.   The upsurge in party membership, and its dominance in the opinion polls—establishing it as the government in waiting—also had one other effect. It helped the party's financial situation. By the end of the 1980s, the party had a running deficit of more than £1 million ($1.66 million). This was exacerbated by the cost of the 1992 election campaign. Under Blair's leadership, membership increased and the party became more attractive to donors. The unions continued to provide the bulk of the party finance—between 1992 and 1997, four unions gave donations of at least £1 million a year each—but the proportion declined. Between 1986 and 1996 the proportion of party funds supplied by the unions declined from two-thirds to one-half. Private business became increasingly important as a source of funds, providing—according to one source—some £15 million ($24 million) over a nine-month period from June 1996.[41] Some individuals are known to have donated more than £1 million each. One donor attracted particular controversy. Bernie Ecclestone, a leading figure in Formula One car racing, made a £1 million donation to the party. When the Government subsequently decided, not long after the 1997 general election, to extend the period for the phasing out of tobacco advertising in racing, there were accusations of a conflict of interest. As a result of the controversy, the party returned Ecclestone's donation to him.

The 1997 election took its toll on party finances. As we have seen, it is estimated that the party spent some £26 million ($41.6 million) on the election. It had a staff of some 250 in a new campaign headquarters (Millbank Tower). After the election, it had a deficit of some £2 million ($3.2 million) and had to reduce the number of personnel. The party also saw some slippage in its membership: In August 1998, it was announced that it had fallen below the 400,000 figure. This was blamed in part on the party's financial situation, as it had no money to launch a new membership drive. The party remained in a strong position—especially so compared with earlier decades—but appeared to have peaked in terms of its financial and organizational strength in 1997.

Most of the party's central income is spent on personnel and organization. The same applies to money raised locally. Like the Conservatives, Labour has local constituency parties. Income raised by local parties varies considerably. Many—over 200—benefit from some funding from the unions. The trades unions used to sponsor candidates but, in order to avoid claims of a conflict of interest by MPs, Tony Blair persuaded the unions to sponsor the local parties directly rather than the candidates. The sponsorship provides a modest but very useful income. Historically, local Labour parties have not been as well funded nor as well organized as Conservative constituency parties. The Conservatives have tended to have far more constituency agents (full-time executive officers). But in recent years the gap has narrowed, if not disappeared, in part because of improvements in Labour's organization, but more importantly, because of the decline in Conservative funding and organization. By 1997, the Labour party had supplanted the Conservative party as the exemplar of what a well organized political party should look like.

THIRD PARTIES

In the postwar years from 1945 to 1970, the principal third party in Britain, and the only one to enjoy parliamentary representation throughout the period, was the Liberal party. Its parliamentary strength was small, but as *the* third party it had no obvious competitors. That ceased to be the case from the 1970s onward.

In the 1970s, the Scottish and Welsh Nationalist parties grew in strength: They had both gained a parliamentary toehold in the 1960s (one seat each) but that grew rapidly in 1974. In 1972, the Ulster Unionists in Northern Ireland, previously affiliated with and, in parliamentary terms, subsumed within the Conservative party, broke away (in protest at the imposition of direct rule in the province) to sit as a separate parliamentary party. The Unionists subsequently witnessed divisions within their own ranks, resulting in the return of MPs representing different Unionist parties.

The situation became even more complicated in the 1980s. In 1981, the Social Democratic party (the SDP), drawing its parliamentary strength from defecting Labour MPs (and one defecting Conservative), was formed. It then entered into an alliance with the Liberal party. It was as an alliance that the two parties contested the 1983 and 1987 general elections. In 1988, the two parties voted to merge. They created the Social and Liberal Democratic party, known popularly as the Liberal Democratic party. A number of SDP members, opposed to the merger, maintained what was known as the Continuing SDP, but that party soon folded. Some disaffected Liberals also refused to merge and maintained the Liberal party, putting forward a number of candidates in the 1992 election.

In 1987, the sole Social Democratic and Labour party (SDLP) MP from Northern Ireland was joined by two more colleagues, thus establishing another new parliamentary party. A Sinn Fein MP, Gerry Adams, had been elected in 1983 and 1987 (though refusing to take his seat in the Commons). He lost his seat in 1992 but was elected again in 1997, along with another Sinn Fein candidate, Martin McGuiness. Both refused to take the oath and so were barred from the House. However, in terms of numbers, they were sufficient to form a parliamentary party.

The extent to which third parties have become more prominent in the House of Commons in recent decades is illustrated by Figure 6.2. Ten parties had members elected to the House of Commons in 1997. (As we have already

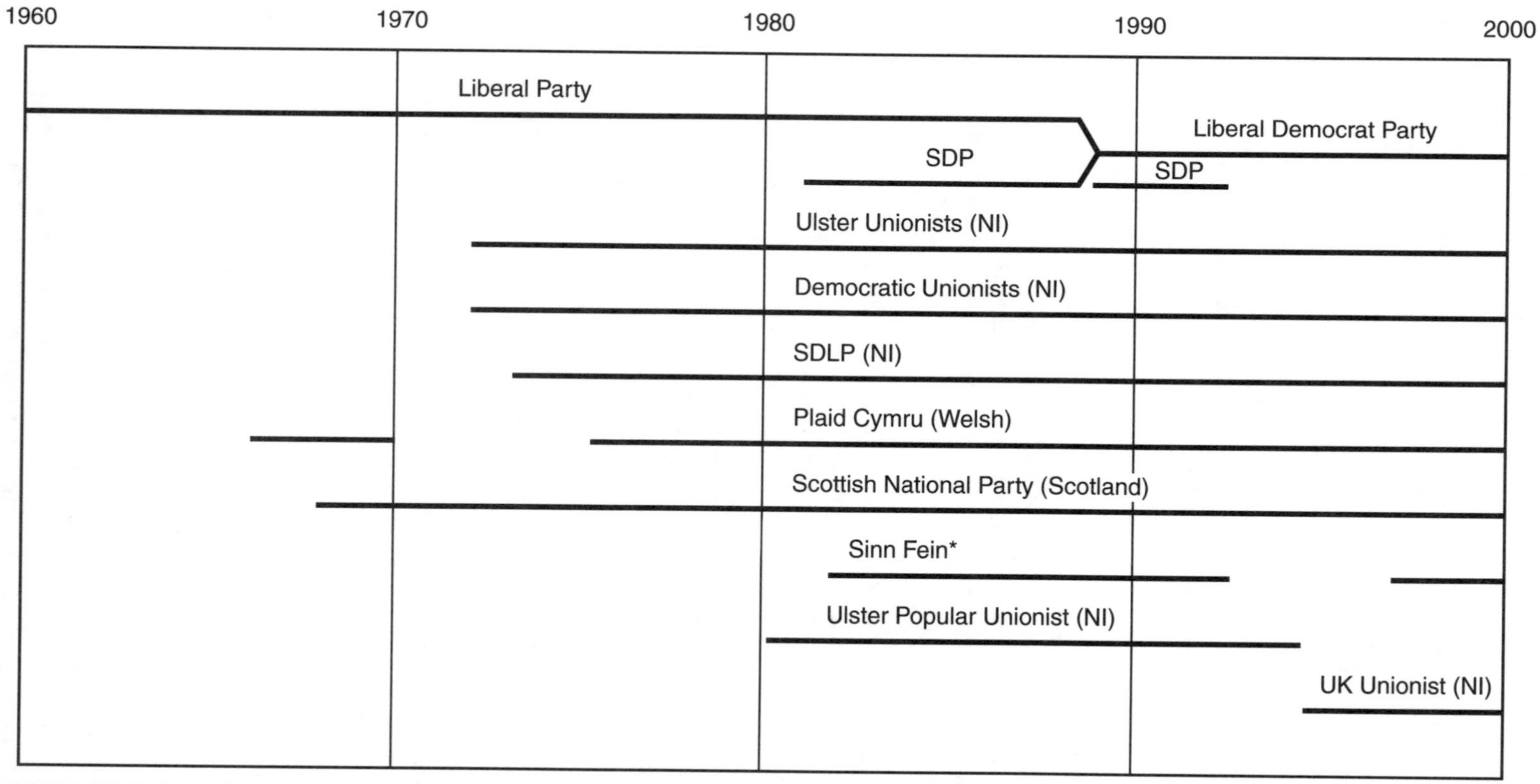

FIGURE 6.2 A Growing Field: Third parties in Parliament, 1960–1997

NI = Northern Ireland
* Did not take seat(s) in the House.

seen, one Independent MP was also elected.) There are other parties that have contested parliamentary elections but failed to win any seats. In 1989 the Green party—formed in 1985 as the successor to the Ecology party—polled unexpectedly well in the European Parliament elections, drawing twice as much support as the Liberal Democrats. In the 1997 election, the newly-formed Referendum party attracted more than 800,000 votes. The UK Independence Party was the only other party to achieve more than 100,000 votes.

The position has become even more complex in recent years because of the election, under an additional member system (AMS), of the Scottish parliament and Welsh assembly and the introduction of a new method of electing members of the European Parliament. As a result of elections to the new assemblies and to the European Parliament, the number of parties able to claim some form of parliamentary representation has increased substantially (see Table 6.4). The European Parliament now has U.K. members from the Green party and the UK Independence party. The Scottish parliament has Scottish Socialist, Independent Labour, and Green representation (albeit only one member each) and the Northern Ireland assembly has members elected from the Alliance party, the Women's Coalition, and various Unionists, in addition to Ulster Unionists and Democratic

TABLE 6.4   Party representation in parliamentary bodies

Party	Number of members elected to				
	House of Commons (1997)	Scottish Parliament (1999)	Welsh Assembly (1999)	Northern Ireland Assembly (1998)	European Parliament (1999)
Labour	419	56	28		29
Conservative	165	18	9		36
Liberal Democrat	46	17	6		10
Scottish National	6	35			2
Plaid Cymru	4		17		2
Ulster Unionist	10			28	1
Democratic Unionist	2			20	1
UK Unionist	1			5	
SDLP	3			24	1
Sinn Fein	2			18	
Green		1			2
UK Independence					3
Progressive Unionists				2	
Alliance				6	
Women's Coalition				2	
Scottish Socialist		1			
Non-party:					
Independent Unionists				3	
Independent Labour		1			
Independent	1				

Unionists. The representation may not be great in terms of the number of seats, but it gives the parties a political toe-hold that previously they lacked.

The Liberal Democrats

The Liberal Democratic party was formed in 1988 by the merger of the long-established Liberal party and the relatively new Social Democratic party (the SDP). By virtue of its age and parliamentary representation, the Liberal party was the senior partner in the merger.

The Liberal party had had a relatively short history as a major political party, spanning less than sixty years. Succeeding the Whigs in the 1860s, it was a major force on the British political scene until the 1920s, when it went into rapid decline. Like the other parties, it is a coalition of interests. The main tenets of Gladstonian Liberalism in the nineteenth century were free trade, home rule for Ireland, economy wherever possible, and social reform where necessary. Within the party there was a radical wing, which placed more emphasis on social reform, as well as an imperialist wing.[42] Returned to government in 1906, the party enacted a number of social reforms, but it proceeded on the basis of no coherent program and was divided on a number of important issues. The second decade of the century proved a disastrous one. The party was beset by such problems as division in Ireland, the suffragettes, and the First World War.[43] It was also rent asunder by a rift between Herbert H. Asquith, the party leader until 1916, and Lloyd George, who successfully displaced him. The rift was never really healed successfully. The party's internal problems and its declining electoral appeal were to reduce its parliamentary numbers. In 1918 the election was won by a coalition consisting of Lloyd George Liberals and the Conservatives. The Conservatives were the dominant partner, though Lloyd George remained as premier. In 1922, Conservative MPs brought the coalition to an end. In the ensuing general election, 62 National Liberal and 54 Liberal MPs were returned. The position improved temporarily in 1923, when 159 Liberal MPs were returned. In 1924 the number returned was only 40. In subsequent elections the number returned was 59 (1929), 33 (1931, 41 Liberal National MPs also being returned),[44] and 20 (1935). In the general elections between 1945 and 1979 the number of Liberal MPs elected varied from 6 to 14. The only occasion in postwar years when it came close to government was during the period of the Liberal-Labour (known as the Lib-Lab) Pact from 1977 to 1978, when it achieved some concessions and the opportunity to consult in return for sustaining the minority Labour government in office.[45] The pact proved unpopular with party activists and was short-lived.

The fortunes of the party appeared to improve in 1981, when it entered into an alliance with the newly formed Social Democratic party. The Social Democratic party was formed in March 1981 when a number of Labour politicians broke away from the Labour party. The new party was led by four former Labour Cabinet ministers, dubbed by newspapers as "the Gang of Four": Roy Jenkins, Shirley Williams, David Owen, and William Rodgers. The last two were already in the House of Commons. The other two, both former MPs, were to return later in by-elections. The party was created with the ostensible aim of "breaking the mold" of British politics.[46] It wanted to get away from the adversary relationships that had characterized British politics, favoring instead consensus government that would represent the center ground of British politics. It favored decentralization, equality, electoral reform, a pay-and-prices policy, and especially membership in the European Community.

The new party attracted support both within the House of Commons and within the country. By the end of 1981, a total of 27 Labour MPs (and one Conservative) had defected to join it. It attracted over 70,000 members, and by December its support in the Gallup poll exceeded that of any other party. It formed an alliance with the Liberal party, and alliance candidates began to score some notable victories in by-elections.[47] Within a year of its formation, it posed a threat to the two main traditional parties.

During 1982 it began to develop its internal organization and to formulate policies. It also witnessed a decline in support. The former may provide a partial explanation for the latter. As the party committed itself to specific policies and as it selected a leader with a distinctive leadership style and appeal, so it began to shed its "catchall" appeal. A contest for the party leadership and a dispute with the Liberals over the allocation of alliance candidatures produced some loss of support. The Falklands campaign also served to rob it of much-needed publicity.

A consequence of these developments was that the alliance entered the 1983 election campaign in third place in the opinion polls. As the campaign progressed and the Labour campaign faltered, alliance support increased. It became a topic of media speculation as to whether Labour or the alliance would come in second to the Conservatives in the number of votes cast. In the end, despite its worst share of the poll for almost 70 years, the Labour party retained second place in the polls and benefited from the concentration of its support. The alliance obtained 26 percent of the votes but suffered from the broadness of its support: Only 23 alliance MPs were returned, 17 of them Liberals and 6 SDP.

In the wake of the election, SDP leader Roy Jenkins resigned and the party elected Dr. David Owen. The two parties remained in alliance but, with a limited parliamentary base, failed to make a dent in public consciousness during the new Parliament. Both alliance partners entered the 1987 election campaign hoping to improve on their 1983 result: The two party leaders—known as "the two Davids" (David Owen and David Steel)—toured the country together to rally support. However, the two parties, and their leaders, failed to make much impact, and both parties were showing internal unease by the end of the campaign. In the election, alliance candidates garnered just under 23 percent of the vote and 22 seats.

Immediately following the 1987 election, Liberal leader David Steel pressed for a merger of the two parties, believing that such a move was necessary if the alliance were to maximize its impact. The move was opposed by David Owen, who decided to step down as SDP leader; he was replaced by SDP MP Robert

Maclennan, who began negotiations with Liberal leaders. Agreement was reached eventually on a merged party: In January 1988 a special Liberal Assembly voted, 2,099 to 385, in favor of a merger. The Council of the SDP followed suit by a vote of 273 to 28. Both parties then held a mail ballot of all members: Liberals voted in favor by 46,376 to 6,365 and the SDP, less decisively, by 18,722 to 9,929. Many SDP members, including David Owen, abstained. The new party was formed with the support of all 17 Liberal MPs but only 2 SDP MPs; the remaining 3 SDP MPs refused to join.

The new party immediately encountered a problem of nomenclature: Liberals were insistent that the name "Liberal" should not be lost. Finally the party chose the name of the Social and Liberal Democratic party. It was not a popular choice, especially with Liberal MPs, and the name was believed to contribute to confusion on the part of electors about the nature of the party. The new party also proceeded to elect a leader. David Steel decided not to stand and David Owen was no longer available. The party elected a relatively new MP, Paddy Ashdown, a candidate with a reputation for dynamism (and some degree of erraticism), in preference to a longer serving MP, Alan Beith, regarded as solid and reliable but lacking in charisma.

The combination of new name and leader appeared to leave electors confused as to what the party was and what it had to offer. The party did badly in local elections in 1988 and 1989 and trailed the Green party in the 1989 European Parliament elections, in which the party got a little over 6 percent of the vote. That performance represented the nadir of the party's fortunes. The party then decided to be called by the name Liberal Democrats. In 1991, Paddy Ashdown had a "good Gulf War": the only ex-serviceman (he had served in the marines) among the party leaders, he appeared frequently on television to provide authoritative comments. Party fortunes appeared to improve. In the 1992 general election, the party got just under 18% of the vote: down on the alliance performance in 1983 and 1987 but better than might have been expected two or three years before. The party was overshadowed after 1992 by Labour's dominance in the opinion polls and, especially after Tony Blair became leader, by Labour's move towards the political center. Former Labour supporters who had defected to the SDP in the early 1980s returned to the fold. In 1997, the party failed to improve on its percentage share of the vote but, because of tactical voting (Labour supporters voting Liberal Democrat in seats in which the Liberal Democrats were the principal challengers to the incumbent Conservatives), the party achieved its best parliamentary representation for more than sixty years: 46 Liberal Democrats were elected to the House of Commons. For the first time in postwar history, the party had a notable presence in Parliament. Though the size of Labour's majority meant that the Liberal Democrats could not have an impact on the outcome of votes, the party shared some policy goals with Labour, especially on constitutional issues, and prime minister Blair set up a Cabinet committee, comprising ministers and some Liberal Democrat MPs, to consider constitutional change. The committee had no decision-making powers but it constituted a significant departure in terms of constitutional practice. The

Liberal Democrats debated as to what extent they should become closer to the Labour party.[48] The realization that the party might hold the balance of power in a future parliament added extra significance not only to their deliberations but also to the calculations of politicians in other parties. In 1999, the party saw greater practical cooperation with the Labour party: in Scotland, where it won 17 seats in the new parliament, it entered into coalition with Labour in order to form a Scottish administration. The leader of the Liberal Democrats in Scotland became deputy first minister (see Chapter 10) and various portfolios were given to the party. At the same time, the party saw a change in leadership. Paddy Ashdown decided to retire in 1999. The party elected in his place a 39-year-old former SDP MP, Charles Kennedy. He supported Ashdown's approach to cooperation with the Labour party. However, a candidate skeptical of further cooperation came a strong second in the ballot. The new leader indicated that there were limits to further cooperation. The party wished to retain its independence and integrity.

Scottish and Welsh Nationalists

Prior to the 1960s the nationalist parties in Scotland and Wales had not proved to be politically important. Their main achievement had been "simply to survive."[49] In the 1960s, both parties—first Plaid Cymru (Party of Wales) and then the Scottish National party (SNP)—achieved a parliamentary toe-hold (each won a seat in a by-election) and then became more significant forces in the 1970s. This was especially so in the case of the SNP.

Favoring independence for Scotland, though being prepared to accept an elected national assembly as a step on that path, the SNP was able to exploit dissatisfaction with Westminster government and to make use of an issue that became salient during this period: North Sea oil. It argued that the oil was Scottish oil and that revenue from it could make an independent Scottish government viable. In Wales, the Plaid argued more for self-government than for independence and was able to play on the fears of the indigenous Welsh population, which felt its heritage to be threatened by English encroachment.

In the October 1974 election, the SNP won 11 seats in Scotland and Plaid Cymru won three in Wales. As nationalist support increased in both countries, it began to constitute a threat to the dominant party in both: the Labour party. The threat was especially strong in Scotland: In addition to winning 11 seats in October 1974, the SNP came second in 35 of 41 Labour-held seats. The Labour government introduced a scheme for elected assemblies in Scotland and Wales, but the proposal was rejected decisively in a referendum in Wales and failed in Scotland: Although 1,230,000 people in Scotland voted for the proposal and 1,153,000 voted against it, the yes vote failed to meet a threshold set by Parliament. The nationalist parties appeared less prominent during the period of Conservative government from 1979 to 1997, though both still maintained a parliamentary presence. Though its number of seats in the House declined, the SNP managed to maintain its share of the poll in Scotland and it had the bonus of winning, and retaining, a seat in the European Parliament. In the 1994 elections to the European Parliament, it doubled its representation. In the 1997 general election, it won 6 seats in the House of Commons—double the number elected in 1992—and, more significantly, took 22 percent of the vote in Scotland (slightly up on its 1992 percentage), establishing it as the second largest party in Scotland. (Conservative support declined, pushing the party out of second place.) The new Labour government's commitment to elected assemblies in Scotland and Wales resulted in legislation creating both bodies (see Chapter 10). The new assemblies provided a new opportunity for the nationalist parties and soon the SNP, under its leader Alex Salmond, mounted a strong challenge in elections to the Scottish parliament, emerging as the second party and denying the Labour party an absolute majority of seats. The SNP won 35 seats—to Labour's 56—in the 129-member parliament. To stave off the SNP challenge, Labour members of the new parliament formed a coalition with Liberal Democratic members in order to form a majority administration. The new parliament offered the SNP a valuable platform. It was now a major player in Scottish politics.

Similarly, in Wales, Plaid Cymru—which won 4 seats in the 1997 general election—established itself as the second largest party in the Welsh assembly, winning 17 seats (to Labour's 28) in the 60-member body. It also achieved a notable success in the 1999 elections to the European Parliament, winning two seats in a body in which it previously had no representation. The two Plaid Cymru members of the European Parliament joined two SNP members. Both nationalist parties thus enjoyed parliamentary representation at three levels—in their home assembly, in the U.K. Parliament, and in the European Parliament.

Northern Ireland Parties

In Northern Ireland the majority of voters vote Unionist, supporting the maintenance of the union with Britain. They have been represented, historically, by the Unionist party. Originally a united party tied to the British Conservative party, it disassociated itself (though in organizational terms not totally) from the Conservative party following the imposition of direct rule in the province by a Conservative government in 1972. It also divided within itself, the two main Unionist parties being the Ulster Unionists and the Democratic Unionists. The Ulster Unionists tend to be more middle class and Anglican and Methodist, whereas the Democratic Unionists, led by fundamentalist Protestant clergyman Ian Paisley, appeal more to working-class Protestants and are more heavily Presbyterian. The Ulster Unionist party is the more dominant of the two: In 1997, it won 10 of the 18 seats in the province, while the Democratic Unionists were reduced from three to two seats. There is also a lone Unionist sitting in Parliament under the banner of the United Kingdom Unionist party, committed to integrating the province into the rest of the United Kingdom.

Within the province, there is also the predominantly Catholic party, the social Democratic and Labour party (the SDLP). In 1992, it achieved its best result, increasing its representation from 3 to 4 seats, winning Belfast West from Gerry

Adams of Sinn Fein, the political wing of the Provisional IRA (see Chapter 9). Adams had been elected for the seat in 1983 and was reelected in 1987 but refused to take his seat. In 1992, the SDLP increased its share of the poll in the province to 24 percent; Sinn Fein's share dropped to 10 percent. Sinn Fein witnessed something of an improvement as it sought to be involved in peace talks following the Downing Street Declaration in 1993. In elections to a Forum to discuss peace plans in 1996, Sinn Fein got 15 percent of the vote. In the 1997 general elections, it increased its share of the poll to 16 percent and won two seats.

The Alliance party, unconnected to the former British SDP/Liberal alliance, is a nonsectarian party that seeks to bridge the gap between the two communities. However, it has never won any seats in the House of Commons and looks unlikely to do so. It won less than 9 percent of the votes in 1992 and less than 8 percent in 1997. However, it did achieve parliamentary representation in 1996 when its leader, John Alderdice, was created a life peer, and it won seats in the new Northern Ireland assembly elected in 1998. Alderdice was elected presiding officer of the assembly.

The cease-fire in the province and the signing of the Good Friday agreement in 1998 (see Chapter 10), resulting in the creation of a Northern Ireland assembly, has provided a new political forum not only for those parties already enjoying representation in the U.K. Parliament but also for the Alliance party (6 seats) and the Women's Coalition (2 seats)—a coalition specific to the province—as well as for Independent Unionists (3 seats) and Progressive Unionists (2 seats) (see Chapter 10). The assembly has not yet taken on a substantial deliberative role—it becomes fully operational when the Secretary of State concludes that sufficient progress has been made to implement the Good Friday Agreement—but it has provided some electoral legitimacy to nine political groupings.

Other Parties

Various other parties contest parliamentary election in the United Kingdom. Most never achieve national prominence. A few do, but usually on a temporary basis. In the 1990s, a few parties contested multiple seats. The eight parties to achieve at least 0.1 percent of the votes cast in the 1997 general election are listed in Table 6.5. As can be seen, each fielded more than fifty candidates. The number is significant, as any party with fifty or more candidates qualified for free air time for a party election broadcast. However, where third parties have achieved prominence in recent years has been in elections to other bodies.

The *Referendum party* was formed by millionaire businessman Sir James Goldsmith to demand a referendum on Britain's future in the Union. Some Conservatives feared that it could damage their electoral prospects. As can be seen from Table 6.5, it was the only minor party to win more than 2.5 percent of the votes cast and, as such, it established itself as the fourth party in England. Its prominence was short-lived: Goldsmith died shortly after the election and the party largely disappeared from view.

TABLE 6.5   Minor parties in the 1997 general election

Party	Votes	% share of poll	Average vote % per seat contested	Candidates	Lost deposits
Referendum	811,827	2.6	3.1	547	505
UK Independence	106,028	0.3	1.2	194	193
Green	63,991	0.2	1.4	95	95
Socialist Labour	52,110	0.2	1.7	64	61
Liberal	44,989	0.1	1.8	54	52
British National	35,833	0.1	1.3	57	54
Natural Law	30,281	0.1	0.7	196	196
Pro-Life Alliance	18,545	0.1	0.7	53	53

SOURCE: D. Butler and D. Kavanagh, *The British General Election of 1997* (Macmillan, 1997), p. 255.

The somewhat longer-established *UK Independence party*, favoring British withdrawal from the European Union, garnered more than 100,000 votes in the 1997 election but held its deposit in only one seat. However, it achieved prominence as a result of the elections to the European Parliament in 1999. It won just under 700,000 votes—7 percent of the poll—which was sufficient for it to win no less than 3 seats (see Chapter 9). This gave it an electoral legitimacy, and a platform, that previously it lacked. Indeed, in terms of the number of seats won, it established itself as the fourth party—after the Conservatives, Labour, and the Liberal Democrats—in the election.

The *Green party* was founded as the People's party in 1973, changed its name to the Ecology party in 1975, and took its present name in 1985. It made little impact until 1989, when it attracted 14.5 percent of the vote in elections to the European parliament. The vote gave it national visibility but its support was not maintained, reverting in subsequent general elections to pre-1989 levels of support. It regained some support in the elections to the European Parliament in 1999. Though not emulating its support of 1989, it nonetheless received 625,000 votes—just over 6 percent of the poll—which, under the new regional list system of election, was sufficient for it to win 2 seats. Like the UK Independence Party, it thus achieved some parliamentary representation through election for the first time in its history. It also obtained a place in the House of Lords when a Liberal Democrat peer switched his allegiance.

The *Socialist Labour party* was, like the Referendum party, a new body created to contest the 1997 general election. It was set up by the leader of the national union of mine workers, Arthur Scargill. It represented the far left in British politics which, by itself, has never fared well in national elections.[50] The achievement of the party was to retain its deposit in three seats. Socialists were, though, able to take some comfort two years later from the elections to the Scottish parliament: One candidate standing as a Scottish Socialist was elected. However, they were able to take little comfort from elections in the same year to the European Parliament: The party garnered fewer than 87,000 votes, just under 0.9 percent of the poll. It was out-polled by the British National party.

The Liberal party is best described as the Continuing Liberal party, formed to represent Liberals opposed to the merger with the SDP. Despite the support of a former Liberal MP, it has failed to make a mark. (Following the merger of the two parties, a Continuing SDP was also formed, including in its ranks three SDP MPs, but it faded at the 1992 election.) In elections to the European Parliament in 1999, it attracted 93,000 votes, less than 1 percent of the poll.

The *British National party* represents the far right, constituting a breakaway movement from the National Front, a right-wing neofascist party that attracts support largely on the basis of opposition to immigration by nonwhites. The party, like the National Front before it, attracted little support in the 1997 general election. Its party election broadcast attracted criticism not only for its message but also for including film footage of black citizens without their permission. As can be seen from Table 6.5, it averaged just over 1 percent of the poll in those seats it contested. Similarly, in the elections to the European Parliament in 1997, it won only 1 percent of the votes cast, not enough to deliver any seats in the Parliament.

The *Natural Law party* emerged as an election-contesting party in 1992. The party expounded the "vedic science" of Maharishi Mahesh Yogi and issued a largely incomprehensible election manifesto. The candidates, some of whom were flown in from abroad, did no campaigning. The party contested 309 seats and lost its deposit in every one; only two candidates actually managed to get more than 1 percent of the votes cast. As can be seen from Table 6.5, it essentially repeated the performance in 1997, achieving an average of 155 votes per candidate. It was also a largely ignored "also ran" in the 1999 elections to the European Parliament.

The *Pro-Life Alliance*—an anti-abortion organization—decided to contest more than 50 seats in the 1997 election, thus giving it a free election broadcast but not many votes, an average of 350 votes per candidate. It lost its deposit in every seat it contested. However, as is apparent from Table 6.5, that is the norm rather than the exception for minor parties in British general elections. For minor parties to gain representation, their best chances lie in contesting elections to other parliamentary bodies.

DECLINE IN PARTY SUPPORT

The past two decades have witnessed major changes in electoral behavior and in support for the two main parties. One of the principal changes that has been variously identified has been a decline in support for the two main parties. What is the evidence for a decline in the two-party system? If there has been a decline, what explains it?

A decline in voting support for both parties has been sketched in the preceding chapter. Ever since the peak of two-party support reached in the 1950s, electors have shown a relative desertion of both main parties. In every general election from 1983 onwards, more than 20 percent of those who voted have cast their ballots for candidates other than Conservative and Labour candidates: In 1950 the figure had been less than 2 percent. As we have already noted, the Labour share of the poll in 1983 was its lowest since 1918. The Conservative party won with its lowest share producing victory since the general election of 1922. In 1997, the Labour party was swept to victory with 43.2 percent of the votes cast—a smaller percentage than it had achieved in the three general elections of the 1950s, when it lost to the Conservatives, and smaller than the percentage that had produced victory (with a smaller parliamentary majority) in 1945, 1964, and 1966. In 1997, the Conservatives achieved their worst share of the poll this century, fewer than one in three of those who voted casting their ballot for the party.

Furthermore, these low percentages are in the context of a lower voter turnout than in earlier decades. If we take the votes cast as a proportion of the total eligible electorate, then the contrast is even more stark (Table 6.6). In the 1950 general election, three-quarters of the electorate (75.2 percent) voted for one of the two main parties. In the 1997 general election, only just over half of all eligible electors (52.6 percent) voted Labour or Conservative—Labour won a massive majority on the votes of 30.8 percent of the electorate. Thus, almost half the electorate either stayed at home or voted for parties other than the Labour or Conservative parties.

Other indicators have also been employed to show a relative desertion of the two main parties. One has been in levels of party identification. There was a decline in levels of "very strong" identifiers, especially among Labour supporters, in the 1970s[51] and relatively low levels of identification in subsequent years.[52] More recent research has revealed considerable fluctuation in identification and found a correlation between identification and voting preferences, suggesting the two may not be discrete phenomena.[53] Identification with Labour increased markedly in the 1990s as it became increasingly popular. If so, the data on identification serves to repeat rather than reinforce our findings on voter behavior. Fluctuating levels of identification reinforce the findings of our previous chap-

TABLE 6.6 Two-party support, 1950 and 1997

Party	Votes won as % of votes cast		Votes won as % of electorate	
	1950	1997	1950	1997
Labour	46.1	43.2	38.7	30.8
Conservative	43.5	30.7	36.5	21.8
Totals	89.6	73.9	75.2	52.6

ter, suggesting that voter attachment to the two main parties is not as strong as it was.

Another indicator has been a decline in membership. The Conservative party claimed a membership of 2.8 million in 1952. That was a high-water mark, but it was still able to claim a membership in excess of 2 million in 1958. The figure declined in the 1960s and 1970s and was probably around the 1 to 1.5 million mark in the 1970s. One estimate put the figure in the late 1980s at just under the 750,000 level. By the mid 1990s, according to one survey, membership was down to around 500,000.[54] Some reports suggested an even lower figure. The Labour party reached its peak in membership at about the same time as the Conservatives, claiming a membership of just over 1 million in 1952. By 1992, its membership was approximately 260,000, the lowest membership figure since 1929. Since then, it has witnessed a sharp increase—peaking, as we have noted already, at just over 400,000 in 1997, and has tailed off a little since then. Even the increase in the three years from 1994 to 1997—phenomenal by recent standards—has not brought it to the membership level it enjoyed in the 1950s.

The two parties in Britain have thus witnessed a decline in support in recent decades. The phenomenon is not one peculiar to the United Kingdom. It is also a feature of the United States. The proportion of the adult population turning out to vote for Republican or Democratic candidates in presidential elections has declined over the past forty years. Voting turnout in presidential elections reached a peak in 1960. Then, almost two out of every three adult Americans went to the polls. In the presidential elections since, and including 1984, the proportion was down to roughly one out of two. And of those voting, not all have cast their ballots for Republicans and Democrats, third-party candidates siphoning off a significant vote in 1968, 1980, and, most especially, 1992. Identification with both parties also has declined.[55] Ticket splitting has also increased, as has the degree of negative voting. According to survey data, in the 1988 presidential election half of each candidate's supporters voted more to stop the other ticket than because they genuinely approved of their choice.

Both countries, then, have witnessed two-party decline. The decline and the comparison should not be pushed too far. Of those who do vote, seven out of ten in the United Kingdom, and usually nine out of ten in the United States, vote for one of the two main parties. The Labour party has managed to reverse the decline in its membership, increasing it by more than 50 percent in three years. Nonetheless, the two main parties do not attract support on the scale that they did in earlier decades. The quarter-century following the end of the Second World War was a period of hegemony by the two parties. The quarter-century since 1970 saw the parties still dominating British politics, but not to the extent they did in the previous 25 years. There was a clear decline in support.

The decline in support is not identical in Britain and the United States. Consequently, explanations for that decline differ. The principal explanations for decline in the United Kingdom can be subsumed under three headings: *structural dealignment*, *policy orientation*, and *performance*. The first two explanations correlate closely with the partisan preferences of those who advance them. The structural analysis tends to be advanced by members of center parties and by a few within each of the main parties. The policy-orientation thesis is advanced predominantly by protagonists *within* the two main parties.

Structural Dealignment

The structural thesis is one we have touched upon already (Chapters 3 and 5). The contention is that the decline in support for the two main parties is the product of the structure of the two-party system. The two parties dominate the political agenda, taking positions that are not congruent with the wishes of most electors. Such a stance is dictated by the electoral system, forcing the parties to compete for the all-or-nothing spoils of electoral victory and, in so doing, to compete vigorously with one another in an adversary relationship. Once in office, a party often must modify or abandon its program when it discovers the resources do not exist to meet the more extravagant of its promises (made in order to outbid its opponent party). There is thus a poor fit between what electors want and what the parties actually provide. Britain, in short, has a dysfunctional party system. As the economic resources to meet manifesto promises have declined, in inverse relationship to the growth of such promises, so voter disenchantment with the two parties—one in government, the other forming the alternative government—has grown. Such voters then have the option of voting for a third party or, given that the electoral system works against third parties, of staying at home on election day. That, on this argument, is what they have been doing for the past quarter-century.

Given that the party system cannot be separated from the workings of the nation's electoral arrangements, it is not surprising that proponents of this thesis advance reform of the electoral system as a primary means of resolving the problem. A system of proportional representation, it is argued, would ensure a fit between voters' wants and public policy as well as increase support for, and participation in, the political system.

The problem with this argument, as Nevil Johnson has observed, is that a decline in support for one or both of the two main parties does not of itself demonstrate a decline in support for the two-party system.[56] Voters may support a particular third party because they wish it to replace one of the existing major parties in a two-party framework. There are no objective data to suggest that electors wish to dispense with what supporters view as the fruits of a two-party system: a clear choice between parties, and a party government with an overall majority. Indeed, there are data that suggest the opposite. Survey data reveal broad, but not deep, support for some change in the electoral system, but not for the consequences such a change would have.[57] Electors dislike the prospects of a Parliament in which no one party has an overall majority. In a poll conducted in the final days of the 1992 general election campaign, 56 percent of those questioned were opposed to a "hung" Parliament.[58] The final objective data are voting figures. Only a minority of electors vote for parties that challenge the two-party system and even those who support third parties do not necessarily oppose a two-party system, preferring the party they support to supplant one of the two main parties. (Even Paddy Ashdown, when leader of the Liberal Democrats, spoke of his party replacing the Labour party as the principal challenger to the Conservatives.) A decline in two-party support should not be equated with a collapse in two-party support. And what decline has taken place has not been consistent. In the 1992 general election, for example, there was an increase both in voter turnout—the second highest turnout since 1959—and in the proportion voting for the two main parties. The 1997 election produced, as we have seen, a poor result in terms of two-party voting. The two results put together means that it is difficult to predict a further decline next time around.

Policy Orientation

This thesis about the two-party decline takes different forms, largely dependent upon where one stands in the political milieu. One form, which may be described as the *consensus thesis*, attributes decline in party support to the consensus policies of postwar decades, when the two parties followed similar Keynesian economic policies. This was the era of the social democratic consensus, or what Samuel Beer termed the Collectivist era.[59] For socialists within the Labour party and neoliberals within Conservative ranks, this consensus was responsible for the decline in support for their parties. It was responsible for that decline for two reasons. First, the policies themselves were deemed inadequate to meet Britain's fundamental problems. Socialists favored more state control; neoliberals wanted a free market economy. Second, the consensual stance of the parties robbed the electors of a clear choice between competing policies. The absence of a clear choice continued into the 1970s, the Conservative government of Edward Heath abandoning a non-interventionist stance and Labour governments pursuing orthodox economic policies.

Those advancing this thesis could point to the decline in two-party support being most marked in the 1970s. For neoliberals in the Conservative party, the pursuit of Thatcherite policies from 1979 onward ensured a clear choice and one that resulted in successive victories in four general elections. The loss of the election in 1997 was blamed on John Major and his failure to pursue distinctive Thatcherite policies; his challenger for the leadership in 1995, John Redwood, was committed to the pursuit of neoliberal policies and predicted disaster if they were not pursued. Socialists in the Labour party attributed Labour's failure in 1970 and 1979 to the absence of a socialist program and its continuing failure in the 1980s to the retrospective evaluation by electors of earlier Labour governments. Voters were continuing to vote on their evaluation of past performance rather than on an evaluation of what was being offered for the future. As Paul Whiteley expressed it, "If centrist policies fail, as they have done for the most part during Labour's tenure in office, no amount of moderation will bring electoral success."[60]

This thesis is challenged by the *extremist thesis*. This contends that a decline in support for both parties was the result of extreme policies pursued by both of the parties. The left-wing programs of Labour in the 1980s, and especially in the 1983 election, resulted in a disastrous electoral performance, the party almost being squeezed into third place by the Liberal/Social Democratic alliance. The Conservative party won three elections under Margaret Thatcher's leadership, but did so despite Thatcherism and not because of it. Electors, on balance, preferred a Conservative government to a Labour one, but they did not support, nor they did move more in the direction of supporting, Thatcherite policies.[61] The policies, particularly the economic policies, pursued by the Thatcher government alienated many voters, resulting in disaffected Conservative supporters switching their support to center parties. Although the Conservative party won the elections, it did so on a low share of the poll. Hence, Conservative victory over Labour masked an underlying decline in support. When both parties moved more toward the center ground, the support for the principal third party declined. A more moderate approach by the Major government, it is argued, helped keep the Conservatives in power in 1992, and a more moderate program helped Labour to a stunning victory in 1997.

Performance

In the preceding chapter, we identified explanations for greater volatility in voting behavior. Explaining greater volatility is not necessarily to explain a *decline* in support for the two main parties. Voters may switch their votes more frequently but the switch could be from one of the two main parties to the other one. However, one of the explanations may have relevance: that of performance evaluation. Voters look to a party to be competent in governing the nation and especially in handling the nation's finances. Traditionally, the Conservatives have benefited from appearing to be a party of governance, that is, a party knowing how to govern the nation effectively. This is important in understanding Conservative success in the 1980s: Even though many of the policies pursued by the Conservative government were not popular, the Conservatives still led in the opinion polls. Electors favored the party because it looked as if it knew what it was doing and was able to deliver economic success.[62] In the eyes of electors, the Conservatives lost this claim to competence in 1992 and never recovered it.

Performance is relevant to explaining a decline in two-party voting in that neither party may be able to deliver what voters want. Two-party voting was at its height at a time of relative economic prosperity for the United Kingdom. It has declined as the capacity of government to meet the economic expectations of citizens has declined. We have already touched upon this phenomenon (Chapter 3). As Richard Rose has argued in *Do Parties Make a Difference?* the party in government can make some difference to economic performance, but not much.[63] A globalization of markets and membership of the European Union further constrain the independent capacity of government to determine outcomes. Thus, whichever party is in the power, it is not going to be able to buck international pressures and markets. If parties, when in office, are not able to deliver the goods expected of them then voters may desert those parties and either support third parties or no parties at all.

Supporters of this thesis argue that it has a better explanatory value than the other explanations. Significant shifts in public policy are notable between elections, as reactions to external developments rather than as a consequence of a change of party in office. The drop in two-party voting appears to bear little correlation to the shifts of parties to the center or the extreme. Two fairly centrist parties faced one another in 1992 and turnout and two-party voting increased; two even more centrist parties faced one another in 1997 and turnout and two-party voting declined.

This explanation does not suggest that what parties do in office is not important—a party may pursue social policies, for instance, that affect many millions of people—but that the impact governments can have on economic trends is limited and that it is competence, especially in handling economic affairs, that determines citizens' evaluations of government. What this suggests is that, absent a significant improvement in the world economy, the two parties may continue to witness a decline in support—or at least see no reversion to the levels of support achieved in earlier decades—and that, if they want to stem the decline, they have to educate electors into expecting less of government. This may prove difficult in a political environment in which others are suggesting that the problem is one of structural dealignment or bad policies. An improvement in economic conditions may mean that one party remains in office for a considerable period of time.

NOTES

[1] See, e.g., D. McSweeney and J. Zvesper, *American Political Parties* (Routledge, 1991) and M. P. Wattenberg, *The Decline of American Political Parties 1952-1992* (Harvard University Press, 1994).

[2] See especially L. Hartz, *The Liberal Tradition in America* (Harcourt, Brace and World, 1955). Also S. M. Lipset, *American Exceptionalism* (Norton, 1996).

[3] L. D. Epstein, "What Happened to the British Party Model?" *American Political Science Review*, 74 (1), 1980, pp. 9-22.

[4] *A Bicentennial Analysis of the American Political Structure* (Committee on the Constitutional System, 1987).

[5] R. H. S. Crossman, "Introduction" to W. Bagehot, *The English Constitution* (Fontana ed., 1963), p. 39.

[6] See J. Vincent, *The Formation of the British Liberal Party 1857-68* (Penguin, 1972).

[7] A. Seldon and S. Ball (eds.), *Conservative Century* (Oxford University Press, 1994).

[8] R. Blake, *The Conservative Party from Peel to Churchill* (Eyre and Spottiswoode, 1970), p. 2.

[9] On the basic tenets, see P. Norton, "Conservatism," in M. Foley (ed.), *Ideas That Shape Politics* (Manchester University Press, 1994), pp. 39-45.

[10] See P. Norton, "History of the Party I: Tory to Conservative" and P. Norton, "History of the Party II: From a Marquess to an Earl," in P. Norton (ed.), *The Conservative Party* (Prentice Hall/Harvester Wheatsheaf, 1996).

[11] P. Norton and A. Aughey, *Conservatives and Conservatism* (Temple Smith, 1981), Ch. 2.

[12] See Norton, "Conservatism," and A. Aughey, "Philosophy and faction," in Norton, *The Conservative Party*.

[13] See R. Rose, "Parties, Factions and Tendencies in British Politics," *Political Studies,* 12, 1964, pp. 33–46.

[14] See P. Norton, *Conservative Dissidents* (Temple Smith, 1978), Ch. 4, and J. Campbell, *Edward Heath* (Jonathan Cape, 1993), Part 4.

[15] The epithet *wet* has different meanings and uncertain origins. In the present context, it derived from Mrs. Thatcher's habit of annotating papers with the word when she wished to indicate that a particular proposal or comment was indecisive, bland, and poorly argued.

[16] "The Thatcher Style," *The Economist,* May 21, 1983, p. 32.

[17] See H. Young, *One of Us* (Macmillan, 1989), pp. 431–458

[18] See P. Norton, "The Conservative Party from Thatcher to Major," in A. King (ed.), *Britain at the Polls 1992* (Chatham House, 1993), pp. 29–69.

[19] I. Crewe, "Electoral Behaviour," in D. Kavanagh and A. Seldon (eds.), *The Major Effect* (London: Macmillan, 1994), p. 109.

[20] See D. Denver, "The Government That Could Do No Right," in A. King (ed.), *New Labour Triumphs: Britain at the Polls* (Chatham House, 1997), pp. 26–38.

[21] P. Norton, "The Conservative Power: 'In Office but Not in Power,'" in King, *New Labour Triumphs,* pp. 99–103.

[22] See Denver, "The Government That Could Do No Right," pp. 15–48.

[23] P. Norton, "Electing the Leader: The Conservative leadership contest," *Politics Review,* 7 (4), 1998, pp. 10–14.

[24] See especially P. Norton, "The party leader," in Norton, *The Conservative Party,* pp. 142–156.

[25] See P. Whiteley, P. Seyd, and J. Richardson, *True Blues: The Politics of Conservative Party Membership* (Oxford University Press, 1994). See also P. Tether, "The party in the country II: Members and organisation," in Norton, *The Conservative Party,* pp. 112–126.

[26] J. Fisher, "Party finance," in Norton, *The Conservative Party,* pp. 158–160.

[27] Fisher, "Party finance," pp. 159, 162.

[28] D. Butler and D. Kavanagh, *The British General Election of 1992* (Macmillan, 1992), p. 260.

[29] M. Pinto-Duschinsky, "Problems arise calculating price of democracy," *The Times,* 14 April 1998.

[30] D. Butler and D. Kavanagh, *The British General Election of 1997* (Macmillan, 1997), p. 242.

[31] Butler and Kavanagh, *The British General Election of 1997,* pp. 27–28.

[32] C. F. Brand, *The British Labour Party* (Stanford University Press, 1965); see also F. Williams, *Fifty Years March* (Odham, n.d.), Part 1.

[33] S. H. Beer, *Modern British Politics,* rev. ed. (Faber, 1969).

[34] H. Pelling, *A Short History of the Labour Party,* 5th ed. (Macmillan, 1976), p. 44.

[35] K. Jefferys, *The Labour Party Since 1945* (Macmillan, 1993), p. 24.

[36] E. Shaw, *The Labour Party Since 1945* (Blackwell, 1996), p. 63.

[37] P. Seyd, "Labour: The Great Transformation," in A. King (ed.), *Britain at the Polls 1992* (Chatham House, 1993), p. 76.

[38] I. Crewe, "Why Did Labour Lose (Yet Again)?" *Politics Review,* 2 (1), September 1992, pp. 2–11.

[39] P. Seyd, "Tony Blair and New Labour," in A. King (ed.), *New Labour Triumphs: Britain at the Polls* (Chatham House, 1997), p. 52.

[40] Seyd, "Tony Blair and New Labour," p. 60.

[41] Butler and Kavanagh, *The British General Election of 1997,* p. 55.

[42] P. Rowland, *The Last Liberal Governments* (Macmillan, 1969), p. 34.

[43] See T. Wilson, *The Downfall of the Liberal Party 1914-1935* (Fontana, 1968), p. 20.

[44] The Liberal National MPs became allied with and were eventually absorbed into the Conservative party.

[45] See A. Michie and S. Hoggart, *The Pact* (Quartet, 1978).

[46] See I. Bradley, *Breaking the Mould?* (Martin Robertson, 1981) and I. Crewe and A. King, *SDP: The Birth, Life and Death of the Social Democratic Party* (Oxford University Press, 1995).

[47] Within months of its creation, it achieved notable victories in Croydon North-West in October, Crosby in November (won by Shirley Williams), and Glasgow, Hillhead, the following March (won by Roy Jenkins).

[48] See D. MacIver, "Political Strategy," in D. MacIver (ed.), *The Liberal Democrats* (Prentice Hall/Harvester Wheatsheaf, 1996), 173-190.

[49] H. M. Drucker and G. Brown, *The Politics of Nationalism and Devolution* (Longman, 1980), p. 167.

[50] The British Communist party, founded in 1921, has had little impact in electoral terms. One Communist MP was elected in 1924, one in 1935, and two in 1945. Since then the party has achieved no parliamentary representation and has never come close to doing so. What power it had in the 1970s and 1980s was through some of its members holding office in certain trade unions. See R. Taylor, *The Fifth Estate* (Pan Books, 1980), p. 325.

[51] B. Sarlvik and I. Crewe, *A Decade of Dealignment* (Cambridge University Press, 1983), pp. 333-334. See also I. Crewe, B. Sarlvik, and J. Alt, "Partisan Dealignment in Britain 1964-1974," *British Journal of Political Science,* 7 (2), 1977, pp. 129-190.

[52] For the 1980s, see G. Heald and R. J. Wybrow, *The Gallup Survey of Britain* (Croom Helm, 1986), p. 14.

[53] M. Brynin and D. Sanders, "Party Identification, Political Preferences and Material Conditions," *Party Politics,* Vol. 3 (1), 1997, pp. 53-77.

[54] *The Times,* October 10, 1994. See also Tether, "The party in the country II: members and organisation," in Norton, *The Conservative Party,* pp. 116-117.

[55] By the mid-1970s, less than two-thirds of Americans identified themselves with either party (compared with 75% in 1964) and only 24% claimed to be "strong" identifiers (compared with 37% in 1964). During the 1970s and early 1980s, the number of independent identifiers outnumbered Republican identifiers. Identification with the Democratic party has continued to decline and about 30% of electors continue to identify themselves as independents. H. W. Stanley and R. G. Niemi, *Vital Statistics on American Politics,* 2nd ed. (CQ Press, 1990), p. 146.

[56] N. Johnson, book review, *The Times Higher Education Supplement,* July 22, 1983.

[57] See P. Norton, "Does Britain Need Proportional Representation?" in R. Blackburn (ed.), *Constitutional Studies* (Mansell, 1992).

[58] *The Times,* April 6, 1992. When given a straight choice between PR or one-party government, or between majority or coalition government, a plurality has tended to favor the existing arrangements: In an exit poll during the 1987 election, 49% were for the existing system, 46% for PR (*The Independent,* June 13, 1987), and in a MORI poll in 1991, 38% were for majority government, 25% for coalition government (*The Independent,* April 25, 1991).

[59] Beer, *Modern British Politics.*

[60] P. Whiteley, "The Decline of Labour's Local Party Membership and Electoral Base, 1945-1979," in D. Kavanagh (ed.), *The Politics of the Labour Party* (Allen and Unwin, 1982), p. 132. See also P. Whiteley, *The Labour Party in Crisis* (Methuen, 1983).

[61] See especially I. Crewe and D. Searing, "Ideological Change in the British Conservative Party," *American Political Science Review,* 82 (2), 1988; R. Jowell, S. Witherspoon, and L. Brook, *British Social Attitudes, Fifth Report* (Gower, 1988) and P. Norton, "The Conservative Party from Thatcher to Major," in King, *Britain at the Polls 1992*.

[62] See Norton, "The Conservative Party: 'In Office But Not in Power,'" in King, *New Labour Triumphs*.

[63] R. Rose, *Do Parties Make a Difference?* 2nd ed. (Macmillan, 1984).

Chapter 7

Interest Groups
Insiders or Outsiders?

Interest groups have commonly been defined as bodies that seek to influence government in the allocation of resources without themselves seeking to assume responsibility for government. This definition is usually employed to distinguish such groups from political parties, which do seek, through electoral success, to form the government. The distinction, though not watertight, is nonetheless a useful one.

Interest group activity and the study of it have, historically, been more apparent in the United States than in Britain. This difference is explicable largely in terms of the different political systems. The United States has been characterized as enjoying a "multiple access" system. A group can seek to influence a particular department or bureau. If that attempt fails, it can lobby the White House. It can lobby Congress. The separation of powers and the relative weakness of political parties—in essence, depriving representatives and senators of a protective party shield to hide behind—make members of Congress worthwhile targets for group pressure. Such pressure is applied continuously on Capitol Hill; well over 20,000 lobbyists are retained by groups of some sort to lobby members of Congress. If pressure in Washington fails, a group can always turn to the state or district to try to rouse support there. Rallies may be organized. A mass mailing to Congress may be instigated. Not surprisingly, such visible activity and its apparent effect have been the subject of serious study and academic debate. The United States has been the breeding ground of group and pluralist theory.

The position in the United Kingdom in terms of group activity has been different. For groups seeking to influence government decisions, the principal focus of activity is the executive: the ministers and officials occupying the government departments. Attempts to lobby Parliament or to a maintain regular contact on a scale analogous to that maintained on Capitol Hill have been notable for their rarity. Many groups have maintained friendly contact with members of Parliament; as we shall see, an increasing number make use of professional lobbyists, but their number is relatively small. Lobbying of MPs is an admission that attempts to influence ministers and their officials have failed. It is often an unprofitable exercise: Failure to influence ministers will frequently be replicated in a house dominated by those same ministers. Interest-group activity has thus tended to be less visible than in the United States.

The relative lack of visibility of group activity should nonetheless not be misconstrued. Group activity in Britain has been difficult to study because it has not been conducted as obviously and as openly as in the United States. And the lack of such obvious public conduct may be indicative of group influence, not weakness. Only if groups fail to influence ministers or officials do they need to go public and concentrate on Parliament and the media. For much of the postwar period, in which group pressure increased, government was able to satisfy the wants of those groups making demands of it as well as of consumers: There was little need for the more influential sectional groups to mount campaigns. In recent decades, important groups have become far more visible in their attempts to influence government. And as group activity has become more visible, the role played by particular groups in the political arena has become a topic of controversy, both academic and political.

TYPES OF INTEREST GROUPS

Sectional Interest and Promotional Groups

Interest groups have been variously subdivided for analytic purposes. One subdivision, the most common and longstanding, is that between *sectional interest* groups and *promotional* groups. The former, as the name implies, are formed to defend and pursue the interests of specific sections of the community, sections usually defined on an economic basis. (Indeed, to emphasize the point, some writers distinguish between economic or producer groups and promotional groups.) Promotional groups exist to promote particular causes, which may draw their support from disparate individuals and are not based on economic divisions within society. There are a number of recognizable interest groups that fall somewhere between the two categories (for example, the Automobile Association) and others that do not easily fall into either category.

Sectional interest groups are usually permanent bodies formed for a purpose primarily other than influencing government. Most are created to provide services of one form or another to their members: for example, negotiating on their behalf; providing legal, social, and insurance facilities; offering advice and information; and providing a forum in which matters of common interest can be discussed and policy determined. Such groups are numerous. They include, for example, trade unions, the Law Society, the National Farmers Union, the Royal College of Nursing, the Police Federation, the British Medical Association, and various employers' associations. Membership in such bodies is normally exclusive, and actual membership is often close to the potential membership. In some instances, membership in a professional body is a requirement for pursuing a particular vocation. Many have their counterparts in the United States: the AFL-CIO, for example, is the rough equivalent of the Trades Union Congress in Britain, and the American Medical Association the equivalent of the British Medical Association.

Whereas sectional groups seek to promote the interests, normally the economic interests, of their membership, promotional groups seek to promote a cause or causes that are not usually of direct economic benefit to their members. The motivation for joining a sectional group is economic, and for joining a promotional group, often moral or ideological. Promotional groups may seek to promote and defend the interests of particular categories of individuals within society (for example, the Child Poverty Action Group, the National Council for One-Parent Families), of particular rights (Liberty, formerly the National Council for Civil Liberties), or of shared beliefs (the Lord's Day Observance Society). Some seek to achieve a specific objective, one often embodied in their title (for example, the Abortion Law Reform Society). A number are essentially defensive groups formed to counter the campaigns mounted by reform movements: For example, the Society for the Protection of the Unborn Child (SPUC) was formed to oppose the pro-abortion lobby, and the British Field Sports Society was created to defend hunting against the activities of the League against Cruel Sports. A number of such groups, by their nature, are little concerned with public policy and rarely engage in political activity. Others, by contrast, often exist for the purpose of pursuing a public campaign to achieve a modification of public policy and the enactment of legislation.

Insider and Outsider Groups

A second subdivision, developed by Wyn Grant, focuses on the relationship between groups and government. This distinguishes between *insider* and *outsider* groups.[1] Insider groups are regarded as legitimate by government and are consulted on a regular basis. Outsider groups are groups that are not regarded by the government as legitimate bodies to consult on a regular basis or do not seek such status. When he first formulated these categories, Grant sought to refine them, offering various subdivisions of each. He subdivided insider groups into prisoner groups (dependent on government, not least for funding, and thus unable to break away), low-profile insiders (working behind the scenes), and high-profile insiders (cultivating public opinion to reinforce their contact with government). Outsider groups he subdivided into potential insiders (working to gain insider status), outsiders by necessity (lacking the sophistication to gain insider status), and ideological outsiders (rejecting the existing political system and therefore not prepared to work within its rules and practices). Other commentators have since formulated alternative or similar distinctions. One set of authors supplemented the insider/outsider dichotomy with a third category: that of thresholder groups.[2] These are groups that oscillate between insider and outsider strategies. Trades unions were offered as examples of thresholder groups, sometimes adopting an outsider approach—standing apart from government—and at other times seeking insider status, wanting to be consulted by government on issues that affected them.

There is a rough correlation between sectional interest and insider groups and between promotional and outsider groups. The sectional interest groups already mentioned, for example, would mostly fall into the insider category and most of the promotional groups into the outsider category. However, the correlation is not exact. Some sectional interest groups may not be consulted regularly by government. Given their concerns, they may not seek to be consulted. A number of promotional groups may have achieved such high public status or may have developed such a specialist knowledge in their field that they are treated as legitimate by government and thus have insider status.

The insider-outsider categorization not only has a political focus but also is dynamic. That is, it admits of a group moving from one category to another. An outsider group may become an insider group. An insider group may produce such poor information or engage in activities that result in government deciding not to consult it, thus consigning it to outsider status. Grant's work thus allows us to see movement in a way that the sectional interest–promotional categorization does not. However, it has a similar limitation. Just as some groups do not fall exclusively within the domain of a sectional interest or a promotional group, so some groups do not fall squarely within the exclusive domain of an insider or outsider group: Both categories have their hybrids.

In this chapter, we shall treat the two sets of categorizations as being complementary rather than competing with one another, utilizing the established distinction between types of groups (sectional interest/promotional) and relating it to group status in relation to government (insider/outsider). For much of the twentieth century, sectional interest groups have been recognized as having achieved, in the main, insider status. Conversely, most promotional groups have been accorded outsider status. However, what we have witnessed in recent years has been a change in the relationship to government. In terms of high policy—policy that is concerned with the economic well-being and security of the nation—sectional interest groups have, to some extent, joined promotional groups in being outsiders to the decision-making process. In terms of medium- and low-level policy, especially policy adjustments and detailed policy implementation, promotional groups have tended to join sectional interest groups in enjoying, in some measure, insider status.

THE DEVELOPMENT OF INTEREST GROUPS

Interest groups in one form or another have existed for many years. Some existed in the fifteenth and sixteenth centuries—for example, various merchant guilds. The earliest, according to R. M. Punnett, was the fourteenth-century Convention of Royal Burghs in Scotland.[3] In succeeding centuries, various groups were formed. Some we would now recognize as sectional interest groups and some as promotional groups. There were various groups established in the nineteenth century to press for parliamentary reform or, in the 1840s, to achieve a repeal of the corn laws. Later on in the century, trade unions and employers' organizations began to be formed. However, the phenomenon of a large and diverse body of permanent, well-organized groups making demands of government is a relatively recent one, largely associated with the growth of government activity, especially in the years after the Second World War. "This surely was inevitable," wrote Robert McKenzie. "Once it had been largely agreed by all parties that the government (national and local) should collect and spend over a third of the national income, tremendous pressures were bound to be brought to bear to influence the distribution of the burdens and benefits of public spending on this scale."[4] Those pressures were channelled especially through and articulated by sectional interest groups. Groups needed government in order to ensure that their members got the share of the economic cake that they desired. Conversely, government needed the groups—for advice, for information, and for cooperation. The relationship became one of mutual dependence. Hence sectional interest groups became, predominantly, insider groups.

As government extended its activities into the economic and social life of the nation, and especially as it began to utilize Keynesian techniques of economic management, it came to depend on information on which it could base both particular and macroeconomic policies. Such information often could be supplied only by sectional interest groups. The groups were also in a position to offer advice. The nearer the actual membership of a group came to its potential membership (all solicitors are members of the Law Society, for example, and 75 percent of full-time farmers are members of the National Farmers Union of England and Wales), the closer the group came to enjoying a monopoly of the expertise and understanding peculiar to that section of society. "If doctors are powerful," writes one observer, "it is not just because of their characteristics as a pressure group but because of their functional monopoly of expertise."[5] Government also became dependent on such groups for cooperation in the implementation of policies. If groups are ill-disposed toward a government proposal that affects them, they have the sanction of withdrawing their support in the carrying out of that proposal. A policy of noncooperation may cause grave and sometimes insurmountable difficulties for government. The 1971 Industrial Relations Act, for example, failed largely because of the refusal of trade unions both to register under its provisions and to recognize the National Industrial Relations Court it created. The act was subsequently repealed. Such instances of noncooperation are rare, a sign not of group weakness but of political strength. Anticipation of opposition from affected groups will frequently induce government to refrain from pursuing a particular policy or, more likely, to seek some modification acceptable to the groups concerned; in 1989, for example, the Conservative government modified proposals for reform of legal services following opposition from the legal profession.

The growing interdependence of government and groups led some observers to view sectional groups as central to policy making. They saw the ideological gap between the parties as having narrowed, with government acting primarily as arbiter between competing group demands, seeking to meet the demands of groups while meeting the expectations of consumers. It was seen as the age of what Beer referred to as the "new group politics."[6] Whereas the electoral contest between parties may appear to emphasize an adversary relationship, the relationship between government and groups was perceived as a consensual one. To proceed with a given policy, government and the affected groups had to reach some measure of accord: One had to influence the other. In the formulation of public policy, government and groups could be seen increasingly as being inseparable.

The twentieth century thus witnessed a remarkable growth in the number of interest groups. The first half of the century witnessed especially the development of sectional interest groups. Insider groups were drawn principally from their ranks. The latter half of the century saw a notable expansion in the number of promotional groups, often single-issue groups. They have generally fallen into the category of outsider groups, though—as we have noted—the two are not synonymous, and some promotional groups have come to be treated as insider groups by government. There is, thus, a remarkable range of interest groups in existence. It is helpful, first, to flesh out the sheer diversity of such groups before addressing their relationship in recent years to government.

Sectional Interest Groups

There are at least several thousand bodies in Britain that constitute sectional interest groups. It is common to look at such groups under the three sectoral headings of labor, business, and agriculture. Although the business and labor sectors have "peak," or umbrella, organizations, they are notable for the number of groups that exist within them.

Labor. The groups within the labor sector comprise primarily trade unions. There are just over three hundred of these. Some are extremely small and specialized, whereas others are large and not confined to a particular industry or trade. Almost 40 percent of unions have memberships of under five hundred. The eight largest unions account for more than half of all union membership. Within the union movement, the older unions representing manual workers (such as miners) have suffered a dramatic decline in membership, and those representing white-collar workers (scientists, teachers, technicians, and other professional employees) have grown rapidly in recent years. The overall trend, though, has been one of decline. In the 1970s, over 40 percent of employed civilian workers were members of trade unions, the percentage reaching over 50 percent (in excess of

12 million workers) by the end of the decade. By 1995, the percentage had declined to 27 percent. The decline was greatest among male workers.[7]

The income of each union comes primarily from membership subscriptions and from interest on invested capital. (Union pension funds are among the major investors in Britain.) Annual subscriptions vary from union to union, ranging from a few pounds a year to in excess of £40 ($64). In return, unions provide a variety of services to members, such as insurance schemes, benevolent funds, discounts on purchases at certain stores, help with house purchases, strike funds, wage negotiations with employers, and the compiling and publishing of information useful to members. More than two-thirds of union expenditure is on working expenses (paying the salaries of full-time officials, rent, and running of headquarters), and most of the remaining one-third is spent on providing various benefits to members.

The "peak" organization for trade unions is the Trades Union Congress (TUC). In 1997, 75 unions were affiliated with it, representing some 6.7 million workers. Although a majority of trade unions are not affiliated, it is a far more inclusive body in terms of the large and important unions than is its equivalent in the United States, the AFL-CIO (the American Federation of Labor–Congress of Industrial Organizations). A number of the largest unions in the United States, such as the auto workers, are not affiliated with the U.S. body. In Britain, the largest unions are in the TUC. Indeed, the 75 affiliated unions represent more than three-quarters of all trade unionists.

The TUC coordinates the activities of its members and represents them in dealings with government. It has a number of specialist departments on topics such as economics and social affairs, and equality and rights; these departments research and compile data and help various specialist committees of the TUC to formulate policy. It provides a service of trade union education and it provides members to serve on various advisory and quasi-governmental bodies. It has an executive body, the General Council, which has 48 elected members and meets seven times a year. The chief executive officer is the General Secretary.

Three pertinent points can be made about trade unions. First, they are largely decentralized. The TUC annual congress constitutes at best a federal body. Individual unions are largely autonomous and often have difficulty in asserting their wishes over local branches. Most industrial work stoppages, for example, are unofficial, which means they take place without the official sanction of the union. (Since the relevant statistics on strikes began to be collected in 1960, unofficial strikes have accounted for more than 90 percent of strikes.) Second, the trade unions have a close relationship with the Labour party, much closer historically than has been the case between any union and party in the United States or in most other European countries. As we have seen (Chapter 6), the trade unions were the largest sponsoring element when the Labour party was formed, and they continue to be its main provider in both income and affiliated membership. This relationship may in part help explain the third feature. Although unions may and do seek to influence government policy on such issues as employment and the economy, union militancy and strikes are used to pursue wage claims rather than political ends. Overtly political strikes or "days of action" are rare; unions rather have looked to the Labour party to achieve their political goals.

Business.   In the business sector, sectional groups are equally if not more diverse. Although there is a well-known peak body for firms in industry, the Confederation of British Industry, it is far from all-encompassing. According to Wyn Grant and David Marsh, "There is a large and complex system of associations which look after the interests of individual industries or, in some cases, the interests of manufacturers of particular products, and many large firms deal directly with government."[8] Finance and the retail sector have their own structures and arrangements with government that are separate from those of the industry sector. "The City," the name given to the interests and institutions that inhabit the square mile of the City of London (Bank of England, the Stock Exchange, the Discount Market, the London Bankers' Clearing House, the commodity markets, insurance companies, and the like), is essentially a separate interest with its own structures and concerns, the latter not always compatible with those of business organizations. Company directors have their own organization in the form of the Institute of Directors (IoD), a highly organized body, with headquarters in Pall Mall, London; it has a somewhat greater free-market orientation than the CBI. There are chambers of commerce throughout the country, though they tend to be most active and effective at regional and local levels rather than on a national scale. In addition, there is a host of trade associations, important ones being bodies such as the Society of Motor Manufacturers.

These examples give some flavor of the diversity of business organizations. The most visible body, that which receives most academic and media attention, is the Confederation of British Industry (the CBI). It was formed in 1965 as a result of the amalgamation of the Federation of British Industries (known, confusingly to Americans, as the FBI), the British Employers' Confederation, and the National Association of British Manufacturers. It sought to bring together the resources of the amalgamated bodies to form a more efficient servicing body and a more effective representative of industry's needs in discussions with government. Indeed, its functions are not dissimilar to those of unions: It provides various services to its members and it seeks—its primary and explicit aim—to represent them in negotiations with government departments and with government generally. It provides advice and assistance on industrial problems; it provides information on such things as technical translation services, and conditions in foreign countries; it produces its own economic reports; and, in practice, it provides a medium through which firms and associations can make new and useful contacts. It seeks to act as a voice for the needs of industry, not only through making representations directly to government and through appointing representatives to various advisory bodies, but also now through its own annual conference, a relatively recent innovation. (The TUC, by contrast, has been holding annual conferences since the nineteenth century.) Its 1999 conference was addressed by all three main party leaders. A survey by Grant and Marsh found that the smaller firms in the CBI joined particularly because of the services it offered, whereas the larger industrial giants tended to join because of its position as a lobbying body on behalf of industry.[9]

Membership in the confederation is broad, though industrial companies are predominant. More than 250,000 public and private companies, and more than 200 trade associations, employer organizations, and commercial associations are members. Of the company members, over 90 percent of them have fewer than 200 employees. Most small firms, though, are not members; the smaller the firm, the less likely it is to be a member. (The Smaller Businesses Association claims to speak for such firms.) The biggest companies are more strongly represented, with about 80 of the top 100 companies in the United Kingdom being members. More than half of the CBI's income comes from the companies with more than 1,000 members (subscriptions being based on a company's salary bill and its U.K. turnover), and more than three-quarters comes from industrial companies. Income is used primarily to finance its staff of just over 300, headquarters in London's Centre Point, 12 regional offices, and an office in Brussels.

The main body within the CBI is its council, a 400-member body drawn from the employer, trade, and commercial associations, the public sector, 13 CBI Regional Councils, and a variety of companies. The council meets several times a year, but most of the work is conducted through a variety of standing committees, particularly the formulation of policy on industrial and economic questions. Within the council, the two most prominent and influential figures are the president, usually an industrialist drawn from one of the major companies, and the director-general, the full-time chief executive, usually drawn from a senior position in industry. As a result of the work of the council, the standing committees, and its regional councils, its claims that more than 2,500 people are involved in the CBI policy-making process.

Politically, the CBI has no formal link with any political party, but it has tended to be closely associated with the Conservative party, the party most closely associated with business. Although the CBI itself has never made any contribution to Conservative party funds, a number of its members are or have been contributors to party funds and, as we have seen (Chapter 6), a significant proportion of Conservative party income nationally derives from business donations. However, the links are now not as strong as they were.

Agriculture.   Although not an inclusive peak organization, the CBI nonetheless is more extensive than any similar body in the United States. Similarly, in the agriculture sector the National Farmers Union of England and Wales (NFU) is the predominant body; in the United States there are more obviously competing bodies in the form of the Farmers' Union, the National Grange, and the American Farm Bureau Federation. The NFU in 1998 had a membership of over

120,000, constituting approximately 70 percent of all full-time farmers in England and Wales. (There are separate NFUs in Scotland and Northern Ireland.) It also has categories of corporate membership (for farmer controlled businesses) and a countryside membership, for people who do not rely on farming for their main income but have an interest in the land (such as smallholders). In 1998, it had 38,000 countryside members. Each member of the NFU pays an annual subscription (a flat fee, plus a payment based on the size of the enterprise) and in 1996 the Union's income from subscriptions was £16.6 million ($26.5 million). The money is used to fund its staff and services as well as education campaigns designed to increase popular understanding of farming.

The NFU is by no means the only body seeking to represent farming interests. The Farmers' Union of Wales, for example, is now recognized by the Ministry of Agriculture as a representative body for the purposes of discussions on the annual farm price review. There are also bodies representing more specialized interests within the broad sector of agriculture, such as dairy producers.

Like its union and business counterparts, the NFU provides various services to members (including advice on legal, planning, and taxation matters) and also represents the interests of members in discussions with government. Unlike the two other sectors, the agriculture sector is covered primarily by one government department, the Ministry of Agriculture, Fisheries and Food, and so the relationship with government is more concentrated and, in many respects, more structured and discreet than is the case with the TUC and the CBI. The ministry and the NFU discuss on a regular basis the annual review of farm prices, and the union is represented on a host of advisory bodies.

Rather like the CBI, the union has a large national council, with the most influential members being the president and the general secretary. Below national level, the main unit of organization is the county branch, an often active and well organized body, particularly in the large agricultural counties. Although farmers are traditionally strong supporters of the Conservative party, the union nationally as well as at county level tends to adopt a strict political neutrality, though this is essentially of postwar origin. Before 1945 (the union was founded in 1908) it was more closely associated with the Conservative party, despite formal assertions of nonpartisanship.[10] Once a body with substantial political clout, the NFU in recent years has had to adopt a more defensive stance against what it sees as government indifference or even hostility towards the interests of farmers and of the countryside.

There is thus a mass of sectional interest groups. The CBI and the TUC in particular serve as umbrella organizations for a vast range of groups and the coverage of each is not exhaustive. There are a large number of bodies that fall outside these particular groupings. Many professional bodies, for example, are not affiliated to the TUC. As we have already noted, most small businesses are not members of the CBI. Diversity is thus a feature of sectional interest groups.

Promotional Groups

Promotional groups are even more diverse than sectional interest groups in that they generally lack umbrella organizations to draw them together. They are notable for their growth in recent years and for their diversity. Most sectors of public policy have seen the growth of such groups.

We have already had cause to touch upon the nature and range of promotional groups. Many are created for altruistic purposes and have charitable status. These include bodies concerned to improve the welfare of particular groups in society. The rubric includes animal as well as human welfare. Among the top one hundred charities by income are bodies such as Oxfam (helping the homeless), Help the Aged, the National Society for the Protection of Children (NSPCC), the Royal Society for the Protection of Animals (RSPCA), the Royal Society for the Protection of Birds (RSPB), and the National Association for the Care and Rehabilitation of Offenders (NACRO). In 1996–97, Oxfam had an income of £121 million ($193.6 million), Help the Aged one of £55.5m. ($88.8 million). Though precluded by their charitable status from engaging in overtly political activities, they still take stands on public policy. Many have their own parliamentary officers; some hire political consultants (lobbyists). Though many charities have been founded in recent decades, some are long established. Some also have impressive membership figures. The RSPB, for example, was founded in 1899 and now has a membership of 967,000. As some commentators have variously noted, this exceeds the combined membership of the three main political parties.

Other bodies, as we have noted, may be formed for ideological purposes and engage in overt political action; some may even engage in direct action. The bodies falling under this rubric are diverse and there is an overlap with the preceding category. Some bodies committed to animal welfare are overtly political bodies. Some confine their activities to working within the political system. Others take to the streets to make their voice heard. Among animal welfare groups, for instance, Compassion in World Farming lobbies MPs and government departments. Members of the League Against Cruel Sports variously disrupt fox hunts. Of groups pressing for gay rights, the leading pressure group, Stonewall, utilizes traditional lobbying methods, while a much smaller fringe group, Outrage, adopts more confrontational tactics. Some groups combine public demonstrations with more traditional methods of leafleting and lobbying politicians.

Some promotional groups are, as we have already noted, formed in response to existing groups. Some appear to be formed as a result of the success of a promotional group in a particular area. The Campaign for Nuclear Disarmament, one of the better known groups for organizing demonstrations and civil disobedience, was founded in 1958. Later years witnessed the formation of other groups, including European Nuclear Disarmament (END), as well as groups supporting the use of nuclear weapons.

One particular area of growth has been in the environmental field. The environmental group Greenpeace is now well established in the United Kingdom, as are a range of other, sometimes quite specific groups. These have included in recent years some direct action groups, including Reclaim the Streets, a group seeking to have streets used by pedestrians rather than motorists.

What emerges from this brief review is the diversity and the sheer extent of promotional groups in British politics. The numbers run into the thousands. Some, like the RSPB, have a large membership. Some have a handful of members. Increasingly, citizens are channelling their interests through organized groups. The postwar development of what Inglehart has termed *cognitive mobilization*[11]—citizens, through improved mass education and the mass media, being more aware of issues—has resulted in a greater interest and involvement in the political process, citizens forming groups to protect or further particular causes. Promotional groups are now a pervasive feature of the political landscape.

RELATIONS WITH GOVERNMENT

In terms of the relationship between interest groups and governments, three periods can be identified. The first period, up to the 1970s, was characterized by the institutionalization of the relationship between government and insider groups; by the development of particularly close relations between government and the peak organizations representing labor and business; and by the growth and political activity of outsider groups. The second period, as we shall see, saw insider groups moving more to outsider status in the sphere of high policy and of outsider groups moving more toward insider status in terms of middle-level and, more especially, low-level policy. The third period has seen the greater fragmentation of power with the creation of elected assemblies in different parts of the United Kingdom. Organized interests now seek to influence public policy through a number of government bodies, and not simply through a single U.K. Government department. What has been a feature of government–group relationships at the U.K level has now become a feature of relationships at other levels of government.

The Period up to 1979

Insider Groups: Institutionalization. As its responsibilities expanded, government came to have greater need of what groups could offer, and the groups, in turn, looked to government for the satisfaction of their demands. This relationship often necessitated frequent contact and increasingly became institutionalized. Groups not only were asked for advice on an informal or nonroutine basis, but also they became drawn into the processes of government by being invited to appoint representatives to serve on advisory bodies, tribunals, and committees of different sorts. This in itself is not a recent phenomenon. The National Health Insurance Act of 1924 provided for the functional representation of specific interests, such as the medical profession, on various committees appointed to administer the system of social insurance. Analogous provisions had appeared in the Trade Board acts of 1909 and 1918.

By the late 1950s, more than a hundred advisory bodies existed under statutory provision. The 1960s and 1970s witnessed the growth of bodies that comprised representatives of the CBI and the TUC as well as representatives of government. Examples of such bodies were the National Economic Development Council (the NEDC, known as "Neddy"), created in 1961 to provide a forum in which representatives of the three could meet to discuss the economy (and since disbanded); the Manpower Services Commission (since disbanded), to promote training and job creation schemes; the Health and Safety Commission, to help regulate and supervise safety and health at work; and the Advisory, Conciliation and Arbitration Service (known as ACAS), to help resolve industrial disputes. At the same time, various bodies at a lower level proliferated in number, to consider more specialized topics and to bring together representatives of the various core (as opposed to peak) groups. Between 1974 and 1978, for example, 11 new governmental bodies were created in the sector covered by the Department of the Environment. These included an advisory group on commercial property development and an advisory board of construction experts.[12] A report on such bodies in 1978 identified more than 1,560 advisory bodies and nearly 500 similar bodies with executive powers (to issue regulations, dispense funds, and carry out similar functions), such as the Manpower Services Commission.[13] Methods of appointment to these disparate bodies varied. In some cases there were statutory requirements to include representatives of particular groups, and in other cases the power was vested with the relevant minister, who could appoint people in a representative capacity (on behalf of a group) or in an individual capacity (drawn from but not officially representing a particular group). What is significant for our purposes is the number of such bodies and the extent to which they were staffed by, and indeed would be unable to function without, members of affected interest groups.

It is important to remember that such bodies constituted the formal, institutional embodiment of the close relationship between insider groups and government departments. Over and above these, there was regular contact between groups and departments through formal and informal meetings, sometimes through formal or informal social gatherings. At the level of regular contact, for example, the National Farmers Union and the Ministry of Agriculture followed well established procedures each year in discussing the annual price review. Each year, the two were in constant touch with one another, indeed "almost hourly contact" according to one study.[14] There was similar contact between other departments and groups within their sphere of responsibility.

What emerges from even this brief review of the institutionalization of group–departmental relationships is its range and diversity, which should not be surprising. Groups, as we have seen, are remarkably diverse, with peak organizations being at best federal or confederal bodies. Government departments are not dissimilar in diversity. Usually a department is divided into a number of functional units. The relevant outside groups will discuss a proposal with the relevant unit—comprising civil servants—and if agreement is reached, the proposal is then "sold" to the department itself before, if necessary, it is put forward for approval at a higher level. Only major policy decisions percolate up to the cabinet for discussion and approval. Most middle- and virtually all low-level policy is made at departmental and subdepartmental levels. There are functional and legal, as well as cultural, reasons encouraging this practice. The range and extent of government policy making is such that the cabinet is able to deal with only a fraction of it. Formally, legal powers are vested in individual ministers (not the cabinet), and for a proposal to be authoritative and enacted, it is often sufficient for a minister to give it formal approval. Furthermore, the political culture favors consensus within these small policy communities of officials and group representatives. Disputes are neither sought nor encouraged. It is to the advantage of both group and civil servants to avoid dissent. Each needs the other, and disputes could jeopardize their relationship as well as pass the problem on for others to resolve. A desire to decide the issue for themselves impels civil servants and the groups to seek agreement. One of the characteristics of the British policy style, according to Jordan and Richardson, is that of "bureaucratic accommodation."[15]

A combination of this diversity and institutionalization has important implications for the nature of policy making in Britain, for it favors incrementalism. This situation has tended to create problems for any government seeking to impose a comprehensive new policy on both its own departments and affected groups. Departments or their various units have often become so closely associated with the groups with which they deal that they tend to represent the interests of the groups to the government rather than (or in addition to) representing the interests of government to the groups. This position, sometimes referred to as a form of "clientelism," results in departments speaking on behalf of different interests and often competing among themselves where those interests are not compatible. Thus, a government determined to cut public expenditure has the task of imposing cuts upon departments that are keen to resist them and that come up with plausible arguments for their own exemption, arguments that have the backing of the department's clientele groups. For example, cuts in the defense budget are likely to be resisted by officials, sometimes the minister (if persuaded by department officials), as well as by the armed services and the various industries that help manufacture and maintain military hardware and equipment. Similarly, cuts in other departments are resisted on analogous grounds, ministers competing to defend their own departmental budgets. For government to impose a comprehensive policy, it has to persuade a variety of policy communities to agree to that policy. Although a party manifesto might provide a government with its plan of action, achieving that plan is a task for which neither the manifesto nor control of a party majority in the House of Commons may be sufficient.

Insider Groups: Tripartism.   By the 1970s, the relationship between governments and groups was institutionalized. This was primarily the case in determining middle-level policy, that is, policy not at the heart of government policy, and low-level policy, that is, the detail for implementing policy. In the 1970s, it was also to become a feature of high-level policy making, with peak organizations being drawn in for discussions with the prime minister and other senior ministers to determine economic policy.

As we have seen, in the 1960s and 1970s, representatives of the CBI and the TUC were variously co-opted onto a range of bodies. In addition, negotiations with government, often at prime-ministerial level, were common; Labour Prime Minister Harold Wilson was keen to consult with the two peak organizations—in 1966, he told the House of Commons it was the government's duty to consult with them—and Conservative Prime Minister Edward Heath sought to arrange a voluntary prices-and-pay policy with both bodies in 1972. However, the relationship became a feature especially of the period from 1974 to 1979.

During this period, there was an especially close relationship between government and the trade unions. The government negotiated with the TUC a "social contract" that entailed the government's introducing various measures (on employment law, for example) favored by the unions, in return for which the unions moderated wage demands. In 1976 the chancellor of the exchequer, Denis Healey, made a 3 percent reduction in income tax conditional on the acceptance of pay restraint by trade unions. The decision invoked a political storm, Conservative and Liberal politicians asserting that the final say on the levying of taxation was being transferred from Parliament to the trade unions.[16] The relationship that developed between government, and especially certain trade union leaders, was seen as an intimate one. By the end of the 1970s opinion polls demonstrated that the unions—and particular union leaders—were considered "too powerful." There were fears that other groups, as well as the public interest, were being excluded from the process; a pluralist system was being stifled by corporatist tendencies.

There was a close relationship at times between the government and the representatives of finance. The CBI, as we have seen, was variously integrated into formal bodies. On other occasions, its support was sought for particular policies. At times, various bodies were drawn together. The government had, in effect, to negotiate with the TUC, the International Monetary Fund, the CBI, the City of London, and (if not negotiate, at least take into account) the House of Commons to achieve the economic policy it wanted.

Various peak organizations were thus variously co-opted, at times on an institutionalized or semi-institutionalized level, into the process of making high-level policy. The nature and frequency of meetings at 10 Downing Street involving union representatives became popularized in the term "beer and sandwich" meetings, implying talks while beer and sandwiches were brought in to sustain the participants. Union as well as business leaders became used to being consulted by government.

Outsider Groups: Greater Activity. The growth and incorporation of insider groups was a particular feature of the period, especially the 1970s. Another was the growth and, by definition, nonincorporation of outsider groups. The growth of such groups we have touched upon already. The period between 1960 and 1979 was a notable period of pressure group formation.

Most outsider groups were, and remain, promotional groups. They fell into the outsider category largely for three reasons. The first reason was the fact that they generally lacked the political clout enjoyed by sectional interest groups. They usually lacked a monopoly of information and expertise, and certainly did not have information and expertise needed by government. As we have already noted, a feature of promotional groups is that there is no exclusive membership. Their potential membership, technically, constitutes the entire population. They have few, if any, sanctions that they can employ against government if it proves unresponsive to their overtures. In short, they were largely without the attributes enjoyed by the sectional interest groups in achieving leverage in their relationship with government. A second reason, specific to the period though not applicable to all groups, was the very newness of the groups. Ministers and officials were wary of groups that had not had an opportunity to establish their credentials. That tendency was likely to have been exacerbated if, in order to attract attention, the groups engaged in public demonstrations. The third reason, specific to a number of groups, was that some groups were ideologically unacceptable. There was little likelihood, for example, that the Ministry of Defense was going to accord insider status to the Campaign for Nuclear Disarmament. Indeed, given the causes promoted by some groups, a government may be keen to keep some of them at arm's length.

To achieve their goals, promotional groups, by virtue of their outsider status, often found themselves compelled to seek support outside the corridors of government departments. This often took the form of trying to attract support from Parliament, either directly or indirectly. Direct contact with MPs took the form of letters or pamphlets sent to all MPs or, in the case of better organized groups, to MPs likely to be sympathetic to their cause and, increasingly, through lobbying of members by group supporters. Sympathetic MPs, some of whom held office in the groups (quite often as honorary vice presidents), variously arranged for delegations from a group to meet with other MPs or even a minister, or else they asked parliamentary questions or, in some cases, introduced private members' bills. For outsider groups, private members' bills were a particularly attractive way of pursuing their cause, especially if the government was unwilling to act. Indirectly, groups sought to influence MPs through mass demonstrations, marches, public meetings, and press releases. In the absence of extremely large numbers or violence, attracting publicity by such means was an uphill struggle. The various means were not mutually exclusive. A campaign would often encompass a demonstration, a petition, or a campaign of writing letters to MPs.

The success of these groups varied considerably. The fact of outsider status did not necessarily doom a campaign to failure. It did mean, though, that the groups had to try much harder than insider groups to make their voice heard within government. Some groups achieved success through private members' legislation in the 1960s, when government was not unsympathetic but was not willing to commit itself publicly to introducing the measures. Several major measures of social reform—on divorce, abortion, homosexuality, the death penalty, and theater censorship—were enacted as private members' bills.[17] Such success, though, was exceptional. Some groups made some headway, achieving some action or concession. Others worked hard but often to little avail, at least in terms of government action.

Many of the features of British promotional groups, and indeed the causes pursued, are not dissimilar to those of U.S. promotional groups. Both benefited in this period from the development of television, which gave them more visual impact through their public demonstrations and lobbies. British groups, though, were—and remain—more limited than their U.S. counterparts by virtue of the strength of party. On an issue about which a party stance was taken, an MP could hide behind his or her party's position in responding to group pressure. It was, and it remains, an effective shield. Promotional groups present no significant threat to a sitting MP. They stand no chance of persuading electors to vote the MP out at the next election, because the party label will normally determine whether the MP stays or goes. Groups will have no leverage through campaign donations: Donations go to parties and, as we have seen, local campaign expenditure is strictly controlled. Occasionally, issues become divisive within parties—for example, capital punishment in the Conservative party or abortion in the Labour party—but rarely do they impinge upon an MP's chosen behavior or continuance as a party candidate. Even where they do, it is not because of group activity. A good constituency MP who remains loyal to party will have little difficulty in ignoring any promotional groups that he or she chooses to ignore.

This is not to argue that MPs did not align themselves with or were not persuaded by promotional groups. Many were associated with such groups and not infrequently served as active advocates of a group's cause. The point is that MPs were in a much stronger position than members of Congress to resist pressure from groups with which they—or their party—were not in sympathy. MPs did not need such groups and rarely could groups be considered a threat to their political survival.

This point is essential to understanding the distinction between insider and outsider groups. If government granted access to a group, it was an insider. If it denied access, it was an outsider. The strength of party made it difficult for a group to achieve access by alternative routes. The government had a supportive majority in the House of Commons. For outsider groups to have any influence on public policy, they need at least government acquiescence. In the United States, the barriers were not so sharp—party was not such a protective shield—and the distinction between insider and outsider status less relevant in explaining the genesis and development of public policy.

By the 1970s, interest groups were thus a major and integral part of the British political process. The period since the 1940s had seen a remarkable growth in the number of groups. The growth was especially marked in the period between 1960 and 1979. Of pressure groups and representative organizations listed in one directory published in 1979, more than 42 percent had come into existence since 1960.[18] Insider groups had a largely institutionalized relationship with government, not usually needing to seek publicity for their activities. Peak organizations enjoyed access at the highest levels of government. Outsider groups, by definition, lacked such access but were vigorous in promoting their cause. However, taking their cause to Parliament was generally viewed as an admission of failure and unlikely to admit of success in a body where the government dominated the proceedings.

The Period of Conservative Government, 1979–1997

Under the Conservative government of Margaret Thatcher, elected in 1979, there was a radical departure from past practice. The divorce from the past was not total. Indeed, we can identify two features of the period, one much commented upon, the other less noted. The first change was radical and much noticed. That was the attempt, at the level of high policy, to exclude groups from policy deliberations. As a result, peak organizations, especially the TUC, moved essentially from insider to outsider status. The second was less noticed. In seeking to influence middle- and low-level policy, outsider groups tended to make greater and more effective use of Parliament—and on occasion achieve some success. Peak organizations, pushed from insider status, also made greater use of Parliament. The consequence was a greater visibility for Parliament and a blurring of the distinction between insider and outsider groups. Lobbying by interest groups, whether insider or outsider, has become a feature of the political landscape.

High Policy: Exclusion.   To achieve its neoliberal economic policy, the Thatcher government began to disengage itself from anything that smacked of corporatist relationships. The goal of a free-market economy was nonnegotiable and corporatism distorted market forces. The government sought autonomy in policy making and, at the same time, wished to restrict bodies seen as employing restrictive practices. The trade unions were seen as a particular target. They moved from the status of insiders to that of outsiders. The government introduced a number of legislative measures to reform the unions, limiting their capacity to strike and to impose closed shops, as well as attempting to break up monopolistic practices in other sectors. "Beer and sandwich" meetings at No. 10 came to an abrupt end.

By withdrawing from bipartite and tripartite relationships, the government removed an obstacle to the realization of goals by other groups. However, by virtue of its free-market orientation, it also became, especially at the level of high policy or any policy that derived from its free market objective, less responsive to demands made by those groups. The government did not assume a position as independent arbiter, and certainly not at the level of economic policy making. In terms of economic policy, policy making was formulated by government and then imposed.

Groups thus faced the problem of how to make their voice heard by government in the making of high policy. As we shall see, they were still heard at the lower levels, but at the upper levels they had notably less input than before. The answer for many groups was, and remains, to engage in extensive, more open, and more professional lobbying—that is, directly and on their own initiative, extolling their cases to decision makers. The years since 1979 have seen the emergence of the lobbyist.

Medium and Low-Level Policy: Inclusion.   One much neglected aspect of the period since 1979 has been the extent to which, at the level at which government departments develop policy, groups retained insider status or acquired insider status. Despite the arm's-length relationship established between government and groups on high policy, there has been continuing contact between departments and insider groups, and a willingness on the part of departments to draw in more outsider groups. Departments continue to need sectional interest groups for information. Ministers have continued to meet with group representatives and to keep abreast of groups' activities and thinking.[19] In consulting on proposed delegated legislation (usually detailed proposals to give effect to particular provisions of Acts of Parliament), departments have consulted widely, including groups that would previously have been categorized as outsider groups. The inclusion of such groups would appear in some cases to be the consequence of the groups having established their credentials as serious organizations with advice that may be helpful. Thus, for instance, Greenpeace—which would have been classed as an outsider group in its early years—now appears on the list of groups sent draft delegated legislation in its area of interest. So extensive nowadays is the consultation with interested groups that there almost appears little relevance, at least at this level, to the distinction between insider and outsider groups.[20]

The nature of this inclusion, though, should not be misunderstood. The inclusion of groups did not necessarily mean that their advice was taken. Nor did it mean that they were necessarily consulted about policy initiatives. For groups to influence public policy, they may need to be proactive, especially if they wish to see a new policy introduced. They may also need to take action to get noticed if other groups are busy making a pitch to ministers. A greater degree of consultation does not necessarily imply that all groups enjoy equal access. Some groups remain better regarded by government than others. Groups may still need, therefore, to lobby politicians. Indeed, that need has arguably been greater as a consequence of two of the developments we have identified. One is the growth in the number of groups. The more groups there are, the more each one has to work harder to get noticed. Furthermore, if groups taking an opposing view are created, the more you have to work to counter their activities. The second development was the stance taken by the Thatcher government towards peak groups. Though the practice of exclusion did not percolate down to all groups, it nonetheless generated the perception that the government was unreceptive to group pressure. Groups, whether insider or outsider, thus felt the need to lobby government to be heard and, to complement that, to lobby Parliament. No group wanted to be left out and therefore lobbying became a marked feature of British politics. It encompassed lobbying of both government and Parliament.

Lobbying Government. Ministers and civil servants remain the principal targets of group lobbying.[21] Groups that are consulted but have not found their views accepted, and groups—often promotional groups—that are not consulted at all, will utilize in-house or professional lobbyists to make their case to the relevant minister or official. Many large companies now have their own in-house parliamentary or public affairs divisions, responsible for relations with government departments and Parliament. Others employ the services of independent political lobbyists, known formally as political consultants. Before 1979, there were hardly any firms of political consultants. By the mid 1990s, there were more than 40 such firms, the largest with about 30 or 40 employees, supplemented by a three-figure number of freelance consultants.

Most big companies and financial concerns—including, for instance, British Airways, Citibank, Procter and Gamble, Unilever, and Boeing—now retain political consultants.[22] The practice of hiring consultants is not confined to commercial organizations. Lobbying firms are also used by sectional bodies such as the Bar as well as by a host of promotional groups, ranging from animal welfare organizations to bodies promoting the social sciences. The work of lobbyists has been supplemented by the appearance of a number of books and guides on lobbying;[23] among those producing such a guide is the CBI. The result has been a more crowded and proactive field of groups seeking to make their existence and their needs known to targeted ministers and officials. The task is facilitated by the fact that political consultancy firms frequently recruit staff from former civil servants and, in some cases, former ministers.[24] Indeed, as we shall see, the hiring of former Labour policy advisers following the election of a Labour government in 1997 was to cause political controversy.

Lobbying Parliament. Lobbying government has added a new dimension to the relationship between groups and government departments. However, much more dramatic has been the growth in parliamentary lobbying. Parliament has always been a target of groups seeking some change in the law, but for much of the twentieth century it has not been regarded as the principal target of those seeking change. Promotional groups have variously used it, sometimes to effect (as with the social reform measures of the 1960s) but usually to no effect. Recognition of the limitations of lobbying Parliament resulted in many sectional groups not even bothering. They had their links with departments; in seeking to achieve some change in policy, those links were necessary and sufficient. The period since 1979 has seen a change in the perceptions, and consequently the practice, of such groups. They have made far greater use of Parliament than ever before.

A survey in 1986 of more than 250 organized groups, ranging from the CBI to small charities, found that one-fifth of them hired political consultants and, more significantly, three-quarters of them had regular or frequent contact with one or more MPs.[25] It is now common for groups to circulate briefing material to MPs and to have officers or lobbyists present during the committee proceedings on a bill. During the passage of one particular bill, more than eighty references were made by MPs on the committee to representations made by outside groups.[26] The MP's daily mailbag now bulges with material from pressure groups.[27] Though ministers and civil servants remain the principal focus of group activity, Parliament constitutes an important and growing target for such activity as well.

There are a number of reasons for this change in group behavior toward Parliament.[28] One, as we have seen, is that groups have looked elsewhere for other channels for getting their views heard by ministers and civil servants. However, Parliament itself has variously added to its own attractiveness. Greater behavioral independence has meant that MPs—and peers—may not only be willing but also more able than before to influence public policy (see Chapter 12). The creation of a series of departmental select committees also has provided a focus for group lobbying. Previously, groups had to rely on finding and using a few sympathetic MPs, and to hope that they might be able to pursue their cause on the floor of the Commons. The opportunities were rare and usually fruitless. Government controlled the parliamentary timetable. Select committees now determine their own agenda and, by concentrating on particular departments, act as magnets for groups seeking to influence those departments. The televising of proceedings has further added to the attractiveness of the institution for pressure groups seeking to put their case before government and the wider public.

Since 1979, lobbying has resulted in some notable instances of policy modification or even withdrawal. The extent of this influence is not amenable to precise quantification: Causal linkages between group lobbying and government action cannot usually be proved. Nonetheless, there have been some significant, and observable, examples of effective group pressure. In the 1980s, the most significant instance was the defeat of the Shops Bill, introduced to liberalize the law on Sunday trading. Pressure groups were active in lobbying both for and against the bill. A coalition of trade unions and religious groups, including the Church of England, lobbied against the bill and employed the services of a lobbying firm. Their campaign was stunningly effective: 72 Conservative MPs voted with Labour MPs against the bill, producing a notable defeat for the government.[29] Other instances are on a less dramatic scale, but encompass changes to bills and to government policy—on issues as diverse as the regulation of financial services, the sale of alcohol at football grounds, and broadcasting.[30] A number of policy proposals implemented by the incoming Labour government in

1997 may also be seen to have their genesis in group pressure, including the policy of banning the private ownership of handguns.[31]

Lobbying the European Union.   Lobbying has not been confined to the U.K. government and Parliament. It also occurs at the level of the European Union. Though the United Kingdom became a member of the then-European Community in 1973 (see Chapter 9), it was only in the 1980s that organized interests began to see the value of lobbying at a supranational level. Direct elections to the European Parliament took place in 1979. The Single European Act, which came into force in 1987, extended the powers of EC institutions. There was a new layer of policy making and one that companies began to realize had potentially major implications for how they operated. More and more firms and trade associations, as well as political lobbyists, began to set up offices in Brussels. The principal political consultancies in London established branches in Brussels. Lobbying of the Directorates General of the European Commission became big business. The Directorates General were accessible bodies and consultation on proposals was usually extensive. At this level, the distinction between insider and outsider groups also appears rather blurred. The institutions of the EC were willing to consider representations from any body with an interest in the subject under consideration.

The lobbying at a supranational level became more intense as the powers of the European Community were extended by the treaty on European Union (the Maastricht Treaty, 1992), creating a three-pillar European Union. For many large organizations—commercial, consumer, and environmental—ensuring that their voices were heard in Brussels became as, and in many cases more, important than getting their cases heard in London.

For organized interests, the access points to the policy-making process thus became more numerous. Instead of simply establishing contacts with Whitehall (U.K. government departments) they now had to establish contacts at Westminster (the U.K. Parliament) and Brussels (the EC Commission and committees of the European Parliament). Not only that, for some there was also another avenue for influencing public policy: the Strand, in London, home of the high court. If groups felt that a government department was acting beyond its legal powers, or in conflict with European law, it could take the case to court and, increasingly, groups did so. Seeking judicial review became, as we shall see, a feature of the period.

Groups thus had to lobby to get their voices heard. Increasingly, they had to compete with other groups to ensure that they were heard. Lobbying thus became the order of the day and it also became more extensive as organized interests entered the field to ensure their case did not go by default.

The Period Since 1997

Lobbying is thus extensive and visible—and has remained so under the Labour government elected in 1997. Groups remain as keen as under a Conservative government to influence policy, ministers continue to adopt an inclusive policy—especially in determining the detail of policy implementation—and political consultancies continue to pitch for business. What has changed in the period since 1997 has been the further fragmentation of power. There are now new layers of government and thus additional sources of lobbying by organized interests.

For groups keen to influence public policy, the sites of policy making have been extended to include Edinburgh (home of the Scottish executive) and Cardiff (home of the Welsh executive). The courts have also increased in significance as a consequence of the incorporation into British law of the European Convention on Human Rights.

The creation of a Scottish parliament and a Welsh assembly has meant that groups with an interest in public policy in Scotland and Wales have to lobby members of the new executives and the elected bodies. The emphasis in both has tended to be one of inclusion, again eroding the distinction between insider and outsider groups. Many lobbying firms now have offices in different parts of the United Kingdom. Because of the powers devolved to Scotland (see Chapter 10), Edinburgh has been the most important site for such firms.

The incorporation of the European Convention on Human Rights (ECHR) also offers new opportunities for organized interests to achieve their goals. Any perceived infringement of rights under the Convention and a body can now take a case to the British courts. Such is the expected impact of the incorporation of the ECHR that judges received training in how to handle such cases. The incorporation of the ECHR provides notable opportunities for cause groups—especially those concerned with civil liberties—to pursue cases through the courts.

Both these developments—the creation of the new assemblies and the incorporation into the British law of the ECHR—will be considered in detail in later chapters. They have been supplemented by further moves toward European integration, most notably with the coming into force of the Amsterdam Treaty in 1999. For the moment, it is sufficient to note them for the purpose of establishing the disparate points of access for groups seeking to influence the policy-making process. A single focus, the preserve largely of insider groups, has given way to several, and those points of access are open to a wide array of groups. The situation is one that organized interests in the United States, used to multiple access points, will have some familiarity with.

EXPLANATIONS OF GROUP BEHAVIOR

Group behavior has thus been notable in the twentieth century, especially the latter half of the century. It has also variously changed. Various models have been formulated to help further understanding of such behavior. The three most important for our purposes are the pluralist, the rational action, and the corporatist. They have some utility for giving shape to group behavior in recent decades.

The Pluralist Model

The basic premise of the pluralist model is that the political system provides an essentially neutral process through which government acts as an arbiter between competing group demands. Within the political process, the essential element is the group, with individuals having the opportunity to join groups and then, through those groups, having some input into the making of public policy. Pluralists emphasize the extent and range of groups, their access to government, and the competition among them.[32] There is presumed to be a balance between groups, no one group enjoying supremacy, with the balance and institutionalized relationship between groups and government providing for stability in the political system and incremental policy making.

The model, like all models, is an ideal one, but one that its proponents believe provides a reasonably close fit with U.S. and British experience. Our description of groups in Britain provides some basis for this assertion. There is a large and diverse range of groups. Their numbers have increased dramatically since 1960. A huge proportion of the population are members of groups. There are many groups with mutually countervailing goals, with government being called upon to choose among their competing demands. Incrementalism has been a predominant feature of policy making. Furthermore, after 1979, groups not only competed more with one another, but government also adopted a more autonomous stance.

The pluralist thesis, however, does not go unchallenged. Marxist and elite theorists dispute the neutral role of government.[33] The extent of balance and participation is also challenged. Insider groups, by definition, have enjoyed greater access to policy makers than do outsider groups. Some sectional groups wield greater influence than others. The City of London, for example, insofar as it represents a coherent single interest, is a powerful body that has few obvious and comparable countervailing groups. During the period of Conservative rule from 1979 to 1997, government may have been more autonomous of groups, at least at the level of high policy, but it did not adopt a neutral stance. Furthermore, group membership is not evenly spread: Group activity is disproportionately a middle-class pursuit. Many groups have not developed democratic structures and extensive member participation.[34] Some have no provision for electing officers nor the means for consulting members: The Automobile Association, for example, claims to speak for motorists, yet has not developed procedures for seeking the opinion of those who join its ranks.

The pluralist model also is criticized for failing to take into account the impact of political parties and of elections in policy making. Parties, as Richard Rose found, may not have a profound impact on economic indicators, but they do have *some* impact.[35] A party in office adopts a particular program and usually manages to implement most of it.[36] Groups thus have to operate within a framework shaped by parties, a feature of the British system that is largely missing in the United States.

The Rational Action Model

This model, deriving in large part from the work of Mancur Olson,[37] interprets group strength as a function of the members' reasons for joining. It contends that people join a group only if a rational calculation of costs and benefits shows that their personal welfare would be improved if they became group members.

Groups that are all-encompassing—that is, are able to negotiate benefits intended only for their members—are in a strong position to recruit members. These groups include professional bodies in which membership is necessary to remain and to progress in a given profession—for example, the British Medical Association and the Law Society. They are well organized and powerful bodies, enjoying influence in relation both to their members and to government.

Groups that are not all-encompassing, that negotiate benefits to be enjoyed by members and nonmembers alike (for example, wage raises), are in a weaker position to recruit members. These include most promotional groups; generally, what they can offer to their members exclusively is advice and information. Such groups tend to be weak and often are poorly organized.

The model is helpful in understanding the "pluralist stagnation" argument advanced by Samuel Beer and others (see Chapter 3). The absence of all-encompassing groups militates against the ability of government and groups to formulate and impose policies in the public interest. The range of groups, which are pursuing the interests of members who have joined to benefit their own and not the public interest, results in a lack of agreement, each group recognizing that by itself it cannot produce the end desired by government for the public good. One group's accepting the need for moderation in wage demands, for example, will have little effect if all other groups do not follow suit. The consequence, according to Beer's analysis, is pluralist stagnation.

This model tends to draw attention to inequalities among groups and hence is not strictly compatible with the pluralist model. Like pluralism, however, it has been subject to a number of important criticisms. It fails to offer an explanation for the existence of well organized and influential promotional interest groups. Olson excludes "philanthropic" groups from his analysis, yet it is these groups that have shown the most rapid expansion in numbers in recent years.[38] The welfare of a promotional group member may not benefit from membership, but the moral or ideological stance of the group moves some people to commit both their time and their money to a particular cause. For example, some members of Greenpeace risk personal injury in their attempts to prevent the slaughter of animals. This model also does not explain extensive membership of sectional groups that negotiate benefits that can be enjoyed by nonmembers. The study of the CBI by Grant and Marsh found that many members, particularly a number of large- and medium-sized firms, were aware that nonmembers could receive some of the benefits (such as research reports) they received as members and that, as members, they did not receive value for money.[39] Many firms had not even attempted to do a cost-benefit analysis of membership.

The Corporatist Model

Of all the models, this is probably the most contentious. Corporatism has been subject to various definitions, but basically it entails a system in which government directs the activities of industry, which remains predominantly in private hands, through the representatives of a limited number of singular, compulsory, noncompetitive, hierarchically ordered, and functionally differentiated interest groups.[40] *Societal* corporatism exists where government tends to be but one participant in a complex of negotiations with such groups. Where government is dominant in the relationship, there exists a form of *state corporatism.*[41]

Britain, on these definitions, has never enjoyed a pure form of corporatism. However, various writers have identified corporatist trends, based primarily on a tripartite relationship of government, employers, and trade unions. They have discerned that in practice this relationship has taken two forms: the co-option of representatives of employers and unions onto various bodies concerned with resolving disputes and discussing economic policy, and informal discussion between ministers and representatives of the CBI and TUC. The 1960s, as we have noted, saw the emergence of structured tripartite bodies such as the National Economic Development Council; discussions between ministers and leaders of unions and employers' bodies were already a feature of political life. Taken to its logical conclusion, tripartism would, as Edward Heath observed, be a relationship in which government, employers, and unions "share fully . . . the benefits and obligations of running the country."[42] It would, in other words, be societal corporatism.

Many writers on corporatism have been divided on its merits. Some see it as a threat to existing representative institutions, with decisions being taken by unelected bodies rather than by the citizens' elected representatives. Adherents to a free-market economy regard corporatism as a direct threat and are vigorous in their condemnation of it. In contrast, some economists and political scientists considered that some form of tripartism, or a more full-blooded form of corporatism, would offer the best way of dealing with Britain's economic problems.[43] They feel that corporatism would allow government to persuade or induce groups to give up the pursuit of narrow goals in favor of the national interest. Marxists provide a somewhat different interpretation: They see corporatism as a device used to defend capitalism and, according to some Marxist analyses, to incorporate the working class into a system dominated by business interests.

Tripartism was much discussed in the 1970s and assumed to be a description of what was happening. However, it was inadequate to explain fully the relationships that developed. Some negotiations, as we have seen, were essentially multipartite or bipartite. Yet, though the concept of tripartism was descriptively inadequate, the period of the mid- to late-1970s clearly witnessed the basic feature of negotiation intrinsic to societal corporatism. The unions in particular, but by no means exclusively, were co-opted into the process of determining public policy. This was in part institutionalized—and much of the institutionalization was on a tripartite basis—and in part based on ad hoc gatherings as occasion demanded.

The Conservative government elected in 1979 was opposed to anything that smacked of corporatism. However, corporatist tendencies in the form of tripartism had failed before Margaret Thatcher entered No. 10. Though tripartism was highly visible and, in the eyes of critics, too strong an influence on public policy, it failed because of its intrinsic weakness. This is where the rational action model is useful in helping us understand what happened. The TUC and CBI were, and remain, loose umbrella organizations, lacking the power to enforce discipline on their members. Not all unions were affiliated with the TUC, and those that were put the interests of members first and the interests of the TUC second. In the autumn and winter of 1978, wage claims were pressed for the benefit of members; a wave of strikes in the public sector followed. Far from being able to exert pressure from the top, TUC leaders were forced by pressure from activists below to repudiate renewal of a national pay policy. Though public opinion was clearly hostile to the industrial action that occurred, individual unions pursued their claims. According to Robert Taylor, workers were striving "through fragmented and localised bargaining, to hold their position relative to workers in other work-places and other industries," seeking at most "to climb a rung or two above those whose pay they traditionally compare with their own."[44] The result was "the Winter of Discontent" and the return of a Conservative government.

Of the various models, then, none is adequate to provide a comprehensive explanation of group behavior in Britain. Each provides some insight and cannot be discarded. The most relevant since 1979 is arguably the pluralist. Groups have become more numerous and they have had to compete more vigorously to have some input into government, a consequence of two developments: the growth in their number and of the position taken toward groups by government. The blurring of the distinction between insider and outsider groups also suggests a greater breadth of access. The fit with the pluralist model is not precise, but the model helps give shape to what is happening.

THE CURRENT DEBATE

The competitiveness engendered by greater pluralism can be seen in positive terms. It entails a greater involvement in political activity by organized interests. More and more citizens are finding some means of access to the political system through those interests. However, there is also a negative side. The system is not perfectly pluralist. Groups have to compete for access and some groups appear to achieve it more readily than others. The methods by which access appears to be gained have led to claims of "influence buying." Such claims have featured prominently in public debate, especially since 1994, leading to demands for a more regulated system of lobbying.

Groups that can afford lobbyists can achieve a degree of access to the political process that is likely to be denied to those without such resources. This criticism was fueled in the 1980s and early 1990s by the fact that many MPs were themselves political consultants, or were hired to advise consultants.[45] In addition, many civil servants were lured away to work for consultants (the Ministry of Defence, in particular, having a reputation as a "revolving door"),[46] thus ensuring that "insider" knowledge was available to clients who retained the consultants. These developments, according to *The Observer,* constituted "worryingly corrosive influences."[47] Criticisms of lobbying grew in volume and led to various investigations by committees of the House of Commons. The issue achieved especial prominence in 1994 when a national newspaper reported that two MPs, approached by an undercover reporter, had agreed to accept £1,000 ($1,600) each in return for asking parliamentary questions. It was immediately dubbed the "cash for questions" affair and generated extensive and enduring negative publicity. A Gallup poll found that 64 percent of those questioned believed that "most MPs make a lot of money by using public office improperly." (In 1985 the percentage giving that response was 46 percent.) Later the same year, another newspaper reported that another two MPs had accepted money from a businessman to ask questions. (Both, by this time, were ministers and, as a result of the story, left office.) The prime minister established a special committee, the Committee on Standards in Public Life, headed by a distinguished judge (Lord Nolan), to examine "current concerns" about standards of conduct of office holders and to make recommendations for changes that "might be required to ensure the highest standards of propriety in public life." In 1995, the committee came up with various recommendations for Members of Parliament.[48] After two heated debates, the House of Commons approved various changes, including the creation of a Parliamentary Commissioner for Standards, a new committee on standards, a code of conduct for MPs, a ban on paid advocacy, and the disclosure of income derived from service as an MP.

Subsequent investigations by the new parliamentary committee ensured that the issue of what was termed parliamentary "sleaze" continued to attract the headlines. One leading lobbying firm, implicated in the affair, went out of business.[49] The issue returned after the election in 1997 of a Labour government. In 1998, claims by a former Labour adviser, now working as a lobbyist, about his access to important figures in government attracted adverse publicity, as did claims that some other Labour advisers-turned-lobbyists had obtained and passed to a client an advance copy of a report of a parliamentary select committee. There were also allegations that a member of the Downing Street policy unit, a former lobbyist, had offered to put a businessman in touch with various people in government. The "cash for access" controversy generated further negative publicity, suggesting privileged access to the political system for those with the money to pay for it. Nor was the newly-elected Scottish parliament immune from such controversy. Shortly after its inception in 1999, accusations of privileged access—or claims to privileged access—were leveled at a lobbyist who was the son of the Secretary of State for Scotland, leading to an inquiry by the parliament.

The negative publicity served to mask the value of lobbying. On balance, lobbyists tend to facilitate rather than impede greater pluralism in the system. A group with a good case to make needs to get that case heard by government. Lobbying makes that possible. The more lobbyists at work, the more crowded the field and the less easy it is for a single group to dominate. The growing availability of freelance lobbyists serves to enhance the pluralist ideal through allowing more and more groups to achieve some greater degree of access to officials and politicians. Groups may not achieve what they want, but they have at least made their voice heard. Politicians and civil servants are well able to recognize lobbying activities and to separate effective argument from weak argument, in whatever form it is presented. Parliamentarians tend to be wary of material presented in too lavish a form. Material of no relevance to them finds its way into the wastebasket.

Lobbying by groups will nonetheless remain a point of controversy. Part of the problem derives from the activity being only partially observable; part derives from the fact that payment takes place for such activity. Given continuing criticism, some formal regulation of lobbyists may take place. (The principal lobbying firms have already introduced an element of self-regulation.) However, lobbying is certain to continue as a growth industry. Whatever the ethics of lobbying, groups are not likely to want to be left behind in the rush to influence public policy.

CONCLUSION

Pressure groups in Britain are numerous and diverse. Insider groups enjoy a frequent and fairly well institutionalized relationship with government departments. For peak organizations, the relationship with government became especially close, and structured, in the 1960s and 1970s, when tripartism became a feature, or at least a partial feature, of policy making. Since then, the field of policy making has become open and crowded. Increasingly, in order to influence policy, groups have resorted to lobbying government, Parliament, the institutions of the European Union, the new assemblies in Scotland and Wales, and the courts. By Capitol Hill standards, the development of lobbying is an extremely modest one, but it is growing and is likely to continue to do so. It offers the prospect of a more, rather than a less, pluralistic system of policy making.

NOTES

[1] W. Grant, *Pressure Groups, Politics and Democracy in Britain,* 2nd ed. (Harvester Wheatsheaf, 1995), p. 15.

[2] See Grant, p. 20.

[3] R. M. Punnett, *British Government and Politics* (Heinemann, 1970 ed.), p. 134.

[4] R. T. McKenzie, "Parties, Pressure Groups and the British Political Process," *Political Quarterly,* 29 (1), 1958.

[5] R. Klein, "Policy Making in the National Health Service," *Political Studies,* 22 (1), 1974, p. 6.

[6] S. H. Beer, *Modern British Politics,* rev. ed. (Faber, 1969), p. 326.

[7] *Social Trends 27* (London: The Stationery Office, 1997), p. 83.

[8] W. Grant and D. Marsh, *The CBI* (Hodder & Stoughton, 1977), p. 55.

[9] Grant and Marsh, pp. 44–50.

[10] P. Self and H. Storing, "The Farmer and the State," in R. Kimber and J. Richardson (eds.), *Pressure Groups in Britain* (Dent, 1974), pp. 58–59.

[11] R. Inglehart, *The Silent Revolution: Changing Values and Political Styles among Western Publics* (Princeton University Press, 1977).

[12] J. Richardson and G. Jordan, *Governing under Pressure* (Martin Robertson, 1979), p. 61.

[13] *Report on Non-Departmental Public Bodies,* Cmnd. 7797 (Her Majesty's Stationery Office, 1980), p. 5.

[14] G. K. Wilson, *Special Interests and Policy Making* (Wiley, 1977), quoted in Richardson and Jordan, p. 114.

[15] G. Jordan and J. Richardson, "The British Style or the Logic of Negotiation?" in J. Richardson (ed.), *Policy Styles in Western Europe* (Allen & Unwin, 1982), p. 81.

[16] P. Norton, *The Constitution in Flux* (Martin Robertson, 1982), pp. 272–275.

[17] See especially P. G. Richards, *Parliament and Conscience* (Allen & Unwin, 1970).

[18] P. Shipley, *Directory of Pressure Groups and Representative Organisations* (Bowker, 1979).

[19] See especially P. Norton, "The New Barons? Senior Ministers in British Government?" paper presented at the Birkbeck College-ESRC-Civil Service Public Service Seminar, British Academy, London, July 10, 1998.

[20] See especially E. C. Page, "Insider and Outsider Groups: An Empirical Examination," unpublished manuscript, 1998.

[21] M. Rush, "Parliament and Pressure Politics—An Overview," in M. Rush (ed.), *Parliament and Pressure Politics* (Clarendon Press, 1990), p. 272.

[22] C. Grantham and C. Seymour-Ure, "Political Consultants," in Rush, *Parliament and Pressure Politics,* pp. 45–84.

[23] As, e.g., D. Wilson, *Pressure: The A to Z of Campaigning in Britain* (Heinemann, 1984); M. Davies, *Politics of Pressure* (BBC, 1985); A. Dubbs, *Lobbying: An Insider's Guide to the Parliamentary Process* (Pluto Press, 1989); C. Miller, *Lobbying* (Blackwell, 1990).

[24] See Grantham and Seymour-Ure, pp. 50–56, 58–59.

[25] Rush, *Parliament and Pressure Politics.*

[26] P. Norton, "Public Legislation," in M. Rush (ed.), *Parliament and Pressure Politics.*

[27] See especially P. Norton, *Does Parliament Matter?* (Harvester Wheatsheaf, 1993).

[28] See P. Norton, "The Changing Face of Parliament: Lobbying and Its Consequences," in P. Norton (ed.), *New Directions in British Politics?* (Edward Elgar, 1991); and P. Norton, "Interest Representation in the House of Commons," in G. Copeland and S. Patterson (eds.), *Parliaments in the Modern World* (University of Michigan Press, 1994).

[29] See P. Regan, "The 1986 Shops Bill," *Parliamentary Affairs,* 41 (2), 1988; and A. C. S. Bown, "The Shops Bill," in M. Rush, *Parliament and Pressure Politics,* pp. 213–233.

[30] See C. Grantham, "Parliament and Political Consultants," *Parliamentary Affairs,* 42 (4), 1989; Grantham and Seymour-Ure, "Political Consultants"; "The Broadcasting Act 1990: A Case

Study," in *Making the Law: The Report of the Hansard Society Commission on the Legislative Process* (Hansard Society, 1993), pp. 372–387.

[31] Opposition to ownership of handguns was organized effectively by the Snowdrop Campaign, drawing on extensive public support following a massacre of children in a school in Dunblane, Scotland, by a deranged gunman.

[32] The principal works on pluralism, now regarded as classics, are R. A. Dahl, *A Preface to Democratic Theory* (Chicago University Press, 1956); and R. A. Dahl, *Who Governs?* (Yale University Press, 1961). See also D. Truman, *The Governmental Process* (Knopf, 1962).

[33] For a Marxist analysis, see R. Miliband, *The State in Capitalist Society* (Quartet, 1973). The classic U.S. elite study is that of C. Wright Mills, *The Power Elite* (Oxford University Press, 1956). Subsequent and more empirical U.S. studies include T. R. Dye, *Who's Running America,* 2nd ed. (Prentice-Hall, 1979); G. W. Domhoff, *Who Rules America Now?* (Prentice-Hall, 1983), and M. Schwarz (ed.), *The Structure of Power in America* (Holmes and Meier, 1987).

[34] R. J. Harrison, *Pluralism and Corporatism* (Allen & Unwin, 1980), Ch. 5; Grant, *Pressure Groups, Politics and Democracy in Britain,* p. 33.

[35] R. Rose, *Do Parties Make a Difference?* 2nd ed. (Macmillan, 1984).

[36] See R. I. Hofferbert and I. Budge, "The Party Mandate and the Westminster Model: Election Programmes and Government Spending in Britain, 1945–85," *British Journal of Political Science,* 22 (2), 1992, pp. 151–182.

[37] M. Olson, *The Logic of Collective Action* (Schocken, 1968); see also, by the same author, *The Rise and Decline of Nations* (Yale University Press, 1982).

[38] See Grant, *Pressure Groups, Politics and Democracy in Britain,* p. 31.

[39] Grant and Marsh, pp. 50–52.

[40] See A. Cawson, "Pluralism, Corporatism and the Role of the State," *Government and Opposition,* Spring 1978, p. 197.

[41] P. C. Schmitter, "Still the Century of Corporatism?" *The Review of Politics,* 36 (1), 1974, pp. 85–131. See also R. Pahl and J. Winkler, "The Coming Corporatism," *New Society,* October 10, 1974, pp. 72–76.

[42] Quoted in Richardson and Jordan, *Governing under Pressure,* p. 50.

[43] See A. Cox, "Corporatism and the Corporate State in Britain," in L. Robins (ed.), *Topics in British Politics* (Politics Association, 1982), p. 128.

[44] Quoted in S. H. Beer, *Britain Against Itself* (Faber, 1982), p. 57.

[45] See M. Hollingsworth, *MPs for Hire* (Bloomsbury, 1991).

[46] S. Berry, "Lobbyists: Techniques of the Political 'Insiders,'" *Parliamentary Affairs,* 45 (2), 1992, p. 229.

[47] *The Observer,* April 9, 1989.

[48] Committee on Standards in Public Life, *Volume 1: Report* (Her Majesty's Stationery Office, 1995).

[49] See D. Leigh and E. Vulliamy, *Sleaze: The Corruption of Parliament* (Fourth Estate, 1997); I. Greer, *One Man's Word* (Andre Deutsch, 1997).

Part III

Governmental Decision Making

CHAPTER 8

The Executive
Government at the Center

The formal process of determining public policy in Britain is dominated by the executive. Once the executive has agreed on a measure, the assent of Parliament can usually be ensured. Parliament is essentially a policy-ratifying rather than a policy-making body. In the United States, by contrast, the executive enjoys no such dominance. The president cannot proceed on the assumption that any proposals he makes can be assured by the assent of Congress. The U.S. political system has been described as a "multiple-access" one. It also may be characterized as a "multiple-check" system. A proposal emanating from one branch of government can be checked—that is, negated—by another. A bill has to overcome a number of very real hurdles in Congress in order to become law. It may be pigeonholed in committee, it may fail to be scheduled by the House Rules Committee, and it may face a filibuster in the Senate. Congress has negating powers that it is prepared to and variously does use; Parliament has negating powers that it can but hardly ever does use. The executive in Britain can make assumptions about legislative support that few U.S. presidents would dare to make.

Viewed in terms of the Constitution and the relationships governed by conventions, the policy-making process in Britain may appear clear and effective. An executive is formed and proceeds to implement a party program with the support of a parliamentary majority. That has been a popular perception, in Britain itself as well as elsewhere. In practice, the process has proved to be more complex and constrained than this picture suggests. Government has usually a majority in the House of Commons but it faces an organized opposition. Unlike in the United States, the cabinet is challenged by an alternative, the "shadow cabinet." Government ministers are "shadowed" by members of the principal opposition party. The strength of a party may deliver a majority to the government but the party system ensures that government is subject, on a regular and organized basis, to critical scrutiny. Government also has to work within an increasingly intricate political environment shaped by public expectations, judicial decisions, group pressures, party commitments, limited resources, the global economy, and a volatile milieu of international relations. The international constraints have become more pronounced as a consequence of membership in the European Union. Furthermore, to talk in terms of the executive as some homogeneous entity is misleading. Rather like the situation in the United States, government comprises a multitude of bodies, each with its own powers and responsibilities, and pursuing its own interests rather than the interests of the government as a whole.

THE STRUCTURE

It is not only the environment external to the executive that is complex and not always (if ever) harmonious. The same may be said of the executive itself. It comprises a tangled web of bodies, powers, and relationships that, in practice, are not easy to discern. They confuse any attempt to delineate clearly how policy is formulated and where power lies within government. At the apex of government stands the cabinet, headed by the prime minister, and below that the individual government departments headed by ministers and staffed by civil servants. But even within the cabinet there exists a complex infrastructure and sometimes shifting relationships. As government has grown, it not only has become more complex but also has experienced problems of political accountability. There is a large body of civil servants. Recent years have seen the growth of semi-autonomous agencies within departments. At the edges of government, there are many nondepartmental public bodies. For the cabinet, itself diminishing in significance, maintaining control of the government body itself has become a formidable task.

In terms of the structure of the executive and the lines of responsibility to Parliament, the formal position is outlined in Figure 8.1. For the purposes of analysis, it is necessary to identify the essential features of the different elements of the executive. The main elements may be subsumed under the headings of the prime minister, the cabinet, ministers, departments, agencies, civil servants, and nondepartmental public bodies, a category encompassing "quangos" (quasi-autonomous nongovernmental organizations), and task forces. The powers, structure, and composition of each element and the relationships among them have become increasingly a matter of controversy.

The Prime Minister

The prime minister stands at the apex of government. The position is a powerful and highly visible one. In the 1960s, there was a largely academic debate as to whether or not Britain had "prime-ministerial government." The debate widened in the 1970s and reached new heights in the eleven and a half years (1979–90) that Margaret Thatcher occupied No. 10 Downing Street (the prime minister's official residence). It has resurfaced, with renewed vigor, under the

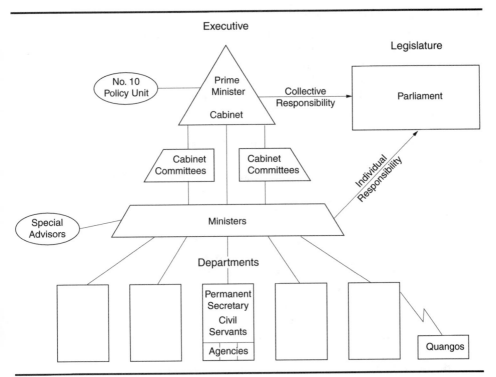

FIGURE 8.1   *The structure of the executive and its relationship to the legislature*

premiership of Tony Blair (1997–). It is now common to find, in both academic literature and the press, accusations that Britain is acquiring a "presidential" form of government.

In the sixteenth and seventeenth centuries, monarchs were often dependent on particular ministers. However, it was not until the eighteenth century that a recognizable first, or "prime," minister began to emerge. George I, the first of the Hanoverian kings, had little interest in British politics, spoke little or no English, and spent six months of each year on the Continent. He left the conduct of affairs entirely to the cabinet, his chosen group of ministers. "This," as Arthur Berriedale Keith observed, "led inevitably to the development of the office of Prime Minister; for, once the King was removed from the cabinet, the natural tendency was for some minister to take his place as a unifying influence."[1] The first minister to be considered—at least by historians—as prime minister was Sir Robert Walpole, from 1721 to 1742. The term itself had been used before and Walpole himself disclaimed it. It came eventually into colloquial but not formal use. Not until the twentieth century was the position to be referred to in a statute. The official position held by most "prime" ministers was that of first lord of the treasury, a position that is still retained by holders of the office. Over time, however, the position of prime minister grew in recognition and in powers. The growth of party government acted as a particular spur to the growth of prime ministerial power. The nineteenth century, as we have seen (Chapter 3), witnessed a transfer of power from the monarch and later from Parliament to the cabinet, a cabinet headed—and chosen—by the prime minister.

The powers that inhere in the office of prime minister are considerable. They are also remarkable for the fact that they exist by convention and not by statute or common law. Prerogative powers, such as the appointment of ministers, reside in the monarch. Statutory powers are vested in individual ministers. The most powerful person in government is the one who wields no legal powers at all.

There are several powers that coalesce to make the prime minister the most powerful figure in government. They are summarized in the list below.

Prime-Ministerial Powers

1. Appoints, moves, and dismisses ministers
2. Dispenses patronage (honors—such as peerages and knighthoods—and various appointments to public office)
3. Chairs the cabinet
4. Determines the cabinet agenda
5. Appoints senior members of the civil service
6. Determines the date of general elections
7. Enjoys the mandate of an election victory
8. Represents the nation at international summits
9. Is a focus of media attention
10. Occupies an office once held by such great figures as Pitt, Gladstone, Disraeli, Lloyd George, and Churchill
11. Is party leader[2]

The best known as well as the most important of these powers are appointment and dismissal. The monarch formally appoints ministers, but by convention she does so on the advice of her prime minister. The reality of who does the choosing is well recognized. Announcements of ministerial appointments are made direct from Downing Street. The prime minister not only chooses who the ministers will be, he or she can also decide when they are no longer to be ministers. Ministerial reshuffles are used by prime ministers to make changes and bring new blood into the cabinet, or the ranks of non-cabinet ministers. They are sometimes controversial, as in July 1962 when Harold Macmillan dismissed one-third of his cabinet and in July 1989 when Margaret Thatcher moved a very unwilling Sir Geoffrey Howe from the Foreign Office to the position of lord president of the council and leader of the House of Commons. The extent of prime ministerial patronage is considerable: There are now more than a hundred ministers and all owe their positions to the prime minister. Nor does the patronage end with ministers. The prime minister in effect chooses new members of the House of Lords, decides other honors (such as the awarding of knighthoods), and can appoint individuals to a range of public positions. He even has the final say, should he choose to exercise it, over the appointments of archbishops and bishops in the established church, the Church of England.

The power to appoint ministers is not unfettered. By convention, ministers must normally be drawn from Parliament and, by convention, predominantly from the House of Commons. (There is no legal requirement that ministers be MPs or peers, and occasionally one post in particular—that of the solicitor general for Scotland—has been filled by a lawyer outside Parliament.) Partisanship dictates that the ministers will be drawn from the prime minister's own party. It is also deemed politically prudent to ensure a reasonable balance of ministers, in terms of both geography—drawing ministers from different constituencies across the country—and the different wings of the party. There are also likely to be senior figures with considerable support among MPs whom the prime minister would find it difficult to exclude, not least because they could become dangerous critics from the back benches. Nonetheless, the extent of the balance is sometimes a little skewed—Edward Heath (1970-74) and Tony Blair (1997-) have each faced accusations of selecting a personally loyal cabinet—and few are willing to challenge the prime minister's judgments. The appointing—and dismissal—power wielded by the prime minister serves to ensure loyalty on the part of ministers and of those MPs who would like to be ministers.

The power to choose ministers is important not only in ensuring ministerial loyalty to the prime minister; it is also a major tool in influencing the direction of public policy. As Maurice Kogan has observed, the authority to appoint, transfer, or dismiss enables the prime minister to allocate values and change or confirm an individual minister's policies.[3] When Margaret Thatcher was prime minister, she ensured that supporters of her neoliberal economic policy occupied the key economic ministries. Tony Blair has been accused of promoting key supporters—"Blairites"—to the cabinet, replacing ministers with less-Blairite credentials.

Power to determine the direction of policy is not confined to the blunt weapon of appointment and dismissal. It derives also from the prime minister's position as chairman of the cabinet. In the nineteenth century John Morley described the prime minister as *primus inter pares* (first among equals) in the cabinet. In practice, the premier's position has always been much more than that. The prime minister (PM) determines when the cabinet will meet and what it will discuss. The prime minister sums up discussion. Very few prime ministers have resorted to taking votes in cabinet. The PM's summing up is therefore crucial. It is that which will determine what is recorded in the minutes. As chairman of the cabinet, the prime minister also determines the extent and composition of cabinet committees, appointed to save cabinet time by discussing and resolving issues before they go to full cabinet. As we shall see, the range of such committees is extensive.

The prime minister's control is not confined to the cabinet. It extends to the rest of Whitehall. The prime minister is minister for the civil service.

The permanent head of the service reports directly to the PM. Power over the appointment of senior civil servants—primarily the permanent secretaries, the civil service heads of each department—rests with the prime minister, not the ministers in whose departments they serve. If a minister wants to have a senior civil servant moved, as occasionally happens, the support of the PM is essential. It is also a potentially risky business: The prime minister might refuse and take the side of the civil servant.[4] Some premiers have taken an active interest in civil service appointments. Margaret Thatcher in particular intervened to ensure that a number of vacancies were filled by high-flying officials rather than by the person second in seniority. Tony Blair has taken an active interest in the management of the civil service and in ensuring that civil servants deliver on the government's promises, in so doing attracting claims that he is "politicizing" the civil service.

The prime minister can also determine the date of the general election (another prerogative power, where the sovereign takes the advice of her prime minister) and, if he leads his party to victory, has the added authority that derives from that victory. Credit tends to accrue to the person at the head of the winning campaign. Edward Heath was often seen as having won the 1970 general election for the Conservatives almost single-handedly, having led his party to an unexpected victory. A similar view was taken of Margaret Thatcher in her three consecutive election victories. By leading his party to its best-ever election victory in 1997, Tony Blair was claimed by commentators to be in an almost invincible position, many Labour members of parliament crediting their victory to his leadership.

As head of government, the prime minister represents the nation at major international summits, the foreign secretary acting essentially in a supporting role. The more frequent such summits—and the number has increased substantially as a result of frequent meetings of the European Council, comprising the heads of government of the member states of the European Union—the greater the visibility of the PM on the international stage. As head of government, the PM also has considerable media visibility at home. He or she is a natural focus of media attention. The PM is a powerful political power—usually the most powerful political figure—and one who occupies an office once held by such towering figures as William Pitt (the elder, and the younger), William Gladstone, Benjamin Disraeli, David Lloyd George, and Winston Churchill. An aura attaches to the office, one now reinforced by security considerations: The PM has to be kept some distance from ordinary public contact. He or she travels with an escort—a very modest escort by U.S. standards, but an escort nonetheless.

The PM is thus a powerful political figure. However, there is one essential component of that power that has not yet been mentioned. The PM is also leader of his or her party. It is that leadership that is a necessary but not sufficient condition for becoming prime minister. (Electoral success provides the sufficient condition.) In office, the fact of being party leader gives the PM the capacity to call on party loyalty and also to utilize the machinery of the party organization. Historically, this has been particularly important on the Conservative side (see Chapter 6), with all party bodies being advisory to the leader and the leader appointing all the senior officers of the party. It has also become increasingly important in the Labour party, Labour leaders in the 1980s and 1990s taking greater control of the party machinery. The confluence of party leadership and the premiership thus makes the PM a tremendously powerful figure. However, it does not render the PM all-powerful. The fact of being party leader is a double-edged weapon. The party, or that part of it that selects the leader, can withdraw its support, as Margaret Thatcher found to her cost in November 1990. Having lost the leadership of the Conservative party, she resigned the premiership.

The prime minister has usually wielded the powers of the office with relatively limited institutional support. There is, formally, no prime minister's "department." The size of the prime minister's office has traditionally been small.[5] However, as chairman of the cabinet, the PM is serviced by the secretary to the cabinet (who is also usually head of the civil service) and the Cabinet Secretariat, which records and monitors cabinet decisions. A number of new units have also been created in the Cabinet Office since 1997 in order to increase central coordination. The prime minister also has the support of a number of advisors. That number is growing. Before the 1970s, prime ministers appointed advisors on an ad hoc basis. In 1970 the Central Policy Review Staff (CPRS), more popularly known as the "think tank," was established. Comprising a small number of political appointees and seconded civil servants, it provided wide-ranging policy advice to the cabinet and the prime minister. However, it was gradually overshadowed by a small body of advisors established to advise the prime minister—the No. 10 Policy Unit—and in 1983 the CPRS was disbanded. Under the premiership of Tony Blair, the No. 10 Policy Unit consists of about a dozen politically-committed specialists on particular subjects, offering party-oriented advice and working directly for the PM.[6] It is complemented by other bodies, including a strategic communications unit to coordinate government announcements. The number of staff in Downing Street has increased notably under the Blair premiership: from 130 in April 1997 to 199 in December 1999.

The prime minister thus has a relatively small but important body to offer advice independent of that coming from ministers and civil servants. It reinforces the PM's capacity to lead within government. The extent to which the prime minister chooses to lead, though, depends very much upon the occupant of the office.

Britain has had 20 prime ministers since 1900 (see Table 8.1). Their approach to the office has varied considerably. Some have been forceful wielders of power, others more emollient occupiers of the office. Some have been driven by a powerful ideological world view, others by the need to satisfy their egos. One useful way to analyze the 20 people who have occupied No. 10 in the twentieth century is to look at their purpose in seeking office. Utilizing this approach, it is possible to identify four prime ministerial types:[7]

Innovators. They seek power in order to achieve a future goal of their own creation and are prepared, if necessary, to bring their party kicking and screaming in their wake in order to achieve that goal.

Reformers. They seek power in order to achieve the implementation of a particular program, but one drawn up by the party rather than by the premier.

Egoists. They seek power for the sake of power; they are concerned with enjoying the here-and-now of office rather than with future goals, and they fight to keep power.

Balancers. They fall into two categories: those who seek power in order to achieve balance, within society and within party, and those who share

TABLE 8.1 Prime ministers since 1900

Took Office	Prime Minister	Party
June 25, 1895	The third marquess of Salisbury	Unionist (Conservative)
July 12, 1902	Arthur James Balfour	Unionist (Conservative)
December 5, 1905	Sir Henry Campbell-Bannerman	Liberal
April 8, 1908	Herbert Henry Asquith	Liberal[1]
December 7, 1916	David Lloyd George	Liberal[2]
October 23, 1922	Andrew Bonar Law	Unionist (Conservative)
May 22, 1923	Stanley Baldwin	Unionist (Conservative)
January 22, 1924	J. Ramsay MacDonald	Labour
November 4, 1924	Stanley Baldwin	Conservative
June 5, 1929	J. Ramsay MacDonald	Labour
August 24, 1931	J. Ramsay MacDonald	National Labour[3]
June 7, 1935	Stanley Baldwin	Conservative[3]
May 28, 1937	Neville Chamberlain	Conservative[3]
May 10, 1940	Winston S. Churchill	Conservative[4]
May 23, 1945	Clement Attlee	Labour
October 26, 1951	Sir Winston Churchill	Conservative
April 6, 1955	Sir Anthony Eden	Conservative
January 10, 1957	Harold Macmillan	Conservative
October 19, 1963	Sir Alec Douglas-Home	Conservative
October 16, 1964	Harold Wilson	Labour
June 19, 1970	Edward Heath	Conservative
March 4, 1974	Harold Wilson	Labour
April 5, 1976	James Callaghan	Labour
May 4, 1979	Margaret Thatcher	Conservative
November 28, 1990	John Major	Conservative
May 2, 1997	Tony Blair	Labour

[1] Coalition from May 1915
[2] Coalition government
[3] National government
[4] Coalition government May 1940–May 1945; national government May–July 1945

the same goal but, rather than seeking power, have it thrust upon them, usually as compromise choices for leader; the latter may be described as conscripts in the office.

These four are ideal types. Some premiers have straddled categories. Others have changed over time: Winston Churchill was essentially an innovator as wartime prime minister but a balancer in peacetime. Purpose has also varied depending upon the context. Tony Blair was an innovator as Labour party leader, forcing a radical change in the culture and organization of the party, but is probably closer to an egoist in his position as prime minister. Nonetheless, the categories are useful for assessing and distinguishing prime ministers. Table 8.2 categorizes the twentieth-century prime ministers. The past 40 years have seen three power-seeking balancers (Macmillan, Callaghan, Major), two egoists (Wilson, Blair), a conscript balancer (Douglas-Home), an obvious innovator (Thatcher), and a premier who straddled the categories of innovator and egoist (Heath). The quest to occupy the office thus draws many different politicians. Which one actually reaches the top of what Disraeli described as "the greasy pole" will affect significantly how the powers of the office are used. Had Michael Heseltine (an egoist-innovator) won the Conservative party leadership—and hence the premiership—in 1990, he would almost certainly have utilized the powers of the office in a very different way from John Major. The cabinet minister seen as a potential successor to prime minister Tony Blair (namely, Chancellor of the Exchequer Gordon Brown) is predominantly an innovator. Practices between premiers have varied considerably. Margaret Thatcher used to badger the cabinet and sometimes summed up discussions at the beginning! John Major allowed the cabinet to operate more as a relaxed seminar, with ministers questioning other ministers. Tony Blair keeps his cabinet meetings as short as possible, with little of importance being discussed.

A particularly determined occupant of No. 10 is likely to achieve more, at least in the short term, than a less determined individual. Nonetheless, however

TABLE 8.2   Typology of prime ministers

| | | | Balancers | |
Innovators	Reformers	Egoists	Power-Seeking	Conscripts
Churchill (wartime)	Campbell-Bannerman	Lloyd George?	Salisbury	Bonar Law
Heath?	Asquith	MacDonald?	Balfour?	Douglas-Home
Thatcher	Chamberlain	Eden	Baldwin	
	Attlee	Wilson	Churchill (peacetime)	
		Heath?	Macmillan	
		Blair	Callaghan	
			Major	

SOURCE: Developed from P. Norton, "Prime Ministerial Power," *Social Studies Review 3* (3), 1988, p. 110.

determined the individual might be, wielding the powers of the office will not necessarily achieve the desired result. Prime ministerial power depends in part upon the skills of the individual in the office. He or she has to engage in "impression management." As Barbara Kellerman put it in the U.S. context, "the president must seem presidential".[8] Similarly, the prime minister must appear prime ministerial. The PM must not only look fit for the office, but also has to have a feel for it, or in other words an intuitive grasp of how to deploy, or not deploy, the powers of the office. Some prime ministers have managed to mold a united cabinet, some have been able to judge what is or is not politically acceptable (a particular skill of Margaret Thatcher's until it deserted her in 1989 and 1990), some have been able to judge the parliamentary and the public mood and to capitalize on it, and some have proved good manipulators of other actors in the political system (the principal skill attributed to Major and, more notably, to his successor, Tony Blair). Few have managed to combine all such skills.

How the skills of the individual are deployed will help determine the extent to which the PM can influence the immediate political environment, encompassing not just the cabinet but also the rest of the executive, the legislature, and other proximate actors. In seeking to influence that immediate environment, the prime minister enjoys a position of superiority but not one of hegemony. The cabinet, individual ministers, civil servants, and the courts are not lacking in powers of their own to influence public policy in the United Kingdom.

Success also depends in part, and sometimes crucially, upon external circumstances over which the prime minister can have little or no control. A recession in the United States or the Far East, ethnic conflict in the former Yugoslavia, a refusal of the U.S. Federal Reserve to lower interest rates, or the uncertain intentions of the president of Iraq can and do have major implications for the United Kingdom. So can decisions of the European Council, over which the PM does have a little more influence, but as one of 15 heads of government. The future of the British prime minister may depend upon events well beyond Britain's shores and hence beyond her or his immediate political reach.

When a determined prime minister has been able to effectively utilize skills to achieve policy goals and when the external environment has proved helpful or benign, the consequence has generally been a prime minister judged as successful. A 1999 poll of historians and political scientists found that Winston Churchill was judged the greatest of twentieth-century prime ministers. Britain's other wartime leader, David Lloyd George, was judged second greatest. The egoist Sir Anthony Eden, who sent forces to try to take control of the Suez canal in 1956—and ran into powerful opposition from U.S. President Eisenhower—was deemed to be the least successful. Innovator Margaret Thatcher came fifth in the poll (see Table 8.3). Her successor, John Major, who presided over a divided party and led it to a disastrous election defeat in 1997, ranked near the bottom. Tony Blair, as the serving prime minister, was excluded from the poll.

TABLE 8.3   Ratings of twentieth-century prime ministers

Prime ministers ranked in order of success

1. Winston Churchill
2. David Lloyd George
3. Clement Attlee
4. Herbert Asquith
5. Margaret Thatcher
6. Harold Macmillan
7. Marquess of Salisbury
8. Stanley Baldwin
9. Sir Henry Campbell-Bannerman
10. Harold Wilson
11. Edward Heath
12. James Callaghan
13. Andrew Bonar Law
14. Ramsay MacDonald
15. Sir Alec Douglas-Home
16. Arthur Balfour
17. John Major
18. Neville Chamberlain
19. Sir Anthony Eden

SOURCE: BBC *Westminster Hour* poll, broadcast December 26, 1999.

The Cabinet

The cabinet is the collective decision-making body of British government. It usually comprises just over twenty members (see Table 8.4), constituting the ministerial heads of all the principal government departments as well as a number of ministers without departmental responsibilities (such as the president of the council and the lord privy seal, titles usually given to the ministers who serve as managerial leaders in the two houses of Parliament). By convention, as we have seen, its members are drawn from, and remain within, Parliament. A minimum of two peers (the lord chancellor and the leader of the House of Lords), and rarely more than four, are appointed to the cabinet. Most members have served a parliamentary apprenticeship, having moved up from the back benches to junior ministerial office and then to minister of state level before being considered for cabinet appointment. It is rare for cabinet ministers to be appointed from the ranks of back-benchers or from people outside the Commons. There have been rare exceptions: In World War II, for example, union leader Ernest Bevin was brought straight into government. In such cases, the normal practice is for the new minister to be created a peer or (less likely nowadays) to be found a safe seat to win in a by-election.

The cabinet, like the position of prime minister, developed in importance during the eighteenth and nineteenth centuries. However, as the monarch's principal body of advisors, it was not particularly efficient. It often had little to

TABLE 8.4   The cabinet, January 2000

Prime Minister, First Lord of the Treasury and Minister for the Civil Service—The Rt. Hon. Tony Blair MP

Deputy Prime Minister and Secretary of State for the Environment, Transport, and the Regions—The Rt. Hon. John Prescott MP

Chancellor of the Exchequer—The Rt. Hon. Gordon Brown MP

Secretary of State for Foreign and Commonwealth Affairs—The Rt. Hon. Robin Cook MP

Lord Chancellor—The Rt. Hon. Lord Irvine of Lairg

Secretary of State for the Home Department—The Rt. Hon. Jack Straw MP

Secretary of State for Education and Employment—The Rt. Hon. David Blunkett MP

President of the Council and Leader of the House of Commons—The Rt. Hon. Margaret Beckett MP

Parliamentary Secretary to the Treasury [Government Chief Whip]—The Rt. Hon. Ann Taylor MP

Secretary of State for Culture, Media, and Sport—The Rt. Hon. Chris Smith MP

Minister for the Cabinet Office and Chancellor of the Duchy of Lancaster—The Rt. Hon. Marjorie ("Mo") Mowlam MP

Secretary of State for International Development—The Rt. Hon. Clare Short MP

Secretary of State for Social Security—The Rt. Hon. Alistair Darling MP

Minister of Agriculture, Fisheries and Food—The Rt. Hon. Nicholas Brown MP

Lord Privy Seal, Leader of the House of Lords and Minister for Women—The Rt. Hon. The Baroness Jay of Paddington

Secretary of State for Trade and Industry—The Rt. Hon. Stephen Byers MP

Secretary of State for Health—The Rt. Hon. Alan Milburn MP

Secretary of State for Scotland—The Rt. Hon. Dr. John Reid MP

Secretary of State for Wales—The Rt. Hon. Paul Murphy MP

Secretary of State for Northern Ireland—The Rt. Hon. Peter Mandelson MP

Secretary of State for Defence—The Rt. Hon. Geoffrey Hoon MP

Chief Secretary to the Treasury—The Rt. Hon. Andrew Smith MP

do; decisions were frequently leaked by waiters (it met for dinner at the home of one of its members); members sometimes slept during meetings; and there was no agenda. In the twentieth century, as the demands on the cabinet grew—public policy becoming both more extensive and more complex—it developed in terms of its political significance and its organization.

The second decade of the twentieth century witnessed a particular improvement in organization as well as an authoritative clarification of what its role was. In 1916 the Cabinet Secretariat came into being, responsible for circulating agenda, papers, and minutes and for monitoring the implementation of cabinet decisions. Previously, implementation had been very much dependent on the memories of ministers, some of whom forgot what had been decided. In 1918 the Machinery of Government Committee delineated the functions of the cabinet to be (1) the final determination of the policy to be submitted to Parliament, (2) the supreme control of the national executive in accordance with the policy prescribed by Parliament, and (3) the continuous coordination and delimitation of the authorities of the several departments of state. This delineation remains extant. It has not been superseded but what has changed has been the cabinet's mode of fulfilling its functions. As the functions became more onerous for a single body meeting once or twice a week, it developed a complex infrastructure. Consequently, there are two vehicles through which the cabinet now operates: cabinet committees and the full cabinet.

Cabinet committees have burgeoned, particularly since 1945. They are formed from the ministers relevant to the area covered by the committee as well as some ministers free of departmental responsibilities. The committees' creation, membership, and chairmanship are determined by the prime minister. They are serviced by the Cabinet Secretariat, which, among other things, provides briefing papers for the chairmen.

Until the premiership of Margaret Thatcher, the committees were shrouded in secrecy. No details were given about them: Officially, they did not exist. Mrs. Thatcher broke with tradition to admit their existence and named four standing committees. Her successor, John Major, took the revelations one step further and authorized the publication of the names, membership, and terms of reference of all cabinet committees, and that practice has been continued. At the beginning of 1999, there were 13 committees and 10 subcommittees (see Table 8.5). Each is usually referred to by coded initials. The committees are supplemented by various committees or groups appointed on an ad hoc basis, and known by the code MISC (miscellaneous) or GEN (general). As can be seen from Table 8.5, in 1999 there were seven ministerial groups, in some cases dealing with essential transient issues such as the millennium date change. The number of ad hoc committees varies over time. In the first six years of her premiership, for example, Margaret Thatcher appointed in total about 150 ad hoc committees—a large number, but fewer than the number created by her predecessors, and less than half the number formed by Clement Attlee during his six-year premiership.[9]

Committee membership ranges in number from six (the committees on defense and overseas policy, Northern Ireland, and the intelligence services) to 20 (the committee on devolution policy).[10] One subcommittee has a membership in excess of 20 (the subcommittee on freedom of information, with 23 members). The committees comprise wholly or almost wholly cabinet ministers: One or two ministers of state serve on some of them. The subcommittees have memberships that mix senior and junior ministers, and ministerial groups have a preponderance of junior ministers in their membership. The committees and subcommittees are chaired by the prime minister or by another senior cabinet minister. Under Tony Blair's premiership, the ministers chairing the most committees have been the deputy prime minister, the chancellor of the exchequer, the president of the council, and the lord chancellor. The president of the council chairs several committees because of the nature of the post.

Decisions emanating from the committees have the same authority as full cabinet decisions, and since 1967, disputes within committees can be referred to the full cabinet only with the approval of the committee chairman. When

TABLE 8.5 Cabinet committees, January 1999

Name and Coded Initials	Chair
Committees	
Economic Affairs (EA)	Chancellor
Public Services and Public Expenditure (PSX)	Chancellor
Environment (ENV)	Deputy PM
Local Government (GL)	Deputy PM
Home and Social Affairs (HS)	Deputy PM
Queen's Speech and Future Legislation (QFL)	President
Legislation (LEG)	President
Constitutional Reform Policy (CRP)	PM
Devolution Policy (DP)	Lord chancellor
Joint Consultative Committee with the Liberal Democratic Party (JCC)	PM
Defence and Overseas Policy (DOP)	PM
Northern Ireland (IN)	PM
Intelligence Services (CSI)	PM
Subcommittees	
Energy Policy (EA(N))	Chancellor
Welfare to Work (EA(WW))	Chancellor
London (GL(L))	Deputy PM
Health Strategy (HS(H))	President
Drug Misuse (HS(D))	Minister for Cabinet Office
Women's Issues (HS(W))	Lord privy seal
Incorporation of European Convention on Human Rights (CRP(EC))	Lord chancellor
Freedom of Information (CRP(FOI))	Lord chancellor
House of Lords Reform (CRP(HL))	Lord chancellor
European Issues ((E)DOP)	Foreign secretary
Ministerial Groups	
Food Safety (MISC 1)	President
Crime Reduction and Youth Justice (MISC2)	Home secretary
Utility Regulations (MISC 3)	Trade secretary
Millennium Date Change (MISC 4)	President
Restructuring of the European Aerospace and Defence Industry (MISC 5)	Trade secretary
Biotechnology and Genetic Modification (MISC 6)	Minister for the Cabinet Office
Better Government (MISC 7)	Minister for the Cabinet Office

Chancellor = chancellor of the exchequer; PM = prime minister; Deputy PM = deputy prime minister; President = president of the council; Trade secretary = secretary of state for trade and industry

important issues are under discussion, it is usual for the designated members to attend, though on other occasions senior ministers can and do replace themselves with their junior ministers.[11] Richard Crossman, subsequently a cabinet minister himself, took the view that the committees detracted from the power of the cabinet,[12] though the more general view is that they serve as a useful complement to the cabinet, lightening its workload, clarifying issues for it, and allowing it to concentrate on the more central and general matters of government.

The full cabinet usually meets every Thursday morning in the Cabinet Room at 10 Downing Street. The government chief whip, though not formally a member of the cabinet, used to attend the meetings, in order to tender advice; in 1998, the new chief whip, Ann Taylor, was made a full member of the cabinet. The chief whip is the minister responsible for ensuring the support of the parliamentary party in parliamentary votes and acts as a channel or communication between the cabinet and its parliamentary supporters. The cabinet secretary (a civil servant) attends and sits on the prime minister's right. The length of cabinet meetings varies. Under some prime ministers, meetings have lasted for one to three hours, with additional meetings, if necessary, on Tuesdays and sometimes other days as necessary. Margaret Thatcher tried to keep meetings to a minimum. Tony Blair also keeps them to a minimum, both in terms of number and duration. Under Blair, meetings sometimes last less than an hour.

The cabinet remains important as the central forum for the resolution of disputes between departments, particularly in the allocation of public expenditure. Ministers usually defend their particular department, often supported on a reciprocal basis by ministers representing other spending departments. Much depends on the personalities involved, not least that of the PM. Some PMs tend to involve themselves in a wide range of items being brought forward by ministers, whereas others content themselves with concentrating on central issues of the economy and foreign affairs, leaving other departmental ministers to get on with their jobs unhindered. The process by which a cabinet determines policy thus varies from PM to PM and, depending on changing political circumstance, may vary during the tenure of office of one PM. The cabinet remains the forum for the resolution of most major issues of public policy, but a number of those issues may effectively be resolved elsewhere, either in cabinet committee or by a meeting of senior ministers. Less central issues usually do not reach the cabinet at all.

As with the position of prime minister, no formal powers are vested in the cabinet: It exists and operates by convention. The most important convention, one that in part governs its behavior as well as its relationship to Parliament, is that of collective responsibility. This convention, which developed during the eighteenth and nineteenth centuries, prescribes that members of the cabinet accept responsibility collectively for decisions made by it. Ministers may argue in cabinet session, but once a decision has been made they are required to support that decision publicly. Any minister failing to support a cabinet decision in public once it had been announced would be expected to resign: Failure to do so would result in the PM requesting that minister's resignation.

The convention is deemed also to dictate the necessity for secrecy to attach to cabinet discussions. The authority of the cabinet and of particular ministers could be undermined if cabinet disputes were made public. Ministers publicly defending decisions with which they are known to have disagreed in cabinet session would weaken the cabinet in trying to ensure implementation of those decisions. A minister's authority and influence could be undermined if it were known that he or she was implementing a policy against which he or she had fought in the cabinet. Nonetheless, recent years have witnessed a weakening of this aspect of the collective responsibility convention, with ministers engaging in semipublic and, for all intents and purposes, public leaks and disagreements, and with some ex-ministers recording cabinet discussions in their memoirs. On two occasions in the Labour government of 1974–1979 the convention was actually suspended in order to allow ministers to vote against government policy in the House of Commons. Both occasions concerned the issue of British membership in the European Community, on which cabinet members were bitterly divided. To avoid the possibility of resignations or the cabinet falling apart, the PM (Harold Wilson in 1975, James Callaghan in 1977) decided to suspend the convention. Although the convention remains extant, it is becoming a difficult one for PMs to enforce.

One other condition dictated by the convention of collective responsibility continues to be followed. A government defeat in the House of Commons on the motion "that this House has no confidence in Her Majesty's Government" necessitates the government's resigning or requesting a dissolution. On March 28, 1979, when the minority Labour government was defeated on a vote of confidence, the PM immediately went to Buckingham Palace to request a dissolution. This requirement stipulated by the convention is one of the few about which it remains possible to generalize with confidence.

Ministers

When a PM forms an administration, he or she is called on to select not only the senior ministers to head the various departments of state, as well as senior ministers without portfolio, but also a host of junior ministers. In addition to a ministerial head, who is usually of secretary of state rank, each department normally has one and sometimes more ministers of state and one or more undersecretaries of state. The PM also appoints a chief whip and 13 or 14 other whips in the Commons as well as a chief whip and five or six other whips in the House of Lords. In total, a little more than one hundred ministerial appointments are now made (see Table 8.6). Despite the demands made of government, the increase in the number of ministers during the course of the twentieth century has been a modest one.

Of the ministers appointed, the most important are, as one would expect, those appointed to head the various departments (see Table 8.4). The significance of junior ministers tends to vary. In past decades, many parliamentary undersecretaries had little to do and often were regarded as constituting something of an insignificant life form within the departments. To some extent, that remains the case today for a number of undersecretaries, known in Whitehall circles under the acronym PUSS (parliamentary undersecretaries of state). The influence of junior ministers within departments tends to depend on the ministerial head. There is a growing tendency for ministers to assign greater responsibility for certain functions to their ministers of state and undersecretaries; when junior ministers attend cabinet committees, they gain some knowledge

TABLE 8.6 Number of government ministers, January 2000

Rank	House of Commons	House of Lords	Total
Cabinet ministers (including PM)	20	2	22
Ministers of state*	28	6	34
Law officers	2	1	3
Undersecretaries of state/ Parliamentary secretaries	23	5	28
Whips (excluding chief whip in Commons)	15	7	22
TOTAL	88	21	109

* Includes the paymaster-general and the financial and economic secretaries to the treasury

of the workings of the higher echelons of government. Nonetheless, disputes between junior ministers and the chief civil servant, the permanent secretary, in a department can be resolved only by the ministerial head, and there remains a tendency for interested bodies to try to influence the senior minister even on matters delegated to junior ministers.

The heads of departments have tended to become even more important decision makers than they were hitherto. Indeed, there is a case for arguing that, far from having prime ministerial or cabinet government, Britain has a form of ministerial government. As demands on government have increased, only the most important matters have percolated up to the cabinet for resolution. Most important decisions affecting a department are made by the minister. The relationship between a minister and the House of Commons and between the minister and his or her department is governed by the convention of individual ministerial responsibility. The convention is important not only for determining who is responsible to whom (civil servants to minister, minister to Parliament), but also for determining who is responsible for what. The cabinet as a body has no legal powers; powers are vested in ministers. When government takes on new responsibilities by statute, powers to fulfill those responsibilities are granted to a minister. "The Secretary of State shall have power to ... " According to Nevil Johnson, "the enduring effect of the doctrine of ministerial responsibility has been over the past century or so that powers have been vested in ministers and on a relentlessly increasing scale."[13]

Ministers, then, are very much at the heart of the government process. Major issues are resolved in cabinet session or directly with the PM and other senior ministers. Other issues are usually but not always resolved at the departmental level. And when issues go to cabinet, it is the minister who is responsible for the document or proposal. Major changes in policy are usually announced through the publication of a "white paper." Such policy documents have to go through the cabinet (discussed in cabinet committee and then presented to the full cabinet), but they are drawn up within departments on the minister's instructions.

Though heavily dependent on their civil servants for information and advice, ministers have an alternative channel of advice in the form of special advisors. Senior and some middle-ranking ministers each have a special advisor. (Some junior ministers also share an advisor.) The advisor is a political appointee—often a high-flying young party activist destined later for a parliamentary seat—who is given temporary civil service status for the period of the appointment. The advisors provide political advice, which civil servants are precluded from doing, and act as conduits for information and advice from party sources and outside bodies. Each is chosen by the minister and serves essentially at the minister's pleasure. Some are political all-rounders, and may follow a particular minister from one post to another; a few (as with the special advisor to the defense secretary) have more specialized knowledge. The number of political advisers increased with the return of a Labour Government in 1997.

Nonetheless, ministers operate under a number of significant constraints. Because of parliamentary, constituency, and various public duties, the time they have to devote to their jobs is limited. Special advisors, despite an increase in their numbers, are often as much overloaded with work as their ministers. Ministers have little time to get to know a department before moving on to another post. It is rare for a minister to serve in the same post for the lifetime of a Parliament. In the decades before 1945, the average tenure of a senior minister was four years. In the latter half of the century the average tenure was approximately two years. As one former cabinet minister put it: "Normally, you're the minister for buttons one day, and secretary of state for string the next. . . . And the first morning, you have to do an interview with Brian Redhead [a radio interviewer] on string, and be an expert!"[14]

Given these limitations, and the sheer volume of business, ministers rely substantially on their civil servants. Many decisions have to be delegated to officials to make in the minister's name. Even matters that do come before ministers may be heavily weighted by the advice of officials and by the manner in which the issue is brought to the minister's attention. Such decisions also have to be taken within the context of limited resources. The minister has to battle with treasury ministers to try to get as big a slice of the government cake as possible. Given economic restraints, it is rarely likely to be enough to meet a department's self-determined needs.

The extent to which a minister is able to achieve desired results is dependent in part on the individual holding the office. As with prime ministers, it is possible to discern particular types of senior ministers. Five types of minister can be identified:[15]

Commanders. They have clear goals they wish to achieve, goals determined by their own personal philosophies, derived from experience or personal reflection.

Ideologues. They seek to achieve particular goals determined by an existing political philosophy.

Managers. They are more concerned with the here and now of political life, of ensuring the efficient running of their departments, implementing existing policies, and variously serving as brokers between competing demands.

Agents. They seek to carry out the desired policy goals of other political actors, such as the prime minister or the civil servants within the department.

Team Players. They are wary of making decisions on their own, preferring to take an issue to cabinet for collective deliberation or, more informally, seeking the advice and confirmation of a team of trusted confidants.

Though commentators have variously argued that ministers have tended to be agents—carrying out uncritically the wishes of the prime minister—or that, under the Thatcher government, ideologues tended to dominate in cabinet, research by this writer has found that commanders and managers tend to be the most prevalent types to serve in cabinet.[16] Ministers will variously adopt the status of agents (a minister may straddle more than one category, depending in large part on the office held), but this will tend to be on particular issues on which they have no fixed view themselves, and are prepared to follow the established departmental line.

Whether ministers are successful in achieving their goals will also depend, as with the prime minister, on their political skills as well as on the wider political environment. Relationships with colleagues, with members of the parliamentary party, with the media, and with the party in the country can be important in helping them, or hindering them from achieving their policy goals and, indeed, their ambitions for higher office. In 1998, one cabinet minister, who had a reputation for indecisiveness and who performed poorly in the House of Commons, was sacked, as was a middle-ranking minister who had clashed with and publicly criticized the civil servants in his department. Some senior ministers, such as Chancellor of the Exchequer Gordon Brown, and Home Secretary Jack Straw had reputations for not only being in control of their departments but also for maintaining close contact with back-bench Labour MPs. The Chancellor, in particular, was widely regarded as being entrenched in office.

Departments

Ministers are appointed to head departments. The way these departments are structured and the responsibilities vested in them can affect the nature of policy making. Departments adopt particular processes. They acquire particular traditions and a distinctive ethos. "Departments matter. They lead lives of their own. As Shirley Williams put it, they have banners to defend on which the departmental traditions and orthodoxy are emblazoned like fading regimental colours in a cathedral—and these are defended against all-comers whether they be pressure-groups, select committees, international organizations or other ministries."[17]

The structure of departments, however, is not static. Structures and responsibilities change. The number of major departments has fluctuated during the twentieth century, ranging from 18 in 1914 to a high of 30 in 1951.[18] Since then, the number has been reduced with the amalgamation of a number of departments. The three departments covering the armed services were merged in 1964 to create the Ministry of Defence (the MOD); in 1968 the Foreign and Commonwealth Offices were merged to form a single department; and two "super ministries"—the Department of Environment and the Department of Trade and Industry (the DTI)—were formed in 1970, the former incorporating the ministries of housing and local government, transport, and public buildings and works. The last two new departments were part of a conscious effort to create the capacity to manage larger resource-consuming programs and to reduce the need for interdepartmental compromise, allowing a single strategy to be pursued within one ministry. In 1997 a massive Department of the Environment, Transport, and the Regions was created, headed by the deputy prime minister, John Prescott.

The move, however, has not always been in one direction. A Welsh Office was created in 1964, Welsh affairs having previously been covered by the Home Office. A new department for Northern Ireland was formed in 1972, again assuming responsibilities previously exercised by the Home Office. A Department of Energy was sliced off from the DTI in 1973 in the midst of the energy crisis of 1973-1974. It existed until 1992, when it was absorbed back into the DTI. Under the Labour government of 1974-1979, Transport was reinstated as a separate department and the DTI was broken up into three departments: Trade, Industry, and Prices and Consumer Affairs. In 1979, under the new Thatcher administration, Prices and Consumer Affairs was returned to the Department of Trade and the DTI subsequently recreated. In 1988, the two components of the Department of Health and Social Security were separated to form individual departments. In 1992 a National Heritage Department (later renamed the Ministry of Culture, Media, and Sport) was crafted from responsibilities—such as sport and broadcasting—held by a number of departments.

Just as large departments have their attractions, so, too, does the splitting off from a large department of a new one. It allows for a more clearly defined administration of a particular responsibility and signals the importance the government attaches to the issue. Such changes, though, are not problem-free. The more frequent the changes, the more confusion among affected groups as to who exercises responsibility in a particular sector. The more new departments are created, the greater the pressure from groups for further departments to be formed in order to recognize the importance of their area of interest. There is pressure, for example, for the creation of a Ministry for Women (supported by the Labour party when in opposition but not implemented when the party came to government) and one devoted to "green" issues.

Changes in the number and responsibilities of departments are thus frequent. The last major changes were made following the 1997 general election with the creation in particular of the vast Department for the Environment, Transport, and the Regions. Departments vary considerably in their range of responsibilities and their size. The largest departments in terms of staff numbers are the Department of Social Security (93,000 civil servants in 1997) and the Ministry of Defence (78,000 civil servants). Among the smallest in staff terms are the Ministry of Health (excluding staff of the National Health Service) and the Department for Culture, Media, and Sport. Small staff numbers, though, do not necessarily mean either limited influence or simple internal structures. The Foreign and Commonwealth Office, for example, has a relatively small number of civil servants—fewer than 10,000—but great political clout and a complex departmental infrastructure.

Each department is normally divided into functional areas. Each functional unit, the division, is headed by a civil servant who typically now has a functional title such as director (they were previously known as assistant undersecretaries of state). Above the units are deputy undersecretaries and, above them, the civil servant responsible for running the department, the permanent undersecretary of state (known as the permanent secretary). He (rarely she) is in effect the chief executive officer of the department and answers directly to the minister. Some departments have a small number of functional units. The Department for Education and Employment, for example, has a handful; the Foreign and Commonwealth Office has more than fifty.

Despite a basic similarity in structure, departments vary considerably in size and functional organization. They are complex organizations. That complexity is now greater as a result of the creation of executive agencies.

Agencies

In 1988, following a report from an efficiency unit set up by the prime minister, the government decided that to the greatest extent possible the executive functions of departments (as distinct from the function of advising ministers) should be carried out by operationally distinct agencies, each with clearly defined tasks and managerial responsibility for carrying out those tasks.

Various sections within departments were identified as suitable for agency status. The initial list was a modest one, both in terms of numbers and responsibilities. The first agency created was the Vehicles Inspectorate, followed by bodies such as Her Majesty's Stationery Office. By early 1990, only 12 agencies, employing just over 10,000 staff, had been created. However, the program then gathered pace and by the middle of 1992, there were 75 agencies, with a staff exceeding 300,000—more than half the total number of civil servants. By 2000, more than 70 percent of civil servants were working in agencies. Most departments have some agencies. They range from the Social Security Benefits Agency, employing 68,000 civil servants, to the small Forensic Science Service, employing fewer than 600.

The agencies are essentially semi-autonomous bodies within government. Each has a tailor-made framework document, setting out its aims and objectives, relationships with ministers and Parliament, and the regimes under which it will work. Performance targets are published.

Each agency is headed by a chief executive, who is also the accounting officer. In other words, the chief executive—not the permanent secretary in the department—is accountable for how money is spent. A majority of chief executives have been recruited by open competition and a number drawn from outside the civil service. They nonetheless remain accountable to ministers, who are then answerable to Parliament for the work of the agencies.

Agencies thus form a considerable component of government departments (see Figure 8.1). They exercise important managerial functions, though remaining a formal part of government departments. The nature of their accountability to ministers and to Parliament, despite the wording of framework agreements, remains ambiguous.[19] Breaking away some measure of executive power does not necessarily march hand in hand with removing political responsibility. The creation of executive agencies has thus created fragmentation in structures and some ambiguity in lines of accountability.

Civil Service

Ministers stand at the political apex of government. They head departments that are staffed by a body of permanent public employees, known collectively as the civil service. At the turn of the nineteenth century there were a little more than 100,000 civil servants. Their number reached a peak in 1979, when there were more than 700,000. By 1991, following government cutbacks and some transfers of bodies such as the Royal Ordnance to the private sector, there were just over 550,000. By 1996 the number was down to 494,000. (The figure does not include employees of nationalized industries or local government, or members of the judiciary or the armed forces.) They serve to provide ministers with advice and to carry out their decisions and to administer the business of government.

The relationship between civil servants and ministers is governed by the principle of individual ministerial responsibility. The minister alone is answerable to Parliament for the department and its activities. The civil service head of each department—the permanent secretary—is answerable to the minister for the work of the civil servants within the department and serves usually as the minister's principal advisor. The convention of ministerial responsibility provides a cloak of anonymity to departmental activities. The advice a minister receives from officials and the manner of its formulation are kept from the public gaze. Knowledge of what goes on in a department, certainly at the higher levels, may be made available only by the minister or by officials acting on the minister's instructions.

Most civil servants carry out the routine tasks of government. About half are engaged in providing services to the public, such as issuing benefits and pensions. The rest carry out service-wide or internal departmental support functions. As we have seen, almost three-quarters are now employed in executive agencies. The number involved in advising ministers is small. The most-senior civil servants have, since 1996, formed "the senior civil service." Posts are evaluated by each department to establish their level of responsibility and pay is determined by each department within certain set salary bands. The number of senior civil servants comprise no more than 20,000 people. At the very top—occupying what used to be the posts of assistant secretaries (equivalent to the U.S. posts of bureau chiefs) upwards—are less than 3,000 people.

It is this small elite of civil servants who advise ministers, prepare briefing papers for them, and ensure that their decisions are carried out. They take great care to brief incoming ministers. During each general election campaign, they study the party manifestos. The moment a new government is returned, they are ready with advice on how to implement its program. Where there is no established policy, officials look to the relevant minister to "take a view"— that is, make a decision. According to a study by Bruce Headey, civil servants prefer ministers who are capable of making decisions, of winning cabinet battles, and of defending their departments from parliamentary criticism.[20] Ministers, for their part, look for officials who will provide them with expert advice, a range of options from which to choose, and the loyal implementation of ministerial objectives and policies. In practice, neither ministers nor officials always get what they want but the formal relationship between the two is well established.

Ministers are political appointees, in office so long as the prime minister wishes them so to be and as long as their party remains in power. Civil servants are permanent public officials, and as such required to be nonpartisan in the performance of their duties. They remain in post regardless of the outcome of general elections. They answer to ministers as ministers and not to ministers as party politicians. They help draft speeches given by the minister acting in a formal ministerial capacity—for example, addressing the House of Commons or a particular body that has invited the minister to speak in a ministerial capacity. They do not assist ministers with purely partisan speeches. Civil servants, for example, do not accompany ministers to party conferences nor to party engagements. Civil servants do not draft replies to letters from members of the public that raise party points. A letter about official policy will receive a reply written by civil servants. A letter asking why the minister's party has or has not done something will be drafted by the minister's special advisor.

Ministers reach office through established party and parliamentary routes. Civil servants reach their positions through open, competitive examination. There is a special recruitment procedure for the senior ranks of the service involving written examinations and an appearance before a final selection board. Competition for places is intense, and those recruited through this procedure tend to be drawn from an intellectual and social elite. Those successful tend to have the highest educational qualifications, with almost one in three having a first-class honors degree. They are also disproportionately male (in 1999 only 18 percent of senior civil servants were women) and drawn from public school and Oxbridge graduates, despite attempts to widen the intake.[21] Recruitment also tends to favor generalists over specialists; that is, there is a tendency to select graduates in the arts and humanities rather than those in the pure or applied sciences. Relatively few science graduates apply and the percentage being successful is small.[22]

Once an applicant is in the service, most training is on-the-job training. Senior civil servants are geared to assisting ministers in the formulation and implementation of policy; traditionally, they have had little—often no—training as managers, even though they have extensive responsibilities for personnel and finance.[23] As one senior civil servant put it in 1987, "the golden route to the top" had been through policy, not management.[24] Recent years have seen various changes designed to inject a greater managerial element. These changes have been grouped under the umbrella term "new public management" (NPM).[25]

The 1980s saw the introduction of the Financial Management Initiative (FMI), designed to utilize management information systems and a range of financial management techniques. One of the principal reasons for the government's decision in 1988 to create executive agencies was to improve management within the civil service, creating a new team of identifiable managers separate from the permanent secretary, who previously was the general manager of a whole department. The Blair government has introduced various units designed to improve coordination and management. These include a performance and innovation unit to monitor departmental progress, an efficiency and effectiveness unit to improve coordination across departments, and a center for policy and management studies, incorporating the civil service college, to help improve training of civil servants. A modernizing-government secretariat has also been established to assist with strategic policy making. An attempt to improve efficiency has resulted also in recruitment to some senior posts through open recruitment—rather than simply through promotion within the civil service—and about 30 percent of senior posts are now open to external candidates. Civil servants are also expected, as we have seen, to meet performance targets.

Senior civil servants nonetheless remain, in most cases, generalists drawn from a particular social background. The similarity in social and educational background has produced a body of public servants that is relatively homogeneous. There is regular contact between senior officials, not only in an official capacity—the various interdepartmental committees and the meetings necessary to prepare material for ministers—but also socially: Senior civil servants are often members of the same London clubs and will sometimes wine and dine together. This homogeneity, and their permanence in office, is often seen as giving civil servants a common and a relatively long-term perspective on policy—relative, that is, to politicians—geared to what one permanent secretary referred to as "the common ground."[26] Civil servants carry out the wishes of their ministers but will be influenced by civil service and departmental norms and their perceptions of that common ground.

Though the homogeneity of the senior civil service is breaking down as greater openness and new methods of recruitment take effect, and civil servants see themselves as being on the defensive in the face of pressure from government to improve performance, the senior civil service remains at the heart of British government.

Non-departmental Public Bodies

Non-departmental public bodies are what in U.S. terminology would be referred to as an offline governmental agency (for example, the Environmental Protection Agency). They are public bodies set up either by administrative act or by statute to carry out various executive actions or to operate in an advisory capacity on a particular subject. Advisory bodies are usually formed to provide government with advice that it cannot get from within its own ranks. Such bodies will normally comprise representatives or appointees of interested groups (see Chapter 7). Bodies with executive powers are often formed in order to establish an arm's-length relationship between government and a particular concern.

Two types of body can be grouped under this heading. The first, and better known, type is known as a "quango." It is an acronym for quasi-autonomous nongovernmental organizations. They are bodies created to establish an arm's length relationship with government, fulfilling tasks that, for reasons of efficiency or for ensuring political neutrality, are deemed best fulfilled by a body other than government itself. Whereas the creation of government agencies represents a separation of functions *within* a department, quangos represent a separation of functions *from* a department. Quangos may be associated with a particular department but are not part of that department.

A number of quangos—nondepartmental public bodies—are long-standing and not confined to the twentieth century.[27] The number increased considerably in the twentieth century and in two periods in particular: in the decades after the Second World War and again after 1968. The growth of government and the welfare state after 1945 spurred the creation of a wide range of nondepartmental public bodies. A report in 1968—the Report of the Fulton Committee on the Civil Service—raised the possibility of adding to their number through the splitting off of autonomous units from departments. The concept of separating functions found favor with the then Labour government and with the governments—first Conservative, then Labour—of the 1970s. Despite party differences, successive administrations were influenced by a prevailing managerialism—that services could be more efficiently provided through a managerial restructuring of government.

Among major nondepartmental public bodies created in the 1970s were the Manpower Services Commission; the Health and Safety Commission; and the Advisory, Conciliation, and Arbitration Service (ACAS). A report in 1980 identified the existence of more than 2,000 such bodies: 489 executive bodies and 1,561 advisory bodies.[28] The former were responsible for spending almost £5,800 million (about $9,000 million) in 1978 and had a staff of about 217,000.

Support for quangos came to an end with the return of a Conservative government under Margaret Thatcher in 1979. They were seen as unaccountable, interventionist, a drain on the public purse, and—when acting in a quasi-judicial capacity—a threat to the rule of law. The government initiated a "quango cull" and within three years more than 440 nondepartmental public bodies had been abolished, with more than 100 scheduled for extinction. As far as possible, remaining quangos were put under the aegis of a particular department, with ministers having responsibility for their efficient and effective operation.

Quangos, though, still remain a significant feature of public activity. Government has not been able to do without them. For various purposes, executive and advisory tasks need to be carried out by bodies that enjoy some degree of independence of ministers and civil servants. The number in existence remains a four-figure one, and ministers continue to announce the setting up of such bodies. Their number include bodies as diverse as the Advisory Committee on Statute Law, the Further Education Funding Council, the Inland Waterways Amenity Advisory Council, the Post Office Users' National Council, and the Unrelated Live Transplant Regulatory Authority. However, such bodies are created on an "as and when" basis rather than as part of a conscious, and favored, strategy.

Whereas quangos, as such, are not seen as being in favor with government as a species of institution, there is another form of nondepartmental public body that is in favor. This is the "task force." Task forces are advisory bodies appointed to offer help to deal with a particular problem. They go under a variety of titles—task forces, reviews, working groups, and expert committees—and differ from quangos only inasmuch as they are essentially temporary bodies (they are disbanded once the problem has been addressed) and are viewed as existing to assist government in dealing with particular problems rather than being established at arm's length to government. Task forces have a long pedigree but they have grown remarkably in number under the premiership of Tony Blair. According to government figures, in April 1999 there were 148 review groups and task forces in existence. However, one study identified 295 task forces and similar bodies as having been created in the first 18 months of Labour government.[29] The disparity in numbers is because of the absence of an agreed definition. What is clear is that the government is keen to establish small bodies of experts and advisors in order to address particular problems; experts are, in effect, co-opted in the governmental process on a temporary basis.

THE CURRENT DEBATE

The bodies that form the executive in the United Kingdom are thus several—and greater in number than before—and the relationships among them, and between each of them and the citizen, complex. The range and complexity of those bodies have given rise to considerable debate, not least about the location of power in government. There are four separate approaches that have emerged. These have sought to locate the crucial decision-making power as resting with the prime minister (the presidential model), senior ministers (the baronial model), civil servants (the bureaucratic model), and with a combination of the different elements of government (power dependency). Each retains its proponents.

The Presidential Model

This thesis contends that power is concentrated at the center, with few if any significant checks on that power. Power has become more concentrated in the hands of government and, within government itself, in the hands of the prime minister. A number of writers, as we have noted, have claimed that Britain now has a form of "prime-ministerial government." The concentration of power in the hands of the PM, according to Labour MP Tony Benn, has gone too far "and amounts to a system of personal rule in the very heart of our parliamentary democracy."[30] This claim has been reformulated in two ways since the 1970s. In 1976, Lord Hailsham coined the term "elective dictatorship" to describe the centralization of power.[31] More recently, academic Michael Foley has been among various commentators to allege that Britain is acquiring a "presidential" form of government.[32] The prime minister, it is claimed, is becoming more detached from government, parliament and the party organization, assuming a detached role as the populist leader of the nation.[33]

Longevity in office, large parliamentary majorities, and a radical program of public policy derived from the prime minister's particular philosophy combined, in the eyes of many critics, to render Margaret Thatcher's premiership an exemplar of "presidentialism." She appointed supporters to head the key economic ministries, used bullying tactics in the cabinet—tactics described by one cabinet minister as "Stalinist"—in order to get her way, and used her powers to "handbag" any institution, including the civil service, that got in her way. (The concept of "handbagging" derives from the observation of one Conservative MP that Mrs. Thatcher could not see an institution "without hitting it with her handbag.")[34] "Her conduct of meetings," recalled one senior minister, "became increasingly authoritarian."[35] In the wake of her third election victory in 1987, she was seen by many, including some within her own party, as politically invulnerable, capable of achieving what amounted to a system of one-woman rule. Texts analyzing the creation of "the strong state" grew in number, claiming that traditional safeguards were being eroded as more and more power became concentrated in the Thatcher government.[36]

The argument that Britain was experiencing a "presidential" form of government reemerged with renewed vigor when Tony Blair entered Downing Street in 1997. Under his premiership, the size of the prime minister's staff has increased, more units have been created inside No. 10, and cabinet meetings are kept to a minimum, each lasting—as we have already seen—less than an hour in duration. 10 Downing Street is now seen as the essential powerhouse of British government, the prime minister's advisers crammed into every available space. The cabinet, dominated by the prime minister's supporters ("Blairites"), is no longer seen as a significant decision-making body. Key decisions are taken by the prime minister, either alone or in consultation with senior ministers. Some decisions are reputedly taken by the prime minister's press secretary, Alistair Campbell, who enjoys the prime minister's confidence and is alleged to have sometimes given orders to cabinet ministers. The prime minister stands detached from government, from Parliament (he rarely attends to vote), and from his own party.

This thesis, though, does not go unchallenged. It is countered by the claim that the position of the prime minister relative to the cabinet and, most important of all, relative to the wider political environment has not changed as significantly as critics claim. The prime minister has always been powerful, but that power has not been exclusive or constant.

The cabinet, meeting once or twice a week, is not a body geared to extensive debate and reflection. Much has been left to the PM and individual ministers. It was ever thus.[37] Instances of strong prime ministerial leadership are to be found as much in the nineteenth century as in the twentieth. Being powerful, though, is not the same as being all-powerful. The cabinet acts as a deterrent, a brake on prime ministers, however strong they may appear or want to be. Margaret Thatcher and Tony Blair have faced cabinet revolts. When Margaret Thatcher could not muster support for her views, "she could then become unbelievably discursive . . . generally going round in circles and getting nowhere. . . . Broadcasting and education were two cases in point."[38] Indeed, her tactics in cabinet were essentially evidence of prime ministerial weakness, not strength. Ministers had to be browbeaten because their support could not be taken for granted. Most of her predecessors—even Churchill in wartime—had faced similar difficulties.

The demands on the prime minister's time are extensive. An increasing amount of time has to be spent abroad, not least at European Union summits.[39] Tony Blair is frequently abroad. The resources at the PM's disposal in No. 10 are limited. Individual ministers have a far greater range of advisers and civil servants. The bolstering of resources in No. 10 by Tony Blair is the product of prime ministerial weakness, reflecting his inability to impose his will on the rest of government. Government is structured on the basis of departments. Tony Blair has expressed his frustration at what he calls "departmentalitis."[40] Many policy decisions, especially at the level of medium- and micro-policy making, have to be left to individual ministers. The PM has limited time and resources to keep abreast of all aspects of government. He also has a limited inclination to do so. Few premiers are policy polymaths. They tend to focus on a limited number of policy areas, usually high policy (affecting the economic well-being and security of the nation). In other sectors, senior ministers are left to get on with their jobs.

Furthermore, the prime minister has a more crowded political environment to cope with. There has been a notable fragmentation of power in recent decades.[41] Interests are more organized than before. Policy-making competence in various sectors has passed increasingly to the institutions of the European Union. Margaret Thatcher sometimes found herself isolated in the European Council; Tony Blair has had a similar experience. The EU has taken up more time of the prime minister as the capacity to affect outcomes has declined. Power has been devolved to elected assemblies in different parts of the United Kingdom. Some of the established institutions, notably the courts, have become more active. Prime ministers have had to use more extensively the weapons in their prime-ministerial armory simply to keep pace with the changes in the wider environment.[42]

The Baronial Model

This thesis recognizes that ministers remain powerful figures, not necessarily collectively but rather individually. The basis for it has been outlined in the section on ministers. Statutory powers are vested not in the prime minister or cabinet but in individual ministers. Indeed, as we have seen, powers have been vested in ministers on an increasingly grand scale. The introduction of large regulatory measures results in more and more order-making powers being given to the relevant minister. Formal powers rest in ministers and, given that most ministers are ideologues, commanders, or managers, are frequently exercised by ministers acting on their own volition.

Indeed, such is the power exercised by ministers that the baronial model has been developed to identify their position within British government.[43] The model stipulates that senior ministers are akin to medieval barons. They have their own territory (the policy sector covered by their department), their own courts (ministries), and courtiers (junior ministers, parliamentary private sector, and advisers). They hold a formal position of power and have their own armies (civil servants). They are formally the tenants-in-chief of the king (the prime minister) but are able to use their power bases to carve out an independent position. They build alliances with other barons and with influential figures at court. The power bases of some barons puts them in a particularly powerful position, making it difficult for the monarch to move against them. Under the premiership of Tony Blair, for example, a number of senior ministers—most notably Chancellor of the Exchequer Gordon Brown—are seen as occupying unassailable positions. Brown is an effective political operator with supporters in the House of Commons, in government, and in the party organization. When ministers are in powerful positions, the prime minister may seek to undermine them through arranging for off-the-record press briefings against them. Various ministers complained about this during the premiership of John Major and presently under the premiership of Tony Blair. Such skirmishes reflect the difficulties that a prime minister has in moving against his own "barons."

The greater the responsibilities of government, the less able the prime minister is to keep abreast of everything that is happening in government. Senior ministers are left to get on with their particular jobs. Indeed, they are largely left to determine the jobs for themselves. One of the most remarkable findings of recent research on the role of senior ministers is that, when invited by the prime minister to take office, they are not told what is expected of them.[44] They are offered the job, accept, and take their leave. When Margaret Thatcher offered Nigel Lawson the post of chancellor of the exchequer, he was given only one piece of advice by the prime minister: "That was to get my hair cut."[45] Ministers thus have considerable scope to carve out their own policy preferences. They are, in effect, offered a particular policy territory and left to shape it as they wish.

Despite perceptions of a powerful premier, journalists variously employ the term *barons* to refer to the position of ministers. Tony Blair has strengthened his body of advisers to try to counter the range of advisers at the disposal of senior ministers. Government is still structured on the basis of departments and those departments are headed by senior ministers. The baronial model is a highly plausible one.

This model, though, also has its critics. The analogy with medieval barons, it is argued, is too pat. Senior ministers, other than the chancellor of the exchequer, are not able to levy taxes, though they are able to exercise considerable power over those within their territory. They can be removed from office by the prime minister. The back benches of the House of Commons are littered with ex-ministers. Furthermore, ministers, just like the prime minister, are under increasing pressures. They occupy a political environment that is increasingly crowded and a policy space over which they exercise less and less unilateral power. They too are constrained by the effects of membership in the EU; this is especially the case with particular ministers, such as the minister of agriculture. They are also constrained by a more active judiciary and by the devolution of power to elected assemblies in Scotland and Wales. The secretaries of state for Scotland and Wales now have little to do. Ministers may not quite resemble medieval barons and, even if they do, they are operating in a shrinking kingdom.

The Bureaucratic Model

For some critics, the problem of government is not to be found with the prime minister and ministers generally. They are, after all, the leaders of a party elected to office. Rather, the problem is seen as being with the nonelected part of the executive: the civil service.

Senior civil servants are seen by critics as having the means to ensure the outcomes they want. Furthermore, those outcomes are criticized for contributing to Britain's poor economic performance. The background of civil servants has produced a body of generalists, with no particular knowledge or understanding of the problems faced by British industry and commerce. Rather, they are guided by some amorphous notion of "common ground"—which, for critics, means the common interest of senior civil servants.

Ministers come and go, but senior officials remain in place. Battles lost by civil servants under one minister can be fought again under another. A new government provides particular scope to refight old battles. By tradition, incoming ministers do not see the papers of their predecessors. This provides senior civil servants with an almost clean ministerial canvas on which to try their persuasive brushwork. During a minister's tenure, officials have various means for influencing outcomes. Ministers look to their permanent secretaries for knowledge of how their departments work. They look to officials for advice and briefing documents. They look to the civil servants in their private offices to control the flow of paperwork that reaches their desks, and also to control their diaries.

Officials thus have the opportunity, should they choose to exercise it, to skew advice in favor of a particular course of action. They can swamp a minister with an excess of paperwork to obscure the importance of a particular document. They can submit important documents at the last minute to prevent time for reflection and outside advice. They can schedule so many meetings that the minister has little time to devote to particular issues. And, if these techniques fail to work, they can brief their counterparts in other departments, engage in some degree of misinterpretation of the minister's wishes, or simply stall until a new minister takes over. "Oh, he won't be here in another year or so" is a phrase that has been heard from the lips of civil servants, including in the hearing of this writer. And adding to their influence in recent years has been British membership in the European Union. Not only has membership entailed increased demands on ministers' time, especially in attending meetings of the Council of Ministers, but it also has given a greater role to bureaucrats. Most of the documents discussed by the council are prepared by officials: Contact between civil servants in the member states and officials in the European Commission is extensive. No sooner had Doug Henderson been appointed minister for Europe in May 1997 than he was on a plane to Brussels, being briefed by his officials. The dispersal of power also makes it increasingly difficult for government to monitor the implementation of policy, especially that which is carried out through EU officials in Brussels.[46]

For ministers, there is thus the problem of ensuring that they have control of their departments. A capable and determined minister will normally enjoy mastery of the department. Even so, that mastery will usually extend only to important issues drawn to the minister's attention or to specific policy goals set by the minister. Other matters, of necessity, will be dealt with at lower levels. If there is a problem with senior officials—"some ministers," as Pyper notes, "operate in an atmosphere of almost continuous tension and conflict with their officials"[47]—then, as we have seen, the minister lacks the power to remove those officials. The matter has to be resolved by the prime minister and it may not necessarily be resolved in the minister's favor. Less forceful, energetic, or intelligent ministers may find themselves guided by the papers and recommendations put before them by officials.

Compounding the problem is the homogeneity of senior officials. Insofar as they seek to influence decisions, they do so in support of what they see as the national interest—or "common ground"—but which critics claim as more the common interests of senior civil servants, the "national interest" often being synonymous with departmental or general civil service interests. The shared background and continuing social contact of officials reinforces both their shared perception of what is needed to maintain the common ground and their influence in order to effect the desired outcome. For critics, outcomes are as bad as the means by which they are arrived at, reflecting the self-assured but limited views of a social elite that has no experience of life beyond public school, Oxford, and the corridors of Whitehall.

The bureaucratic model has found favor among politicians on the left and right. Many of the left have tended to see the civil service as an inherently conservative body, likely to stifle the radical ambitions of a Socialist government. Margaret Thatcher, a Conservative premier with a radical policy, also tended to see the civil service as an impediment to change. She brought to the premiership a strong animosity toward the civil service, born of her neoliberal philosophy and of her own ministerial experience in the early 1970s: She had experienced poor relations with officials when she was education secretary. As one permanent secretary told Peter Hennessy, "She doesn't think clever chaps like us should be here at all. We should be outside, making profits."[48]

However, this thesis is also challenged. The civil service, it is pointed out, is not quite the monolithic entity it is sometimes made out to be. Departmental ethos and attitudes differ. The Environment Department, for example, has a reputation for being a fairly open one, whereas the Home Office has a reputation for excessive secrecy. Insofar as there is a civil service ethos, it is one that compels compliance with ministers' wishes. The relationship between ministers and officials is often more congenial and collegial than it is conflictual. Civil servants may argue a point in preliminary discussions, but once ministers have decided they then carry out whatever has been decided. "In my view," recorded one member of Margaret Thatcher's cabinet, "a good cabinet minister can always get what he or she wants out of the Civil Service."[49] This view was echoed by other ministers who served in government from 1979 to 1997; indeed, it appeared to constitute the prevailing view. Far from keeping officials at arm's length, some ministers drew more civil servants into meetings to discuss proposals. Civil servants may not always like the substance of what a minister decides, but—as Bruce Headey found in a seminal study of minister-civil service relations—they do like ministers capable of making decisions.[50] And, once the decision is made, they implement it. One energetic junior minister recalled the occasion when she summoned officials to discuss a big event she was organizing to promote health education. "I realized then just how disciplined some civil servants are when faced with a pesky minister with 'ideas.' It must have taken a lot of effort for the one who had to run the thing to keep saying 'Yes, Minister,' but bless her cotton socks, she did it."[51]

Furthermore, the changes that have taken place in civil service recruitment and organization have meant that civil servants feel more under threat than in control of the affairs of government. Most civil servants are now working in agencies, senior jobs are increasingly being opened up to external candidates, and departments are being set targets to meet. Every permanent secretary has been asked "to ensure that their department has the capacity to drive through achievement of the key government targets and to take a personal responsibility for ensuring that this happens."[52] Claims of the politicization of the civil service have been fueled during the Blair government, especially as a result of the centralization of media relations in Downing Street and by the departure of many departmental press officers (career civil servants). The perceptions of civil servants that underpinned criticism in the 1970s and 1980s no longer have the force they did. When he was president, Gerald Ford declared that the presidency "was not so much imperial as imperiled." By the end of the twentieth century, some civil servants could be forgiven for expressing a similar view about the civil service.

The Power Dependency Model

The power dependency model has been advanced by R. A. W. Rhodes.[53] Though developed to cover principally center–local relations, it is relevant for the relationships between the different bodies of government at national level. It contends that any organization is dependent upon other organizations for resources and that in order to achieve their goals, organizations have to exchange resources. In short, no body can operate as an exclusive entity. It depends on others to achieve outcomes just as other bodies may have to rely on it to assist them to achieve what they want to achieve. The prime minister has his own resources but is dependent on senior ministers and on civil servants to get what he wants. Ministers have to acquire allies in cabinet committees to ensure that their proposals are accepted. Civil servants need ministers to win battles in cabinet and with the treasury. Though the prime minister and senior ministers may have formal powers, they need more than these powers to ensure they get the outcomes they desire. Indeed, this approach is not dissimilar to Richard Neustadt's thesis of presidential power: for a president to get his way, he has to persuade others that what he wants is in their interests as well.[54] Formal powers are but one of the weapons in the arsenal needed to achieve particular outcomes. Professional reputation and popular support are other important weapons.

The power dependency thesis offers a complex and less hierarchical model than that advanced by the presidential model. It suggests that prime minister, ministers, and civil servants have an interactive and mutually dependent relationship. That mutual dependence was well drawn out by Headey in his study of minister–civil servant relationships. It is also illustrated by what happens in determining high policy. The prime minister needs to consult with the relevant minister or ministers. Briefing papers are provided by civil servants. When the prime minister faces the House of Commons at prime minister's question time, he is armed with briefing material called in by the parliamentary questions section in 10 Downing Street. That section has only three staff members. It is heavily dependent on departments. In large measure, the prime minister is only as good as the material supplied by the various departments. No. 10 sometimes has to chase departments when the briefing material is not up to snuff.

The model can be widened. Ministers may be dependent on outside bodies for assistance in achieving the implementation of policy decisions. Departments may be dependent on sectional interest groups for information, advice, and cooperation. Interest groups may be dependent on ministers making decisions favorable to their interests. Ministers may build a parliamentary support base in order to ease the passage of contentious measures. MPs may support a minister in order to build goodwill for when they need the minister to make a decision favorable to their constituencies.

This model is highly plausible. It views government as a complex network rather than a set of fairly disparate and discrete entities. However, it is not immune from criticism. It does not necessarily help explain who is principally responsible for determining a particular outcome. Extensive empirical study is necessary to discover that. It does not help explain outcomes that result from unilateral actions of the prime minister or ministers, nor outcomes achieved by actors adopting a confrontational rather than an alliance-building stance. As various ministers recorded, Margaret Thatcher was not noted for building alliances in the cabinet. The statutory powers vested in ministers means that, in many cases, they can (and do) act unilaterally. Certain ministers have built reputations for making decisions without reference to anyone else. One senior minister under the Thatcher and Major governments—Kenneth Clarke, who held two of the senior offices of state (home secretary and chancellor of the exchequer)—was well known for his single-handed decision making. He was not prone to listen to others.

The power dependency model points to the complexity of governmental decision making. The criticisms of the model suggest that the reality of decision making is even more complex than the model suggests.

CONCLUSION

What is clear from our analysis is that it is misleading to refer to "the executive" as a monolithic body. It consists of a sophisticated and complex infrastructure, with relationships that are neither static nor easy to discern. There is no one part of the executive that can be identified clearly and unambiguously as the body for the making of public policy.

In so far as generalization is possible, one can identify a continuous and significant flow of advice and policy recommendations between officials and ministers, with the policy-making process resembling—insofar as a coherent shape can be ascribed to it—a pyramid, as shown in Figure 8.1. Policy is formulated and agreed on at different levels. What may be termed high policy (such as economic policy) is usually made at the level of prime minister and cabinet; medium-level policy (a new initiative on transport safety or school examinations, for example) at the ministerial level within departments; and low-level, or day-to-day incremental, policy at the civil service level, often in consultation with those representatives of outside groups who, together, form policy communities (Chapter 7). This last category probably accounts for the bulk of public policy or, perhaps more accurately, policy adjustments.[55]

Even this threefold delineation must be treated with caution. The boundaries are far from clear-cut. Contact between ministers and officials is extensive and continuous and, as posited by the power dependence model, few decisions are taken in isolation. The more important, and the more extensive, the policy the greater the involvement of all elements of government. On other occasions, important issues may, for reasons of time or security, have to be decided quickly or secretly by a few ministers. Minor issues may suddenly achieve public prominence and move up the decision-making ladder. Some decisions may, in effect, move down the ladder as a consequence of a lazy or not overly bright minister deferring to officials. The extent to which this happens, given the secrecy that still attaches to the process of government, is difficult to determine. All that one can say with confidence is that the process may resemble a pyramid, but that pyramid may be rather misshapen.

Furthermore, the structure and processes of government are not static. Not only are they variously modified—sometimes radically—but also they remain the subject of demands for further change. As we have seen (Chapter 3), some of the explanations offered for Britain's poor economic performance are political—most notably, in the context of this chapter, the concentration of power in central government and, within that government, in the hands of the prime minister. Others have identified problems within that central government in terms of the civil service and the processes employed for determining public policy. The nub of the argument can be simply put. For critics of the existing political system, that system has not served the country well. For defenders, it constitutes a system that is, despite its complexity, both coherent and accountable.

NOTES

[1] A. B. Keith, *The British Cabinet System,* 2nd ed. by N. H. Gibbs (Stevens & Sons, 1952), p. 14.

[2] Derived from B. Donoughue, *Prime Minister* (Jonathan Cape, 1987); and A. King, "The British Prime Ministership in the Age of the Career Politician," in G. W. Jones (ed.), *West European Prime Ministers* (Frank Cass, 1991).

[3] M. Kogan, *The Politics of Education* (Penguin, 1971), p. 35.

[4] There have been various instances recorded of ministers failing to get their way. Barbara Castle and Tony Benn both encountered problems in trying to get prime ministerial support in battles with senior officials in their departments (Castle when transport minister, 1965-1968, and Benn as industry secretary, 1974-1975, and energy secretary, 1975-1979). Ministers appear to have had more success under more recent prime ministers.

[5] See especially G. W. Jones, "The Prime Minister's Aides," in A. King (ed.), *The British Prime Minister,* 2nd ed. (Macmillan, 1985), pp. 72-95.

[6] Prior to the Blair premiership, the Policy Unit comprised a mix of political appointees and individuals seconded from the civil service and outside organizations.

[7] P. Norton, "Prime Ministerial Power," *Social Studies Review 3* (3), 1988, p. 110; see also P. Norton, "Prime Ministerial Power: A Framework for Analysis," *Teaching Politics 16* (3), 1987, pp. 325-345.

[8] B. Kellerman, *The Political Presidency* (Oxford University Press, 1984), p. 37.

[9] P. Madgwick, *British Government: The Central Executive Territory* (Philip Allan, 1991), pp. 73-74.

[10] The membership and terms of reference may be found in *Dod's Parliamentary Companion 2000* (Vacher Dod Publishing, 2000), pp. 439-450.

[11] J. Barnett, *Inside the Treasury* (Andre Deutsch, 1982), p. 27.

[12] R. Crossman, "Introduction" to W. Bagehot, *The English Constitution* (Fontana, 1963 ed.).

[13] N. Johnson, *In Search of the Constitution* (Methuen, 1980), p. 84.

[14] "The Typhoon Hits Hong Kong," *Sunday Times Magazine,* August 30, 1992, p. 21.

[15] P. Norton, "Barons in a Shrinking Kingdom? Senior Ministers in British Government," in R. A. W. Rhodes (ed.), *Transforming British Government* (Macmillan, 2000).

[16] P. Norton, "Barons in a Shrinking Kingdom?"

[17] P. Hennessy, *Whitehall* (Secker & Warburg, 1989), p. 380.

[18] See Sir R. Clarke, "The Machinery of Government," in W. Thornhill (ed.), *The Modernization of British Government* (Pitman, 1975), p. 65.

[19] T. Butcher, "Improving Civil Service Management: The Next Steps Programme," *Talking Politics 3* (3), 1991, pp. 110-115; P. Norton, "Getting the Balance Right," *The House Magazine 18* (585), March 8, 1993, p. 16.

[20] B. Headey, *British Cabinet Ministers* (George Allen & Unwin, 1974).

[21] See R. Pyper, *The Evolving Civil Service* (Longman, 1991), p. 98; G. Drewry and T. Butcher, *The Civil Service Today* (Blackwell, 1988), pp. 71-72.

[22] Drewry and Butcher, Table 3.9, p. 71.

[23] See Hennessy; J. Garrett, *Managing the Civil Service* (Heinemann, 1980).

[24] Quoted in Butcher, p. 111.

[25] See The Select Committee on the Public Service, *Report,* HL Paper 55 (The Stationery Office, 1998), pp. 34-35.

[26] Sir Anthony Part, speaking on an Independent Television program, "World in Action," January 7, 1980.

[27] See P. Holland, *The Governance of Quangos* (Adam Smith Institute, 1981), pp. 10-12.

[28] *Report on Non-Departmental Public Bodies,* Cmnd. 7797 (Her Majesty's Stationery Office, 1980).

[29] A. Barker, I. Byrne, and A. Veal, *Ruling by Task Force* (Politico's, 1999). See also the debate on Task Forces in the House of Lords, February 23, 2000, *HL Deb.* Vol. 610, cols. 234-270. In the debate, the minister of state at the Cabinet Office said there were 46 task forces and 270 ad hoc reviews and advisory groups. See also *Reinforcing Standards: Sixth Report of the Committee on Standards in Public Life,* Vol. 1: Report, Cm 4557-I (The Stationery Office, 2000), pp. 123-124.

[30] T. Benn, "The Case for a Constitutional Premiership," *Parliamentary Affairs 33* (1), 1980, p. 7.

[31] Lord Hailsham, *Elective Dictatorship* (BBC, 1976).

[32] M. Foley. *The Rise of the British Presidency* (Manchester University Press, 1993).

[33] For an invaluable summary of these characteristics, see G. P. Thomas, *Prime Minister and Cabinet Today* (Manchester University Press, 1998), pp. 77-80.

[34] J. Critchley, *Westminster Blues* (Futura, 1986), p. 126.

[35] N. Lawson, *The View from No. 11* (Bantam, 1992), p. 128.

[36] As, for example, A. Gamble, *The Free Economy and the Strong State* (Macmillan, 1988); C. Graham and T. Prosser (eds.), *Waiving the Rules* (Open University Press, 1988); and P. McAuslan and M. J. McEldowney (eds.), *Law, Legitimacy and the Constitution* (Sweet & Maxwell, 1985).

[37] Norton, "Prime Ministerial Power," p. 114.

[38] Lawson, p. 128.

[39] P. Madgwick, *British Government: The Central Executive Territory* (Philip Allan, 1991), p. 142.

[40] P. Webster and J. Sherman, "Straw chosen to relaunch the New Deal message," *The Times,* Jan. 23, 1998.

[41] J. Greenaway, S. Smith, and J. Street, *Deciding Factors in British Politics* (Routledge, 1992), pp. 236-238; P. Norton, "In Defence of the Constitution," in P. Norton (ed.), *New Directions in British Politics?* (Edward Elgar, 1991), pp. 153-160.

[42] Norton, "Prime Ministerial Power," pp. 113-114.

[43] P. Norton, "The New Barons? Senior Ministers in British Government," *Goldsmiths College Public Policy Paper* (Goldsmiths College, 1998); Norton, "Barons in a Shrinking Kingdom?".

[44] Norton, "The New Barons?" pp. 10-11.

[45] Lawson, p. 249.

[46] Greenaway, Smith, and Street, p. 237.

[47] Pyper, p. 43.

[48] Hennessy, p. 592.

[49] N. Ridley, *"My Style of Government"* (Fontana, 1992), p. 41.

[50] Headey, *British Cabinet Ministers.*

[51] E. Currie, *Life Lines* (Sidgwick & Jackson, 1989), p. 161.

[52] Government White Paper, *Modernising Government,* Cm 4310 (The Stationery Office, 1999), p. 6.

[53] R. A. W. Rhodes, *Control and Power in Centre-Local Government Relationships* (Gower, 1981); R. A. W. Rhodes, *Understanding Governance* (Open University Press, 1997), pp. 36-40.

[54] R. E. Neustadt, *Presidential Power* (Free Press, 1990 ed.).

[55] See especially Greenaway, Smith, and Street, Ch. 10.

CHAPTER 9

The European Union
Government above the Center

Prior to the 1970s, the United Kingdom had entered into various treaty obligations with other nations. It was a founding member of the United Nations Organization. It had joined the North Atlantic Treaty Organization (NATO). It
signed, though at the time did not incorporate into domestic law, the European
Convention on Human Rights. It participated in the various rounds of the General Agreement on Trade and Tariffs (GATT) to reduce barriers to free trade. At
no time, though, did it hand over to a supranational body the power to make
regulations that were to be applied within the United Kingdom and be enforceable as law.

This situation was to change on January 1, 1973. On that date the United
Kingdom became a member of the European Community. Forty-two volumes
of legislation promulgated by institutions of the European Community were incorporated into British law. Under the provisions of the 1972 European Communities Act, future legislation emanating from the Community was to be incorporated as well. Further treaties led to an expansion of the Community,
both geographically (more countries became members) and in terms of responsibilities. Under the terms of the Treaty on European Union (TEU), which
took effect in 1993, a European Union was formed. The Union comprises three
"pillars"—the first pillar is the European Community, the second is cooperation in foreign and security policy, and the third is cooperation in dealing with
justice and home affairs.

The United Kingdom is thus a member of a body that is expanding, both
quantitatively and qualitatively, and one for which the United States has no
equivalent. Though the United States is now part of the North American Free
Trade Agreement (NAFTA), there is no supranational body in North America
able to make law that can be imposed in the United States against the wishes of
the president and Congress, and no supranational body interpreting that body

of law. In this respect, the USA is not unusual. It is the member states of the European Union that are in a unique situation.

FROM COMMUNITY TO UNION

The European Community, the first pillar of the Union, formally comprises three bodies: the European Steel and Coal Community, the European Atomic Energy Community (Euratom), and the European Economic Community (the EEC). The Steel and Coal Community, formed in 1951 under the Treaty of Paris, placed iron, steel, and coal production in member countries under a common authority. Euratom and the EEC were created under the Treaty of Rome and came into being on January 1, 1958. Euratom was designed to help create a civil nuclear industry in Europe. The EEC formed a common market for goods within the community of member states. The three bodies were merged in 1967 to form the European Communities, known now by the singular term, the European Community (the EC).

Britain declined to join the individual bodies when they were first formed. The Labour government in 1951 found the supranational control of the Steel and Coal Community to be unacceptable. The succeeding Conservative government was not initially attracted by the concept of the EEC. The economic and political arguments for joining, which weighed heavily with the member states, did not carry great weight with British politicians. Britain was still seen as a world power. It was enjoying a period of prosperity. It had strong political and trading links with the Commonwealth. It had a "special relationship" with the United States. It had stood alone successfully during World War II. Lacking the experience of German occupation and the need to recreate a polity, Britain was not subject to the psychological appeal of a united Europe, so strong on the continental mainland.[1] Neither main political party was strongly attracted to the idea of a union with such an essentially foreign body. The Conservatives still hankered after the idea of empire, something that had died as a result of the war (Britain could no longer afford to maintain an empire and the principle of self-determination had taken root) and something for which the Commonwealth now served as a kind of a substitute. Labour politicians viewed with distrust the creation of a body that they saw as inherently antisocialist, designed to shore up the capitalist edifice of Western Europe and frustrate any future socialist policies that a Labour government in Britain would seek to implement. It was one of the few issues on which the leader of the Labour party, Hugh Gaitskell, found himself in agreement with left-wingers within his own party.

The attitude of the British government toward the EEC, at both a ministerial and official level, was to undergo significant change in 1960. Britain's economic problems had become more apparent. Growth rates compared poorly with those of the six member states of the EEC (France, Germany, Italy, Holland, Belgium, and Luxembourg). There was a growing realization that having lost an empire, Britain had gained a Commonwealth. That Commonwealth, however, was not proving as amenable to British leadership as many Conservatives had hoped, nor was it proving to be the source of trade and materials that had been expected. Even the special relationship with the United States was undergoing a period of strain. The "special" appeared to be seeping out of the relationship. Some anti-Americanism lingered in Conservative ranks following the insistence of the White House that Britain abort its operation to occupy the Suez Canal zone in 1956, a distrust still not wholly dispelled. The sudden cancellation by the U.S. administration in 1960 of the Blue Streak, a missile that Britain had ordered and intended to employ as the major element of its nuclear defense policy, awakened British politicians to the fact that in the Atlantic partnership, Britain was very much the junior partner. The U.S. administration itself began to pay more attention to the EEC, and President John F. Kennedy made clear to his friend and distant relative, Prime Minister Harold Macmillan,[2] "that a British decision to join the Six would be welcome."[3] The option became one that had an increasing attraction to Britain.

Politically, the EEC was seen as a vehicle through which Britain could once again play a leading role on the world stage. Economically, it would provide a tariff-free market of 180 million people, it would provide the advantages of economy of scale, and it was assumed that it would encourage greater efficiency in British industry through more vigorous competition. Political and economic advantages were seen as inextricably linked. Economic strength was necessary to underpin the maintenance of political authority.[4] "If we are to meet the challenge of Communism," Macmillan wrote to Kennedy, "[we must show] that our modern society—the new form of capitalism—can run in a way that makes the fullest use of our resources and results in a steady expansion of our economic strength."[5] On July 31, 1961, he announced to the House of Commons that Britain was applying for membership.

The first application for membership was vetoed in January 1963 by the French president, General Charles de Gaulle. He viewed British motives with suspicion, believing that Britain could serve as a vehicle for the United States to establish its dominance within the EEC. A second application was lodged in 1967, this time by the Labour government of Harold Wilson.[6] Agreement to open negotiations was reached eventually in 1969. Negotiations began under the newly returned Conservative government of Edward Heath in 1970. Relations between the British and French governments on the issue were now more amicable, de Gaulle having resigned the presidency in 1969, and no French veto was imposed. Negotiations were completed in 1971 and the British government recommended entry on the terms achieved. On October 28, 1971, following a six-day debate, the House of Commons gave its approval to the principle of membership on the terms negotiated. The vote was 356 in favor, 244 against. Both parties were badly divided. Of Labour members of Parliament, 69 voted with the Conservative government in favor of entry and a further 20 abstained from voting. Of Conservatives, 39 voted with the Labour opposition against entry, and 2 abstained. It was the most divisive vote of the Parliament.

At the beginning of 1972, the Treaty of Accession was signed, and the European Communities bill, to give legal effect to British membership, was given a second reading on February 17. To ensure its passage, Prime Minister Heath made the vote one of confidence. Despite that, the majority for the bill was a slim one of only 8, Labour MPs largely uniting against the bill and being joined by some Conservatives. The bill faced sustained opposition from Labour members and a number of dissident Conservatives, but it completed its remaining stages without amendment and was given a third reading on July 13.[7] The United Kingdom became a member of the European Community on January 1, 1973.

Britain's membership in the EC has been anything but uneventful. Following the return of a Labour government in 1974, the terms of membership were renegotiated and the renegotiated terms put to—and approved by—the electorate in Britain's first nationwide referendum in 1975. In the referendum, 17,378,581 people voted to remain in the EC on the terms negotiated; 8,470,073 voted no. Many commentators interpreted the result as putting Britain's membership beyond further dispute. However, it did not stop conflict taking place over Britain's role within the Community. After the return of a Conservative government in 1979, Prime Minister Margaret Thatcher argued that Britain's financial contribution to the EC was too high and pressed for a reduction. After several heated meetings with other EC heads of government, agreement was reached in 1984, with the United Kingdom receiving refunds on previous years' payments and with a new system to operate in the future. In 1986 the Thatcher government agreed to the terms of a new treaty, known as the Single European Act. This strengthened the institutions of the EC in measures designed to achieve a single market. However, the effects of the treaty were seen by opponents as weakening the member states. This appeared to be a view that Thatcher herself came to share. In 1988, she made a speech signaling her opposition to developments within the Community and to monetary union within the Community. She defined a role for the EC that was at odds with that envisaged by leaders of other member states. She was committed to achieving a single market but opposed to any moves designed to create a supranational government that could impose its will on member states. Her "so far and no further" stance left her often in a minority of one at EC summits and badly split the Conservative party.

Thatcher's unwillingness to modify her negative stance was a contributory factor in her loss of the party leadership in 1990 (see Chapter 6). Her successor, John Major, adopted a more emollient approach and had some success in negotiations on a new Community treaty, the Treaty on European Union, more commonly known as the Maastricht Treaty, in 1991. The bill to give effect to the treaty in British law proved difficult (opponents were spurred to mount a spirited campaign against the bill following the rejection of the treaty in a referendum in Denmark),[8] but it was eventually passed. The issue, however, divided the Conservative party and Major had to contend with a vocal and determined section of his party that opposed further European integration and, in particular, opposed U.K. membership in a single European currency. Major had negotiated an "opt out" (or, as Major put it, an "opt in") provision for the United Kingdom as part of the Maastricht treaty: The United Kindgom was not committed to joining a single currency, but could opt to join it if it wished. The stance of the Major government was one of "negotiate and decide" (popularly portrayed as "wait and see") but some Conservatives wanted him to rule out any prospect of British participation. In the run-up to the general election in 1997, a large number of Conservative candidates departed from the party line and expressed their opposition to membership in a single currency.

The election saw the return of a Labour government and a different stance to the issue of European integration. The Labour party had moved from vehement opposition to membership in the EC—in its 1983 manifesto it had advocated withdrawal from the Community—to a position where, in the mid 1990s, it was seen as the more "Euro friendly" of the two parties. It favored a positive engagement in the European Union. Shortly after coming to office in 1997 it was involved in the negotiation of a new treaty, the Amsterdam Treaty, that further extended the policy-making capacity of the Union. Ministers sought to portray a more positive approach to EU affairs than that taken by their Conservative predecessors. Nonetheless, the United Kindgom continued to be seen as a skeptical member of the Union—willing to say "no" when other leading member states were in agreement—and the issue of European integration and, especially, participation in a single currency has remained very much on the political agenda.

British membership in the EC, now the EU, has had major constitutional, economic, and political implications. The issue of "Europe" has always been a contentious one. It divides both main political parties and it is an issue very much on the agenda of political debate.

Constitutional Implications

As we have already had cause to note (Chapter 4), membership in the European Community added a new dimension to the British constitution. Under the provisions of the European Communities Act, existing EC law was to have general and binding applicability in the United Kingdom, as was all subsequent law promulgated by the Communities. Section 2(1) of the act gives the force of law in the United Kingdom to "rights, powers, liabilities, obligations, and restrictions from time to time created or arising by or under the Treaties." Section 2(4) provides that directly applicable EC law should prevail over conflicting provisions of domestic legislation. The effects of membership and the provisions of the act were several. Membership introduced two new decision-making bodies into the ambit of the British polity: The Council of Ministers and the Commission. It restricted the role and influence of Parliament in matters that came within the competence of the Communities. It injected a new judicial dimension to the constitution. Disputes concerning the treaties or legislation made under them were to be treated by the British courts as matters of law, with provision for their referral to the European Court of Justice. And it allowed for British representation in the European Parliament, albeit until 1987 a body with very limited powers.

The constitutional implications were a matter of controversy at the time Britain joined the EC. Equally controversial were the implications of subsequent treaties. The Single European Act (the SEA) took effect in 1987. The provisions necessary to give effect to it in British law were enacted by the 1986 European Communities (Amendment) act. The SEA was introduced in order to facilitate the achievement of a single market: Though that was the goal of the European Economic Community, it had proved difficult to achieve. The SEA created a shift in power relationships *within* the institutions of the EC as well as *between* the institutions of the EC and the member states. Under the SEA, the European Parliament not only was designated as a parliament (its formal title previously was the European Assembly) but also was given a more powerful role in the EC lawmaking process. Previously its role was solely advisory. To allow for the approval of the measures necessary to achieve the single market, provision for the Council of Ministers to determine issues by qualified majority voting (QMV) was extended. Under QMV, each member state has a number of votes, the number varying according to the size of the country, and a set number of votes is necessary to approve a proposal. QMV replaced the usual practice of agreeing measures on the basis of unanimity. The use of QMV made it possible for measures to be passed despite the opposition of a small number of member states. By the end of the decade, British ministers had sometimes found themselves outvoted under this procedure.

The Treaty on European Union (the Maastricht Treaty), negotiated in 1991, signed in 1992 and taking effect in 1993, established the European Union and established economic and monetary union as an objective of the Community. It also enhanced the powers of the European Parliament through introducing a new co-decision procedure. Under the procedure, the parliament cannot force the Council of Ministers to adopt a measure but it can block a measure. The treaty also embodied the principle of subsidiarity, stating that in areas outside its exclusive competence, the Community "shall take action . . . only and in so far as the objectives of the proposed action cannot be sufficiently achieved by the Member States." Britain interpreted this as limiting the centralizing tendencies of the EC. Others took a different view, seeing it as a legitimation of the Community extending its reach. Opponents pointed out that it would still be at the level of the Community that the decisions would be made as to what should fall within the scope of subsidiarity.

The Amsterdam Treaty, which took effect in 1999, further strengthened the position of the European Parliament by making more treaty provisions subject to the co-decision procedure. This is now the procedure more used than any other. The treaty also further extended the policy-making competence of the Community. Provision for qualified majority voting was also extended, including to some areas under the second pillar (foreign and security policy) of the Union. The Commission also acquired new rights in respect of immigration and asylum policy. The policy areas now falling within the competence of the European Union are extensive.

The effect of these treaties has thus been to create a powerful supranational decision-making entity with fundamental implications for the constitution of the U.K. Membership in the EU constitutes an important part now of the British constitution, but it is a part that does fit well with other basic tenets. As we have seen, it serves to undermine, though formally not destroy, the doctrine of parliamentary sovereignty. Law can be promulgated by the institutions of the EC and that law has effect in the United Kindgom, even though the British minister may have voted against it in the Council of Ministers. If British law conflicts with the provisions of EC law, the courts are to give precedence to the EC law. In the *Factortame* case in 1990–91, the European Court of Justice held that British courts could, in effect, suspend acts of Parliament that appeared to breach EC law, until such time as a final judgement was made. In the *EOC* case in 1994 the courts struck down a provision of British law as being contrary to EC law. The position of the courts is further strengthened as the policy-making competence of the EU is extended. It is also strengthened by moves to create new rights within the EU.

The British Parliament, like other national parliaments, has no formal role in the European lawmaking process. It remains important when new treaties are negotiated: Member states have to give their approval through their usual constitutional procedures. Parliament has to approve bills to give effect to treaty changes. However, it has no power to block or amend legislation made under the treaties. European regulations have direct and binding effect; directives are binding as to their ends but each member state may decide the form of implementation. All that Parliament can do to affect measures promulgated by the institutions of the EU is to consider draft documents to be submitted to the Council of Ministers and to influence the relevant minister prior to meetings of the Council of Ministers. Both houses of Parliament have established committees to undertake scrutiny of EU documents.[9] The scrutiny they undertake is generally regarded as good, not least compared with that undertaken by most other national parliaments, but they serve essentially as advisory bodies in the process. Though a declaration appended to the Maastricht Treaty, and a protocol attached to the Amsterdam Treaty, encourage greater involvement by national parliaments, no place in the decision-making process is accorded to them.

Economic Implications

The economic attractions for joining the EC were, as we have seen, a major influence in Britain's applying for membership. The Community offered, in trading terms, a "common market" (the popular name for the EEC), one which has assumed increasing significance for the British economy. Enlargement—there are now 15 member states—has resulted in a market of 370 million consumers, a market that accounts for 40 percent of world trade.

Before membership, most U.K. trade was with countries outside the EC. Since joining, British exports to the EC increased and trade grew faster with EC states than it did with the rest of the world. In 1973, 36 percent of U.K. trade was with EC countries; in 2000, the figure was 58 percent. The U.K. exports more than four times as much to other member states as it does to the United States. The country also has attracted significant inward investment. Of overseas investment in the EU, 30 percent comes to the United Kindom. Britain also receives money from what are known as the Community's structural and cohesion funds.

The structural funds are made up of the European regional development fund, the European social fund, the guidance section of the European agricultural guidance and guarantee fund, and the financial instrument of fisheries guidance. These provide grants towards regional economic infrastructure projects, vocational training, adaptation of agriculture and fisheries structures, and measures to promote competitiveness in regions dependent on declining industries. The cohesion fund, which came into force in 1994, provides grants to four "cohesion" countries (Spain, Portugal, Greece, and the Republic of Ireland) to assist with transport infrastructure and environmental projects. The United Kindgom receives money from the structural funds to assist with economic development and regeneration, especially in Northern Ireland, Merseyside, and the Highlands and Islands of Scotland. Funding is also received to assist more generally with retraining and helping the unemployed into work. In 1999 it was agreed that the United Kindom would receive over £10 billion ($16 billion) between 2000 and 2006 from the structural funds.

The agricultural fund has proved contentious. The guarantee part of the fund supports the Common Agricultural Policy (the CAP) for which the United Kingdom has sought, and achieved, various reforms. Britain has a highly efficient agricultural sector, especially in comparison with other member states. The CAP has favored price supports rather than cheap food, thus working to the benefit of countries with large farming communities, such as France. The guidance part of the fund, forming part of the structural funds, is designed to help finance the modernization of farming and to provide income support in rural areas.

The EC also administers a number of other funds and programs, such as one to provide assistance with energy research and development, and it also encompasses the European Investment Bank. Created under the Treaty of Rome, the bank operates on a nonprofit basis to grant loans and guarantees that facilitate the financing of new investment and projects concerned with modernization. It is now the largest international financing institution in the world. There is also now the European Central Bank (ECB), which was appointed in 1998 to oversee monetary policy once a single European currency was in place. The single currency— the "euro"—was brought into being on January 1, 1999. Eleven member states were deemed to have met the criteria necessary to participate. The exchange rates of the currencies of these states were irrevocably locked on that date.

The single currency proved highly controversial in the United Kindgom. Those who were already skeptical of British membership of the EU attacked it as undermining Britain's capacity to decide its own fate. They pointed out that when in 1990 Britain had joined the European exchange rate mechanism (ERM)—linking the value of the pound to other European currencies—it had proved disastrous. Membership had not saved the pound from an attack by currency speculators in 1992 and the United Kindgom had to withdraw from the ERM. The skeptics argued that British membership had not delivered the economic benefits claimed for it. The cost of imports from the EU far exceeds the value of exports and in the late 1990s exports to the rest of the world increased while trade with EU states actually declined. The largest single investor in the United Kingdom remained the United States (just as the United Kindgom remained the largest single investor in the States). Joining a single currency, they argued, would lead to harmonized taxation throughout the EU, which would drive up the tax burden in the United Kingdom. It would also drive up borrowing costs, undermine the competitiveness of the City of London as the world's leading financial marketplace, create a major burden in funding pensions (other major EU countries having "unfunded" pensions) and lead to instability in the nation's trading relationship with the rest of the world. Supporters of joining the single currency argued that it would bring stability through ensuring a stable marketplace within the EU. It would also likely result in a fall in interest rates and inflation. It would get rid of exchange rate transaction costs and make Britain an attractive location for foreign investors. Lower interest rates, it was claimed, would increase competitiveness and reduce unemployment. Opponents pointed out that during the period that Britain was in the ERM, unemployment doubled.

The single currency itself did not fare well in its first year of introduction. It was intended that it should have an exchange rate of just under 1.20 euros to the dollar. It got off to a poor start with a dispute as to who should head the European Central Bank and attempts by Germany to have interest rates cut to revive its flagging economy. By the end of 1999, the exchange rate was down to 1 euro to the dollar, a fall in value of 20 percent. By June 2000, the exchange rate had fallen below 1 euro to the dollar and was trading at 0.94 euros to the dollar. Both the dollar and the pound remained strong currencies. Opponents of British membership in a single currency have taken this as reinforcing their case. Supporters maintain that joining the single currency will be good for British business, a strong pound making it difficult for British exporters to find markets overseas.

The United Kindgom has not exercised its power to "opt in" to the single currency. The Labour government of Tony Blair adopted a not dissimilar stance to that of its Conservative predecessor. It was committed to joining when the conditions appeared right. It was generally accepted that it would be some time for Britain to meet the necessary "convergence" criteria for joining, the British economy operating on a different cycle from that of other member states. As we shall see, the issue remains a highly divisive one in British politics.

Political Implications

British membership in the Community has had political implications in terms of U.K. domestic politics. It remains a contentious issue. However, it has wider political implications—that is, in terms of the member states acting together as a political power bloc. That, as we have seen, was one of the motivations for Britain joining the Community. For Britain, the prospect of EC member states acting together looked increasingly attractive as other avenues for maintaining a world status (the Commonwealth, the "special relationship" with the United States) receded in significance.

In the event, the United Kindgom has supported moves towards creating the mechanisms for greater cooperation but has sometimes clashed with other member states in reaching decisions through those procedures. The United Kindgom, as a member state, was a party to the treaties extending the policy competence of the EC and to creating the new pillars under the Maastricht treaty. The second pillar created a new mechanism for discussing and deciding foreign and security policy. Consultation among member states had taken place before 1987 under an informal process known as European political cooperation (EPC): This was given formal recognition under the Single European Act. The Maastricht treaty took it one stage further. It institutionalized the process of cooperation. However, a feature of the second and third pillars was that they remained outside the normal procedures of the EC: Decision making was to be intergovernmental rather than through the institutions and decision-making processes of the EC. What this meant in particular was that decision making would be by unanimity and with the EC Commission, and other EC bodies, not having the same rights of involvement as they did under the first pillar. The Amsterdam Treaty saw some moves towards bringing some elements of the second pillar closer to the first. Under the Amsterdam Treaty, certain decisions under the second pillar can be reached by qualified majority voting. A new post, that of high representative for the common foreign and security policy, was also created. It was designed to give foreign and security policy a higher profile. The high representative was to be supported by a policy planning and early warning unit, set up to monitor and analyze developments and to produce assessments and options papers. As we have seen, there were also changes in the sector of domestic policy, with new powers for immigration and asylum policy shifting to the institutions of the EU.

The Treaty of Rome included the goal of moving towards an "ever closer union" and these various treaty changes were seen as a move toward achieving such a union. In the United Kindgom, opinion has remained divided on the goal of an ever closer union. This, in the view of many within the EU, has been behind the United Kingdoms's objection to various policies brought forward by the Commission. However, it has also been claimed to be a product of a different approach to policy making. In Chapter 2, we noted the approach to problem solving in the United Kingdom compared with some other European countries. Whereas the English adopt an empirical approach, the continental approach tends to be rationalist. In the context of EU policy making, this is reflected in the principal member states favoring rather broad formulations (such as "ever closer union"), while Britain favors more precise measures with the mechanism for implementation and achievement clearly laid out. This produces some disparity both in decision making and in implementation. Britain will prove difficult at times in policy making, sometimes to the exasperation of other member states, but prove very good in implementing measures once they are agreed. Other countries, such as Italy and France, will move quickly to agree to measures which they subsequently treat as essentially aspirational, implementing them how and when they think appropriate, if at all. By the end of 1999, not all measures necessary to achieve a single market had been implemented by member states. The best implementation rates were achieved by the United Kindgom and Denmark, the two countries regarded as the most "Euro-skeptic" within the EU.

Though many supporters of the EU favor moves toward full political union, this is a goal largely resisted in the United Kindgom. There are concerns over moves that would give the EU greater powers over domestic lawmaking. Successive British governments have been wary of moves that would transfer powers in certain areas. British ministers have not been afraid to argue their case in the Council of Ministers. In one dispute, the Conservative government of John Major went so far as to adopt an "empty seat" policy: Ministers refused to attend meetings, which in many cases meant decisions could not be taken. As a result, Britain has acquired a reputation within the EU as "an awkward partner."[10] Though relations appeared to improve under the Labour government elected in 1997, the perception remains, with ministers sometimes opposing proposals brought forward by the Commission. The perception is, in many respects, misleading. The United Kindgom is often in agreement with other member states. On occasion, it is used as a surrogate by other member states, their representatives asking British ministers to voice their opposition for them. Nonetheless, the perception shapes attitudes towards the United Kindgom, and domestic conflict about Britain's role in the EU continues to fuel the perception.

INSTITUTIONS OF THE EU

The main bodies of the EU are the European Council, the Council of Ministers, the Commission, the European Parliament, and the Committee of Permanent Representatives. There are also various other judicial and advisory bodies.

The *European Council*, more commonly known as the "European Summit," comprises the heads of government of the member states. Though already a regular feature, it was not until the Single European Act that it was given treaty status. Under the act, it was to meet twice a year. Formally, it has no decision-making powers—its decisions have to be agreed and implemented through the Council of Ministers—but it is the most powerful body within the EU in terms of high policy.

The *Council of Ministers*—formally titled the Council of the European Union—comprises the ministers from the member states whose portfolios cover the subject under discussion. Thus a proposal covering agriculture will be considered by the council comprising agriculture ministers. (In practice, it would be more appropriate to refer to *councils* of ministers.) The demands made of the council vary according to the subject. The Council of Foreign Ministers and the Council of Finance Ministers meet more often than do the others. The council seeks to proceed on the basis of consensus and tacit agreement. Even before the passage of the Single European Act, various matters could be resolved through qualified majority voting. Some measures are subject to simple majority voting or to unanimity. Under the so-called Luxembourg compromise of 1966, a country may veto legislation if "very important interests" (in effect, vital national interests) are involved. However, this is a highly contentious provision, with no clear agreement on what is actually entailed. It is not clear that the Luxembourg compromise could now be invoked.

The Council of Ministers has limited powers to initiate measures. Rather it discusses and agrees to measures placed before it. The body principally responsible for initiating measures is the *Commission*. This constitutes the bureaucracy of the EU. It has a staff of about 15,000 and is headed by a College of Commissioners. The 20 commissioners are drawn from the member states (the larger states—France, Germany, Italy, Spain and the United Kindgom—each appoint two Commissioners and other states each appoint one) though each takes an oath not to seek to represent national interests. They are headed by a commission president. The president is chosen by the heads of state in the European Council and is then subject to approval by the European Parliament. The commissioners meet once a week to adopt proposals, finalize policy papers, and make other decisions required of the commission.

The commission serves a five-year term and is responsible for initiating most policy proposals as well as for ensuring that the provisions of the treaties are complied with. It is also responsible for implementing policy decisions. It operates through 36 directorates-general. Each commissioner has responsibility for one or more directorates-general. The directorates-general undertake widespread consultation before coming forward with a proposal for the commissioners. There is extensive contact with firms and other organizations affected by EU decision making and many bodies have offices in Brussels, where the commission is based. Lobbying of the commission by outside organizations is well developed.

The members of the commission are frequently people who have held high political office in their home country. In 2000, the two British members of the commission were Neil Kinnock, former leader of the Labour party, and Chris Patten, a former cabinet minister and the last British governor of Hong Kong. However, the commission was hit by controversy in 1999. In December 1998 a commission official, Paul van Buitenen, made allegations of fraud and mismanagement within the EU. The same month the EP refused to approve the EU's accounts for 1996. The accusations led to an investigation by a special team of investigators. They issued a damning report, naming a number of commissioners for failing to exercise proper control and, in the case of the commission president, for allowing "a state within a state" to develop. Some commissioners were accused of favoritism in making appointments. Following publication of the report, the entire commission resigned, though some were then kept on to complete their terms. The president of the commission, Jacques Santer, former prime minister of Luxembourg, was replaced by Romani Prodi, an academic and former prime minister of Italy. Neil Kinnock, who was untainted by the scandal, was given responsibility for tackling fraud and mismanagement.

Until the passage of the single European act, the *European Parliament* was an advisory body in dealing with EC legislation. It did have two formal, but rather blunt, powers: One was to reject the budget, which it did employ (and continues to), and the other was to force the resignation of the commission *en bloc* (something it was to later threaten in 1999). In the legislative process, though, it was called upon only to offer an opinion on a proposal emanating from the commission. That opinion was then passed on to the Council of Ministers to consider. The parliament could have some effect by failing to offer an opinion, but when it did offer one there was no obligation on the council to accept it.

The position of the parliament was strengthened by the Single European Act and by succeeding treaties. The SEA designated the parliament as a parliament (though it had previously styled itself the European Parliament, its formal title was the European Assembly) and it introduced the cooperation procedure. This gave the parliament a more significant role in certain types of legislation, principally that aimed at achieving a single market. A "second reading" was introduced. If the parliament amended or rejected the position taken by the council after the first reading (the traditional procedure), the commission re-examined and resubmitted the proposal. The council could then only amend, reject, or reinstate a proposal rejected by the parliament by unanimity.

The Maastricht Treaty introduced a new and more powerful procedure, the co-decision procedure. If the council and parliament could not agree after two readings, a conciliation committee was formed; if no agreement was reached, the council version prevailed unless the parliament voted it down. The co-decision procedure thus gave the parliament the capacity to block a measure. It was also given additional power under the assent procedure: Under this, the consent of the parliament is necessary for treaties bringing new members into the Union. The Amsterdam Treaty further strengthened the position of the parliament. Under the Maastricht Treaty, the co-decision procedure only applied to a small number of legislative proposals. Under the Amsterdam Treaty, it was extended to cover most of the areas previously covered by the cooperation procedure. It became the most common procedure. The cooperation procedure was retained largely for single market measures. The original procedure, the opinion of the parliament being sought, still applied for proposals in the agriculture sector.

The parliament has thus become a significant political actor in the EU. It has proved willing to exercise its powers and to press for more. It wants to be able to initiate proposals as well as to have its powers extended to cover all areas of EU responsibility. Though it seeks to cooperate with national parliaments, it is wary of moves that would involve national parliaments encroaching on its areas of responsibility. Some national politicians have argued the case for a second chamber within the parliament, with members drawn from the parliaments of the member states: The EP has been a vigorous opponent of the proposal. It tends to see itself as a form of first chamber, with the Council of Ministers being a second chamber; The commission is the executive.

The other principal body in the process is the *Committee of Permanent Representatives*, known as COREPER. This has the responsibility for preparing the work of the Council of Ministers and for carrying out tasks assigned to the council. As the name implies, it comprises official representatives (classified as ambassadors) from the member states, each assisted by a staff of diplomats and officials seconded (released from regular duty and temporarily assigned elsewhere) from the national civil service. COREPER studies a proposal on behalf of the council, isolating any problems associated with it. If the committee reaches agreement, it is usual for the council to adopt the proposal without further discussion.

These bodies are supplemented by a number of advisory bodies with members drawn from different organizations within the member states. The *Economic and Social Committee*, based in Brussels, offers opinions on commission proposals as well as on broader issues affecting society. The members are drawn from workers, employers, and consumers' organizations. The United Kingdom has 24 members on the 222-member body. The *Committee of the Regions*, which also has 222 members, was established under the Maastricht Treaty. It comprises members drawn from regional and local authorities. Members are appointed by national governments for four-year terms. There is now a legal obligation for the Committee to be consulted on various matters that concern the regions. There is also a large number of committees appointed to oversee and advise on the implementation of policy, the operation of these committees collectively being called *comitology*.

There are a number of other bodies standing outside the normal decision-making process. The *European Court of Justice*, based in Luxembourg, ensures that EC law is observed in the interpretation and application of the treaties, and this court can itself interpret EC law. Its judgments are binding on member states and enforceable through the national courts. There is also now a *Court of First Instance* to help reduce the burden on the court in a limited number of areas.

The *Court of Auditors* exists to exercise a watchdog function on the EU's financial practices. Its reports are usually "qualified," meaning that it is not satisfied with all the accounting practices. The *European Ombudsman* investigates allegations of "maladministration" leveled against an EU institution by an EU citizen. The Ombudsman has wide ranging powers of inquiry and can, in certain cases, require the production of all documentation that he requires. He may also draw cases to the attention of the European Parliament.

The EU thus has a range of powerful institutions. The structure of decision making within the EU is unusual, indeed unique. It bears no relationship to existing political systems. Whereas most countries of Western Europe are used to a parliamentary form of government—with the executive being chosen through elections to the legislature—there is no equivalent procedure in the EU. Nor do the institutions of the EU bear any relationship to a presidential system of government. The executive within the EU—the commission—is an appointed and not an elected body. This, coupled with the fact that the European Parliament had, until recently, very limited powers—and still lacks the power to initiate measures—has led to claims that there is within the institutions of the EU a "democratic deficit." Though the EP has seen its powers increase, turnout in elections to the parliament have decreased. A low turnout does little to counter claims of a democratic deficit.

ELECTIONS TO THE EUROPEAN PARLIAMENT

The European Parliament, as we have seen, is an increasingly powerful body. It is also a peripatetic body. It works principally through 17 standing committees and these meet in Brussels. However, it holds most of its plenary sessions in Strasbourg, France. Its secretariat is located in Luxembourg, though many staff are based in Brussels. (The Parliament employs a total of 3,850 people and its budget in 2000 was £610 million [$976 million].) Three weeks are given over to committee meetings, followed by one week for plenary meetings. Each month, a mass of papers and other material is moved from Brussels to Strasbourg to be ready for the plenary session.

The parliament now has 626 members and is directly elected. Before 1979, the members were appointed from the members of the national parliaments of the member states. Direct election was introduced in 1979. The parliament is elected for a five-year term. There have thus been five elections to the parliament: in 1979, 1984, 1989, 1994, and 1999. From 1979 to 1994, the number of MEPs elected from the United Kindgom was 81. In 1994, following an enlargement of the size of the parliament, the number was increased to 87. Though there have been attempts to create pan-European political movements, the elections are essentially fought in each country by national parties. Indeed, the issues that dominate at European elections tend to be national rather than European, the elections being used as a means of passing opinion on the national government.

In the first two elections to the EP, the Conservative party did especially well, benefiting from the fact that the party was doing well in the opinion polls. In 1989 and 1994 it suffered a reversal in its fortunes, losing most of the seats it held (see Table 9.1). In 1984 the party held 45 out of 81 seats. In 1989 it was reduced to 32 members, and in 1994 it fell to only 18 members. In the run-up to the 1994 elections there was speculation that it might not even get 10 members elected. The Labour party became the dominant party, achieving the election of 45 members (MEPs) in 1989 and 62 in 1994, its members playing a leading role within the Socialist Group in the parliament.

In the 1999 elections, a new method of election was used. From 1979 to 1994, the nation had been divided into single-member constituencies and the first-past-the-post method of election employed. (The exception was Northern Ireland where, because of the particular problems of the province, the three members were elected under the single transferable vote system.) The EU was committed towards finding a uniform system of election, and the new Labour government elected in 1997 introduced a bill to provide for the use of a regional

TABLE 9.1 Number of MEPs elected from the United Kingdom

Party	Election				
	1979	1984	1989	1994	1999
Conservative	62	45	32	18	36
Labour	17	32	45	62	29
Liberal Democrat	0	0	0	2	10
Scottish National	1	1	1	2	2
Plaid Cymru	0	0	0	0	2
UK Independence	0	0	0	0	3
Green	0	0	0	0	2
Democratic Unionist*	1	1	1	1	1
SDLP*	1	1	1	1	1
Ulster Unionist*	1	1	1	1	1

* MEPs elected from Northern Ireland under the single transferable vote

list system of elections. This was employed in 1999. Each region was allocated a set number of members, and voters went to the polls to vote for a particular party rather than for individual candidates. The results of the election were disastrous for the Labour party, giving the Conservative party a boost at a time when it was still notably lagging behind Labour in the opinion polls. The Conservatives won 36 seats (a gain of 18), while Labour's representation went down from 62 to 29. It was Labour's worst result since 1979.

The 1999 election was also notable for the success of third parties. The Liberal Democrats achieved double figures in terms of the number of members elected. The Green Party, which had won almost 15 percent of the popular vote in 1989 but no seats, gained representation for the first time, as did the UK Independence party—committed to British withdrawal from the EU—and Plaid Cymru. There were now 10 U.K. parties with seats in the European Parliament.

The election was also characterized by a low turnout. The election campaign was generally charaterized as a non-campaign.[11] Though the parties campaigned, electors did not seem particularly interested. During elections to the European Parliament, most voters in the United Kingdom have stayed at home. In 1979 the turnout was 32.7 percent. It was roughly the same in 1984 and increased slightly in the two subsequent elections (Table 9.2). In 1999 it was 24 percent. Though most other EU countries achieved a higher turnout, there was an EU-wide downward trend. The EU-wide turnout was 49 percent, a figure boosted by the fact that in some countries voting is compulsory. For the first time, most electors in the EU did not bother to go to the polling booths. As the powers of the European Parliament have increased, the interest in it among citizens appears to have decreased.

Within the parliament, the Conservative MEPs sit as part of the center-right Group of European People's Party (Christian Democrats) and European Democrats. With 233 members, this is now the largest group in the parliament. The Labour MEPs sit as part of the Socialist Group. The Group used to be the largest group in the EP, but following the 1999 elections, it slipped—with 180

TABLE 9.2   U.K. turnout in European Parliament elections

Year	Votes cast	Turnout (%)
1979	13,446,083	32.7
1984	12,998,274	32.6
1989	15,893,408	36.8
1994	15,847,417	36.8
1999	10,681,080	24.1

SOURCE: D. Butler and M. Westlake, *British Politics and European Elections 1999* (Macmillan, 2000), p. 213.

members—into second place. The Liberal Democrats sit as part of the 51-strong European Liberal Group.

THE CURRENT DEBATE

The issue of European integration has been notable for the divisions it has created in British politics. Neither of the main parties has maintained a consistent stance on the issue and neither has ever been united in its stance. The issue has been identified as the "fault line" of British politics, with the capacity to split parties asunder.

The Labour party was initially opposed to British membership in the EC, then moved to support membership in the 1960s. In the early 1970s it opposed membership on the terms negotiated and then supported membership after it won office in 1974 and had an opportunity to renegotiate the terms. In the early 1980s, with a leftward shift in the party, it swung heavily against membership. Under the leadership of Neil Kinnock, John Smith, and Tony Blair it moved towards embracing membership and the benefits that it was perceived to bring. Many trade unions also shifted their position. Having previously been hostile or skeptical, they began to see the EC as a means of achieving economic and social rights for workers. By the time of the 1997 election, Labour had established itself as a "Euro-friendly" party. The party's election manifesto declared that, though it was opposed to a European federal super-state, it would offer leadership in Europe.

The Conservative party was initially hostile to membership, but—as we have seen—shifted its position in the early 1960s. It was under a Conservative prime minister, Edward Heath, that the United Kindgom became a member of the EC. Heath remained committed to the concept of European integration. His successor as Conservative leader, Margaret Thatcher, campaigned for a "yes" vote in the 1975 referendum but, after becoming prime minister in 1979, adopted an increasingly skeptical position. In 1988, she launched a sharp attack on further moves toward European integration. In a speech to the College of Europe in Bruges, she attacked the idea of a supranational government capable of imposing its will on the member states. "We have not successfully rolled back the frontiers of the state in Britain," she declared, "only to see them re-imposed at a European level, with a European super-state exercising a new dominance from

Brussels."[12] Her strident stance attracted the support of many Conservatives but it dismayed others. Her attack on the European Commission at the dispatch box of the House of Commons in 1990 sparked her deputy prime minister to resign. That resignation was to trigger a train of events resulting in Thatcher's loss of the party leadership (see Chapter 6). Her successor tried to keep the divided wings of the party together, but it proved a difficult task. Achieving passage of the European Communities (Amendment) Bill in 1992—to give effect to provisions of the Maastricht Treaty—proved difficult, the bill being passed in the summer of 1993, a year after it was intended to be passed. The party was badly divided on the issue of a single currency and entered the 1997 election as a divided party. After the election, the new party leader, William Hague, took a more Euro-skeptic stance and committed his party to opposing membership in a single currency for the lifetime of that and the subsequent parliament. In the 1999 European Parliament elections, he adopted the slogan of "In Europe, not run by Europe." At the end of 1999, the Conservative shadow foreign secretary spoke of negotiating an amendment to the Treaty of Rome.

There are essentially four groupings within the Conservative party that can be identified on the issue of Europe. It is possible to refine the categorization even further, but this fourfold typology is sufficient to indicate the nature, and intensity, of the debate. There are similar groupings in the Labour party, but it is the divisions within Conservative ranks that have attracted the most attention. The first category is that of the *anti-Europeans*. These are people who opposed British membership in the EC and continue to oppose it. The main objection has tended to be on constitutional grounds: They oppose the loss of sovereignty that comes with membership. They have also argued that it does not bring great economic gains either and that Britain would be well able to survive outside the EU. The second category is the *Euro-skeptics*. These are people who support membership in the EC for the purposes of achieving a single market. However, their goal is the removal of trade barriers. They are opposed to any moves toward political union and the creation of a supranational government. They argue that the EC has moved beyond the initial aims of a common market. Since the 1980s—especially since Margaret Thatcher's 1988 Bruges speech—they have joined with anti-Europeans to oppose further moves toward European integration, opposing especially the Maastricht treaty in 1992 and 1993. The third category is that of *Euro-agnostics*. These are people who have no ingrained ideological stance on the issue but are driven by what they see as being in the interests of the nation, and the party, at any particular time. In the late 1980s, they tended to turn against Margaret Thatcher, believing her stance was harming British interests. In the 1990s, they have moved toward a more hostile stance, especially on the issue of a single currency. The fourth and final category is the *Europhiles*. These are people who have a principled commitment to European integration and favor moves toward economic and monetary union. They campaign for Britain to enter the single currency.

In the early 1970s, the anti-Europeans were a small minority in the party. Since then, they have been joined in their opposition to further integration—

and especially in their opposition to a single currency—by the Euro-skeptics and the Euro-agnostics. Only the Europhiles continue to press for further integration, and they constitute a minority—about one-fifth—of the parliamentary party.[13] The Europhiles, though, have the advantage of including some well-known political figures, including a former prime minister (Edward Heath), a former deputy prime minister (Michael Heseltine), and a former chancellor of the exchequer (Kenneth Clarke). Their numbers, though, may be declining on the issue of a single currency. Some politicians previously classed as Europhiles, including a former minister close to Edward Heath, have expressed their opposition to the U.K. joining a single currency.

By 2000, there were two debates going on about "Europe." One was on the issue of the single currency. We have already touched upon the economic arguments surrounding a single currency. As we have seen, the euro came into being—at least on paper—in 1999. (Though coins were being minted, they were not in circulation.) The Labour government took the stance that it would join when the convergence criteria were met, and its 1997 election manifesto committed it to holding a referendum on the issue before joining. Various bodies were set up to advocate British membership. A "Britain in Europe" movement was formed to bring together politicians and business figures to explain the advantages of a single currency and to counter arguments against the EU made by opponents. The organization was supported by some top business figures, such as the chief executive of Unilever, who favored monetary union. A group of business people in the City of London who were strongly committed to economic union formed a body called Europe 21. Established organizations, such as the European Movement, bringing together Europhiles from different parties, also took up the cause of the single currency. Other bodies in support included various Conservative pro-European groups (Conservative Group for Europe, Tory Reform Group, Conservative Mainstream) and Labour groups (Labour Movement for Europe). Some business groups also expressed support for Britain joining the single currency. The Confederation of British Industry expressed some support for joining, but it did not campaign and there were known to be divisions among its members on the issue. The British Chambers of Commerce also expressed support, but again, did not campaign on the issue.

Opposition to membership in a single currency came from several bodies. Various established Euro-skeptical bodies (Bruges Group, European Foundation) opposed it and were joined by several new organizations. A number of leading business figures formed "Business for Sterling" to argue the case for retaining the pound. Some politicians, previously regarded as supporters of European integration, formed "New Europe," supporting British membership in the EU but opposing monetary union. The leading figures included a former Labour foreign secretary (David Owen), a former Labour chancellor of the exchequer (Denis Healey), and a former Conservative cabinet minister (Lord Prior). A "Democracy Movement" was launched from the remnants of the Referendum party (see Chapter 6); other bodies coming into being included "Cafe-Conservatives Against a Federal Europe," "the Keep the £ Campaign," and "the Labour Euro-safeguards Campaign."

Opposition to, or disquiet about, membership in a single currency was also voiced by the Institute of Directors and the Federation of Small Businesses.

The debate was thus engaged. Though there was significant elite support for membership in a single currency, there was little popular support for membership. Opinion polls showed a majority of respondents opposed to British membership in a single currency. MORI polls found that opposition peaked in 1995 and 1996, when 60 percent of respondents said they would vote against Britain joining a single currency in a referendum. However, throughout the 1990s, a majority of those asked consistently said they would vote against it (Table 9.3). Apart from September 1998, when it was 49 percent, the proportion was always 50 percent or more. Even if the government were to strongly urge that Britain should join a single currency, more people would still be opposed than in favor. In September 1999, 37 percent said they would vote in favor if the government strongly urged in favor, but 49 percent said they would vote against. Business people were also divided. One MORI poll in 1999 found that opposition among the chief executives and directors of businesses employing 11 or more people had increased. In 1998, 23 percent of those questioned thought it would be best for their company if Britain never joined a single currency; in 1999 the figure was 37 percent. The proportion thinking Britain should join as soon as possible fell from 26 to 19 percent.[14]

Whereas there was pressure to move Britain toward joining the single currency, there was another debate going on. This was generated by opponents of the European Union who wished to go in the opposite direction. They wanted Britain to withdraw from membership. In the late 1970s, whether or not Britain should remain in the EC was a live issue. More people favored leaving the Community than favored staying in. However, the position changed markedly in the 1980s. A majority clearly favored staying in. As can be seen from Figure 9.1, the percentages favoring staying in were fairly substantial. That appeared to put the issue beyond doubt. Debate switched from whether Britain should be a member to what it should do as a member. However, as Figure 9.1 shows, the gap between those favoring and opposing British membership narrowed in the 1990s. In April 1997, as many favored getting out (40 percent) as favored staying in (40 percent). Since then, a small majority has supported staying in. In June 1999, 41 percent supported staying, 37 percent

TABLE 9.3 Attitudes toward a single currency

Q. If there were a referendum now on whether Britain should be part of a single European currency, how would you vote?

	Nov. 1991	Nov. 1994	June 1995	Nov. 1996	Oct. 1997	Sept. 1998	July 1999	Sept 1999
In favor	33	33	29	22	27	30	27	31
Against	54	56	60	64	54	49	58	53

SOURCE: MORI, *British Public Opinion*, Vol. 22, no. 8, Oct. 1999, p. 6.

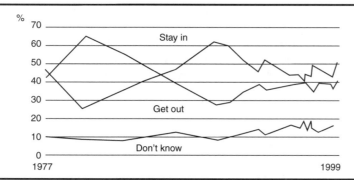

Q. If there were a referendum now on whether Britain should stay in or get out of the European Union, how would you vote?

FIGURE 9.1   British attitudes toward British membership in the EU

Base: c. 1,000 or 2,000 aged 18+ per survey
SOURCE: MORI.

favored getting out. In October 1999, 51 percent favored staying in and 41 percent wanted Britain to get out.

As we have seen, in the European Parliament elections in 1999, three members of the UK Independence party were elected. Various bodies were set up to make the case for withdrawal. These included a "Campaign for an Independent Britain," run by two anti-Europeans: Labour peer Lord Stoddart of Swindon and Conservative MP Sir Richard Body. As we have seen, the Britain-in-Europe movement was established not only to explain the advantages of a single currency but also to counter the arguments of those opposed to Britain's membership in the EU itself. Michael Heseltine, at the launch of Britain in Europe in October 1999, declared (and in so doing had a sideswipe at his former leader, Margaret Thatcher): "Whether we like it or not, what happens in Europe is inseparable from what happens to our own trade, employment, investment, and industry. You can't wield a handbag from an empty chair."[15] Opponents of membership argued that, like many other independent countries, the United Kingdom would be able to survive on its own. Indeed, they argued that the moves toward globalization in trade rendered organizations like the EU less relevant. They favored cooperation among independent nation states, rather than imposition through a supranational body. There was no common ground between the two sides.

CONCLUSION

The U.K. has been a member of the EC, now the EU, for almost 30 years. Membership has had profound constitutional, economic, and political implications for the nation. Support for membership grew in the 1980s and the EU appeared to be forward-looking as it moved toward the realization of a single market. In the 1990s, the issue of "Europe" returned to the political agenda as the EU moved toward a single currency. Britain did not join, and popular opinion was against joining. Opponents of membership of the EU, who had been in a notable minority in the 1980s, started gaining some ground in debate in calling for Britain to leave the EU. Though there is little likelihood of a British government favoring withdrawal, the fact that the issue is on the political agenda reflects British ambivalence towards European integration.

NOTES

[1] See A. King, *Britain Says Yes* (American Enterprise Institute, 1977), pp. 2–7.

[2] The nephew of Macmillan's wife had married John Kennedy's sister Kathleen.

[3] M. Camps, *Britain and the European Community 1955–1963* (Oxford University Press, 1964), p. 336.

[4] See the comments of E. Heath, *Our Community* (Conservative Political Centre, 1977), p. 4.

[5] H. Macmillan, *Pointing the Way* (Macmillan, 1972), p. 310.

[6] On the first two applications, see R. J. Lieber, *British Politics and European Unity* (University of California Press, 1970); and U. Kitzinger, *The Second Try* (Pergamon, 1968).

[7] See P. Norton, *Dissension in the House of Commons 1945–1974* (Macmillan, 1975), pp. 395–398; and U. Kitzinger, *Diplomacy and Persuasion* (Thames and Hudson, 1973), Ch. 13 and Appendix 1.

[8] The treaty was later approved in a second Danish referendum.

[9] See P. Norton, "The United Kingdom: Political Conflict, Parliamentary Scrutiny," in P. Norton (ed.), *National Parliaments and the European Union* (Cass, 1996); P. Giddings and G. Drewry (eds.), *Westminster and Europe* (Macmillan, 1996).

[10] See S. George, *An Awkward Partner* (Oxford University Press, 1990).

[11] D. Butler and M. Westlake, *British Politics and the European Elections* (Macmillan, 2000), Chs. 6 and 7.

[12] M. Thatcher, *Britain and Europe* (Conservative Political Centre, 1988), p. 4. This pamphlet constitutes the text of Thatcher's speech.

[13] See P. Norton, "The Conservative Party: 'In Office but not in Power,'" in A. King (ed.), *New Labour Triumphs: Britain at the Polls* (Chatham House, 1998), p. 94.

[14] MORI, *British Public Opinion*, Vol. 22, no. 9, pp. 1 and 4.

[15] *The Guardian*, October 15, 1999.

Chapter 10

The New Assemblies
Government Beyond The Center

The United States is a federal nation. As such, autonomous and constitutionally protected powers are vested in both federal and state government. Article 1, section 8, of the Constitution enumerates the powers of Congress. The tenth amendment stipulates that powers not delegated to the United States by the Constitution, nor prohibited by it to the states, "are reserved to the States respectively, or to the people." The Constitution thus prescribes and protects two layers of government. Below those two levels there is a third: local government.

The position in the United Kingdom stands in marked contrast to that in the United States. Recent years have seen some notable changes in subnational government, with elected assemblies being created in Scotland, Wales, and Northern Ireland. However, the new structure differs from that of the United States in three ways.

First, as we have seen in Chapter 4, the United Kingdom remains formally a unitary state. The unitary state has sometimes been described as a union state, a number of countries having been brought together under a single crown and parliament. However, it is a unitary state in that state power resides at the center. The Queen-in-Parliament is the constitutionally supreme organ of power. New layers of government are created by an act of Parliament and can be removed by an act of Parliament. Thus, for example, Northern Ireland had a Parliament at Stormont, just outside Belfast, for 50 years, from 1922 to 1972. That parliament was established by an act of Parliament and, as we shall see, it was suspended and later abolished by an act of Parliament.

Second, the devolution of powers to elected assemblies in different parts of the United Kingdom has been termed asymmetrical devolution. Not all parts of the U.K. have elected assemblies. Elected assemblies have been established in the least populated parts. The bulk of the population live, as we have seen in Chapter 1, in England. There is no elected assembly for England. Although some governmental bodies operate at a regional level in England, there are no elected assemblies in the English regions.

Third, the method of election employed for the elected assemblies differs from that used for elections in the United States and for elections to the House of Commons. The changes that have taken place in the United Kingdom have meant that the framework of government at the beginning of the twenty-first century differs markedly from that which existed throughout the twentieth century. However, it has not moved very much in the direction of the form of government that exists in the United States. As we shall see, there are some in the United Kingdom who would like it to do so.

The devolution of power to Scotland and Wales differs from that to Northern Ireland, which—as we have mentioned—has recent experience of its own parliament, and so deserves separate consideration. The history in each case is important for explaining the creation of the new assemblies. Given that, as we have mentioned, some governmental bodies operate at a regional level in England—and there is pressure for the creation of elected assemblies in the English regions—we shall look briefly at regional government in England.

SCOTLAND AND WALES

Electors in Scotland went to the polls in May 1999 to elect the members of a Scottish parliament, a parliament with legislative and tax-raising powers. On the same day, electors in Wales went to the polls to elect members of a Welsh assembly, a body with power to determine the allocation of the Welsh budget. The last time that Scotland had a parliament was nearly three hundred years before. It ceased to exist when the Act of Union was agreed, the Scottish and English parliaments being superseded by a single British Parliament. The Welsh had never previously had an assembly. Pressure for the creation of both bodies built up in the last four decades of the century and culminated in referendums in Scotland and Wales in 1997 and the passage in 1998 of the Scotland Act and the Government of Wales Act.

Demands for Devolution

The demands for some form of "home rule" for Scotland and Wales were not confined to the latter decades of the twentieth century. The Liberal party advocated the more radical proposal of federalism during most of its history.[1] Some form of home rule for Scotland and Wales had been advocated by the Scottish National (SNP) and Plaid Cymru (PC) parties, respectively, since their formation earlier in the twentieth century, but the main achievement of the two parties prior to the 1960s was simply to have survived. This situation was to change in the 1960s, when each party won one seat at a parliamentary by-election and also made gains in local elections. The apparent growing strength of nationalist sentiment was sufficient to encourage the Labour government to establish a

Royal Commission on the Constitution; announced in 1968, it was appointed in 1969 and reported in 1973. It recommended some form of devolved government. By this time there had also emerged what A. H. Birch referred to as the "eruptive factor,"[2] North Sea oil. The SNP was able to play on the argument that the location of the offshore oil fields meant the oil was Scotland's as much as anyone's and that revenue from it would be sufficient to make a Scottish government viable. By playing on the expectation of a rising middle class in Scotland, whose expectations had been left unfulfilled by the Westminster government, the SNP began to make electoral inroads into the strength of both main parties. By playing on the cultural fears of the Welsh people, the PC had some impact in Wales. In the February 1974 general election, the SNP won 7 of the 71 Scottish seats and the PC won 2 of the 36 Welsh seats. In the October general election, the SNP increased the number of seats won to 11 and the PC to 3. Of the SNP's 11 seats, 9 were won from the Conservatives but the party had come second in 35 out of 41 Labour-held seats. In total number of votes received, it was the second largest party in Scotland.

The Labour government that was returned to office in 1974 saw the prospect of the SNP developing into the dominant party in Scotland and, in so doing, ruining Labour's chances of winning future elections (both Scotland and Wales constitute important electoral bases for the party; see Chapter 5). To respond to the nationalist challenge, the government put forward proposals for a form of devolved government in both Scotland and Wales and eventually achieved passage of bills providing for an elected assembly in each of the two countries, the Scottish assembly to have greater powers than that of the Welsh. However, the proposals ran into opposition from the Conservative party. Many Labour members also found them unpalatable. A number were opposed to devolution, seeing it as a step on the road to eventual independence. Some MPs from the north of England disliked devolution because they felt it would effectively discriminate against regions that were not to have similar assemblies. Given the opposition to its proposals, the government agreed that the devolution proposals would be submitted to referendums in Scotland and Wales. MPs carried amendments, against the government's wishes, stipulating that 40 percent of eligible voters had to "yes" vote in each referendum for devolution to take place.

The referendums in Scotland and Wales were held on March 1, 1979, and were preceded by vigorous campaigns in the two countries. In Wales, it appeared that the prospect of devolved government aroused suspicion among non–Welsh-speaking inhabitants—the majority—and was not gaining overwhelming support. In Scotland, the debate was keenly fought between pro- and antidevolutionists. Some opponents feared devolution would constitute the thin end of the wedge, leading to an eventual breakup of the United Kingdom; supporters argued that it was necessary in order to maintain the unity of the kingdom. On March 1, 950,330 voters in Wales voted "no" to the devolution proposals; only 243,048 voted "yes." In Scotland, the result was a close one: 1,230,937 people voted "yes," and 1,153,502 voted "no." Although a slight majority of those who voted had opted for the devolution proposals, the number voting "yes" did not constitute 40 percent of all eligible voters. As a consequence, the Cabinet decided not to proceed with devolution, a decision that precipitated Nationalist MPs withdrawing their support from the government. This loss of Nationalist support deprived the government of a majority in a vote of confidence on March 28, 1979. The result was a general election and the return of a Conservative government. In the new Parliament, the government introduced the relevant motions for the repeal of the two acts and both motions were carried.

In the wake of the 1979 general election, it looked as though devolution was no longer an important issue on the political agenda. The SNP won only two seats in the election, as did Plaid Cymru. The new government was not keen to pursue the issue—Prime Minister Margaret Thatcher being a notable opponent of devolution—and other issues came to the fore. However, from the early 1980s onward, the subject began to reemerge as a feature of debate. Initially, much of the running was made by the Liberal party and then the newly formed SDP. In alliance, the two parties pressed for elected assemblies in Scotland, Wales, and the English regions. This commitment was reiterated in 1988, when the two parties merged to form the Liberal Democratic party. The Labour party, which had maintained a commitment to some form of devolution throughout the decade, also committed itself—following its policy review of 1987-1989—to support ten regional assemblies in England as well as assemblies in Scotland and Wales. There was also some pressure within Conservative ranks for some devolution of power to a Scottish assembly. Calls for such a policy became more pronounced from Scottish Conservatives following the party's disastrous showing in the 1987 general election, when it won only 10 of the 72 seats. The marginal improvement in the party's position in 1992—winning 11 seats—did not still calls for some form of elected assembly. However, the official Conservative policy remained opposed to devolution, Prime Minister John Major being just as firm an opponent as his predecessor. The government emphasized the importance of the union and pursued a limited political initiative in the context of that union: In 1993, it strengthened the position of the Scottish Office and a number of parliamentary bodies responsible for Scottish affairs.

The calls for some form of devolution continued to be heard, especially in Scotland. When European Community leaders met for a summit in Edinburgh in December 1992, more than 25,000 people marched through the streets to demonstrate in support of Scottish home rule. Much was made of the fact that Scotland was governed by a Conservative government, even though a majority of MPs elected from Scotland were Labour MPs. The same case was made in Wales. In the 1997 general election, all main parties except for the Conservative party supported devolution. In its election manifesto, the Labour party declared that "we will meet the demand for decentralisation of power to Scotland and Wales, once established in referendums." As soon as possible after the election, it declared, legislation would be introduced to provide for referendums. The party proposed a Scottish parliament with lawmaking powers—taking control of those matters controlled by the Scottish Office (the government department for Scotland)—and limited powers to vary rates of taxation. The Welsh assembly would not have powers to enact primary legislation nor to vary tax rates. Instead, it would have powers of secondary legislation (order-making powers granted by act of Parliament) and have control of functions carried out by the Welsh Office (the government department for Wales). Once the proposals had been approved in the referendums, bills would be brought forward to establish the new bodies.

The Labour party won the 1997 general election by a decisive margin. The Conservative party suffered a massive loss of seats, notably so—as we have seen (Chapter 5)—in Scotland and Wales, where it failed to win any seats at all. The new Labour government promptly introduced legislation to provide for referendums. There were no threshold requirements: a simple majority was to suffice. The referendums were held in September 1997. Voters in Scotland had two questions to answer, whether they agreed with the proposal for a Scottish parliament, and if they supported having a parliament with tax varying powers. Voters in Wales were asked whether they agreed or not with the government's proposals for a Welsh assembly.

The arguments advanced in favor of devolution centered on both consent and effectiveness. Decisions taken in Scotland and Wales by elected government, it was argued, would be more efficient and effective because of a better appreciation of the area—its needs as well as its resources—and additionally, would enhance consent by being closer to the people. Power would be removed from a distant government at Westminster and given—restored, in the Scottish case—to the people. Devolving governmental responsibilities would also serve to reduce pressure on central government and on Parliament. Both government and people, it was felt, would benefit.

Against this, Conservatives, as well as some Labour MPs, expressed the fear that devolution could lead to a breakup of the United Kingdom. They also opposed it on the grounds that it would introduce another expensive and unnecessary layer of government and that it would exacerbate economic inequality between the regions. Economically, it was argued, wealthy regions would fight to retain as much of their wealth as possible. Among the poorer parts of the United Kingdom to suffer would be Scotland and Wales; their small populations and limited resources made them economically dependent on the rest of the United Kingdom. The argument, in short, was that more government was not necessarily better government.

The "yes" campaign made most of the running in both countries, especially in Scotland. On September 11, voters in Scotland voted decisively—albeit in a turnout lower than in general elections—in favor of a Scottish parliament and in favor of a parliament with tax-varying powers. The voters in Wales went to the polls on September 18. As the figures in Table 10.1 reveal, the result in the province—where the turnout was only 50 percent—was not so decisive. By a

TABLE 10.1 Referendum results: Scotland and Wales, 1997

Scotland	A Scottish Parliament	Tax-varying Powers
Agree	1,775,045 (74.3%)	1,512,889 (63.5%)
Disagree	614,400 (25.7%)	870,263 (36.5%)
Turnout: 60.4%		

Wales	A Welsh Assembly
Yes	559,419 (50.3%)
No	552,698 (49.7%)
Turnout: 50%	

majority of a 6,721 (0.6 per cent of the poll), they voted for the assembly. There was a notable regional divide. Counties in the eastern half of Wales showed majorities voting against and counties in the western half had majorities voting in favor.

Following the yes vote in both referendums, the government introduced legislation to set up a Scottish parliament and a Welsh assembly. The Scotland Act and the Government of Wales Act were enacted in 1998. The former provided for an elected Parliament in Scotland and the latter for an elected assembly in Wales, with elections to take place to both bodies in 1999.

The Scottish Parliament

The parliament has power to legislate on all matters other than those that are explicitly reserved to the U.K. Parliament. Under Schedule 5 of the Scotland Act, the principal reserved matters are the Constitution (a rare reference in statute, given that—as we have seen—there is no codified document), foreign affairs, defense, the civil service, financial and economic matters, national security, immigration and nationality, trade and industry (covering such matters as competition and consumer protection), broadcasting, energy (nuclear energy, coal, gas and oil), social security, and employment. Although social policy as such is not a reserved matter, particular social issues are reserved to the U.K. Parliament, notably abortion and the misuse of drugs. By virtue of the doctrine of parliamentary sovereignty, the U.K. Parliament has the power to legislate on any matters that fall within the competence of the Scottish parliament, but it is assumed that it will be become a convention that the U.K. Parliament will only do so with the consent of the Scottish parliament.

In practice, this means that the Scottish parliament can legislate on a wide range of issues. They include the environment, education, health, agriculture, local government, the police, housing, planning, economic development, tourism, the courts, criminal justice and most aspects of the criminal and civil law, and some aspects of transport. The parliament also has the power to vary the standard rate of income tax by 3 pence in the pound. In addition, various matters that are reserved have been devolved to the Scottish parliament to administer. This is known as executive devolution.

The parliament is elected for a fixed four-year term. Elections take place on the first Thursday in May every four years, though there are circumstances in which an election can take place at another time. The parliament has 129 members, 73 elected for individual constituencies on the first-past-the-post method of election and 56 additional members drawn on a proportional basis from party lists drawn up for each of eight larger regions. In the elections to the parliament, each elector is able to cast two votes: one for a constituency MSP (member of the Scottish parliament) and one for the party of their choice.

Once the parliament is elected, a Scottish executive is formed. The head of the executive is the first minister—in effect, a prime minister for Scotland—and the first minister nominates other ministers and junior ministers. (Two law officers—the lord advocate and the solicitor general for Scotland—also serve as members.) The first minister is formally appointed by the queen, but the nomination has to be approved by the parliament. The first minister's nominees for other ministerial offices also have to be approved by the parliament before they are submitted to the queen. The ministers forming the executive operate on the basis of collective responsibility. They work, like the U.K. government, through departments (see Chapter 8). Where there are some subjects that cut across departmental responsibilities, cabinet committees are formed. Ministers are serviced by the civil service, in essence the civil servants that were previously employed in the Scottish Office.

The first election to the parliament took place on May 6, 1999. At one stage during the election campaign, the Scottish Nationalists appeared to be pulling ahead of the Labour party. Labour fought back to gain the lead in the opinion polls, but it was not expected that Labour would—as at one time looked possible—gain an absolute of the votes or of the seats in the parliament. In the election, Labour emerged as the largest single party, but it failed to gain an absolute majority. The results were:

Labour	56
SNP	35
Conservative	18
Liberal	17
Scottish Socialist	1
Independent Labour	1
Green	1

The Green party had gained its first parliamentary seat. The Independent Labour MSP was a member of the U.K. Paliament who had been denied nomination as a Labour candidate for the Scottish elections and so decided to defy his party and stand as an independent. In the event, he achieved the best constituency result in the election.

The outcome of the election meant that the Labour party either had to form a minority government or else form a coalition with another party. In the event, it pursued the option of a coalition with the Liberal party. After some intense negotiations, a coalition was formed and various policies agreed on. One particular policy (on tuition fees for students at Scottish universities) looked as if it would prevent agreement being reached, but a compromise was eventually negotiated. Labour MSP Donald Dewar, who previously sat in the cabinet as secretary of state for Scotland, became first minister. The new executive comprised Dewar, ten ministers, and 11 junior ministers. The portfolios were divided between Labour and Liberal MSPs, with the leader of the Scottish Liberals, James (Jim) Wallace, becoming deputy first minister and minister for justice.

The new executive began to exercise its powers on July 1, 1999. It soon found itself embroiled in a number of controversial issues. The release of a psychopathic killer from a Scottish hospital led to a promise that the executive would act to prevent any repetition, but it then emerged that other releases were imminent. A willingness to consider the use of motorway tolls (essentially alien to the United Kingdom, apart from on certain bridges and tunnels) attracted opposition. There also emerged the prospect of conflict with the Westminster government over financial support for the ailing farming industry. The first three bills introduced in the Parliament by the executive were a Public Finance and Accountability Bill, an Abolition of Feudal Tenure Bill, and an Adults with Incapacity Bill. Other issues being addressed included a ban on fox hunting, and a ban on smoking in public places.

The Parliament established a regular routine, the normal parliamentary week being 2:30 to 5:30 P.M. on Mondays, 9:30 A.M. to 5:30 P.M. on Tuesdays, Wednesdays, and Thursdays, and 9:30 A.M. to 12:30 P.M. on Fridays. Extensive use began to be made of committees, with Tuesdays and Wednesdays being given over to committee meetings. The committees are listed in Table 10.2. They are permanent and have wide-ranging remits, being permitted to consider and report on any matters within their field of competence. Thus, for example, the terms of reference of the Local Government Committee are "to consider and report on matters relating to local government." They are thus able to consider proposed bills, statutory instruments (orders made under the authority of an act), European Union legislation, the conduct of the executive, and issues of public policy. They have the power to summon evidence and a great deal of time is spent taking oral evidence from witnesses, including members of the executive. So forceful was some of the questioning of ministers in the first few months of the committees' existence that in November 1999 there were press reports that the executive was considering seeking to curb the work of the committees.

TABLE 10.2   Committees in the Scottish Parliament

Audit
Procedures
Public Petitions
Standards

Education, Culture, and Sport
Enterprise and Lifelong Learning
Equal Opportunities
European
Finance
Health and Community Care
Justice and Home Affairs
Local Government
Rural Affairs
Social Inclusion, Housing, and Voluntary Sector
Subordinate Legislation
Transport and the Environment

The Welsh Assembly

The Welsh assembly has no powers to make primary legislation or to vary rates of taxation. What it has done, in effect, is to take over powers previously vested in the cabinet minister responsible for Wales (the secretary of state for Wales). The assembly has the power to "develop and implement policy" in a number of areas, including agriculture, culture, economic development, education, the environment, housing, social services, and transport. Though it cannot enact primary legislation, it can exercise the power—previously vested in the secretary of state for Wales—to promulgate secondary legislation, that is, orders permitted to be made under a parent act of Parliament.

The assembly, like the Scottish parliament, sits for a fixed four-year term. It has 60 members. These are elected by the same method (the additional member system) as members of the Scottish parliament. Forty members of the assembly are elected for individual constituencies by the first-past-the-post method of election and 20 additional members are drawn on a proportional basis from party lists drawn up in four regions.

Once elected, the assembly elects a first secretary. The first secretary then selects a number of assembly secretaries who are responsible for particular policy sectors, such as health and education. Collectively, they form an executive committee, the assembly cabinet, which is responsible to the assembly. The first secretary and the assembly secretaries are assisted by a civil service, essentially the civil service that previously worked in the Welsh Office, the department headed by the secretary of state for Wales. The assembly works through regional and subject committees, members being elected to committees to reflect party strength in the assembly.

The first elections to the assembly took place on the same day as elections to the Scottish parliament—May 6,1999. Labour, as expected, emerged as the largest party in the assembly. The results were:

Labour	28
Plaid Cymru	17
Conservatives	9
Liberal Democrats	6

Plaid Cymru thus firmly established itself as the second party in Wales. The assembly elected as first secretary Alun Michael, at the time the secretary of state for Wales; he resigned his cabinet post in order to take up his new position. He proceeded to appoint assembly secretaries, all drawn from the ranks of Labour members of the assembly. There was no attempt to form a coalition. Labour members decided to form what, in effect, was a minority government. One early controversy was the appointment of a vegetarian as the assembly secretary responsible for agriculture, an appointment that was not popular with some meat-producing farmers.

The queen formally opened the new assembly on May 26 and it began to exercise its powers with effect from July 1, 1999. One early problem was the prohibition on the sale of beef still on the bone. The sale of beef on the bone had been banned in the United Kingdom, prior to devolution, for health reasons (there was thought to be a remote possibility of catching "mad cow" disease) and the decision had proved unpopular. The U.K. government decided in 1999, on professional advice, to get rid of the ban. Because agriculture was not a reserved power, it could not lift the ban in Scotland and Wales. The Welsh assembly, along with the Scottish parliament, decided—also on professional advice—that the ban should not be lifted. The U.K. government was reluctant to act without the support of the devolved assemblies. Its reluctance to act unilaterally raised questions as to the purpose of devolution. The ban was lifted at the beginning of December 1999.

NORTHERN IRELAND

The demands for a new form of government in Northern Ireland have borne little relationship to the demands for devolution in Scotland and Wales. The problems of Northern Ireland are particular to the province. Those problems have aroused perplexity, incredulity, and misunderstanding in other parts of the United Kingdom as well as abroad. (Indeed, the failure of some Americans to comprehend the problems of the province has been a bone of contention both within Northern Ireland and in government circles.) The debate about the future of the province is longstanding: It has existed ever since Northern Ireland came into being. The last three decades of the twentieth century were marked by violence and by the persistence of those engaged in the debate adopting mutually exclusive positions. By the end of the 1990s, a political solution had been negotiated, but the negotiations had been long and tortuous—conducted against a background of mistrust and continuing conflict—and the capacity of the new governmental arrangements to survive was uncertain. Hope was tempered by doubt.

Background

The history of Ireland has been a depressing and troubled one extending over many centuries and marked by bitter conflict between the English and the Irish and, within Ireland, between indigenous Catholic Irish and Protestant Scottish Presbyterian settlers. The Irish uprising in 1916 forced the U.K. government to recognize Irish demands for self-determination. In 1920 the Westminster Parliament passed the Government of Ireland Act, which provided for home rule in the country and created two parliaments: one for the six northern counties, part of the region of Ulster, and one for the remaining 26 counties. The provisions for the southern counties were stillborn. The continuing troubles in the country resulted in the Treaty of Ireland of 1922, which realized the Irish Free State. Ireland was partitioned and the provisions of the 1920 act applied in the new province of Northern Ireland. A bicameral parliament was established at Stormont, from which an executive was drawn. The new government of the province exercised a number of devolved powers and, in exercising those powers, was not much hindered by the Westminster government. British politicians were not keen to be drawn again into the infructuous bog of Irish politics.

The province of Northern Ireland was created at the forceful behest of the Protestant community of the North. Largely derived from Scottish Presbyterian stock, it had no wish to be engulfed within a Catholic Irish state. Within the new province, it was dominant. It was not, though, the only community within the province: One-third of the population was Catholic. The religious divide between the two communities was reinforced by social, economic, and educational differences as well as by centuries of ingrained animosity. Catholic children were educated in Catholic schools, were taught Irish history, played Gaelic games, and lived in Catholic communities. Protestant children were taught British history, played non-Gaelic games, lived in Protestant communities, and were taught to regard Catholics as threatening to the existence of the province. Catholics, in turn, looked on Protestants as being gravely in error. The divisions ran deep. The Protestants continued proudly to celebrate the victory of Protestant William of Orange in the Battle of the Boyne in 1690. Indeed, in the new province the anniversary of the victory was made a public holiday.

Northern Ireland after 1922 became for all intents and purposes a one-party province. The Unionists party, representing the Protestants, regularly won two-thirds of the seats at Stormont (there was little alternation of seats from one party to the other) and formed the government, enjoying uninterrupted power. Despite occasional violence by the self-styled Irish Republican Army (the IRA), which wanted a united Ireland and was prepared to engage in terrorist activities to achieve it, the Stormont government enjoyed sufficient coercive powers to impose its will and did so in a manner that favored the Protestants. Catholics were discriminated against in the allocation of houses and jobs and were forced to live in an environment where they felt themselves to be second-class citizens. There was little they could do within the existing political structure, a position analogous to that faced by African Americans in the deep south of the United States.

"The Troubles"

The position in the province was to change in the latter half of the 1960s. A new, relatively liberal Unionist prime minister, Terence O'Neill, sought better relations with the Republic of Ireland, a move that caused consternation in the more traditional ranks of his party. On the Catholic side, the steps taken by the O'Neill government were seen as being too little and too late. A civil rights movement sprang up in the province, inspired by the experience of the United States. The Civil Rights Association was formed in 1967 and was joined the following year by a more revolutionary organization, the People's Democracy. The two groups engaged in tactics designed to provoke a violent response in the hope that this would draw attention to the plight of the Catholic minority in the province. They organized demonstrations and marches. These resulted in a vigorous reaction from the police force, the Royal Ulster Constabulary, as well as from various Protestant groups. Clashes between protesters and their opponents erupted into civil disorder that the police and their auxiliary forces, the so-called B-Specials (despised in the Catholic community), were unable to contain. In August 1969, at the request of the Northern Ireland cabinet, the Westminster government sent troops to the province to maintain order. In return for such action, the government insisted on phasing out the B-Specials and introducing full civil rights for Roman Catholics. Ensuring that the latter demand was complied with was another matter.

The arrival of troops was initially welcomed by Catholics in the province. However, the use of troops to support the civil authorities—in other words, the Protestant government and the police—and the search of Catholic areas for arms produced a rapid dissipation of that support. A "shooting war" broke out between the IRA and the British army in February 1971. In August the British government decided to intern without trial suspected IRA leaders. Instead of lessening the violence, the action appeared to exacerbate it: Internment aroused greater sympathy for the IRA cause among the Catholic community, and the interned leaders were replaced by more extreme followers. At the same time, tension increased between the Stormont and Westminster governments, the former contending that the latter was not doing enough to counter the activities of the IRA. The Stormont government even made a request for troops in the province to be put under its control. The request was denied.

Violence in the province became more marked toward the end of 1971, with more than a hundred explosions a month. In the first two months of 1972, 49 people were killed and another 257 injured as a result of bombings and gunshots. In an attempt to break the deadlock in the province, the Conservative government at Westminster decided to pursue some form of political initiative. The government's proposals included periodic plebiscites on the issue of the border, a start to the phasing out of internment, and the transfer of responsibility for law and order from Stormont to London. The last proposal proved unacceptable to the Northern Ireland cabinet, which made clear that it would resign if the proposal was implemented. In consequence, Prime Minister Edward Heath informed the House of Commons on March 24, 1972, that the British government was left with no alternative but to assume full and direct responsibility for the administration of Northern Ireland until such time as a political solution to the problem of the province could be achieved. To give effect to the government's decision, the Northern Ireland (Temporary Provisions) Bill was quickly passed by Parliament, enjoying the support of the Labour opposition as well as of the Liberals. The new act suspended the Stormont parliament and transferred its powers to the Westminster government. A new Northern Ireland Office was established under a secretary of state.

Attempts to Achieve a Solution

The task of succeeding Northern Ireland secretaries has been twofold: to try to maintain security within the province, doing so in a way that will not alienate either community (the Protestant community by not doing enough, the Catholic by doing too much), and at the same time to seek a political solution that is acceptable to both. Various political initiatives have been attempted since 1972, each usually failing to mobilize the cross-community support necessary to sustain it. The initiative coming closest to success emerged in the 1990s. The initiatives in the intervening period variously provided initial hope, only to be dashed by the actions of politicians and others in Northern Ireland.

The first attempt to reach a solution—a power-sharing elected assembly in 1974—was destroyed by a province-wide strike organized by the Protestant Ulster Workers Council. The new Labour government in London was unwilling to use its coercive powers to try to break the strike. The executive resigned. It had lasted four months. An elected constitutional convention in 1975 failed to break the deadlock: The Unionist-dominated body issued a report favoring a Stormont-type cabinet government—that is, a reversion to government by the majority party, unhindered by any form of power sharing—which was rejected by the government. A reconvened convention failed to reach agreement. A conference convened at the beginning of 1980 was boycotted by the Ulster Unionist party. A proposal to create an advisory council of elected officials drawn from the province, to fulfill advisory and reporting functions until such time as a more durable settlement could be reached, was stillborn. It was overshadowed by hunger strikes of IRA prisoners in the Maze prison (demanding various concessions, including the reintroduction of "political status") and by a recommendation from former prime minister James Callaghan that the province develop into a "broadly independent State." In 1982 an attempt was made to introduce a form of "rolling devolution." This involved the election of a 78-member assembly under a system of proportional representation. The concept of rolling devolution allowed the assembly to propose at any time the transfer of executive responsibilities for any particular department to its own jurisdiction. The ultimate objective was full devolution, but to be achieved at a pace made possible by the assembly itself. In practice, the assembly proved short-lived. The elections to it, in October 1982, provided a publicity coup for Sinn Fein, the political wing of the Provisional IRA: It garnered one-tenth of the first-preference votes cast and saw five of its candidates elected. SDLP as well as Sinn Fein candidates elected to the assembly boycotted its sittings. Only Unionists attended. In March 1986 they decided not to fulfill the assembly's statutory functions in protest of the Anglo-Irish Agreement. Three months later the government decided to disband the assembly; like its predecessors, it had fallen foul of the lack of consensus it was designed to counter.

The Anglo-Irish Agreement

The Anglo-Irish Agreement was the product of the discussions that had taken place under the aegis of the Anglo-Irish Intergovernmental Council. Signed at Hillsborough Castle in Northern Ireland on November 15, 1985, by the British prime minister, Margaret Thatcher, and the *Taoiseach* (prime minister) of the Irish Republic, Dr. Garret Fitzgerald, the agreement had three essential elements. Under Article 1, both governments recognized that "any change in the status of Northern Ireland would only come about with the consent of the majority of the people of Northern Ireland." This was the first time the Irish government had given legal recognition to Northern Ireland's right to self-determination. The British government hoped this part of the agreement would help make the whole document acceptable to the Unionists. The second element was embodied in Articles 2 to 8, which established the Intergovernmental Conference, chaired by the secretary of state for Northern Ireland and the foreign minister of the republic. Through the conference, the republic was enabled to raise issues on the administration of the province that were of particular concern to the minority community. The committee was an advisory one, with a small secretariat. It became a particular target for Unionist opposition. The third element, covered by Articles 6, 7, and 9, provided for greater cross-border cooperation on security matters, and security became a subject regularly discussed at meetings of the conference. The agreement also dealt with a number of other topics, including the creation of an Anglo-Irish parliamentary body, and this came into being in February 1989.

The first and third elements of the agreement proved insufficient to make it acceptable to the Unionist parties. To them, the Intergovernmental Conference allowed a foreign government the opportunity to interfere in the affairs of the province and constituted a "thin end of the wedge," the first step toward forcing the province into a united Ireland. In protest, all 15 Unionist MPs in the province resigned their seats in December 1985, fighting by-elections as a means of demonstrating popular opposition to the agreement. The move was a partial success: One Unionist failed to achieve reelection; the rest were returned, including Enoch Powell in the highly marginal seat of Down South (he lost the seat in the 1987 general election). Their next step was to refuse to fulfill the statutory functions of the Northern Ireland assembly, in effect signing the assembly's death warrant. Their actions failed to dent the government's resolve to persist with the agreement.

Five years after the signing of the agreement, the British government could point to a notable increase in cross-border coordination on security matters. It was also able to claim that the number of deaths and injuries each year attributable to the security position in the province was running well below that of the 1970s. Unionists could point to the fact that the biggest decline predated the agreement taking effect. There was greater contact between the British and Irish governments, with the Irish government agreeing to make some changes to its extradition policy, a contentious issue on which the British government had been pressing for reform for some years. On the British side, various measures had been introduced to meet some of the fears and demands of the nationalist community: an independent commission for complaints against the police, a fair employment act, the extension of the franchise for council elections, and the removal of special protection for the Union flag. Relative to the previous initiatives, the agreement—in terms of substance and longevity—constituted the most successful initiative taken by the British government since the imposition of direct rule.

Despite the Anglo-Irish Agreement—or, in the view of some of its opponents, because of it—the situation in the province remained tense. Ninety-three people were killed in 1988, the same number as in the previous year. The government sought to go beyond, and build on, the agreement in order to reach a political solution.

New Talks

By the end of the 1980s, the IRA was losing support in the nationalist community, not least because of some of the killings it carried out, including 11 people killed by bombs in a Remembrance Day ceremony and a little girl who was shot. The new secretary of state for Northern Ireland, Peter Brooke, signaled a willingness to talk and, on March 26, 1991, he announced to the House of Commons that the basis for formal talks involving all the constitutional parties in the province had been established—the first such talks since the collapse of the convention in 1976. The parties accepted that the talks should concentrate on the establishment of new institutions for governing the province, the relationship between those institutions and the Republic of Ireland, and the relationship between the British and Irish governments. Bilateral meetings between the secretary of state and the various parties began in April 1991, followed—after various delays—by a full meeting in June. Delays and disagreement hampered the talks and in July they were brought to a conclusion. Mr. Brooke told the House of Commons that, despite the ending of the talks, the plenary sessions had demonstrated that there were grounds for resuming the talks later. The resumption took place—under his successor, Sir Patrick Mayhew—in April 1992, when discussions were held on the first of the three elements: the institutions of government in the province. In July, the talks moved on to intergovernmental relationships. The round table talks ended in November 1992 without reaching overall agreement. The government continued discussions, mostly on a bilateral basis, with the Northern Ireland parties; and separately with the Irish government on matters of mutual interest, including constitutional issues, under the auspices of the Anglo-Irish Intergovernmental Conference.

The Downing Street Declaration

The leader of the SDLP, John Hume, opened discussions with the leader of Sinn Fein, Gerry Adams, to see if some settlement might be possible. Discussion also took place between the British and Irish governments. The contact between the governments was to result in a joint declaration on December 15, 1993. Known as the Downing Street Declaration, the statement made clear that the consent of a majority of the people in Northern Ireland was required before any constitutional change could come about. The two governments agreed that, following a cessation of violence, democratically mandated parties that had established a commitment to exclusively peaceful methods, and that had shown that they would abide permanently by the democratic process, would be free to participate fully in democratic politics and to join in dialogue in due course between the governments and the political parties on the way ahead.

The text reiterated Northern Ireland's statutory constitutional guarantee and reaffirmed that the British government would uphold the democratic wish of a greater number of the people of Northern Ireland on the issue of whether they preferred to support the Union or a sovereign united Ireland. On this basis the British government reiterated that it had no selfish strategic or economic interest in Northern Ireland, and that, were a majority in Northern Ireland to wish it, the government would introduce legislation to bring about a united Ireland. For their part the Irish government accepted that it would be wrong to attempt to impose a united Ireland in the absence of the freely given consent of a majority of the people of Northern Ireland. The Irish government also confirmed that in the event of an overall settlement, they would put forward and support proposals for change in the Irish Constitution, which would fully reflect the principle of consent in Northern Ireland.

The Downing Street Declaration helped create a new political situation, with some notable consequences. In August 1994, the IRA announced a "complete cessation of military operations." This was followed in October by a cease-fire by the loyalist paramilitary bodies. The British government proceeded to enter into talks with the different parties. In February 1995, the British and Irish governments published two papers under the title *Frameworks for the Future.* The documents were discussion papers and outlined what an overall settlement might look like. "A Framework for Accountable Government" described the British government's idea for possible new democratic institutions in Northern Ireland. It envisaged an assembly of 90 members, elected by proportional representation and including a system of checks and balances. "A New Framework for Agreement" outlined a shared understanding between the two governments as to how relations within the island of Ireland and between London and Dublin might be based on cooperation and agreement to the advantage of all. The new *Taoiseach* (John Bruton) said that changes to Articles 2 and 3 of the Irish Constitution envisaged in the document would remove any jurisdictional or territorial claim of legal right over Northern Ireland contrary to the will of the people.

Both governments followed this up in November 1995 with the launch of the Twin Track Initiative, the aim of which was to create the conditions necessary for substantive talks to begin early 1996. The initiative established an international body to examine the decommissioning of illegal arms and to undertake preparatory talks designed to establish, if possible, the basis for all-party negotiations. Former U.S. Senator George Mitchell was invited to chair the body. The International Body published its report on January 24, 1996. It concluded that the paramilitaries would not decommission any arms prior to all-party negotiations; set out six principles to which it said all parties should adhere, including a commitment to the fundamental principles of democracy and nonviolence; set out guidelines on decommissioning; and suggested a number of confidence-building measures including, if it were broadly acceptable, an elective process, to take negotiations forward.

The British government accepted the report but the peace process suffered a setback the following month, when the IRA ended its cease-fire and exploded a bomb in Canary Wharf, in London's Docklands, causing massive damage and resulting in two fatalities. The two governments decided to move ahead with all-party negotiations, following a broadly elective process, but with Sinn Fein's participation dependent on an unequivocal restoration of the IRA cease-fire and all parties agreeing to the Mitchell principles of democracy and nonviolence. Elections were held on May 30, 1996, and ten parties were elected to take part in initial negotiations and in a new deliberative Northern Ireland Forum. Multiparty talks opened in June, but with Sinn Fein—one of the ten parties—excluded. Time was taken up with agreeing how to proceed before the focus moved to decommissioning of arms. No conclusion was reached. The new forum was also convened, but Sinn Fein, which was eligible to sit, declined to do so, and the SDLP withdrew from participation.

The Good Friday Agreement

The 1997 general election intervened. The new Labour government announced its intention that substantive negotiations should begin in September 1997, with a view to reaching a conclusion by May 1998, when the final outcome would be put to the people of Ireland, north and south, for approval in concurrent referendums. The government also outlined its position in meetings between British officials and representatives of Sinn Fein. On July 19, 1997, the IRA announced an unequivocal restoration of the cease-fire. After six weeks, the government decided that the cease-fire met the conditions it had set and admitted Sinn Fein to the negotiations. Sinn Fein affirmed its commitment to the Mitchell principles. The two governments also announced the creation of an Independent International Commission on Decommissioning.

All-party negotiations took place from October 1997 through to April 1998. At various points, they looked under threat because of incidents of sectarian violence. However, agreement was reached on April 10, 1998. The agreement—dubbed the Good Friday Agreement—replaced the Anglo-Irish Agreement and was based on the three strands that had formed the basis of the talks.

The first, dealing with the arrangements for the governance of Northern Ireland, resulted in a proposal for an 108-member Northern Ireland assembly, elected by single transferable vote (STV). It would have responsibility for all legislative and executive matters within the domain of the existing six Northern Ireland government departments. Safeguards were built in to ensure that all sections of the community could participate. There would be an executive committee, with a first minister and a deputy first minister.

The second, dealing with the whole of Ireland, proposed the creation of a North-South Ministerial Council to bring together those with executive responsibilities in Northern Ireland and the Irish government "to develop consultation, co-operation and action within the island of Ireland—including through implementation on an all-island and cross-border basis—on matters of mutual interest within the competences of the Administrations, North and South." Among areas identified for cooperation were agriculture (animal and plant health), education (teacher qualifications and exchanges), transport (strategic planning), environmental protection, tourism, inland fisheries, and urban and rural development.

The third, dealing with relations between Britain and Ireland, proposed a British-Irish Council—dubbed the Council of the Isles—"to promote the harmonious and mutually beneficial development of the totality of relationships among the peoples of these islands." It was to comprise representatives of the British and Irish governments, devolved institutions in Northern Ireland, Scotland, and Wales, as well as the Isle of Man and the Channel Islands. It also proposed a British-Irish Intergovernmental Conference, which would subsume the Anglo-Irish Intergovernmental Council and the Intergovernmental Conference established under the 1985 Anglo-Irish Agreement. The conference would bring together the British and Irish governments "to promote bilateral co-operation at all levels on all matters of mutual interest within the competences of both governments."

The agreement also included sections on rights, safeguards, and equality of opportunity. It reaffirmed the commitment to "the total disarmament of all paramilitary organizations," the intention being to achieve decommissioning within two years of the agreement being endorsed in a referendum. Both governments also agreed to put in place mechanisms for an accelerated program for the release of prisoners—affiliated to organizations maintaining an unequivocal cease-fire—convicted of certain specified offenses. Both governments would sign a new British-Irish Agreement, replacing the 1985 Anglo-Irish Agreement.

The agreement also identified the timetable for progress. A referendum was to be held in both Northern Ireland and the Republic on May 22, 1998, and, if majorities supported the agreement, elections to the Northern Ireland assembly would take place on June 25. This program was maintained. On May 22, people both north and south of the border endorsed the Good Friday Agreement by massive majorities (Table 10.3). One exit poll showed that support was most pronounced in Northern Ireland among Catholic voters: 96 percent voted yes. Though most Protestant voters voted in favor, the percentage was not so overwhelming: 55 percent voted in favor, and 45 percent voted against.

Following the referendum, the parties than geared up for the assembly elections in June. In the elections, the Unionists, in different guises, ended up with the bulk of the seats. The results were:

Ulster Unionists	28
SDLP	24
Democratic Unionists	20
Sinn Fein	18
Alliance	6
UK Unionists	5
Independent Unionists	3
Progressive Unionists	2
Women's Coalition	2

TABLE 10.3   Results of the referendum on the Good Friday Agreement, 1998

	Yes	No
Northern Ireland Turnout: 80.9%	676,966 (71.1%)	274,879 (28.9%)
Republic of Ireland Turnout: 66.5%	1,401,919 (94.4%)	83,141 (5.6%)

The assembly met for the first time on July 1, 1998. It elected the leader of the Ulster Unionist Party, David Trimble, as first minister-designate. Seamus Mallon of the SDLP was elected as deputy first minister-designate. The assembly subsequently met to establish various committees.

The referendums and the election to the assembly represented a particular high point in the peace process. In subsequent months, problems were encountered with the issue of decommissioning. The IRA failed to decommission any weapons and the Unionists began to press for a halt to the release of IRA prisoners, and for the exclusion of Sinn Fein members in the executive committee, until some weapons were decommissioned. In 1999, the situation deteriorated with no movement on the issue of decommissioning. So-called punishment beatings (the IRA using physical violence against members of the nationalist community who had transgressed its rules), the murder of a Catholic taxi driver, and alleged IRA involvement in gun smuggling from the United States, led to claims that the IRA cease-fire was breaking down. Relations between the Unionists and the Secretary of State for Northern Ireland Marjorie ("Mo") Mowlam became increasingly strained. Seamus Mallon resigned as deputy first minister-designate on July 15. By August, the situation was looking bleak. Relations between the Ulster Unionists and the Northern Ireland secretary had all but broken down.

However, the situation improved in the autumn. Mo Mowlam was replaced as Northern Ireland secretary by Peter Mandelson, a confidant of the prime minister, and Senator Mitchell was recalled to broker negotiations between both sides. It looked as if the talks might flounder, but agreement was eventually reached, the Unionists agreeing to an executive being created ahead of decommissioning of weapons, but apparently with assurances being given by the British government as to what would happen if the IRA failed to meet its commitment to decommission. David Trimble managed to carry his governing Ulster Unionist Council with him in supporting the deal.

On November 30, 1999, the secretary of state laid the order establishing an executive in the province. It was approved by Parliament within a matter of hours. A quarter of a century after the last occasion on which a power-sharing executive had been attempted, a ten-member executive was brought into being. David Trimble took up the post as first minister and Seamus Mallon was persuaded to return and to take up the post of deputy first minister. The remaining posts were allocated among the parties. Sinn Fein obtained two of the posts, its leading figure—Martin McGuinness—becoming minister for education. It was the first occasion that Sinn Fein had accepted a role in the governing of the province. The new executive got under way (it met for the first time on December 2), though with some internal conflict—the two Democratic Unionist ministers vowing not to attend executive meetings with Sinn Fein ministers present until the IRA decommissioned weapons—and some uncertainty as to whether the IRA would deliver on the promise to decommission. The executive nonetheless constituted a new departure for the province, with politicians who once would not have come together in public now working together in government. The cooperation proved short-lived. A failure to make progress on the decommissioning of arms resulted in the suspension of the executive at the beginning of 2000. Following further negotiations, it was brought back into being in May 2000.

The new form of government in the province is closer to that of Scotland than to that of Wales. As in Scotland, executive and legislative powers are devolved. The assembly works through committees. Apart from occasional ad hoc committees and two "domestic" committees (the Committee to Advise the Presiding Officer and the Committee on Standing Orders), ten departmental committees have been established. These are listed in Table 10.4. The committees parallel the ten executive departments.

Resolving the Conflict

Though the new form of government in Northern Ireland has some similarities to the form of devolved government in Scotland, there the similarity ends. The situation in Northern Ireland, in terms of the history leading to the new arrangements, stands out from that in Scotland and Wales. Scotland and Wales were characterized by demands for some form of "home rule" or even, in the case of Scotland, independence. In Northern Ireland, there were some demands for home rule, primarily from Unionists, who—as we have seen—had dominated politics during the period that the province did have home rule, from 1922 to 1972. However, a section of the population wanted not home rule but incorporation into another country. For a section of the population in Northern Ireland, the province was part of the United Kingdom and they were determined that it should remain as such. Another, smaller (though, in demographic terms, growing) section of the population believed the province should be part of a united Ireland. This situation had no parallels in Scotland and Wales. It created a unique situation, spawning, as we have seen, violence for more than

TABLE 10.4 Departmental committees in the Northern Ireland Assembly

Agriculture and Rural Development
Culture, Arts, and Leisure
Education
Enterprise, Trade, and Investment
Environment
Finance and Personnel
Health, Social Services, and Public Safety Committee
Higher and Further Education, Training, and Employment
Regional Development
Social Development

two decades. It also created a constitutional conundrum: how to find a political solution acceptable to parties that adopted mutually exclusive positions.

The problem has not been the absence of proposals for a constitutional solution. For 30 years, from 1969 to 1999, the problem was one of mobilizing the support of the nationalist *and* Unionist populations behind any one of them. At least eight different constitutional options were proposed during this period (see Table 10.5). *Direct rule* existed from 1972, but proved unacceptable to all the parties involved. It was seen as what it was, a political expedient. The parties were agreed that the province should move from direct rule to another form of government, but could not agree on what form that alternative should take. *Self-government via majority government*—of the sort that existed from 1922 to 1972—was pushed for by the Unionists in the years following the suspension of the Stormont parliament but was unacceptable to the British and Irish governments as well as to the nationalist community. It would allow for a Unionist hegemony that is anathema to the nationalists. *Redrawing the border* was seen as impractical and morally unacceptable. It would not solve the basic problem. Although there are Catholic and Protestant communities in Northern Ireland—and they have become more starkly defined in recent years, "mixed" communities having declined in number—they nonetheless exist in each of the six counties of the province. *Integration* with the rest of the United Kingdom was not acceptable to the nationalists and was not favored by the British or Irish governments. Though the British government recognized Northern Ireland as part of the United Kingdom, as long as the majority in the province wished to remain part of the United Kingdom, it recognized that there were features that distinguished it from other parts of the United Kingdom. *Independence* for the province was not seen as economically viable and had little support. *Federalism,* advocated by some Catholics and by Michael Sheane in *Ulster and the German Solution,*[3] was a compromise that was acceptable neither to the Unionists nor to the IRA. For the former it went too far and for the latter not far enough. *Unification* with Ireland was the goal of the IRA but was the one thing that Unionists were adamantly op-

TABLE 10.5 *Constitutional options for Northern Ireland*

- Direct rule—the province being governed by the U.K. government
- Self-government with a majority government, similar to that which existed from 1922 to 1972
- Self-government through a power-sharing executive, different parties holding office in the executive
- Redrawing of the border, moving large sections of the province with Roman Catholic populations into the Irish Republic
- Integration with the United Kingdom, putting the province on a par with any other part of the United Kingdom
- Independence, letting Northern Ireland became a nation state
- Federalism, letting Northern Ireland become a federal state within a federal Ireland
- Unification with the Republic of Ireland

posed to. The IRA did not want the province to remain part of the United Kingdom. Unionists did not want it to become part of the Republic of Ireland.

That left one option: *self-government based on power-sharing.* This proved popular with the British government but, as we have seen, attempts to create a power-sharing executive variously ran afoul of Unionist opposition. It also encountered opposition from the SDLP, who were willing to consider it only within the context of an "Irish dimension." It did not prove a viable option during the 1970s and 1980s. As we have seen, not until the 1990s did the situation change and only after protracted and often fraught negotiations did a power-sharing executive eventually emerge.

What changed in the 1990s was that there was a recognition by the IRA that it was losing political support and that, while it could continue a military campaign, it was not likely to achieve a united Ireland. For its part, the British government, aware that it was proving impossible to destroy the IRA militarily, was keen to exploit the situation to press for a political solution. On the Unionist side, there was a recognition that the demographic situation in the province was reducing the gap between the size of the Protestant and Unionist communities and that there might be some merit in seeking a political accommodation within the context of Northern Ireland, as a way of maintaining the integrity of the province. The result was contact between the British government and Sinn Fein and a willingness on the part of many, though by no means all, Unionist politicians to participate in talks.

The result of these talks, leading to negotiations—which at times were on-off negotiations—was, as we have seen, the Good Friday Agreement and the election of a Northern Ireland assembly. The agreement provided the Irish dimension sought by the SDLP. It gave Sinn Fein an opportunity to become part of the political process: exclusion from the executive committee led it to refer to its "democratic mandate." The agreement gave the Unionists the opportunity to have a more direct say in the running of the province.

However, the conflicts that emerged in the wake of the election of the Northern Ireland assembly also pointed to the continuing difficulties of achieving and maintaining a new constitutional solution. Not all Unionists supported the Good Friday Agreement: the Democratic Unionists, led by MP Ian Paisley (see Chapter 6) were vehemently opposed to it. So too was the smaller UK Unionist Party led by MP Robert McCartney. There was also a more widespread wariness on the part of many Unionists. Unionist politicians were wary of the "Irish dimension" and did not trust the IRA: The failure of the IRA to decommission weapons prior to the formation of the executive committee, and continued sectarian violence, was taken as confirmation of their worst fears. The release from prison of convicted murderers—including the man convicted of the 1984 bombing of the Grand Hotel in Brighton, where the prime minister, Margaret Thatcher, was staying, and in which five people were killed—caused considerable unease, including among many British politicians. Sinn Fein feared that they were being squeezed by Unionist demands for decommissioning to precede any further progress.

Even with the creation of a Northern Ireland executive in December 1999, a momentous development given the configuration of opinions that we have outlined, there was the recognition that the basic conflict would remain. One section of society in Northern Ireland—the majority—wished to remain part of the United Kingdom. Another section did not. That was, and is, the basic conundrum at the heart of the politics of Northern Ireland.

REGIONAL GOVERNMENT IN ENGLAND

Scotland, Wales, and Northern Ireland now have devolved assemblies. England has no devolved assemblies. There is no English parliament nor are there any elected regional authorities. The Labour party, in its 1997 election manifesto, promised "in time" to introduce legislation to allow people, region by region, to decide in a referendum whether they wanted directly elected regional government. The closeness of the result in the Welsh referendum in 1997 came as something of a surprise to ministers and appeared to discourage them from moving quickly to introduce the legislation. The emphasis appeared very much to be on "in time."

However, though there are no elected tiers of government at the regional level in England, there are a number of nonelected governmental or quasi-governmental bodies. Various factors have contributed to governmental functions being fulfilled at a regional level. Among the more important pressures have been administrative convenience, the need to involve more local authorities, technical advantages, the desire to dissociate central government from certain decision-making activities, and pressure from groups and professional bodies seeking some degree of regional autonomy in their sphere of activity.[4] Recent years have seen the number of government or public bodies operating at such a level decrease, the consequence of the Conservative government's privatization policy. Various public utilities, which previously had an extensive regional organization (the regional water authorities being the most extensive), are no longer in the public sector. However, regional government has acquired a new significance with the creation of regional development agencies.

Eight government departments have some organization at the regional level, either as an integral part of the department or as part of a service for which the department is responsible. The Prison Department in the Home Office, for example, has a regional organization. Within the Lord Chancellor's Department, courts are organized on a circuit—that is, regional—basis (see Chapter 14). Apart from government departments, a number of other public bodies also have a regional organization. The National Health Service, for example, operates at two levels, the district and regional level. Regional health authorities (RHAs) have responsibility for regional planning, resource allocation, major capital building work, and certain specialized hospital services that are more appropriately administered on a regional basis. (Various private companies, such as utilities, are also organized on a regional level.) There is thus some regional aspect to government in England. This has been extended by the creation of regional development agencies (RDAs).

The Regional Development Agencies Act, enacted in 1998, established an RDA in each of nine regions. Each agency is designed as a small body—with 8 to 15 members drawn from the region and being business-led—with responsibility for furthering economic development and regeneration; promoting business efficiency, investment, and competitiveness; promoting the development and application of skills; and promoting sustainable development. Each RDA has power to develop its own approach. Each brings together various regeneration programs previously vested in a number of bodies, including government regional offices. Each is expected to force partnerships with other bodies in the region.

The RDAs are financed mostly from public funds. They have the status of nondepartmental public bodies and are answerable to ministers and to Parliament. However, provision is also made for the RDAs to be scrutinized by regional interests. Voluntary regional chambers were envisaged, drawing on regional interests and local councils, and under the act, power is given to the relevant minister to designate a chamber as the body to constitute the focus for consultation about the work of the RDA. These voluntary chambers were seen as a substitute for elected regional government and, indeed, as potential stepping stones to elected regional assemblies. Various such chambers now exist. The Yorkshire and Humberside regional assembly, for example, is especially active in pressing for further regional development and for moving toward an elected parliament for the region.

There is thus a layer of government operating at a regional level in England. The value of a regional tier is both managerial and economic. Membership of the EU adds a further spur, creating opportunities for regions to seek funds from the different EU funding agencies (see Chapter 9). However, the regional structures that do exist vary in size and authority. The regions differ in size, both spatially and demographically. They also differ in terms of their definition. There is no agreement on what constitutes the regions of England. Some parts of the country have a clear regional identity; others do not. This, as we shall see, has some political significance.

THE CURRENT DEBATE

The creation of the elected assemblies in Scotland, Wales, and Northern Ireland has not provided settled constitutional solutions. That is apparent, as we have seen, in the case of Northern Ireland. However, it is also the case in Scotland and Wales. In Scotland, the Scottish National Party views devolution as a means to an end (that is, independence) rather than an end in itself. It therefore pushes for independence. The potential for clashes between the Scottish parliament and the Westminster Parliament also suggests a likelihood of pressure for more constitutional reform, or at least some constitutional adjustment. Such clashes are likely to provide political ammunition for the SNP. In Wales, there is a problem in that, as the referendum result in 1997 showed, a large proportion of the Welsh population did not want the Welsh assembly. However, some people in Wales not only did want a Welsh assembly, they wanted a Welsh assembly with more powers than it has been given. They favor a body more on a par with the Scottish parliament, with legislative and even tax-varying powers. Given the strength of the national parties in both the Scottish and Welsh bodies, demands for a greater say for each are likely to continue.

However, the situation in Scotland and Wales has major political implications for England. Following devolution, there was a growing awareness that England and the English regions had nothing comparable. A question raised some years before by a Labour MP, Tam Dalyell—and known, after the name of Dalyell's then-constituency, as "the West Lothian question"—came very much to the fore. That was, how could MPs from Scotland sitting in the U.K. Parliament vote on matters that applied only to England when MPs sitting for English seats could not vote on matters that applied only to Scotland? MPs from Scotland could vote, for example, on bills dealing with transport in England, but English MPs could not vote on bills dealing with transport in Scotland, because that was a devolved subject. One partial solution advanced by some politicians was to reduce the number of Scottish seats in the U.K. Parliament. Another, advanced by Conservative leader William Hague in 1999, was that bills that dealt solely with English matters should be voted on only by English MPs.

A more radical solution, advanced by a number of Conservative MPs, was that England should also have its own elected parliament, leaving the Westminster Parliament to deal with U.K.-wide matters such as defense and the currency. This, it was argued, would ensure equity, ensuring that England was on a par with the other parts of the United Kingdom. It would serve to produce, in effect if not formally, a federal structure.

Whereas a number of Conservative MPs favored an English parliament, some Labour and Liberal Democrat politicians favored a regional solution—that is, elected parliaments in the English regions. As we have seen, there have been some moves in this direction with the creation of voluntary regional assemblies. The regions covered by the RDAs could develop in such a way as to each have their own elected assembly. This, it is argued, would be equitable, given that—in population terms—English regions would be more comparable in size to Scotland and Wales than would be the case if there was a single English parliament.

The arguments for an English parliament or regional parliaments are variously challenged. The objection to an English parliament is practical and political. It raises practical problems because of the population size of England. It would be a skewed form of federalism, with one parliament representing the bulk of the population of the United Kingdom. Fears are also expressed that it might increase the pressure for a breakup of the kingdom, encouraging the different parts to think in terms of independence. According to supporters of the union, the U.K. provides for strength in numbers: The whole is greater than the sum of the parts. Disaggregate the different parts of the kingdom and you weaken it immeasurably.

The problems with the proposal for regional government are that local opinion is divided on the subject and that in some parts of England there is no obvious regional identity. A MORI poll in 1999 found that those favoring giving greater power to the regions outnumbered those opposing it (47 to 30 percent).[5] However, when it came to giving power to one's own region, opinion was divided. In the southeast of England, more were against an elected regional assembly than were for (47 against 37 percent). There was a small majority against the idea in the northwest, and opinion was evenly divided in Yorkshire and Humberside. The only regions where there was a large majority favoring elected assemblies were London (which subsequently got its own elected authority) and the northeast. Not only was opinion divided, there was the problem of determining the boundaries of the regions. Though some regions had fairly clear boundaries and a regional identity (such as Yorkshire, a county big enough to constitute a region), in others it was difficult to discern obvious regions. The "southeast" of England was not a natural region in terms of economic activity or in terms of the perception of residents. It would also constitute a doughnut shape, circling Greater London. Creating artificial regions, it was argued, would encourage local animosity, rather in the way that creating new counties in 1974 had encountered strong local opposition.

Proposals for change are thus clearly on the political agenda. Mobilizing a majority behind any one of them is the difficult task.

CONCLUSION

The closing years of the twentieth century saw a remarkable change in the constitutional landscape of the United Kingdom. For most of the century, there was no elected tier of government in Britain between the national government and local government. That changed at the end of the 1990s with the introduction of devolved assemblies. In 1998, the people of Northern Ireland (who had an elected parliament from 1922 to 1972) voted for a Northern Ireland assembly. In 1999, both Scotland and Wales got elected assemblies and, through them, a new form of executive government.

However, there was nothing uniform about the devolution of powers to these new bodies. The United Kingdom, as we have noted, acquired what was termed asymmetrical devolution. The Scottish and Welsh assemblies were elected by the same electoral process but were given different powers. The Northern Ireland assembly was elected by a different electoral system from that of the Scottish and Welsh assemblies. The form and operation of the Northern

Ireland assembly and its executive committee were prescribed by statute in a way that was particular to the province. And, the most marked element of the asymmetry, there was, and is, no elected assembly for England or for the regions within England. This has meant that debate about the form of government for the different parts of the United Kingdom remains on the political agenda.

NOTES

[1] David Steel refers to the commitment to such a policy as stemming from Gladstone's pamphlet of 1886 that argued for a reform of government consistent with the aspirations of the individual nations in Great Britain. D. Steel, "Federalism," in N. MacCormick (ed.), *The Scottish Debate* (Oxford University Press, 1970), p. 81.

[2] A. H. Birch, *Integration and Disintegration in the British Isles* (Allen & Unwin, 1977).

[3] M. Sheane, *Ulster and the German Solution* (Highfield, 1978).

[4] See B. W. Hogwood, "Introduction," in B. W. Hogwood and M. Keating (eds.), *Regional Government in England* (Oxford University Press, 1982), pp. 10–12.

[5] The question, asked in March 1999, was also open to the objection that it was not neutral, given its opening statement: "As you may know, there will be elections to a Scottish Parliament and a Welsh assembly next May. Do you support or oppose giving greater powers of government to regions in England?" The results were published in *The Economist,* March 26, 1999.

Chapter 11

Local Government
Government Below the Center

Local government is a well-established feature of political life in Britain. The same can be said of local government in the United States. However, where Britain differs from the United States is in terms of the history and status of local government as well as in changes made to the structures of local councils. Those changes have sometimes been motivated by the need to achieve greater administrative efficiency. Others have been motivated by a political impetus to limit the powers or actions of local government. Such changes demonstrate the extent to which local government in Britain is very much subordinate to Parliament. Though there is a fairly pervasive commitment to the principle of local governance, the form that such governance takes is determined by acts of Parliament. Recent decades have been notable for the number of acts passed that are changing the shape of local government in the United Kingdom.

THE CHANGING STRUCTURE OF LOCAL GOVERNMENT

There were local communities with leaders in Anglo-Saxon times. Counties and boroughs existed when the first parliament was summoned in the thirteenth century. From around the fifteenth century, three types of civil authority were well established: the parish (based on the church parish), responsible for law and order and for the poor; the borough, essentially a town granted a royal charter and enjoying certain privileges, including the right to self-administration; and the shire (county), responsible for some degree of general oversight and administration.[1] Industrialization created pressures on local government, making it difficult for existing structures to cope with the scale of urban development and attendant problems of disease and crime. The response was initially piecemeal, but there was a major reform in 1880. This created a uniform two-tier system of local government.

The first tier consisted of county boroughs, exercising control over all local government services within their boundaries, and county councils, each exercising control over certain local government services within the county (other than in county boroughs within their borders). Below the county councils was the second tier: municipal boroughs, urban districts, and rural districts, each exercising limited functions. Within rural districts, there was an additional layer of local government in the form of parish councils, each exercising very limited functions.

As demands on government grew further in the twentieth century—especially in the decades following the Second World War—and the responsibilities of local government expanded, there was pressure for further reform. After a period of little change, local government witnessed a period of significant change, and continues to do so. The last four decades of the twentieth century saw several major reforms.

Local government in Greater London was reformed in the 1960s: A Greater London Council (GLC) was created to deal with issues such as planning, roads, overspill housing, and other needs affecting the whole of the Greater London area. Responsibility for most local authority housing, and certain other services, was retained by the 32 borough councils within the GLC area.

Local government in the rest of England, and in Wales, was reorganized in 1974. The 1972 Local Government Act, which took effect in 1974, created a new two-tier system. It established 47 county councils, each with responsibility for education, transport, most highways, planning housing, personal social services, libraries, police, fire service, garbage disposal, and consumer protection. Below them a second tier of more than 300 district councils was created, each with responsibility for town planning, environmental health, building and housing management, and various registration and licensing functions. The act also created new local government structures in highly urbanized areas: Six separate metropolitan counties were created and, below them, 36 metropolitan districts. The metropolitan counties had the same responsibilities as county councils, except for education, personal social services, and libraries, which passed to the metropolitan districts. The metropolitan counties and districts also shared responsibility for certain amenities, such as parks, museums, and airports. Below the two tiers, provision for parish councils was retained.

In Scotland, under the provisions of the 1973 Local Government (Scotland) Act, a two-tier division was also created, between regional and district councils. Nine regional councils were established, but because of the concentration of population in the western lowlands of Scotland, one region—Strathclyde—contained more than half of the country's population.

The reorganization was designed to create a system of local government to last for the foreseeable future. It failed to live up to expectations. The spending and actions of some local councils also generated political controversy. The result has been frequent and piecemeal changes.

The reorganization proved costly and did little to enhance consent for government: There was little apparent increase in citizens' awareness of local authority responsibilities. Attempts to achieve an efficient managerial structure also encountered problems, councils variously reverting to old styles of management (committees based on established service, for example) rather than maintaining a new style (committees based on expenditure functions). Certain features of the reorganization created resentment. Inhabitants of counties that had been dismembered or abolished were often vehement in their vocal opposition to the changes. So too were former councilors and other citizens in the boroughs that were reduced to parish council status. Within some of the new counties, a number of boroughs resented and continue to resent the dominance of larger cities. Local government thus achieved no settled state.

Reforms under a Conservative Government

Change was a significant feature under the Conservative government elected in 1979. The government clashed with many local authorities, especially the Labour-controlled GLC and metropolitan counties. The government wanted to limit public spending, and local government expenditure was one of the major features of public spending that exceeded government targets. In 1983–1984, for example, GLC spending exceeded grant-related expenditure (the amount government considered it should spend) by 81 percent. The need to limit public spending was accorded priority over the commitment to the principle of local autonomy, and various measures were introduced to limit the spending of local councils. However, the GLC and many other Labour-controlled councils also constituted an additional thorn in the government's flesh as a result of campaigns that they waged on particular political issues. The GLC, under its leader Ken Livingstone, supported campaigns on a wide range of issues—usually opposed to government policy—and funded organizations (such as feminist and gay groups) that the government regarded as inappropriate recipients of public funds. By 1983, because of the government's annoyance at such activities, it promised to introduce a bill to abolish the GLC and the six metropolitan councils. The commitment was embodied in the party's 1983 election manifesto and was carried through two years later in the 1985 Local Government Act. The GLC and the metropolitan councils ceased to exist on March 31, 1986. The functions of the metropolitan councils were dispersed to metropolitan boroughs and to joint authorities to run police, fire, and passenger transport services. The functions of the GLC were given to the 32 London boroughs. As we shall see, the Conservative government also introduced a raft of measures to change the powers and responsibilities of local government.

The absence of an authority to cover the whole of London proved unpopular with opposition parties and with many London residents. The bifurcation of responsibilities between county and district councils created by the 1972 act continued to cause resentment and some confusion. Some of the new counties created by the 1972 act remained unpopular with residents. A number of cities resented having no more than district council status. This sense of dissatisfaction influenced the political parties. Both the Conservative and Labour parties committed themselves to a further reform of local government, and in 1992 the

Conservative government achieved passage of a new Local Government Act. The act created a new local government commission to review local government structures and boundaries. The commission began work in the autumn of 1992. 1t adopted a peripatetic approach, visiting different parts of the country and conducting inquiries to discover local opinion. It was initially expected to be radical and to make extensive recommendations for unitary, rather than the existing two-tier, authorities. However, the Commission lost momentum and it ran into some trouble with government. Nonetheless, as a result of its work, various county councils were abolished and replaced by a number of unitary authorities (all the functions of local government being vested in a single authority). The outcome was the creation of 46 new unitary authorities. "The result was to be a patchwork. Local government in England would now be characterized by the term 'hybridity'.... This did not look to be a particularly stable mix."[2] In Scotland and Wales, the position was very different. Instead of an extensive review, the government imposed a new uniform system of unitary authorities in each country. As from 1996, Scotland has had 32 unitary authorities and Wales 22.

Reforms under a Labour Government

The Labour government returned in 1997 was committed to devolution and to reform of the system of government for London. Devolution (see Chapter 10) is important in this context in that it resulted in the new Scottish parliament being given responsibility for local government. The Scottish parliament is thus free to reform Scottish local government, should it wish to do so. It is no longer a matter for the Westminster Parliament. In its election manifesto, the Labour party also promised—subject to a referendum of voters in London—to establish an elected mayor and strategic authority for the capital. The referendum was held on May 7, 1998, and—as can be seen from Table 11.1—produced a massive "yes" vote, albeit on a small turnout. The Greater London Authority Act was passed in 1999, with elections for the mayor and the 25-member authority scheduled for 2000.

The change in the governance of London, though, constituted the only change in local government structure promised by the Labour government. Its other changes, as we shall see, were essentially to the powers and responsibilities of local government. It also envisaged some change in the internal organization of councils, favoring a move to a more cabinet-style of government, similar to that existing at national level.

TABLE 11.1   Referendum result in London, 1998

I agree that there should be a London-wide assembly and a directly elected mayor:		
Yes	1,230,715	72.0%
No	478,413	28.0%
Majority	752,302	44.0%
Electorate: 5,014,567		
Turnout: 34.1%		

The 1960s and 1970s thus witnessed important changes to the structure of local government in Britain. The changes did not prove permanent. The last two decades of the century saw significant, piecemeal changes. The result has been a patchwork system of local government. That patchwork is shown in Map 11.1. However, it has not been only the structure of local government that has changed. As we shall see, there have been major changes in powers and finance.

MAP 11.1   Local government in England: Counties and unitary authorities, April 1, 1998

ELECTIONS AND MEMBERS

There are approximately 20,000 councilors. They are elected for four-year terms, with no limit on the number of terms one can serve. Not only is there a patchwork of local councils in England, there is also a patchwork of elections. County, London borough, some unitary and shire district councils (and all parish councils) have whole council elections every four years. In each of the three years between the county council elections, all metropolitan districts, some unitary authorities, and some shire districts elect a third of their members.

The franchise to vote in local elections is essentially the same as that for national elections; citizens age 18 or over who are resident in the area on the qualifying date. (Members of the House of Lords, who cannot vote in elections to the House of Commons, can vote in local elections.) Candidates in local elections must be citizens age 21 or over and be resident in the local authority area or have resided in premises in the area for the preceding 12 months or, in that 12 months, have had their principal place of work in that area. No one may be elected to a council of which he or she is an employee. This prohibition was extended in 1988 by an act prohibiting senior council officials from being elected as councilors in any authority.

Election procedure is essentially the same as that for national elections. (In 1979 and 1997 the two actually coincided, a general election taking place the same day as local elections.) Although elections are fought ostensibly on local issues, candidates at other than parish council level now usually stand under a party label, a tendency that increased in postwar years and was given added impetus by the reorganization of the 1970s. Large authorities are now such significant bodies of public expenditure and policy making that the national parties cannot afford to ignore them. Party has become the most important variable influencing the voting behavior of those electors who bother to cast a vote (turnout, as in local elections in the United States, is low, about 40 percent of eligible voters and declining); local elections are viewed as an annual opportunity to pass judgment on the incumbent national government. Once a party has an absolute majority of seats on a council, it takes control. The person who chairs a council—in towns and cities, it is the mayor—is not usually the party leader. The leader of the council is the person who exercises power. If no party achieves an absolute majority, the result is either an attempt at minority government by the largest single party or shared control by two of the parties (usually, though not always, Labour and the Liberal Democrats). The party in government nationally is expected to lose council seats during the midterm of a Parliament—the Conservative party while in government in the 1990s experienced massive losses in local government elections; a net gain of seats by the governing party is hailed as a considerable victory.

Although councilors are elected on party labels and usually operate within coherent party groupings, with elected officers and whips, they behave differently depending on local circumstances. Given that the needs and demands of communities vary, local parties temper their responses accordingly. The councilors themselves tend to be disproportionately male and drawn from nonmanual occupations. Survey research in the 1990s suggested that nearly 80 percent were over 45 years old, a third had retired, and only 24 percent were women.[3] The likelihood is greater now than it was prior to the mid-1970s that they will have a university education. Since 1972, councils have been empowered to pay members attendance allowances. No salaries are paid, though the attendance allowance can sometimes be the equivalent of a small wage, amounting in the case of some councils to several thousand pounds a year. In the city of Hull, for example, the standard allowance at the beginning of 1999 was just over £7,000 ($11,200).

What motivates individuals to seek election to local councils is not at all clear. Some appear to see it as a stepping-stone to higher things (a number are subsequently selected as parliamentary candidates); some do it out of a desire to further the aims of their party; some do it out of a sense of civic responsibility (to be found also in the performance of a wide range of other local activities, such as serving on the local magistrates' bench and doing voluntary social work); some do it to enhance their status in the community; and some, possibly a majority, do it for the simple reason that they were inveigled into running by friends or local party activists. Because of the number of councilors to be elected and the level of public indifference toward local government, local parties frequently have difficulty recruiting candidates to contest elections. In some areas, it might be described as a seller's rather than a buyer's market.

Most of a councilor's time is given over to the plenary and committee meetings of the council. A government consultation paper on local government published in 1998 reported the finding of one survey that a councilor spent an average of 97 hours per month on council work, two-thirds of which was spent on preparing for, traveling to, and attending council meetings. The document also reported the conclusion of one official body (the Audit Commission, established to make efficiency studies of local government and other public bodies) that "too much of a burden is placed on councillors, often unproductively, by committee meetings." The consultation paper also noted that, while 70 percent of councilors in a recent study felt that representational work directly with the community was their most important role, they spent an average of only 30 percent of their time on it.

Some councilors also devote themselves to activities that are beyond the law. Corruption has been an occasional problem in local government. There have been various high-profile scandals in recent decades. Some cases have involved councilors who are serving on particular committees, such as planning committees, accepting bribes from contractors in return for approving contracts. Other cases have involved councilors submitting false expense claims or using council funds to go on trips that are not strictly necessary to fulfilling their official duties. Some councilors have also operated at a level that is not strictly illegal but is not necessarily regarded as legitimate by electors, such as receiving free tickets for particular events. In the 1990s, a number of cases attracted particular media attention. In the town of Doncaster, for example, a number of councilors were arrested and convicted for misusing council funds or making false claims. This case, dubbed "Donnygate," was one of several that served to reflect badly on local government.

Two explanations have been offered for the level of corruption identified in local government. One is the fact that the decision-making structure of local government means that a small number of local, identifiable individuals make important decisions: They are visible and accessible to local firms and companies. (This contrasts with members of Parliament who, individually, have little scope to influence important decisions.) The other is the fact that many local councils are dominated by one party. This dominance, it is argued, facilitates an arrogance of power on the part of those in the majority party. There is a tendency to believe that they can do what they want or get away with misusing funds.

Allegations of corruption are investigated by the police. Allegations of maladministration (the term is not formally defined, but means, essentially, a failure to observe due process) are investigated by a public official known as the Local Government Ombudsman. (There are separate ombudsmen for England, Scotland, Wales, and Northern Ireland.) Complaints may be made directly to the ombudsman by citizens. The ombudsman has powers of investigation and can recommend remedies in cases where maladministration is held to have occurred. There are no formal powers of enforcement,[4] though if a local authority continues to refuse to comply with a recommendation for redress, the ombudsman can require it to publicize the reasons for its failure to comply. In 1998–99, the local government ombudsmen received 15,869 complaints, a 6 percent increase over the previous year and an all-time high. Education was the subject of more complaints than ever before. Nearly 6,000 complaints were about the handling of housing issues.

In 1999, the government introduced legislation that would require councils to establish standards committees to consider complaints against councilors for failing to comply with ethics guidelines. The intention, as we shall see, was that these bodies should be independent or quasi-independent bodies. Some councils, such as Hull City Council, established such committees ahead of the legislation. The committee set up by Hull is composed of well-known local citizens who are not members of the council. It is chaired by this writer.

POWERS AND FINANCE

Local councils enjoy no constitutionally protected autonomous powers and can exercise only those powers vested in them by law. Their scope for branching out into areas of activity for which they have no specific statutory authority is limited: Under the 1972 Local Government Act, they could levy up to a 2p (pence) rate for generally whatever purpose they wished; under the 1988 Local

Government and Housing Act, this amount was replaced by a per-adult limit (£5 per adult, for example, in the case of London borough and metropolitan district councils). In addition to having to work within statutorily defined limits, councils are also constrained within the confines of powers held and policies pursued by national government. Ministers have various statutory powers to make orders as well as to issue circulars to local authorities giving guidance on the implementation of government policy.

The limitations upon local government are considerable and these were extended during the period of Conservative government from 1979 to 1997. During that period, more than fifty acts of Parliament were passed affecting local government. As we shall see, various spending restrictions were imposed and the domain of local government control constricted. Local authorities are nonetheless major spenders and employers. Approximately two million people are employed by councils in England and Wales. More than a quarter of all public spending is done by local government. Each year, local councils spend in total in excess of £40 billion ($64 billion). The figure for 1999–2000 is closer to £50 billion ($80 billion). Of the service expenditure by local councils, about 40 percent is spent on education. Personal social services account for another 18 percent. Local authorities thus constitute significant economic units.

Local authorities derive their revenue from three principal sources: a central government grant, known as the standard spending assessment (SSA); income from services provided by the authority; and a local tax. The income from services constitutes the smallest of the three sources. The central government grant, having been the largest element and then declined, has become again the dominant source. Just over 20 percent of income derives from the local tax. Most of the rest comes from central government.

Though the local tax accounts for only a small proportion of local government income, it has proved to be the most controversial of the three sources. Until 1990, it took the form of an annual tax on real estate, based on a notional property value; each house had a rateable value and the local authority determined how much to levy each year. Known as "the rates," the system was replaced at the end of the 1980s, and has had two successors.

The Conservative government returned in 1979 took the view that the rating system was inherently unfair; a single person in a house paid the same rate as did a large family living next door, the former helping subsidize the services consumed by the latter. It decided to replace the rates with a community charge, immediately dubbed the "poll tax," levied on individuals rather than on property. Because everyone (with very few exceptions) would pay all or part of the new tax, the government argued that it would increase local accountability—because everyone would have a vested interest in how the council spent their money.

The new tax was brought in first in Scotland in 1989, and in England and Wales the following year. It was accompanied by a uniform business rate (UBR), set centrally by government, replacing the business rate that had been set by councils and that had varied significantly from one authority to another. The new tax proved extraordinarily unpopular, its introduction sparking mass demonstrations and London's worst riot in recent decades. It was one of the contributory factors to Margaret Thatcher's loss of the leadership of the Conservative party (see Chapter 6): She had seen it as the flagship of her legislative program and was not prepared to contemplate its demise.[5] She was replaced by a leader who was willing to let it die, and in 1992 a new measure was approved by Parliament, replacing the poll tax with a "council tax." This new tax was based on actual property values (grouped into bands, a house falling in the top band—band A—paying the highest level of tax), but with a reduction for people living alone. It came into effect on April 1, 1993.

These changes in local government finance constituted part of a wider body of reforms introduced by the Conservative government. The government was concerned especially to acquire powers to limit local authority spending. In 1981 the grant given to councils that exceeded the government's spending targets was reduced. In 1982, the power of councils to raise supplementary rates (that is, additional rates levied after the rate for the year had been set) was abolished; and, after the government was returned for a second term in 1983, power was also taken to impose a maximum limit on the rates that could be levied by big-spending authorities. The government used its powers rigorously to penalize councils exceeding spending limits.

The government also sought to limit the powers and functions of local government. State schools were given the opportunity to opt out of local authority control (though only a small proportion chose to do so). The role of local government in the health service and in the oversight of certain bodies, such as the police, was reduced. The domain of local councils was also constricted by the government's policy of allowing the tenants of council housing (public housing) to buy their houses. In the late 1980s the government also began to place an emphasis on making local government services more competitive, the aim being to increase efficiency and secure greater value for money. Competitive bidding was encouraged and, indeed, increasingly required by law. Under this system, local government services are put out to tender and private firms are able to compete for the contract. The purpose of these various changes was to end the role of councils as "universal providers." Local councils were meant to become "enabling authorities," buying services rather than providing the services themselves through their own workforce.

The overall effect of these changes was to limit the role and powers of local government. The changes also had political consequences. As we have seen, the poll tax proved massively unpopular. The limitations imposed on local councils also proved unpopular, in that they were seen as an attack on local democracy. Whereas the government had effectively demonized certain Labour-controlled councils in the early 1980s—characterizing them as "loony left councils"—the demonization failed to have much impact in the 1990s, public sympathy flowing now in favor of local government, rather than against it.

The Labour government elected in 1997 moved, as we have seen, to create a new Greater London Authority. It did not move to change radically the structure of local government. However, it did move to lessen the controls on local government. It removed the requirement to put services out to tender, but instead required councils to obtain "best value." It encouraged innovation and also partnership with other local bodies. It also changed the method of determining the standard spending assessment and started a consultation process to see if local democracy could be revitalized. It was keen to achieve a more vibrant local government, but without necessarily having to undertake a comprehensive scheme of reform.

Local government in Britain thus changed significantly in the last decades of the twentieth century. It seems likely to continue changing on a piecemeal basis. Various academics have developed different models of local government, but none appears to have been embraced wholeheartedly by British government. One leading scholar, R. A. W. Rhodes, identified, at the beginning of the 1990s, four scenarios for local government: *centralization* (power being concentrated at the center); *the contract authority* (local government contracting with others for the provision of services); *community government* (a revival of the preeminence of local government as the institution of government beyond Whitehall); and *differentiation* (an extension of institutional fragmentation).[6] Rhodes himself inclined most to the differentiation scenario, despite the pressures—as we have seen—under Conservative governments to achieve some element of centralization as well as the creation of the enabling, or contract, authority. The chapter in which Rhodes summarized his approaches was entitled "Now Nobody Understands the System: The Changing Face of Local Government." The position that he sketched then remains largely the case today. Despite various changes, differentiation—continuing institutional fragmentation—remains the most plausible description of local government.

THE CURRENT DEBATE

As we saw in Chapter 10, devolution of power to the elected assemblies in Scotland, Wales, and Northern Ireland has generated political debate. So too has local government. In large part, this stems from the various changes of recent decades, especially those introduced by the Conservative government in the period from 1979 to 1997. However, it is also the subject of debate as to how it can be revitalized. As we have seen, turnout in local elections is poor. It is also getting worse. Britain shares with the United States the worst turnouts in local elections in the western world. In most countries in western Europe, turnout in local elections ranges from 60 percent upward. In Britain and the U.S., a turnout of 40 percent is nowadays considered good. In recent years, the turnout in Britain has dipped below 40 percent (except in 1997, when the local elections took place at the same time as the parliamentary elections). In

1999, it reached an all-time low. Turnout was less than 29 percent. In some council areas, less than a quarter of voters bothered to go to the polls. In some individual wards, the turnout fell below 15 percent. There is thus seen to be a crisis in terms of local democracy. This has been exacerbated by various high-profile cases of corruption in local government.

Various schemes of reform have been advanced and the Labour government elected in 1997 began exploring which might be worth pursuing. Among proposals that it was keen to encourage was a reshaping of the way local councils were organized.

Among the more radical proposals for reform was the introduction of elected mayors. As we have seen, the Labour government elected in 1997 was committed to an elected mayor for London. When the Labour party was in opposition, it had moved toward embracing the proposal for elected mayors for other councils. However, in its 1997 election manifesto it expressed its support only for pilot schemes in different councils. Opponents of the proposal envisaged the potential for conflict between an elected mayor and an elected council, encouraging stalemate or skewed outcomes. However, the proposal was popular. In a 1998 MORI poll, 68% supported referendums so that people in cities could decide whether they wanted an elected mayor. When asked about an elected mayor in their own city, two-thirds of respondents in the cities surveyed supported the proposal.[7]

Another proposal, one which Parliament approved in 2000, was to introduce a new structure that more resembled national government, with a cabinet and with committees of scrutiny to check what the cabinet was doing. This, coupled with committees designed to develop links between council and residents in particular areas, was intended to generate greater interest in local government. It was also designed in part to address the problem found in some of the councils dominated by one party: that is, an arrogance of power. The use of scrutiny committees was intended to ensure that party leaders were subject to more regular review than was the case under the existing system. Alongside this change, as we have already noted new structures were also proposed to ensure greater probity on the part of members. The police could investigate cases of alleged illegal activity (such as falsifying expense claims). And cases of alleged maladministration—where there had been some mistake or delay in processing a particular matter—could be referred for investigation by an official appointed to investigate such cases, namely the local government ombudsman. However, there were few or no procedures for dealing with questionable but not illegal conduct on the part of councilors. To cover this gap, a new structure, based on standards committees, was included in the legislation. The standards committees, composed predominantly of local people independent of the council, were to investigate claims made by members of the public that councilors had not complied with a new code of conduct.

Various other proposals, designed to encourage greater participation in government elections, have included changing the method of election, changing the voting day from a Thursday to a Sunday, allowing voting by telephone, and placing polling booths in places like supermarkets. Opinion polls suggested that some of these proposals would be popular, but they also tapped views that indicated they may have a limited utility. A MORI poll in April 1998 asked respondents about their attitude to voting at local elections. The responses failed to suggest any one particular reason why people failed to vote. Some 17 percent of respondents said "I don't believe it will make a difference to local taxes and services" and 10 percent said "my vote doesn't make any difference." As multiple responses were permitted, it is likely that there was overlap between the two. No other single response (apart from "other" and "don't know/no opinion") achieved a double-digit response. "The voting system is not fair" attracted the agreement of only 5 percent of those questioned. "I'm too busy to get along to vote" was chosen by only 4 percent. None of the responses pointed in the direction of any particular scheme that would provoke a substantial increase in voter turnout. When questioned about particular proposals, voting by telephone, extending the voting period, and having polling booths in supermarkets were considered more likely than not to make the respondents vote. Voting by other means (such as via digital television or the Internet) or voting on a Saturday would also make some respondents more likely to vote, though for most respondents they would not make a difference. Perhaps most interestingly, given the support for elected mayors, only 21 percent said that having an elected mayor would make them more likely to vote; 11 percent said it would make them less likely to vote. Almost as many would be less likely to vote as would be more likely if voting was held on a Sunday.[8] Various experiments were carried out in a number of local authority areas in the local elections in May 2000. All-postal ballots appeared to make a difference to turnout. Other schemes, such as allowing voters to vote on earlier days or to vote in supermarkets, had no appreciable impact.

The conundrum faced by politicians is one of deciding how to get voters more interested in government other than national government. As we saw in Chapter 10, turnout in elections to the new assemblies in Scotland and Wales is low. And as we saw in Chapter 9, turnout in elections to the European Parliament is low. Turnout in local government elections is the worst of all. And, the problem is getting worse.

NOTES

[1] T. Byrne, *Local Government in Britain* (Penguin Books, 1981), p. 26.

[2] K. Young and N. Rao, *Local Government Since 1945* (Blackwell, 1997), p. 217.

[3] Commission for Local Democracy, *Taking Charge: The Rebirth of Local Democracy* (Municipal Journal Books, 1995), p. 12.

[4] Though in Northern Ireland a complainant can seek a court order for an appropriate remedy where a grievance is upheld by the ombudsman.

[5] See P. Norton, "The Conservative Party from Thatcher to Major," in A. King (ed.), *Britain at the Polls 1992* (Chatham House, 1993), pp. 43–45.

[6] R. A. W. Rhodes, "Now Nobody Understands the System: The Changing Face of Local Government," in P. Norton (ed.), *New Directions in British Politics* (Edward Elgar, 1991), pp. 83-112.

[7] MORI, *British Public Opinion,* November 1998, p. 3.

[8] MORI, *British Public Opinion,* May-June 1998, p. 5

Part IV

Scrutiny and Legitimation

Chapter 12

Parliament
Commons and Lords

The United States has a bicameral legislature. In legislative matters, each house is the equal of the other.[1] Both houses are chosen by popular vote, albeit by differently defined constituencies. They are elected separately from the executive, and members of the two houses are precluded by the Constitution from holding any civil office under the authority of the United States. There is a formal separation between the executive and the legislative branches not only in personnel but also of powers. Congress displays the characteristics of what Michael Mezey has aptly termed an "active" legislature: Its policy-making power is strong and it enjoys popular support as a legitimate political institution.[2] Each house is master of its own timetable and proceedings.

In their behavior, not least in their voting behavior, senators and members of the House of Representatives are influenced by party, more so than is sometimes popularly supposed.[3] Nonetheless, though party is an important influence, it is not an exclusive one. Members of Congress are responsive to other influences. The political landscape bears the bodies of senators and representatives who, regardless of party, fell to the wrath of their electors because of their neglect of their constituencies or because of their stance on a particular issue. Although the initiative in policy making has passed largely to the executive, Congress remains an important part of the process. As Michael Foley and John Owens have noted, there was a seesawing of power between president and Congress in the nineteenth century. "Although the power of the president was augmented exponentially in the twentieth century—notably during and after Franklin Roosevelt's presidency (1933-45)—the period has witnessed a similar see-sawing in the pre-eminence and power of the two branches."[4] The past century has witnessed various periods of congressional dominance.

The United Kingdom also has a bicameral legislature, but there the similarity ends. Of the two houses, only one—the House of Commons—is popularly elected. Members of the upper house, the House of Lords, are not elected: Until 1999, most members served by virtue of having inherited their seats. The two houses are no longer equal: The House of Commons as the elected chamber enjoys preeminence and can enforce its legislative will over the upper house under the provisions of the 1911 and 1949 Parliament Acts (see Chapter 3). The executive, or rather the political apex of the executive (i.e., ministers), is drawn from Parliament—there is no separate election—and its members remain within Parliament. The executive dominates both the business program (deciding what will be debated and when) and the voting of Parliament, party serving as the means of that domination. Party cohesion is a feature of voting in the House of Commons. (The same is largely true of the House of Lords, though fewer votes take place there.) Party is the determining influence in the election of a member of parliament (MP) and it is normally the determining influence in his or her parliamentary behavior. Parliament exhibits the features of what Mezey has termed a "reactive" legislature: It enjoys popular support as a legitimate political institution but enjoys only modest power, if that, in policy making. Discussion of "the decline of Parliament" has been a characteristic feature of political discourse in Britain for many years.[5] MPs have on occasion been known to look with envy across the Atlantic at the power and influence of their U.S. counterparts.

The reasons for executive dominance of the legislature in Britain have been sketched already (Chapter 3). For part of the nineteenth century, Parliament exhibited the characteristics of an "active" legislature. The 1832 Reform Act helped lessen the grip of the aristocracy and of the ministry on the House of Commons (seats were less easy to buy, given the size of the new electorate), allowing MPs greater freedom in their parliamentary behavior. Debates in the House could influence opinion and the outcome of votes was not a foregone conclusion. This period was short-lived. The 1867 Reform Act and later acts created a much larger and more demanding electorate. With the passage of the 1884 Representation of the People Act, most working men were enfranchised. Electors were now too numerous to be bribed, at least by individual candidates. The result was that "organized corruption was gradually replaced by party organization,"[6] as one observer puts it, and both main existing parties were developed from small cadre parties to form mass-membership and complex organizations. Party organization made possible contact with the electors. To stimulate voting, candidates had to promise something to electors, and electoral promises could be met only if parties displayed sufficient cohesion in parliamentary organization to ensure their enactment.

Institutional and environmental factors combined to ensure that the pressures generated by the changed electoral conditions resulted in a House of Commons with low policy influence. Competition for the all-or-nothing spoils of a general election victory, the single-member constituency with a plurality method of election, and a relatively homogeneous population (relative to many other countries) would appear to have encouraged, if not always produced, a basic two-party as opposed to a multiparty system. One party was normally returned with an overall parliamentary majority. Given that the government was drawn from and remained within Parliament, the electoral fortunes of MPs depended primarily on the success or failure of that government. Government was dependent on the voting support of its parliamentary majority both for the passage of its promised measures and for its own continuance in office. Failure of government supporters to vote against a motion expressing "no confidence" in the government or, conversely, not to vote for an important measure that the government declared a "matter of confidence" would result in a dissolution. Within the House of Commons, party cohesion quickly became the norm.

Internal party pressures also encouraged MPs' willingness to defer to government. A member was chosen as a party candidate by the local party and was dependent on it for renomination as well as for campaign support. Assuming local party loyalty to the party leadership (an assumption that usually but not always could be made), local parties were unlikely to take kindly to any consistent dissent from "their" members. The norms of the constitution and of party structures also encouraged acquiescence. There were no career channels in Parliament alternative to those of government office, and a place in government was dependent on the prime minister, the *party* leader. Achieving a leadership position in the House meant, in effect, becoming a minister.

The nature of government decision making as well as the increasing responsibilities assumed by government also had the effect of moving policy making farther from the floor of the House. The conventions of collective and individual ministerial responsibility helped provide a protective cloak for decision making within the cabinet and within departments. Only the conclusions of discussions could be revealed. Furthermore, as government responsibilities expanded and became more dependent on the cooperation of outside groups (see Chapter 7), government measures came increasingly to be the product of negotiation between departments and interest groups, who then presented those measures to Parliament as packages already agreed on. As the demands on government grew, these "packages" increased in extent and complexity. The House of Commons was called on primarily to approve measures drawn up elsewhere and for which it had neither adequate time, resources, or knowledge to submit to sustained and informed debate.

Parliament thus came to occupy what was recognized as a back seat in policy making. This is not to say that it ceased to be an important political body. The government remained dependent on Parliament for its support, and both houses continued to provide significant forums of debate and scrutiny. Nelson Polsby has distinguished between transformative legislatures (enjoying an independent capacity, frequently exercised, to mold and transform proposals into law) and arena legislatures (providing a formal arena in which significant political forces could express themselves).[7] The British Parliament can most appropriately be described as having moved from being a transformative legislature in the second third of the nineteenth century to an arena legislature in the twentieth. The U.S. Congress, by contrast, has remained a transformative legislature.

THE HOUSE OF COMMONS

The events of the nineteenth century that served to transfer power from Parliament to the executive served also to ensure the dominance of the House of Commons within the triumvirate of monarch, Lords, and Commons. The Commons constitutes the only body of the three that is popularly elected. Indeed, its dominance has become such that there is a tendency for many to treat "House of Commons" and "Parliament" as almost synonymous terms. The attention accorded it by the media and outside observers is far more extensive than that accorded the House of Lords. It has a greater "working" membership and more importance is attached to the functions it is expected to fulfill.

Members

The House of Commons has a much larger membership than its U.S. equivalent. It has 659 members, each elected to serve a particular constituency (see Chapter 5). The size of the House has varied, ranging from a twentieth-century high of 707 members (from 1918 to 1922, subsequently reduced because of the loss of most Irish seats) to a low of 615 (from 1922 to 1945). Since 1945, the size of the House has increased gradually as a result of the recommendations of the Boundary Commissions.

There is no formal limit on the number of terms an MP can serve. (Nor, unlike in the United States, is there any pressure to impose term limits.) The average length of service in the British Parliament is much longer than that in other Western legislatures. As can be seen from Table 12.1, in the early 1990s the average length of service of a British MP was 20 years. This compared with just over 11 years for a U.S. senator and 12 years for a member of the House. The figure is an average. Some MPs serve for only one or two terms, leaving the House usually as a result of electoral defeat: The 1997 general election produced a large number of electoral casualties. Others (as with some members of the U.S. Congress) serve for several decades. It is not uncommon for MPs representing safe seats to sit in the House for 30 years or more. Sir Winston Churchill sat in the House for a total of 62 years.[8] The MP with the longest continuous service in the House is given the courtesy title of "Father of the House." Since 1992, the title has been held by former prime minister Sir Edward Heath, an MP since 1950. In 2000, he celebrated 50 years of continuous service in the House.

The House elects one of its members as speaker. The speaker is normally drawn from the majority party in the House, though once in office may serve in succeeding Parliaments despite a change of government. The House departed from this practice in 1992. Indeed, it broke from tradition in two ways. Although a Conservative government was returned to office, the House elected a Labour MP to the speakership. (The previous speaker had retired at the end of the preceding Parliament.) Furthermore, that Labour MP was a woman (Betty Boothroyd), the first female speaker in the history of Parliament. The speaker, once elected, disclaims any party affiliation and serves as an independent presiding officer. Though she or he enjoys important powers of discipline and some business management, much of the speaker's activity is governed by precedent, most of it embodied in

TABLE 12.1   The average length of legislative service, 1994

Country	Average length of service (years)
Canada	6.5
France	7
Denmark	7.8
Germany	8.2
Israel	11
United States (Senate)	11.1
United States (House)	12.2
New Zealand	13.1
Japan	15
United Kingdom	20

SOURCE: A. Somit and A. Roemmele, "The victorious legislative incumbent as a threat to democracy: a nine nation study," *American Political Science Association: Legislative Studies Section Newsletter*, Vol. 18 (2), 1995.

the handbook of parliamentary practice, known as *Erskine May* (after the clerk in the nineteenth century responsible for its initial compilation); the speaker is also advised by the clerks, the full-time officers of the House of Commons. Three other members of the House are appointed to serve as deputy speakers. The deputy speakers retain their party labels, but—like the speaker—they serve as impartial officers of the House and do not normally take part in votes.

Since 1945, MPs have become notably more middle class. Before World War II, and for a little time thereafter, the Parliamentary Labour party (the PLP) boasted a significant proportion of MPs from working-class backgrounds, often miners; the Conservative ranks were swelled by members of aristocratic families and very wealthy industrialists. As parliamentary work has become more demanding, and as salaries and resources have improved, more members drawn from the professions and from academia have entered the House. Today most MPs have university degrees and enter the House after a spell in business or the professions. Tables 12.2 and 12.3 show the backgrounds of members returned to the House in 1997. An increasing number are drawn from careers in the political world, such as party researchers, parliamentary officers for pressure groups, and political lobbyists. Some are drawn from jobs that have been pursued as a temporary expedient, essentially to provide a base while pursuing election to the House of Commons. Of the new Conservative MPs elected in 1997, 40 percent had previously held political posts. Such politicians have been characterized by Anthony King as "career politicians"—people who live for politics.[9] Career politicians have always existed in British politics, but they have grown in number in recent decades. They enter Parliament as soon as they can and pursue careers as parliamentarians. Critics contend that such MPs have little knowledge of the world outside the political domain; their defenders point out that they enter the House well versed in the ways of government and hence are in a good position to influence government on behalf of their constituents.

MPs are more numerous than members of the U.S. House of Representatives. There is also another notable difference. MPs, compared with their U.S.

TABLE 12.2   The educational background of MPs, 1997

Type of Education	Conservative	Labour	Liberal Democrat
Elementary	—	—	—
Elementary +	—	2	—
Secondary	5	48	5
Secondary + poly/college	9	86	6
Secondary + university	42	215	16
Public school	9	2	1
Pub sch + poly/college	9	5	2
Pub sch + university	91	60	16
Total	165	418	46
Oxford University	46	41	11
Cambridge University	38	20	4
Other universities	49	214	17
All universities	133	275	32
Eton	15	2	1
Harrow	—	—	—
Winchester	1	1	—
Other public schools	93	64	18
All "public" (i.e. private) schools	109	67	19

SOURCE: Derived from B. Criddle, "MPs and Candidates," in D. Butler and D. Kavanagh (eds.), *The British General Election of 1997* (Macmillan, 1997), Table 10.3, p. 203.

(and indeed most Western) counterparts, have generally been underpaid and under-resourced. The payment of salaries to MPs is a twentieth-century phenomenon—first introduced in 1912, when the princely sum of £400 ($640) was paid annually—and has generally lagged behind legislative salaries elsewhere and behind salaries of middle-level managers in the United Kingdom. Even in 1964 an MP enjoyed a salary of only £3,250 (just over $5,000). Apart from their salaries, MPs were provided with free travel between the constituency and London. They were provided with little else. Most MPs had no offices (they had to make do with school-type lockers) and for research and information were dependent on the facilities of the Commons' Library, a body with limited staff. There were no secretarial or research allowances. A number of MPs could not afford to hire secretaries and some replied to constituents' letters in longhand.

Conditions have variously improved since then. Acquisition and conversion of various buildings close to the Palace of Westminster—coupled with the building of a large new office block, named Portcullis House—has meant that every MP has an office. Some of the offices are spacious and well equipped. Some are small and relatively barren. The more fortunate MPs have secretaries in adjoining offices. (Because MPs' offices are allocated by the party whips and secretarial offices allocated by the Sergeant at Arms' Office—an administrative department of the House—a Member's office can sometimes be some distance from the secretary's office; in some cases, they are in separate buildings.) A secretarial allowance—of £500

TABLE 12.3 The occupational background of MPs, 1997

Occupation	Conservative	Labour	Liberal Democrat
Professions			
Barrister	20	12	4
Solicitor	9	17	2
Doctor/dentist	2	3	4
Architect/surveyor	2	—	—
Civil/chartered engineer	—	3	1
Accountant	3	2	1
Civil servant/local govt.	5	30	2
Armed services	9	—	1
Teachers			
University	1	22	2
Polytechnic/college	—	35	1
School	7	54	4
Other consultants	2	3	1
Scientific/research	1	7	—
Total	61	181	23
	(37%)	(45%)	(50%)
Business			
Company director	17	7	2
Company executive	36	9	7
Commerce/insurance	7	2	1
Management/clerical	1	15	1
General business	4	4	—
Total	65	37	11
	(389%	(9%)	(11%)
Miscellaneous			
Misc. white collar	2	69	1
Politician/pol. organizer	15	40	5
Publisher/journalist	14	29	4
Farmer	5	1	1
Housewife	2	—	—
Student	—	—	—
Total	38	139	11
	(23%)	(33%)	(24%)
Manual workers			
Miner	1	12	—
Skilled worker	—	40	1
Semi/unskilled worker	—	2	—
Total	1	54	1
	(1%)	(13%)	(2%)
Grand Total	165	418	46

SOURCE: Derived from B. Criddle, "MPs and Candidates," in D. Butler and D. Kavanagh (eds.), *The British General Election of 1997* (Macmillan, 1997), Table 10.4, p. 205.

($800)—was introduced in 1969 and has since been increased to cover research as well as secretarial support: It is now known as the office cost allowance and at the end of the 1990s stood at just over £50,000 ($80,000) a year. Allowances have also been introduced to cover the cost of living away from one's main residence; for MPs representing seats in the capital there is a London supplement. Members have travel passes, with some provision made for spouses. Library facilities have also been expanded, in terms of personnel and resources. There is a computer retrieval system known as POLIS (parliamentary on-line information system) and greater use is now made of computer facilities and of the Internet. (The proceedings of the House as well as parliamentary publications are available on the Internet.) The office cost allowance now proves sufficient to employ two secretaries (an increasing number of MPs have a constituency-based secretary in addition to a Westminster-based secretary, though both are not necessarily full-time) and to buy in some research assistance. An MP's annual salary was increased by 26 percent in 1996 when MPs voted, against government advice, to increase it from just over £34,000 ($54,400) to £43,000 ($68,800), with future increases linked to a formula based on civil servants' pay. In 1999, an MP's salary was £47,008 ($75,200). MPs have thus seen a marked improvement in their resources and in their salary in recent decades. The increase in salary in 1996 helped bring them up to the level of some, but not all, of their Western counterparts. Relative to the situation in the United States, the provision remains modest. Some MPs look with envy (others, believing in frugality, with some distaste) at the position across the Atlantic.

The limited pay and resources provide little incentive for MPs to stay on the back benches. If one becomes a minister, one is able to exercise political power. One also enjoys the pay and perks of ministerial office. Ministers are paid separate ministerial salaries, enjoy the trappings of office (chauffeur-driven car, ministerial offices, and staff) and, as MPs, continue to receive their parliamentary salary and office cost allowance. At the beginning of 1999, Cabinet ministers sitting in the House of Commons were each entitled to—though did not accept in full[10]—a salary of £106,716 ($170,750) a year, a figure that included their parliamentary salaries (the prime minister and lord chancellor had higher salaries; cabinet ministers in the House of Lords, other than the lord chancellor, had lower ones). However, following the lead given by the prime minister, they did not take the increases awarded taking office, leaving them with a salary of £90,267 ($144,400). Ministers of state received £77,047 ($123,200) and junior ministers £69,339 ($110,900), again with ministers in the Lords—and thus with no constituency responsibilities—receiving less.

The other notable difference between members of the House of Commons and members of the House of Representatives is that already touched upon at the beginning of this chapter: Voting behavior. Members of the House of Representatives, as we have noted, are influenced by several sources. Party is important but not always the most important. With MPs, party is the dominant influence. If the parties issue a whip—in other words, declare a party line on an issue—then MPs will vote loyally with their party. In recent years, party voting has shown something of an increase in the U.S. Congress but, by international standards, party voting remains extraordinarily weak. In the years after 1970, party voting in the House of Commons was less pronounced than in previous decades. MPs proved more willing to vote against their own side on more occasions, in greater numbers and with more effect. However, the change was relative. Party cohesion remained a notable characteristic of voting in the House and it continues to do so. Even the most rebellious of MPs votes with his or her party in more than 90 percent of all votes. The gap between the House of Representatives and the House of Commons in voting behavior is not as wide as it once was, but the remarkable feature is not the narrowing of the gap but simply the fact that it remains a veritable gulf.

Functions

The Commons, like other legislatures, is a multifunctional body: That is, it fulfills a variety of tasks in addition to the defining task of legislatures (that of giving assent). The most important twentieth-century functions of the Commons are those of providing the personnel of government, of legitimation, of debate, and of scrutinizing and influencing government. The list is not exhaustive, nor are the functions mutually exclusive.

Parliament provides the personnel of government—that is, ministers; by convention, most ministers, including the prime minister, are drawn from the Commons. This function is largely a passive one in that the House itself does not do the choosing. The outcome of a general election determines which party will form the government, and the prime minister chooses who will fill which ministerial posts. Even so, the institution is important because membership is a prerequisite for appointment to office. In the United States, there are multiple routes to the top: The president can draw members of his administration from a wide range of positions. They do not have to be drawn from the Senate or the House. In the United Kingdom, the prime minister has a small pool from which to draw. Parliament holds a virtual monopoly on the supply of politicians for ministerial office. Furthermore, the House provides an important arena in which ministerial aspirants can demonstrate their political abilities. It also constitutes an important testing ground for ministers once they are appointed. Ministers remain members of the House. They have to cope with the demands of a sometimes rowdy chamber and of supporters who may be less than happy with ministers' performances at the Commons' dispatch box. A poor performance may hamper, on occasion even destroy, a ministerial career.

Legitimation is fundamental to the existence of Parliament. It constitutes the core defining function of the institution and is the oldest function of the House of Commons. Government requires the formal assent of Parliament both for the passage of legislation and for the grant of money. Given the government's control of a parliamentary majority, such assent is normally forthcoming. The giving of this assent, however much it may be taken for granted, fulfills an important symbolic role. It constitutes the elected assembly giving the seal of approval on behalf of the citizenry. Furthermore, it is important because the

House retains the power to deny that assent. It may hardly ever use the power, but the option to do so remains. Parliament also provides what has been termed latent legitimation for government. By meeting regularly and uninterruptedly, by subjecting public policy to debate and questioning, and by being seen to do so, Parliament serves to legitimize the government. Citizens know that Parliament is there, carrying out tasks on their behalf.

The function that is the most obvious manifestation of an arena legislature is that of debate. Parliamentary debate forms a central mechanism for scrutinizing and attempting to influence government, but serves also as an important safety valve. The House provides an authoritative forum in which different and often conflicting views in society can be given expression. The most structured expression is through political parties, but MPs can also use the chamber to raise the concerns of other groups in society and to express the specific views of constituents. The power of the House to debate was established early in its history. The capacity of members to debate has been developed over several centuries. As an arena legislature, the emphasis has been on debate in the chamber. Debate takes place in public session and with ministers present to hear what is said. It also takes place according to extensive and well-established rules.

The House itself is not the government, but government is drawn from it and remains answerable to it. The House is thus uniquely placed to subject government to scrutiny, and to seek to influence it, on behalf of the citizenry. The means of scrutiny and influence are varied. They can be divided into those used for legislation and those employed for executive actions.

Legislation

Legislation is subject to a well-defined procedure once it has been submitted for parliamentary approval (see Table 12.4). First reading constitutes the formal introduction of a bill. At this stage, it is not debated. Indeed, it does not even exist in printed form. Once formally introduced, it is printed and set down for its second reading. Compared with the analogous procedure in the U.S. Congress, the second reading is distinct in two significant respects. First, it is the government that determines when the debate will take place. (With the exception of 20 "opposition days," and certain days given over to debates on reports, private business, private members' bills, and motions, the government has control of the parliamentary timetable.) The cabinet approves legislation to be placed before Parliament and a cabinet committee (the Queen's Speech and Future Legislation Committee—see Chapter 8) decides the program for the forthcoming session. Second, the debate in plenary session precedes the committee stage. On second reading, the principle of the bill is debated and approved. Only after it has received its second reading is it referred to a committee for consideration of its specific provisions.

Second reading debates follow a set pattern. With a government bill, a minister makes a speech outlining and justifying the bill. A member of the shadow cabinet then makes a speech in response, outlining the stance of the opposition. There will then usually be a speech from the relevant spokesperson on the Liberal

TABLE 12.4   Legislative stages in Parliament

Stage	Where Taken	Comments
First reading	On the floor of the house	Formal introduction; no debate
Second reading	On the floor of the house*	Debate on the principle
[Money resolution: Commons]	On the floor of the house	
Committee	In standing committee in the Commons unless house votes otherwise (certain bills taken on the floor of the house); almost invariably on the floor of the house in the Lords. Considered clause by clause; amendments may be made.	
Report	On the floor of the house**	Bill reported back to house; amendments may be made.
Third reading	On the floor of the house	Final approval; no amendments possible in the Commons
Lords (or Commons) amendments	On the floor of the house	Consideration of amendments made by other house

* In the Commons, noncontentious bills may be referred to a committee.
** If a bill is taken in committee of the whole House and no amendments are made, there is no report stage.
SOURCE: P. Norton, *Does Parliament Matter?* (Harvester Wheatsheaf, 1993), p. 73.

Democrat benches. There then follows a series of speeches by back-benchers, alternating between the two sides of the House. Technically, members are called to speak by catching the speaker's eye, though in practice they will have notified the speaker in advance and will have received some indication as to whether or not they will be called. Speeches are usually prepared in advance and so those taking part usually offer set-piece presentations. To call it a "debate" is thus somewhat misleading. Also, in practice, there are often few MPs present to engage in debate. Attendance falls following the speeches from the front benches. In some debates a back-bencher may be speaking to only a handful of MPs in the chamber. More members tend to come in toward the end of the debate, with closing speeches made from the two front benches—the front-benchers responding to the points made during the debate. The question ("That the Bill be read a second time") is then put and, if some members shout "No," a vote takes place. All votes are roll-call votes with members going into voting lobbies on either side of the chamber. As long as a government has an overall majority, the House will vote for the bill. During the whole of the twentieth century, there were only three occasions when a government lost a bill on second reading and only one of those occasions did a government have an overall parliamentary majority.

At committee stage, bills are considered by standing committees. The name is a misnomer: They are appointed on an ad hoc basis. A committee will be appointed to consider a specific bill and then, having completed its deliberations, ceases to exist in that form. (Committees are known by letters of the alphabet, such as Standing Committee A, and once a committee with the letter A has finished its deliberations, a new Standing Committee A will be appointed to consider another bill—but the members of the committee will be different.) Each committee has a membership of between 16 and 50 members, usually now 18 members for all but the largest and most contentious bills. They meet to discuss bills clause by clause and to consider amendments to each clause. In practice, their ability to amend and influence the content of measures is circumscribed. Once the House has approved the principle of the measure, a committee cannot make any changes that run counter to the principle embodied in the bill. The greatest constraints, however, are political. The format adopted at committee meetings is an adversarial one: Government MPs sit on one side, opposition MPs on the other. Debate is usually along party lines, as is voting. The result is that the amendments that are carried are almost always those introduced by ministers. (One or more ministers from the relevant department are always appointed to the committee.) Because most bills discussed by standing committees are introduced by the government, the main purpose of introducing government amendments is to correct drafting errors, improve the wording, or, more substantially, to meet points made by outside groups or meet points made by MPs that the government finds acceptable.

Standing committees thus differ considerably from their U.S. counterparts. They have no power to summon witnesses or evidence,[11] they are presided over by an impartial chairman (an MP drawn from a body of MPs appointed for their ability to chair such meetings), and they are confined in their deliberations solely to the content of bills. They have no power to undertake inquiries or to discuss anything other than the bill before them. The government's majority on a standing committee is in proportion to its majority in the house as a whole. Hence, as long as it has a majority in the House, it is ensured a majority on such committees. The result is that bills usually emerge from committees relatively unscathed. Unlike U.S. congressional committees, standing committees are not a burial ground for bills. Rather, they serve as temporary transit points in their passage.

Once a standing committee has completed its deliberations, a bill is then returned to the House for the report stage, during which the House may make further amendments. This stage is not dissimilar to the committee stage and the government may use it to introduce amendments that it had not been able to introduce in committee (for example, to meet points raised in committee but for which it had not had time to formulate a precise amendment). The outcome of votes on amendments is the same as in committee. Government amendments are normally carried. Amendments introduced by private members are usually defeated, unless they find favor with the government. The acceptance rate is similar to that in committee.[12]

All bills considered in standing committee go through a report stage. Certain important bills, such as those introducing constitutional change (for example, reform of the House of Lords), have their committee stage on the floor of the house. If they emerge from this stage without amendment, there is no report stage: They proceed immediately to third reading. At third reading, the House gives its final approval to a measure. Debate at this stage is usually shorter than on second reading (it may be dispensed with altogether), and it must be confined to the content of the bill. Suggestions for amendments are out of order.

Once the House has approved third reading, the bill is sent to the House of Lords. (The exceptions, of course, are any bills that originate in the Lords.) If the Lords make any amendments, these are then sent to the Commons. The House debates these amendments, usually on a motion to agree or disagree with them. If the House disagrees with a Lords amendment, this fact—along with the reasons for the disagreement—is communicated to the upper house. The House of Lords then usually concurs with the Commons and does not press its amendment. Once a bill has passed both houses, it is sent for the Royal Assent.

Government bills dominate the legislative timetable. This is hardly surprising given the onus placed on government to initiate measures and the fact that the government controls the timetable. Between 25 and 55 government bills are introduced and passed each year (see Table 12.5). In recent decades, the number of government bills has not increased markedly, but the length of the bills has. Bills are longer and more complex than before and so require substantial parliamentary time.

Opportunities for private members to introduce bills of their own are limited. Certain Fridays each session (usually ten) are set aside to discuss private members' bills. So limited is the time available and so great the number of members wishing to introduce bills that a ballot is held each parliamentary session (that is, each year), and the resulting 20 top members have priority in introducing bills. In practice, only about the first six whose names are drawn will stand much chance of achieving a full debate for their bills, and even then there is no guarantee of the bills being passed. The opportunities available for a substantial or contested bill to get through all its stages during private members' time on Fridays are small. Such a bill will normally need more time than is available and will be dependent on government's finding time in its own timetable. The government is thus in a position to determine the fate of most private members' bills. It can deny such bills the necessary time to complete the required legislative stages or it can persuade its supporters to defeat them in a parliamentary vote. As a result, most private members' bills cover matters that are not politically contentious and are unlikely to arouse the opposition of government. A fairly high number of such uncontentious bills, usually involving little or no debate, are passed; 65 in the 1987-1992 Parliament and 87 in the 1992-1997 Parliament (see Table 12.5).[13] A further important constraint is that such bills cannot make a charge on the public revenue. Only ministers can introduce bills that make such a charge.

Hence, the scope for legislative initiative by private members is limited but not nonexistent. Occasionally, a private member may introduce a bill on an important issue toward which the government is sympathetic and for which it is prepared to find time. This was the case especially in the 1960s, when a number of major social measures—reforming the laws on abortion, divorce, homosexuality, and the death penalty—were enacted through private members' legislation. The government left it up to the House, providing time where necessary in order for members to reach decisions. However, the period was exceptional.

TABLE 12.5 1992–1997 Parliament: Bills introduced

| | Government | | Private Members'* | |
Session	Passed	Failed	Passed	Failed
1992–1993	52	0	15	150
1993–1994	25	0	16	51
1994–1995	37	1	17	96
1995–1996	43	0	17	72
1996–1997	37	0	22	54
Total	194	1	87	423

* The number of private members' bills excludes bills introduced in the House of Lords but never brought to the Commons.
SOURCE: Calculated from House of Commons, *Sessional Information Digests* 1992–1997 (Her Majesty's Stationery Office).

Since then, governments have been reluctant to find time for such bills. Rather, private members' bills are introduced as a way of raising issues. Debate on a bill allows for different views to be aired: It may even influence the government to introduce a bill of its own. If back-benchers are keen to achieve a change in the law on an important social issue, they are more likely now to table an amendment to a government bill than introduce a private member's bill.[14]

The number of days the House spends in session each year is shown, for the 1992–1997 Parliament, in Table 12.6. About one-third of its time is taken up with debate on government bills. Less than five percent of its time is spent discussing private members' bills. Most of the rest of the time is given over to scrutinizing, in one form or another, the actions of government.

TABLE 12.6 House of Commons: Sittings and parliamentary questions, 1992–1997

| | Parliamentary Session | | | | |
	1992–1993	1993–1994	1994–1995	1995–1996	1996–1997
Number of days sitting	240	154	159	146	86
Number of hours sitting	1,933	1,258	1,313	1,278	717
Average length of sitting day	8hrs 3min	8hrs 10min	8hrs 16min	8hrs 45 min	8hrs 21min
Parliamentary questions:					
Oral*	7,134	4,559	4,903	4,464	2,622
Written**	55,992	41,496	42,570	48,429	18,165

Note: The first session was a long one following a general election; the last session was a short one, brought to a close by the calling of a general election.
* Questions appearing on the Order Paper for oral answer
** Questions receiving written reply in *Hansard* (official report of the proceedings)
SOURCE: Figures derived from House of Commons, *Sessional Information Digests* 1992–1997 (Her Majesty's Stationery Office).

Executive Actions

Ministers and civil servants spend most of their time pursuing and administering policies and programs for which legislative authority has already been given or for which authority is not necessary (for example, policies pursued under prerogative powers). Hence, the formal approval of Parliament is not required. Nonetheless, the House of Commons subjects such actions to scrutiny. Various devices are employed for this purpose, principally parliamentary questions, debates, select committees, early day motions, and—outside the formal procedures—correspondence and private party meetings.

Parliamentary Questions.   Question Time is a feature of the House of Commons for which there is no parallel in the Congress of the United States. It has its origins in the eighteenth century and it entails the regular appearance of ministers, including the head of government, in the House to answer questions submitted by back-bench MPs. (The rough equivalent in the U.S. Congress would be for cabinet secretaries and the president to appear regularly on the floor of the House or Senate to answer questions, such sessions taking place several times a week.) Question Time in the House of Commons takes place each parliamentary sitting day, Monday to Thursday. (There is no Question Time when the House sits on a Friday.) Though sometimes referred to as "Question Hour," the session does not usually last a full hour. On the first three days of the week it begins shortly after 2:30 P.M. and concludes promptly at 3:30 P.M. On Thursdays, it begins shortly after 11:30 A.M. and concludes at 12:30 P.M. It is subject to well-defined procedures.[15] Ministers answer questions on a rota (rotation) basis, each principal minister coming up on the rota every four weeks. The prime minister has a regular slot, answering questions for 30 minutes from 3:00 to 3:30 P.M. on a Wednesday.[16]

Each MP is restricted in the number of questions he can submit (no more than two on any given day), though the number submitted remains substantial. It is not uncommon for the number of questions tabled to a senior minister, such as the chancellor of the exchequer, to exceed 100. As time only exists for about 20 questions to be dealt with in one Question Time, the questions are selected by a random "shuffle." The shuffle used to be done manually but is now done by computer. As there is not time to answer all the questions put down for oral answer, only those highly placed in the shuffle are printed on the daily Order Paper (see Figure 12.1).

At Question Time, the MP whose question has come to the top in the shuffle rises and says, "Number One, Madam Speaker." The minister then rises to answer the question. Questions are submitted two weeks in advance, so ministers come armed with relevant information or responses compiled by their civil servants or special advisors and normally give prepared answers. Once the answer has been given, the speaker will then call on the MP who asked the question to put a supplementary, or follow-up, question. It is at the speaker's discretion as to how many supplementaries are allowed. If a member of the opposition front bench rises to put a supplementary, he or she enjoys priority over back-benchers. Having allowed one or more supplementaries—and rarely more than three or four—the speaker then calls the MP in whose name the second question stands. The MP rises, says, "Number Two, Madam Speaker," and the process is repeated. Questions that appear on the Order Paper but are not reached receive instead written answers that appear in *Hansard,* the official report of proceedings.

MPs also have the option of submitting questions for written answer. These are more numerous than questions tabled for an oral answer at Question Time: In a typical session, more than 40,000 will be tabled (see Table 12.6). The answers, along with the questions, are published in *Hansard.* Written questions are popular as a means of eliciting statistics and other material that cannot easily be given in oral form. Oral questions, by contrast, are used to elicit statements and comments on government policy and matters that MPs think might embarrass (or, if the MP is on the government side, help) government or generate favorable attention back in the constituencies.[17] Prime minister's Question Time has become a particular vehicle for the partisan clash between the parties, and especially between the prime minister and the leader of the opposition. Because the prime minister has no departmental responsibilities, questions have to be general—or "open"—in nature. The most common is to ask the prime minister to list his engagements for the day (see Figure 12.1), thus leaving MPs free to raise almost any issue in supplementary questions. Through this technique, opposition MPs try to catch the prime minister out by asking difficult questions which he may not be anticipating.

Debates.   As we have seen, debate is central to the House of Commons. Various types of debate are held on the floor of the House of Commons. The most important can be classified as general debates, held to discuss particular government policies. These are usually of just over three or seven hours' duration. They start once any business after Question Time, such as ministerial statements, is concluded. A half-day debate lasts usually until 7:00 P.M. and a full day's debate until 10:00 P.M. Such debates take place on motions tabled by the government (for example, on motions to approve particular policies or to take note of particular documents) or, on 20 "opposition days," by opposition parties (the official opposition decides the topic on 17 days, the third largest party—presently the Liberal Democrats—on the other three days). General debates are also held at the beginning of the parliamentary session on the Debate on the Address. Following the Queen's Speech opening the new session, in which government policy for the year is announced, a five-day debate is held. Formally, it takes place on an address to the queen, thanking her for her gracious speech, but in practice it covers particular government policies. One day, for example, is normally given over to a discussion of foreign affairs.

The other main type of debate is the adjournment debate. In practice, there are two forms of adjournment debate. One is the same essentially as a general debate; the only difference is that no substantive motion is before the house. Instead, a motion to adjourn is put down as a way of allowing debate to range freely on a topic for which the government has no specific policy or action that it

Oral Questions to the Secretary of State for Wales

*1 Mr Win Griffiths (Bridgend):   What representations he has received about the Care Standards Bill [Lords] in the last month. (118432)

*2 Miss Anne McIntosh (Vale of York):   When he last met the Minister of Agriculture to discuss compensation for farmers in Wales in relation to the high value of the pound. (118433)

*3 Mr Jon Owen Jones (Cardiff Central):   What discussions he has had with Assembly Secretaries concerning the implications of the Housing Green Paper in Wales. (118434)

*4 Mr Eric Pickles (Brentwood and Ongar):   By how much, in real terms, the cost of running his office, or its predecessor, in (a) London and (b) Cardiff has changed since May 1997. (118436)

*5 Ms Julie Morgan (Cardiff North):   What representations he has received about the Care Standards Bill [Lords]. (118437)

*6 Mr Nicholas Winterton (Macclesfield):   When he last met the First Secretary to discuss the Government's legislative programme and its impact on rural communities in Wales. (118439)

*7 Mr Elfyn Llwyd (Meirionnydd Nant Conwy):   What representations he made to his Cabinet colleagues on the Second Report of the Welsh Affairs Committee Session 1999–2000 on the Transport Bill and its Impact on Wales (HC 287); and if he will make a statement. (118440)

*8 Mr Michael Fabricant (Lichfield):   When he will next meet the Agriculture Secretary to discuss Welsh dairy farming. (118441)

*9 Mr John Bercow (Buckingham):   What estimate he has made of the number of people who have left the New Deal for Young People and returned to state benefits within 12 months. (118443)

*10 Mr Gareth Thomas (Clwyd West):   If he will make a statement on the reform of local government in Wales. (118444)

*11 Mr Alan W. Williams (Carmarthen East and Dinefwr):   If he will make a statement on the outcome of the meeting in Cardiff on 7th April of the Joint Ministerial Committee on reform and modernisation of the health service. (118445)

*12 Sir Sydney Chapman (Chipping Barnet):   What estimate he has made of the impact of the provisions of the Local Government Bill [Lords] on the cost of remuneraton of councillors in Wales. (118446)

*13 Mr Andrew Robathan (Blaby):   What recent discussions he has had with the First Secretary on NHS waiting lists in Wales. (118447)

*14 Mr Martin Caton (Gower):   What representations he has received about the Learning and Skills Bill [Lords]. (118448)

*15 Mr Huw Edwards (Monmouth):   What recent discussions he has had with the First Secretary about health funding in Wales. (118449)

*16 Mr David Heath (Somerton and Frome):   What recent discussions he has had with the First Secretary on the policy of the National Assembly concerning genetically-modified crops. (118450)

*17 Mr John Smith (Vale of Glamorgan):   What discussions he has had with the First Secretary about education funding in Wales. (118451)

... [Other Questions follow, up to Question 26]

At 3:00 P.M.

Oral Questions to the Prime Minister

*Q1 Mr Nick St. Aubyn (Guildford):   If he will list his official engagements for Wednesday 19th April. (118462)

*Q2 The Reverend Martin Smyth (Belfast South):   If he will list his official engagements for Wednesday 19th April. (118463)

*Q3 Sir Robert Smith (West Aberdeenshire and Kincardine):   If he will list his official engagements for Wednesday 19th April. (118464)

*Q4 Mr Barry Gardiner (Brent North):   If he will list his official engagements for Wednesday 19th April. (118465)

*Q5 Mr Desmond Swayne (New Forest West):   If he will list his official engagements for Wednesday 19th April. (118466)

... [The same question is repeated, up to Question 20]

FIGURE 12.1   Questions on the House of Commons Order Paper, April 19, 2000
SOURCE: Her Majesty's Stationery Office.

wishes to be approved. In short, it is a useful means of sounding out the opinion of the House. At the end of such debates, the motion to adjourn is generally negatived without a vote. The other type of adjournment debate is known as the half-hour adjournment debate and is held at the end of each day's sitting. These debates allow an MP, chosen usually after a ballot, to raise an issue, usually of constituency interest, for about 15 minutes, and allow the relevant minister (traditionally a junior minister) about 15 minutes to respond to the points made. After exactly 30 minutes have elapsed, the House is automatically adjourned. These short debates take up little time but are extremely popular with back-bench MPs, allowing them to raise constituency problems or important but nonparty issues (for example, problems such as gambling, drug misuse, or the transferability of pensions). MPs raising the issues normally give ministers advance information of the points they intend to raise, thus allowing for a full reply to be prepared.

There are one or two other forms of debate, the most important but rarely employed being that of the emergency debate. A member can ask leave to move the adjournment of the House "for the purpose of discussing a specific and important matter that should have urgent consideration." If the MP can convince the speaker that the matter (1) deserves urgent attention, (2) falls within the responsibility of government, and (3) cannot be raised quickly by another procedure, then the debate may be granted. If the debate is granted, it takes place the next day (or the following Monday if granted on a Thursday) or, if the speaker considers that the urgency of the matter justifies it, that same evening at 7:00 P.M. In practice, the speaker tends to dislike the interruptions to scheduled business caused by such debates, and few are granted: on average, only about four a session. They nonetheless constitute a useful safety valve, allowing members to discuss an important topic on occasion that the government had not proposed to bring before the House.

Of these various types of debate, general debates take up the most time. About 10 percent of the House's time is taken up with debates on government motions. The format of such debates is similar to that of second reading debates. A government minister moves the motion; a member of the opposition front bench responds; then back-bench MPs speak, called alternately from each side of the House. In practice, as with second reading debates, any "debate" thus takes place among very few members. Most speeches are delivered from prepared notes and often have little relevance to the speeches that have preceded them. Nonetheless, any member wishing to have a speech printed in *Hansard* has to be present, catch the speaker's eye, and deliver it. There is no procedure in debate analogous to the American practice that allows for material to be inserted in the official record without it having been presented verbally in the chamber.

The opportunity for debate has also been extended recently. In 1999, the House approved what are called "meetings in Westminster Hall." A large meeting room (the Grand Committee Room, just off Westminster Hall) is used, in effect, as a parallel chamber. Meetings are held there at set times on three days of the week to discuss noncontentious issues. Meetings can be held while the House itself is sitting and every MP is entitled to attend. The meeting room itself differs from the chamber in that the seating is arranged in a semicircular fashion, with desks rather than continuous benches, and with the chair sitting on a raised dais. As such, it resembles more the U.S. Senate than the British House of Commons. It is used in order to extend the opportunities for MPs to raise issues of concern. Wednesday morning debates, for example, take the form of several short adjournment debates. Like the half-hour adjournment debates at the end of each sitting, they are useful in that each debate receives a response from a minister. Like the half-hour adjournment debates, they receive little if any publicity and attract only a few MPs.

Select Committees. Away from the floor of the House, the most important device employed for the scrutiny of the executive is that of select committees. Select committees are appointed to consider particular matters referred to them by the House. They have no responsibility for the formal scrutiny and approval of bills (that is the function of the separate standing committees, unlike the procedure in the United States, where the two responsibilities are combined in congressional standing committees). They can be divided into two types: domestic and investigative. Domestic committees deal with matters internal to the House, such as procedure, privileges and catering. Investigative committees consider issues of public policy and the conduct of government. Our primary concern here is with investigative select committees. Such committees have been variously utilized in past centuries, but not on any consistent or comprehensive basis. Over the past two centuries, only two investigative committees have existed as important committees for any length of time. One is the Public Accounts Committee, first appointed in 1861 to ensure that public expenditure was properly incurred for the purpose for which it had been voted. Over time the committee has interpreted more widely its terms of references, conducting value-for-money exercises and investigating possible negligence. The committee has developed a reputation as a thorough and authoritative body, its recommendations resulting in government action to implement them or to provide a reasoned response to them. Traditionally, the committee is chaired by an opposition MP. The other important committee was the Estimates Committee. Unlike the Public Accounts Committee, it no longer exists. It was first appointed in 1912 and, after being suspended from 1914 to 1921, existed until 1971. It was appointed to look at the annual estimates and to consider ways in which policies could be carried out more cost-efficiently. It was not supposed to consider the merits of policies, but after 1945 began to venture into areas that could not be described as solely administrative. However, it was hampered by limited resources both in staff and in terms of the information presented to it by government. In 1971 it was replaced by a larger committee, the Expenditure Committee, itself divided into functional subcommittees. This committee disappeared in 1979, when a new system of committees was introduced.

The Select Committee on Nationalized Industries was formed in 1955 and a number of similar committees formed in the latter half of the 1960s. These later committees were disparate in the range of areas covered and vulnerable to government displeasure: One—a committee on agriculture—was wound up after encountering Foreign Office opposition to an inquiry it wanted to carry out in Brussels. In 1978, a Commons procedure committee recommended that if Commons scrutiny of the executive was to be effective, a new committee system was necessary, created on a systematic and permanent basis. Pressure for the creation of such a committee system built up within the house, and in 1979 the new Conservative leader of the house, Norman St. John-Stevas, brought forward motions for the appointment of the recommended committees. By 248 votes to 12, the House approved the creation of such committees to "examine the expenditure, administration, and policy of the principal Government Departments and associated public bodies." Twelve committees were agreed upon, though a further two—covering Scottish and Welsh affairs—were added shortly afterward. There have been some variations in numbers since. Following the 1997 general election, 16 committees were appointed. The committees are listed in Table 12.7. They are generally referred to as departmental select committees, thus distinguishing them from other investigative select committees of the House, such as the European Scrutiny Committee (looking at European Union documents), the Environmental Audit Committee (looking at the extent to which government policies contribute towards environmental protection) and the PAC, which do not monitor particular departments.

The committees have faced a number of problems. Most committees have 11 members and each usually meets once a week for about 90 minutes. Of necessity, each has to be selective in its choice of topics for investigation and in deciding whether to opt for short- or long-term studies, and whether to focus on policy, estimates, or administration (few have opted for estimates).[18] They have limited resources: usually one or two full-time clerks each, secretarial support, and, in some cases, one or two specialist assistants (graduates with specialist knowledge, appointed usually on a fixed-term contract), with some specialist advisors drawn from outside institutions and paid on a daily basis. The committees have the formal power to "send for persons, papers and records" (in effect, to summon oral and written evidence), but that is of limited use in ensuring the attendance of ministers and other parliamentarians. (An order to attend, if ignored, can be enforced only by a resolution of the House, which is unlikely to be forthcoming against the wishes of government.) Civil servants attend on behalf of their ministers and cannot express personal opinions or reveal any internal advice given to ministers. The relationship of the committees to the floor of the house is limited. There are very limited opportunities on the floor of the House for reports to be debated. Only a handful are debated each year, principally on three "estimates days"; some others are discussed now in the meetings in Westminster Hall. Other reports may be mentioned ("tagged") on the Order Paper when a relevant debate occurs and occasionally there may be a special debate on a particular report, but there is no automatic procedure under which a committee can ensure its report is considered by the House. And, ultimately, the government may choose to ignore the recommendations of the committees. Though the government is committed to publishing a response to each report within two months (a target not always met), it is not committed to taking any further action on them.

Yet, despite these limitations, the committees have proved to be major improvements on their predecessors. They are more extensive and thorough in their scrutiny, have operated as identifiable and often cohesive units, and have attracted the enthusiasm of members. They are usually well attended and—unlike most

TABLE 12.7   House of Commons: Departmental select committees, January 2000

Committee	Number of Members	Chairman
Agriculture	11	Peter Luff (Con.)
Culture, Media and Sports	11	The Rt. Hon. Gerald Kaufman (Lab.)
Defence	11	Bruce George (Lab.)
Education and Employment	16	
Education subcommittee	12	Barry Sheerman (Lab.)
Employment subcommittee	7	The Rt. Hon. Derek Foster (Lab.)
Environment, Transport and Regional Affairs	17	
Environment subcommittee	11	Andrew Bennett (Lab.)
Transport subcommittee	11	Gwyneth Dunwoody (Lab.)
Foreign Affairs	12	Donald Anderson (Lab.)
Health	11	David Hinchcliffe (Lab.)
Home Affairs	11	Robin Corbett (Lab.)
International Development	11	Bowen Wells (Con.)
Northern Ireland Affairs	13	The Rt. Hon. Peter Brooke (Con.)
Science and Technology	12	Dr. Michael Clark (Con.)
Scottish Affairs	11	David Marshall (Lab.)
Social Security	11	Archy Kirkwood (Lib. Dem.)
Trade and Industry	11	Martin O'Neill (Lab.)
Treasury	13	The Rt. Hon. Giles Radice (Lab.)
Treasury subcommittee	12	Sir Michael Spicer (Con.)
Welsh Affairs	11	Martyn Jones (Lab.)

Con. = Conservative, Lab. = Labour, Lib. Dem. = Liberal Democrat

standing committees—there is demand to join them. They have proved to be prolific: In the 1992–97 Parliament, they issued a total of 453 reports. In the first session of the new Parliament elected in May 1997, they issued 110. In the second session (1998–99) they issued 121. The transport subcommittee alone issued 21. Examples of reports issued by other committees are listed in Table 12.8. (Committee reports are published in paper form and are also available on the Parliament web site.) They have attracted more extensive media attention than their predecessors and they have become significant targets for representations from outside groups, something that never happened before. By their evidence-taking—and most committee sessions are used to take evidence from ministers, civil servants, or representatives of outside bodies—they have served to obtain information that otherwise would not be on the public record and also have served to inform debate. By taking evidence from outside bodies, they have provided the House with additional advice, or as an alternative, to that offered by government. They also have provided groups with an authoritative forum in which to make their views known and get them on the public record. They have sometimes served to have some influence on public policy. That impact has varied from committee to committee and is not amenable to precise quantification (government will not always give committees credit for a particular proposal) but there is some evidence of influence.[19] At one point in the mid-1980s, when the government did attempt to quantify the number of committee recommendations it had accepted in a single

TABLE 12.8   Select committee reports, session 1998–99: Foreign affairs and health

Committee	Substantive Reports
Foreign Affairs	Foreign policy and human rights
	Sierra Leone
	European Union enlargement
	Gibraltar
	Foreign and Commonwealth Office Resources
	South Caucasus and Central Asia
	Kosovo: interim report
Health	The relationship between health and social services
	Primary care groups
	Future NHS staffing requirements
	Long term care of the elderly
	The regulation of private and other independent healthcare
	Procedures related to adverse clinical incidents and outcomes in medical care

SOURCE: House of Commons, *Sessional Information Digest 1998–99* (Her Majesty's Stationery Office, 1999).

year, the number totaled 150. It has to be recorded, though, that the recommendations accepted were not on matters of high policy and constituted a minority of the recommendations made by the committees. The most typical response is not to accept or reject a recommendation but to say that it is under review.

Early Day Motions.   Early day motions (EDMs) are put down by members, technically for debate "on an early day." In practice, there is no time available to debate them. Rather, given that they are published, they serve as a means of expressing a written opinion. Members can and do add their signatures to such motions and the number of names a motion attracts serves as some indication of opinion within the House. A large number of signatures may occasionally influence the government to take action or may seriously embarrass it. In 1992, the "fresh start" motion on the European Community signed by nearly 70 Conservative MPs (see Chapter 10) signaled the growing disquiet about the Maastricht Treaty on the Conservative benches. Such occasions, though, are rare. The impact of EDMs is limited by the large number tabled, now more than a thousand a year, and by the range of topics covered. Some are essentially flippant or congratulatory (congratulating some prominent figure on a recent achievement, for example), whereas others express opinions on important issues of policy. (The text of these motions, like select committee reports, are available via the Parliament web site.) Members are free to submit and to sign as many motions as they like. Some rarely do so; others have a reputation for signing every motion with which they have some sympathy. (At least one has been known to sign two motions that were mutually exclusive.) As a result, the significance of such motions is effectively diluted.

Correspondence.   Members do not rely solely on formal procedures. They can and do write to ministers, normally to elicit information and to convey the grievances, demands, and opinions of constituents and of different interests. Letter writing is an extensive activity, with between 10,000 and 20,000 letters a month being written by MPs to those of their number who are ministers. When a constituent writes to an MP, the MP will normally pass the letter on to the minister, requesting a response; there are printed cards available for the MP to use. A letter from an MP receives priority within a government department. A letter from a member of the public normally receives a reply from a civil servant. A letter from an MP must by convention be replied to by a minister. An MP's letter thus ensures that the particular issue reaches the minister's desk. In replying, ministers are not subject to the same time and partisan constraints that apply on the floor of the House. A detailed response can be and often is given, and this is then sent by the MP to the constituent. As we shall see, in writing to ministers, MPs are acting as important links between citizens and ministers. It is also a time-consuming activity.

Private Party Meetings.   Both the Conservative and Labour parliamentary parties have a reasonably extensive organization. Apart from weekly plenary meetings of the party, each has a series of party committees. The Conservative committees have tended to meet more regularly and be more active than Labour committees. Such committees cover particular sectors—foreign affairs, finance, trade and industry, and so on—and meet to listen to invited speakers, to discuss forthcoming business, and to question ministers (or, in opposition, opposition front-benchers). Meetings are in private, thus providing an opportunity for plain speaking between back-benchers and front-benchers. Each Conservative committee meeting is normally attended by a whip. If the party is in government and there are serious expressions of dissent on a particular issue, this is reported back to the chief whip and, if the dissent is serious and on a major issue, to the cabinet. If a Conservative minister encounters problems with the relevant back-bench committee, this may cause the minister to modify or even abandon the particular policy (more likely the former) and may harm the minister's reputation and future career prospects. Any Conservative MP can attend a Conservative committee meeting, and a large attendance can often signal widespread concern or dissent. (Attendance is normally fairly low, with numbers often not reaching double figures.) Following the return of the Labour party to power in 1997, Labour back-bench committees have tended to be more active than before; they were helped by a change in the rules of the parliamentary Labour party (PLP) imposing a greater duty on front-benchers to consult with the committees. Some ministers, such as the chancellor of the exchequer, Gordon Brown, have reputations for being very good at consulting the relevant committee. On the Conservative side, attendance at meetings is poor, partly reflecting the greatly diminished size of the parliamentary party (it was halved in number as a consequence of the 1997 general election), and some committees do not meet regularly.

These, then, constitute the primary devices available to members of Parliament to debate and scrutinize the actions of government. Most such devices are long-standing ones, though used more often in recent years than they were previously. Others are of recent origin. Together, they demonstrate that the relationship between Parliament and government is highly institutionalized. However, there is another vital relationship: that between Parliament and citizen.

LINKS WITH THE CITIZEN

MPs are elected, like members of the House of Representatives, in single-member districts (constituencies). The link with a locality has existed ever since the thirteenth century, when leading figures from the shires and then boroughs were summoned by the king. The constituency role of the MP has grown in significance since the growth of a mass electorate and has become especially pronounced in recent decades. MPs are notably constituency-active. They spend time in their constituencies, fulfilling civic, party, and parliamentary roles. Virtually all hold what are known as constituency "surgeries": publicly-advertised meetings when constituents can come along and discuss issues in some detail. The average MP will hold at least two surgeries a month. In constituencies that are geographically large, an MP will often hold surgeries in different parts of the constituency. Such surgeries can, on rare occasions, be dangerous (early in 2000, an MP was attacked by a sword-wielding constituent and the MP's assistant was killed)[20] and, more pervasively, they are time-consuming. However, the most significant and most time-consuming aspect of the MP–constituency link is through correspondence. Constituents write to their MPs and they do so on an increasing scale.

The growth of the welfare state in the latter half of the twentieth century meant that there was greater likelihood of citizens having some grievance against a public body. The expansion of mass education and the growth of the mass media contributed to a greater awareness of the political system and the availability of the local MP. Writing to the local MP also has a "ripple" effect: Other constituents hear about it and then they do likewise. More recently, Parliament has also become more visible to the citizen. Since 1989, television cameras have been permitted to record proceedings. The text of *Hansard,* and a mass of other parliamentary material, is published on the Internet. Citizens thus have a greater awareness of Parliament and they have written to their MPs on an ever-increasing scale. The development in recent years of word processors and fax machines (and, more recently, electronic mail) has facilitated that contact. As we shall see, interest groups have also made greater contact with MPs. The result has been a massive increase in MPs' mailbags. In the mid-1960s, the number of letters flowing into the Palace of Westminster averaged 10,000 a week. By the mid-1990s, the figure was 40,000 *a day.* Some MPs receive several hundred letters each week.

MPs have to cope with this volume of correspondence with, as we have seen, relatively limited resources. However, they feel that they do have to cope with it. Constituency correspondence takes priority in an MP's office. There is a parliamentary convention that an MP must reply to a letter written personally by a constituent. MPs reply not only because they feel that they have to but because they want to. Constituency work generates job satisfaction (by getting something done for a constituent—even if it is only obtaining an authoritative reply from a minister—an MP tends to feel something has been achieved) and is also increasingly seen as a means of bolstering support. Electors vote for a party but there is some evidence that MPs can attract a limited "personal" vote.[21] By working hard in the constituency, an MP may prevent supporters from peeling off and voting for another party. This may make a difference in some highly marginal seats. For most MPs it will not make any difference to the outcome, but the perception that it might do so motivates them to work hard in the constituency.[22]

Between 10 and 15 percent of constituents are believed to communicate with their member of Parliament. Survey data also show that, in the event of a harmful measure being considered by Parliament, most constituents "would" write to their MP—the most popular course of personal action—and a plurality believe that this constitutes the "most effective" course to take.[23] Most of those who do write to the MP usually want an explanation or confirmation that something is in hand.[24]

MPs pursue constituency casework through a variety of means. They may table a question or they may even raise the matter in a daily adjournment debate. However, the most common means of pursuing casework is through correspondence with ministers. Writing to ministers following receipt of constituents' letters is also a time-efficient process of communication for MPs; it is a task undertaken at a time convenient to them, or at least less inconvenient than other means—such as questions for oral answer—that require their presence at a particular place at a particular time. If a minister's reply proves unsatisfactory to the member, then these other devices may be used. It is also a private means of communication, allowing the minister to reply without feeling the need to be defensive.

Evidence suggests that contact with MPs produces a positive evaluation on the part of constituents.[25] It also appears to contribute to a general perception that the local MP is doing a good job. When asked if the local MP was doing a good job, MORI polls in the 1990s found that roughly twice as many respondents gave a positive than a negative response, and the figures remained unchanged while evaluations of the House of Commons itself declined.[26]

The MP's role has changed over the years and the MP is now far more constituency active.[27] MPs are also more active because of the work of interest groups. Citizens come together in groups to defend their interests and to promote particular causes (Chapter 7). Such groups have variously lobbied MPs to take action on their behalf, but the primary focus of such activity has been government. Though government remains the focus of group activity, interest groups have increasingly made use of Parliament in recent years. Government after 1979 appeared to adopt an arm's length relationship to interest groups. The existence of more and more groups created a more competitive environment. Parliament also looked more attractive because of the creation of departmental select committees. MPs also appeared more willing to express their own views a little more than they previously did.[28] Groups started developing contacts with MPs and, as we have seen (Chapter 7), groups now inundate MPs with briefing material and requests to take action. We have recorded the findings of a 1986 survey of more than 250 organized interests that found that three-quarters maintained regular or frequent contact with MPs. Of those maintaining such contact, over 80 percent had asked MPs to table parliamentary questions for them, and most had asked members to table motions and amendments to bills, and arrange meetings for them at the House of Commons (see Table 12.9). As we noted in Chapter 7, the use of professional lobbyists—little known before 1979—is now common. Contact with MPs has generally elicited a positive evaluation by the groups. In the 1986 survey, more than 90 percent of those groups that maintained regular contact deemed it to be useful or very useful. Of those that had attempted to influence legislation through an MP, 55 percent rated their efforts as quite or very successful; less than 6 percent rated their efforts as unsuccessful.[28]

The work of MPs on behalf of citizens, either as individual constituents or drawn together in groups, is increasingly extensive and time-consuming. It is work that appears to be appreciated by those who make contact with the MP. However, it has generated two problems. One has been the workload for MPs. There is an opportunity cost to dealing with all the correspondence they receive. By devoting so much time to constituency work, there is the danger that they may not have the time to fulfill their collective functions (such as scrutinizing legislation) effectively.[30] The other is that by working on behalf of interest groups, MPs have at times appeared to face a conflict of interests, putting the interests of a group (especially one that may be paying them a fee) ahead of the interests of their constituents. There was a particular controversy caused in 1994 by the "cash for questions" scandal, resulting—as we have seen in Chapter 7—in the creation of the Committee on Standards in Public Life and the acceptance of various recommendations made by that committee. As a result, MPs are now subject to a code of conduct for MPs; they are prohibited from advocating any cause for which they receive payment; and they have to comply with extensive rules on the disclosure of interests and outside income derived from their position as members of Parliament. A Parliamentary Commissioner

TABLE 12.9   Use made of MPs by interest groups*

	Answering "yes"	
Q: Have you ever asked an MP to:	Number	%
Put down a parliamentary question?	157	83.1
Table a motion?	97	51.3
Introduce or sponsor a private member's bill?	70	37.0
Table an amendment to a bill?	117	61.9
Arrange a meeting for you or your organization at the House of Commons?	148	78.3
Arrange a dinner or reception or similar function at the House of Commons?	78	41.3
Arrange a meeting with a minister?	94	49.7
Total respondents	189	

* From a 1986 survey of 253 organized interests. Responses of 189 that maintained regular or frequent contact with MPs.

SOURCE: M. Rush, *Parliament and Pressure Politics* (Oxford University Press, 1990), p. 281.

for Standards exists in order to advise on the rules and to investigate allegations of any breaches of the rules. She reports to a committee of the House, the Committee on Standards and Privileges. Various MPs have fallen afoul of the rules on disclosure, including leading figures of both main parties, and have been reprimanded or have apologized to the House. In more extreme cases, members have been suspended from service in the House for short periods. Though the rules are designed to improve the public image of the House of Commons, they have also had one negative effect. Some MPs complain that complying with the rules—in terms of the paperwork involved—is time consuming, thus adding to their already overburdened schedule.

THE HOUSE OF LORDS

The House of Lords is unusual in three respects and unique in a fourth. It is unusual in that it is a second chamber. Most countries have unicameral rather than bicameral legislatures. However, it is not unusual among Western legislatures, where second chambers tend to be the norm rather than the exception. It is unusual also in the size of its membership. Prior to a reform in 1999, it had just over 1,200 members. (There is no fixed number for membership.) Though this did not render it unique, it did render it exceptional among Western legislatures. Even after reform, it retains a large membership: 666 members at the end of November 1999, a number that has since increased to just over 700. It is unusual also in that it has a wholly appointed membership. Citizens do not elect any members of the second chamber. Though unusual in this respect, it is not alone. There are some other second chambers that are wholly appointed, most notably the Canadian senate. However, it is unique in that it has had a membership based predominantly on the principle of inheritance. Until 1999, the majority of members of the House of Lords—known as peers—served by virtue of having inherited their positions. Most members were hereditary peers.

The House has its origins in the court of Anglo-Saxon kings and their Norman successors. The king summoned to court his leading churchmen and his chief barons (who were the great landholders). The tradition developed of summoning the heir on the death of a baron and so the practice of an hereditary membership developed. From the time of the restoration, the hereditary peers outnumbered the churchmen. In the nineteenth century, the number of churchmen—known formally as the Lords Spiritual—was fixed at 26.

Though the principle that the House of Commons should initiate tax-raising measures was conceded in the fifteenth century, in other respects the two Houses were equal. However, the House of Lords was gradually forced in the nineteenth and early twentieth century to accept a subordinate position in its relationship with the House of Commons. The reason for this is clear. It was well stated by the Earl of Shaftesbury during debates on the 1867 Reform Bill. "So long as the other House of Parliament was elected upon a restricted principle," he declared, "I can understand that it would submit to a check from a House such as this. But in the presence of this great democratic power and the advance of this great democratic wave it passes my comprehension to understand how an hereditary House like this can hold its own."[31] Although not altogether swept away by this "great democratic wave," the House was at least to be swamped by it. It could not maintain a claim to equal status with the elected House, a house elected on an ever-widening franchise.

It is clear that the House of Lords cannot sustain a claim to being a representative chamber. Peers represent no one but themselves: Their writs of summons are personal. No member serves by virtue of popular election. It has thus had to accept a position as a subordinate chamber. It has undergone various reforms in order to adapt it to the changed circumstances. In the first half of the twentieth century, there were reforms to limit its powers. In the second half of the century, there were reforms to change its composition.

The changes to its powers were brought about by the Parliament Acts of 1911 and 1949. The 1911 Act stipulated that the House could delay a non-money bill for no more than two parliamentary sessions (in effect, two years) and could not delay a money bill (one certified by the speaker as dealing exclusively with money) at all. A money bill becomes law one month after being sent to the Lords, regardless of whether the House passes it or not. The 1949 Act reduced the delaying power from two sessions to one session. The House thus has the power to delay a bill for no more than one year.

The changes to its composition took place through three acts: the 1958 Life Peerages Act, the 1963 Peerages Act, and the 1999 House of Lords Act. The 1958 act introduced life peerages: These were peerages that, as the name suggests, were to exist only for the lifetime of the holder. They were introduced to try to strengthen the House by bringing in new people, especially those who found the principle of the hereditary peerage unacceptable. The creation of life peerages, rather than hereditary peerages, very quickly became the norm. Between 1964 and 1999, only three hereditary peerages were created. By the mid 1990s, the proportion of hereditary peers to life peers was approximately 2:1. However, life peers were, relative to their numbers, disproportionately active, both in the chamber and in the committee work of the House.[32] The introduction of life peerages, coupled with a new willingness on the part of peers from the late 1960s onward to fulfill the functions ascribed to the House,[33] had a notable impact on the activity of the House. It met for more days, had longer sittings than before, and witnessed a notable rise in attendance. The rise in attendance has been steady, decade by decade. As Figure 12.2 shows, by the end of the 1990s the average daily attendance exceeded 400, representing approximately one-third of the membership. About 800 peers—about two-thirds of the membership—attended one or more sittings each year. The extent of the activity of the chamber in recent years is shown in Table 12.10.

The 1963 Peerages Act provided the means for hereditary peers to renounce their inherited titles. Though peers did not have to attend the House of Lords (and many did not do so, either for reasons of infirmity or because they were busy doing other things) they could not give up their titles. This was a problem to some peers, and more especially to their heirs, if they wanted to be elected to the House of Commons: Members of the House of Lords cannot be

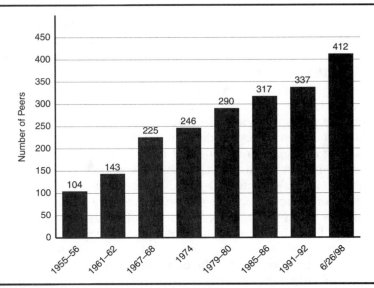

FIGURE 12.2   Average daily attendance in the House of Lords, 1955–1998
SOURCE: House of Lords, *Annual Reports and Accounts 1998–99* (Her Majesty's Stationery Office, 1999), p. 11.

elected to the Commons. The 1963 Act allowed Tony Benn, a Labour MP who had succeeded to his father's peerage, to return to the Commons; it also allowed the Earl of Home to accept the position of prime minister—he renounced his title and was elected to the Commons.

The 1999 Act was, historically, the most significant. Introduced in 1999 by the Labour government of Tony Blair, it sought to remove all hereditary peers from membership of the House of Lords. An amendment accepted during the passage of the Bill allowed 92 to remain. The Bill became the House of Lords Act in

TABLE 12.10   Activity of the House of Lords, 1995–1998

	Sittings of the Lords (by calendar year)			
	1995	**1996**	**1997***	**1998**
Sitting days	145	149	125	163
Number of hours for which the House sat	917	1029	816	1211
Average length of sitting (hrs./mins.)	6:20	6:54	6:32	7:26
Average daily attendance	373	376	394	428
Number of divisions (votes)	113	111	78	161

* General election year
SOURCE: House of Lords, *Annual Reports and Accounts 1998–99* (Her Majesty's Stationery Office, 1999), p. 37.

November 1999. At the start of the new parliamentary session shortly thereafter, more than 600 hereditary peers were no longer members. The membership of the reformed House at the start of the session totaled 666, including the 92 hereditary peers. The vast majority of the membership now comprised life peers, not hereditary peers. The effect also had a notable political consequence. The Conservative party enjoyed disproportionate support among hereditary peers and had done so since the end of the eighteenth century. The removal of hereditary peers from the House of Lords was sought not only because of the fact that they were hereditary but also because they produced a political imbalance in the membership of the House of Lords. The removal of most hereditary peers reduced the Conservative strength in the House, though still leaving it as the largest single party (see Table 12.11). The number of Labour peers was increased in March 2000 when a list of 33 new life peers was announced, the vast majority of them Labour supporters. Other peerages were announced at other points in the year.

The House of Lords has thus changed dramatically in recent years. However, it remains a nonelected chamber and it continues to perform the same functions as it has performed for most of the past century. It is a House that is clearly subordinate to the elected chamber and, as such, it seeks to fulfill functions that complement, rather than challenge, the work of the first chamber.

Membership and Function

What, then, is the nature of the membership and what functions does the House perform?

Members. The members of the House of Lords tend to be male, middle- or upper-class, and middle- and old-aged. Because life peerages tend to be awarded to people who have achieved some distinction in life, they are usually conferred on people who are in their fifties or older. It is rare for life peerages to be conferred on people who are still in their thirties. One exception was in 1998 when a life peerage was given to a 34-year-old television mogul, Waheed Alli. I was elevated to the peerage in 1998 at the age of 47. Because peerages are for life, the

TABLE 12.11 The changing party composition of the House of Lords, 1999–2000

	Number of peers	
Affiliation	**January 1, 1999**	**March 1, 2000**
Conservative	473	232
Labour	168	182
Liberal Democrat	67	54
Cross-bench	322	161

Cross-bench peers are those who are not affiliated with a particular party. The numbers exclude the 26 Lords Spiritual (two archbishops and 24 bishops who sit in the House) and certain other peers.

House has a number of very elderly members. Among the active members of the House in 2000 were former Labour cabinet minister Lord Longford (born 1905), former law lord Lord Wilberforce (born 1907) and former Conservative MP and minister, Lord Renton (born 1908). By the nature of the institution, members tend to be middle- or upper-class. When hereditary peers dominated, it had a much more upper-class flavor, many hereditary peers owning large estates. The membership tends to be male and white, though not exclusively so. Only in recent decades have women entered the House and still constitute a minority of members: At the beginning of 2000, there were 105 women in the House. Several peers of different ethnic background, and indeed different nationalities, sit in the House; Commonwealth citizens can be created peers and several have been elevated to the peerage. For example, Baroness Dunn of Hong Kong Island is, as her title implies, from Hong Kong; Baroness Gardner of Parkes is Australian; and Baroness Howells of St. Davids was born in Grenada. Lord Alli is the only openly gay peer.

The membership tends to be drawn from a range of professions and from people who have served in the House of Commons and in government office. The House has a reputation for the expertise that it is able to draw on when a particular subject is debated. For example, when the House debated the state of British universities in December 1999, the debate was initiated by the chancellor of Oxford University. The House has several professors as members as well as chancellors and some present and former vice chancellors (the equivalent of presidents) of universities, peers who serve on the courts of universities, and some who have served as education ministers. The minister replying to the debate in December 1999 was herself a former academic. The nature of the House—best described as a full-time House of part-time members—is such that it has members who are current experts. One does not necessarily have to give up an existing job in order to become a member of the House of Lords. For example, I have retained all my existing university duties while also regularly attending the House of Lords.

It would, in any event, be difficult to make a career as a member of the House of Lords. Members receive no salaries. They are entitled only to allowances, and fairly modest allowances. (Ministers are paid salaries as are certain officers of the House, as well as the leader of the opposition and the opposition chief whip.) In mid-2000, peers could claim a daily attendance allowance of £36 ($58), a secretarial allowance of a similar amount, an overnight accommodation allowance of just over £80 ($128), and reimbursement of travelling expenses. Members have to attend the House in order to claim the allowances; officials of the House keep a note of who is present in the chamber each day.

Functions.   Given that it is not an elected body and that it occupies a subordinate position in relation to the House of Commons, what functions are performed by the House? For one thing, as we have seen, it provides some of the personnel of government. No fewer than two but usually no more than four peers are chosen to be cabinet ministers. Up to 15 more may be chosen as junior ministers, with six or seven also being appointed as government whips. There is an advantage to the government in having some ministers in the House of Lords. It enables the government to defend itself in the House. It also produces ministers who have no constituency responsibilities and therefore who can spend more time in their departments than ministers who, as MPs, have constituency responsibilities. It also enables the prime minister to draw into the ranks of ministers people who have not sought elective office: Someone can be appointed a minister at the same time as a peerage is conferred on that person. Prime minister Tony Blair has made a number of such appointments.

The other functions may be subsumed under the broad rubric of scrutiny and influence (of legislation and of executive actions), of providing a forum for public debate, and, formally, of legitimation. The House also has a unique judicial function as the highest domestic court of appeal, a function in practice now exercised by a judicial committee (see Chapter 14). These may be identified as the main functions of the House. Of them, one—that of legitimation—has been circumscribed both by the provisions of the Parliaments acts and by the acceptance by peers of their politically surbordinate status.

Recognizing their undemocratic nature, members of the Lords have refrained from seeking to challenge the House of Commons. There have been occasional periods of bad feeling between the two houses, notably in the period of Labour government from 1974 to 1979 and, to some extent, since 1997, but the upper house rarely seeks to press an amendment—let alone delay a measure—when it is clear that the Commons is not prepared to support it. As a result of an agreement between the two front benches in the 1945–1950 Parliament, the official opposition in the Lords does not force a vote on the second reading of any bill promised in the government's election manifesto. A government is usually ensured of the upper house approving (or rather, not opposing) the principle of any measure it proposes.

Given the Lords' reluctance to challenge the government on the principle of measures, the House concentrates instead on scrutinizing the specific provisions of such measures. Bills pass through the same legislative stages as in the Commons, though committee stage is taken on the floor of the House rather than in standing committee. Consideration of a bill in the Lords allows for discussion of many provisions that may not have been debated fully in the Commons, for what may be termed technical scrutiny (ensuring that the specifics of a measure make sense and that they are correctly drafted), and for the introduction of further amendments. Of amendments made to bills during their passage through the House, the majority are introduced by the government, though frequently in response to prompting or amendments tabled by other members of the House. Most amendments made by the Lords prove acceptable to the Commons. Of those that do not, the Lords rarely seeks to press any.

Under the rubric of scrutiny of legislation may now be included scrutiny of draft legislation emanating from the European Union (see Chapter 10). It is a function shared with the House of Commons, but one that the Lords is generally credited with fulfilling especially effectively. The function is fulfilled primarily through the Select Committee on the European Union and six subcommittees. The subcommittees cover different subjects and make greater use than does the Commons of specialist advisors and outside witnesses. Each subcommittee comprises two or more members of the main committee and several co-opted members, appointed because of their presumed expertise in the area. Whereas the Commons committee goes for breadth in coverage, the Lords committee opts for depth, looking at selected proposals in some detail. The nature of the inquiries, coupled with the expertise of the members, means usually that reports are detailed and authoritative, and are generally acknowledged as such, including by those working in the institutions of the European Union. The reputation of the House for its work in EU legislation is now well established and widely recognized.[34]

Apart from scrutinizing bills introduced by government (and draft EU legislation), the House seeks also to scrutinize the actions of the executive. The procedures available to do this are similar to those employed in the Commons: debates and questions. The House spends about one-fifth of its time on general debates, though not all are confined to discussion of government actions and policy. The procedure for asking questions differs somewhat from Commons procedure. At the start of the day's business, only four oral questions may be asked, though supplementary questions are permitted. Question time is a maximum of thirty minutes, which means that there is roughly seven or eight minutes for each question. This provides time for several supplementary questions, more than is possible on a single question in the Commons. At the conclusion of a day's business (or in what is known as the dinner hour, usually between 7:30 and 8:30), what is termed an "unstarred question" is taken (see the question from Lord Bradshaw in Figure 12.3). These are questions (previously submitted, like all questions) on which a short debate may take place before a minister replies. As in the Commons, written questions may also be put down, and the answers are published in the Lords' *Hansard*. In the Lords, unlike the Commons, all questions are addressed to Her Majesty's government and not to individual ministers.

The House also makes some use of committees for scrutinizing the executive and public policy. The number is not great but the work tends to be of high quality. There are a number of what may be termed domestic committees, covering the internal administration of the house and its privileges, and a number of investigative committees. It has sessional (i.e., permanent) committees on science and technology, notable for the expertise of its members,[35] and on delegated powers and deregulation. The latter committee looks at bills after they are introduced to examine the powers to be delegated to ministers and reports on whether the delegation is appropriate or not. The committee was founded in 1994; its recommendations have been acted on by successive governments. The House also appoints committees for inquiries into different subjects. In recent years, the House has appointed committees to consider the public service and the monetary policy committee of the Bank of England. It has also on occasion formed a joint committee with the Commons to consider issues of common concern.

The other main function that may be ascribed to the Lords is that of providing a forum for debate of important public issues. A similar function, of course, may be ascribed to the Commons. The difference between the two is that the Lords allows greater scope for the discussion of important topics that are not the subject of contention between parties. The Commons concentrates on partisan

---

NOTICES AND ORDERS OF THE DAY
TUESDAY 18TH APRIL
At half-past two o'clock

*The Lord Judd—To ask Her Majesty's Government whether, in view of recent reports by the Chief Inspector of Prisons on the effects of solitary confinement and on the treatment of young offenders, and following two suicides in Leicester prison on 21st March, they will now instigate a policy review of the role of prisons in the rehabilitation and wellbeing of prisoners in the United Kingdom.

*The Lord Campbell of Croy—To ask Her Majesty's Government whether, in order to reduce fraud, they will in future require all local authorities to arrange with the Post Office for housing benefit correspondence not to be re-directed to other addresses, as already arranged in the present voluntary scheme.

*The Lord Chalfont—To ask Her Majesty's Government whether they have entered into any arrangement to provide support for an American national missile defence system if the United States government should decide to establish such a system.

*The Lord Renton—To ask Her Majesty's Government whether they will negotiate with those governments which signed the 1951 Geneva Convention Relating to the Status of Refugees with a view to its revision.

Deputy Chairmen of Committees—The Chairman of Committees to move, that the Viscount Falkland and the Lord Geddes be added to the Panel of Lords appointed to act as Deputy Chairmen of Committees for this Session.

Powers of Criminal Courts (Sentencing) Bill [HL] *(Consolidation)*—Third Reading [The Lord Chancellor]

Financial Services and Markets Bill— Further consideration of Report [The Lord McIntosh of Haringey] [*12th Report from the Delegated Powers Committee*]

The Lord Bradshaw— To ask Her Majesty's Government whether they will consider paying members of the Special Constabulary.

FIGURE 12.3 Questions on the House of Lords Order Paper, April 18, 2000
SOURCE: Her Majesty's Stationery Office.

issues, with little time for discussion of subjects outside the realm of party debate. Wednesdays in particular are given over to general debates (usually two on each Wednesday) and peers initiate debates on a wide range of subjects, usually those on which they have some specialized knowledge.

Possibly the most significant role played by the House in acting as a forum of debate is as a safety valve. By avoiding replication of the party debate in the Commons, it allows for the occasional public debate on topics that might otherwise not receive an airing in an authoritative public forum. For some outside interests, making their voices heard through such a forum is all that they desire. The House of Lords has achieved a reputation for discussing on occasion important social issues and for helping ease onto the political agenda topics that might otherwise have been kept off. In recent years, for example, it has proved a valuable forum for those seeking to introduce constitutional reform.

The nature of scrutiny and debate in the Lords means that it attracts considerable interest from interest groups. Peers do not have constituents, so they do not receive the same volume of mail as MPs. Nonetheless, their mailbag can be considerable as a result of individuals and interest groups writing in order to try to have some input into a particular debate or consideration of a particular bill. Peers have greater opportunities than MPs to speak. (Peers sign up to speak in debates and a speakers' list is published in advance. All peers who have put their names down are listed and speak in the order listed. Whereas a back-bench MP only gets to make an average of four substantial speeches in the House each year, an active peer can make as many speeches in as many weeks.) Not surprisingly, therefore, lobbyists see the House of Lords as an important supplementary channel—and sometimes not so supplementary—to that of the Commons for getting an issue raised and onto the political agenda. Of organized interests questioned in 1986, 70 percent had used the House of Lords to make representations or to influence public policy; of those using the house, four out of five had regular or frequent contact with one or more peers.[36] It is quite common before or during committee stage of a bill for peers to receive briefings from bodies that have a particular interest in the bill. Given the expertise of peers in particular areas, and the fact that the government is not necessarily assured a majority in the event of a vote, ministers are usually prepared to engage in a discussion with peers and can be persuaded to accept an amendment. As a result, the House of Lords can sometimes be a more worthwhile focus of attention for interest groups than the House of Commons.

THE CURRENT DEBATE

In historical perspective, debate on parliamentary reform has tended to be more intense—and to generate the introduction of more measures of reform—when focused on the House of Lords. In recent years, however, both houses have become targets of radical proposals for change.

The House of Commons

In the 1960s a number of Labour MPs and academics, notably Professor Bernard Crick, were active in pressing for parliamentary reform and especially for procedural change. The dominance of the government over Parliament, they argued, was too great. The House of Commons lacked the facilities to subject the government to sustained scrutiny; MPs were too badly paid, lacked adequate research facilities, and were constrained by archaic procedures.[37] Even as an arena assembly, the House was performing badly. What was needed, they argued, were reforms that would allow the House to engage in more effective scrutiny through investigation and debate. To such an end, they advocated the greater use of select committees, longer sittings of the House, better pay and research facilities for members, modernization of parliamentary procedure, the broadcasting of debates, and more opportunities for emergency debates. Such reforms, it was contended, would allow the House the opportunity to subject government to public scrutiny and to keep it responsive to public feeling, thus maintaining consent for the political system (the house doing the job expected of it) without jeopardizing the effectiveness of government (the government retaining its parliamentary majority). A strong government, declared Professor Crick, was compatible with a strong opposition.

In the 1970s pressure for limited internal reform of the House began to give way to calls for more radical change. A convergence of two developments may

help explain why this happened. One was the failure of a number of internal reforms implemented in the latter half of the 1960s and early 1970s. Various reforms
were attempted but few proved effective or lasting. The relationship between the
House and the part of it that formed the government remained essentially unchanged—hence an impetus for more far-reaching reform. This was reinforced by
a second development. The 1970s witnessed greater economic and political tur-
moil than had existed in the previous decade. The country's economic position
worsened, and the two general elections of 1974 produced governments elected
with less than 40 percent of the votes cast and an apparent and significant shift
away from the two main parties (see Chapters 5 and 6). A combination of these
developments fostered more rigorous and critical analyses of the House of Commons and its relationship to the country's economic and political malaise.

The radical reformers, led by academics such as S. E. Finer and S. A. Walkland,
were intent on ripping away what they saw as the inaccurate and misleading
gloss that previous writers had placed on the role of the House.[38] They assailed
the House as having clung to nineteenth-century practices and beliefs during a
period that witnessed major economic and social change (the welfare state and
the managed economy), the swelling of bureaucracy, and the trend toward a corporate economy. It had failed to adapt and to keep pace with such developments. The electoral system encouraged the return of one party with a majority
of seats, and party discipline within the House assured the resulting party government of a parliamentary majority for whatever it proposed. The result was a
dysfunctional parliamentary system. It was a system that undermined rather than
reinforced political authority. The House was incapable of subjecting government to scrutiny, let alone having any tangible impact on public policy.

Such an analysis led reformers to advocate electoral reform. The basis of
their argument and its implications were discussed in Chapter 5. Electoral reform would produce, according to its exponents, a more representative House
of Commons. On the basis of existing voting behavior, no one party would
achieve an overall majority, thus forcing a coalition of the political center or a
minority government responsive to other parties in the House. The House of
Commons would continue to provide most of the personnel of government, to
subject government to (more effective) scrutiny and influence, and to legitimate the government and its measures. The most significant difference would
be that the House itself would have a greater claim to legitimacy in fulfilling
those functions and would, in its behavior, be more consensual. As we have seen
in Chapter 5, the issue has become a significant feature of political debate, especially following the election of a Labour government in May 1997.

Pressure for radical reform has become more prominent, but it has not totally eclipsed continuing demands for internal reform. Indeed, such demands
have become more pronounced in recent years. The experience of the departmental select committees and the televising of proceedings have been used to
demonstrate the usefulness of change within the institution. There are demands
for further change, including a reform of the legislative process. These demands
have emanated from a number of MPs and from bodies such as the educational

charity the Hansard Society, which produced a major report in 1993 advocating extensive change to the existing legislative process.[39] The debate assumed a new vigor in the late 1990s. The House established a Select Committee on the Modernization of the House of Commons. It made various recommendations to strengthen the legislative process and the scrutiny of EU legislation. However, its work was overshadowed by recognition of the power wielded by government. The Labour party was returned to office in 1997 with a massive overall majority of 179. Labour MPs were issued pagers and received regular messages telling them how to vote and what messages to convey. The government proved keen to see the passage of major pieces of legislation, if necessary keeping MPs at work late into the night to get the measures through. Recognition of the need for reform of the House, to enable it to more effectively scrutinize and influence government, led to various calls for change. In 1999, the Hansard Society established a new commission, under a former leader of the House of Commons, to examine the subject of parliamentary scrutiny. The commission was appointed for a two-year period to engage in extensive investigation. Also in 1999, the leader of the Conservative party, William Hague, appointed a Commission to Strengthen Parliament, chaired by me and with three former cabinet ministers as members, in order to propose changes to strengthen the House in calling government to account. The commission reported just before summer 2000 and made an extensive range of recommendations for change to parliamentary structures and procedures.[40] It sought to strengthen the different elements of the House, including the opposition, parliamentary parties, committees, and individual members. In 2000, the Liaison Committee of the House of Commons, comprising essentially the chairmen of select committees, also issued a report advocating a reform of the select committees. In particular, it sought to create a career structure within the committees as an alternative to government office. Its report was titled "Shifting the Balance: Select Committees and the Executive."

The debate about reform also increasingly took on board the argument that I had been advancing since the 1970s:[41] Namely, that attitudinal change is a prerequisite for effective structural and procedural change. MPs have to demonstrate the political will to embrace change. Without that will, blueprints for reform will remain precisely that. If the will exists, MPs can generate the structures and the resources necessary for fulfilling a more participant role, without jeopardizing the capacity of a government—a party government—to govern. A House of Commons in which the government can normally be assured a majority, but a majority it cannot take for granted, is the most effective way of ensuring the existence of a government that can govern but that is responsive to the elected House of Commons. However, recognizing that fact is not the same as ensuring that the political will exists. There are limited opportunities to achieve parliamentary reform: Political will is a prerequisite. There also needs to be a window of opportunity (usually at the beginning of a Parliament) and a reform program behind which MPs can mobilize.[42] These conditions existed in 1979 when the departmental select committees were established. They have not come together since. The Hansard Society Commission and the Commission to Strengthen Parliament have produced reform programs. What is now needed is the window of opportunity and, above all, the political will to implement them.

The House of Lords

Though reform of the House of Commons is an important issue, it has been overshadowed by debate about what to do with the House of Lords. The House has rarely been free of proposals for reform. As we have seen, various reforms have been enacted, the most recent being the removal of most hereditary peers from membership of the House in 1999. The 1999 reform was seen as an interim measure. The Labour government made clear that it wished to remove hereditary peers as the first stage of a two-stage reform process. In stage two, it wanted to make the House, according to its 1997 election manifesto, "more democratic and representative." At the beginning of 1999, under pressure from the opposition (which claimed the government did not want to have a "stage two" reform), it appointed a Royal Commission on the Reform of the House of Lords to advise on what form the second stage should take. The commission, chaired by a Conservative peer, Lord Wakeham, reported in January 2000.[43] It favored a chamber of 550 members, with most members appointed and a minority to be elected. It wanted the appointed members to be chosen by a powerful and independent Appointments Commission, each serving 15-year terms. Because the members of the Royal Commission could not agree on how many members should be elected, they offered three options. Under option A, 65 members would be elected (based on party voting in a general election); under option B, 87 members would be elected (the election taking place at the same time as European Parliament elections, with one-third of nations and regions electing their members); and under option C, 195 members would be elected (the election also taking place at the same time as European Parliament elections, with one-third of members being elected in each nation and region). Most members of the commission favored option B. The report received a critical press. Some critics attacked it for not going far enough. Some parliamentarians claimed that it went too far. In a debate in the House of Lords on March 7, 2000, the government announced that it broadly accepted the recommendations of the commission. However, it was clear that no action was likely in advance of the next general election.

The future of the House of Lords thus remains a topic of political debate. There is no clear agreement on what form it should take in the future. Indeed, four separate approaches to reform can be identified. These can be termed the four R's: retain, reform, replace, and remove altogether.

Retain.   This approach favors retaining a wholly appointed chamber.[44] It accepts the need to introduce procedures to prevent excessive political patronage but argues that appointment allows the House to retain its existing strengths. That is, it is a House of expertise and experience, with members able to offer informed advice in a way that would not be possible with an elected chamber, which would produce a body of career politicians similar to the Commons. An appointed chamber ensures that the primacy of the elected first chamber is maintained and, as such, maintains accountability within the political system. As such, it is claimed to be the most democratic option if democracy is defined as the translation of the popular will into legislative outputs. The chamber continues to fulfill functions complementary to the first chamber, rather than competing with it. The existing House, it is argued, adds value to the political process, and that should be retained.

Reform.   This approach involves taking the existing House and modifying it rather than replacing with a completely new chamber. It seeks to retain some of the strengths of the existing House while conferring some element of electoral legitimacy. This was the approach favored by the Royal Commission. Other bodies also have advocated a part-elected chamber, though the proportion to be elected varies. Supporters argue that this approach offers the best of both worlds: It combines the expertise of appointed members while bolstering its authority through an element of election. Critics claim that it produces the worst of both worlds, creating a two-tier membership and the potential for conflict between the two tiers.

Replace.   This approach wants to do away with the existing House and replace it with a new chamber.[45] Most advocates of this approach want to have a wholly- or almost wholly-elected chamber. Advocates claim that this would give the chamber the legitimacy it presently lacks and enable it to challenge the first chamber—hence, in effect, the government. This would limit an overly powerful government. It is also claimed to be the most democratic option if democracy is defined in terms of election. Opponents argue that it would introduce the potential for gridlock within the political process and, in effect, rid the system of its accountability. In the event of conflict producing undesirable outcomes, whom do the electors hold accountable? And what value is there in having a second chamber of career politicians, essentially replicating the first chamber? Some advocates of a new second chamber do not want an elected House but instead want a functional chamber: that is, one composed of representatives of different groups in society. This has little support and critics point that it is difficult to achieve (how to decide which groups should have representation?) as well as undesirable, giving a position of power to special interests.

Remove altogether.   This approach favors getting rid of the House of Lords and not replacing it with anything. Unicameral legislatures, as we have noted, are common, so why should not the United Kingdom follow suit? Advocates claim that the only reason the House of Lords continues to exist is because of the inadequacies of the House of Commons. If the House of Commons was reformed effectively, there would be no need to have a second chamber. The purpose of a second chamber, it is claimed, is contestable. If the second chamber simply agrees with the first chamber, it is superfluous. If it conflicts with it, it is objectionable.

This approach has some advocates but is not widely held. There is general though not universal support for having a second chamber.

There is no consensus favoring any particular approach to reforming the House of Lords. There are various supporters of retaining a wholly appointed House, and they are to be found in both houses of Parliament. The "reform" approach is favored by the Royal Commission and by the Labour government. The "replace" approach is favored by some senior figures in both Houses: Most Conservative MPs are believed to favor an elected second chamber. There are some supporters of a functional chamber and of a unicameral legislature (and some writers who favor selection by lot) but they are in a notable minority. What Lord Wakeham has called "the center of gravity" on the issue appears to hover somewhere between leaving the situation as it is and having some element of election. The issue has yet to be resolved. The absence of a consensus may mean that the "retain" option wins by default. The present House of Lords is seen as an interim House. However, the House of Lords following the passage of the 1911 Parliament Act was seen as an interim House. (The preface to the 1911 Act envisaged a move towards an elected chamber.) That "interim" House lasted for nearly 90 years. The present "interim" chamber may be a long-term one.

CONCLUSION

Parliament continues to enjoy popular support as a legitimate political institution. It is the institution from which the political apex of government is drawn and from which government derives its popular legitimacy. It has the characteristics of an arena assembly, seeking through debate to subject government to scrutiny and some measures of influence, and providing the broad limits within which government may govern.

Recent decades have witnessed claims that neither popular support for it as a legitimating political body nor its modest powers has been as great as was previously believed. The mode of election and the adversary relationship between two parties have been identified as undermining the claim of the House of Commons to be a representative assembly. The unelected basis of the Lords continues to be used as sufficient reason for denying the house any claim to be considered an appropriate political institution. Party hegemony has been identified as constricting Parliament's ability to exercise even the modest powers ascribed to it. A consequence of these factors has been pressure for change within the House in order to restore to Parliament both popular support and the political will to exercise modest powers in the making of public policy. Pressure for more radical reform is on the agenda. What has been lacking among proponents of radical reform has been agreement as to what form change should take. Although many may agree on ends, agreement as to means is notably absent. Electoral reformers seek to generate a parliamentary system that reflects and seeks to generate consensus. In their preference for their own scheme of reform, consensus is the one thing they lack.

NOTES

[1] However, under Article 1, section 7(1), of the U.S. Constitution, all revenue-raising bills must originate in the House of Representatives.

[2] M. Mezey, *Comparative Legislatures* (Duke University Press, 1979), Ch. 2.

[3] See the useful summary in M. Foley and J. E. Owens, *Congress and the Presidency* (Manchester University Press, 1996), pp. 163–167.

[4] Foley and Owens, p. 3.

[5] The perception of decline was popularized by the scholar-statesman Lord Bryce in the 1920s. See P. Norton (ed.), *Legislatures* (Oxford University Press, 1990), Ch. 3. Bryce was British ambassador to the United States 1907–13.

[6] R. H. S. Crossman, "Introduction," to W. Bagehot, *The English Constitution* (Fontana, 1963 ed.), p. 39.

[7] N. Polsby, "Legislatures," in F. I. Greenstein and N. Polsby (eds.), *Handbook of Political Science*, Vol. 5 (Addison-Wesley, 1975). See also Norton, *Legislatures,* Ch. 7.

[8] Churchill sat in the House from 1900 to 1964, with a break between 1922 and 1924. He was Father of the House from 1959 to 1964.

[9] A. King, "The rise of the career politician in Britain—and its consequences," *British Journal of Political Science,* Vol. 11, 1981, pp. 249–285. See also P. Riddell, *Honest Opportunism* (Hamish Hamilton, 1993).

[10] Following a lead given by the prime minister, cabinet ministers did not accept the salary increases awarded to them since the Labour party came to power. This meant that at the beginning of 1999 cabinet ministers each accepted a salary of £90,267 instead of the £106,716 to which each was entitled. Perhaps not surprisingly, the lead given by the prime minister was reported to be unpopular with some members of the cabinet.

[11] There is an exception in that certain standing committees—special standing committees (SSCs)—can be appointed with power to take evidence. They have rarely been used, though there is pressure for their more regular employment.

[12] See P. Norton, "Legislation," in M. Rush (ed.), *Parliament and Pressure Politics* (Oxford University Press, 1990), pp. 186–188.

[13] See D. Marsh and M. Read, *Private Members' Bills* (Cambridge University Press, 1987).

[14] See P. Cowley (ed.), *Conscience and Parliament* (Frank Cass, 1998).

[15] See H. Irwin, D. Kennon, D. Natzler, and R. Rogers, "Evolving Rules," in M. Franklin and P. Norton (eds), *Parliamentary Questions* (Oxford University Press, 1993), pp. 194–207.

[16] This half-hour slot was introduced in May 1997. Before then, the prime minister answered questions in two 15-minute slots each week, one on Tuesday and the other on Thursday.

[17] See P. Norton, "Questions and the Role of Parliament," in Franklin and Norton, *Parliamentary Questions,* pp. 194–207.

[18] See D. Judge, *Parliament and Industry* (Dartmouth, 1990), pp. 176–184.

[19] See, e.g., G. Drewry (ed.), *The New Select Committees,* rev. ed. (Oxford University Press, 1989); M. Jogerst, *Reform in the House of Commons* (University Press of Kentucky, 1993); and D. Hawes, *Power on the Back Benches?* (S.A.U.S., 1993).

[20] In November 1981 an Ulster Unionist MP was shot dead by a terrorist while conducting a constituency "surgery." While physical attacks on MPs are very rare, many MPs are normally accompanied by a councillor or assistant, partly to take notes or assist in dealing with a case, but also as a form of security.

[21] See especially P. Norton and D. Wood, *Back from Westminster* (University Press of Kentucky, 1993).

[22] See P. Norton, *Does Parliament Matter?* (Harvester Wheatsheaf, 1993), Ch. 9.

[23] R. Jowell and S. Witherspoon, *British Social Attitudes: The 1985 Report* (Gower, 1985), p. 12.

[24] R. Rawlings, "The MP's Complaint Service," *Modern Law Review,* 53, 1990, p. 44.

[25] Norton, *Does Parliament Matter?* pp. 156–157.

[26] MORI, *State of the Nation,* 1995 (MORI, 1995).

[27] P. Norton, "The Growth of the Constituency Role of the MP," *Parliamentary Affairs,* 47 (4), 1994, pp. 705–720.

[28] Norton, *Does Parliament Matter?* Ch. 10.

[29] M. Rush (ed.), *Parliament and Pressure Politics* (Oxford University Press, 1990), pp. 282, 285.

[30] See Norton and Wood, *Back from Westminster,* Ch. 3.

[31] *Parliamentary Debates (Hansard),* Vol. 188, cols. 1925–1926 (1867).

[32] See N. Baldwin, "The House of Lords: Behavioural Changes," in P. Norton (ed.), *Parliament in the 1980s* (Blackwell, 1985), pp. 96–113; C. Grantham and C. M. Hodgson, "The House of Lords: Structural Changes," in Norton, *Parliament in the 1980s,* pp. 114–135.

[33] Baldwin, "The House of Lords: Behavioural Changes," pp. 96–113.

[34] See P. Norton, "The United Kingdom: Political Conflict, Parliamentary Scrutiny," in P. Norton (ed.), *National Parliaments and the European Union* (Frank Cass, 1996), pp. 92–109; D. Shell, "The House of Lords and the European Community, 1990–91," in P. Giddings and G. Drewry (eds.), *Westminster and Europe* (Macmillan, 1996), pp. 159–190.

[35] See P. D. G. Hayer, "The Parliamentary Monitoring of Science and Technology in Britain," *Government and Opposition,* 26, 1991, pp. 147–166; C. Grantham, "Select Committees," in D. Shell and D. Beamish (eds.), *The House of Lords at Work* (Oxford University Press, 1993), pp. 282–307.

[36] Rush, *Parliament and Pressure Politics.*

[37] B. Crick, *The Reform of Parliament* (Weidenfeld and Nicolson, 1964). See also P. Norton, *The Commons in Perspective* (Martin Robertson, 1981), pp. 203–204.

[38] See especially S. E. Finer (ed.), *Adversary Politics and Electoral Reform* (Wigram, 1975).

[39] The Hansard Society, *Making the Law* (Hansard Society, 1993).

[40] The Report of the Commission to Strengthen Parliament, *Strengthening Parliament* (Commission to Strengthen Parliament, 2000).

[41] See especially P. Norton, "The Norton View," in D. Judge (ed.), *The Politics of Parliamentary Reform* (Heinemann Education, 1983).

[42] P. Norton, "Independence Without Entrenchment: The British House of Commons in the Post-Thatcher Era," *Talking Politics,* Vol. 6 (2), 1994, pp. 80–87.

[43] Royal Commission on the Reform of the House of Lords, *A House for the Future,* Cm 4534 (The Stationery Office, 2000).

[44] See P. Norton, "Adding Value to the Political System," evidence to the Royal Commission on The Reform of the House of Lords. The evidence is published on the CD-ROM that accompanies the report of the Royal Commission.

[45] See I. Richard and D. Welfare, *Unfinished Business* (Vintage, 1999).

CHAPTER 13

The Monarchy
Above the Fray?

In the United States, the head of state is the president. In the United Kingdom, the head of state is the monarch. Both fulfill certain formal duties associated with the position. Beyond that there is little similarity between the two. In terms of history, determination of incumbency, powers, and current responsibilities, the U.S. presidency and the British monarchy have virtually nothing in common. The president is both head of state and political head of the administration. He operates directly and personally at the heart of the political decision-making process. The monarch, as head of state, stands above political decision making. In political terms, he or she serves not to decide but primarily to perform a symbolic role. The president serves by virtue of election; the monarch reigns by virtue of birth.

The monarchy is the oldest secular institution in Britain. It predates Parliament by some four centuries and the law courts by three centuries. The present monarch is able to trace her descent from King Egbert, who united England under his rule in A.D. 829. The continuity of the institution has been broken only once, during the period of military rule by Oliver Cromwell in the seventeenth century. There have been various interruptions in the direct line of succession, but the hereditary principle has been preserved since at least the eleventh century. The succession itself is governed by certain principles of common law and by statute. The throne descends to the eldest son or, in the absence of a son, the eldest daughter. By the Act of Settlement of 1701, affirmed by the Treaty of Union in 1707, the Crown was to descend to the heirs of the granddaughter of James I, Princess Sophia; this line has been confirmed by later acts.

For several centuries, there was no separation of powers: executive, legislative, and judicial powers were exercised by the king. With the growth of Parliament (and its power of the purse) as well as the courts, the direct exercise of these functions progressively declined. As we have seen (Chapter 3), the conflict between king and Parliament in the seventeenth century resulted in the Settlement of 1688–89 and the establishment of what was essentially a limited constitutional monarchy. The monarch nonetheless remained at the head of government, in practice as well as formally. Those responsible for the Bill of Rights of 1689 wanted "a real, working, governing king, a king with a policy,"[1] albeit a king governing with the consent of Parliament. The centrality of the monarch to governing was to decline in the eighteenth century with the king's increasing dependence on his ministers. During this century, one can see the divorce of the positions of head of state and political head of government, formerly united in the person of the king. The former remained with the king, the latter in practice became vested in his chief minister. The withdrawal of the monarch largely but by no means exclusively from active participation in political life was to be a marked feature of the succeeding century. Queen Victoria's reign (1837–1901) marked the transition from a monarch still active in political life to one fulfilling primarily a formal role, part of what Bagehot had identified as the "dignified" part of the Constitution.[2] The twentieth century has realized the move toward a politically neutral monarchy, standing now well removed from the partisan fray of party government.

The years since 1688 have witnessed various landmarks on this path toward a neutral monarchy divorced from active partisan decision making. The last occasion on which a monarch vetoed a piece of legislation was when Queen Anne did in 1707, the last time a monarch dismissed a ministry was in 1834, and the last occasion on which the monarch clearly exercised a personal choice in the selection of a prime minister was Queen Victoria's summoning Lord Rosebery in 1894. (Monarchs have on occasion subsequently had to exercise a choice in the selection of prime ministers but, as we shall see, have acted under advice.) The last monarch to attempt to veto cabinet appointments, with some measure of success, was Queen Victoria. She was also the last monarch to be instrumental in pushing successfully for the enactment of particular legislation: On at least two occasions she virtually initiated legislation, the 1874 Public Worship Regulation Act and the 1876 Royal Titles Act.[3] She may also be described as the last monarch to indulge, albeit within a limited circle, in partisan expression. Initially a Whig, she became for all intents and purposes a vehement Conservative; she clearly adored her Conservative prime minister, Benjamin Disraeli, and made little secret of her utter disdain for the Liberal leader, William Gladstone. Partisan expression declined significantly under her successors. Indeed, according to Frank Hardie, this was a notable feature of the first half of the twentieth century: "Since 1901 the trend towards a real political neutrality, not merely a matter of appearances, has been steady, reign by reign."[4]

The result of these developments has been that twentieth-century monarchs have come to occupy a position in which they are called on to fulfill two primary tasks. One is to represent the unity of the nation. The other is to carry out certain political functions on the advice of ministers. The weakness of the monarch in being able to exercise independent decisions in the latter task has ensured the strength of the monarchy in fulfilling the first.

The Crown in Britain is the symbol of supreme executive authority. It serves essentially as a substitute for the concept of the state, a concept not well developed in Britain and one that has not made an impact on the national consciousness. The monarch is the person on whom the Crown is constitutionally conferred. Various public duties are carried out in the name of the Crown (for example, public prosecutions) and, as the person in whom the Crown vests, the monarch's name attaches to both government and the armed forces. The armed services are Her Majesty's Services. Her Majesty is commander in chief. People go to war to fight for "queen and country." The government is Her Majesty's government, ministers are Her Majesty's ministers. Even the opposition in Parliament is titled Her Majesty's Loyal Opposition. Postage stamps and coins bear the queen's image. (British postage stamps are unique: The monarch's head substitutes for the name of the nation.) The queen personifies what for Americans is represented by the Stars and Stripes.

In order that the queen may embody the unity of the nation, it is imperative that she not only abstain from partisan activity but also be seen to abstain, indeed be seen to transcend political activity. The political functions she performs, such as the appointment of the prime minister, the appointment of ministers, the dispensing of honors, and the assent of legislation, are governed by convention. She acts on the advice of her ministers and is recognized as so acting. When the Queen's Speech is read from the throne on the opening of Parliament, the speech is handed to the queen by the lord chancellor and subsequently handed back to him, signifying that it is the government's responsibility. Government is carried on in the name of the queen and not by the queen.

The formal exercise of political functions by the monarch serves a useful purpose. It provides a sense of duty for government (fulfilling duties as Her Majesty's ministers is a reminder that they are in office to perform a service to the nation) and it provides a significant sense of continuity. Governments may come and governments may go, but the queen continues to reign. When Queen Elizabeth II ascended to the throne in 1952, Winston Churchill was prime minister. She has been served by nine different prime ministers. By being the person to whom prime ministers submit their resignations and who summons the new premier, the monarch gives a sense of continuity, one that arguably could not be provided by any other form of head of state in a free society.

The continuity provided by the monarch has another and, from the perspective of government, very useful aspect. Each prime minister has a regular audience with the queen, usually at least once a week when the sovereign is in London; under a practice initiated by Harold Macmillan, the PM sends in advance a list of points he or she would like to raise. The queen receives the minutes of cabinet meetings and cabinet committee meetings. She also receives copies of important Foreign and Commonwealth Office documents. According to her various prime ministers, she is an assiduous reader of all such papers. Apart from more than 40 years' experience of meeting with her prime ministers, the queen is also head of the Commonwealth and has traveled extensively, building personal links with other heads of state. This experience she can and does bring to bear in her meetings with the prime minister, doing so in a nonpartisan context (raising issues in the form of questions) and in an environment where the prime minister does not have to deal with an opponent or political rival. The audience provides the premier with a unique opportunity, as Sir Ian Gilmour expressed it, "to explain decisions and policies to a disinterested observer in the fullest privacy."[5] Successive prime ministers have attested to the value of such meetings. According to Harold Macmillan, "the Queen was a great support, because she is the one person you can talk to."[6] Labour prime ministers Harold Wilson, James Callaghan, and Tony Blair expressed similar views. Speaking at the time of the queen's golden wedding anniversary in November 1997, Tony Blair said that he enjoyed his weekly audience with the queen not simply because of her experience, but because she was an "extraordinarily shrewd and perceptive observer of the world. Her advice is worth having."[7] The only two prime ministers with whom relationships have reputedly been a little cool have been, ironically—given Conservative support for the monarchy—Conservatives Edward Heath and Margaret Thatcher; the queen, according to some reports, was distressed at the strains that Mrs. Thatcher's refusal to endorse sanctions against South Africa was placing on the Commonwealth. The queen attaches much importance to her role as head of the Commonwealth; according to a 1988 Gallup poll, so do most of her subjects.

Prime ministers have reason also to be grateful to the monarch for the fulfillment of various formal duties. In the United States, the president as head of state has to fulfill a number of time-consuming tasks, including receiving new ambassadors, presenting medals, and attending a number of formal nonpolitical functions. The president is not trained to carry out these tasks and the time given over to them is at the expense of time that could be used for running the administration. In Britain, the symbolic tasks are carried out by the monarch or, in some cases, by other members of the royal family. The physical distinction between head of state and head of government allows for ceremonial duties to be carried out by someone schooled for the task and eliminates the conflicting time demands faced by any political leader who is also head of state.

By being scrupulously neutral in performing her duties, the queen is able to fulfill her task of representing the unity of the nation. The hereditary principle in this context is a benefit rather than a hindrance. It helps provide a monarch prepared for the task, one free of the partisan implications that can inhere in the election of a head of state. A hereditary monarchy, as a number of observers have pointed out, serves also to prevent the growth of competing dynastic families. By fulfilling her duties in the way that she does, the queen serves also to overcome any perceptions of incompatibility between a hereditary monarchy and a presumed democratic society. Indeed, there are those who see the monarch as fulfilling an essential role to protect democratic institutions.[8] In the unlikely event of an attempt to impose military or otherwise nondemocratic government, the monarch would be the most effective barrier to its realization. A monarch, as Gilmour observed, can engage the affections and loyalty of the armed forces more readily than can a president.[9] Almost paradoxically, the monarchy serves as a backstop, an ultimate safeguard, to protect those political institutions that have superseded it as the governing force in the United Kingdom.

The importance of these various functions has been confirmed by the public. A 1988 Gallup poll found that more than 80 percent of respondents judged the uniting, or figurehead, functions of the queen, and her immediate family, to be very or quite important. Eighty-two percent attached importance to uniting the people "despite their political, economic and class differences" and more than 90 attached importance to representing the United Kingdom at home and abroad. More than 70 attached importance to maintaining the political neutrality of the armed forces.

What may be termed the core functions of the monarch thus enjoy widespread recognition. The Gallup poll also found other functions widely ascribed to the queen and her family. Recent years have witnessed a growing debate about the royal family. There has been relatively little debate about the core functions. The extent to which members of the royal family have fulfilled the other functions has been a matter of considerable comment.

THE CURRENT DEBATE

For much of the twentieth century, the monarchy was not a major topic of public debate. The king (George VI) and his family proved especially popular during the Second World War, remaining in Buckingham Palace (which was partially bombed) and visiting bomb-damaged areas of the country. His successor, his daughter Elizabeth II, achieved particular popularity in the 1960s and 1970s, initiating royal "walkabouts" (talking and shaking hands with people in the street) and opening up the activities of the monarchy to the public gaze, relative to past and sometimes obsessive secrecy. The twenty-fifth anniversary of the queen's accession to the throne in 1977 was marked by widespread public events throughout the country.

However, there have been occasions when the monarchy has been the subject of controversy and critical comment. The most significant occasion in the twentieth century was in 1936 when the new king, Edward VIII, wanted to marry an American divorcee, Wallis Simpson. The marriage was opposed by the British government and by the archbishop of Canterbury. The problem was not that Mrs. Simpson was an American but that she was divorced (and had remarried). The king was the supreme governor of the Church of England and in the eyes of the church Mrs. Simpson was still married to her first husband. The king had to choose between the throne and Mrs. Simpson. He chose the latter and abdicated. The abdication crisis caused political controversy—some politicians, such as Winston Churchill (then out of office), backing the king's desire to marry and stay on the throne, others seeing Edward's actions as irresponsible and a threat to the institution of the monarchy. Support for the institution was largely restored by his brother, the duke of York, who succeeded him, becoming George VI.

The second most significant period of controversy was that of the 1990s. Both 1992 and 1997 proved particularly difficult years for the queen and her family, with questions being raised about the cost and the position of the monarchy and the royal family. The critical nature of the debate raised some doubt about the long-term future of the institution.

The main areas of debate concerning the monarchy can be subsumed under three heads: (1) the monarch's exercise of certain political powers not clearly governed by convention, (2) the cost and activity of members of the royal family, and (3) the future of the monarchy. The first is a continuing but not prominent one, and has been overshadowed since the early 1990s by the second and third.

The Exercise of Political Powers

There is a continuing debate about the powers of the queen not clearly governed by convention. As we have seen, the exercise of most of the political powers vested in the monarch *is* governed largely by convention. In most cases, this entails the queen's acting on the advice of her ministers. However, certain important powers remain vested in the monarch that on occasion may require a choice among alternative options, a choice not clearly dictated by convention. The most obvious and important power involved here is that of choosing a prime minister.

It is a convention of the Constitution that the queen will select as prime minister that person whom she considers capable of ensuring a majority in the House of Commons. In practice, this usually creates no problems. If a party obtains an overall majority in a general election, the queen summons the leader of that party. But what happens if there is no party leader to be summoned or if no party is returned with an overall majority at a general election? The first possibility no longer faces the queen, though until recently it did. Until 1965, the Conservative party had no formal mechanism for choosing a leader. The leader was expected to "emerge" following soundings of one sort or another within the party. In the event of a Conservative prime minister's retiring with no successor immediately apparent, or with different contenders for the succession, the choice was left to the monarch. In 1957 the queen was faced with summoning someone to succeed Sir Anthony Eden as prime minister. After consulting with senior statesmen, she sent for Harold Macmillan instead of, as many assumed she would, R. A. Butler. In 1963 she was confronted with the difficult task of appointing a prime minister in succession to Macmillan. After taking the advice of her outgoing prime minister, she summoned Lord Home (or Sir Alec Douglas-Home, as he quickly became after renouncing his title in order to seek a seat in the House of Commons). The choice was a controversial one and, though the decision was essentially that of Macmillan, it embroiled the Crown in political controversy. The prospect of any repetition was avoided when the Conservative party in 1964 introduced a procedure for the election of the party leader. The party was thus in a position to elect a leader and avoid the queen's having to make a selection on its behalf.

The second possibility, a party having no overall majority, is a real one. The outcomes of a number of general elections, most notably and most recently that of 1992, have been far from certain. What should the queen do in the event of no party having an overall majority? Usually the position does not entail her having to make a decision. The outgoing prime minister formally remains in office until resigning and may therefore seek to strike a deal with a third party (as Edward Heath attempted to do, unsuccessfully, with the Liberals in February 1974). But what if the prime minister is unacceptable to the third party but another leader—drawn from the same party—might be? Does the queen summon that leader or does she summon the leader of the opposition? In such a situation she would be saddled, as David Watt put it, "with a highly controversial and thankless responsibility."[10] It is one she would almost certainly prefer to do without.

One other power that has produced a similar debate is the power to dissolve Parliament. The usual practice is for the prime minister to recommend a dissolution to the queen and for Her Majesty to accede to that request. There is some doubt, though, as to whether it is a convention for the queen to accede automatically to that request. In the event of a government losing its parliamentary majority through defections or a major party split, and the prime minister's preference for a dissolution rather than forming a coalition with a third party is opposed by the Cabinet, would the queen be justified in withholding her consent to a dissolution? If the prime minister wanted a dissolution following a major defeat in the Commons, but his cabinet colleagues did not,[11] what should the queen do? Lord Blake, a constitutional historian, has argued that in such or similar circumstances the queen would not be obliged to grant a dissolution.[12] When the Tribune Group, a left-wing body of Labour MPs, argued in 1974 that the prime minister had an absolute right to determine the date of the election, a senior minister responded, "Constitutional lawyers of the highest authority are of the clear opinion that the Sovereign is not in all circumstances bound to grant a Prime Minister's request for a dissolution."[13] The problem is one of determining the circumstances that would justify the queen's denying a dissolution, and whether, whatever the circumstances, such an action could be taken without seriously damaging the queen's reputation for being above the partisan fray. "For the monarch," wrote Kingsley Martin, "the only safe rule is always to follow the Premier's advice."[14] If that rule were accepted as a convention, it would ensure that the queen's actions were predictable, putting her beyond claims of partisanship. However, the problem presently is the absence of agreement that such a rule exists.

One alternative, advocated by Labour MP Tony Benn, is for the power of dissolution (indeed, all prerogative powers) to be transferred to the speaker of the House of Commons. This, Benn notes, would avoid the queen's being drawn into the heart of political debate, transferring instead the power to someone who "knows the Commons intimately and is therefore specially qualified to reach a judgment about the appropriate moment for granting a dissolution and who is most likely to command a majority."[15] The case was reiterated in a Fabian pamphlet in 1996, written by a Labour parliamentary candidate, and in a pamphlet from the left-wing think tank *Demos* in 1998.[16] There is also evidence of some popular support for the proposal. A MORI poll in August 1998 found that 49 percent thought the powers should be removed, against 45 percent who thought they should be retained. The difficulty with the proposal is that it would not solve the problem but rather transfer it. As we saw in Chapter 12, the speaker is a neutral figure, and to exercise the power of dissolution would draw the speaker into "the heart of political debate." The speaker is no more keen to jeopardize her claim to being above the partisan fray than is the queen.

There thus remain certain circumstances in which the queen may be called on to exercise a choice. Such circumstances could, and almost certainly would, draw the queen into political controversy. Such circumstances are, though, exceptional.

The Cost and Activity of Members of the Royal Family

The crown vests in the monarch and there are certain tasks that only the monarch can perform. However, many public duties of the monarch can be, and are, performed on her behalf by members of her family. Members of the royal family can be deputed to represent the queen abroad and at various state functions. They will also often be invited themselves to perform public duties, such as opening a factory or hospital or acting as patron of a charity.

The work of members of the royal family has generally been in a positive light. There have been few criticisms of the queen or of her mother, Queen Elizabeth the Queen Mother (widow of George VI) who continues to fulfill public engagements despite celebrating her one hundreth birthday in August 2000. However, the conduct of other members of the royal family has come in for criticism. In the early 1990s, the activities of various "royals" led to public criticism of the amount of public money spent on the royal family. This criticism reached a peak in 1992. In the latter half of the 1990s, the activities of members of the royal family (including, on this occasion, the queen herself) led to accusations of detachment from the rest of the country. This criticism reached a peak in 1997.

The costs incurred in fulfilling public duties by the queen and most other members of the royal family have traditionally been met from the Civil List. For the queen, this covers such items as staff costs and the cost of state dinners and other functions.[17] For other members of the royal family, lesser sums have been provided to cover staff and related expenses. (The exception is the prince of Wales, whose income derives from the duchy of Cornwall.)[18] In 1990, to avoid an annual public debate on the amount to be paid through the Civil List, agreement was reached between the queen and the government that the size of the list should be set at £7.9 million a year (just under $13 million) for a decade (for the current position, see Figure 13.1 on page 358). When other costs were included that were not covered by the Civil List but paid instead by government departments, such as the maintenance costs of royal castles (more than £25 million—$40 million—in 1990–1991) and of the royal yacht *Britannia* (£9 million—$14.4 million), the annual public expenditure on the monarchy was estimated to be almost £60 million (£96 million).[19]

Three criticisms of such spending had been expressed for a number of years. The first was that the Civil List was large in absolute terms. The 1990 settlement marked a significant increase on previous years, designed to take account of inflation in future years. Even in 1988, 40 percent of respondents in a Gallup poll expressed the view that the monarchy cost "too much."[20] The second was that the country did not get particularly good value for the money from certain members of the royal family, especially junior members. A 1989 MORI poll found that senior members, such as the queen, the Prince of Wales (Prince Charles), and the Princess Royal (Princess Anne) were judged to be hard working and cost-effective. However, when asked which two or three members of the royal family represented the worst value for the money to the British taxpayer, 37 percent identified Sarah, Duchess of York, and 23 percent identified her husband, Prince Andrew; they were followed by the queen's sister, Princess Margaret, and the queen's youngest son, Prince Edward.[21] Many critics tended to view such "hangers on," as they were often described, as serving no useful purpose. Third, there was criticism of the fact that the queen received money from the Civil List despite enjoying a large personal fortune—a fortune on which she paid no tax. The queen is reputed to be one of the richest women in the world. (Her wealth has been estimated by some publications, including *Fortune* magazine, as running into several billion pounds, though this figure includes national treasures held in perpetuity on the nation's behalf by the monarch, such as the crown jewels, and which she is not at liberty to sell; her real personal, and disposable, wealth is believed to be closer to £100 million ($160 million) though even this figure was described by the Lord Chamberlain in 1993 as "grossly over-stated.") When income tax was introduced in the nineteenth century, Queen Victoria volunteered to pay tax and did so; in the twentieth century, the tax liability was whittled down and George VI reached agreement with the government to remove any tax burden from his successors. Various calls were made, not least by left-wing MPs critical of the institution of monarchy, for the queen to be subject to income tax.

These criticisms became more prominent in the latter half of the 1980s, in large part because of the antics of several younger—and newer—royals, such as the duchess of York, who was portrayed as enjoying frequent sojourns in expensive ski resorts in preference to fulfilling mundane public duties at home, and at the end of the decade because of the increases in the Civil List at a time of recession. However, they were to reach a new level of intensity—eventually invoking action by the queen—in 1992.

Criticism of the royal family became pronounced—generating intense, and often highly critical, media coverage—as a result of several independent developments. The first was the separation of the duke and duchess of York and the subsequent publication of photographs showing a topless duchess in intimate proximity to a Texan friend, described as her "financial advisor," with her children present. The second was speculation about the state of the marriage of the Prince and Princess of Wales. The speculation was fueled by publication of a book about the Princess of Wales that portrayed her as the vulnerable wife in a difficult royal environment, not helped by a largely intolerant and distant husband.[22] The princess was variously alleged to have allowed, even encouraged, friends to talk to the author in order to put out her side of the story. Some of the prince's friends later retaliated, seeking to put out his side of the story. Media attention became intense following the release of a tape of an intercepted telephone conversation held some time previously between the Princess of Wales and a male admirer, referred to on the tape as "Squidgy."

Then came a separate development that appears to have been crucial in making 1992 what the queen was to describe as an *annus horribilis* (a horrible year, translated by one tabloid headline writer as "a bum year"). On November 20, St. George's Hall of Windsor Castle was destroyed by fire. The national heritage secretary announced that the government would meet the cost of repairs—believed to be at least £50 million ($80 million)—as the castle was uninsured. The public response was strongly negative. Out of 30,283 callers to a television program, 95 percent said the taxpayer should not have to pay the entire bill. A Harris poll found three out of four respondents believing that ways should be found to cut the cost of the royal family. The normally loyal *Daily Mail* asked: "Why should a populace, many of whom have had to make huge sacrifices during this most bitter recession, have to pay the total bill when the Queen, who pays no taxes, contributes next to nothing?"[23] Six days after the fire at Windsor Castle, the prime minister announced in the House of Commons that the queen "some months ago" had initiated discussions on changing her tax-free status and removing all members of the royal family, except herself, the duke of Edinburgh, and the Queen Mother, from the Civil List. The announcement served to meet much of the immediate criticism. The queen also announced that Buckingham Palace would be opened to the public and that income from doing so would be used to pay for the restoration of St. George's Hall.

Though criticism of the cost of the royal family peaked in 1992, the personal relationships of members of the royal family continued to attract media attention and were to produce a crisis of their own in 1997. The separation of the Prince and Princess of Wales was announced by the prime minister in December 1992. Unlike the separation of the duke and duchess of York, this separation raised a number of constitutional questions. In announcing it to the House of Commons, the prime minister emphasized that the separation as such had no constitutional implications. The prince remained heir to the throne and would in due course become king, and there was no reason, said the prime minister, "why the Princess of Wales should not be crowned Queen," a statement that—according to *The Economist* attracted "a murmur of disbelief."[24] Though the prime minister's statement was correct in constitutional terms, "the thought of them kneeling together before the Archbishop of Canterbury at the sacred moment of coronation now seems wildly implausible."[25] A survey in December 1992 found that 65 percent of those questioned thought it would be wrong for the princess to become queen if the couple were still separated.[26] The issue became academic when, apparently on the prompting of the queen, the couple decided to divorce. The divorce took effect in 1996.

The status and role of the Princess of Wales became a matter of public debate. (Upon her divorce she lost the prefix of "her royal highness" and became simply "Diana, Princess of Wales.") Her relationships became a matter of media interest, as did those of the Prince of Wales. In a television interview, the prince admitted he had committed adultery while married. (It transpired that he had a mistress, Camilla Parker-Bowles, who—at the time—was also married.) In a later interview, the princess made a similar admission, though saying that it happened after it was clear that the marriage was over. The princess promoted various high-profile causes (such as banning the use of land mines) but also withdrew for a time from public activity. She was seen as a tragic figure and achieved something of an iconic status. In August 1997, she was killed in a car accident in Paris. She immediately became greater in death than in life. (Some commentators saw parallels with the death of President John F. Kennedy in 1963. As with Kennedy's death, many people remember exactly what they were doing when they first heard the news of what had happened.) There was an immediate and intense outpouring of popular grief, which was not confined to the United Kingdom.

Her death also resulted in a public relations fiasco for the royal family. The Prince of Wales went to Paris to collect the body of his former wife, but the queen and other leading members of the royal family remained at Balmoral Castle, the royal holiday home in Scotland. The failure to return to London attracted intensely critical comments in the media. So too did the fact that the flag was not flown at half-staff at Buckingham Palace. (Because the queen was not in residence there was no flag flown, so all that people saw was a bare flagpole.) There was a public perception that the royal family was detached from what was going on and was not sharing, or certainly not leading, the national grief. This had a serious negative impact on public perceptions of the monarchy. By the time the queen returned to London, and made a televised address, the damage had been done. The funeral of the Princess of Wales was the occasion for unprecedented scenes of grief and a funeral oration in Westminster Abbey from the princess's brother, the Earl Spencer, which was interpreted as an attack on the royal family. It was a low point for the monarchy.

The royal family has since recovered from those low points of the 1990s. The royal finances are better organized and also open. The Civil List (Figure 13.1) continues to fund the expenses of the Queen, Prince Philip, and Queen Elizabeth the Queen Mother. Other expenditure is now met by grants-in-aid: a property grant-in-aid to cover the cost of maintenance of royal palaces and a travel grant-in-aid to cover transportation costs on official duties. Annual accounts are published and efficiency savings have been made in recent years. (The property grant-in-aid has been reduced and savings made on transportation costs.)[27] A "Way Ahead" group has been formed, comprising the leading members of the royal family (principally the queen, her husband Prince Philip, and the Prince of Wales) and senior officials, to discuss how to modernize the monarchy and adapt to changing conditions. One of the outcomes of such discussions has been a more visible and "popular" schedule for the queen, visiting people in their homes, visiting a supermarket, and travelling on the underground. She, and other leading members of the royal family, continue to undertake an extensive range of public duties. Such activities appear to have stemmed the criticism leveled at the monarchy. However, the criticisms of recent years appear to have fueled a greater skepticism about the long-term future of the institution.

FIGURE 13.1   The Civil List

The Civil List is the sum provided by Parliament to meet the official expenses of The Queen's Household so that Her Majesty can fulfil her role as Head of State and Head of the Commonwealth. It is not in any sense 'pay' for The Queen.

The Civil List dates back to the Restoration of the Monarchy in 1660, but the current system was created on the accession of George III in 1760, when it was decided that the whole cost of civil government should be provided by Parliament in return for the surrender of the hereditary revenues (principally the net surplus of the Crown Estate) by the King for the duration of the reign. Revenue from the Crown Estate amounted to £113.2 million in 1997/98 and this was paid to the Treasury.

About 70 per cent of Civil List expenditure goes to pay the salaries of staff working directly for The Queen. Their duties include dealing with State papers, organising public engagements and arranging meetings and receptions undertaken by The Queen. The Civil List also meets the costs of functions such as the Royal Garden Parties (Her Majesty entertains over 48,000 people each year) and official entertainment during State Visits.

The Civil List is set by Parliament as a fixed annual amount of £7.9 million for a period of up to 10 years. The Household is currently succeeding in containing Civil List expenditure within inflation, however, and the resulting surplus is being carried forward to reduce the amount of the Civil List for the next 10-year period.

The budget for each year's projected net Civil List spending is reviewed by the Treasury, which audits the accounts and verifies that the Household's financial management is in line with best practice. Details of expenditure are published.

SOURCE: The British Monarchy web site, http://www.royal.gov.uk/today/civillst.htm.

The Future of the Monarchy

The continued existence of the monarchy has been challenged by various politicians and writers. The institution has been attacked as anachronistic and undemocratic, a bastion of privilege and conservatism unsuited to the late twentieth century, and certainly unsuited to the twenty-first century. Various Labour MPs have variously put the case for abolition, as have writers Tom Nairn in *The Enchanted Glass* (1988) and Edgar Wilson in *The Myth of the British Monarchy* (1989). They have been joined since 1994 by the influential weekly magazine, *The Economist.* To Wilson, the various arguments put forward to support the monarchy are essentially myths, generated to justify the existing order. Far from being neutral, he contends that the institution is arbitrary "and exercises a pernicious influence."[28] To *The Economist,* the monarchy "is the antithesis of much of what we stand for: democracy, liberty, reward for achievement rather than inheritance." It was, it declared, "an idea whose time has passed."[29] Such critics believe the functions fulfilled by the queen as head of state could equally well be carried out by an appointed or an elected president. A number of Labour MPs have expressed support for a presidential system, albeit one based on the German rather than the U.S. model: that is, with a head of state (the president) separate from the head of government. Most countries have a nonhereditary head of state. So, they ask, why not Britain?

Supporters of the monarchy have defended it on the grounds that the monarch fulfills functions that could not be carried out as well (or at all) by an elected or nominated head of state. An elected head of state, it is argued, could not perform the uniting task as well as the queen—in part because election would be potentially divisive and in part because he or she would not have been prepared for the office in the way that an heir to the throne is prepared. The queen stands above political activity in a way that others are unlikely to emulate, and her experience would be difficult to match, especially by presidents serving for fixed terms of office. For defenders, the pageantry of the office is a positive rather than a negative aspect of its existence, contributing both to a sense of pride in the nation and—at a more materialistic level—acting as a powerful incentive to tourists to visit Britain. According to Harold Macmillan, who took a romanticized view of the monarchy, replacing the queen with a president would be disastrous. He expressed himself in characteristic style:

> Imagine if at this moment, instead of the Queen, we had a gentleman in evening clothes, ill-made, probably from Moss Bros., with a white tie, going about everywhere, who had been elected by some deal made between the extreme Right and the extreme Left! Then we would all wait for the next one, another little man, who is it going to be? "Give it to 'X,' you know he's been such a bad Chancellor of the Exchequer, instead of getting rid of him, let's make him the next President." Can you imagine it? I mean, it doesn't make sense, that would be the final destruction of colour and life and the sense of the past in this country, wouldn't it?[30]

Critics would respond that Macmillan's analysis has not necessarily been borne out by experience elsewhere. The response of supporters of the monarchy would doubtless be that Britain is not "elsewhere."

Defenders of the monarchy have also contended that it is efficient. By general consent, the queen is hard working and fulfills her duties well. The issue of cost has now been addressed, even if not to everyone's satisfaction, and there is now greater transparency and efficiency in the royal finances. Supporters also point out that many of the costs attributed to the monarchy—such as the maintenance of national monuments—were costs that would have to be borne by the public purse regardless of whether one had a monarch or not. They have also contended that, on balance, the nation makes a profit out of the monarchy. Since the 1760s, as noted in Figure 13.1, each monarch has surrendered income from Crown lands in return for a Civil List. Income from crown lands exceeds the amount of public money spent on the monarchy. When this is coupled with the benefits derived from tourism and from the trade accruing from foreign tours—members of the royal family drumming up trade in a way an elected head of state could not—then the nation benefits financially from the monarch and the activity of members of the royal family.[31] Critics retort that the money from crown lands is now effectively public money anyway, that tourists would still come to Britain (the national monuments would still exist), and that trade does not necessarily follow the crown. The prime minister and other senior ministers can do a good job drumming up trade and are in a stronger position to offer government-backed incentives.

The controversies surrounding the royal family in recent years, and especially in 1992 and 1997, have served to dent but not to destroy support for the monarchy. Critics made some headway but did not carry the majority with them. The early 1990s saw an increase in the number of people favoring the abolition of the monarchy. Before 1992, less than 15 percent of people questioned wanted to get rid of the monarchy. At the end of 1992, the figure stood at 24 percent. That, however, was a high point in support for abolition. The majority of respondents favor retaining the monarchy. Given a choice between monarchy and a republic, about three-quarters usually opt for the monarchy. As Table 13.1 shows, support since 1973 has recovered slightly. Despite the death of Diana, Princess of Wales, most people continue to support the institution.

The figures, however, masked a notable skepticism about the value and future of the monarchy. In 1987, 73 percent of those questioned in a MORI poll thought Britain would be worse off if the monarchy was abolished. In December 1992, the figure collapsed to 37 percent. About 42 percent thought it would make no difference. By 1997, the percentage thinking Britain would be worse off had shown a marked increase, with 55 percent giving that response. Only 27 percent thought it would make no difference. However, what is clear is that the percentage saying the country would be worse off was still not at the level of 1987. There is also a notable increase in the proportion of the population that is doubtful about the long-term future of the monarchy. Even many who support it think that it will not exist in fifty years' time. In 1992, for the first time more people thought that the monarchy would not exist in 50 years' time than thought it would (42 to 36 percent). Since then, the number thinking it will not last 50 years has continued to outnumber those thinking it will (Table 13.2). Indeed, by the end of 1998 the figures were not very different from those of 1992.

The debate about the future of the monarchy thus shows a mixed picture. Most people want the monarchy to continue but are doubtful that it will survive for more than a few decades. The royal family has moved to bolster its position. The queen retains public support. Prince Charles has also regained much

TABLE 13.1 Attitudes toward the monarchy

Q. Would you favor Britain becoming a republic or remaining a monarchy? (%)

	April 1993	Jan. 1994	Dec. 1994	Sep. 1997	Aug. 1998	Nov. 1998	June 1999
Republic	18	17	20	18	16	18	16
Monarchy	69	73	71	73	75	73	74
Don't know	14	10	9	9	9	9	10

SOURCE: MORI, *British Public Opinion*, XXII (6), August 1999.

TABLE 13.2   Attitudes toward survival of the monarchy

Q. Looking to the future, do you think that Britain will or will not have a monarchy in fifty years? (%)

	Jan. 1990	Feb. 1991	May 1992	Dec. 1992	Feb. 1996	Dec. 1996	Sept. 1997	Nov. 1998
Will	69	55	46	36	33	33	30	33
Will not	11	21	30	42	43	48	45	42
Don't know	20	23	24	22	24	19	25	25

SOURCE: MORI, *British Public Opinion*, 21 (10), December 1998, p. 5.

of the support he lost in the early 1990s and following the death of Diana, Princess of Wales. In 1991, 82 percent of those questioned in a MORI poll thought he would make a good king. By February 1996 this was down to 46 percent. It picked up to 50 percent in the first half of 1997 but fell to 42 percent in the month following Diana's death. By November 1998, 63 percent thought he would make a good king. Also bolstering the position of the monarchy is the fact that Prince Charles' heir, Prince William (elder son of Charles and Diana, born in 1982), who will succeed to the throne on the death of Charles, enjoys great popular support. Prince Charles is also credited with doing a good job in bringing up his two sons: In November 1998, 75 percent of respondents thought he was doing a good job; only 7 percent thought he was doing a bad job. There has thus been something of a restoration of popular respect for Prince Charles. His relationship, now a semipublic one, with Camilla Parker-Bowles continues to excite media interest, both at home and abroad, but his own position as a respected public figure, capable of taking on the responsibilities of the throne, now seems to be secure.

CONCLUSION

The queen fulfills the task of representing the unity of the nation as well as carrying out certain political tasks largely but not wholly governed by convention. Her role as a political actor is circumscribed, necessarily so in order for her to fulfill her unifying role, and any real choice she is called on to exercise is the product of circumstance and unclear conventions and not of any personal desire on her part. She carries out her duties assiduously and continues to maintain the support of the population. Recent years, however, have been problematic. At times, she has not been particularly well served by members of her family, and the funding of the monarchy (and, more especially, members of the royal family) has proved controversial. Survey data reveal a change in mood toward the monarchy but not a collapse of support. The challenge for the monarchy is one of adapting, and it is in the process of doing so. Despite the problems of recent years, it is not in danger of imminent demise. Whether it does exist in 50 years' time depends on how well it adapts.

NOTES

[1] F. W. Maitland, *Constitutional History of England*, quoted in H. V. Wiseman (ed.), *Parliament and the Executive* (Routledge and Kegan Paul, 1966), p. 5.

[2] W. Bagehot, *The English Constitution* (Fontana, 1963 ed.), p. 61.

[3] F. Hardie, *The Political Influence of the British Monarchy 1868–1952* (Batsford, 1970).

[4] Hardie, p. 188.

[5] I. Gilmour, *The Body Politic*, rev. ed. (Hutchinson, 1970), p. 317.

[6] A. Horne, *Macmillan*, Vol. II: 1957–1986 (Macmillan, 1989), p. 168.

[7] Tony Blair, quoted in *The Times*, Nov. 21, 1997.

[8] See V. Bogdanor, *The Monarchy and the Constitution* (Oxford University Press, 1995).

[9] Gilmour, p. 313.

[10] D. Watt, "If the Queen Has to Choose, Who Will It Be?" *The Times*, December 11, 1981.

[11] The constitutional position in the event of such a scenario was raised in late 1992 after the prime minister's aides signaled that the PM might make a particular vote on the Maastricht bill (see Chapter 9) a vote of confidence, thus necessitating a dissolution or the resignation of the government in the event of the vote being lost. This course of action was reported not to enjoy the support of his cabinet colleagues. In the event, the vote was not made one of confidence, though it was believed the prime minister himself would resign if the vote was lost. The government won the vote with a majority of 3.

[12] Lord Blake, *The Office of Prime Minister* (Oxford University Press, 1975), pp. 60–61.

[13] E. Short, quoted in Blake, p. 60.

[14] K. Martin, *The Crown and the Establishment* (Penguin, 1963).

[15] *New Socialist*, August 1982, reported in *The Daily Telegraph*, August 27, 1982.

[16] P. Richards, *Long to Reign Over Us?* (Fabian Society, 1996); T. Hames and M. Leonard, *Modernising the Monarchy* (Demos, 1998).

[17] Private expenditure as sovereign, such as gifts to visiting dignitaries, is met from the Privy Purse (the income from the duchy of Lancaster), and personal expenditure as an individual, such as wedding or Christmas gifts, is met from the queen's personal wealth.

[18] Prince Charles, among other titles, is duke of Cornwall, and the duchy encompasses a number of revenue-generating estates. In 1991, income from the duchy exceeded £2 million ($3.2 million).

[19] "Should One Pay Tax?" *The Economist*, January 25, 1992, p. 36.

[20] *Gallup Political Index*, Report No. 341, January 1989, p. 10.

[21] MORI, *British Public Opinion*, February 1989, p. 5.

[22] A. Morton, *Diana: Her True Story* (Simon & Schuster, 1992).

[23] *The Daily Mail*, November 24, 1992. For a summary of the chronology, see "Seven Days That Shook the Crown," *The Sunday Times*, November 29, 1992, p. 11.

[24] "Admitting the Obvious," *The Economist*, December 12, 1992, p. 25

[25] Ibid., p. 25.

[26] "Royal Survey," *The Sunday Telegraph*, December 13, 1992, p. 2.

[27] The property grant-in-aid was £19.6 million ($31.3 million) in 1996–97 and £16.4 million ($26.2 million) in 1997–98. The travel grant-in-aid in 1997–98 was £19.4 million ($31 million) but only £17.3 million ($27.6 million) was actually spent.

[28] E. Wilson, *The Myth of the British Monarchy* (Journeyman/Republic, 1989), p. 178.

[29] *The Economist*, 22, October 1994.

[30] Quoted in A. Horne, *Macmillan*, Vol. II: 1957–1986 (Macmillan, 1989), pp. 170–171.

[31] See P. Norton, "The Case Against Abolition," *Social Studies Review*, 4 (3), 1989, p. 122.

views to a mass audience. For political parties, and for organs of the state, the Internet offers a highly efficient way of communicating with citizens. It also offers a means of communication free of an intermediary. The political parties have developed their web sites, putting out information that television and radio may not have bothered to report or may have reported only partially. No. 10 Downing Street has its own web site, as do the monarchy and government departments. The Downing Street web site not only contains the latest announcements from No. 10, magazine features, and a policy forum, but also carries a regular broadcast from the prime minister. The monarchy web site, like the Downing Street web site, has tended to be at the forefront of web site development and has proved extremely popular. Parliament also has its own web site, though members of Parliament have been somewhat slower than their counterparts in America to recognize the value of having their own web pages.

The Internet is also a means for those who have been denied access to print and broadcast media to make their views known. These include groups whose activity is outlawed or deemed socially unacceptable. Hate groups of various kinds are able to post material on the Internet and to make contact with others who share their views. Contact through the Internet may also be used by groups to organize demonstrations and direct action. Anarchist groups that engaged in riots and civil disturbance in London in April 2000 are believed to have communicated through the Internet.

The development of the Internet has been rapid. More and more households have a computer and have the potential for Internet access. In 1996 only 16 percent of households in the United Kingdom had a home computer. By 1997, the figure was 26 percent.[5] The Internet is a major form of communication. Like newspapers and television, political communication only forms a small part of what it is about. Where it differs from the more traditional forms of communication is that it is unmediated, offering the individual or group the opportunity to disseminate material without the interference of a third party. Access to the Internet offers unrivalled opportunities to select and read material that was previously unavailable or not easily available.

POLITICAL INFLUENCE

The mass media, by the content and method of their communicating or failing to communicate information, can exert tremendous political influence. Political evaluations and actions of politician and citizen are based on receipt of information. How that information is portrayed and transmitted can significantly affect both the evaluation and the action taken on the basis of that evaluation.

The political information transmitted by the mass media is, of necessity, limited. Newspapers do not have the space nor broadcasting media the air time to transmit comprehensive coverage of daily events (nationally or worldwide) of political significance. Nor do they have the inclination to do so. Although newspapers and the broadcasting media constitute the primary means of transmitting political information to a mass audience, they do not exist exclusively or indeed even primarily to fulfill such a function. Television and radio are essentially media of entertainment. Newspapers may make some claim, by virtue of the written word, to be more a medium of information, but the information transmitted is not usually on the subject of political behavior. Although the so-called quality newspapers (*The Times, Financial Times, Daily Telegraph, Independent,* and *Guardian*) devote a significant proportion of space to reporting and commenting on political events, the mass readership papers do not.

Indeed, the trend has been away from covering political items to what publishers consider human-interest stories. In postwar decades, news coverage in the mass-circulation dailies has decreased significantly.[6] The tabloid newspapers have generally expanded human-interest content, entertainment features, sports, and home and family articles.[7] The greater the circulation war between papers, the greater the emphasis on these human-interest features, which constitute the most consistently read part of newspapers. One study of the main topics gaining media coverage in 1998 found that about 28 percent of the coverage was devoted to disasters and accidents and 10 percent to sports. Politics as a category got 8 percent of coverage, the same coverage as was accorded to crime. Royalty attracted 5 percent of the coverage, a substantial coverage relative to that given to politics as a whole.[8] The competition for a decreasing market has also produced competitions and greater emphasis on short items and color pictures.

Television has also seen some reduction in political coverage. Various current affairs programs disappeared in the 1990s or were transferred to late-night slots. By 1999, television was covering Parliament less than it was a decade previously, when the cameras were first allowed into the House of Commons. ITV moved its flagship news program, *News at Ten* from its established ten o'clock slot to eleven o'clock, with an accompanying decline in audience. Budget cuts also meant that some news and current affairs programs had to cut down on carrying features that were expensive (such as outside broadcast reports) and concentrate instead on cheaper studio-based items. Regional companies also saw similar cutbacks. One regional company shifted from having a weekly evening current affairs program to a monthly program broadcast on a Sunday morning and run, as one insider put it, "on a shoe string."

Nonetheless, the role of the mass media in transmitting political information remains of vital significance. Indeed, the significance of newspapers and television as media of communication has increased over the past century not only because of the size of the audiences but also because of the increase in sophistication of communication technology. Television, in particular, was important because of its immediacy. Not only can various happenings—a bomb blast, politicians arguing with one another—be portrayed visually and in sound, but they also can be transmitted shortly after or even at the time of happening. Receiving information with such immediacy, and in such a form, can affect viewers' evaluations in a way not possible when this medium of communication did not exist. As Hedley Donovan queried once in *Time* magazine: "Could the Civil War have survived the 7 P.M. news? Could George Washington have held his command after a TV special on Valley Forge?"[9] Media coverage of the Vietnam War clearly affected the American public's perception of the wisdom, or lack of it, in such an action. In Britain, recognition of the implications of media coverage influenced the government in its actions and its control of information during the Falklands War in 1982. The government controlled the means of transmitting news from the Task Force to Britain, and facilities for the quick transmission of television pictures were not made available. To have shown on television during the conflict "pictures of the sort of realism that the Americans had during the Vietnamese war," to be seen by servicemen's families, would, in the words of one commanding officer, "have had a very serious effect" on troop morale.[10] Pictures of dead servicemen—or of captured officers being paraded by enemy forces—have greater emotional impact than a written report. Pictures of human suffering may engender a desire for action. Media coverage of particular events such as riots may extend beyond constituting an impartial recording of those events to being an alleged instigator of them. There have been accusations in some conflicts of skirmishes being staged, or of the presence of a camera crew inciting, unwittingly or otherwise, disorder. The activities of the media themselves may constitute political issues.

The way in which information is channeled, then, is not neutral in its effect. The mass media, in short, exert political influence. This influence may be primary, that is, affecting the recipient of the communication. It may be secondary, affecting a party independent of the communication process (e.g., a politician whose capacity to achieve a particular action is limited by public reaction to news of a certain event as, for instance, President Lyndon Johnson in the Vietnam War). The influence of the media may be seen as especially important in terms of the legitimacy of the political system, the partisan support of electors, and the behavior of politicians. The influence exerted in each case may be described as that of enhancing, of reinforcing, and of constraining, respectively.

The media fulfill a function of latent legitimation of the political—as well as the social and economic—system.[11] By operating within that system and accepting its norms, newspapers and television help to maintain its popular legitimacy. When a political crisis arises, journalists and TV reporters descend upon ministers and MPs for comment, hence accepting and reinforcing the legitimacy of those questioned to comment on the matter at hand. The media have studios in a building (known by its address—4 Millbank) just across the road from Parliament. What political leaders do in a public and often in a private capacity is considered newsworthy. News of an affair creates a media frenzy. So too does family news. When one leading Labour politician, Clare Short (appointed to the Cabinet in 1997) was reunited with her long-lost son (given up for adoption when he was a baby) it made the headlines. So too did the news in 1999 that the prime minister's wife, Cherie Blair, was expecting her fourth child at the age of 45. The movements of Diana, princess of Wales, attracted extensive media attention, not just in the United Kingdom. Though her activities were viewed on occasion as undermining the monarchy, her status derived from the very fact that she had been married to the Prince of Wales. Her death in a car accident in August 1997 was the occasion for a massive outpouring of grief. By according status to politicians and other occupants (or even the spouses of occupants) of public office and to the institutions they occupy and represent, the media serve to reinforce the legitimacy of such bodies. Where a body does not enjoy popular legitimacy, the media probably could not create it. Where it does exist, however, they can and do reinforce it by the very nature of their activities.

At times, certain media may also fulfill the more conscious role of overt legitimation. At times of national crisis, some newspapers consider it not only their duty but also that of their readers to support the national effort, and vigorously exhort their readers to provide such support. One example that has passed into folklore was that of a number of national newspapers, most notably the *Sun*, during the Falklands War in 1982. Reporting of the war was merged with vigorous, not to say crude, editorializing in support of the British effort, any critics being roundly condemned as unpatriotic. The broadcast media, by virtue of their charters, sought to take a more detached position.

On party political preferences, the media may be seen as having primarily a reinforcing effect. This is in line with the findings of various studies of the effect of mass communication. Persuasive mass communication, according to Klapper's classic study, tends to serve far more heavily in the interests of reinforcement and of minor change than of converting opinions.[12] As one analyst of the British media put it, "the media do more towards corroborating opinion than creating it."[13] There is a marked tendency for the recipients of communications to indulge in a process of selective exposure, perception, and retention. This phenomenon was borne out by Butler and Stokes's study in Britain on the effects of newspaper reading.[14] Most readers chose a newspaper whose partisan stance was in line with their own stance or, for young people, with that of their parents; when the children absorbed and accepted the preferences of their parents, they continued to read the same newspaper.

The effect of reading any given partisan newspaper was characterized by Butler and Stokes as "magnetic": "Readers who are already close to their paper's party will tend to be held close; those at some distance will tend to be pulled towards it."[15] A similar finding emerged from a study by Dunleavy and Husbands. In their analysis of media influence on voting in 1983, they found that the greater the exposure to Conservative newspapers, the greater the likelihood to vote Conservative. The relationship remained strong even when social class was controlled for. "Within all the class categories used the Conservative vote is some 30 percentage points lower among people primarily exposed to non-Tory messages than it is amongst readers of the Tory press, a high level of association that has few parallels amongst either social background or issue influences. The difference is even more marked when we compare the two extreme groups, those exposed to a predominantly Tory message and those receiving a predominantly non-Tory one; the differences in Conservative support range from 36 to

58 points."[16] The relationships they established were, they concluded, too close to be attributable solely or even mainly to partisan self-selection. Hence, according to their analysis, newspaper reading can have a political influence. The beneficiary of such influence has been, at least until 1997, the Conservative party. Even so, the extent of the influence should not be exaggerated. As John Curtice and Holli Semetko pointed out in their analysis of the 1992 general election, "only 38 per cent of the readers of the *Sun,* supposedly the most stridently pro-Conservative newspaper, voted Conservative."[17] And as Margaret Scammell and Martin Harrop argued in their study of the press in the 1997 general election, the impact of the press in changing votes was marginal. As they wrote: "the *Sun's* endorsement of Tony Blair was certainly remarkable evidence of the success of his political project, but like the rest of the press, the *Sun* was following opinion more than creating it."[18] The press may serve to reinforce opinions, perhaps even shape them over time, but have limited impact in getting readers to switch their allegiance.

Media coverage may serve to have a constraining effect on politicians' behavior. To achieve their aims, politicians must be able to communicate with others, at what may be described as the horizontal level (i.e., with fellow politicians, civil servants, and other policy makers) as well as the vertical (i.e., politician to the public). They must also at times ensure the noncommunication of material. Most politicians crave the attention of the media. Such attention enhances their legitimacy and provides them with the means to influence others. Political behavior may often be geared, in consequence, to the needs of television and newspapers. Press conferences are now *de rigueur* during election campaigns. (They are not so necessary at other times, because Parliament provides ministers with an authoritative and structured forum for communicating their views, an important facility not available to the president and cabinet secretaries in the United States.) Texts of speeches are given in advance of delivery to journalists and TV reporters. Meetings are organized so as to present a good televisual effect and also timed to meet newspaper deadlines or to get onto the early television evening news. The Labour party during and since the 1997 election has been credited with bringing these techniques to a new level of sophistication. It created its own media center, the Millbank Media Center, and has used it to ensure that its message is effectively disseminated to the media.

The effect or presumed effect of the televising of particular politicians may even influence the careers of political leaders. A politician whose words in print may be persuasive may come across as hesitant and bumbling on television; he or she may not be photogenic. When the television cameras entered the House of Commons in 1989, Margaret Thatcher was judged to come across well on the screen, whereas her Labour rival, Neil Kinnock, came across as negative and hectoring. Since 1997, Conservative leader William Hague has been credited with a superb performance at Prime Minister's Question Time but portrayed as performing poorly on the public platform. It is also common now for politicians to give more attention to how they appear. Margaret Thatcher had voice training. Leading politicians have "makeovers," their appearance (haircut, dress) being groomed by professional advisers. Politicians are thus constrained not only in how they behave in seeking to put across a particular message but also in how they look and how they present themselves before the television cameras.

The media may constrain a politician also in terms of the substantive actions or policies he or she may wish to pursue. Knowledge that one's activities may be observed and reported may deter a minister, for example, from engaging in a policy or particular action that is thought to be unpopular or likely to incur the wrath of one's colleagues or supporters. In both the Falklands War in 1982 and the Gulf War in 1991, policy makers were keen to achieve a quick military victory with as few casualties as possible. They were conscious that reports of heavy losses or a long, drawn-out, and indecisive campaign could have an effect on public morale similar to that of media coverage of the Vietnam War. Civil servants and other public officials may decide not to pursue a particular line, albeit a secret one, for fear that details may be leaked to the press and television. The effect of media reporting may thus limit the options that policy makers believe are open to them.

Thus despite their not seeking to act primarily as channels of political information and influence, the mass media in Britain constitute an integral part of the political process. Through reading newspapers and watching television (or listening to radio), citizens receive information that helps shape and reinforce their political attitudes and that, by its presentation, reinforces the legitimacy of the political system and may at times help modify their attitudes. By similarly reading newspapers and watching news and current affairs programs, politicians are aware of the material that is being communicated to the public. Their perceptions of the likely impact of this material may influence their behavior, even if the communication does not have the impact expected.

The media also serve to communicate information to political leaders on how particular policies and programs are being received. Investigative work by journalists or television researchers may present new public evidence on a particular issue. The reporting of evidence researched by others, the coverage of demonstrations, or the publication of opinion polls commissioned by the newspaper or program serve to inform both the public and political leaders of attitudes and responses to policies and the actions of policy makers. The Labour government of Tony Blair is known to employ focus groups to monitor reaction to its policies but it also pays close attention to opinion poll data. Blair is reported to be especially sensitive to shifts in the government's popularity.

The mass media, by which we mean radio, television, and newspapers, are thus significant. The Internet also has significance, but in a somewhat different way. It may have consequences similar to those of the mass media. As we have seen, established bodies such as the monarchy, government, and political parties can use it to make information available. However, it is also a subversive element in that anyone who can create a web site can put information into the public domain. A range of bodies and indeed individuals exploit the opportunity to put their views on the Internet. These include bodies that are not part of the established political or social framework. Internet users may have difficulty finding and selecting material that is of use to them. Whereas the mass media make, in effect, a choice for the reader or viewer (you shall have the opportunity to read or to see only this), the Internet user is effectively left to make a choice from an increasing mass of material. There is no mechanism by which the citizen's view of society is shaped by intermediaries. By accident or design, the Internet user may come across views or material that shape his perception in a way that would not be possible through watching television or reading a newspaper. In practice, the most significant political consequence appears to be that it enables those who wish to access material previously unavailable (such as from neo-Nazi groups) to do so. The very fact of its dissemination may also give such groups, in the eyes of their supporters, a credence they previously lacked.

THE CURRENT DEBATE

The media serve to convey information. They also form part of contemporary political debate. There are four criticisms that are leveled against the media: that they intrude unduly on privacy, that they are politically biased, that they manufacture news, and that they allow unsavory material to be broadcast or printed.

Privacy.　There is a potential conflict between the freedom of the press and the right to privacy. Achieving a balance between the two is not easy. The media are often accused of invading privacy. The activities of the popular press in particular in obtaining stories has proved a cause of controversy. The harassment of individuals by journalists and television crews—camping outside their homes, constantly telephoning, pursuing them down the street whenever they venture out—has been a cause of serious complaint, ranging from pursuit of aged and innocent relatives of figures in the public eye to the engulfing of certain members of the royal family and those close to them. The pursuit of the Princess of Wales prior to her marriage and during her first pregnancy aroused the ire of Buckingham Palace, as did speculation about the state of her marriage following publication of a book about the princess—*Diana: Her True Story*—in 1992. The princess also sometimes complained about media intrusiveness following her divorce. She was trailed by photographers up to and including the time of her fatal accident in Paris in 1997. The Prince of Wales also on one occasion made a formal complaint about media coverage of his elder son, Prince William. The use of money to elicit exclusive stories has similarly incurred public criticism, particularly in instances when it has been employed to obtain evidence from witnesses involved in pending court cases. It has been likewise with the practice of making up "interviews" from disparate quotations already on the public record and the publication of private or intrusive photographs.

　　Extensive criticism has also been generated by many of the stories that have resulted, the press having considerable license to criticize and abuse. The position has been exacerbated by the limited means available to those attacked by the press to achieve a redress of grievance. The only means available are to sue for libel or to report the matter to the Press Complaints Commission. (Or, in the case of television, the Broadcasting Standards Commission.)[19] Neither is considered a particularly effective course of action. For individuals, the cost of pursuing a case through the courts is, in most cases, financially prohibitive. (Legal aid is not available in such cases.) Only those with personal wealth are in a position to sustain a lengthy libel action.[20] Newspapers have the resources to defend themselves against any libel actions and in recent years have put up some vigorous defenses. Reporting cases to the Press Complaints Commission is a course of action available to all. The problem here is lack of powers available to the commission. A nonstatutory body established by the newspaper industry, it came into being on January 1, 1991, replacing the Press Council. It has a smaller membership than its predecessor and a stronger code of practice, and it can investigate and adjudicate on complaints against newspapers. Of nearly 3,000 complaints received each year, less than 5 percent require adjudication by the full commission: The rest are resolved prior to that stage. (In 1998 there were 2,601 complaints, most about inaccuracy in reporting, and only 86 required adjudication by the commission.) If the commission upholds a complaint, the paper concerned is committed to publishing the commission's statement. However, such reports are not necessarily printed in a prominent position and are sometimes treated with contempt. Critics also point out that the code of practice it polices was drawn up by the newspapers and has no statutory force, and that seven of the 16 members of the Commission are senior newspaper editors.

Public lack of confidence in the press is reflected in the low standing of journalists. In a 1999 poll, journalists were ranked bottom of the pile of those whom people would trust to tell the truth. Whereas 91 percent of those questioned would trust doctors to tell the truth, only 15 percent would trust journalists to tell the truth.[21] Some 79 percent would not trust them to tell the truth. Distrust of the press has led to various demands for more effective means of redress. These have included providing legal aid in libel cases, strengthening the law on defamation, providing an enforceable right to reply, and creating a statutory right to privacy. An official report in 1990—the Calcutt report—said that if the press did not put its own house in order, then statutory restraints should be introduced. The press responded with the creation of the Press Complaints Commission and the appointment of in-house "ombudsmen" to adjudicate readers' complaints. These changes failed to satisfy many of those pressing for an effective policing mechanism. In another report in 1992, Sir David Calcutt recommended greater statutory regulation. An inquiry was undertaken by a House of Commons select committee and an attempt was made—unsuccessfully—to reform the law through the mechanism of private members' legislation. Demands for action usually fall afoul of fears about the effect on press freedom—a cause championed, naturally, by the media—and by the difficulties of producing measures that are enforceable.

Political bias.   There is controversy as to the political influence of the mass media. Fulfilling the function of latent legitimization has attracted criticism from left-wing bodies opposed to the existing political system. They see the media as buttressing opposition to change. Radical critics such as the Glasgow University Media Group have argued that rather than devoting space to the activities of the royal family or to interviewing MPs, television and newspapers should give greater coverage to the activities and the opinions of factory workers and the unemployed. Such criticism from the Left of the political spectrum is an enduring feature of debate, but on occasion criticism is leveled by government and other elements of the existing political system. Such criticism often stems from media coverage of bodies and activities that are opposed to the existing political order. In particular, reporting on the Irish Republican Army (IRA) in Northern Ireland, and especially the interviewing of IRA leaders and sympathizers, has sometimes generated a strong reaction from political leaders in Britain. The response of the media, especially the broadcasting media (which are most sensitive to criticisms from government sources), is that coverage does not imply approval and that to fail to report what is going on in the province would constitute a form of censorship.

Criticism of the media function of legitimation has extended, more obviously, to its overt attempts to reinforce the legitimacy of particular institutions or of specific actions. Opponents of the monarchy decry the extent not only of coverage given the royal family by the media but also the editorializing and some degree of sycophancy in its support. When in April 2000 the BBC revealed that it did not intend to provide live coverage of a parade in honor of the one hundredth birthday in August of Queen Elizabeth the Queen Mother, two tabloid newspapers attacked the BBC in lead front-page stories. And just as the media may be accused of indulging in overt attempts at legitimation, various media—especially certain newspapers—are accused also of seeking to deny the legitimacy of certain bodies and types of activity. Among groups portrayed as being in some respect not legitimate, and hence deserving of public disapproval, are "new age" travelers, strikers, demonstrators, communists, homosexuals, and individuals dubbed "social security scroungers" who manage to obtain social security payments to which they are not entitled.

On occasion, the media have also come under pressure from the government of the day for failing to indulge in more overt approval of particular actions. This has been notable at times of national crisis, especially when British troops have been in action abroad: for example, during the Falklands War in 1982. Though some newspapers were enthusiastic in their support of the British action in the Falklands, some media—notably television—were accused of treating Argentinean news releases as being on a par with those of the British and of seeking to present in a neutral fashion both sides of the dispute. The BBC came in for special condemnation from Conservative MPs when a *Panorama* program devoted itself to a study of the Conservative critics of the action. Such programs were taken by some Conservatives as reinforcing their belief that the BBC was manned by left-wing sympathizers.

Less dramatically and more pervasively, the media also come under pressure from government to give favorable coverage to domestic government policy and the actions of ministers. Editors and reporters come under pressure to provide similar positive coverage for opposition parties and other political actors. However, the government of the day has the advantage of being what it is—the government. What it does is deemed newsworthy, more so than the activities of opposition parties. Increasingly, government is accused of indulging in "spin doctoring," that is, trying to give a particular "spin" to events that is favorable to its position. As soon as some news breaks, government press officers are busy phoning news editors to provide the government's particular interpretation of events. Prime minister Tony Blair has a press secretary, Alistair Campbell, who wields considerable power over ministers and who shapes and controls the government's response to events. The government came in for considerable criticism following its election in 1997 for trying to politicize the government press service, with a number of career press officers in government departments being removed or resigning. Opposition parties have criticized both the coverage the government receives and the extent to which the stories, and the political agenda, are shaped by the spin doctoring of the Downing Street press office.

Political bias in the media thus takes different forms. There is a bias in favor of established institutions and a bias toward—and against—certain groups in society. There is some partisan bias, especially on the part of newspapers. Critics also ascribe some bias to the broadcast media, though the criticism sometimes comes from both Left and Right. The Left regard the broadcast media as inherently conservative. Many on the Right complain of an anti-Conservative bias in the BBC. There is also a perceived media bias in favor of the government of the day. That bias, according to Conservatives, has been pronounced during the premiership of Tony Blair. Whereas Conservative ministers used to cultivate newspaper proprietors, Labour politicians have cultivated news editors. The Labour government has benefited from the size of its parliamentary majority and a continuous lead in the opinion polls in the years since it was elected to government. The media gravitate toward the government as the source of important stories, and editors do not wish to lose their sources. The Blair government has exploited that fact possibly more ruthlessly than any of its predecessors.

Creating news.   Other criticisms of media influence have centered on the media's ability to set the agenda of political debate and on the extent to which events may be manufactured for the benefit of media coverage. The former is an important but possibly overstated point. By selecting certain materials and events to cover, newspapers and news programs can influence the agenda of political debate. However, for that debate to be sustained, the media have to find some apparently solid base on which to pursue it and it has to be considered a salient issue by those who participate in the debate. If an issue fails to elicit a response or, worse still, produces a counterproductive response (readers or viewers objecting to the line taken), then media coverage may be affected accordingly—that is, the issue may not be pursued or the editorial policy may be changed. In the case of newspapers, it is important to recall that their primary concern is to sell copies. Taking an unpopular political line that could jeopardize sales of the newspaper would be unlikely to find favor with the proprietors. Although the significance of the media in helping set the agenda of political debate is great, the preceding qualification is important. They rarely can help influence that debate by operating in a political vacuum.

The accusation that events are created for the benefit of media coverage is an important and contemporary one. Clearly, politicians and others, as we have seen, modify their actions to try to ensure media coverage. Where controversy arises is in the cases of violent demonstrations or specific acts of violence being carried out, allegedly, to attract media attention. By being present on the streets of Belfast during the time of "the troubles," or during riots in Trafalgar Square in London, television crews have been criticized for encouraging—not actively, but passively, by virtue of their presence waiting for something to happen—the stoning of troops or police by rioters. Again, it is important to stress that rioting is unlikely to take place merely for its own sake (so-called "copycat" rioting is rarely sustained), but had camera crews not been present, the incidents that occurred might not have been as extensive or as violent as they were. The problem for the media, primarily the broadcast media, is deciding what to do in such circumstances. Once rioting has begun, they can hardly ignore it. Yet, once present at the scene, they are open to claims that their presence served to instigate continued or renewed rioting. The problem was not helped by claims in the late 1990s that some skirmishes in overseas conflicts, such as Sierra Leone, were reenacted for the benefit of the cameras.

Publishing offensive material.   Though there are, as we have seen, some legal constraints on what may be printed or broadcast, editors have considerable freedom in deciding what to publish. What they publish sometimes attracts criticism for going beyond the bounds of what is socially and politically acceptable. Some material is deemed politically unacceptable, for instance printing information about how to make a bomb or security arrangements for a public figure. Some material is deemed socially offensive. This tends to be the more extensive category. Such material does not fall afoul of the objection that it invades privacy but rather that it is degrading and is offensive to the reader or viewer. Some newspapers publish pictures of seminude women, television channels occasionally screen programs with simulated violence or sex, and some media carry stories that are deemed offensive to particular groups in society. Sexually explicit material is available on video, and the Internet has created access to a range of unregulated material. Among the established mass media, the *Sun* newspaper has a longstanding reputation for its topless "page three girls." Channel 5 has acquired a reputation for screening programs portraying sex. In 1999 there was particular criticism of a fictional program, "Queer as Folk," broadcast on Channel 4, that vividly portrayed sexual activity among homosexual men. Complaints are variously made to the Broadcasting Standards Commission and the Press Complaints Commission. The biggest contemporary concerns are whether or not there is a link between the portrayal of physical and sexual violence on the television or film screen and its occurrence in real life and with the impact of the Internet. Though research has rarely found proof of a causal link between violence on screen and in real life, some high profile cases of murder, in which the assailant has watched a particular film, have fueled popular beliefs that there is such a link. Problems encountered with children being able to watch unsuitable programs on television are now writ large in terms of what they can access on the Internet. Whereas individuals can complain about a television program, and there are mechanisms for limiting what is shown, there are no established avenues for complaining about, or limiting, what is available on the Internet.

CONCLUSION

The mass media in Britain play a significant, indeed vital, role in the political process. They serve to communicate information to a large audience. By virtue of the way in which they present that information, they can and do exert influence on attitudes toward the political system, on partisan support, on attitudes toward particular issues, and on politicians' behavior. They help set the agenda of political debate. Not only do they help communicate contemporary political debate, they are themselves in part the subject of that debate. They remain the subject of criticism, not least (but by no means exclusively) on grounds of political bias and their limited coverage of politics. Though constituting the primary means for communicating political information to a mass audience, the national newspapers and the broadcast media remain first and foremost commercial concerns intent on maintaining readership and viewing figures. To achieve a large audience, they are predominantly media of entertainment. Indeed, they are moving even further in that direction, facing accusations of a "dumbing down" of quality as they compete in a more fragmented and competitive marketplace. In 2000, the most-watched television programs remained, as had been the case in previous decades, soap operas: *Coronation Street,* on ITV (the longest running soap opera on British television), and *Eastenders,* the BBC's answer to *Coronation Street.* To the media, their output is meeting the demands of the market. To critics, they are pandering to the lowest common denominator.

NOTES

[1] J. Whale, *The Press and the Media* (Fontana, 1977), p. 86.
[2] S. Peak and P. Fisher (eds.), *The Media Guide 1999* (Fourth Estate, 1999), p. 28.
[3] *Britain 1998: An Official Handbook* (The Stationery Office, 1998), p. 501.
[4] Andrew Wiseman's Television Room, via Media UK Internet Directory.
[5] *Social Trends 99* (The Stationery Office, 1999), p. 212.
[6] C. Seymour-Ure, *The British Press and Broadcasting Since 1945* (Blackwell, 1991), pp. 129–133.

[7] J. Curran and J. Seaton, *Power without Responsibility: The Press and Broadcasting in Britain,* 4th ed. (Routledge, 1991), p. 116.

[8] Figures from Durrants as reproduced in Peak and Fisher, *The Media Guide 1999,* p. 30.

[9] "Fluctuations on the Presidential Exchange," *Time,* November 9, 1981, p. 60.

[10] *The Handling of Press and Public Information during the Falklands Conflict,* First Report from the Select Committee on Defence, Session 1981–82, HC 17-I (Her Majesty's Stationery Office, 1982), p. xiv.

[11] See Curran and Seaton, p. 126.

[12] J. Klapper, *The Effects of Mass Communication* (Free Press, 1960), pp. 15–18.

[13] J. Whale, *The Politics of the Media* (Longman, 1977), p. 85.

[14] D. Butler and D. Stokes, *Political Change in Britain* (Penguin, 1971), pp. 281–300.

[15] Butler and Stokes, p. 291.

[16] P. Dunleavy and C. T. Husbands, "Media Influences on Voting in 1983," in J. Anderson and A. Cochrane (eds.), *A State of Crisis* (Hodder & Stoughton, 1989) pp. 291–292.

[17] J. Curtice and H. Semetko, "Does it Matter What the Papers Say?" in A. Heath, R. Jowell and J. Curtice, with B. Taylor, *Labour's Last Chance: The 1992 Election and Beyond* (Dartmouth, 1994), p. 44.

[18] M. Scammell and M. Harrop, "The Press," in D. Butler and D. Kavanagh, *The British General Election of 1997* (Macmillan, 1997), p. 184.

[19] The Commission was established in 1997 to replace two existing bodies, the Broadcasting Standards Council and the Broadcasting Complaints Commission.

[20] Among those who have done so are Jeffrey (now Lord) Archer, the novelist and former deputy chairman of the Conservative party, who successfully sued the *Star,* and Elton John, the singer, successful in a major action against the *Sun,* settled out of court for a seven-figure sum. See Seymour-Ure, pp. 228–229.

[21] MORI, *British Public Opinion,* Vol. XXII, 1, 1999, p. 1. The poll was conducted in January 1999.

Part VI

Conclusion

CHAPTER 16

Flux and Strength
A Book with Two Themes

The British polity has witnessed major changes in recent years. Those changes have been pronounced in the past three decades and especially in the years since 1997. The constitutional and political landscape of Britain looks very different at the start of the twenty-first century from that which existed in the 1970s and even at the beginning of the 1990s. It is impossible not to be struck by the extent of the change. The *British Polity* was first published in 1984. In preparing this, the fourth edition, chapters had to be rewritten or revised several times to keep abreast of what was taking place. This chapter itself bears testimony to the extent of change. The title remains the same as in earlier editions—I wish to address two themes—but the content is different.

The two themes developed in earlier editions were those of change and continuity. They remain appropriate themes for this edition. However, in this chapter, I wish to develop two arguments about continuity. The first is essentially objective: That is, to identify the extent to which continuity is a feature of the British polity. The second is subjective: That is, to argue that the greater the continuity the better.

The British polity has been moving in a direction that will be familiar to American readers. Reformers have been pressing for a political system in which power is dispersed: Dispersed among different branches of government—executive, legislative, and judicial—and dispersed among different levels of government. They have been pressing for a system in which the rights of citizens enjoy some degree of constitutional protection, those rights embodied in a formal, and judicially protected, document. They have, in recent years, achieved a measure of success. In American eyes, these developments may appear both unremarkable and unobjectionable. Why should the United Kingdom not move towards features that are well-established, indeed at the core of, the American polity?

I shall argue that the basic and long-established features of the "traditional" British constitution have served the nation well and offer benefits that the new constitutional framework sought by reformers cannot offer. The moves away from that traditional constitution have undermined a system that has worked well. The changes have also distracted attention from what should be the real debate about the British polity: That is, how to adapt to changes in the international environment. The challenges to the British polity come not from within its shores but from beyond its shores.

THE EXTENT OF CHANGE

The extent of change is clear from the foregoing chapters. As we have seen in Chapter 4, there have been two major waves of constitutional change. The first wave derives from Britain's membership in the European Union. Membership has had significant constitutional, economic, and political consequences (Chapter 9). Membership has served to undermine the core doctrine at the heart of the British constitution: that of parliamentary sovereignty. The second wave began in 1997, following the election of a Labour government. The new government introduced a number of measures of constitutional change. Elected assemblies have been created in Scotland, Wales, and Northern Ireland (Chapter 10). London also now has an elected mayor and strategic authority. These changes followed referendums, no longer novel constitutional devices but still unusual ones. The new bodies have been elected by electoral systems that depart from the system used for British parliamentary elections. The government also achieved passage of the Human Rights Act, incorporating the European Convention on Human Rights into British law. That incorporation, combined with membership in the EU and the devolution of powers to the new assemblies, has introduced a new judicial dimension to the constitution (Chapter 14). As we have seen in Chapter 4, this list is not exhaustive. There have been other measures,[1] including a change in the membership of the second chamber of Parliament. The two waves continue to flow and to overlap. There is to be another intergovernmental conference to consider further institutional reform within the European Union. There are demands for an elected second chamber. There is pressure for the further use of referendums, not least on the issue of reform of the electoral system for parliamentary elections and on a single European currency.

The fact of change is clear. The changes have been described in the preceding chapters. As we have also seen, there have also been notable changes in the social and political landscape. Our focus is the changing constitutional landscape. To put the change in context, we have to understand the demands for change.

DEMANDS FOR CHANGE

The constitution was not a subject of much debate in the quarter century after the end of the Second World War. The country had emerged victorious. Its institutions, including Parliament, had continued to function during the conflict.

Postwar decades witnessed relative economic prosperity (see Chapter 3). The political system appeared to function well. Britain had an effective two-party system and only a small percentage of citizens failed to vote in elections. The Westminster model of government was rarely discussed, other than occasionally for the purpose of praise and for recommending its emulation elsewhere. It was variously exported to newly independent colonies.

The situation was to change in the 1960s and, more especially, the 1970s. As we have seen (Chapter 3), the country saw an economic downturn. It lagged behind its European neighbors. Northern Ireland witnessed the beginning of "the troubles" (see Chapter 10). Stagflation became a feature of the 1970s. At one point the annual inflation rate topped 25 percent. There were two general elections in one year, neither producing a notably decisive outcome. The proportion of voters going to the polls declined, as did the proportion voting for either of the two main parties (Chapter 5). There was a growing perception that the political system was dysfunctional. In the view of an increasing number of critics, it was not sufficient to replace one party in government with another. The system itself was seen as part of the problem. There were various demands for constitutional reform. Initially, these demands were rather disparate. There was little experience of discussing the constitution as a constitution: The tradition of constitutional discourse, which has sometimes been a feature of the nation's history, had disappeared in the years after 1945. There were calls for a new electoral system and for a Bill of Rights but these were not integrated into intellectually coherent approaches to constitutional change. This was to change in the 1980s.

During the 1980s, it was possible to discern a number of emerging approaches to constitutional change. Seven approaches have been identified: These are shown in Figure 16.1. Each approach had its advocates. The high-Tory approach was not prominent but it had its supporters. The 1970s had seen some form of tripartite cooperation between government, business, and labor (Chapter 7) and advocates of the group approach wanted this to be taken further. The socialist and Marxist approaches were variously articulated in magazines and pamphlets and had some articulate supporters. The socialist approach had a particular influence in the Labour party in the early 1980s. The party's manifesto in the 1983 general election was essentially a socialist manifesto, advocating— among other things—British withdrawal from the European Community (see Chapter 6). The "new right" approach also came to the fore. There were various new-right think tanks coming up with new ideas and publishing pamphlets. The deputy director of the Institute of Economic Affairs—a long-established think tank—argued the case for a "free market written constitution." The approach found a high profile supporter in the leader of the Conservative party, Margaret Thatcher. Though she supported the basic constitutional framework—she was essentially an adherent to the traditional approach—her support for the free market nonetheless meant that she had no qualms about tackling vested interests that interfered with the operation of the market. The liberal approach gained momentum in the 1970s and 1980s. It was supported by the Liberal party and the successor Liberal Democrat party but acquired new adherents as more people became critical of existing constitutional arrangements. In 1988, the

---

High Tory

Believes that the conveniences of existing arrangements are preferable to the unknown. Argues that the constitution has evolved organically and cannot be improved by artificial change. It is opposed not only to major reforms—such as electoral reform and an elected second chamber—but also to minor changes to existing arrangements. Its stance on any proposed reform is thus predictable: It is against it.

Socialist

Believes that the political system should be geared to realizing the wishes of the people. This approach favors reform, but a particular type of reform. It seeks strong government, but a party-dominated strong government, with adherence to the principle of intraparty democracy and the concept of the mandate. It wants to shift power from the existing "top-down" form of control (government to people) to a "bottom-up" form (people to government), with party acting as the channel for the exercise of that control. It favors limiting the powers of the prime minister, sweeping away privileged positions (monarchy, unelected members of a second chamber), and the use of more elective processes, both for public offices as well as within the Labour Party. It wants, for example, the election of members of a Labour cabinet by Labour MPs. It is wary of, or opposed to, reforms that might prevent the return of a socialist government and the implementation of a socialist program. For government to carry through socialist policies, it has to be free of constitutional constraints that favor or are dominated by its opponents.

Marxist

Sees the restructuring of the political system as largely irrelevant, certainly in the long run, serving merely to delay the collapse of capitalist society. Government, any government, is forced to work in the interests of finance capital. Whatever the structures, government will be constrained by external elites, and those elites will themselves be forced to follow rather than determine events. The clash between the imperatives of capitalism and decreasing profit rates in the meso-economy determine what capitalists do. Political structures will be changed in order to facilitate the hegemonic position of capitalism. Constitutional reform, in consequence, is not advocated but rather taken as demonstrating tensions within the international capitalist economy.

Group

Favors a consensual policy-making process, incorporating organized interests. Argues that an integrated process can facilitate a more stable economic system and therefore seeks the co-option of functional interests into the governmental process. Supporters of this approach have cited countries such as Germany as examples of what can be achieved. This approach, in its pure form, favors a functional second chamber as well as a right for organized interests to be consulted on policy proposals in their sector.

New Right

Believes in the superiority of the free market. State intervention in economic affairs is viewed as illegitimate and dangerous, distorting the natural forces of the market and denying the consumer the freedom to choose. The state should therefore withdraw from economic activity. This entails a contraction of the public sector, with state-owned industries being returned to the private sector. If institutions need reforming in order to facilitate the free market, then so be it: Under this approach, no institution is deemed sacrosanct.

FIGURE 16.1   Approaches to constitutional change

Liberal

Derives from traditional liberal theory and emphasises the centrality of what Giovanni Sartori in *Democratic Theory* terms "the theory and practice of individual liberty, juridicial defence and the constitutional state." It views the individual as increasingly isolated in decision making, being pushed aside by powerful interests and divorced from a highly centralized governmental process that is dominated by a single party. The individual has no means of protection, hence the need for radical constitutional change. In its pure form, the approach embraces federalism, a system of proportional representation for parliamentary elections, an entrenched Bill of Rights, and an elected second chamber, with the new constitutional structure codified in a written constitution. These changes would shift power from government to the individual. The only reform about which it is ambivalent is the use of referendums, some adherents to this approach seeing the referendum as a device for oppression by the majority.

Traditional

Draws on Tory theory in its emphasis on the need for strong government and on Whig theory in stressing the importance of Parliament as the agent for setting the limits within which government may act. These emphases coalesce in the Westminster model of government, a model that is part descriptive (what is) and part prescriptive (what should be). Government, in this model, must be able to formulate a coherent program of public policy, with Parliament scrutinizing the actions and the program of government and providing the limits within which government may govern. This approach stresses the importance of the House of Commons as the deliberative body of the nation, citizens exhibiting a contingent deference to the deliberative wisdom of Parliament. The approach opposes any change that damages the basic features of the Westminster model but is not opposed to changes designed to strengthen the model.

FIGURE 16.1   (continued)

SOURCE: Adapted from P. Norton, *The Constitution in Flux* (Blackwell, 1982) and P. Norton, "The Constitution." in B. Jones (ed.), *Politics UK*, 4th ed. (Pearson Education, 2000).

tercentenary year of the Glorious Revolution of 1688, a new reform movement, Charter '88, was formed to draw together those who supported a new constitutional settlement for the United Kingdom. The organization, as its name implies, subscribed to a charter of reforms, at the heart of which was a written constitution, and invited supporters to sign up to the charter. By 1991 it had attracted 25,000 signatures. It published pamphlets and papers as well as organizing meetings: It attracted media attention, especially from one of the broadsheet newspapers, the *Guardian*. The traditional approach favored the Westminster model of government and during this period was powerful, not so much through advocacy but through its adherents being in government. The approach attracted support especially, though not exclusively, from Conservatives, and the Conservative party was in government. Some of the most articulate supporters of the traditional approach were seated around the Cabinet table.

The situation was to change in the 1990s. In the first half of the decade the debate started to polarize around two of the approaches. The high-Tory approach had never been too prominent and did not make any of the running in debate. Events in central and eastern Europe, coupled with the changes made to the Labour party under the leadership of Neil Kinnock and John Smith

(Chapter 6), undermined the prominence and the credibility of the Socialist and Marxist approaches. The group approach had been overshadowed by the new-right approach and was further marginalized by the Labour party moving towards an acceptance of the market economy. The new-right approach lost its icon when Margaret Thatcher lost the leadership of the Conservative party in 1990. Though her successor, John Major, pursued her economic policies, he was—in terms of the constitution—committed to the traditional approach. The liberal and the traditional approaches were the beneficiaries of the changes. Some notable intellectuals on the left of the political spectrum, including the editor of the journal *Marxism Today,* threw their support behind Charter '88. High Tories made common cause with supporters of the traditional approach in opposing radical change. The traditional approach also found supporters articulating the case for the Westminster model. Previously, it had been assumed that by engaging in debate with supporters of Charter '88 it would raise the profile of the reform movement: It was hoped that by ignoring the movement it would decline and disappear. When it was clear that this was not going to happen, traditionalists began to put their heads above the political parapet and argue their case. Among those doing so were Cabinet ministers such as foreign secretary Douglas Hurd and education secretary John Patten.[2] The prime minister, John Major, was also a powerful advocate of the traditional approach, arguing especially against devolution and in favor of the existing union.

The 1990s thus saw an important debate taking place on constitutional change. There were powerful arguments advanced for and against change. The Liberal Democrats were wedded to a new constitutional settlement for the United Kingdom. The Conservatives, the party in power, were wedded to the existing Westminster model of government. The Labour party favored some change and in 1997 it was elected to power and began, as we have seen (Chapter 4), to implement measures of constitutional change. Those changes we have identified throughout this volume. However, the changes that have taken place have not replaced the Westminster model of government with another. Instead, as we mentioned in Chapter 4, what Britain has is a modified Westminster model of government.

The Labour party in the 1980s and 1990s moved away from the socialist approach to constitutional change. It embraced some of the liberal agenda. The more time the party spent as the "out" party in British politics, the more attractive some element of constitutional change began to appear. If the party could not prosper under the existing constitutional arrangements, perhaps the time had come to consider new constitutional arrangements? The party was also opposed to what it saw as the effects of a centralized and arrogant government. It began to advocate some change to the existing constitution. It was committed to devolution of powers to Scotland and Wales, not least because in Scotland the Scottish National party was the chief challenger to its dominant position and it wanted to undermine the SNP's position. It began to advocate a charter of rights and many members began to see some merit in changing the electoral system for parliamentary elections. The party's manifesto in the 1992 general election moved the party in the direction of the liberal approach but fell short of embracing all the elements of that approach. Its manifesto in the 1997 general election was similar, though arguably not moving quite as far as the 1992 manifesto. The 1992 manifesto was the high point of Labour's advocacy of anything approaching the liberal approach. However, the closest the liberal approach came to realizing its goals was in 1997, when Labour was elected to power. As we have seen, some of the things it wanted were introduced by the Labour government.

However, the Labour party has never fully embraced the liberal approach. Though it was the "out" party in British politics for 18 years, from 1979 to 1997, it was nonetheless the alternative party of government. As the 1990s progressed, it became apparent that it was likely to become the "in" party. It was therefore wary of committing itself to measures that could limit in when it was in government. As we have seen, when returned to government, it introduced various measures of constitutional change, including devolution, the incorporation of the European Convention on Human Rights, and reforming the composition of the second chamber. What is equally important to note, though, is what the government did not do. It did not move to destroy the doctrine of parliamentary sovereignty. Parliament retains the powers to abolish or change the elected assemblies in the different parts of the United Kingdom. (As we saw in Chapter 10, the secretary of state for Northern Ireland early in 2000 exercised the powers given him by Parliament to suspend, albeit temporarily, the Northern Ireland assembly.) The courts cannot strike down acts of Parliament as being contrary to the European Convention on Human Rights. The government set up a commission on the voting system (Chapter 5) but did not move to hold a referendum on the voting system. Though it managed to remove most hereditary peers from membership of the House of Lords, it did not move to replace an unelected second chamber with an elected chamber (Chapter 12). Though supporting the Amsterdam treaty, the treaty was somewhat less radical than earlier treaties (Chapter 9) and, although projecting itself as being "Euro-friendly," the government was not prepared to commit itself to membership in a single European currency. In short, the government was careful not to destroy its capacity to gets its way, ultimately, through utilizing its parliamentary majority.

The support of the Labour government for the liberal approach to the constitution was thus, at best, highly qualified support. It did not embrace the approach, it did not wholly discard the traditional approach, and it failed to generate an approach of its own. It was accused of adopting a stance that was essentially disparate and discrete, similar to that taken by people advocating constitutional change in the 1970s: They saw particular problems and addressed them, but failed to put them in any intellectually coherent approach to change. When asked in Parliament—by this writer—what approach the government adhered to, and what form of constitution it wanted to see in place in five or ten years' time, ministers were silent. The constitution of the United Kingdom is being changed, but not according to any particular principle or goal. Hence, as we have seen, the country now has not a new constitution but a modified—critics claim a vandalized—Westminster model.

The nature of the change introduced by the Labour government creates problems for the political parties. In the case of the Labour party, the problem is immediate. For the Conservative party, the problem is prospective. The problem can be gleaned from our foregoing comments. Though it has introduced various changes, the Labour government cannot fit them into a coherent approach to constitutional change. In a debate in March 2000 on reform of the House of Lords, the government announced that it would broadly accept the report of the royal commission that it had set up to consider reform (Chapter 12). In a contribution to the debate, I pointed out that the government had announced what it intended to do but had failed to say where it thought it was actually going. The minister responding to the debate failed to say where the government thought it was going. No minister has been able to explain the type of constitution that the government would like to see in place in the twenty-first century.

For the Conservative party, the problem is prospective. It has been able to adopt a consistent stance in response to the measures of constitutional reform introduced by the Labour government: It has opposed them. It managed to get ahead in debate in opposing the government's proposals for reform of the second chamber. It also mounted an effective campaign against the report of the commission on the voting system. However, it faces a problem in the future: What is a Conservative government to do in response to the constitution that it inherits? There is a recognition that it cannot go back to the situation as it existed before 1997. Conservative leader William Hague has accepted that devolution is a feature now of the British polity. Does, then, a Conservative government seek to conserve that which exists at the time that it takes over? Or does it seek to reform the constitution, perhaps seeking to strengthen the features of the Westminster model insofar as it is possible to do so without completely reverting to the pre-1997 position? The latter is the more likely, though it is difficult to articulate what form the changes will take when the constitution is still changing under a Labour government.

For the Liberal Democrats, the problem is one of tempering principle with expediency. The party supports the liberal approach to the constitution. Intellectually and morally, it has no problem with that stance. However, it would also like to be in government. Recognizing that this may not be possible on its own, it is prepared to cooperate with another party. In 1996 it formed a joint consultation committee with the Labour party.[3] In 1997, a cabinet committee, drawing together ministers and leading members of the party, was formed. There is the prospect that the party could hold the balance of power in a future Parliament in which no one party holds an absolute majority. Recognition of this fact is believed to motivate Tony Blair in maintaining a dialogue with the Liberal Democrats. Recognition that there is no guarantee of a "hung" Parliament means that the Liberal Democrats cannot afford to be too demanding in their negotiations with the Labour party. The dilemma they face is shown in respect to electoral reform. The party is deeply committed to a system of proportional representation and has variously claimed that a commitment to introduce it would be a precondition of any future pact with the Labour party. However, it has proved willing to modify its position, and in 2000 it was reported that it had accepted that there would be no referendum on the electoral system before the next general election and the prime minister had decided against implementing the report of the commission on the voting system. The party leaves itself open to the accusation of abandoning its principles in favor of achieving political power.

The parties thus face problems in addressing constitutional change. The nature of constitutional change also means that the debate about the future shape of the constitution has not let up. There remains something of a polarization around the liberal and traditional approaches. There are those arguing that the United Kingdom must have a new constitutional settlement. Then there are those who argue that the Westminster model has served the nation well and that, as far as it is possible to do so, it should be retained. A modified Westminster model is not as good as the Westminster model, but it is better than the alternatives.

THE LIBERAL APPROACH

The liberal approach stresses the centrality of the individual and limited government. Its advocates argue that the political system was able to meet its goals in the nineteenth century. The scope of public policy was essentially limited, primarily to the defense of the nation and the maintenance of the Queen's peace. There were various checks and balances in the system, not least with each House of Parliament enjoying powers to block measures of the other. The political rights of the individual were being extended, especially through reform of the franchise. The balance within the constitution prevented an electoral majority from oppressing minorities or individuals.[4] The concepts of limited government and of the rights of the individual were well established. Even in the First World War there was apparently opposition to providing armed escorts to merchant ships on the grounds that this interfered with the freedom of the captains to determine their own courses.

While such a situation pertained, the liberal approach was not a radical one. However, the situation changed in the last quarter of the twentieth century. There was the perception that individual liberties were under threat, not just from government but from other public bodies and private organizations. A government, secure in its parliamentary majority, was able to get whatever measure it wished enacted. In the 1960s and 1970s it listened to organized interests; after 1979, it was accused of not listening to any particular interests. In the formulation of public policy, individuals were ignored. Governments fought to bolster their position, pushing through whatever they wanted against the vocal opposition of their political opponents. Both parties sought to out-promise the other in general elections, the winner then committed to policies that might be expensive to fulfill.

Institutions were becoming divorced from citizens and increasingly unable to protect them and act in their interests. As institutions failed to deliver what was expected of them, so—as we noted in Chapter 2—trust in the effectiveness and equity of government began to decline. The less it was trusted, the less able it was to proceed on the basis of cooperation. Power became more centralized in order to enable government to get its way. The result, according to critics such as Samuel Beer, was a "collapse" in the civic culture. As we saw in Chapter 2, the empirical basis for this claim was to be found in the decline in voter turnout, in party membership, in popular support for a change in the system of government, and in perceptions of a centralization of power. Lord Hailsham in 1976 coined the phrase "elective dictatorship." This was taken by reformers as a fair characterization of the system of government. The "dictatorship" became more pronounced as the "elective" element diminished, parties gaining power on a minority of votes. Surveys showed that most people thought that the system of government needed "a great deal" of improvement or could be "improved quite a lot." As we saw in Chapter 2, in 1991, 63 percent gave those responses. In 1995 the figure had increased to 75 percent.

According to adherents of the liberal approach, the political system was thus dysfunctional. It needed fundamental reform in order to restore the centrality of the individual. The approach stressed decentralization of decision making. This would limit an overmighty government and allow greater opportunities for citizens to engage in decision making. Greater participation, it was argued, would help maintain consent for the political system as well as improve the quality of decision making: Decisions would be taken closer to those affected by the decisions. The approach also stresses the use of checks and balances in the political system: Power should be made to counteract power. Each institutional element of the system should be strengthened. In the legislature, this meant an elected second chamber. It also meant a powerful judiciary; the rights of the individual could be protected through a bill of rights, with those rights then being enforced through the courts. An entrenched bill of rights would put rights beyond the reach of simple majorities in the two Houses of Parliament. The approach also stresses the need for consensus, moving away from the hegemony (and hence the arrogance) of a single-party government. To this end, it seeks the end of an adversary system in which parties compete with one another for the all-or-nothing spoils of election victory.

The liberal approach thus embraces a new constitution for the United Kingdom. We have outlined already the measures it proposes. It favors decentralization through a devolution of powers or—in the pure form of the approach—federalism. It favors building up checks and balances through an elected second chamber and a more powerful judiciary. It wants to protect rights through an entrenched bill of rights. It believes that consensus will be encouraged through the use of a new electoral system for parliamentary elections. A new system, it argues, will deny any one party a majority of seats, thus forcing a coalition of parties to form the government. It wants the new constitution to be codified, that is, to be embodied in a written constitution. There have been various attempts to craft such a constitution.[5]

Advocates of the liberal approach support most of the changes introduced by the Labour government but they want to see the changes taken further. As we have seen, the government has moved only partially in the direction of the liberal approach. It has not abandoned the Westminster model. Supporters of the liberal approach want it to abandon that model and to introduce measures to give effect to a liberal constitution of a sort familiar to Americans. Indeed, it may seem strange to American eyes that there is opposition to introducing such a constitution. The opposition is powerful and, I shall argue, persuasive.

THE TRADITIONAL APPROACH

Those who support the traditional approach argue that the liberal approach derives from a false analysis and that it mistakes the real problems facing the nation. Further, it argues that the Westminster model of government has delivered benefits that cannot be matched by the liberal, or any other, model. The Westminster model is the most appropriate for the United Kingdom.

The extent to which the liberal argument rests on a false premise was touched upon in Chapter 2. Those arguing that there has been a collapse of the civic culture in Britain rely too heavily on data that will not bear the weight given them. Britain has not seen a collapse of attitudes and values from some golden age to a new dismal age. If there ever was anything approaching a "golden age" it was to be found in the quarter-century following World War II— certainly not before—and that period of stability and relative economic prosperity produced particularly high levels of pride in institutions, a pride tapped by Almond and Verba in *The Civic Culture*. Those heady and exceptional days may be past, but the basic orientations toward cooperation and problem solving are not. The civic culture remains intact. Britain is a pluralist society, more pluralist than ever before.[6] The culture remains essentially a deferential one, but that deference—as we have argued—is contingent. If government goes beyond what is acceptable, various mechanisms still exist to check it. That is allied with the empirical approach to problem solving and cooperation. If things appear to be going too far, then efforts are made to find a practical solution.

It is this empirical approach that is emphasized by the traditional approach to the constitution. The essentials of the system remain sound. The data that support this claim were variously identified in Chapter 2. Levels of trust in the state are higher in the United Kingdom than in Germany, America, Spain, Italy, or France (see Table 2.1). There are also high levels of trust in different professions in society: As we saw in Chapter 2, there are especially high levels of trust in the armed forces, a figure not matched by other countries that were surveyed. As we also saw, the highest levels of national pride in the 1998 *British—and European—Social Attitudes* survey were to be found in Britain, ahead of Spain, Sweden, and Germany.

There is also a higher level of political participation in the United Kingdom than in many other Western countries. That participation is usually peaceful participation. As we mentioned in Chapter 2, the MORI State of the Nation poll in 1995 found that 55 percent of those questioned had signed a petition in the preceding two or three years; only 7 percent had taken part in a demonstration, picket, march, or sit-in. Furthermore, contrary to the claims of advocates of the liberal approach, those levels have not declined in recent years. MORI surveys have shown that levels of participation have not changed dramatically over the past three decades. Table 16.1 reveals the extent to which participation levels are best described as stable. If there is a "decline" in the civic culture, then that is not apparent

TABLE 16.1   Socio-political activity in the United Kingdom, 1971–1999

Q. Which of these things on the list, if any, have you done in the last two or three years?

A. Voted in a general election
B. Helped on fund-raising drives
C. Urged someone to get in touch with a local councillor or MP
D. Urged someone outside my family to vote
E. Made a speech before an organized group
F. Presented my views to a local councillor or MP
G. Been an officer for an organization or club
H. Written a letter to an editor
I. Taken an active part in political campaigning
J. Stood for public office

	A %	B %	C %	D %	E %	F %	G %	H %	I %	J %	None %
1971	77	22	13	18	12	10	15	6	3	1	16
1972	74	22	14	18	11	11	14	6	4	—	17
1973	68	19	14	18	9	11	12	6	3	1	23
1974	80	18	13	23	8	10	11	4	3	1	14
1975	(Not available)										
1976	77	24	16	20	11	12	14	6	4	1	14
1977	76	26	16	18	11	12	15	5	4	1	15
1978	68	26	15	18	12	11	15	6	3	—	19
1979	75	26	18	25	12	15	13	5	3	1	15
1980	74	28	16	19	12	13	14	7	3	1	n/a
1981	72	28	16	19	11	12	10	5	3	1	n/a
1982	69	31	17	17	14	13	14	6	3	1	17
1983	79	30	17	24	15	15	16	6	4	1	12
1984	74	26	16	19	13	15	14	6	4	1	17
1985	72	28	17	17	13	16	13	7	4	1	17
1986	71	33	18	18	16	17	16	7	4	1	17
1987	79	33	20	25	17	15	15	8	4	1	11
1988	74	35	19	20	16	15	15	7	4	1	14
1989	72	34	18	19	15	15	12	8	3	1	16
1990	69	35	20	18	15	15	14	8	3	1	16
1991	63	32	18	16	17	15	13	7	3	1	19
1992	80	32	18	22	17	14	12	6	3	1	11
1993	76	31	17	16	16	14	11	7	4	1	14
1994	73	27	18	15	15	14	11	8	3	1	16
1995	69	37	21	18	19	17	16	9	3	1	15
1996	70	32	17	16	17	16	14	8	3	1	17
1997	75	33	18	22	18	15	15	9	4	1	14
1998	76	29	16	17	17	15	14	7	3	1	15
1999	75	25	14	14	15	14	12	7	3	1	16

SOURCE: MORI, *British Public Opinion,* 22 (1), Jan–Feb. 1999

from citizen participation in public affairs. Some forms of participation may not be indulged in by many citizens, but that is not evidence of decline and, as we have mentioned, participation levels in the United Kingdom tend to be higher than elsewhere.

None of this is to argue that the United Kingdom does not face a number of social and economic problems. We have touched upon these in the preceding chapters. There are also political problems. There has been a decline in the membership of the political parties. People are devoting their energies to organized groups—often single-issue groups—rather than to the political parties. There are low levels of turnout in elections to local councils and to the European Parliament. Although traditionally exhibiting low levels of turnout, the electoral turnout among young people is about a third less now than it was in the 1970s. However, where supporters of the traditional approach take issue with advocates of the liberal approach is in the explanation for these phenomena. They argue that the causes are not structural: They are not specific to the political institutions of the United Kingdom. A decline in party membership—and greater attachment to single-issue organized groups—is an international phenomenon. It is as much a feature of the United States as it is of the United Kingdom. Low turnouts in local elections are not confined to Britain: A similar phenomenon exists in the United States, most voters staying at home in off-year elections. Many countries saw a low turnout in the 1999 elections to the European Parliament. There are problems, but to ascribe them to a dysfunctional political system in the United Kingdom is misleading. So ascribing them detracts from attempts to identify the real cause of the problem.

The analysis of existing arrangements by advocates of the liberal approach is thus deemed to be flawed. The existing system is not a cause of the problems it identifies. Far from being part of the problem, traditionalists argue that the existing system remains, if anything, part of the solution. It offers a number of benefits that other systems cannot offer, and by moving away from it, one is likely to undermine rather than bolster support for the political system. The attributes of the system as a whole are not dissimilar to those ascribed to the electoral process (see Chapter 5). Fundamentally, the system delivers a high level of accountability to the electors. There is one body—the party-in-government—that is responsible for measures of public policy. Electors therefore know whom to blame, or to praise, for public policy. If they disapprove, they have the option of getting rid of the party-in-government and replacing it with another. Too much emphasis in debate is placed on the "hiring" aspects of elections and not enough on the "firing" aspects. The essence of democracy, according to Sir Karl Popper, is the capacity of citizens to get rid of the body in power and to do so in a peaceful way:

> In *The Open Society and its Enemies* I suggested that an entirely new problem should be recognized as the fundamental problem of a rational political theory. The new problem, as distinct from the old 'Who should rule?', can be formulated as follows: how is the state to be constituted so that bad rulers can be got rid of without bloodshed, without violence?[7]

The electoral system of the United Kingdom was, as Popper recognized, central to ensuring that citizens can remove a party from government. There is less potential than in continental systems, which employ forms of proportional representation, to stay in office through post-election bargaining despite a slump in electoral support. Furthermore, the system usually delivers a decisive method of election. A party can be swept out of office on election day, and on the following day a new prime minister and government are in place. There is no lengthy hiatus while parties haggle over who is to be in power. Unlike in the United States, there is no lengthy transitional period between election and taking office. There may be a change of party but there is continuity in government.

The problems associated with a new electoral system are to be found in the experience of Scotland and Wales. Under the form of additional-member system employed in Scotland, the elections produced no one party with an overall majority. The consequence was a coalition between the largest party, the Labour party, and Liberal Democrats—the party that actually came fourth in the elections. If electors do not like public policy—the product of post-election bargaining—whom do they hold to account at the next election? In Wales, there is a minority Labour administration, Labour being in power though lacking an absolute majority in the assembly. If there is a stalemate between the Assembly and the administration, whom do electors blame for the absence of policy?

The experience of Scotland and Wales also points to the dangers of moving away from the centrality of an accountable party-in-government at Westminster. The more layers of elected government there are, the less accountable each one becomes. Electors are uncertain as to which layer of government is responsible for what, and if one layer of government cannot deliver because it is blocked by another, then there is the danger of a decline in support for the system of government. Some levels of government may also be undermined if electors fail to attach significance to them. There are problems with elections to local councils in the United Kingdom as well as elections to the European Parliament. One distinguished public servant, Lord Dahrendorf—a member of the House of Lords, but previously a government minister in Germany—has queried whether the European Parliament is any more legitimate now under direct elections than it was when its members were appointed from national parliaments.

The existing system is also responsive. Ministers know that they may be turned out of office at the next election. They are therefore sensitive to public opinion and to shifts in that opinion. There is thus a closer link between electors and elected than is the case in many continental countries, where politicians can act without being unduly concerned by shifts in opinion, knowing that they are likely to be able to negotiate their way back into government after the next election. The system is also transparent. A party is elected to office on the basis of a program that it placed before the electors at the election, and that program provides the framework for action: Political parties have a good record in implementing election promises. The program is, above all, a published program; electors have a benchmark against which to assess government.

The existing system also provides representation at both a general and a particular level. The general is delivered through parties, the particular through the individual member of Parliament. The MP is the essential link between citizen and government. Constituency representation is an integral part of the existing political system and is reinforced by the political culture. For the purpose of expressing grievances and demands to government, contacting one's MP is the most popular form of personal action and is judged to be effective. MPs serve as important safety valves as well as grievance chasers on behalf of citizens.[8] The essence of the relationship between MP and citizen has been well summarized by Ivor Crewe: "The further away the local Member is from the constituency . . . the less the public approve. People want to have their Member . . . . Familiarity appears to breed content."[9] However, the general representation acts as a constraint on an abuse of the relationship. Party provides a crucial shield for MPs, protecting them from undue influence by outside groups. The political system is not open to special interests in the way that it is in the United States.

The political system in the United Kingdom is essentially stable as well as effective and flexible. It is not necessarily more stable nor more effective than some other systems, but they are central features of the system. The attributes of the system are threatened by the reforms advocated by the liberal approach. A dispersal of power, be it to devolved assemblies, the institutions of the European Union, or an elected second chamber, undermines accountability. Giving power to the courts moves power from the people's elected representatives to unelected jurists: Political decisions are decided not by a political process but by a judicial process. Though there is an acceptance of political questions being resolved by judicial means in some other polities, including the United States, it is alien to the British political culture.

Democracy, like representation, is subject to different definitions. Some define it in terms of process: that is, election. So defined, there is a case for dispersing power to different elected bodies. On that definition, the United States is a highly democratic polity. However, if democracy is defined in terms of translating popular will into legislative output, then the United States is far from democratic. There is often a mismatch between what most electors want and what Congress delivers. In the words of Hibbing and Theiss-Morse, one would be "hard-pressed to design a Congress that less accurately reflected the process preferences of the people than the one we see in the mid-1990s."[10] On this definition, it is the United Kingdom that is democratic. The measures advocated by the liberal approach are designed to temper rather than reinforce this democratic element.

The traditional approach thus emphasises the accountability of the existing arrangements and the fact that there is no popular support to move away from it. Though majorities can be found in surveys for particular items in the liberal reform agenda, there is no popular support for a new political system. Constitutional change is accorded no priority by electors and does not feature in the list of issues deemed to be the most important issues facing the nation. To traditionalists, advocates of the liberal approach offer a false prospectus and the more the United Kingdom moves in that direction the less the nation benefits.

EXTERNAL CHALLENGES

The capacity of the United Kingdom to determine issues is under challenge, but less from internal pressures than from external developments. One of these is membership in the European Union. We have already discussed some of the implications (Chapter 9). The United Kingdom is in danger of acquiring what amounts to a written constitution through its membership in the EU: The treaties establishing the European Communities and the European Union form something of a "higher law." That higher law derives its authority from an act of Parliament. Formally, the doctrine of parliamentary sovereignty remains in place. Parliament could repeal the 1972 European Communities Act. The effect would be to take Britain out of the EU, since the United Kingdom would no longer be able to fulfill its treaty commitments. However, such a withdrawal is unlikely. The United Kingdom thus has to address how to adapt its constitutional arrangements to membership in the EU without allowing greater encroachment on its domestic policy-making arrangements.

The other external development is subsumed under the heading of globalization. A liberalization in capital markets has meant a global capital market. There has been something of a globalization in terms of communications and, to a lesser extent, in terms of trade. Governments have limited capacity to affect markets. The British government discovered that, to its cost, in September 1992 when it was forced to withdraw from the European exchange rate mechanism (ERM). There is a certain inherent conflict in the stance taken by neoliberals in the United Kingdom. On the one hand, there is an embrace of the free market and hence globalization in trade and capital. On the other, neoliberals are at the forefront of opposition to the seepage of policy-making power from British government to the European Union, arguing the merits of decision making by the nation state. Yet a global market implies, indeed necessitates, some weakening of the nation state.[11] The nation state loses some of its capacity to determine outcomes; indeed, according to some critics, the nation state is beginning to crumble.[12] The inherent conflict in the neoliberal approach was exemplified by Margaret Thatcher when she was leader of the Conservative party, and it was a feature of what was termed Thatcherism (see Chapter 6). The Labour party has moved some way toward the Conservative approach: It has accepted the imperatives of a market approach and, although claiming a positive attitude toward European integration, has made clear its opposition to moves to create a United States of Europe. Under Tony Blair, the party has embraced what it has termed "The Third Way," a position somewhere between capitalism and social democracy,[13] but the essence of the approach has not been fleshed out in detail. For the political parties in Britain, there is the challenge of coping with developments external to—though also encompassing—Britain's shores. The challenges are not peculiar to the United Kingdom.[14]

CONCLUSION

At times of economic, social, or political difficulty, there has been a tendency—not confined to the United Kingdom—to look to constitutional change as a palliative or a means of dealing with the difficulty, of producing a system capable of being effective and resolving problems. At the time of the depression in the 1930s, for example, the implications for the constitution were noted by Conservative leader Stanley Baldwin. "There is bound to be unrest," he said, "when more questions are being put than statesmen can answer. Within the House of Commons itself there is a growing sense of the need for overhauling the ship of state."[15] Disappointment with the working of representative government, he observed, was no new thing. "It recurs periodically and we are in one of the fermenting periods now. It may be uncomfortable but it is not surprising."[16]

The years after the Second World War in Britain witnessed a period of stability and—especially in the 1950s—relative economic prosperity, with little debate consequently about constitutional arrangements. As the economic condition of the nation worsened in the 1960s, calls for change in structures began to be heard. Those calls became more strident in the 1970s and 1980s. Various blueprints for constitutional reform, including a new constitution, were devised. In the 1990s, much of the debate focused on the liberal and traditionalist approaches. The closing years of the decade saw several reforms being carried through. The nature of the debate is not unusual in the context of British history. What is disputed is the extent to which change is necessary and how Britain should respond to wider changes in the global environment.

NOTES

[1] See R. Blackburn and R. Plant (eds), *Constitutional Reform* (Addison Wesley Longman, 1999).

[2] See, e.g., J. Patten, *Political Culture, Conservatism and Rolling Constitutional Change* (Conservative Political Centre, 1991).

[3] The committee agreed on a report on constitutional reform. *Report of the Joint Consultative Committee on Constitutional Reform* (1997).

[4] P. Norton, *The Constitution in Flux* (Blackwell, 1982), p. 276.

[5] See, e.g., the Institute of Public Policy Research, *A Written Constitution for the United Kingdom* (Mansell, 1993).

[6] See P. Norton, "In Defence of the Constitution," in P. Norton (ed.), *New Directions in British Government?* (Edward Elgar, 1991), pp. 154–160.

[7] Sir K. Popper, "The Open Society and its Enemies Revisited," *The Economist,* April 23, 1988.

[8] See P. Norton, *Power to the People* (Conservative Policy Forum, 1998), p. 3.

[9] I. Crewe, "Electoral Reform and the Local MP," in S. E. Finer (ed.), *Adversary Politics and Electoral Reform* (Wigram, 1975), p. 322.

[10] J. R. Hibbing and E. Theiss-Morse, *Congress as Public Enemy* (Cambridge University Press, 1995), p. 161.

[11] See, e.g., T. Banuri and J. B. Schor, *Financial Openess and National Autonomy* (Oxford University Press, 1992). I am grateful to D. J. Skelton, "'EMU and the Neo-Liberal Project': The Decapitation of Parliamentary Democracy," undergraduate dissertation, University of Hull, 2000, for this source and for the clarity with which it develops the point embodied in this paragraph.

[12] K. Ohmae, *The End of the Nation State—The Rise of Regional Economies* (Free Press, 1995).

[13] See A. Giddens, *The Third Way: The Renewal of Social Democracy* (Polity Press, 1998).

[14] Bob Woodward recounts how President-elect Clinton came to realize that the success of his economic program rested on the Federal Reserve and the bond market. B. Woodward, *The Agenda* (Simon and Schuster, 1994), p. 84.

[15] S. Baldwin, *The Torch of Freedom,* 4th ed. (Hodder & Stoughton, 1937), p. 50.

[16] Ibid.

Select Reading List

This is neither a bibliography of works used nor a comprehensive survey of available literature. Rather, it is a brief guide to the main and, in particular, the most recent texts available for student use. Chapter endnotes provide a pointer to further reading for students whose intellectual appetite is not satiated by what follows.

PART I: INTRODUCTION

Various reference works provide useful facts and figures on contemporary Britain. The most regular and helpful of these are *Britain: An Official Handbook,* published annually by The Stationery Office (TSO), and *Social Trends,* compiled annually by the Central Statistical Office and also published by TSO. G. Parry, G. Moyser, and I. Day, *Political Participation and Democracy in Britain* (Cambridge University Press, 1992) provides an extensive analysis of political participation and attitudes toward participation in Britain. D. Cannadine, *Class in Britain* (Yale University Press, 1998) looks at the history of class.

The history of Britain is treated in numerous works, including the 15-volume *Oxford History of England,* published by Oxford University Press. There is also a highly acclaimed political history, *The British Political Tradition,* by W. H. Greenleaf, published in three volumes: *Vol. 1: The Rise of Collectivism* (Longman, 1983), *Vol. 2: The Ideological Inheritance* (Longman, 1983), and *Vol. 3: A Much Governed Nation* (Longman, 1987). A number of works also offer a historical perspective in analyzing political developments and the nation's problems. See D. Marquand, *The Unprincipled Society: New Demands and Old Politics* (Fontana, 1988); A. Gamble, *Britain in Decline,* 4th ed. (Macmillan, 1994); W. Self, *The State We're In* (Jonathan Cape, 1995); and

R. English and M. Kenny (eds.), *Rethinking British Decline* (Macmillan, 1999). On various explanations for Britain's economic performance, see A. Cox, S. Lee, and J. Sanderson, *The Political Economy of Modern Britain* (Edward Elgar, 1997). For analyses focusing on political developments, see A. Marr, *Ruling Britannia* (Michael Joseph, 1995) and D. Kavanagh, *The Reordering of British Politics* (Oxford University Press, 1997).

PART II: THE POLITICAL ENVIRONMENT

Several publications put the constitution in a political context. Among the more recent are P. Madgwick and D. Woodhouse, *The Law and Politics of the Constitution* (Harvester Wheatsheaf, 1995) and V. Bogdanor, *Power and the People* (Victor Gollancz, 1997). For a study of the working of constitutional arrangements, see R. Brazier, *Constitutional Practice,* 2nd ed. (Oxford University Press, 1994); P. Hennessy, *The Hidden Wiring* (Gollancz, 1995); and C. Munro, *Studies in Constitutional Law,* 2nd ed. (Butterworths, 1999). For a discussion of the reforms proposed or introduced since 1997, see J. Beatson, C. Forsyth, and I. Hare, *Constitutional Reform in the United Kingdom: Practice and Principles* (Hart Publishing, 1998) and R. Blackburn and R. Plant (eds.), *Constitutional Reform* (Longman, 1999). On the implications of constitutional change, see R. Hazell (ed.), *Constitutional Futures* (Oxford University Press, 1999). Works that are central to the current debate on the constitution—taking a particular stand on its strength and weaknesses—are listed under Part VI.

Election results, and details of candidates, are published after each general election in *The Times Guide to the House of Commons* (*The Times*). The standard works of analysis on British general elections are those published in the Nuffield election series, authored or coauthored by D. Butler and published after each election. The most recent edition is D. Butler and D. Kavanagh, *The British General Election of 1997* (Macmillan, 1997). Two other works also cover the 1997 election: A. King (ed.), *New Labour Triumphs: Britain at the Polls* (Chatham House, 1998) and A. Geddes and J. Tonge (eds.), *Labour's Landslide* (Manchester University Press, 1997). See also G. Evans and P. Norris (eds.), *Critical Elections* (Sage, 1999) which puts the 1997 election in the context of electoral change.

The electoral process is dealt with comprehensively in R. Blackburn, *The Electoral System in Britain* (Macmillan, 1995). National campaigning is addressed in D. Kavanagh, *Election Campaigning* (Blackwell, 1995). Constituency campaigning is well covered in D. Denver and G. Hands, *Modern Constituency Electioneering* (Cass, 1997). On electoral change, see P. Norris, *Electoral Change Since 1945* (Blackwell, 1997) and D. Denver, *Elections and Voting Behaviour in Britain,* 2nd ed. (Macmillan, 1998). There is an annual review, *British Elections and Parties Review,* published by Cass, which offers valuable analyses. D. Denver et al., *British Elections and Parties Review,* Vol. 8 (Cass, 1998) is especially useful on the 1997 election. D. Denver et al., *British*

*Elections and Parties Review,*Vol. 9 (Cass, 1999), covers, among other topics, partisanship and voting.

In the debate on the electoral system, the seminal work for reformers has been S. E. Finer (ed.), *Adversary Politics and Electoral Reform* (Wigram, 1975). On proposals for change, see *The Report of the Independent Commission on the Voting System,* Cm 4090-I (The Stationery Office, 1998), and P. Dunleavy, H. Margetts, B. O'Duffy, and S. Weir, *Making Votes Count* (Democratic Audit, 1997). The arguments for change are summarized in M. Linton and M. Southcott, *Making Votes Count* (Profile Books, 1998) and the arguments against in P. Norton, *Power to the People* (Conservative Policy Forum, 1998).

The classic but now dated work on political parties is R. McKenzie, *British Political Parties,* 2nd ed. (Heinemann, 1964). Recent introductory texts are R. Garner and R. Kelly, *British Political Parties Today,* 2nd ed. (Manchester University Press, 1998); J. Fisher, *British Political Parties* (Macmillan, 1999); and S. J. Ingle, *The British Party System,* 3rd ed. (Pinter, 2000). A seminal study of the effect of political parties in office is R. Rose, *Do Parties Make a Difference?* 2nd ed. (Macmillan, 1984), providing an effective rejoinder to the thesis of adversarial politics advanced by Finer in *Adversary Politics and Electoral Reform.*

On the history of the Conservative party, see R. Blake, *The Conservative Party from Peel to Major* (Arrow Books, 1997) and J. Ramsden, *An Appetite for Power: A History of the Conservative Party since 1830* (HarperCollins, 1998). An extensive treatment of the party's history, support, and organization is provided in A. Seldon and S. Ball (eds.), *Conservative Century* (Oxford University Press, 1994) and P. Norton (ed.), *The Conservative Party* (Prentice Hall/ Harvester Wheatsheaf, 1996). P. Whiteley, P. Seyd, and J. Richardson, *True Blues* (Clarendon Press, 1994) provides a fascinating study of the party's membership. S. Ludlam and M. J. Smith (eds.), *Contemporary British Conservatism* (Macmillan, 1996) offers a useful collection of analytical essays.

For a history of the Labour party, see H. Pelling and A. J. Reid, *A Short History of the Labour Party,* 11th ed. (Macmillan, 1996); E. Shaw, *The Labour Party Since 1945* (Blackwell, 1996); and A. Thorpe, *A History of the Labour Party* (Macmillan, 1997). For a more extensive treatment, see B. Brivati and A. Heffernan (eds.), *The Labour Party: A Centenary History* (Macmillan, 2000). On the party's philosophy, see G. Foote, *The Labour Party's Political Thought,* 3rd ed. (Macmillan, 1997). On "New" Labour, see B. Brivati and T. Bale (eds.), *New Labour in Power* (Routledge, 1997); L. Martell and S. Driver, *New Labour* (Polity, 1998); and S. Ludlam and S. J. Smith (eds.), *New Labour in Power* (Macmillan, 2000). On the goals of the Labour party under Tony Blair, see A. Perryman (ed.), *The Blair Agenda* (Lawrence and Wishart, 1996); A. Giddens, *The Third Way: The Renewal of Social Democracy* (Polity, 1998); and A. Giddens, *The Third Way and its Critics* (Polity, 2000).

On the Liberal party and its successor see D. MacIver, *The Liberal Democrats* (Prentice Hall/Harvester Wheatsheaf, 1996) and C. Cook, *A Short History of the Liberal Party,* 5th ed. (Macmillan, 1998). On the Social Democratic Party, see

I. Crewe and A. King, *SDP* (Oxford University Press, 1995). Also see A. Sykes, *The Rise and Fall of British Liberalism* (Longman, 1997).

On the development of group influence in British politics, see the seminal works of S. H. Beer, *Modern British Politics* (Faber, 1965; 3rd ed. 1982) and K. Middlemass, *Politics in Industrial Society* (Andre Deutsch, 1979). See also J. Richardson and A. G. Jordan, *Governing under Pressure* (Martin Robertson, 1979). On the contemporary role of pressure groups, see R. Baggott, *Pressure Groups Today* (Manchester University Press, 1995) and W. Grant, *Pressure Groups and British Politics* (Macmillan, 2000). On the relationship between business and politics, see W. Grant, *Business and Politics in Britain,* 2nd ed. (Macmillan, 1993). See also G. Jordan and W. Maloney, *The Protest Business?* (Manchester University Press, 1997). The relationship of Parliament and pressure groups is covered in M. Rush, *Parliament and Pressure Politics* (Oxford University Press, 1990) and P. Norton (ed.), *Parliaments and Pressure Groups in Western Europe* (Cass, 1998), Ch. 2.

PART III: GOVERNMENTAL DECISION MAKING

Though there are a great many works on individual prime ministers, works on the premiership as such are notable for their rarity. The principal introductory texts are A. King (ed.), *The British Prime Minister,* 2nd ed. (Macmillan, 1985); D. Shell and R. Hodder-Williams (eds.), *Churchill to Major: The British Prime Ministership since 1945* (Hurst, 1995); and G. P. Thomas, *Prime Minister and Cabinet Today* (Manchester University Press, 1998). On the development of the office, see R. Blake, *The Office of Prime Minister* (Oxford University Press, 1975). On the support and advice available to the prime minister, see J. M. Lee, G. W. Jones, and J. Burnham, *At the Centre of Whitehall* (Macmillan, 1998) and D. Kavanagh and A. Seldon, *The Powers Behind the Prime Minister* (Harper-Collins, 1999). On the argument that there is a "presidential" premiership, see M. Foley, *The Rise of the British Presidency* (Manchester University Press, 1993). The premiership is considered in comparative perspective in G. W. Jones (ed.), *West European Prime Ministers* (Frank Cass, 1991).

For a good historical work on the Cabinet, see J. P. Mackintosh, *The British Cabinet,* 3rd ed. (Stevens, 1977). More recent works covering the Cabinet include S. James, *British Cabinet Government* (Routledge, 1992); M. Burch and I. Holliday, *The British Cabinet System* (Prentice Hall/Harvester Wheatsheaf, 1996); and M. J. Smith, *The Core Executive in Britain* (Macmillan, 1999). On ministers, see R. Brazier, *Ministers of the Crown* (Clarendon Press, 1997). K. Theakston, *Junior Ministers* (Blackwell, 1987), explores a much neglected aspect of British government. On developments within the central system of government, see R. A. W. Rhodes (ed.), *Transforming British Government* (Macmillan, 2000). Revelations about the workings of cabinet and government departments are also provided by ministerial memoirs. Among the more useful are three by former chancellors of the exchequer: N. Lawson, *The View from*

No. 11 (Bantam, 1992); G. Howe, *Conflict of Loyalty* (Macmillan, 1994); and N. Lamont, *In Office* (Little, Brown, 1999). Also worth consulting are memoirs by former prime ministers: M. Thatcher, *The Downing Street Years* (HarperCollins, 1993); E. Heath, *The Course of my Life* (Hodder & Stoughton, 1998); and J. Major, *The Autobiography* (HarperCollins, 1999). The books by Lamont and Major show how it is possible to look at one event (withdrawal from the exchange rate mechanism in 1992) in completely different ways.

The civil service is explored exhaustively in P. Hennessy, *Whitehall* (Secker & Warburg, 1989). More succinct analyses are offered by K. Theakston, *The Civil Service Since 1945* (Blackwell, 1995); K. Dowding, *The Civil Service* (Routledge, 1995); C. Pilkington, *The Civil Service in Britain Today* (Manchester University Press, 1999); and R. Pyper, *The British Civil Service* (Macmillan, 1999). A critical analysis of what has happened to the Whitehall model of government is offered by C. Campbell and G. K. Wilson, *The End of Whitehall* (Blackwell, 1995).

There are also now numerous publications on the politics and institutions of the European Union and on Britain's position in the EU. On the history of Britain's approach to European integration, see S. George, *An Awkward Partner*, 2nd ed. (Oxford University Press, 1994) and H. Young, *This Blessed Plot* (Macmillan, 1998). On the institutions and the future of the EC, see A. Stevens, *The Administration of the European Union* (Macmillan, 2000); N. Nugent, *The Government and Politics of the European Union,* 4th ed. (Macmillan, 1999); and D. Dinan, *Ever Closer Union?* 2nd ed. (Macmillan, 1999). The principal works on the European Parliament are M. Westlake, *A Modern Guide to the European Parliament* (Pinter, 1994) and R. Corbett, F. Jacobs, and M. Shackleton, *The European Parliament,* 3rd ed. (Catermill, 1995). On the 1999 European Parliament elections, see D. Butler and M. Westlake, *British Politics and European Elections 1999* (Macmillan, 2000).

On politics in the different parts of the United Kingdom, there are several introductory works. On devolution itself, see V. Bogdanor, *Devolution in the United Kingdom* (Oxford University Press, 1999). On developments in Scotland, see A. Brown, D. McCrone, and L. Paterson, *Politics and Society in Scotland,* 2nd ed. (Macmillan, 1998) and, by the same authors, *The Scottish Electorate* (Macmillan, 1998). An early guide to the Scottish Parliament is provided in B. Taylor, *The Scottish Parliament* (Polygon, 1999). There is also an annual *Scottish Government Yearbook,* published by Edinburgh University Press. There are numerous works on the politics, problems, and future of Northern Ireland. Among the more recent are A. Aughey and D. Morrow (eds.), *Northern Ireland Politics* (Longman, 1996); P. Bew, H. Patterson, and P. Teague, *Northern Ireland Politics Between War and Peace* (Lawrence and Wishart, 1997); P. Rose, *How the Troubles Came to Northern Ireland* (Macmillan, 1999); and P. Dixon, *The Politics of Northern Ireland* (Macmillan, 2000). See also the seminal work by R. Rose, *Governing without Consensus* (Faber, 1971).

Useful texts on local government include K. Young and N. Rao, *Local Government Since 1945* (Blackwell, 1997); D. Wilson and C. Game, *Local*

Government in the United Kingdom, 2nd ed. (Macmillan, 1997); J. Stewart, *The Nature of British Local Government* (Macmillan, 2000); and T. Byrne, *Local Government in Britain,* 7th ed. (Penguin, 2000). Also useful on the changing nature of local government is G. Stoker, *British Local Governance: Theory and Practice* (Macmillan, 2000).

PART IV: SCRUTINY AND LEGITIMATION

The principal introductory works on Parliament are P. Norton, *Does Parliament Matter?* (Harvester Wheatsheaf, 1993); A. Adonis, *Parliament Today,* 2nd ed. (Manchester University Press, 1993); and P. Silk and R. Walters, *How Parliament Works,* 4th ed. (Longman, 1998). Parliamentary questions are considered in M. Franklin and P. Norton (eds.), *Parliamentary Questions* (Oxford University Press, 1993). The relationship between Parliament and the European Union is covered in P. Giddings and G. Drewry (eds.), *Westminster and Europe* (Macmillan, 1996). The relationship between Parliament and the law is dealt with in D. Oliver and G. Drewry (eds.), *The Law and Parliament* (Butterworths, 1998). The constituency role of MPs is considered in P. Norton and D. Wood, *Back from Westminster* (University Press of Kentucky, 1993). How Parliament deals with "conscience" issues, such as abortion and homosexuality, is covered in P. Cowley (ed.), *Conscience and Parliament* (Cass, 1998). On the contemporary problems facing Parliament, and the arguments for reform, see P. Riddell, *Parliament Under Pressure* (Gollancz, 1998) and *Strengthening Parliament* (The Commission to Strengthen Parliament, 2000). Biographical details of every MP and peer can be found in the annual edition of *Dod's Parliamentary Companion* (Vacher Dod Publishing), which also contains a mass of useful data on Parliament, agencies, and government departments.

The most recent and useful works on the House of Lords are D. Shell, *The House of Lords,* 2nd ed. (Harvester Wheatsheaf, 1992); D. Shell and D. Beamish (eds.), *The House of Lords at Work* (Oxford University Press, 1993); and P. Carmichael and B. Dickson (eds.), *The House of Lords: Its Parliamentary and Judicial Roles* (Hart Publishing, 1999). See also *A House for the Future,* The Report of the Royal Commission on Reform of the House of Lords , Cm 4534 (The Stationery Office, 2000). The House of Lords is put in comparative perspective in M. Russell, *Reforming the House of Lords: Lessons from Overseas* (Oxford University Press, 2000).

There are many works dealing with the problems of the royal family but few good works putting the monarchy in a political context. The principal scholarly work is V. Bogdanor, *The Monarchy and the Constitution* (Oxford University Press, 1995). B. Pimlott, *The Queen* (HarperCollins, 1996) provides an excellent biography of Queen Elizabeth II. Recent critiques of the monarchy include P. Richards, *Long to Reign Over Us?* (Fabian Society, 1996) and T. Hames and M. Leonard, *Modernising the Monarchy* (Demos, 1998).

PART V: ENFORCEMENT AND FEEDBACK

There are several works, usually entitled *Constitutional and Administrative Law,* that provide introductions to the English (and sometimes the Scottish) legal system, as well as the broader constitutional context. Recent examples include A. W. Bradley and K. D. Ewing, *Constitutional and Administrative Law,* 12th ed. (Longman, 1997) and A. Carroll, *Constitutional and Administrative Law* (Financial Times/Pitman, 1998).

On the debate surrounding judges, the courts, and the legal system, see J. Rozenberg, *The Search for Justice* (Hodder & Stoughton, 1994). For a radical critique of the judiciary, see J. A. G. Griffith, *The Politics of the Judiciary,* 5th ed. (Fontana, 1997). On the implications of membership of the European Union for the courts, and the role of the House of Lords in its judicial capacity, see B. Dickson and P. Carmichael (eds.), *The House of Lords: Its Parliamentary and Judicial Roles* (Hart Publishing, 1999). On the impact of devolution and of the incorporation of the European Convention on Human Rights (ECHR) for the courts, see the Summer 1998 and Summer 1999 issues of the journal *Public Law.* On the incorporation of the ECHR, see also the Government White Paper, *Rights Brought Home,* Cm 3782 (Home Office, 1998). C. Walker and K. Starmer (eds.), *Miscarriages of Justice* (Blackstone Press, 1999) reviews the nature of the criminal justice system and cases of miscarriages of justice in the United Kingdom.

There is a growing volume of literature on the role and effect of the mass media. Among the more recent publications are C. Seymour-Ure, *The British Press and Broadcasting since 1945,* 2nd ed. (Blackwell, 1996); J. Eldridge, J. Kitzinger, and K. Williams, *The Mass Media and Power in Modern Britain* (Oxford University Press, 1997); J. Curran, *Power Without Responsibility: The Press and Broadcasting in Britain,* 5th ed. (Routledge, 1997); and A. Reading and J. Stokes, *The Media in Britain: Current Debates and Development* (Macmillan, 1999). C. Shaw, *Deciding What We Watch: Taste, Decency and Media Ethics in the UK and the USA* (Oxford University Press, 1999) offers a comparative study of ethics. The role of the media in the 1997 general election campaign is explored in I. Crewe, J. Bartle, and B. Gosschalk, *Political Communications* (Cass, 1998).

PART VI: CONCLUSION

There are now several books and pamphlets that take a particular approach to constitutional change. Works that had a particular influence in the 1970s were S. E. Finer (ed.), *Adversary Politics and Electoral Reform* (Wigram, 1975); and Lord Hailsham, *Elective Dictatorship* (BBC, 1976). Recent critical literature has included A. Wright, *Citizens and Subjects* (Routledge, 1993); W. Hutton, *The State We're In* (Jonathan Cape, 1995); A. Barnett, *This Time: Our Constitutional Revolution* (Vintage, 1997); and S. Weir and D. Beetham, *Political Power and Democratic Control in Britain* (Routledge, 1999). The main defense of existing arrangements is offered in the conclusion to P. Norton (ed.), *New Directions in British Politics?* (Edward Elgar, 1991); J. Patten, *Things To Come* (Sinclair-Stevenson, 1995); and A. Lansley and R. Wilson, *Conservatives and the Constitution* (Conservative 2000 Foundation, 1997). See also P. Norton, *Power to the People* (Conservative Policy Forum, 1998).

Glossary

Back-bencher. A member of either house of Parliament who is neither a government minister nor a spokesperson for the opposition. The name derives from where the members sit: on the back benches.

Barrister. A specialist lawyer who appears on behalf of clients in superior courts and is retained through a solicitor.

Big Ben. The clock housed in the clock tower of the Palace of Westminster. (The clock tower itself is sometimes referred to, inaccurately, as Big Ben.) Various explanations have been offered as to why the clock is so named. Some ascribe it to the name of a popular boxer at the time it was installed, others to the first commissioner of works, Sir Benjamin Hall. A light shines above the clock tower whenever either House of Parliament is sitting at night.

Bill. A measure introduced into Parliament for enactment as law. It has to go through several stages. It remains a bill until such time as it receives the royal assent. At that point, it becomes an Act of Parliament.

"The bill." A colloquial name for the police. See "bobby."

Black rod. The Gentleman Usher of the "Black Rod" is an official of the House of Lords who has responsibility for security and administration. He is commonly called "Black Rod" even though this refers formally to his baton of office. He summons the House of Commons to attend the House of Lords when the queen opens a new session of Parliament.

"Bobby." Colloquial name for a policeman (not used much now) that was derived from the first name of the home secretary, Sir Robert Peel, who was responsible for the creation of the (metropolitan) police force in 1829. The police are also sometimes known by other colloquialisms, most notably nowadays "the bill" (now the title of a popular TV police series), but also "the filth," "rozzers" (hardly ever used now), and "pigs."

Buckingham Palace. The official London residence of the queen. When the prime minister "goes to the palace" for an audience (i.e., meeting) with the queen, the reference is to Buckingham Palace.

By-election. The election to return a member of Parliament (MP) in a constituency in which a vacancy has occurred (usually because of the death or resignation of the incumbent). A vacancy can be filled only by means of an election. By agreement between the parties, the precise date of a by-election is usually determined by the party that previously held the seat. Like general elections, by-elections are traditionally held on a Thursday.

Chequers. The official country residence of the prime minister, located close to London, near Princes Risborough in Buckinghamshire. It was given to the nation by Lord Lee of Fareham in 1917.

Chief constable. The professional head of each police force, except in London, where the metropolitan and City of London forces are each headed by a commissioner.

Chiltern Hundreds. Technically, a member of the House of Commons cannot resign. To give up a seat in the House, a member has to apply for a nominal office of profit under the Crown which then disqualifies the member from remaining in the House. Traditionally, the two offices used for this purpose are that of the steward or bailiff of Her Majesty's Three Chiltern Hundreds of Stoke (known simply as the Chiltern Hundreds) or the steward of the manor of Northstead. To say that an MP "has applied for the Chiltern Hundreds" means that he or she is, in effect, resigning.

The City. The City of London, occupying one square mile in the heart of London; it is the traditional home of the Bank of England, the stock exchange, and the nation's other financial institutions.

Clerk of the House of Commons. The senior official in the House of Commons who advises the Speaker and other members of the House on procedure and who has responsibility for a large part of the administration of the House. The clerk is the corporate officer as well as the accounting officer for the House. He is supported by other clerks. When sitting at the Table in the House, he (never yet she) wears a black robe and a wig, as do other clerks sitting at the Table.

Clerk of the Parliaments. The senior official in the House of Lords, the equivalent to the Clerk of the House of Commons. He is responsible also for the accuracy of the texts of acts of Parliament and is the custodian of the records of both Houses of Parliament.

Collective ministerial responsibility. The answerability of all members of the government to Parliament for decisions made by the cabinet.

Commonwealth. A voluntary association of independent states and territories. The Commonwealth evolved from the British Empire and exists now to provide cultural, sporting, and some political links among member states. The queen is head of the Commonwealth.

Constituency. An electoral area equivalent in nature to a congressional district. Each is known by a geographical name rather than by number. Each constituency elects one member of Parliament.

Contest an election. To stand for election.

Conventions of the Constitution. Informal constitutional rules treated as binding by those to whom they are directed.

Delegated legislation. Orders made by ministers under the authority of an act of Parliament. They usually take the form of what are known as Statutory Instruments.

Devolution. The devolving of powers from national government to subordinate assemblies.

Dispatch Box. The Table in each House of Parliament has two dispatch boxes on either side. These are used to store papers but are employed by speakers on the two front benches to rest their notes when addressing the House.

Dissolution. The closing, or dissolving, of Parliament to prepare for a general election, that is, the election of a new Parliament.

Division lobbies. The voting lobbies in the two houses of Parliament. When members vote (divide), they enter lobbies on the two sides of the chamber; the "aye" lobby is to the right of the presiding officer, the "no" lobby to the left. In the House of Commons, the terminology is "aye" or "no"; in the House of Lords it is "content" and "not content."

Downing Street. A small cul-de-sac off Whitehall housing three principal houses—numbers 10, 11, and 12. No. 10 is the official London residence of the prime minister, No. 11 the official London residence of the chancellor of the exchequer, and No. 12 houses the office of the government chief whip in the House of Commons. All three have interconnecting doors. No. 10 also has interconnecting doors to the cabinet office in Whitehall.

Elector. A registered voter.

Empire. The British Empire comprised countries under British sovereignty (though some were self-governing) and in 1918 it encompassed well over a quarter of the human race and more than a quarter of the world's land surface. It began to wither as various dominions gained independence. From the 1920s onward, it came to be called the British Commonwealth of Nations, now known simply as the Commonwealth.

Erskine May. The manual of parliamentary procedure—"the parliamentary bible"—the full title of which is *Erskine May's Treatise on the Law, Privileges, Proceedings and Usage of Parliament.* Sir Thomas Erskine May was a nineteenth-century clerk of the House of Commons. The book is now in its twenty-second edition, published in 1997; new editions are compiled by clerks under the direction of the clerk of the house. It is relied upon by parliamentarians but has no binding force.

Field a candidate. To put up a candidate for election.

Fleet Street. A street in central London, a continuation of the Strand (off Trafalgar Square), that traditionally has housed the main national newspapers. The name is still used to refer to the British press, even though no national newspapers are still based there; the last newspaper left in 1989. Most have relocated in the docklands area of east London.

Free votes. Parliamentary votes in which parties have not formally requested their members to vote in a particular way.

Front-benchers. The front bench on the government side of the House of Commons (known as the Treasury bench, and extending halfway down the chamber) is by custom reserved for ministers, and the equivalent bench on the opposition side of the house is reserved for spokespersons of the official opposition party. Hence, those who occupy them are known as front-benchers. Front benches also exist in the House of Lords.

General election. The election of a new House of Commons.

Going to the country. The calling of a general election; hence "the prime minister has decided to go to the country" means that the premier has requested a dissolution and the election of a new House of Commons.

Hack. A colloquial name for a journalist.

Hansard. The name given to the official report of the proceedings in both Houses of Parliament. The name derives from the early nineteenth century, when T. C. Hansard took over Cobbett's Parliamentary Debates. The business was sold in 1889 but the name of Hansard remained associated with the publication and, since 1943, *Hansard* has appeared on the cover of the official report.

Head of government. Political head of the executive. In the United Kingdom, the prime minister.

Head of state. Ceremonial leader of the nation. In the United Kingdom, the queen.

Individual ministerial responsibility. The answerability of ministers to the Crown (formally) and to Parliament (politically) for their official actions and those of civil servants within their particular departments.

Law lords. Judges appointed to membership of the House of Lords to enable the House to fulfill its judicial function as the highest domestic court of appeal.

Lord chancellor. A political appointee (a member of the cabinet) who is head of the judiciary. He is also formally the presiding officer of the House of Lords, though this entails the exercise of no significant powers.

Lord chief justice. A senior, professional judge who heads both the Queen's Bench Division of the High Court and the Criminal Division of the Court of Appeal.

Manifesto. A party's election platform, embodied in a written document.

Master of the rolls. A senior, professional judge who presides over the Civil Division of the Court of Appeal.

Member of Parliament (MP). A member of the House of Commons. No such designation applies to members of the House of Lords, who are known by their titles.

Ministry. A government department or the government collectively.

"New" Commonwealth countries. A term employed to refer to Asian and African countries that were granted independence by Britain in the 1940s, thus distinguishing them from the "old" Commonwealth countries of Canada, Australia, and New Zealand.

New Labour. The name applied to the Labour party under the leadership of Tony Blair.

New Scotland Yard. See "Scotland Yard."

Officials. A reference usually, though not exclusively, to civil servants.

Oxbridge. The universities of Oxford and Cambridge.

Palace of Westminster. The buildings, originally a royal palace, that house Parliament. Strictly speaking, its correct title is the New Palace of Westminster. The Old Palace was largely destroyed by fire in 1834.

Peer. A member of the peerage (i.e., a lord). There are two types of peer: hereditary peers (who inherit their titles) and life peers (who hold their titles for their lifetime only).

Peerage. A lordship. Though holders of peerages are known collectively as lords, there are five ranks: barons, viscounts, earls, marquesses, and dukes. Hereditary peers hold different ranks, but all life peers are created as barons.

Premier. Alternative term used to refer to the prime minister.

Private members. All members of Parliament who are not ministers. The term is not synonymous with back-benchers, as opposition front-benchers are private members.

Public schools. A term used, confusingly, to denote private schools. Schools in the public sector are usually referred to as state schools. Leading public schools include Eton and Harrow.

Quango. Quasi-autonomous nongovernment organization.

Rt. Hon. (Right Honorable). This title—as, for example, the Rt. Hon. Tony Blair MP—denotes a member of the Privy Council. The council, historically, was an important advisory body to the Crown but is now largely ceremonial in nature. However, membership in the council is still important because members can receive state secrets. All members of the cabinet and other senior ministers are sworn in as members of the Privy Council. Once sworn, they remain members for life.

Scotland Yard. The headquarters of the metropolitan police force, presently titled New Scotland Yard. The name derives from the location of the original headquarters— Scotland Yard, Westminster (just off Whitehall). It now occupies a modern building in Broadway, Westminster, close to the Home Office.

Second reading. Parliamentary debate on the principle of a bill before it is considered in detail by a committee.

Serjeant at Arms. Officer of the House of Commons with responsibilities for security, enforcing the orders of the House, and some administration.

Speaker. The presiding officer of the House of Commons, selected by the house from among its members. The speaker has the power to select members for debate (through "catching the speaker's eye"), to select amendments for debate, and to discipline members, though all within fairly well-defined limits and procedures. After election to the post, the speaker ceases to be a member of a political party (seeking reelection at a general election simply as "the speaker"), operates as a nonpartisan figure, and leads an isolated parliamentary existence.

Spin doctors. Politicians and their aides who seek to give a particular interpretation ("spin") to a news story that is favorable to their position, often by phoning or seeing journalists in advance of the story breaking.

Swing. An average measure of the changes in the percentages of the vote received by the two major parties in successive elections.

Tabling a motion. The act of submitting a motion for debate. This is a positive move—the start of a process—and should not be confused with the U.S equivalent, which means to shelve a motion.

Thatcherism. A term used to denote the philosophy espoused by Margaret Thatcher when she was leader of the Conservative party. It combines a neoliberal economic philosophy with an emphasis on maintaining social standards.

Third Way. A philosophic approach adopted by Labour prime minister Tony Blair and his supporters, denoting a way that goes beyond capitalism and socialism.

Tory. A colloquial name for a member of the Conservative party, deriving from the name of the party, the Tory party, from which the Conservative party evolved in the 1830s. The term also refers to a specific strand of thought within British conservatism.

Ulster. The northern nine counties of Ireland form the historic region of Ulster. However, the name Ulster is often used, especially by Unionists, to refer to the northern six counties that now constitute Northern Ireland. Since Northern Ireland was formed, it has been common to refer to it as a province of the United Kingdom.

Upper house. The House of Lords. (The House of Commons is the lower house, though it is rarely referred to as such.)

Vote of confidence. A formal motion expressing confidence (or no confidence) in the government, or a vote on a motion on which the government has declared that, if defeated, it will resign or request a dissolution. Such motions are normally discussed only in the House of Commons.

Wapping. An area in the docklands of London to which a number of national newspapers have relocated from Fleet Street.

Westminster. A district in London. The name is usually employed to refer to the Palace of Westminster, where the two houses of Parliament are located.

Westminster Hall. Part of the Palace of Westminster, the hall was originally a great hall of the king's palace and a place where justice was dispensed. It was built in the eleventh century and remodeled in the fourteenth century. It survived the fire of 1834 that destroyed the rest of the Palace of Westminster. King Charles I was tried in Westminster Hall. Today it is used occasionally for exhibitions and state events.

Whipped votes. Votes in Parliament in which the parties have requested their members to vote in a particular manner. Such requests are issued through a weekly written document known as the written whip. The request in the whip is given emphasis by underlining. The most important votes during which all party members are expected to be present and vote in unison are underlined three times. The term "three-line whip" derives from this practice. If there is a free vote (see above), there is no underlining.

Whips. Apart from the weekly written whip, there are members of each parliamentary party designated as whips. They act as channels of communication between party leaders and back-benchers, and largely as business managers. They are responsible for ensuring that party members know what business is being transacted and that they are present to vote when necessary and, on occasion, to speak when insufficient members have volunteered to take part in a debate. Contact between the whips' offices, especially the government and opposition chief whips, is known as contact "through the usual channels."

Whitehall. London street, between the Palace of Westminster and Trafalgar Square, traditionally housing government departments. The name is still employed to denote the environment occupied by ministers, and especially civil servants, even though most departments are now located elsewhere.

Whitehall Mandarins. The name employed on occasion to refer to the senior civil servants in government departments.

Woolsack. The seat on which the Lord Chancellor sits to preside over meetings of the House of Lords. It is stuffed with wool and was designed originally to show the importance of wool to the wealth of the nation.

Index